My Complete Story
of the Flute

Revised and Expanded Edition

My Complete Story of the Flute

The Instrument
The Performer
The Music

Leonardo De Lorenzo

TEXAS TECH UNIVERSITY PRESS

Library of Congress Cataloging-in-Publication Data
De Lorenzo, Leonardo, 1875-1962.
    My complete story of the flute : the instrument, the performer, the music / by Leonardo De Lorenzo. — Rev. and expanded ed.
        p. c.m.
    Includes bibliographical references and index.
    ISBN 0-89672-277-5. — ISBN 0-89672-285-6 (pbk.)
    1. Flute. 2. Flute players. 3. Flute music—History and criticism. I. Title.
ML935.D47 1992
    788.3—dc20   92-8525
                                                          CIP
                                                          MN

92 93 94 95 96 97 98 99 00 / 9 8 7 6 5 4 3 2 1

Texas Tech University Press
Lubbock, Texas 79409-1037 USA

Contents

~~~~~~

Acknowledgments

It was a dream of Leonardo De Lorenzo to publish a second edition of *My Complete Story of the Flute* that would include the three addenda he had written. That his dream is coming to fruition is due to concentrated effort on the part of many dedicated people. The National Flute Association has been working toward this goal for many years. Susan Berdahl, who prepared the introduction and the index, has been the principal source of information and motivation. This publication would not have been possible without her efforts.

To Arthur Ephross goes the credit for the initial impetus for this volume. Betty Mather, as president of the association, established the Special Publications Committee, which has been responsible for managing the details of publication. Members Susan Berdahl, Ann Fairbanks, David Lasocki, Erv Monroe, Mary Jean Simpson, and Nancy Toff have all been quick with their advice and support and are due much appreciation. Association treasurer John Solum has been of vital assistance in clearing the financial way to publication. Susan Miller and Wendell Broom of Texas Tech University Press are due a special word of thanks for their creative efforts.

To them, and to all who have been so very generous in the loan of rare and valuable material to be used in this publication, many, many thanks.

Michael C. Stoune, Chair
Special Publication Committee

De Lorenzo and the Flute Canon

A Bibliographic Note

by NANCY TOFF

My Complete Story of the Flute is a book whose very title inspires disbelief, suspicion, or at least skepticism. Indeed, an author who terms his own work "complete" is committing an act of arrogance, if not naïveté. How can any single volume encompass the *complete* story of the world's oldest instrument? It cannot, of course. The savvy reader, therefore, will place the emphasis not on *Complete*, but on *My*. And that is exactly why De Lorenzo's book is so valuable: It provides the author's very personal account of his instrument, for he is part performer, part historian, part gossip, part teacher. As a European-trained musician who went on to a distinguished career in the United States, De Lorenzo had a view of the flute world that is well worth knowing. As such, his book provides a unique perspective on American flute playing at midcentury, including a fascinating glimpse at the generation of flute players that was about to achieve prominence.

Originally published in 1951, De Lorenzo's *My Complete Story of the Flute* quickly earned a permanent place among the relatively small number of books and magazines that record the history of the flute and flutists. This heritage is hinted at by De Lorenzo's own acknowledgments to Emil Medicus's magazine *The Flutist* and to the books of Welch, Goldberg, Rockstro, Fitzgibbon, Sconzo, and Dayton C. Miller. But exactly where does his book fit into the flute canon, as literary critics might style the historical literature? What are its roots? How is it unique? And why does it continue to be a valuable, if not definitive, historical document?

For purposes of bibliographical logic, "comparing apples to apples," this discussion excludes several categories of material: the primary literature of the instrument—pedagogical works such as those of Hotteterre and Quantz, mechanical treatises such as Boehm's *The Flute and Flute Playing*, and ephemera such as manufacturers' literature; secondary literature such as museum catalogs; biographies and autobiographies of flutists, flutemakers, and composers; and monographs and doctoral dissertations on specific aspects of the flute. All of these are exceedingly valuable sources in their own right, but are intended for a more specialized readership. De Lorenzo falls rather into the category of "popular" literature on music: though the biographical reference section is something that probably only another flute player could love, much of the book is accessible to a general readership.

The first modern work in the secondary literature on the flute appeared in 1826 and was revised a decade later. Entitled *A Word or Two on the Flute*, it was written by W. N. James, the publisher of several London flute periodicals.[1] After a lengthy chapter on the flutes of antiquity, slightly shorter ones titled "English and German Flutes" and "The Capabilities of the German Flute," and brief ones on various aspects of flute playing technique—"Articulation," "The Best Modes, or Keys, for the Flute," and "Tone and Expression,"—James presents "The Performers of the Present Day" —Nicholson, Tulou, Ashe, Drouet, Berbiguier, Gabrielsky, et al.— seventeen men, all Europeans.

The first American book about the flute was *An Illustrated History of the Flute* by the New York flutemaker Alfred G. Badger, the first American manufacturer of the Boehm flute.[2] Badger's book was released in 1853 and revised in 1854, 1861, and 1875. The first two sections, on the mechanism of the instrument, are taken quite directly from British flute maker Richard Carte's 1851 publication, *Sketch of the Successive Improvements Made in the Flute*.[3] But there are also sections on the "primitive" flute of "the ancients," "Hints as to the Proper Method of Studying the Flute," and, most importantly, "Flute in America." Badger's account of the early history of the Boehm flute in the United States, in which he describes his methods of marketing the new instrument and the sometimes rocky road to its acceptance, is a unique first-person resource. Endorsements from leading American flutists, along with copious advertisements for Badger's flutes and music, provide additional data.

Christopher Welch's *History of the Boehm Flute*,[4] published in 1883, contains extremely valuable information on the mechanical development of the instrument. The book includes the 1882 biographical essay on Boehm by Professor Carl von Schafhäutl, with whom Boehm studied acoustics, and is particularly notable for its coverage of the infamous Boehm-Gordon controversy. A second edition, twice the length of the first, appeared in 1892 and continued the colloquy; the third edition, published in 1896, is perhaps the most exhaustive single account of Boehm's work. Welch mentions flute playing in the United States only as it relates to sadness at Boehm's death.

The first truly comprehensive reference work on the flute was published in 1890: Richard Shepherd Rockstro's *A Treatise on the Construction the History and the Practice of The Flute including a Sketch of the Elements of Acoustics and Critical Notices of Sixty Celebrated Flute-Players*.[5] A second edition appeared in 1928. Rockstro's book was the first thorough mechanical history of the instrument, though it betrays his anti-Boehm bias, a matter that has been discussed extensively in Welch's second edition and elsewhere. His biographical section begins circa 1640 with Philbert and proceeds to Robert S. Pratten's work in the late 1860s. The emphasis is on the period 1730 to 1868, with the major nineteenth century British flutists receiving most space. There is not an American in the pantheon.

Henry Clay Wysham, an orchestral flutist in Boston and Baltimore before he moved to the San Francisco area, published a slim but stylishly written volume, *The Evolution of the Boehm Flute*, in 1898.[6] Abundant quotations from Shakespeare, Dickens, and the Greek classics apply a literary veneer; the text is punctuated throughout by none-too-subtle encomia to the products of his publisher, the instrument maker C. G. Conn. Quoting liberally, but with attribution, from other writers, Wysham details the mechanical history of the instrument, including four chapters on Boehm, one on "The Noble Army of Patentees," and one each on "The Material for Flutes" and "The Embouchure."

Chapter 9, "Lady Flute-Players," cites only three: Miss May Lyle Smith, whom Wysham styles "Queen of America's Flutists," Miss Annie G. Lyle of San Francisco, and Miss Cora Cardigan (Mrs.

Louis Honig) of London. Wysham's final chapter on virtuosi includes a predictable cast of characters: Boehm, Franz Doppler, Giulio Briccialdi, Anton Bernhard Fürstenau, and Paul Taffanel. He notes with some horror in his glowing review of Taffanel that the French maître did not merit any mention in Rockstro's book. Wysham was the first writer to cover the American flute-playing scene, including biographies of Sidney Lanier of Baltimore, John Summers Cox of the Sousa band (with useful information on his Badger and Rudall, Carte instruments), Edward Heind'l [Heindl] of Boston and Charles [Carl] Wehner of New York, both students of Boehm; Charles Molé of the Boston Symphony; and Otto Oesterle of the New York Philharmonic and Theodore Thomas Orchestra. Wysham quotes valuable critical excerpts and provides detailed information about the instruments used by these players. This small but informative volume, which is the closest we have to an immediate progenitor to De Lorenzo, has not yet been reprinted in a modern edition.

In 1906, Adolf Goldberg, a Berlin businessman, brought out *Porträts und Biographien hervorragender Flöten-Virtuosen, -Dilettanten und -Komponisten,*[7] a remarkable collection of "cabinet"-size cards containing photographs and short biographies of 409 flutists and 91 composers for the flute. Though the subjects were primarily German, the set does include leading flutists of the French school: Taffanel, Louis Fleury, Philippe Gaubert, Gaston Blanquart, and Georges Barrère (listed as solo flutist of the Colonne Orchestra and member of the Paris Opéra orchestra, though he had moved to New York in 1905).

Goldberg also cites a number of prominent American flutists of the era: J. S. Cox, whose biography reads, in its entirety, "Famous American flute virtuoso" (whereas Frederick the Great rates seven card-sides), Edward Heindl, Sidney Lanier, Ary van Leeuwen, Leonardo de Lorenzo [*sic*], the brothers André and Daniel Maquarre; Otto Oesterle, Carl Wehner, Eugene Weiner (of Boston, New York, and the Theodore Thomas Orchestra), Hugo Wittgenstein, principal flute of the Metropolitan Opera in New York, and Henry Clay Wysham. And a curiosity: a single female flutist, Miss May Lyle Smith, identified only as a student of Eugene Weiner in New York.

The Goldberg collection is particularly notable as an iconographic artifact: The portraits provide a rich lode of information on the types of instruments played by leading players of the day in an era when a wide variety of Boehm system and old system instruments, notably the German-style "Reform" flutes, were competing for customers.

In 1914, H. Macaulay Fitzgibbon published *The Story of the Flute*,[8] part of the now-rare *Music Story Series*, a set that described the various instruments and other musical topics for a general audience. A second edition of the Fitzgibbon volume appeared in 1928. It had the obligatory section on Flutes of the Ancients, an accessible history of the instrument's mechanical development, and chapters on the military fife, piccolo, alto and bass flutes, flute in the orchestra, and music for the flute. Chapter 13, "Famous Flautists," begins with the early French players and is divided into British and foreign sections. There is a separate chapter on "Woman and the Flute," in which these recondite creatures are referred to as "flautistes." The Americans of the species include Miss May Lyle Smith of New York and Miss Marguerite de Forest Andersen of Maryland, for whom Cecile Chaminade orchestrated her *Concertino*. Chapter 16, consisting of all of six pages, is entitled "Flute in America and Australia." Fitzgibbon makes brief reference to some random newpaper notices and gives a paragraph each to John Kyle, Otto Oesterle, Carl Wehner, Edward Heindl, John S. Cox, Sidney Lanier, Eugene Weiner, Alfred Quesnel, and Charles Molé. Some unusual chapters cover "The Flute in English Literature-Poet Flautists"; "Curiosities of the Flute"; and "Flutes of Oriental and Savage Nations" (including American Indians). Discussion of the French school ends with Taffanel. There are a few pages of tightly cropped portraits, some of which have instruments visible.

D. Ehrlich's *The History of the Flute from Ancient Times to Böhm's Invention*,[9] self-published in New York in 1921, is a slim, pocket-size book subtitled "Including Detailed Instructions concerning Embouchure, Tone, Technique, Proper Breathing, Phrasing, Execution, Harmonic-Tones; also Miscellaneous Matters of Interest, and Biographies of Famous Flutists." An introductory chapter deals with legends about the flute, its popularity around the world, some primitive ethnomusicology, and the early history of the instrument. Succeeding chapters deal with Boehm's innovations, the design of various parts of the flute and how to assemble it, tone, practice techniques, breathing, vibrato, harmonics, phrasing, maintenance and repair of the instrument, and the relative merits of closed and open G-sharp systems. Chapter 17, "Flute Teachers and their teaching methods," contains some sound advice, beginning with the warning that "Not everyone who is a flutist can teach." The miscellaneous matters alluded to in the book's subtitle include the "glide," an expressive technique championed by the English flutist Charles Nicholson; the crutch, a left-hand support designed by Boehm; "Effect of colds upon the lips or through strong tea or smoking"; hard pads; false teeth; and one-armed flutists. The biographical chapter cites the usual suspects, but also includes a number of players in the United States: Philip Ernst, John Kyle, Sidney Lanier, Otto O[e]sterle, Carl Wehner, and Eugene Weiner.

Fortunato Sconzo's *Il Flauto e i Flautisti* (1930)[10] provides a useful and comprehensive set of biographies, again spanning flute history. Curiously, all proper names are translated into the writer's native Italian, so that Claude Paul Taffanel is rendered Claudio Paolo Taffanel, and Johann Joachim Quantz as Giovanni Gioacchino Quantz. There are no Italianized Americans, however.

Herbert Kolbel's *Von der Flöte*,[11] published in 1951—the same year as De Lorenzo's book—and revised in 1966, includes generous biographical coverage, beginning with the Hotteterre family and working its way through the centuries to Marcel Moyse. The Germans and the French take center stage (in separate sections); Englishmen such as Nicholson appear briefly; Americans are excluded.

The flute book most contemporaneous with De Lorenzo's, and thus a particularly interesting work with which to compare it, is Adrien Girard's *Histoire et Richesses de la Flûte*.[12] Published in a limited edition of 1,500 copies in Paris in 1953, it is a beautifully designed and illustrated volume that was described recently with some understatement by one rare-book dealer as "très rare et très recherché." After a brief history of the instrument, Girard provides an international survey of flute makers and a generous acknowledgment of the excellent work of the American makers Haynes and Powel [*sic*]. A survey chapter entitled "Les ressources de la flute" covers basics of flute playing and the chamber literature. Chapter 4 is a biographical dictionary of flutists beginning with French flutists of the Middle Ages through Barrère and Gaubert. Other than an allusion to Barrère's emigration to the United States in 1905, there is no coverage of American flutists, nor of post-Barrère Europeans. Perhaps the most interesting feature of this outstanding book is the "genealogical" chart of the French school of flute playing. The concluding chapter is a catalog of flute literature. A discography is an invaluable source of early recordings, including those of several Americans: Julius Baker, Phillip Kaplan, William Kincaid, Paul Renzi, Martin Ruderman, and John Wummer. A number of the illustrations came from the Dayton C. Miller Flute Collection.

Girard's *Histoire* is very much a work of objective scholarship, revealing nothing of its author's personality. De Lorenzo's book, by contrast, is the written incarnation of its author. It is replete with typographical errors and internal contradictions that a more "professional" writer—or his editor—should have corrected. Moreover, the lack of an index (and footnotes and bibliography) betrays the fact that the author, however passionate and well informed about his subject, was no academic. Sadly, this omission has (until the present edition) made the book less useful than it could be. But the lack of scholarly apparatus should not obscure the true worth of the book.

De Lorenzo divided his book into four parts. The first, which describes the physical aspects of varous members of the flute family, is a typically idiosyncratic, anecdotal account. Though many of his anecdotes are charming, others are no doubt apocryphal. The straightforward objective information, likewise, should be used advisedly by the scholar, as there are numerous orthographic and factual errors. For example, De Lorenzo states that "The first flute manufactured in the workshop of Boehm had the improved key mechanism characteristic of the instrument which bears his name. This was in 1828." Later in the text, however, De Lorenzo correctly states that Boehm applied his new fingering system to the flute in 1832.

Part 2: "The Performer," is the longest and by far the most valuable section of the book, because it provides a truly unique view of American flute playing in the midtwentieth century. The "Biographies of Pioneers" cover much the same territory as Sconzo, Goldberg, and the other sources credited in his acknowledgments. But De Lorenzo continues his dramatis personae up to his own time, concluding with John Wummer of the New York Philharmonic, Arthur Lora of the NBC Symphony and Metro-politan Opera, and Carmine Coppola, also with NBC. This is a generation that is relatively unknown to young flute players today; these distinguished players made far fewer solo recordings than their successors, and their anonymous playing must be sought out on orchestral recordings.

The thumbnail biographies are perhaps the most interesting, because they include not only De Lorenzo's own generation— Philippe Gaubert, Georges Laurent, the Maquarre brothers, Ary van Leeuwen—and those just a bit younger—Marcel Moyse and William Kincaid—but also the next generation. This up-and-coming group became the leading flutists of the professional generation who are now our own *eminences grises*: Frances Blaisdell, Julius Baker (described by De Lorenzo, who taught Baker at Eastman, merely as a young American flutist), and John Krell, to name a few.

The "thumb nail biographies" in the first addendum (1954) include the young Doriot Anthony [Dwyer], as well as Geoffrey Gilbert, Louis Moyse, Aurèle Nicolet, Pierre [sic] Rampal, and various "dilettantes" who happened to have corresponded with the author, thereby earning themselves a place in printed posterity.

The second addendum, published in 1955, lists as the leading contemporary flutists such names as Maximilien Schwedler, proponent of the German reform flute in the late 19th century; Fernand Caratgé, the French flutist who edited numerous pedagogical works for Leduc; and Frederick Bennett Chapman, author of a short instructional book on the flute published by Oxford University Press. The Americans include a number of names well known today: Julius Baker and Paige Brook (recently retired from the New York Philharmonic), John Krell (retired piccoloist of the Philadelphia Orchestra), Walfrid Kujala (long-time piccoloist of the Chicago Symphony), Claude Monteux, Ed. E. Powell (son of flute-maker Verne Q. Powell), Los Angeles studio flutist Sheridon Stokes, and Meredith Willson, best known as composer of *The Music Man*.

The third addendum (1957) includes Luisa [Louise] di Tullio of Los Angeles, James Politis of the Metropolitan Opera Orchestra, Andrew Lolya of New York, Peter Lucas [Lukas] Graf of Germany, Sidney Zeitlin of the Minneapolis Symphony, and a reprise of Pierre Rampal.

A short section on the amateur flutist contains random nuggets such as proof that despite popular legend George Washington did not play the flute. And for organologists, the next section contains such useful information as a listing of players who declined to switch to the Boehm flute from the old system.

Part 3 of the main book is rather short and covers "A Thing or Two About Flute Music." The real fun of De Lorenzo's book comes in the fourth section, "Reminiscences of a Flutist," and the sections of the addenda that the author aptly terms "Other Interesting Material." That is exactly what it is: some true, some not; some humorous, some mildly offensive by today's standards (in his treatment of American Indians and Asian peoples, for instance). In this regard, De Lorenzo is one in spirit with his friend Emil Medicus, the Asheville, North Carolina, flutist-entrepreneur who published *The Flutist* magazine from 1920 to 1929. But just as the "Miscellaneous" category is often a treasure to the historical researcher, so De Lorenzo provides much useful if uncategorized data: flute club concert programs, which give us otherwise ephemeral information on trends in repertoire; orchestral flute section rosters, which provide institutional and individual history; anecdotes about players' instruments, which document the evolution of both the instrument and performance practice; odd bits of discography; and so forth. This amalgam is firmly in the tradition of the commonplace book—a collection of quotations copied into one's journal or diary—but here made available to a much wider audience.

In the forty years since the publication of *My Complete Story of the Flute*, there have been several important books on the instrument, principally Rene LeRoy's *Traité de la flûte* (1966),[13] which covers acoustics, mechanical design, and pedagogy; Philip Bate's *The Flute* (1969),[14] largely a mechanical history; Raymond Meylan's *La*

Flute (1974),[15] a more culturally oriented history with lavish color plates; Gustav Scheck's *Die Flöte und Ihre Musik* (1975),[16] a learned treatise on the history of the instrument, the physiology of flute playing, and analyses of landmarks of the literature; and the present writer's *The Development of the Modern Flute* (1979),[17] a mechanical history of the instrument, and *The Flute Book* (1985),[18] a reference guide to the instrument, its performance, and its repertoire. The definitive biographical dictionary of the flute and flutists has yet to be compiled, however. *Follow the Pipers*,[19] a rather random directory of American flutists, was an admittedly amateur effort published by Aldine K. Burks in 1969. Andrew Fairley's *Flutes, Flautists & Makers* (1982)[20] is a derivative work full of inaccuracies. And so, unlikely as it may seem given the continuing high level of interest in the flute, De Lorenzo still has the last, though out of date, word in the biographical arena.

In assessing the overall value of De Lorenzo's book, one might do well to quote from the dust jacket of the first edition: "a storehouse of information about flutes and flutists from ancient times to today, studded with odd facts, unusual facts, illuminating facts, as well as a veritable mine of anecdotes." One might also add, "untrue facts," but as the dust jacket concludes, the book is "an inexhaustible source of information and entertainment." The reader armed with the proverbial grain of salt has much to digest and to savor.

NOTES

1 W. N. James. *A Word or Two on the Flute*. Edinburgh: Charles Smith & Co., 1826. 2nd ed. London: R. Cocks and Co., 1836. Reprint: London: Tony Bingham, 1982.

2 A. G. Badger. *An Illustrated History of the Flute*. New York: Firth, Pond & Co, 1853. 2nd ed.: New York: Firth, Pond & Co., 1854. 3rd ed.: New York: Firth, Pond & Co., 1861. 4th ed.: New York: Firth, Pond & Co. 1875.

3 Richard Carte. *Sketch of the Successive Improvements Made in The Flute*. 3rd ed. London: Rudall, Rose, Carte & Co. and Keith and Prowse, 1855.

4 Christopher Welch. *History of the Boehm Flute*. London: Rudall, Carte & Co., 1883. 2nd ed., rev.: London: Rudall, Carte & Co., 1892; Reprint: New York: McGinnis & Marx, 1961. 3rd ed., rev.: London: Rudall, Carte & Co., New York: G. Schirmer, 1896; Reprint: Wolfeboro, N.H.: Longwood Press, 1977.

5 Richard S[hepherd] Rockstro. *A Treatise on the Construction the History and the Practice of the Flute*. London: Rudall, Carte & Co., 1890. 2nd ed., rev. London: Rudall, Carte & Co., 1928. Reprint: London: Musica Rara, 1967; Boston: Milford House, 1973; Buren, Netherlands: Frits Knuf, 1987.

6 Henry Clay Wysham. *The Evolution of the Boehm Flute.* New York: C. G. Conn, 1898.

7 Adolf Goldberg. *Biographieen zur Porträts-Sammlung hervorragender Flöten-Virtuosen, Dilettanten und Komponisten.* Berlin: privately printed, 1906. Reprint, ed. with foreword by Karl Ventzke: Celle: Moeck, 1986.

8 H. Macaulay Fitzgibbon. *The Story of the Flute.* London: Walter Scott Publishing Co., New York: Charles Scribner's Sons, 1914. 2nd ed., rev.: London: William Reeves Bookseller; New York: Charles Scribner's Sons, 1928.

9 D. Ehrlich. *The History of the Flute From Ancient Times to Böhm's Invention.* New York: author, 1921.

10 Fortunato Sconzo. *Il Flauto e I Flautisti.* Milan: Ulrico Hoepli, 1930.

11 Herbert Kölbel. *Von der Flöte.* Köln: Staufen-Verlag, 1951. 2nd ed., rev.: Kassel: Bärenreiter, 1966.

12 Adrien Girard. *Histoire et Richesses de la Flûte.* Paris: Librairie Gründ, 1953.

13 René LeRoy. *Traité de la flûte, historique, technique, et pédagogique.* Paris: Editions Musicales Transatlantiques, 1966.

14 Philip Bate. *The Flute: A Study of its History, Development and Construction.* London: Ernest Benn; New York: W. W. Norton, 1969.

15 Raymond Meylan. *La Flûte: Les grandes lignes de son developpement de la préhistoire à nos jours.* Lausanne: Editions Payot, 1974. *The Flute.* Translated by Alfred Clayton. London: B. T. Batsford; Portland, Ore.: Amadeus Press, 1988.

16 Gustav Scheck. *Die Flöte und Ihre Musik.* Mainz: Schott, 1975.

17 Nancy Toff. *The Development of the Modern Flute.* New York: Taplinger, 1979. Reprint: Urbana: University of Illinois Press, 1986.

18 Nancy Toff. *The Flute Book.* New York: Charles Scribner's Sons; London: David and Charles, 1985.

19 Aldine K. Burks. *Follow the Pipers: A Guide to Contemporary Flute Artists and Teachers.* Westfield, N.Y.: author, 1969.

20 Andrew Fairley. *Flutes, Flautists & Makers.* London: Pan Educational Music, 1982.

Leonardo De Lorenzo
A Biographic Note

by SUSAN BERDAHL

Success really began for Leonardo De Lorenzo when as an Italian immigrant in 1910, he was offered the coveted position of principal flutist with the New York Philharmonic Orchestra. Carl Wehner, veteran solo flutist of that organization, who had befriended the itinerant Italian, came to him and said, "The position of solo flute with the New York Philharmonic is yours if you want it, but you must promise me *never to answer back to Mahler*. He is a sick man and very unpleasant." De Lorenzo recalled that, obedient to his mentor's wishes, the only time he ever dared answer Mahler was when the famous conductor-composer called him "Lorenzo" one day (after his name had been misspelled in the program as "de Lorenzo" with a lowercase *d*), and then it was only to request the correction with a polite "De Lorenzo, please, Maestro." Prior to his good fortune in receiving the New York Philharmonic position, De Lorenzo had known many years of hard work and hard times.

Born in Viggiano (Potenza) in the province of Lucania, Italy, on August 29, 1875, De Lorenzo began his love affair with the flute at the age of eight when he started to play on a simple six-key Italian flute. He soon graduated to one with thirteen keys. He was considered a professional flutist at the age of sixteen, and as such he set sail to America to seek his fortune. He eventually landed a steady job as a flutist at a hotel in Cerulean Springs, Kentucky, for meager wages. In 1896, somewhat discouraged, he returned to Italy to serve in the Italian army where he was assigned to the military band at Alessandria under the direction of Giovanni Moranzoni, father of the famous conductor of the Metropolitan Opera. It was during his military service that De Lorenzo first tried his hand at composition, beginning what years later became his famous pedagogical work *Nine Grand Studies*. Following military service,

De Lorenzo resumed his wandering musician's lifestyle, traveling in Germany, Italy, England, and South Africa. In Cape Town, South Africa, he played all sorts of occasional jobs before landing his very first symphony orchestra job at the age of twenty-five. It was in Cape Town in 1903 that he made the switch from the old to the Boehm system flute, tutoring himself from Clinton's method. De Lorenzo ordered a two-piece wooden Boehm system flute with open G-sharp from the famous London Rudall-Carte firm. He continued to play this particular instrument throughout his long career; he was a life-long adherent of the wood flute.

Several years later, in 1907, De Lorenzo left South Africa and returned home to Italy to complete his formal musical study at the Naples Conservatory. Though he passed all of his exams for the diploma the first year, he pursued advanced studies for almost two more years. Throughout the years of traveling, De Lorenzo took flute lessons wherever and with whomever he could. At home in Italy, his earliest flute lessons on the simple system had been from Giacomo Nigro, whom De Lorenzo later convinced to switch to the "Bohemian flute" as Nigro referred to it. While at the Naples Conservatory, De Lorenzo studied flute with Alfonso Pagnotti, one of Krakamp's best pupils, and composition with Camillo De Nardis.

In 1909, at the age of thirty-four, he set sail for America for the second time. Now a trained and experienced flutist, he met with great success. After his auspicious first year as principal flutist with the New York Philharmonic in 1910, he began a three-year association with the New York Symphony under Walter Damrosch, where he had the almost thankless and impossible job of substituting for the godlike Georges Barrère when Barrère was away on solo and ensemble tours.

By 1917, just six years after establishing himself in New York, De Lorenzo had achieved national prominence in the United States. He was honored magnificently by the newly organized Los Angeles Flute Club on February 4, 1917, with a "musical" scheduled for the purpose of "honoring Leonardo De Lorenzo, flute virtuoso and composer." The dedication in the program reads, "It is our pleasure to make Mr. Leonardo De Lorenzo our first distinguished guest, also our first 'Honorary Member.' We feel highly honored by his dedication to the Los Angeles Flute Club of this latest composition, a Fantasy for flute and piano." This was just the first of many tributes to De Lorenzo from the Los Angeles Flute Club. Among the flute notables who were subsequently to be so honored by this club were Dayton Miller, Georges Barrère, William S. Haynes, and Verne Q. Powell.

From New York, De Lorenzo went on to the solo flute positions in the following orchestras: the Minneapolis Symphony (1914-19), the Los Angeles Symphony (1919-20), the Los Angeles Philharmonic (1920-23), and the Rochester Philharmonic (1923-35). During his Rochester Philharmonic tenure, he was simultaneously Professor of Flute at the Eastman School of Music. In 1935, he retired formally from professional flute playing and teaching, planning to spend his retirement composing for and writing about the flute. Upon receiving De Lorenzo's letter of resignation, Howard Hanson, director of the Eastman School of Music, responded with the following letter expressing his regret and best wishes:

Dear Mr. De Lorenzo:

I am sorry to have your letter, and I have purposely delayed in accepting your resignation. I gather, however, from our various conversations as well as from your two communications that you really feel that it could be best for you personally to resign, and therefore, for this reason, I accept with much regret your resignation. You have done a great work in the Eastman School, and have left a deep impression both as a personality and as a distinguished musician and educator. You place will be difficult to fill, and you may rest assured that you will always have an affectionate place in the hearts of all of the Eastman School people.

With my deepest thanks for your long and invaluable service, I am yours sincerely,

Howard Hanson, Director

De Lorenzo wrote about 300 musical works consisting of flute solos, chamber music, etudes, and exercises. About one-third of these works were published during his lifetime and were known and performed all over the world—South Africa, Japan, Europe, Australia, Canada, and South America, as well as the United States. He wrote a few easy solos, but most of his solo and chamber output is technically demanding, probably because he often played his own works in concert. De Lorenzo was admired for his technical prowess. His pedagogical works, also very difficult, are designed to develop extraordinary technical facility. His chamber pieces for flute quartet and flute quintet are perhaps the most often performed works and are now included on many high school state contest lists in the United States.

The *Divertimento flautistico* for five flutes, Op. 75, was highly acclaimed, by the audience as well as by the press in its auspicious debut on June 28, 1935, at the Eastman School of Music, marking the occasion of De Lorenzo's retirement and therefore final appearance at the venerable institution. The final number on the program, the piece was performed from manuscript by De Lorenzo and four of his students. The audience consisted of the music faculty and the director, Dr. Howard Hanson. This piece was one of the first important original flute ensemble pieces to feature the alto flute in G. The slow movement, "Serenata Breve a Pan," consists of an exposed alto solo. Of all the movements, it had been composed first and had been performed separately. (Rex Elton Fair broadcast the piece from the University of Nebraska on January 17, 1923.) Years later, De Lorenzo scored a version of this lovely movement for bass flute in C in the place of the alto flute in G. At a concert in California, De Lorenzo had the solo part played twice, once with alto flute and a second time with bass flute solo. De Lorenzo was very influential in promulgating the use of the lower flutes. In addition to writing for the bass C and G alto flutes, he continually programmed works using these instruments with his famous Eastman flute ensemble of the 1930s. The group was the first to incorporate the C bass flute, a Rudall-Carte with a special crook (pictured herein following page 144).

Though *My Complete Story of the Flute* is De Lorenzo's only book, it is by no means his first attempt at writing. Throughout his career he contributed numerous articles on flute topics, which were published in various journals, and advertising pamphlets and as part of his pedagogical books. Around 1911, he began a long and fruitful alliance with the Carl Fischer Company of New York, which eventually published many of his solos and his well-known method book, *L'Indispensabile*. De Lorenzo authored a column entitled, "Famous Flutists of the Past and Present" which appeared in Fischer's journal the *Metronome*. The column featured biographies of many famous artists such as Giulio Briccialdi, Eugene Walckiers, Heinrich Soussman, Benôit Berbiguer, Anton Bernhard Fürstenau,

Julius Manigold, Ernesto Koehler, Carl Wehner, Adolph Terschak, W. Lewis Barret, Ferdinand Büchner, Jean Louis Tulou, Friedrich Kuhlau, John Lemmoné, Theobaud Boehm, Cesare Ciardi, Eugene Portre, Johann Joachim Quantz, Frederick the Great, Johan and Philip Fahrback, Wilhelm Popp Popp, Emil Prill, Paul Taffanel, Paul Wetzger, Albert Fransella, Rudolph Tillmetz, and Friedrich Dulon. De Lorenzo relied on his voluminous correspondence with flutists all over the world for these biographies, supplementing his first-hand accounts with material from *The Flute* by Richard Sheperd Rockstro. Many of these biographies were reprinted and/or amended for the journal *The Flutist* which was published during the 1920s by Emil Medicus. De Lorenzo also wrote original articles for *The Flutist* and for *Etude* magazine. One should not overlook the many interesting essays, covering a wide range of subjects having to do with flute playing and flute history, that are found within De Lorenzo's extensive pedagogical treatises. For example, an extensive biographical list (based in part on Adolph Goldberg's collection of portraits and biographies) of eminent flutists, composers, teachers, amateurs, and inventors connected to the flute is included in Part 2 of his *L'Indispensible*. De Lorenzo also contributed to Carl Fischer's various advertising pamphlets, sheet music covers, and the company catalogs called "Facts Worth Knowing about Flutes and Piccolos." For these he wrote short pieces on flute history, advice on flute playing, very short biographies of flutists, and entertaining stories about flutists, as well as endorsements for the German Rittershausen flutes that Fischer sold.

While traveling the world as a young flutist, De Lorenzo established lifelong friendships with flutists everywhere. These musicians of widely differing nationalities and styles of playing made deep and lasting impressions on De Lorenzo. He sustained personal friendships through enlightening correspondences for years with many celebrated flutists such as Ernesto Kohler, Edward De Jong, Abelardo Albisi, Professor Franceschini of Rome, Jules Manigold, Tommaso Giorgi, Victor Safronoff, John Lemmoné, Georges Barrère, and Carl Wehner. From information gleaned from these letters, De Lorenzo gathered biographical material for his early articles and ultimately for *My Complete Story*.

These relationships had far-reaching effects; from these men he learned not only about their musical activities, but also about many of their noteworthy colleagues and pupils. From Wehner, for example, he learned about Sidney Lanier; from Franceschini, he learned about Ciardi and Briccialdi; and from Safronoff, he learned about Kretschmann and Bücher. And in turn, De Lorenzo made us, the flutists of posterity, privy to those fascinating firsthand personal reports, which he saved and recorded in *My Complete Story*. Many of these flutist-composers dedicated works to De Lorenzo: Ferdinand Bücher, Ernesto Koehler, Paul Wetzger, Rudolph Tillmetz, Leopoldo Pieroni, John Lemmoné, Joseph La Monaca, Gilberto Gravina (great-grandson of Franz Lizst), Ary Van Leewen, Joseph Piastro, Joseph La Violette, Aldoph Weiss, Mario Castelnuovo-Tedesco, and Alferio Mignone. De Lorenzo loved to dedicate pieces to his friends, virtuosos and amateurs alike. During the last few months of his life, while he was blind and bedridden, De Lorenzo dictated a letter to be sent to Archie Wade, officer of the Los Angeles Flute Club, regarding the dedications of his most recent publications (the series called "New Composition in the Modern Idiom" published C. F. Peters in 1960):

> It may interest you to know that one is dedicated to Dr. Selders of Texas who has recently retired. He is an enthusiastic flutist, and practices four hours daily. he owns two silver flutes, one gold flute, one platinum flute and has recently ordered another platinum flute.
>
> Another composition is dedicated to Mrs. Trowbridge, government employee and fine flutist, who has recently changed from closed G# to open G# flute.
>
> The third dedication is to Prof. A. Tassinari who taught at Santa Cecilia Academy in Rome for many years and is now retired. He was Gazzeloni's teacher.
>
> And the fourth, an Allegro Concerto, I should like to dedicate to you.

De Lorenzo died before these compositions came out and his dedications were never officially inscribed in the printed versions.

In addition to the letters to and from flutists, flutist-composers, and other personal friends, De Lorenzo maintained an intense correspondence schedule with all prominent flute writers and historians of his day: Dayton Miller, Emil Medicus, John Finn, H. Macaulay Fitzgibbon, and Christopher Welch. De Lorenzo corresponded with John Finn for more than thirty years and with Emil

Medicus for more than forty. These men shared books, articles, and information and each helped the others politically by offering glowing testimonials to their latest work. For example, De Lorenzo exchanged an early copy of his *Nine Studies* in return for copies of Welch's *History of the Boehm Flute* and *Shakespeare and the Flute*. When Welch died in 1915, it was Finn who wrote the sad news to De Lorenzo. About this time, De Lorenzo arranged for the publication of an excerpt of Fitzgibbon's first edition to be published in Fischer's *Metronome*. De Lorenzo also supplied corrections and additional information for Fitzgibbon's second edition, especially data pertaining to the flute and flute playing in the United States. Emil Medicus was the only correspondent yet alive by the time De Lorenzo was working on the final stages of this book. Naturally, De Lorenzo consulted Medicus on the various aspects of the work. Emil Medicus approved the biography "Medicus" after having De Lorenzo revise and eliminate certain parts which he found offensive. De Lorenzo asked for permission to use material from *The Flutist* and in particular, requested photographs. Of course, Medicus supplied him generously with many (De Lorenzo had furnished a number of these photos to Medicus in the first place) and graciously granted the permissions. De Lorenzo's correspondence with both Emil Medicus and Dayton Miller is preserved as part of the Dayton C. Miller Collection of the Library of Congress.

After retiring to California at the age of sixty from his posts as professor of flute at the Eastman School of Music and principal flutist of the Rochester Philharmonic, Leonardo De Lorenzo and his devoted wife, pianist Maude Petersen, began in earnest to organize his vast collection of clippings and writings on the flute into book form. Over the years, much of the material was pasted systematically into scrapbooks and annotated neatly in his florid English script in words so precise that one is surprised to realize that English was his second language. De Lorenzo had saved items "not just flutistic, but of general interest" since 1902, having begun during his early professional days in Cape Town, South Africa. In letters to friends since the early 1920s, he had expressed definite plans to write the first American book of biographies of flutists in the style of Richard Sheperd Rockstro, John Finn, and H. Macaulay Fitzgibbon. By 1947, he had completed *My Complete Story of the*

Flute, a book that turned out to be much more than a mere compilation of biographies. The book was to be published by a Los Angeles firm that specialized in metaphysical books. This publisher went out of business, however, before the book came out, but not before De Lorenzo had advanced money toward the publishing expenses. Dr. Joseph and Sudie Andrews Breco of Hollywood, close personal friends of the De Lorenzos, kindly stepped in and undertook the sponsorship. A New York publisher was found, but more delays occurred because this firm demanded a prepublication fee of $10,000 (a much higher figure than the first company had wanted) to cover the extra expense of the many photographs in the book. Eventually the contract was finalized with Citadel Press by July of 1950. The book appeared early in 1951, selling for six dollars a copy (twelve dollars deluxe). It eventually sold out. During the 1950s it was widely reviewed and praised in prominent newspapers and music journals such as the *Los Angeles Times*, the *Minneapolis Star*, the *Library of Congress Quarterly*, the *Christian Science Monitor*, the *International Musician, Symphony, Etude, Musical America, Quarterly Notes, Ricordiana, Redondo Beach Daily Breeze, Music Teacher, Palos Verdes News, Notes,* and *Musical Times*. The book also was listed in the *New York Times* "Book Reviews." An excerpt from the book was reprinted in the *Christian Science Monitor* (May 25, 1953).

De Lorenzo was called upon many times to give lectures on subjects from his book. Twice in 1958, he gave a lecture entitled "A Talk on the Flute," taken from material in *My Complete Story*. It was presented first to the Los Angeles Flute Club and later to the Association of University Women's Club of Santa Barbara. A short version of this talk is published in each of the C. F. Peters publications of De Lorenzo's compositions that appeared in the 1960s just after his death.

Though his reputation as one of the most eminent flutists and flute pedagogues of this century was well established long before 1951, the appearance of *My Story of the Flute* which prompted a flurry of formal recognitions of De Lorenzo and his many contributions. Immediately after the book came out, he was decorated by the Italian government with the Knighthood of Merit, and the World Academy of Artists and Professionalists named him an honorary member. In 1953, he was awarded the honorary doctorate in music by the Washington International Academy of Rome. Around this same time, De Lorenzo was elected Padrino (godfather) of the newly formed flute club in Milan, Italy. In addition, he was honored twice by the Los Angeles Flute Club, which organized performances of some of his musical compositions on June 28, 1953, and August 29, 1955 (the occasion of his eightieth birthday).

Though the book was an immediate success, De Lorenzo continued working on it: He arranged leftover materials and gathered new data. The first addenda was put out in 1954 and was delivered gratis with the purchase of the book. De Lorenzo intended that the materials included in the addenda become an integral part of a later edition. A second addenda, dedicated to Mrs. De Lorenzo, was printed in 1955 and was given "in gratitude to all those who have sent their beautiful letters of encouragement . . ."; and yet a third came out in 1957 when he was eighty-two years old. A number of photographs had been gathered for the second edition, but they were bequeathed to friends upon De Lorenzo's death.

In this second edition (1992), the addenda have not been integrated into the original text since it is not known exactly how De Lorenzo would have proceeded with this task. Rather, they have been appended in order at the end and are indexed together with the whole of the original book. The index was made expressly for this edition, there having been none in the first.

One of De Lorenzo's copious scrapbook albums, formed the basis for *My Complete Story* and consisted of 250 large pages of interesting reading matter with many illustrations. He referred to the scrapbook, which he had started before the turn of the century, as his "Encyclopedia of Learning and Information," and it was to have contained newspaper clippings on every conceivable subject. In 1953, De Lorenzo presented it with more than two hundred of his published and unpublished compositions, manuscripts of music by other composers, music books, flutes, and art relating to the flute in a formal dedication ceremony and concert on behalf of the Los Angeles Flute Club to the Hancock Foundation of the University of Southern California. He added continually to these collections until his death on July 29, 1962.

De Lorenzo's only stipulation to the gift was that the items be housed all in one place under the name Temple of Pan and that, if possible, a flute festival or annual flute concert be held in association with it. One regrets that these collections have been dispersed. The original flute collection consisted of only six specimens: a nose flute from the Philippines, a nineteenth century Austrian Schwegel fife, a Boehm system flute by Alfred Badger dated 1866, a Buffet piccolo from the mid-nineteenth century, the Rudall-Carte wood flute that De Lorenzo played for more than fifty years, and a German six-keyed flute by an anonymous maker. Several other instruments were added later. Besides the original manuscripts of compositions by De Lorenzo himself and composers such as Mary Carr Moore, Abelardo Albisi, and Quinto Maganini, other notable items in the collection are a collection by Carl Wehner, a pupil of Theobald Boehm, of autographs and photographs of flutists; original artworks of Louis Maurer, a lithographer on the staff of Currier and Ives; and a coin bearing the likeness of Frederick the Great, dated 1757 and which De Lorenzo kept in his flute case for many years. A small number of De Lorenzo manuscripts were not donated to USC and can be found in the Dayton C. Miller Collection of the Library of Congress in Washington.

Though this book was written from a personal, biographical perspective, it transcends such a limited view largely because the author himself, in his own thirst for every kind of knowledge about his instrument, its players, and its music, pursued a lively trans-global correspondence and friendships with many of the world's greatest musicians. In this book, De Lorenzo enhances information somewhat randomly from personal letters, musical programs, photographs, and newspaper clippings, with pertinent excerpts from journal articles and flute books then out of print and inaccessible. The result, though it may be lacking in modern scholarly appeal and perfectly accurate typography, is nonetheless an irresistible and humor-filled volume thoroughly accessible to any reader, musician or not. It has been enjoyed by such luminaries as President Truman and Grace Hemmingway. Yet, despite its popular appeal, no scholar can afford to overlook it. The book's many references to primary sources point readers of a scholarly bent toward a variety of possible tacks. Much of the important material, such as the biographical sketches of contemporary flutists and information on first performances of well-known flute pieces, is unavailable elsewhere. Though anecdotal in character, the biographies of many of the famous flutists and their immigrant pupils chronicle the assimilation of the various European national schools of flute playing into a respected American school. Though there is much more to the book than the title would imply, De Lorenzo's autobiography is not insignificant in itself. While telling his own story, he manages to give us a first-rate glimpse of musical thought during the first half of the century through the vision of a largely self-taught, highly independent and determined Italian-American immigrant, who rose from the most humble musical beginnings with his old-system flute to a prestigious career as solo flutist with America's greatest musical institutions.

My Complete Story of
The Flute

THE INSTRUMENT · THE PERFORMER
THE MUSIC

by Leonardo De Lorenzo

THE CITADEL PRESS, INC.

NEW YORK · 1951

MANUFACTURED IN THE UNITED STATES OF AMERICA
BY THE COLONIAL PRESS INC., CLINTON, MASS.

xxxii

To the Memory of My Beloved Mother

STELLA VINCENZA ALBERTI DE LORENZO
(1849–1907)

Preface

~~~~~~

This work on flutes and flutists has been on my mind for a number of years. I knew I would not be able to even begin putting together the material which I have garnered from here and there into book-form until I retired from active professional life.

Somehow, even after retiring in 1935, I procrastinated and postponed it until a few months had elapsed in the year of 1945. In the interim, the lovable Dr. Dayton C. Miller, famous physicist, flute lover, historian, and collector, passed on. The master flutist, Georges Barrère, is no more on this planet, and the great virtuoso and composer, Ary van Leeuwen, was stricken with partial paralysis and was unable to play his beloved flute any longer. Thus, of the veterans—a Frenchman, a Dutchman, and an Italian—I, who am apparently nearly whole, shall try to tell the story.

The title of this book could well have been *Reminiscences of a Flute Player*, but I prefer to put the emphasis on the flute itself.

In looking over my scrapbook I found some material which I could not resist using in its entirety—I felt that possibly many would like to share it with me, and so if I have quoted others a little too freely it was with that thought in mind.

If many of my bits of information, accumulated through long and patient research, are not acknowledged by source, it is only because it was not possible to do so; I humbly apologize to those writers whose names I do not know.

Following is a list of books, musical papers, magazines, etc. which have furnished me with valuable information:

Grove's Dictionary of Music and Musicians
International Who's Who in Music
Elbert Hubbard's *Little Journeys*
Pierre Key's *Musical Who's Who*
Who's Who Today in the Musical World
International Cyclopedia of Music and Musicians
Musical America
Musical Courier
Musical Quarterly
Etude
Musica d'Oggi
New Standard Encyclopedia of Knowledge (Frank H. Vize-telly)
Donald N. Ferguson's *A History of Musical Thought*
Will Durant's *The Story of Philosophy*
Edward McCurdy's *The Mind of Leonardo da Vinci*
Wesley La Violette's *Music and Its Makers*
Emil Medicus' *The Flutist*
Italo Piazza's *Breve dissertazione storico-critica sul flauto*
Pedro de Assisi's *Manual do flautista*.

It goes without saying that I helped myself freely from the works of Christopher Welch, John Finn, Adolph Goldberg, Richard Shepherd Rockstro, Macaulay Fitzgibbon, Fortunato Sconzo, Dr. Albert Schneider, and Dr. Dayton C. Miller.

A word of thanks for some translations from the German goes to our friend, Francesca Mann (Mrs. Theodor Mann).

It goes without saying that the help of my wife has been invaluable: it is very doubtful if this book could have been successfully completed without her assistance and encouragement.

I also wish to express my indebtedness to the editorial assistance of David Ewen, eminent musicologist and writer on music.

Villa Pan-by-the-Sea
Palos Verdes Estates, California
1950.

Table of Contents

LIST OF ILLUSTRATIONS

Indian Flute Band

Glinsky Safronoff and His Pupils
(Moscow, September 1929)

John Amadio   John Amans
George Drexler   Ernest Liegl

Leonardo De Lorenzo and His Pupils
(Eastman School of Music, 1932)

Philippe Gaubert   Claude-Paul Taffanel
Louis Fleury   Jean Louis Toulou

FOLLOWING PAGE 304

The Rochester Philharmonic Wind Quintet

René Le Roy   Henry C. Woempner
Arthur Lora   Joseph Mariano

Friedrich Kuhlau   Giulio Briccialdi
Emil Prill   Friedrich Dulon

Expressionless Group of 1886

The American Composers Woodwind Quintet

Marcel Moyse   Arrigo Tassinari
Jacques Ibert   Lambert C. Flack

xl

"Density 21.05"

"Il Velivolo" (The Airplane) Preludietto volante in la minore

Ruth Freeman	Harriet Peacock
Frances Blaisdell	Mildred Hunt Wummer
Vincenzo Demichelis	Ferruccio Arrivabene
Joseph La Monaca	Franz Doppler
Paul Wetzger	Julius Manigold
Michel Vita	Louis Maurer

Pan Playing the Transverse Flute

Sydney Flute Club

Dr. Joseph G. Breco

Leonardo De Lorenzo

Introduction

by WESLEY LA VIOLETTE, Mus.D.

Since unremembered time, the flute has been a symbol of man's "longing to touch the skirts of the dim distance"—an echo of his yearning for far-away things.

Here Leonardo De Lorenzo has garnered many mementos of the flute's history, its players, and the music they have played. He has not neglected the technical aspects of the instrument at the cost of general information; nor has he neglected the phases of particular interest to the flutist in order to interest the layman or the musician in some other field. All interests are included.

No one knows why one person likes to read about the flute, while another likes to play it. The author has recognized the interest of both, and has captured that which is as much a tribute to his understanding of human beings and artists as it is to his own artistry.

The human understanding is interwoven with the professional and he presents material for the performer as well as the listener. He has not forgotten that artists are human, and that many laymen have the same sensibilities as the artist but have not projected them in the field of art. The author's own relish for the material of art and life has involved him in many delectable experiences that he shares with the reader. The sharpness of his own susceptibilities has enabled him to delineate some of the more subtle aspects of his observations on the artists and culture of his time.

Whether you are a flute player, a music lover, or just blessed with a curiosity for life and the joy it holds, you will find much to interest and stimulate you in the pages of this book. Its author has been a recognized flutist for many years in symphony orchestras here in America and in other countries and has brought to this work not only a wide technical knowledge as an artist, but also a background of rich experience as a human being dealing with music and musicians.

The book should fill an important place in the literature of music. More than one reader will get a chuckle from some of the reminiscences. There is a sly sense of humor that flavors many of the anecdotes, and much musical knowledge savors the entire book. It is scholarly without being pedantic or dull, and it is discerning and penetrating without being bitter and caustic. Flutists will need to have it; and music lovers will want it for their libraries.

Los Angeles, 1949.

Part One

THE FLUTE

I | A Short History of the Flute

The wind played upon the river reeds, whose sigh was like music. One day, so long ago that it is lost in the mist of antiquity, someone plucked a reed, notched it with a crude implement, and blew upon it. To his infinite delight, he heard a musical sound. Was it thus that the primitive pipe—the rudimentary flute—came into existence?

Ancient flutes were known in China, Japan, India, and Egypt long before the dawn of Greek civilization. Primitive flutes have been found in Egyptian tombs, dating centuries before the Christian Era; more than any other musical instrument, the flute was depicted in early Egyptian wall paintings. The ancient flute was called "Nay." It was a long, thin, straight pipe held obliquely and blown across the open end held slightly at an angle. Other ancient Egyptian instruments, though commonly called flutes, were most likely played with reeds. However, even after omitting those instruments which were actually reed instruments but which have been translated as flutes, there are still left certain kinds of very ancient flutes which belong unmistakably in the legitimate flute family.

The best known of the ancient wind instruments is the Pandean pipes, or Pipes of Pan, or Syrinx, which achieved fame in

3

Greece. The single primitive pipe could produce only a single tone. To play a scale, or a melody, a series of hollow reeds of graduated lengths were tied together in a row, or sometimes in a bundle; by blowing across the open end of the reeds, the Greeks could produce musical sounds. They did not know they had invented an instrument. They, therefore, created a legend in which this honor went to the god Pan. According to this legend, Pan pursued the nymph Syrinx; as he was about to clasp her in his arms, she turned into reeds, out of which he fashioned the first pipes of Pan.

This ancient instrument could not produce a smooth progression from one tone to the next, because the instrument had to be shifted for each of the tones. There was, therefore, a need for a single pipe upon which all the notes of the scale (or melody) could be played. It was discovered before long that if a series of holes were bored into the side of the pipe, and if properly spaced, and covered by the fingers, the equivalent of a whole series of pipes could be realized. Blown without a reed such a pipe is a flute.

The double flute was used by the ancient Assyrians, Egyptians, Greeks and Romans; it is depicted in their works of art more frequently than the single pipe. This flute consisted of two distinct pipes, sometimes with a single mouthpiece. Usually the two pipes were not in unison. The melody as a rule was played on the longer, deeper pipe (called the male); the accompaniment, pitched higher than the melody, was played on the shorter pipe (female). When both were played together it was referred to as "married playing."

An Egyptian mural painting (a copy of which exists in the British Museum), dating from before 1300 B.C., represents a woman playing a double flute at a festival honoring the God Ptah. The Hebrews also had a double flute—the "Mashrokitha." We find double flutes also depicted on Indian monuments, such as the "Sanchi Tope Gate," *circa* 100 A.D.

The favorite wind instrument of the Greeks, however, was the "Aulos." It was primarily a reed-blow instrument; however, the name also included the reedless Pan's pipes and flute. (When, therefore, mention is made in Greek writings of the

4

flute, it is difficult to know whether the reed-blown instruments, strictly speaking not flutes, or the reedless pipes, are referred to.) Considerable controversy has been inspired over the question as to whether the transverse flute was known to the Greeks and Romans. If known, it surely found less favor than the reed instruments. Transverse flutes were known to the Chinese and Japanese from time immemorial. The Chinese "tsche" is the only ancient instrument which resembles our flute and which was sounded by the breath passing directly from the lips of the performer through the aperture in the instrument. The "tsche" is a transverse flute made of bamboo. Both ends of the instrument are closed; the mouth-hole is in the middle, at each end of which —at equal distances—are three finger holes as large as the bore. Great antiquity is claimed for the "tsche" by Chinese authorities who give *circa* 2637 B.C. as the date of origin. It is, indeed, interesting to speculate whether the European transverse flute is derived from this Chinese instrument. In India, the transverse flute was also known at a very early period. Some carvings of the god Krishna on various ancient monuments in Buddhist temples of Central India (*circa* 50 B.C.) contain representations of transverse flutes.

THE FIPPLE FLUTE. After the prolonged silence following the disappearance of the ancient Greeks, Romans, and Egyptians, the first flute to make its appearance was a vertical flute. Less skill was required in blowing if a "beak" or mouthpiece were added; consequently, this flute became known as the fipple flute, or *flute-à-bec*, and achieved considerable popularity in Western Europe. The fipple flute was so called because a plate, or plug, was inserted into the mouth which was partially blocked, narrowing the tube. In England this instrument was known as the "Recorder." In those days, "to record" meant to warble—to sing like a lark. The name was appropriate—for the instrument produced soft, sweet, mellow tones and had a facility for trilling. It was distinguished from other fipple flutes by the number of finger-holes: eight, seven for the fingers, and one in the back for the thumb. This instrument was built in various sizes from bass to soprano; different families of recorders were kept apart, each set in a case of its own. In 1511, when Henry VIII was on the

5

throne, the recorder was at the zenith of its popularity in England. The King, who practised every day on the flute, had a wonderful collection of instruments, more than 154; how many of these were lip flutes and how many recorders it is difficult to say.

By the end of the 17th century, the recorder was called flute, later the common flute; in France it was known as *flute-douce* or *flute-à-bec* to distinguish it from the German or transverse flute. It was used frequently by Handel and Bach in their scores. In Handel's orchestra it existed side by side with the German flute, giving the composer opportunities to exploit the varieties of flute color. Handel was usually careful to specify which flute he wanted calling the common flute, *"flauto,"* and the German flute *"traversa," "traversiera,"* or *"traverssiere."* When the orchestra was remodeled by Haydn only the transverse flute was retained.

THE TRANSVERSE FLUTE. The origin and early history of the transverse, or sideblown, flute is shrouded in mystery. Sources of information being few and imperfect, we know scarcely anything about it. Some authorities claim that it is comparatively modern; on the other hand, evidence exists that the transverse flute was known in Europe early in the Christian Era. If it did exist in pre-Christian Europe, it disappeared completely for several centuries, until reintroduced from Byzantine sources. Such knowledge as we possess of the early Christian period is derived chiefly from illuminated manuscripts and paintings.

Guillaume de Machaut (born *circa* 1300), a Provençal poet, musician, and composer, includes *"flauster traversiennes"* in a list of instruments of his period in *La Prise d'Alexandrie*. This would appear to be the earliest known mention of the transverse flute in literature. In 1511 we find the first engraving by Virdung. It was well-known in the time of Galileo. And in *The Life of Gargantua* by Rabelais (written in or about 1535) we find Gargantua playing on an *Alleman* (i.e. German) flute. However, the instrument then known in France as a German flute was called the *"Schweytzerpfeiff"* (Swiss pipe), or the *"Zwerchpfieff"* (Transverse pipe) in Germany.

This instrument, said to be of Swiss origin, is generally believed to be the earliest form of the transverse flute in medieval

6

Europe. It seems to have been developed more by the Germans than by any other people; but it was the French who produced the first great performers.

By the time of Agricola (16th century), flutes were made in a complete family (or choir) of four voices; consorts, or concerted groups, of flutes were popular. These early flutes were usually shown in illustrations and engravings: a cylinder of equal diameter throughout, with very small finger-holes and no joints. They were made of wood (generally boxwood) with a round mouth-hole (not until about 1724 do we find the oval mouth-hole). We cannot know its actual sound; but its unquestioned popularity, in spite of its crude construction and limited capabilities, lead us to believe that its unique charm of tone was always present to some extent. Like the recorder, the transverse flute was, at first, without holes for accidental notes; it was pierced only for the major diatonic scale in which it was made, and there were no keys. Six of the holes issued from its six-finger holes; the seventh was produced through the open end of the tube when all the holes were closed.

We come now to the first really significant improvement in the flute: the addition of a new finger-hole, giving D-sharp, produced by covering a closed key with the little finger of the right hand. This occurred in or about 1660, and the origin is unknown. Philibert, a famous French flutist, was the first one to distinguish himself on this improved flute. He was followed by La Barre and the renowned Hotteterre le Romaine. The latter is said to have been the first to play the transverse flute in the Opéra in Paris in or about 1697, in a work by Lully.

It is a curious episode in the history of the flute that constant opposition arose to suggestions for improving the instrument by piercing the tube with additional finger-holes. There were at this period no holes for the four notes of the chromatic octave; to produce these notes the player had to muffle or flatten the note above the accidental needed by closing one or more of the holes that were below the one from which came the note he wished to change. These notes were so impure, feeble, and out-of-tune as to cause the flute (and those who played it) to be held in contempt by other musicians. When Scarlatti was asked to hear

7

Quantz (the leading flute-player of his time) it is said his reply was that he did not like woodwind players because they never played in tune. Yet the one-keyed flute held its ground for about a century. It was considered perfect, and all deficiencies in performance were attributed to the player.

Quantz, while studying in Paris in 1726, made an interesting improvement in the flute by adding a second closed key to the foot-joint, thus making a difference between D-sharp and E-flat and at the same time improving the other notes. With the exception of these two keys, Quantz' flute seems to have been like others of his period. It consisted of four pieces, and there were five extra second joints of different lengths for altering the pitch. Quantz left elaborate directions for improving the imperfect notes. Sometimes he recommended turning inwards or outwards of the flute; sometimes he advised the partial closing or opening of certain holes to correct defects he evidently considered remediable. Although Quantz does not appear to have thought of effecting any radical improvement in the instrument, there is no doubt he made the finest use of the limited resources at his command. More than any other musician of his time, he not only popularized the flute but made it worthy of performing the finest music.

The demand for holes for the chromatic notes became, at last, too insistent to be further ignored. About forty years after Quantz had added the E-flat key, holes were bored for F-natural, G-sharp, and B-flat, and covered with keys. (The exact year when this occurred is unknown.) Between 1770 and 1780, flutes with new keys, although unrecognized in Paris and Berlin came into use in London. They were first introduced by Tacet and Fiorio both of whom had the courage to revolt and to adopt a flute with no less than six keys. Their example was quickly followed by others in England, and—eventually—the new flute came into use in Europe.

The advantages conferred on the transverse flute by completing the chromatic octave was formidable. The instrument was now pierced with holes for all the semitones but one (C-2 key); that key was not generally adopted until about the beginning of the next century when the six-keyed flute was superseded by the eight-keyed flute.

The improvements made by Quantz, Blavet, Tromlitz, Petersen, Monzani, and Cappeller—down to Cappeller's pupil, Boehm —have made the flute the most nearly perfect of all wind instruments.

The progress of the instrument may be observed in representative collections, such as the one on exhibit in the Metropolitan Museum of Art in New York City.

From a simple tube with the ventages so placed as to be within convenient reach of the fingers, the flute has become— after centuries of patient research and experiment—a scientifically proportioned instrument. As the flute has a greater number of ventages than any individual possesses fingers, the greatest achievement of the contemporary flute-maker has been to invent a system of keys with a cleverly contrived mechanism which has eliminated all technical difficulties.

Only a few of those whose inventions helped make the flute the wonderful instrument it is today have been mentioned above; but it is to one man in particular that the world at large owes a debt of profound gratitude. All flutists revere his name and memory, and worship at his shrine. To them he seems to have been possessed of almost superhuman power. He was Theobald Boehm. It was he who developed the flute from an imperfect, poorly toned and unsatisfactory instrument in all respects to the remarkable one which today bears his name and is used in all parts of the civilized world. Besides having possessed rare mechanical genius, Boehm was a remarkable virtuoso, teacher, and composer. His life was one of rare usefulness and unselfish devotion to improving flute-building and flute-playing. So much has been said and written about this unique man that virtually every musician is familiar with his history.

Of the innumerable so-called improvements on the Boehm flute, only two are outstanding. The original open G-sharp flute was converted into a closed one by Dorus which, though not approved by Boehm, is nevertheless widely used. And Briccialdi added the very important B-flat key or lever (left-hand thumb).

9

The respective merits of the closed G-sharp and the open G-sharp flutes have long been subjected to heated debate. The advocates of the latter contend that the scale is more logical with the open G-sharp, not only because one vent is opened at a time in the chromatic scale, but also because it has the advantage of one opening less which, on the closed G-sharp flute, weakens an important note: the third E.

The French-model flute, with holes on the finger plates, is used by many excellent flutists, while others of equal eminence prefer the standard or closed-finger plates. Will the flute of the future be of a single-system like the violin, for example, with all flutes constructed of the same material, whether that material be wood, gold, platinum, or a combination of all three? Such a development would, at least, end all debates!

II | *The Family of Flutes— And Some Members*

THE FLUTE FAMILY: (Pan pipes, nose flutes, Chinese bamboo flutes, etc. do not belong in this family).

Concert Flute.

Ottavino, or *Flauto Piccolo* (piccolo or small flute).

Flute in G: A fourth below, sometimes called the tenor flute, contralto flute, or (erroneously!) bass flute. This is the most beautiful and the most successful of the entire family of flutes next to the concert flute or piccolo.

German Flute, or *Flute Allemande*.

Flute d'Amour in A-flat (or minor-third below).

Albisiphone: bass flute in C played vertically and also called the *flautone*.

Bass Flute in C, or *Flautone* (played transversely).

Flute à Bec, or Flageolet.

Flute Discant, or Flageolet in F (fourth above).

English Flute, or Flageolet.

Ancient, or Kazoo Flute, also called Eunuch.

Terzino di flauto in Mi bemolle (a military band-flute in E-flat).

Flautino, or *Quartino di Flauto in F* (a military-band flute a fourth higher.

11

Ottavino, or *Flauto Piccolo All'Ottava* (piccolo an octave higher).

*   *   *   *

FLUTE IN G. This beautiful instrument has been called by various names—notably bass flute, tenor flute, contralto flute, and *flute-d'Amour*. I think it should be called simply Flute in G. It is easy to play, and its ever-increasing popularity is justified. Its relation to the flute is the same as the bass-clarinet to the clarinet and the English horn to the oboe. America manufactures the finest of these flutes. Among the many composers who have written beautifully for this instrument was Maurice Ravel.

As soon as I came to the Eastman School of Music in 1923, I asked that institution to purchase a Flute in G. They did— and, consequently, they have an excellent instrument. When one of the two conductors there learned that a Flute in G had been acquired, he brought out a new composition by the English composer, Arthur Bliss, a Suite emphasizing flute passages and in which the Flute in G is accompanied by the strings in a magnificent solo. The second flutist became quite upset when he saw the music. The conductor then turned to me and said: "Mr. De Lorenzo, will you do me the favor of playing the solo on the Flute in G?" I hesitated, explaining that the Flute in G was a closed G-sharp and I played on an open G-sharp instrument. "I know that you can do it," the conductor insisted, "even if there is a little difference in the manipulation. Please—I shall be grateful to you."

I brought the instrument to my studio, dismissed my pupils, and went to work for the entire afternoon on the solo passage. However, the suite also had a number of important solos for the ordinary flute, and thus made the interchange from the one flute to the other extremely difficult. Fortunately, since the Suite was intended for a "Little Symphony Concert," there was only one rehearsal, which suited me. Before the concert, I was almost tempted to emulate the German flutist, Wilhelm Barge (Reinecke's *Undine* Sonata is dedicated to him) who always prayed to God before performing at an important concert. The performance, I am happy to relate, went well—so well that the piece was repeated (the second time the performance was some-

12

what less perfect because I had meanwhile been fingering my own flute!). The conductor asked me to stand up twice, and thanked me by saying: "Bravo, I knew that you could do it beautifully!" I must confess here and now that there *was* a minor slip in my playing in the first number following the Flute in G solo, but, apparently, it went unnoticed.

The man responsible for the popularity of the Flute in G in motion-picture studios in Hollywood is Robert Russell Bennett, that excellent composer and arranger who is known to flutists for his splendid *Rondo Capriccioso* for four flutes. Bennett wrote a short solo for the Flute in G, with orchestral accompaniment, when working for one of the studios. The directors were so delighted with the novel and beautiful effects produced by that instrument that they asked Bennett to write more. Other studios followed suit, with the result that flute players in Hollywood went scurrying in search of a Flute in G.

Now that I am on the subject of Robert Russell Bennett and his flute quartet, I would like to tell a story about it. One afternoon, with four advanced students, I was rehearsing this quartet for a radio performance and for a later concert at Kilbourn Hall. I requested the four young players to do their very best in this work which I said was one of the finest in the literature for the flute. The second flutist said: "Mr. De Lorenzo, will you allow me to express my opinion?" I knew that the young musician was unsympathetic to the work, so I said: "You may—but do you think you are good enough a musician to pass judgment? However—let us hear your verdict." "Well," was the response, "I really don't know how to put it, but there is something very unsympathetic about it. I guess it's *too* American."

BASS FLUTE IN C: All the flute students at the Eastman School of Music had the privilege of playing on the fine flute in G owned by that institution; and young composers there began introducing the instrument into their scores, both in chamber-music and symphonic works. However, many students had never seen a real Bass Flute in C, and requested me if I could possibly procure one. As at that time (1930) there were none in America, I ordered one from England—as I had previously received a pamphlet from an English flute firm describing its beautiful sounds and ease of production. The pamphlet claimed that this instrument was so easy to use that one could play all flute duets, with another playing on the ordinary flute. I also knew that Dr. Dayton C. Miller had recently acquired one for his flute collection. When the instrument finally arrived, after several months, I was notified by the custom house that the duty would be more than $100.00. I tried to explain that the instrument was meant for educational purposes, that none were manufactured in this country—but my arguments were to no avail. When I received the instrument, one of the keys had been torn off—in inspection, I presume. I had it repaired as soon as possible, but it never worked so well as the firm claimed it would. There was always a leak some place and the low notes would not play. I had it looked over two or three times but, although it was put into somewhat better shape, the low C-sharp and C-natural never were really satisfactory. However, I did manage to play on it quite well, and once or twice played a little piece for our friends in Beverly Hills. Unlike the bass-clarinet, the English horn, and the contrabassoon, all of which are usually made of wood, this bass flute is made of metal, and is easily overblown.

The following story about the Bass Flute in C was told to me by a violinist-friend who, though usually reliable in all things, is somewhat careless of facts in his story-telling. Nevertheless he assures me that this story actually took place when he was a member of an orchestra:

A famous American symphony orchestra (not, he emphasized, the New York Philharmonic-Symphony; and the conductor was not Toscanini) made a tour of Europe, playing many novelties including a work of Ravel in which a short but prominent solo for Bass Flute in C appears. "This little solo," the violinist said, "consisted only of three notes in the lower register of the huge flute—A-flat, D, C. The first two notes were accompanied by muted strings, but the lowest C was by itself at the end of that movement." The personnel of the orchestra had three flute players. Since several other players had been added for this important tour, it was decided to have one musician devote himself entirely to the Bass Flute in C and that short solo, so that he would not have to change from that instrument to the regular

14

flute in C. After a number of rehearsals in New York, the orchestra came to Paris. The night of the concert arrived; one could see that the performer on the Bass Flute in C was nervous and worried. At the concert itself, only the first note came out fairly well; the second was a whisper and faded out immediately. The lowest C did not come out at all! And this musician had been engaged to play those three notes, and for this purpose had been brought all the way from America! No wonder that he made a vow that as long as he lived he would never again look at a Bass Flute! If it was any consolation for the poor musician, the Musicians' Union collected for him the fee for the entire tour.

In commenting on the above story—which may be true or false—I should like to add that the Bass Flute has never been a success. Why, then, not relegate it to the oblivion it deserves— in the company of such other forgotten flutes as "the little flute in the 22nd" which Monteverdi (1567-1643) used in his opera *Orfeo?* (That little imp sounded three octaves higher than written!) Unless someone invents a Bass Flute which will not make the life of its performer miserable, it might be wise to forget it entirely.

THE GIORGI FLUTE. The *Scientific American* of December 18, 1897 gives the following description of the Giorgi keyless flute and the experiences of the inventor in this country:

This flute has a mouthpiece curved in the direction of the length of the flute, with a mouth-hole on its top, and a resounding chamber extending below the line of communication between the mouthpiece and the body of the flute. It has all the eleven holes necessary to the chromatic scale, each hole being adapted to be closed independently without cross-fingering, and keys are not necessary. The mouthpiece is at the upper end of the pipe, along which the air is blown straight, the notes being of perfect intonation and quality of sound from the lowest to the highest.

Signor Giorgi was professor of the flute in the Royal Academy, of Florence, Italy, for five years. At the same time he was Secretary of the Philharmonic Society of Florence. He received the Grand Prix at the Bologna International Musical Exposition in

1888, a medal at the Paris Exposition in 1889, and one at the Chicago Exposition in 1893. It was while exhibiting his new and improved flute at the World's Fair that the following extraordinary events occurred:

The flute (rich in ornament) was shown with other instruments in the Canadian section of the Manufacturers' Building, in a handsome showcase. One morning, soon after the publication of the prizes, the showcase in which the flute had been exposed was found broken open. The flute was gone. The police made every effort to uncover the thief but were unsuccessful.

A few days later, Giorgi began receiving one letter after another which stated that the thieves (signed "The Modern Robin Hood" or "Friar Tuck") were two wealthy men who had taken the flute on a wager. They would return it, but only on certain conditions. These conditions—while repugnant to the artist— were complied with, and he received the flute back within a reasonable period. All the letters received by Giorgi on the subject of his flute were printed by hand.

After the flute had been restored, Giorgi brought it to the San Francisco Mid-Winter Fair. The exposition opened on Saturday, January 27. On the following Monday, the 29th, the flute disappeared in the same mysterious way it had done in Chicago. The police could find no clue; and the flute was never again seen.

Having several engagements as soloist, Giorgi was obliged to get another instrument. As he understood the Boehm system he secured one of C. G. Conn's "wonder" flutes, made of silver, but with gold keys. This he guarded constantly. At a charity concert, for the benefit of sufferers from the Spanish inundation, the flute disappeared just when Giorgi was about to leave the room. This time—after a few days' search—the instrument was found in the possession of a lady of high social standing, who had taken it only as a joke, having heard repeatedly the stories of previous robberies. Although Giorgi forgave this theft, he formed very peculiar ideas of the manners and customs of this country, and he left directly for Europe—with no little relief, no doubt!

Finding himself unable to avenge himself on his friends, "The

16

Modern Robin Hood" and "Friar Tuck," Giorgi soon set himself the task of constructing a flute which—with the addition of the beautiful tone and intonation of the first instrument—could be produced so cheaply and simply as to provide little temptation to either thieves or practical jokers.

III A Thing or Two About Flutes

I. OF ANTIQUITY

Confucius played melancholy tunes on his flute.

*   *   *   *

The Egyptians had a long flute, called the "Nay." It was held transversely, and was of such length that the player's arms were stretched out to their full length, extended downwards.

*   *   *   *

A curious bronze flute with a wood or reed core was excavated in Karanis, near Cairo, Egypt, in August 1930 by Michigan University Archaeologists. Coins of gold, silver and copper were found in great numbers. There were also many private letters and portions of Greek literary text. Among the latter, a roll containing a considerable part of Homer's Iliad was found just in front of the oven belonging to a granary. There were two stone temples, one dedicated to the Egyptian gods Pnepheros and Petesouchos, the other to Sarapis. The bronze flute, apparently, had been in good company all those years.

19

Pliny, in his treatise *Naturalis Historia* (which he presented to the Emperor Titus in 77 A.D.) wrote that "all that human art has thought out in the torturing music of the flute, may be found in a bird's little throat!"

*   *   *   *

With the introduction of the flute in the Pythian games, the art of playing it well became a matter of noble competition throughout Greece. No Pythian games were complete without flute players. The word *Pythaules* was coined, meaning a distinguished flute soloist—in distinction to *Choraules*, a flutist accompanying the chorus. In Roman times, even the *Choraules* was honored, was feted as a victor, with his laurel wreath appearing on his tombstone.

*   *   *   *

The sacrificial flutes of the Etruscans were made of boxwood; the concert flutes were of lotus wood, asses' bones.

*   *   *   *

Pliny says that Midas was the inventor of a flute called *libia obliqua*, or *vasca*, which had a small tube (almost at right angles to the main pipe), and contained a reed through which the player blew holding the instrument sideways.

*   *   *   *

The flute of Telaphanes of Samos is said to have had equal power over man and brute.

*   *   *   *

Olympus, a Phrygian poet and composer (in or about 630 B.C.) was credited by Plato, Aristotle and Plutarch with the introduction of the flute into Greece from Asia.

*   *   *   *

Aristotle said that, at first, the flute was considered an ignoble instrument, only suitable for mean people and not for free men. After the defeat of the Persians, however, it was much valued,

20

and it became a disgrace for a gentleman not to be able to play it.

* * * *

Boethius was the most copious of the Roman writers on music, including the flute. His most voluminous treatise is called *De Institutione Musica.*

* * * *

The oldest tradition of the art of flute playing points to the Peloponnesos in accord with the charming legend recounting that the flute of Marsyas was driven by the waves of the sea to Sicyon, and there found by a shepherd lad. As late as the days of Pausanius (5th century B.C.) this flute was still shown in a temple of that city.

* * * *

Among its devotees have been many historical personages of the past: Pharaohs, Emperors, Kings, Princes, and other noblemen, generals, poets, statesmen, scientists, famous composers, men of affairs, etc. Some of these enthusiastic dilettanti were excellent performers.

* * * *

The first wind instrument mentioned in the Bible is believed to be identical with the "Pandean Pipes." It was well-known to the Greeks under the name of "Syrinx," being made with from three to nine tubes, but usually with seven (a number also mentioned by Virgil). It is known in China as "Koantfee," with twelve tubes of bamboo; and was used by the Peruvians under the name of "Huayrapuhura," being made of cane and of a greenish steatite or soapstone.

* * * *

The flute was a symbol of death and mourning in both ancient Rome and Egypt, as no funeral (pretentious or simple) was conducted without a band of flutists. When Nero said, "Call me the flute players," it signified that death sentence had been meted out to some unfortunate member of his official family. Flutists were so well remunerated—and lived so luxuriously —that a proverb was born: "To flute players nature gave brains,

21

there's no doubt; but alas! 'tis in vain, for they soon blow them out."

* * * *

The excessive and exaggerated popularity of the flute in ancient times of glory for Greece and Rome led to so violent a reaction that soon after the fall of Rome the cultivation of the instrument was looked upon as a special sin by the Canons of Saint Paul. Flute players who had enjoyed prosperity and luxury were now excommunicated and denied baptism! The flute regained its popularity, but it took more than a thousand years.

* * * *

Terpander of Arcadia and Ardalos (7th century B.C.) were the first to practise singing to the sound of a flute.

Terpander, a professional Greek musician, was born at Antissa, in the island of Lesbos. He went to Sparta, and in 676 was crowned victor in the first musical contest at the feast of Apollo Carneius. He established there the first musical school in Greece, and is credited with the enlargement of the compass of the lyre to an octave. Terpander was the first to set poetry regularly to music.

* * * *

In Volume VIII of *Wonder Book of World's Progress* by Henry Smith Williams (Funk and Wagnalls, 1935), five interesting illustrations of the flute, and its ancient history, are to be found. On page 84, there is "Pan and Apollo." Pan is teaching Apollo to play on his Pan pipes. On page 134, there is "A Puppet Show at Pompeii," picturing a long-bearded old man manipulating puppets on a long string to the amusement of two maids and a youth, and a little boy looking over the wall; the music is furnished by a young man playing on a double flute. On page 138, there is "Roman Festival," portraying a sort of Bacchanal in which everyone appears to be having a hilarious time; the music is provided by two young ladies, one playing the lyre, the other a double flute. On page 154, "Tiberius at Capri," an Emperor is found seated under a gorgeous pergola, entertained by a number of charming young ladies and young children with what appears to be a tiger nearby stretched out on the floor with

22

an air of unconcern; the music is again provided by a young lady playing the double flute. Finally, on page 169, is pictured Aurelius Prudentius, "Chief Christian poet of the early church"; a lyre and a double flute are again to be seen played by two young ladies with a Saint next to them, giving the benediction.

*   *   *   *

I would like to reproduce here a part of an article about ancient instruments by P. J. Nolan published in *Musical America* some years ago:

"A flute fashioned centuries ago from a human tibia, and now seared and yellow with age, sounded its limpid, clear notes to a little group of listeners in a New York apartment the other day. The melody, a call down the ages to the stress and tumult of this modern city, was plaintive in its significance, for it linked two great epochs of civilization, separated by hundreds of years. The flute was found in explorations in the land of the Incas; but it is possible, of course, that it is a relic of an even earlier race. Who can say that the melancholy cry of this flute may not have been a message from the Lost Atlantis?

"The tones were surprisingly clear; as clear, perhaps, as when the flute was first sounded in the festal dances of the antique people to which it originally belonged. As the listeners throught of the strange history of the instrument, the simple notes were thrilling in their effect. The modern apartment and the roar of traffic vanished, as one's imagination took flight to the days of the dynasty of benevolent despots in Peru, and to still more remote days, to which belong speculations of that mystery of the plateau of Lake Titicaca in the Andes, with its ruined monoliths, the origin and history of which were unknown even to the Incas.

"The player of the flute was Daniel Alomia Robles, who devoted a quarter of a century of his life to the investigation of the Inca civilization; and this instrument was only one of a unique collection from the Inca period, or before it, which Mr. Robles exhibited to his deeply interested audience. There were many other flutes, or quenas, either of bone or cane; there were sets of Pan pipes, and there were quaint little three-note instru-

23

ments crudely resembling birds, and made of terra cotta. One small flute he received as a gift from the government of Bolivia, and others he found in explorations in the tombs of Peru.

"What a world of speculation was conjured up by the tones of this ancient flute! Far back into the pre-Christian era runs the tradition of races which inhabited Peru. On the shores of Lake Titicaca, to the south of the territory which the Incas occupied, are the ruins of a great city. The people who built that city, long before the foundation of the Incan empire, were not only skilled masons and draughtsmen, but they possessed a secret which was known to the Egyptians—that of employing cyclopean masses of stone in the construction of huge edifices like the pyramids. One of the stones found among these ruins weighed 170 tons. How were these enormous blocks of stone transported from quarries, and piled into position? How was that great doorway at Tiahuanacu set up, with its highly ornamented and elaborately carved facade? Who built at Cuzco, on Sachsahuman Hill, that gigantic and imposing fortress, the origin of which is as securely wrapped in mystery as is the origin of the Tiahuanacu ruins? Did this stalwart race of men come from Egypt, bringing with them the skilled craftsmanship they had acquired in that country? What fascinating speculation is this! Were the ears of some of these builders charmed by the simple notes of the flute heard in that New York apartment the other day? Perchance these were the craftsmen of the Lost Atlantis, who have left as their legacy to future ages only a few musical instruments and the giant monoliths scattered about an Andean plateau."

*　　*.　　*　　*

The Emperor Hwang Ti (B.C.) of China set his ministers to cutting bamboo tubes which could be blown to imitate the notes of the Phoenix birds.

*　　*　　*　　*

Flutes have been excavated from the ruins of Egypt, Greece, Asia Minor, India, Jerusalem, Mesopotamia, Palestine, Etruscan and Roman towns, including Rome proper. Only recently (in 1928) the original Pan's Pipes or Syrinx's scale was excavated in

24

Greece, and in 1930 a curious bronze flute lined with cane was unearthed in Karamis, near Cairo.

*   *   *   *

II. OF EXOTIC LANDS

The word "flute" is said to be derived from "fluta," a lamprey or small eel taken in the Sicilian seas, having seven holes, just below the gills, precisely the number of those on the old flute. There is a most interesting and peculiar phenomenon of nature in Spain called Vista Oriental de les Flautes. It consists of a group of long-pointed stone peaks in close formation, resembling a bunch of flutes in an astonishing manner.

*   *   *   *

It is almost beyond human comprehension that the gentle and beautiful flute could ever have been associated with cruel superstition and barbarism. Yet the following article reveals only too forcefully to what depths man has descended in the past in his unspeakable stupidity:

"For the great festival of Tezcatlipoca, the handsomest and noblest of the captives of the year had been chosen as the incarnate representative of the god, and paraded through the streets for public admiration dressed in an embroidered mantle, with plumes and garlands on his head and a retinue like a king; for the last month, they married him to four beautiful girls representing four goddesses; on the last day, wives and pages escorted him to the little temple of Tiacochcalco, where he mounted the stairs, breaking an earthenware flute against each step; this was a symbolic farewell to the world, for as he reached the top he was seized by the priests, his heart torn out and held up to the sun, his head spitted on the tzompantli (stake), and his body eaten as sacred food, the people drawing from his fate the moral lesson that riches and pleasure may turn into poverty and sorrow."

*   *   *   *

Another instance of mingling the flute with absurd superstition: "On the middle Septik River, the male brown-skinned

25

savages of the Prince Alexander Mountains play on bamboo flutes which women are not allowed to see or even guess that it is a human who produces sound. It is supposed to be such a mysterious music that as soon as the women hear it they run. The men, at times, sit whole nights long, playing on these long bamboo flutes and beating their drums; a (slight) price to pay, they think, to insure that their children shall grow tall, strong . . . and fearless!"

*   *   *   *

A newspaper item syndicated by the United Press, and originating in San Francisco, California: "There is a spot on the globe where a man can get a wife just by trading a battered old flute. The story of this junk-dealer's paradise was related here by Dr. Margaret Mead, anthropologist and assistant curator of the American Museum of Natural History of New York, when she arrived after a year with a tribe of New Guinea cannibals and head-hunters. After disembarking at Aitape and traveling 280 miles up the Septik River, Dr. Mead found herself in the country of the Mundugamors, a nation some 1,200 strong. She studied their habits and described the most curious of these. Tribal leaders, who had eight or ten wives, bartered cousins and sisters for mates; or, in case there was a shortage of female relatives, a flute. Among other curiosities, Dr. Mead lists the usage of green snail shells for currency; women marrying at an average age of seventeen; and an arrangement whereby women do all the work, while men strive to amuse themselves."

*   *   *   *

According to H. Macauley Fitzgibbon in *The Story of the Flute*: "In India, flute players were usually men of lower caste, the one exception being made in favor of the nose-flute used by the Brahmins. The snake-charmers used a double-pipe, blown through the nose, called 'Toomerie' or 'Poongee.' Numerous nose-flutes are to be met with in Borneo, South America, Java, Siam, Fiji, above all in Ataheite (where the natives often spend the whole day lying in hammocks playing pipes and flutes), and the Polynesian Islands. Melville, in Typee, describes these curious instruments (called 'Vivo') thus: 'The nose-flute is longer than the ordinary fife, is made of a beautiful scarlet-colored reed, and has four or five stops (fingerholes) with a larger hole near one end, which latter is held just underneath the left nostril. The other nostril being closed by a peculiar movement of the muscles of the nose, the breath is forced into the tube and produces a soft dulcet sound. Sometimes the right nostril of the player is closed by the thumb of the right hand whilst its fingers stop the fingerholes. They are often adorned with lines and figures scorched on the surface, and sometimes with human hair.' Also the fierce Paupens—who are very fond of music—use nose flutes, Pan pipes, Jew's harps, flutes and drums, all of their own fabrication."

*   *   *   *

The affinity of religion and the flute, with some Indian tribes were, in pre-Columbian times, positively synonymous, as the following will show:

"God of the flute—Blue flute people—Flute and Prayer of the desert god—Reed flutes and flutes of high Mystery—The Spirit leader of the Flute ceremony—The Secret order of the Flute, instituted—Prayer Flute of the far desert—The Sign of the Flute of the gods—The worship of Pan—The Music of the desert gods is the music of the flute; let it not be silenced by trumpets of brass made by White men who conquer." The above sentences and many others are to be found throughout the book *The Flute of the Gods* by Marah Ellis Ryan (The Copp, Clark Co., Limited, Copyright 1909 by Frederick A. Stokes Co.).

It was difficult for the Indians to understand why the main attraction of the white men, when they invaded their country, was gold, which the natives called Sun Father or Yellow Metal. "It must be," the Indians said, "strong medicine and very precious to them." It was not possible for them to make clear that the virtue of the yellow metal was not a sacred thing; only a thing of barter as shell beads or robes might be.

Some tribes of cannibal Indians, who had neither seen or heard of a flute or religion, and who fought continuously all

27

other Indian tribes as well as the new white intruders, were so ferociously barbarous that they stole young women from all other tribes but their own not, however, for sexual pleasure, which was a minor consideration, but in order to breed babies for them to eat, as they were gluttons for tender human flesh. N.B. see *Admiral of the Ocean Sea*, by Samuel Eliot Morison (Atlantic Monthly Press, 1942).

*   *   *   *

The following is taken from an undated newspaper clipping in my collection of articles on flutes and flute-playing:

"Since music is peculiarly divine to the Hindus, the Brahmin must undergo a severe sacrifice in the second quarter of his life. He must abstain from music, singing, dancing, gaming."

Though the instrument is not divine, it may be the subject for taboo:

"Among the Taiyal and Tsuou tribes in the Malay Peninsula the nose-flute holds this position: Its use is taboo except on the most solemn occasions, such as the celebration of a victory. It is played through one nostril only: in New Zealand, the right nostril; in Tahiti, the left. Getting a good tone is difficult; personally, I have been unable to get any."

Domineering man warns the women away from the nose-flute in Formosa, and from the drum in Lapland. Among the Mafulu people of New Guinea, the work of making a drum has to be done over again if a woman happens to look on it even accidentally.

*   *   *   *

As late as the end of 1919, a noted explorer who sailed for the Amazon River, South America, made a fortunate escape from an unknown jungle inhabited by a race more barbarous than the South Sea savages. All the women, except the favorite wife of the chief, are excluded from eating the human flesh. The arm bones are made into flutes. The forearm and fingerbones are dried and used to stir kawam, or soup. And teeth, and often the fingers, are made into necklaces so that the spirits can never use them in paradise.

28

The great flute collection of the late Dr. Dayton C. Miller (now in the Library of Congress in Washington, D. C.) has an interesting specimen.

Australia and New Zealand claim the unenviable honor of possessing the majority of flutes made from human bones!

Several interesting articles on these gruesome flutes appeared some years ago in the *Evening Post* of Wellington, New Zealand; others, in a newspaper from Sydney, Australia. The whole story of these flutes is so repulsive and fantastic that—silence is golden!

* * * *

The flute of Basutoland, South Africa, is made from crow's feather, a bit of dried gut, and a piece of plank. But the cows love it. The herdsman never calls them. When it is time to return home, he merely pipes a tune and the cattle gather around him, and he then leads them quietly back home, still playing.

* * * *

A Yaqui Indian, Manuel Ayala, plays flute and drum at the same time, an example of complicated rhythms of Guadalupe.

* * * *

Netsuke is the Japanese art of miniature comic-carving. There is a Netsuke in ivory not more than an inch tall, showing the elegant Chinese Emperor, Ming Huang, seated on his throne, teaching his consort, Yank Kwei-fei, to play the flute. She is playfully dumb, he is adoringly exasperated. It is carved underneath as well, and the bottom of the feet and impressions of the sitters in the cushions of the throne arouse gales of laughter (from *Challenge* by Upton Close).

* * * *

In the 1931 Agricultural Exposition series of stamps issued by the former Italian colony of Tripolitania, there was one for twenty-five centesimi picturing an Arab musician playing a simple flute.

29

"Taumatawkakatangihangakauotanenuiarangikitanatahau" is a beautiful hill in New Zealand. It means: "The hill upon which Rangi sat and played the flute to his lady-love."

* * * *

A small shepherd's pipe which had been clutched in the hand of a dead child for some six thousand years was unearthed by excavations under the direction of Dr. E. A. Speiser of the University of Pennsylvania at Tepe Gawra in Northern Iraq, Persia.

* * * *

Flutes made from the jaws of bears were found recently by Prof. Brodar of Cilli, Jugoslavia. It is believed that primitive man fashioned the flutes 25,000 years ago. They are in the Museum of Natural History in that country.

* * * *

In the Special Issue of *Musical America* (February 1946) there is an interesting picture of a "Bolivian Orchestra in Native Costume." Out of fifteen performers, eight are playing on the pandean pipes. Seated on the floor are two young women playing on other quaint instruments, but, on the ground near them can be seen at least five small vertical flutes.

* * * *

"A brilliant new generation of painters invades U. S. Galleries." This headline appeared in *Life* Magazine (June 3, 1946). Three pages were devoted to Feliciano Pena, Chavez Morado (two pictures), Rufino Tamayo, David Sigueiros, Alfonso Michel, and Rufino Tamayo's "The Flute Player." It seems to be an atrociously ugly piece of modern art. The great figure of the flute player is that of a distorted Indian-Negro in the nude, with his ribs sticking out, and what appears to be a huge mandolin at his feet and a bowl of fruit, makes for such a lugubrious picture that my wife said: "Be sure not to have it in any other room but the basement, the garage, or the—dog-house!" However, we are assured that Rufino Tamayo is one of the most famous of contemporary Mexican artists. A pure Zapotec Indian, born in

Caxaca, Tamayo spent most of his life in Mexico and is now living in New York. There he continues to turn out wild but subtly painted canvases which are reminiscent of ancient Mayan ritual art.

Because of the exaggerated irregularities of "The Flute Player" (his nostrils are so wide that a small egg could be inserted in them!), it has been variously described as a "veritable monstrosity," and a "masterpiece of modern art."

The Aztec are Indian people who settled in Mexico about 1100. Their powerful kingdom with the capital where Mexico City now stands, and its language, still survive. They knew about astronomy and a method of reckoning time.

They worshipped many gods and used picture writing. Their priests and medicine men had great powers and human sacrifices were demanded. However, when these credulous people first saw white men arrive they knelt, thinking they were all gods. They soon changed their minds when Cortez, in 1519, brutally destroyed this once great Empire. One of their prehistoric pueblo palaces in New Mexico contained 500 rooms and was situated on nearly twenty-six acres of land, which, in 1923 was declared by the United States Government a National Monument.

The Mayans were American Indian people of Central America. They were a docile race with a considerable sense of spirituality and highly artistic, as is shown by the ruins of their great cities in Yucatan, Cambeche, Guatemala, Honduras, etc., where they enjoyed an advanced civilization for over 2000 years. Their impressive architectural remains at Copan, Quirigua, Palenque and other places reminds one today of their grandeur. They had also a remarkable system of chronology reaching back to the sixth century B.C. and which was recorded in a peculiar glyphic script not yet wholly deciphered.

Two books from which may be gathered considerable historical information are titled: *The Flute of the Gods* (Mayan) by Marah Ellis Ryan, published by the Copp, Clark Company, Toronto in 1909, and *Flute of the Smoking Mirror* (Aztek) by Frances Gillmor, published by the University of New Mexico Press in 1949. In religious and sacrificial functions both people used vertical flutes of clay. It seems that the Aztec, the oldest

31

civilization of the two, was the most superstitious to a point of incredible barbarism. The following are a few of the names of their kings, priests, caves, mountains, etc.: Nezahualcoyotl (the Poet-King whose name means Hungry Coyote), Tzinacanoztoc (name of a cave), Ixtlilxochitl, Matalcihuatl, Tozquentzin, Huitzilihuitl (Humming Bird), Azcapotzalco, Azalxochitl, etc. Both these books have interesting illustrations. There seems to be also a ghastly affinity between these two people in the ritual of sacrifice. In both, the young person chosen for sacrifice must smash a flute on each step before he reaches the place of his doom where the medicine man will slash his breast open and tear out his heart.

Of the few other American pre-Columbian civilizations, the Incas and its empire, dating from about 1230 and which covered what is now Peru and part of Bolivia and Chile, it lasted until 1533, when Pizarro overthrew it. Its area was 2000 miles long and about 500 miles wide. The Incas irrigated and manured the soil, had considerable knowledge of agriculture and worshipped the sun. Its capital was Cuzco and the ruins of palaces, temples, statues, decorations and good roads puts them on the level with both the Aztec and the Mayans. They also used flutes of bone and terra cotta. However, although just as superstitious as the other two, the Incas, in their rituals, were not as barbarous as the Aztec and the Mayans.

As I was in doubt as to the historical accuracy of some of the statements about the Aztec and Mayans, I wrote to Miss Frances Gillmor, the author of *Flute of the Smoking Mirror*, who is teacher at the University of Tucson, Arizona, and an authority on the matter.

The following two letters, I think, will be of interest:

"November 11, 1949

"Dear Mr. De Lorenzo:

"Your letter of last summer went first to the University of New Mexico Press, then to Tucson where I teach at the University of Arizona, and then to Mexico where I was spending the summer. It finally caught up with me in Mexico City. I did see that you were sent a *Flute of the Smoking Mirror* as soon as I got back to the

United States, but I am sorry that I have let the letter itself go so long unanswered.

"As you will have discovered by now there are scattered references to flutes through the book. Nezahualcoyotl is referred to as Flute of the Smoking Mirror, because of the prayer offered at the time of their coronation by the Aztec kings. They prayed to be the flute of Texcatlipoca, the god whose name literally meant smoking mirror, for the obsidian shield carried by the image on the pyramids, which reflected light far off. The ceremony is described in Chapter II with many quotations from the long speech and prayer given on this occasion by the kings as recorded by Fr. Bernardino de Sahagun, the great Franciscan 16th century recorder of Aztec life and ceremony and customs. (Vol. 2, Lib. VI, cap. 9 and 10, in the Robredo edition, Mexico, 1938).

Also you will have noticed occasional references to the prisoner who was prince for a year, and then climbed the steps of the pyramid, breaking his clay flutes step by step, until he reached the top and was sacrificed to Tezcatlipoca. (p. 94 and 124) Sahagun also records this ceremony in Vol. I, Lib. II, Cap. 24. After the victim of the sacrifice was selected to die in the fiesta a year hence, he lived a life of luxury for a year. He went through the streets of the city playing his flute, and carrying flowers and incense. Eight pages accompanied him wherever he went. For the last twenty days of his life he was given four beautiful girls. When the day of the great fiesta arrived, he went with the girls and his attendants in canoes through the canals and lakes around the city of Tenochtitlan, now Mexico City. Finally he left them, and alone climbed the steps of the pyramids, choosing his own time to die. As he climbed, he broke the clay flutes which he had played in his year of happiness, a flute to each step, until they were all gone. Then on the top of the pyramid at the temple, he was bent backward over the sacrificial stone, his breast cut with a knife, his heart torn out and offered to the sun.

Fray Diego Duran in the sixteenth century in his Historia de las Indias de Nueva—Espana, describing the same ceremony, gives a great deal of attention to a ceremony with flutes ten days before the sacrifice. Out on the pyramid, dressed like the god, came a man with roses in his hands and "a little flute of clay of a very sharp sound." He played the flute to the east and to the west and to the north and to the south. When he had finished playing his flute to the four directions, all within hearing put a finger in the ground, and picking up a little earth put it in the mouth and ate it, and prostrating them-

33

selves, wept, and called on the darkness of the night and on the wind, begging them that they should not leave them without help nor forget them. "On hearing the flute the robbers or the fornicators or the homicides, or any kind of delinquents were so filled with fear and sadness that some cut themselves in such a manner that they could not conceal having been in some manner delinquent"—evidently a reference to the piercing of the nose and ears in penitence which was a usual practice. On hearing the flute the soldiers prayed for victory and many captives. The ceremony took place ten days before the sacrifice, and in the intervening days the flute was blown to the four directions so that all might hear and eat earth and bewail their sins. (All of this is summarized from Duran, Vol. 2, p. 100 in the Ramirez edition, published in Mexico in 1867.)

I don't know why the flute should be so particularly identified with the fiesta of Tezcatlipoca. He was the principal god of the Aztecs. In one way or another many of the others are identified with him in the picture writing or early authorities, and are made to be either manifestations of forms of him—including the God of the With and the By, whom Nezahualcoyotl worshipped, and the god of music. He is described as Dreaded Enemy, Wind of Night. He had to do with war.

I hope these facts will be of aid to you.

Sincerely yours,
(signed) Frances Gillmor

George C. Vaillant, *Aztecs of Mexico,* Doubleday Doran & Company, 1941, has a few mentions of flutes that might interest you including this sentence: "The two-tone and one-tone drums could emit sonorous rhythms, but the bone and clay flutes pipe pitifully and are not gauged to a fixed scale" (p. 167)."

*   *   *   *

"November 26, 1949

"Dear Mr. De Lorenzo:

"By all means use my letter any way you wish. I am glad that the flute information in it fitted in with your needs. I was afraid you would be disappointed when you read Flute of the Smoking Mirror and found that it wasn't all about flutes!

"There are one or two points on the page which you sent me which are not quite exact. Marah Ellis Ryan's *The Flute of the Gods* is about Hopi, not Maya, civilization. The Hopis live in northeastern Arizona. I looked the book up in the library to be sure that my mem-

34

ory of it was not in error, and see where the introduction might confuse people, because many similarities are pointed out between the Maya civilization and the Pueblo Indians of New Mexico and Arizona. However, they are many centuries and many miles apart, and are not looked upon as the same people. Similarly the references to cliff ruins in New Mexico in your material I think should be avoided. The word Aztec is cheerfully applied in areas far beyond the Aztec Empire of Central Mexico, but not with scientific accuracy. We even have a Montezuma's Palace in Arizona—but Montezuma would be astonished.

There is also a statement that the Aztec civilization was older than the Maya. That is just turned around. The Maya were much earlier, and the Aztec derived much from them—their calendar for instance, which was an incomplete version of the Maya calendar.

I thought perhaps I should clarify these points in connection with that rather specialized field.

With all good wishes, Sincerely yours,

(signed) Frances Gillmor."

*   *   *   *

In many places in Central and South America, flutes of all kinds are used: Pan pipes, vertical flutes, nose flutes, primitive transverse flutes, flutes with keys, and Boehm flutes of wood, ivory, bone (monkey, ass, human) and metal, including gold and platinum. Among these places are: Panama, Venezuela, Colombia, Paraguay, Uraguay, La Plata, Costa Rica, Guiana, Ecuador, Peru, Chile, Bolivia, Brazil, Rio de Janeiro, Buenos Aires, Natal and Argentina.

*   *   *   *

A silver flute made in Shanghai, China (with the name of the manufacturer in Chinese on the head joint) was brought to Palos Verdes Estates by Townsend Conover, botanist and algologist, who intends to become a first-class flute dilettante.

*   *   *   *

Andu is the name of "The Head Catcher." He is a native of the jungle of Assam and is an expert player on the keyless transverse flute.

35

The Musical Mountain: Reg Ruwan, a white sandy hill near Kabul Afghanistan, produces regularly the sound of flutes, castanets, and drums.

* * * *

In 1932, the Belgian Congo government issued an extremely interesting stamp of 40 centimes showing two gaily dressed natives bedecked in gaudy skirts of native cloth, playing on short wooden flutes which have only seven notes. These flutes produced a plaintive wailing sound, apparently without rhythm! The stamps were eagerly sought after by philatelists everywhere.

* * * *

A strange sect of Buddhist priests wanders about the countryside of Japan playing bamboo flutes, and begging for alms. In order that their friends might not recognize them they wear baskets on their heads hiding their faces.

III. RANDOM NOTES

The Los Angeles Southwest Museum (Highland Park) has two flutes that are believed to have been among the first musical instruments played on this continent. They were found in 1930 in excavations at the gypsum cave, near Las Vegas, Nevada. They are described in detail and illustrated by the Curator, Dr. M. R. Harrington.

* * * *

Gymnorlindetibicen is a flute bird (an Australian shrike) which derives its name from its clear note.

* * * *

Flute-mouths, on the other hand, is a family of marine fish, remarkable for the elongation of the front bones of the head into a pipe bearing the small mouth at its apex.

* * * *

The famous platinum flute of the late Georges Barrère, the first instrument of that material ever manufactured, is now the property of a wealthy dilettante who paid $4,000 for it.

A few years ago, the antiquarian value of the flute of Frederick-the-Great (upon which he played for Johann Sebastian Bach) was placed at $20,000!

* * * *

From *Don Quixote* by Cervantes: "The flutes give forth a soft, pleasing tone which, as it was not overborne by human voice, had a tender amorous effect."

* * * *

Dorus (1812-1896) contrived the change from the original open G-sharp key of the Boehm flute to the closed G-sharp to accommodate players on the old system flute.

* * * *

Giorgi invented a keyless flute (c. 1890). It was constructed on a scientific basis so that the most difficult music could be played; like many others, it is now forgotten.

* * * *

I thought the eternal Boehm-Gordon controversy (famous over a half century ago) was settled once and for all when Christopher Welch's authoritative book, *History of the Boehm Flute* appeared in 1896 in its third and complete edition. I was evidently wrong. Only some years back (November 1945), I was surprised to read in an article in a musical magazine devoted to wood-wind instruments that "Boehm is not the real inventor of the modern or the so-called Boehm flute . . . Its authentic inventor was a Swiss by the name of Gordon; therefore, the modern flute should be called the 'Gordon flute' instead."

To be sure, the author of this article never investigated very deeply. It is probable that he read Rockstro's book, *The Flute*, and was influenced, like many others more than half a century ago, into believing that Gordon was the victim of injustice!

* * * *

A friend of Christopher Welch, who played an old wooden flute, having become subject to fancies and fearing that he was about to die, said to a friend: "I shall soon be in Heaven, and then I shall play the golden flute; but mind, it must be lined with wood!"

*   *   *   *

Rockstro, Welch, Finn and Fitzgibbon

Richard Shepherd Rockstro* (1826-1906)—originally Rackstraw—is the author of one of the greatest books written on any musical instrument: "A Treatise on the Construction, the History and the Practice of The Flute, including a sketch of the elements of Acoustics and critical notices of sixty celebrated flute players," published in 1890 by Rudall, Carte and Company, London, England.

It is to be regretted that there is a serious blot on this otherwise excellent work which has quite ruined its true value. Rockstro openly accuses Boehm of being an impostor and of stealing the invention of the new flute from the real inventor, Captain Gordon, and it was a pity this sad mistake was made as this otherwise magnificent book must have taken a great part of its author's life to complete. Rockstro died suddenly of heart failure one morning while on a walk.

Fortunately for the honor and integrity of that great man Theobald Boehm, a few years later another Englishman, Christopher Welch, after a thorough research, disproved the charge and cleared the matter in his fine book *The History of the Boehm Flute*. Welch accuses Rockstro of professional jealousy.

The Rockstro book fell into my hands in 1903 at the time when I changed from the old flute to the new and I still recall the shock it gave me to read therein that Boehm had stolen the invention from Captain Gordon! A short time thereafter a pupil brought me the new book by Welch which I devoured in a single day! I was so enthusiastic about it that I couldn't resist writing a letter of admiration and thanks to its author and also

---

* Not to be confused with William Smith Rockstro, his brother, who was also an eminent musician and historian. He was a friend and pupil of Mendelssohn and Hauptman. He wrote *A General History of Music*. Also the life of Handel and Mendelssohn. He composed madrigals, piano pieces, books on singing and an oratorio *The Good Shepherd*. He was born in England in 1823 and died there in 1895.

forwarding him a copy of my newly published *Nine Etudes*. After a few weeks I was pleasantly rewarded by a beautiful letter from Mr. Welch and an autographed copy of his famous book and also the booklet *Hamlet and the Recorder*, which consists of a very interesting lecture on that subject. In his letter to me he thanked me for the *Nine Etudes* and said they were beautiful but as for himself, he was afraid his flute playing days were over! Later I was to learn I had been unusually fortunate as Mr. Welch, due to his advanced age and poor health, seldom wrote to anyone.

The Rockstro book of about 670 pages was published through subscriptions and in the list of subscribers a number of familiar names may be seen: W. L. Barrett, Richard Carte, John Finn, Captain Fitzgibbon, Paul Taffanel and Christopher Welch.

It is of interest that Rockstro's daughter, Georgina M. Rockstro, who also played flute, translated the greater part of the biographical information collected and the whole of the extract, from the German and the Italian.

Christopher Welch (1832-1916), besides the book already mentioned in defense of Boehm, wrote *Six Lectures on the Recorder* and other flutes in relation to literature. This is Welch's *Opus Magnum* of 457 pages and is published by Henry Frowde, Oxford University Press of London, New York, Toronto and Melbourne. This is undoubtedly one of the most monumental books of research on any musical instrument. It has numerous excellent illustrations and on page 44 is an interesting picture of a "Contrabass flute" with pedals! This colossal flute was sent from England to one of the kings of France. It has had a well deserved rest for several hundred years and it is to be hoped no one will be foolish enough to disturb its slumber for a long time to come. This unique and extremely interesting book should be in every flute lover's library. Referring again to the booklet by Welch, *Hamlet and the Recorder*, which I mentioned previously —I shall discuss it a little more in detail later as it contains much that is of unusual interest to the flute playing world.

John Finn (1856- ?): England has cause for pride to be able to call her own three men of the caliber of Rockstro, Welch and Finn, who did so much for the flute. The first, Rockstro, was a professional flutist but the other two were just enthusiastic flute dilettanti. But, probably, it is not fair to Finn to put him in the amateur class because he was an extremely fine player and was, by many, considered semi-amateur and as able as many first-class professionals. Several well known flute composers, including myself, have dedicated their works to him. Mr. Finn, like his lifelong dear friend Christopher Welch, devoted all of his leisure time to flute research and gave numerous lectures, mostly illustrated with the playing of the instruments in question. He also wrote many articles on "Some Eminent Flute Players" published in the monthly magazine *Musical Opinion and Trade Review.* Also in *Musical News* in The Student's Page he contributed many interesting articles entitled "The Flute and Flute Playing." One of the finest contributions to the flute by John Finn is: "Recorder, Flute, Fife, Etc." It is 43 pages long and published as part of an elegant book *English Music* (1604 to 1904) by The Walter Scott Publishing Company Ltd., London; New York: Charles Scribner's Sons, 1906.

It was my privilege to have corresponded with John Finn for over thirty years and the stimulus it gave me remains as a pleasant memory.

H. Macaulay Fitzgibbon (18— ?): is very well known in America for his *The Story of the Flute* which appeared about forty years ago and also for the many articles on "Flute and Flute Playing" he contributed to various English musical magazines and in America to *The Flutist.* Although Fitzgibbon is Irish, he was a captain in the English army in World War I. A great lover of the flute, flutists, its literature and history, Fitzgibbon never allowed to pass an opportunity to take part in solo or ensemble that included the flute. When the second and enlarged edition of his book came out a number of years ago, he graciously sent me an autographed copy of it. I had already purchased two copies of the first edition, one of which I presented to a brother of mine, also a flutist, and just married.

I had admired Fitzgibbon's enthusiasm in all his writings. I therefore could not understand that in one of his articles published separately and entitled "Some Brief Notes on the Flute," he says: "Franz Doppler, the famous flutist and composer, was a great friend of Schubert." Now, let us investigate the kind of friendship that could have existed between the two. When Schubert died in 1828, Doppler was a child of four! Unless Schubert had been an intimate of the Doppler family (of which there is no record), and played hide-and-seek with the child, that great friendship is illusory!

Soon after the appearance of *The Story of the Flute,* I wrote the author pointing out a few inaccuracies and some omissions. When the second edition appeared (in or about 1938) he said that America's two most noted flutists were Lorenzo (sic!) and Maganini! Had he never heard of Barrère and Van Leeuwen? Not to mention those of the newer generation—but not too young to be included in the new edition: Kincaid, Laurent, Wummer, Lora (who replaced the late Georges Barrère at the Juilliard School of Music), and a few others in America: Moyse, LeRoy (the latter toured America recently) and others in France? Had Fitzgibbon never heard of two important artists old enough to be included in the first edition of his book, namely, Philippe Gaubert and Georges Fleury? Finn wrote to me enthusiastically about Fleury, who visited England often.

One other point: how could Briccialdi be considered the Paganini of the flute if he had been guilty of all the defects or shortcomings mentioned by Fitzgibbon? I have met a number of noted flutists who had known Briccialdi personally. They all agree that he was a grand person, and a rare and unusual artist!

*　　*　　*　　*

In more than one period in England the playing of the flute was considered indispensable to nearly every gentleman's education. One of these was the time of Lord Byron (the irresistible) who played the flute. The following is a quotation from an article that appeared in *Musical America* in 1926: "The storm of Byronicissimus that swept England reinforced the craze, the glorious Apollo himself having been a notable flutist." Naturally all this extravagance did not pass without reproof! Browning speaks of a candlestick-maker blowing his brains into a flute, and calls its note a "fife-shriek."

Nicola Alberti (1877-   ) of Chicago and Los Angeles, devised a very ingenious flute with revolving inner tube, so that one could play in any pitch from C to D-flat. Consequently, the performer had both the flute in C and that in D-flat in one instrument. It could also be played either closed or open G-sharp by turning a screw. When the flute was shown to a New York manufacturer of wind instruments, he told the inventor: "Very clever and very ingenious indeed but . . . to put on the market such an instrument would be against my own business because, instead of selling two flutes I would be selling one." However, the inventor had no difficulty in patenting it and, in 1915, received the gold medal at the San Francisco Exposition, but his interesting flute has since passed into oblivion; it surely deserved a better fate. Alberti who, in his younger days was a professional flutist, is related to the writer, and his sister-in-law, Catherine Birch Alberti, is an able and enthusiastic flute dilettante whose husband, Henry J. Alberti, is a valued member in the cello section of the Los Angeles Philharmonic Orchestra.

Dr. Dayton C. Miller, famous physicist, was an enthusiastic flute dillettante and inventor of the Phonodeik . . . an instrument for making photographic records of sound waves. It was his theory that the history of the flute and that of the human race went hand-in-hand, and are inseparable and indispensable to each other. He planned to write a series of books on the subject. Unfortunately, Dr. Miller's many activities and untimely passing prevented him from consummating this work. It surely would have made for interesting reading.

*   *   *   *

One of my most cherished possessions is a remarkable "Study of Pan" playing the transverse flute. This was presented to me on my seventieth birthday by its creator, the famous sculptor, Edgardo Simone, at my "Villa Pan by the Sea" in 1944. The conception is bold and audacious, for not only is Pan playing a transverse flute, but the position of the flute is on the left instead of the right. When questioned, Simone said it was not a mistake but done consciously for esthetic reasons. He said further he had no hesitation in making a violinist hold the violin in his right

42

hand if he required that effect. (Edgardo Simone, incidentally, was a great master, who received innumerable decorations here and in Europe. This great artist died in Hollywood on December 19, 1948 at the age of 56.)

A friend of mine, while looking through my album of clippings pointed to a newspaper cutting with a picture of Radie Britain, and said: "Who is this beautiful woman?" Abstractly I answered: "She is the wife of my Pan, and she is an excellent composer." After a few seconds' hesitation, my friend said: "Exactly what do you mean—the wife of your Pan?" "Oh!" I exclaimed, "I beg your pardon. I meant she is the wife of the creator of my Pan—Edgardo Simone. She is one of America's newer generation of women composers and a very successful one, having won several awards, and having had several major works performed by several leading orchestras. 'Casa del Sogno' ('House of Dreams'), their home in Hollywood, is a veritable museum of art.

*   *   *   *

"Pastorale" is a magnificent and impressive piece of sculpture in white marble by the same Edgardo Simone. It portrays the power of music to tame the wildest of beasts. A handsome youth plays on his flute while two leopards gaze up at him, entranced by the music. (A composition for orchestra by Simone's wife, Radie Britain, was inspired by this sculpture, which won first prize in an art exhibit in Los Angeles in January 1946.)

*   *   *   *

Pictures and statues on the subject of flutes and flutists, including mythological characters (Athene, Pan, Euterpe, etc.), and the legendary contest of Marsyas and Apollo (in which the former was skinned alive by his victorious opponent) were made by numerous great artists, notably Phidias, Praxiteles, Bellini, Michelangelo, Tintoretto, de Heore, Van Limborgh, Van Santvoort, Spitzwed, Peter, Rodin, Hals, Rubens, Van Dyke, Rembrandt, and many others. This list of artists also includes our own contemporary mystic, Roerich, who has pictured "Krishna Playing the Flute." "The Singing Teacher" by Springer is a colorful painting depicting a quaint custom in the Harz Mountains of

43

Germany where the celebrated canary birds are frequently taught trills and runs by constant repetition of the notes of a flute.

*　　*　　*　　*

Of all the world's great poets, the one who honored the flute most is William Shakespeare. It will suffice only to quote the following, from *Hamlet*, to illustrate Shakespeare's knowledge of and interest in the flute:

> "Will you play upon this pipe?
> Govern these ventages with your
> Fingers and thumb, give it breath
> With your mouth, and it will discourse
> Most eloquent music."

*　　*　　*　　*

Tchaikovsky, Berlioz, Donizetti, Suppé, Millöcker, Setaccioli, and Borodin were among the composers who played the flute.

*　　*　　*　　*

The following is taken from an article by Henri Malhèrbe in *Le Temps*, a Paris newspaper:

"Anatole France had the sense of music to a high degree. He knew little of the rules of composition; in his youth music was taught only to specialists. Victor Hugo, Gustave Flaubert, the Goncourts, treated the esthetics of instrumentation with scorn. Anatole France seldom went to concerts; at home he had no instruments of music. When Henry Büsser went to La Bechellerie (his country house) to give an audition of the score he had written for 'Les Noces Corinthiennes' he was obliged to send for a piano several miles away. Nevertheless, the discourse of Anatole France gave the effect of song: this great writer was at the source where all music takes its beauty. The composers were not mistaken when the books of Anatole France made them conceive the possibility of lyrical adaptation.

"Anatole France orchestrated his works in the manner of Chateaubriand, Victor Hugo, and Lecomte de Lisle. One must not take him too seriously when he speaks of music through the angel Mirar, who has become Théophile, writer of operettas, for the love of Bouchette,

44

a divette of the café concerts. But under the play of humor one can pierce the serious purpose.

"Here is France's description of a concert of flutes in the woods of Montmorency: 'The gardener poured wine for his guests, and when they had sipped and exchanged compliments, Zita said to Nectaire, "I pray you play something on the flute, you will please the friend I have brought with me." The old man consented immediately; he marshaled his thoughts in a musical discourse full of grace and audacity. He spoke of love, of fear, vain quarrels, the laugh of conquest, the peaceful light of intellect, the arrows of the mind burying their golden points in the monsters of ignorance and hate. He spoke of joy and grief bending their twin heads to the earth, and of desire, the creator of worlds.

" 'The night listened to the flute of Nectaire; Maurice lit a cigaret, the flame flickered one moment and eclipsed the sky and its stars, then died, and Nectaire sang that flame on his inspired flute. The silver voice rose and said: "The flame was a universe which accomplished its destiny in less than a moment. In its limits were suns, planets; Venus-Uranus measured the orbits of gloves wandering in infinite space; at the breath of Eros, first born of gods, plants, animals, thoughts were created. In the twenty seconds between the life and death of this universe, civilizations have flourished, empires have dragged their long decadence, mothers have wept and toward the silent skies have mounted the songs of love, the cries of hate and the sighs of victims. In proportion to its smallness, that universe has lasted as long as the one of which we see the atoms shining on our heads; they are both reflections of the infinite."

" 'And as the clear tones cut the charmed air, the earth changed to vapor, the stars became rapid orbs, the Great Bear flew in pieces, Orion broke its belt, the Polaris left its magnetic axis, Sirius, which throws its incandescent flame to the horizon, changed color, vacillated, and in a second expired; the perturbed constellations grouped themselves into new formations, which in their turn vanished. By its incantations, the magic flute had shortened the life and movement of that universe which to men and angels had seemed immovable.' "

* * * *

Sidney Lanier (1842-1881), lawyer, poet, flutist, was very modest about his flute playing and many times confessed he was not yet the complete master of his instrument, but his friends insisted he was "the greatest flutist in the world." They probably did not know that at that time many of the world's greatest players upon the flute were in their prime! e.g., Boehm, Briccialdi, Taffanel, the Doppler brothers, Ciardi, Radcliff, Terschak, and others. In a letter to his father from Baltimore, November 29, 1873, he says:* "I have given your last letter the fullest and most careful consideration. After doing so I feel sure that Macon is not the place for me. If you could taste the delicious crystalline air, and the champagne breeze that I've just been rushing about in, I am equally sure that in point of climate you would agree with me that my chance for life is ten times as great here as in Macon. Then, as to business, why should I, nay, how *can* I, settle myself down to be a third-rate struggling lawyer for the balance of my little life, as long as there is a certainty almost absolute that I can do some other thing so much better? Several persons, from whose judgment in such matters there can be no appeal, have told me, for instance, that I am the greatest flute player in the world; and several others, of equally authoritative judgment, have given me an almost equal encouragement to work with my pen. (Of course, I protest against the necessity which makes me write such things about myself. I only do so because I appreciate the love and tenderness which prompt you to desire me with you that I will make the fullest explanation possible of my course, out of reciprocal honor and respect for the motives which lead you to think differently from me). My dear father, think now, for twenty years, through poverty, through pain, through weariness, through sickness, through the uncongenial atmosphere of a farcical college and of a bare army and then of an exacting business life, through all the discouragement of being wholly unacquainted with literary people and literary ways—I say, think how, in spite of all these depressing circumstances, and of a thousand more which I could enumerate, these two figures of music and of poetry have steadily kept in my heart so that I could not banish them. Does it not seem to you as to me, that I begin to have the right to enroll myself among the devotees of these two sublime arts, after having followed

* From *Sidney Lanier* by Edwin Mims.

them so long and so humbly, and through so much bitterness?"

Carl Wehner often talked to me about Sidney Lanier whom he had met many times. He remembered him very well as a "good flute player and a great, polished gentleman." In fact, because of his gentleness, great consideration and kindness at all times, some thought him effeminate. However, the following incident will refute that: "He had some of the Southerner's resistance to anything like insult. A story is frequently told in Baltimore of the way in which Lanier resented the conductor's words to a young lady at a rehearsal of the Peabody Orchestra. Irritated in his undisciplined musician's nerves, the conductor vented that irritation in a rude outburst towards a timid young woman who was playing the piano, either with orchestra or voice or in solo. In an instant Lanier's tall, straight figure shot up from his seat and, taking the chair which he had occupied in his hand, he said: 'Mr. ——, you must retract every word you have uttered and apologize to that young lady before you beat another bar.' There was no mistake of his resoluteness and determination, and Mr. —— retracted and apologized; the orchestra went on only after the same had been done. Sidney Lanier often used to say that his flute playing had helped to mitigate the disease (tuberculosis) of which he was a victim. He laughed in the face of death, and each new acquisition in the realm of music and poetry had been a challenge to the enemy. Lanier prophesied America's great symphony orchestra, for in 1877 he said: "When Americans shall have learned the supreme value and glory of the orchestra, . . . then I look to see America the home of the orchestra and to hear everywhere the profound messages of Beethoven and Bach to men. All the signs of the times seem to point to this country as the scene of the future development of music . . . It only needs direction, artistic atmosphere, and technique in order to fill the land with such orchestras as the world had never heard." At the suggestion of Theodore Thomas and Leopold Damrosch, Lanier was chosen to write the words for a "Cantata" of the Centennial Exhibition in Philadelphia for which Dudley Buck wrote the music. Of the numerous fine poems of Lanier the following three are the most successful: "Corn," "The Symphony," and "Psalm of the West." Lanier died at 39 years of age in the same year as Boehm at 88, Briccialdi at 63, and Lobe at 84.

Because of the importance and the unusual personality of Sidney Lanier I wish to reproduce a small portion of an article which appeared in the *New York Times Book Review* of October 20, 1946 written by Henry Steele Commager under the title *A Gallant and Heroic Figure* which is a review of *The Centennial Edition of the Works of Sidney Lanier:*

"Four volumes of this edition of Lanier's writings are devoted to his letters. The major part of these are to his wife, Mary Day, to the father and brother who adored him and helped support him, to his publishers and business associates; a few are addressed to the literary friends, such as Father Tabb, to Paul Hayne, to Bayard Taylor and others. While these letters enable us to elaborate the picture we already have of Lanier, they will not require any change in the basic features of the portrait and Aubrey Stacke will need to add only minor revisions to that admirable biography he gave us over ten years ago. The letters tell, for the most part, a story of a sentimental, love-sick and art-sick young man, of an endless struggle to find work, of concern with music and literature—a touching story of frustrated ambition and unfulfilled genius. Those in the first volume are probably the most entertaining and some of them will be eye openers. For though young Lanier was undoubtedly a Galahad, he was something also of a heart-breaker. He was, at one time—so these letters tell us—engaged to two girls and in love with a third who became his wife. On one day he could write to that Virginia Hankins whom he had met at Bacon's Castle in Virginia, 'I proclaim now in your ear that I love you faithfully and loyally, that you are my One Dream of Roses,' and so forth, and the next day send an impassioned love poem to Mary Day. He simply could not help falling in love with girls, or stopping his pen from writing sentimental nothings. That they *were* nothings is clear; for Lanier was a very honorable and pure young man. Indeed, there is so much self-conscious honor and purity in Lanier that psychological interpreters might be forgiven if they suspected the worst. These letters offer no basis for such a suspicion; one is sometimes tempted to wish that they did.

48

Hamlet and the Recorder

The following, taken entirely from Christopher Welch's booklet of the above title and sent to me many years ago by Mr. Welch himself is, without doubt, the most notable and one of the most interesting writings on the flute and flute-playing.

I wish also to state that the entire booklet of some thirty-five pages was the result of a lecture in which T. Lea Southgate, Esq. was *In the Chair*, and the date is April 8, 1902. Since it is out of print, I believe many flutists would enjoy having it here.

HAMLET AND THE RECORDER

by Christopher Welch, M.A. *Oxon*

"The Plays of Shakespeare have been handled by the naturalist, the botanist, the ornithologist, the angler, the lawyer, the physician, and the divine, but never, as far as I can discover, by one who has brought to bear on them a study of the flute. Yet Shakespeare has honoured the flute as he has honoured no other instrument. In *Hamlet* he has brought it on the stage, displayed it to the audience, and discoursed on its music, its structure, and its manipulation.

"This afternoon I will break new ground: I will bring before you the views of a flute-player on the well known scene.* I shall suggest a change in the way of mounting it, express an opinion on how it might be played, and comment on the technical phrases it contains. . . .

"The King, the Queen, the Court, the Players—all are gone. Hamlet, his doubts dispelled, his suspicions confirmed, is left alone with Horatio in the silent hall. His tempest tossed soul now longs for the solace of sweet sounds, Shakespeare's balm for the wounded spirit: 'Come,' he exclaims, 'some music; come, the recorders . . . come, some music.' Music is so inseparably associated in many minds with mirth, that this sudden and seemingly ill-judged call for it is often regarded as a mad freak. But, if it be madness, it is not without method. Be it observed that Hamlet does not call for the shawms, for the cornets, or for the

---

* *Hamlet*, Act III, Scene 2.

hautboys, although any finger-holed instrument would serve the purpose to which the flute is ultimately put. Nor does he call for a recorder. He called for the recorders; for a band, or concert of recorders. . . .

"'Enter the Players with Recorders' . . . Who were the Recorder Players? At this stage of our inquiry a question presents itself. For what recorder players did Hamlet call? Does the stage direction, 'Enter the Players with Recorders' signify 'Enter the Actors Furnished with Recorders' or does it mean 'Enter the Recorder players with their Instruments?' Did Hamlet expect the Players, who had just been acting before the King, to reappear as recorder-players, as seems generally to be taken for granted, or did he intend professional flute players—such, for instance, as may have come with the Players in the capacity of musicians to the Company, or the recorder-players in the Danish Court Band, to be summoned to the Hall? . . .

"There were no less than six recorder-players in the English Royal household as late as the reign of Charles I . . .

"A *flute-player's view of the Recorder Scene*

"If the Recorder Scene were carried out according to what seems to a flute player to be Shakespeare's intention, it would be conducted as follows: At least four recorder players—a discant, an alto, a tenor, and a bass—would come upon the stage. The semblance of the instruments they carry in their hands would vary in length, the longest being, roughly speaking, rather less than four, the shortest, than two, feet long* . . .

"Although there would on no account be less than four recorder players, if it were desired, a large number might appear. In the collection belonging to Henry VIII there were three sets of four, two of six, one of seven, three of eight, and two of nine recorders; the Hengrave case contained seven; early in the seventeenth century, according to Praetorius, a full flute band comprised twenty-one instruments, including a double bass flute at least seven or eight feet long; and there is reason for believing,

---

* There are a number of excellent pictures of all length recorders in Welch's booklet. Some are called "The Chester Flutes" others "Recorders After Agricola" and yet others "Recorders After Virdung" and "Recorders belonging to Messrs. Rudall, Carte & Company."

50

as I have shown, that as many as thirty or forty fipple flutes were sometimes played together . . .

"*An Objectionable Proceeding of Some Hamlets*

"An act is sometimes seen when *Hamlet* is played, which has only to be named to be condemned. I allude to the offering up of the recorder as a sacrifice to the gods in the gallery by snapping it asunder, and throwing the fragments on the stage. What can be pleaded in justification of the practice, it is hard to say. Can madness, real or feigned, be an excuse for disfiguring by a display of unbridled passion a reproof couched in a form so often chosen by Him who spake as never man spake? Ought Hamlet, who has likened himself to the recorder, demolish his own image? Is it right that, for the sake of a theatrical *coup*, Hamlet should be degraded from the gentleman of Shakespeare's creation into a petulant and destructive rowdy? To realize the enormity of the solecism involved we have only to imagine (if the imagination would go so far) that when the Queen's private band was in the drawing room at Windsor Castle, the Prince of Wales, in his youth, had asked Richardson* for his flute to illustrate a remark he was about to make, and, when he had done with it, had smashed it and thrown it away, instead of returning it to the owner. Such wanton violence, however appropriate it might be to the disposition of Richard III, accords ill with the sympathetic nature of the sensitive Hamlet. He would be the last to inflict a needless wound on the feelings of even the humblest of his fellow subjects. To a musician, be it remembered, his instrument is a cherished object: in his hands it becomes a living being, able to express, and seeming to share, his joys and sorrows. The feeling of affection with which it is regarded, may, in a highly wrought temperament, be heightened into a real passion. Thus Paganini, on seeing his violin taken to pieces for the purpose of repair, is said to have displayed the manifestations of acute suffering shown by the tenderhearted when witnessing a surgical operation on one they love . . .

---

* Joseph Richardson (1814-1862) one of England's finest flutists and composers. He was also one of Christopher Welch's flute teachers. Richardson played on a Nicholson flute, a greatly improved old system instrument.

" '*I know no touch of it*' (I cannot play a note on it) '*Govern these ventages.*'

"To a flute player the most interesting sentence of the passage we are discussing is in Hamlet's next speech. Shakespeare there sums up the art of flute playing, declaring it consists in the government of the holes with the fingers, and the quickening of the instrument with the breath: 'Govern these ventages with your fingers and thumb, give it breath with your mouth, and it will discourse most eloquent music . . .'

"Shakespeare elsewhere speaks of *breathing* life into a stone, and St. Augustine refers to the *breath* blown into the flute as if it were the spirit or soul of the instrument. 'Si unus flatus,' he said: 'inflat duas tibias, non potest unus spiritus implere duo corda?' The metaphorical figure which attributes to the breath of the flute player the power of creating life is expressed in all its fullness by Tertullian. The worthy Father denies that when we blow the flute, we convert the instrument into a human being, although we *breathe* into it as the Deity *breathed his soul* into man. A similar thought, which, as I have said, roused the wrath of the matter-of-fact Sir John Hawkins, is found in the wild rhapsodies of Fludd, who represents the Supreme Being vivifying the universe, as the flute player gives life to his instrument with his breath. Fludd introduces a drawing, reproduced by Sir John, of a fipple flute, and says, '*as this instrument does not sound*, is not moved, nor has any virtue in its own nature, and by itself *without a moving spirit*; so also neither can the world, or the parts of the world, move or act by themselves, without the stirring of an infinite mind. As, therefore, the highest mind, God, at the top of the whole machine . . . makes the structure of the world produce his music . . . so also when *the musician blows life,*' etc. The same notion is expressed by St. Paulinus of Nola, in a passage just alluded to; but the conception is not confined to Christian thought nor, indeed, to the thought of our hemisphere. An idea so similar to Shakespeare's that Carl Engel was struck with the resemblance is to be found in a prayer offered up by an Aztec prince on his accession to the throne: 'I am thy flute,' he said, addressing the deity, 'reveal to me thy will; *breathe into me thy breath* like into a flute, as thou has done to my predecessors on the throne. As thou has opened their eyes, their ears, and their mouth to utter what is good, so likewise do to me.'

"The flute, thus brought to life, proceeds in its turn to *breathe*:

> The *breathing* flute's soft notes are heard around,
> And the shrill trumpets mix their silver sound.
>
> —POPE

Discussion

The Chairman. (T. Lea Southgate, Esq.):

"Ladies and gentlemen, I am sure you must have heard with much interest, indeed I might say delight, from this paper the result of Mr. Welch's long studies upon the flute and the instruments which belong to that family. He has not only carefully analyzed the interesting scene of *Hamlet* and the recorders in Shakespeare's play, but he has told us something about the flute in ancient times, quoting from his extensive reading in the works of the early writers of Rome who spoke about the instrument. I almost wondered that he had not gone a little farther and told us that in Rome there was a college of flute players; possibly some day he will extend his researches and let us hear something about that, for I am sure it would interest us all to know that music was so methodically cultivated and looked after among the Latins in ancient days." . . .

The answer by *Mr. Welch*:

"I will touch in the briefest possible way on some of the questions asked—to discuss them in detail would take up more time than the paper I have just read. First, a word on the College of Flute Players. The guilds, or clubs, called colleges, at Rome were corporations which could hold property, sue, and be sued. They were very numerous. There were Colleges of Magistrates, of Praetors, of ugurs, of Priests of the different temples, as well as of persons engaged in various trades. Amongst those who played on wind instruments there was a College of horn blowers (Aeneatorum), of Trumpeters (Liticinum) and Corneters (Cornicinum); but far more important was the College of flute players (Tibicinum), for it provided the music for the temple service. The duties, or labour, as Ovid calls them, of a Temple

53

Flute player were much heavier than those of a church organist. At a sacrifice he was required to play, not only before the sacred rite began, whilst the hymns were sung, and when the congregation were leaving the temple, but at the libations and the consecration of the victim, and, indeed, at other times during the service, in order to appease and soothe the deity, so as to induce him to accept the sacrifice, hear the prayers, and grant the petitions. In fact, amongst the Greeks, if no sign of divine favour was vouchsafed, the player was expected to keep on with a voluntary until a favourable omen appeared. On account of the holiness of the office, great honours were bestowed on the players by Numa Pompilius, the founder of the College. Those on duty in the Temple of Jupiter Capitolinus had the right of taking food (jus vescendi) in the sacred edifice. An attempt was once made to deprive them of the privilege, whereupon the College left Rome in a body and retired to Tibur, so that there was no one left to play at the sacrifices. Fears of an outburst of divine wrath were aroused, as the priests were sacrificing without flute music, and the Senate, in alarm, sent ambassadors to the Tiburtines, asking them to assist in restoring the flute players to the Romans. The Tiburtines, having in vain besought them to return, are seriously credited with having had recourse to a ridiculously incredible stratagem. They are said to have invited them to a banquet, and, having plied them with wine till they lost their senses, to have thrown them into carts, in which they were carried back to Rome, so that when, at daybreak, they regained consciousness, they found themselves in the Forum, surrounded by a crowd of citizens, overjoyed at their return, and begging them to remain. I have attempted to trace this tissue of historical nonsense to its source, but I will not detain you with my proposed explanation, for if you will turn to the volume of our proceedings which contains my former paper I will refer you to a drawing of a great Bass recorder, which I have conjectured might have been given by Henry VIII to a King of France. It is of such immense size that the player worked two of the keys with his feet. I have also reproduced an engraving from Praetorius, giving a back and front view of an ordinary great, or contrabass, recorder without

54

pedals, and have printed a complete list of the one hundred and fifty-four flutes which belonged to Henry VIII. . . ."

I sincerely hope I have acknowledged very clearly that the material of *Hamlet and the Recorder* is from the pen of that worthy gentleman of letters and enthusiastic flute dilettante, Christopher Welch.

I also wish to repeat that the booklet was published in 1902 by Mr. Welch himself and, if he were alive today, I am quite sure he would not object to my numerous quotations because very few, if any, of the new generation have ever heard of Mr. Welch's booklet on *Hamlet and the Recorder*.

It was our privilege to have as our neighbor for several years one of God's true gentlemen—Mr. Sydney L. Brock. Mr. Brock was a retired merchant from Denver and Oklahoma but he was also writer, philosopher, painter, cabinet maker and music lover. His was a rare and beautiful soul—always deeply interested in his fellowmen, and when he passed from this scene the world was much poorer.

I like to think back now to the happy times we had with Mr. Brock and his charming wife, way up on Summit Ridge, Beverly Hills, making music for ideal listeners.

Soon after we met he told me that his father, who had known and shaken hands with Abraham Lincoln, had been a flute dilettante and he himself had played on his father's flute as a young man. "But," Mr. Brock said, "that poor instrument has been neglected so many years it refuses to make music now, and also it has a bad crack on the head joint." However, as it is, I treasure it for it is now mine. His widow gave it to me as a keepsake after he had passed on—also one of his beautiful paintings, "An Italian Villa in Hollywood."

Palos Verdes Estates is privileged to have among its residents Dr. and Mrs. Dennis Smith, enthusiastic lovers of art and music. Mrs. Smith is also a fine poet and through long residence in China has a deep knowledge of its culture. She brought to my home two most interesting Chinese instruments. One was a bamboo flute upon which her gardener, while sitting in the garden of her Chinese home, used to play the most haunting melodies and which she persuaded him to give to her when she left for America.

The flute is about five inches longer than our concert flute. The mouth-hole, at the top end, as it is played vertically, is so small that at first I thought it to be a nose flute. It is beautifully varnished and has eight vents, five in front and three in the back—one for the left thumb, and the other two, way below, cannot be reached! The upper part of the flute is ornamented with many Chinese hieroglyphics. The other instrument is called "She-ng" and is known in the Western world as the "Chinese reed organ." It is of ancient origin, and was invented about 2850 B.C. There are three parts to the ordinary kind, the mouth-piece, the body and the tubes. The body is made of wood or a gourd about the size of a cup and the tubes are inserted into the upper part of the body. The "She-ng" of today usually has seventeen pipes of five lengths. It produces soft, harmonious tones. The "She-ng" was used at Confucian worship and court ceremonies.

An organ builder of Copenhagen (Kratzenstein), who lived the latter half of the eighteenth century, after seeing the "She-ng" made an organ with free reeds and this led to the invention of the accordion and harmonium and the reed organ in Europe.

*　　*　　*　　*

The Best Material for the Flute?

While I have played on a wood flute all my life I have never been stubbornly against a metal instrument, whether of silver, gold, platinum or any other material. I have heard grand players on both wood and metal and it wouldn't be fair for me to take one side or the other, although I confess that I play better on a wood flute, simply because I have played on one all my life. A famous flutist once was asked, probably for the hundredth time: "What is the difference between the silver flute and the wood flute?" The artist, who played on a metal flute, pretended he didn't understand the real meaning of the question and said: "That is a silly question; why you ought to know that the difference between a silver flute and a wood flute is in the fact that one is of metal and the other of wood!"

The questioner, apologizing for not having made himself clear, said: "I am sorry but what I meant was: What is the difference in the tonal quality of the two instruments, and why is it that a few years back one could see quite a number of wood flutes played by both professionals and amateurs and now one sees a wood flute as often as one sees a white elephant?"

The famous flutist said: "Well, the difference is in the man behind it!" To this answer some agree and others do not. To be sure, no one, an ordinary music lover, a connoisseur of tone or an orchestral conductor ever told Barrère in all his career that he should play on a wood flute.* And you may be sure that Carl Wehner would never have allowed any one to dictate to him about changing to a silver flute!

The heated argument in regard to the best material for the best tone is not a new one. As far back as Frederick-the-Great (1712-1786) the same argument must have existed, because, although Quantz made most of the flutes for his royal pupil of wood, it is known that that monarch possessed several instruments of other material, including several flutes of glass and one of amber! Of course, the argument in favor of the metal flute is that it requires less care, less breath to play and it responds with greater ease especially in the high register. The wood flute, according to those who favor the metal flute, is coarse, hard to blow, particularly in the higher register and . . . the fear of finding it split any time one may look at it. Besides, it requires much more breath and a long phrase can be played, most assuredly, easier with the metal flute!

All these drawbacks are dismissed by the advocates of the wood flute with a . . . "ba-a-h! Nonsense!" and they are (or were) ready to challenge any player on a metal flute on anything; a pianissimo passage or fortissimo on any register of the instrument and any long phrase! These old-fogey players of a wood flute have even the impudence to say that Ciardi could play four measures of a sustained Adagio on his old boxwood flute in one breath and, believe it or not, could be heard in the low register while the orchestra was playing fortissimo!

---

* What would have happened under Gustav Mahler who would tolerate only wood flutes?

The same old-fogey players of a wood flute would get red in the face if anyone would not admit that the metal flute, while good and almost sonorous in the lower register, in the high notes is shrill, metallic, thin, not at all flute-like and with numerous other defects ad infinitum! Besides, they would add, Briccialdi was considered one of the world's greatest players—on any instrument, according to Rockstro—and composed his best works, including his grand opera *Leonora de' Medici* before he changed from the old system wood flute to the new system made of metal.

*   *   *   *

A well known flute manufacturer in 1933 came to my studio in the Eastman School of Music one afternoon "just for a little chat," he said, "before leaving town in a couple of days." He was a fine and sympathetic gentleman. "The purpose of my visit to you," he said, "is this: of all the finest artists of the flute in America you are the only one who still uses the wood flute! Could I induce you to change, not to an ordinary silver flute, because I know that would not be attractive, but to an excellent gold flute? You would have to give me your wood flute; not that I am interested personally in the instrument, but because I should like to present it to Dr. Dayton C. Miller for his great collection."

My answer was: "I would be glad to accept your gold flute, use it in my studio and, probably, play it in the symphony now and then, but to deprive myself entirely of my own grand instrument, which was made for me in London over thirty years ago and with which I have been inseparable, cannot be done! In regard to having it join Dr. Miller's great collection, I have been thinking that, eventually, that is just where I want my instrument to be, but at present it is a trifle premature. I yet feel in my prime and, therefore, am not in a particular hurry!"

The visit with the head of that well known flute firm was extremely cordial. I invited him the next morning to hear a flute quartet and my own *Divertimento Flautistico* for five flutes with flute in G and piccolo, which I had recently completed, and after a spaghetti dinner in my home, we parted the best of friends! Alas! that was the last time I was to see him.

In telling this little story to a friend some time ago he remarked: "I am a bit skeptical that he intended to give you a gold flute for your wood flute just to increase Dr. Miller's collection. He was a fine man and a better business man but he has never given a gold flute as a present to anyone in his life and I am sure he would never give one away, if he could, where he is now!" "Well," I said to myself, "that was the second gold flute I missed." The first was when visiting Berlin in 1926, I learned that Adolph Goldberg, the wealthy flute dilettante and with whom I had corresponded for a number of years, had just passed on. He had presented several gold flutes to his friends and well known artists who had played for him, among whom were Emil Prill and Ary Van Leeuwen.

A couple of years after the flute manufacturer's visit I played Griffes' beautiful *Poem* for flute and orchestra on an American Composer's program to a capacity audience in the Eastman Theatre. It was recorded during the performance without my knowledge and when I later heard the record I was convinced in my own mind that I was still in my prime at 58 and my flute was not yet ready for any collection.

Part Two

THE PERFORMER

I | Biographies of Pioneers

(NOTE: These pioneers of the flute are presented in chronological order.

Many of the following complete biographies are taken from Richard Shepherd Rockstro's *The Flute*, now out-of-print for many years. I have used these, giving full credit to their author, with the intention of giving present-day flutists the privilege of reading Rockstro's distinguished pieces on the pioneers of the flute, written almost a century ago. Where contemporary musicological research has proved some of Rockstro's dates and facts to have been inaccurate, they have been revised. Those pieces not signed by Rockstro's initials (R.S.R.) were written by me.)

LOEILLET, JEAN-BAPTISTE: born at Ghent on November 18, 1680, was one of the most noted among the early players on the one-keyed flute. He was also an excellent performer on the harpsichord, and an industrious composer. In 1702, he went to Paris where he had several of his compositions published. In 1705, we hear of him in England, and, as far as I have been able to discover, he was the first performer on the so-called German flute who visited this country. On his arrival he was appointed principal flutist in the Haymarket. This building, then just completed, was styled the Queen's Theatre until the accession of George the First in 1714; from that period it was known as the King's Theatre, which title it retained until the death of William the Fourth in 1837.

The orchestra was at first under the direction of William Corbett, a celebrated violinist, and leader of the court band. We are told by Sir John Hawkins that the first so-called opera performed was nothing better than a collection of Italian airs adapted by Thomas Clayton to the words of an English drama, entitled *Arsinoe, Queen of Cyprus*, which was written for the purpose by Motteux.

In 1710 an entirely new band was engaged, and Loeillet then devoted himself chiefly to giving lessons on the harpsichord and the flute. In this occupation he achieved distinguished success, and he eventually became one of the most celebrated teachers in London. He also gave weekly concerts at his own house, in Hart Street, Covent Garden, and did much towards the improvement of the musical taste of the English people. The music of Corelli was first performed in London at these concerts.

Loeillet died on July 19, 1730, having amassed a fortune of $80,000.

The following list of his works for the flute, which is more ample than that given by Gerber, is compiled from the catalogue of the British Museum.

Six Sonatas for a variety of instruments, viz., for a common Flute, an oboe or Violin, also for two German Flutes with a Bass for the Violoncello and a Thorough-bass for the Harpsichord. Opera prima. London.—XII. Sonatas or Solos for a Flute with a Thorough-bass for the Harpsichord or Bass Violin. Op. 2da. London.—XII. Sonatas or Solos for a Flute with a Thorough-bass for the Harpsichord or Bass Violin. Op. terza. London. —VI. Sonates à une Flute Traversiere, un Haubois, ou Violon, et Basse Continue. Op. 5, Livre premier. Amsterdam.—VI Sonates à deux Flutes Traversieres, Haubois ou Violons. Op. 5, livre second. Amsterdam.—Six Sonatas of two parts, fitted and contriv'd for two Flutes. London.—XII. Sonatas in three parts, six of which are for two Violins and a Bass; three for two German Flutes, and three for a Hautboy and common Flute, with a Bass for the Violoncello and a Thorough-bass for the Harpsichord. London. (R.S.R.)

HOTTETERRE, LOUIS: surnamed "Le Romain" on account of his having resided in Rome during his youth. The time and place of the birth of this eminent flute-player were long involved in obscurity, but M. Jules Carlez (1877) has furnished almost positive proof that he was born in Evreux, between the years 1640 and 1650. Louis was the third son of Henri Hotteterre, the celebrated wind-instrument maker of Paris, who was born about the year 1610. The father was an excellent musician, and under his able tuition the sons acquired great skill both as performers and constructors. Besides the founder of the family, the Hotteterres known to fame were Nicholas (familiarly known as Colin and particularly celebrated as a bassoon-player), Jean, Louis (Le Romain), Jacques-Jean and Martin, but whether all these were sons of Henri is uncertain.

M. Carlez says: "The Hotteterres were wind-instrument makers who combined with their great skill as artisans talents no less great as instrumental performers. Their collective reputation should therefore have been doubly increased, but alas! in what estimation were orchestral musicians, however skillful and deserving they might have been, likely to have been held in the France of Louis XIV? The mere fact that the name of the Hotteterres has survived may therefore be taken as sufficient proof of their merits."

Borjon, in his *Traité de la Musette* (Lyon 1672), thus speaks of this remarkable family: "The Hotteterres have achieved the highest distinction in this country as composers, performers and manufacturers. The father is a man of really unique skill in the construction of all kinds of musical instruments of boxwood, ivory and ebony, such as musettes, flutes, flageolets and hautboys. . . . The sons are by no means inferior to him in the practice of this art, and they are also admirable musicians."

The talents of the Hotteterres received substantial recognition from the King; the father became the appointed manufacturer of wind-instruments to the Chapel-royal and *"la musique du roi,"* and the sons were installed as court musicians, Louis being dignified by the title of *"flute de la chambre."*

In 1683 Henri Hotteterre died at St. Germain-en-Laye, and the five inheritors of his name continued to exercise their profession in Paris and at Versailles. Four of them, Nicholas, Jean, Louis and Jacques-Jean, figured among the *"douze grands hautbois et violons de la Grande-écurie."* These took part with the "chamber-musicians" and the *"violons du cabinet,"* in all the royal ceremonials at which music was required, including the *"lever du roi"* on New Year's Day, on the first of May and on the feast of Saint Louis.

Amongst the treasures of the museum of the Paris Conservatoire is a precious, and perhaps unique, specimen of the work of Henri Hotteterre, bearing his name. This is a flute-à-bec of brown wood, with broad ivory mountings and with one key. Unfortunately the trade-mark is not to be deciphered, but it is plain enough to be distinguished from the anchor branded on a basse de flute-à-bec which is in the same collection and which bears the single name "Hotteterre." The last mentioned instrument was believed by the late M. Chouquet to be the work of Nicholas.

The most distinguished member of the Hotteterre family was undoubtedly Louis, "Le Romain," and he it was who first had the honor of playing the transverse flute in the orchestra of the Paris Opéra; this was in the year 1697. Some extracts from his most celebrated work, *Principes de la Flute traversiere, etc.,* first printed in Paris not later than 1699. An edition of this book, with the portrait of Hotteterre, published in 1707, also in Paris, is believed by Fétis to be the second. A counterfeit was printed at Amsterdam in 1708; another in 1710, and two others without date. The third Paris edition was published in 1726, and the last in 1741. An edition in Dutch by Abraham Maubach was published in 1728 at Amsterdam, and several imperfect translations into English were published in London without any acknowledgment of the name of the author. The *Journal de Trévoux,* announcing the publication of the edition of 1707, remarks: "The name of the author is a sufficient guarantee for the excellence of the work. This skilful flute-player is well acquainted with all the secrets of his art."

Louis Hotteterre died at an advanced age, for in 1722 he still retained his court appointment, and his latest work was published in 1738, but the precise date of his death is unknown.

Besides the celebrated *Principes*, he is known to have published the following works, which were all printed in Paris:

I*er* livre de pieces pour la flute traversiere et autres instruments, avec la basse. Op. 2.—Sonates en trios, livre 1, etc. Op. 3. —Ire suite de pieces a 2 flutes. Op. 4—2e livre de pieces, etc. Op. 5—2e suite de pieces a 2 flutes avec une basse ajoutee separement. Op. 6.—Les tendresses bachiques, solo pour la flute traversiere.—Brunettes pour 2 flutes.—Rondes ou chansons a danser pour la flute.—Menuets en duos pour deux flutes ou deux musettes.—Duos choisis pour deux flutes ou deux musettes.— L'Art de preluder sur la flute traversiere, sur la flute a bec, sur les hautbois et autres instruments de dessus, avec des preludes tout faits sur tou les tons dans differents mouvements et differents characteres, etc., 1712.—Methode pour la musette, contenant des principes par le moyen desquels on peut apprendre a jouer de cet instrument de soy-meme au defaut de maitre, 1738. (R.S.R.)

PHILBERT: was a celebrated Parisian musician of the seventeenth century. Little is recorded concerning him beyond the important fact that he was the first to achieve distinction as a player on the transverse flute with one key. This we have on the authority of J. J. Quantz: "The first in France to distinguish himself, and to gain popular admiration by his performance on the improved instrument, was the renowned Philbert, the hero of so many singular adventures."

Being a man of lively disposition and engaging manners, Philbert became a great favourite of Louis the Fourteenth and his courtiers, whom he amused as much by his singing and his good-natured mimicry, for which he appears to have had a peculiar talent, as by his excellent flute-playing. In the delightful essay on ancient and modern music, by Laborde and Roussier (1780), particular stress is, however, laid upon the fact that Philbert was not a professional jester. In addition to his other accomplishments he possessed great skill in gardening, especially in raising flowers. The poet Laines was his intimate friend, and it is related that one day when he had been highly entertained by Philbert, he exclaimed: "You have amused me so much that I will immortalize you!" The next morning he sent him the following poem:

"Cherchez-vous des plaisirs? allez trouver Philbert,
Sa voix, des doux chants de Lambert,
   Passe au bruit eclatant d'un tonnerre qui gronde,
Sa flute seule est un concert;
La fleur nait sous ses mains dans un affreux desert,
   Et sa langue féconde
   Imite en badinant tous les peuples du monde.
Si dans un vaste pavillon
Il sonne le tocsin, ou fait un carillon,
   En battant une poele a frire,
Le heros immortel, que nous reverons tous,
Devient un homme comme nous;
   Il éclate de rire.
Cherchez-vous du plaisir? allex trouver Philbert,
Sa flute seule est un concert."

(R.S.R.)

DENNER, JOHANN CHRISTOPH: was born in Leipsig on August 13, 1655. At eight years of age he was taken by his father, a working horn-tuner, to Nuremberg, in which city the family settled. The boy was at first intended to follow the trade of his father, but he soon developed a passion for music, as well as for the construction of instruments of the class known as the "wood-wind," and having learned, without assistance, the rudiments of music he began to make flutes and various reed-instruments. In this art he eventually acquired such skill that his fame extended even to distant lands. He was particularly celebrated for his accuracy in tuning.

Fuerstenau (1834 post) relates that Denner was the first to make important improvements in the transverse flute, as he is well-known to have done in the flute-à-bec; that his sons travelled with chests of such instruments through Europe as far as Constantinople, and that his flutes were even sent by the aid of the missionaries into China.

Besides his celebrity as a maker of all sorts of wood-wind instruments, in which he introduced great improvements, Denner was famous as a player on the flute. About the year 1690 he invented the clarionet.

The museum of the Paris Conservatoire possesses a flute-à-bec which bears the name of Denner in conjunction with that of C. Ruykel. Denner adopted as his trade-mark a laurel between the initials J. D.

This able artist and constructor died at Nuremberg on April 20th, 1707, leaving two sons who added to the fame of their father's business, and who were excellent performers on the various instruments that they constructed. (R.S.R.)

BUFFARDIN, PIERRE GABRIEL: One of the most celebrated flutists of his time was born in France in 1690. He was first flutist of the Royal orchestra at Dresden from 1715 to 1749. When Quantz visited Dresden in 1716 he was much impressed by the excellence of the Dresden orchestra and the playing of Buffardin, and took lessons from him for four months. Buffardin died in Paris in 1768. (R.S.R.)

QUANTZ, JOHANN JOACHIM: This excellent musician and distinguished flute player, born at Oberscheden in Hanover on January 30th, 1697, was the son of a blacksmith named Andreas Quantz, and at nine years of age was compelled to work at his father's trade. Being left an orphan in the spring of 1707, he was enabled to relinquish this calling, for which he entertained a strong aversion, through the kindness of his uncle, Justus Quantz, court musician and tailor, of Merseburg in Saxony, by whom he was adopted, and from whom he began to learn the rudiments of music. Three months later, Justus Quantz died, and was succeeded in his appointment by Johann Adolf Fleischhack, with whom young Quantz remained for seven years and a half, at first as a pupil and afterwards as an assistant, but the progress that he made in music, during this time, was due solely to his "Burning love for knowledge," as he received no material aid from his master. The first instruments that he studied were the violin, the hautboy and the trumpet; he also acquired some knowledge of all the wind instruments of the period, as well as of the violoncello and the viola da gamba. He received lessons on the harpsichord, and learned the rudiments of harmony from a relative named Kiesewetter, but his principal instrument was the violin, and on that he practiced with great assiduity.

In June, 1714, the boy set out on his travels, and journeying from one town to another, he at last arrived at Dresden, where he wished to settle. Being unable to support himself in that city, he went to Radeburg, and there he obtained employment from one Knoll, the chief musician of the town. Quantz, in his autobiography, gives a graphic account of a terrible thunder-storm which soon afterwards occurred, and which caused the total destruction of Radeburg by fire. Poor Knoll was ruined by this disaster, and by his advice, Quantz went to Pirna, where he became assistant to a musician named Schalle, who often sent him to fulfill engagements in Dresden.

After a variety of adventures, including a return to Fleischhack at Merseburg, Quantz gladly accepted the offer of a permanent engagement from Heine, a musician of some note in Dresden, and returned thither in March, 1716. Dresden was then crowded with musical celebrities; the Royal Orchestra was in its zenith, and the young student, as much astonished as delighted at the performance of the famous artists whom he then had the privilege of hearing for the first time, "soon found the duties of a musician to consist of much more than the mere blowing of notes written by the composer." During his stay in Dresden his zeal for music became redoubled, and he strove with all his might to become a worthy member of so brilliant an assembly.

Court-mourning causing a discontinuance of music for three months, in 1717, Quantz travelled through Upper and Lower Silesia, to Mahren and to Vienna, returning in October of the same year, by way of Prague, to Dresden. In March, 1718, he was engaged to play the hautboy in the Royal Chapel at Warsaw, at a salary of a hundred and fifty thalers, with board and lodging. He returned to Dresden early in the following year, and then came what he describes as a great change in his life: the adoption of the flute as his chief instrument. During four months' tuition by Buffardin, then the principal flute player in Dresden, he mastered the technicalities of the instrument of his choice and became skilled in the execution of florid music, but it was under the guidance of Pisendel, the royal Concertmeister, whose friendship he had been fortunate enough to obtain, that he learned to render a slow movement with true expression. Quantz eagerly embraced every opportunity of studying the various styles of the numerous eminent singers and instrumentalists whom it was his good fortune to hear, and the excellence of the musical taste that he eventually acquired is manifest in his celebrated work of 1752, as well as by the golden opinions that he won from all who heard him play.

The scarcity of original music for the flute induced Quantz to turn his attention earnestly towards composition, and by intense application, under the guidance of the excellent Pisendel, he soon became well versed in harmony and counterpoint, and acquired considerable facility in writing.

Nearly every year he went to Poland, and in 1722 his salary was increased to two hundred and sixteen thalers. While he was in Warsaw some of his patrons, chiefly Prince Lubomirsky and Abt Roseroschewsky, persuaded the King of Poland and Elector of Saxony to send him to Italy. On receipt of the news of the King's consent, Quantz lost no time in returning to Dresden, but on his arrival there he found that it had been decided, on the advice of Baron von Seyfertig who had long been his friend, that he was too young to go. Though bitterly disappointed at the time, he afterwards recognized the wisdom of this decision.

In July, 1723, Quantz journeyed, with the lutist Weiss and the Prussian Kapellmeister Graunn, to Prague in order to take part, as hautboyist, in the performance of the grand opera *Constanza e Fortezza*, composed by Fux, on the occasion of the coronation of the Emperor Charles the Sixth. The composer was suffering from gout, and was therefore unable to conduct the performance of his opera, but by the Emperor's command, he was brought in a litter from Vienna to Prague, and was able to be present at the first representation of his opera. One hundred singers and two hundred instrumentalists were engaged in this performance, which took place in the open air, and which Quantz describes as truly magnificent. During his visit to Prague he heard the famous violinist, Tartini, whose fine tone and marvellous command of his instrument he greatly admired, but with whose style he was disappointed.

The performance of the opera being at an end, Quantz returned to Dresden. In 1724 his long-cherished desire to visit Italy was gratified, and on May 23, he started his journey, arriving in Rome on June 11. There he received instruction in counterpoint for six months from Francesco Gasparini. On January 13th, 1725, he left Rome for Naples, and in that city he met his countryman, Hasse, afterwards chapelmaster to the King of Poland, with whom he formed a close and lasting friendship. Hasse was then studying counterpoint under the illustrious Alessandro Scarlatti, and Quantz wished to be introduced to the great master, but Scarlatti at first refused to receive him, saying to his pupil: "My son, you know that I cannot endure wind-instrument players; they all blow out of tune." Hasse, however, succeeded eventually in obtaining permission to introduce his friend, and the veteran contrapuntist not only consented to listen to the flute player, but accompanied him in a solo, and was so much pleased with his performance that he actually composed two solos expressly for him. The kind of flute on which Quantz played at this time proved that he must indeed have been a skillful musician so to have overcome the imperfections of such an instrument and to satisfy his exacting auditor.

Quantz left Naples on March 23, having narrowly escaped being assassinated, and returned to Rome, where he remained until October 21, then, after declining numerous offers of permanent engagements, he journeyed to Florence, Livorno, Bologna, Ferrara, Padua, Venice, Modena, Reggio, Parma, Milan, and Turin. On June 23, 1726, he left Italy, and went by way of Mont Cenis, Geneva and Lyons to Paris, arriving on August 15. He was not at all favorably impressed by the Parisian operatic performances which seemed to him exceedingly poor in comparison with the splendid musical displays that he had been accustomed to hear. He writes: "The acting, for which the French are

72

eminently qualified, the decorations of the stage, and the dancing, were the most attractive features of the opera. The orchestra was bad; the performers played more from memory and by ear than from notes, and they were kept in time by the strokes of a large stick." In a footnote to an English translation (1790) of a portion of the *Parallele des Italiens et des François, etc.*, appears the following account of the Parisian method of beating time: "The Master of the Musick in the Opéra at Paris had an Elboe-chair and Desk placed on the Stage, where, with the Score in one Hand, and a Stick in the other, he beat Time on a Table put there for the purpose, so loud, that he made a greater Noise than the whole Band." Quantz was, however, delighted with the French flute players, especially with Blavet, of whose warm friendship and numerous acts of kindness he writes in terms of grateful acknowledgment. It was during his residence in Paris, in 1726, that he made the memorable addition of a second closed key to the foot-joint, not only to make the difference between D-sharp and E-flat, but also to improve other notes.

On March 10, 1727, he left Paris for London, arriving on the 20th of the same month. He was so anxious to visit this city that he did not ask permission from his master, the King of Poland, for fear of being refused, he therefore "dared to make the journey without asking." Here he heard Handel's opera *Admetus*, in which the leading parts were performed by the three great singers, Faustina Bordoni (afterwards married to his friend Hasse), Francesca Cuzzoni (the refractory lady whom Handel threatened to throw out of the window for refusing to sing his music) and the male mezzo-soprano, Francesco Bernardi, commonly called Senesino. "The orchestra was composed mostly of Germans, but it comprised a few Italians and a couple of Englishmen." Quantz considered the opera lovely, and the performance, under the leadership of Castrucci and the direction of Handel, extraordinarily fine. At that time considerable animosity existed between the respective partisans of Bordoni (or, as she was generally called, Faustina) and Cuzzoni, and the celebrated feud was raging between the supporters of the rival composers, George Frederick Handel and Giovanni Bononcini, concerning which John Byrom wrote:

"Some say, compared to Bononcini,
That Mynheer Handel's but a ninny;
Others aver that he to Handel
Is scarcely fit to hold a candle.
Strange all this difference should be
'Twixt Tweedledum and Tweedledee!"

The flute players at the opera house, then called the King's Theatre, were Wiedemann (mentioned by Dr. Burney as a fine player) and Festin, an Englishman. Quantz says that he had the good fortune to obtain introductions to several families of rank, and that he received numerous invitations, including a most pressing one from Handel, to settle in England, but he determined to return to the service of his "King and master." He left England on June 1, 1727, travelling through Holland, Hanover and Brunswick to Dresden, where he arrived on July 23, and at once renewed his intercourse with his "dearest friend Pisendel."

In March, 1728, Quantz received an appointment in Electoral Chapel at Dresden, though in what capacity does not clearly appear. At this time, he entirely relinquished the practice of the hautboy, as he found that it interfered with his flute playing. In the following May he went with Baron von Seyfertig, in the suite of the King of Poland, to Berlin, where, at the desire of the Queen of Prussia, he remained some months in company with Pisendel, Weiss and Buffardin. The Queen wished to retain his services at a salary of 800 thalers, but his master would not permit him to accept the offer, though he allowed him to go to Berlin twice a year to give lessons on the flute to the crown prince, afterwards Frederick the Second. On the death of the King of Poland, in 1733, his successor, Frederick Augustus, retained Quantz in his service at the same salary that had been offered to him by the Queen of Prussia, granting him permission to continue giving lessons to the crown prince, and also to visit Bayreuth occasionally in order to give instruction to the Margrave of that place. In 1734, Quantz published his first six sonatas for the transverse flute. On June 26, 1737, he married Anna Rosina Carolina Schindler, the daughter of a captain in the Bavarian army, and the widow of a court musician. Two years later, on account of the difficulty of getting good flutes, he began to bore and tune them himself.

In 1741, soon after the accession of Frederick-the-Second to the throne of Prussia, Quantz was offered by that prince, and gladly accepted, an appointment for life as court musician at a salary of two thousand thalers, besides special payment for his compositions and a hundred ducats (£46 13s. 4d.) for every flute that he finished for the King. He was "to receive orders from no one but His Majesty," and his duties were not only to play in the orchestra, but to attend the King daily; to play duets with him or to try over new concertos; to write a constant supply of new music, and to beat time to the concertos performed, generally by the King, at the concerts held nightly in the palace.

In 1752, Quantz invented the wooden tuning slide for the headjoint of the flute, and in the same year he published the important *Essai*. The French translation of the work, which was printed at the same time as the German edition, was no doubt intended to flatter the King's well-known preference for the French language and his pretended ignorance of German. It will be remembered that the proceedings of the Berlin Academy were printed in French.

The chief pupils of Quantz, besides the King of Prussia and the Margrave of Bayreuth, were J. Jos. Frd. Lindner, a nephew of Pisendel; G. W. Kottowsky of Berlin; Augustin Neuff of Graz in Steyermark, and the well-known Georg Gotthelf Liebeskind of Altenburg.

The closing sentences of Quantz's interesting autobiography (1754) are as follows: "This is the history of my life, and a relation of the way in which an all-wise Providence enabled me to fulfill the almost hopeless desire that I entertained for so many years; namely, to make my fortune either in Dresden or Berlin. My wish has been realized in both those cities, and I have to thank God and his gracious Majesty that I am able to subscribe myself, in sound health and prosperity, Johann J. Quantz, Potsdam, August, 1754."

After thirty-two years of a happy and honorable career at the Prussian court, Quantz died at Potsdam on July 12, 1773, in his seventy-seventh year. He was a most indefatigable and prolific composer. Amongst his works were: three hundred flute concertos, the last of which was completed by the King; two hundred flute solos; twenty-six sonatas for flute and harpsichord; numerous duets for two flutes; thirty-nine trios, mostly for two flutes with bass; studies, caprices, preludes and solfeggi for the flute; duets for hautboy and viola; trios and quartets for various instruments; church music; secular songs and other vocal works, including a Serenata.

The greater part of Quantz's music remained in manuscript in the possession of the King. (R.S.R.)

BLAVET, MICHEL: was born at Besançon on March 13, 1700. He was the son of a turner, and for some years followed the trade of his father. Having accidentally become the possessor of a flute, he taught himself to play upon that instrument, and his progress was so rapid that he soon became the finest flute-player in France. Choron relates that a dog, which always became frantic with rage on hearing anyone else play the flute, manifested the greatest delight at Blavet's performance.

When he was twenty-three years of age Blavet went to Paris, at the solicitation of the Duc de Levis; there he gained an immense reputation, and received an appointment as principal flute in the orchestra of the Opéra. So great was the estimation in which he was held as a solo-player, that his acceptance of this post was regarded as an act of some condescension. Many of the contemporaries of this popular favorite, including Voltaire, seem to have vied with each other in their expressions of admiration for his genius. Marpurg speaks of him as a virtuoso of the highest excellence who preserved his innate modesty notwithstanding the unbroken popularity that he enjoyed, and who was always willing to recognize the merits of his rivals. Marpurg says that Blavet was a left-handed player, but that he never attempted to persuade others to hold the flute as he did, and that although he had composed many solos for his instrument, he played the music of other composers as frequently as he did his own.

During the reign of Frederick-the-First, Blavet visited Prussia, and the Crown Prince, afterwards Frederick-the-Second, was so much pleased with his performance on the flute that he offered him a permanent appointment, which was, however, declined. On Blavet's return to Paris, the Prince de Carignan provided him with an income, and apartments in his own house. Blavet afterwards became musical director to the Comte de Clermont, in whose service he remained until his death.

Quantz, during his visit to Paris in 1726, heard Blavet, Lucas, the two brothers Braun, Naudot, and other eminent players on the one-keyed transverse flute. He considered Blavet the best of all, and he writes of him: "His amiable disposition and engaging manners gave rise to a lasting friendship between us, and I am much indebted to him for numerous acts of kindness."

Blavet died in Paris on October 28, 1768, regretted by all who had known him.

Among his compositions for the flute are the following:

Premier oeuvre, contenant six Sonates pour deux flûtes traversières, sans basse. Paris, 1728; Premier, et deuxième, Recueil de pièces: petits airs, brunettes, menuets, etc., accommodés pour les flûtes traversières, etc. Paris; Sonatas or Duets for two German flutes or violins. London. (R.S.R.)

MAHAUT, ANTON: was a distinguished flute-player of Amsterdam from 1737 to 1760. He was also a composer of some celebrity, his published works consisting not only of concertos, sonatas, duets and trios for the flute, but also of symphonies, and Dutch, French and Italian songs. He is, however, chiefly remembered as the author of an important work entitled: *Nouvelle méthode pour apprendre en peu de temps à jouer de la flute-traversière, à l'usage des commencans et des personnes plus avancées* (Amsterdam, 1759). Fétis describes this méthode as "one of the first truly methodical works that have been published for the flute." I have been unable to procure a copy of it for inspection, although I have searched most diligently, both in London and in Paris, I am therefore unable to form any opinion as to its merits.

In 1760 Mahaut found himself so hopelessly in debt that he fled from his creditors to Paris, where he took refuge in a convent, and soon afterwards died. (R.S.R.)

FREDERICK-THE-GREAT: Frederick-the-Second was born on the 24th of January, 1712, at Berlin, and died on the 17th of August, 1786, at Potsdam. He was King of Prussia, a poet, composer and skillful performer on the flute.

In a republican country and during democratic times, royalty loses its aureole; yet proper and profound respect is due to the memory of the man who not only excelled in war, but encouraged the fine arts and devoted himself to composition and to the mastering of the most charming musical instrument.

"Frederick-the-Great as a Musician" was the theme of a most excellent paper by Arthur M. Abell. To emphasize the important part this monarch played in the development of musical art at his time, we quote the following paragraphs:

It would be almost impossible to overestimate the importance to Prussia, and indeed to all Germany, of Frederick's mission as a musician. The beginning of his reign marked the beginning of Berlin as a center of music, and it is well known that the Prussian capital exerted a powerful influence on other cities during Frederick's life. The musical awakening of towns like Magdeburg, Halle, Stettin and many other cities, for instance, dates from this period and is traceable directly to the influence of music at Frederick's court.

Frederick began the study of music at the age of seven, taking instruction on the clavichord from one Heyne, who was at that time organist of the Berlin Cathedral. Heyne was a dry old pedant and Frederick's natural love for music was not greatly stimulated by his narrow instruction. However, the practice he acquired in writing four-part chorales stood him in later years in good stead, when he himself began to compose. Frederick never revealed any great sympathy for the clavichord, nor did he attain to any high degree of skill on the instrument, although he played it more or less all his life. It was not until 1728, when he visited the court of August the Strong, at Dresden, that Frederick's great love for music was given the impetus that later made him so famous in the art. At Dresden the youth, then sixteen years old, heard opera for the first time. The playing of the finished orchestra, the soulful and artistic singing, the brilliancy of the decorations and costumes made an indelible impression on the

Prince. But what impressed him more than all these was the flute playing of Johann Joachim Quantz, the greatest flute virtuoso of his day. A month after this visit to Dresden, Quantz came to Berlin to give a concert at the court. On this occasion the Crown Prince Frederick was so carried away by Quantz's flute playing that he then and there decided to choose the flute as his favorite instrument and from that time on until the very last, it remained his faithful friend.

A great deal has been written about the violent opposition shown by Frederick's father to his musical studies. At first, however, the King was not opposed and he even endeavored to persuade Quantz to leave Dresden and take up his abode in Berlin. Not succeeding in this, he had Quantz come to Berlin twice a year and remain several weeks each time and during these visits the famous flutist gave lessons to the Crown Prince every day. Frederick's enthusiasm for music in general and for the flute in particular soon became so marked that he neglected his other studies and this aroused the opposition of his father, for he desired above all things to make a soldier of his son. By nature, Frederick had not the slightest inclination for militarism; on the contrary, he hated the very sight of a uniform and the daily drills were inexpressibly tedious to him. That he actually did neglect his general studies for the flute is unquestionably a fact and his father finally forbade him music altogether. From that time on he had to practice and have instruction in secret. Nor did the king have any sympathy for Frederick's predilection for poetry and for French literature. Despotic by nature, he took not the slightest cognizance of the fact that his son was differently constituted from himself and he demanded implicit obedience. All this opposition, however, far from killing the boy's devotion to music, served merely to fan the flame. Father and son became more and more estranged, until finally the break came that resulted in the Crown Prince's attempted flight with his friend Katte. His father often said: "Fritz is a pipe player and a poet. He cares naught for soldiering and will spoil all my work." The following letter, written to Frederick by his father some time before the break between the two is interesting and characteristic:

79

"Whenever we are out hunting or traveling, you always prefer to be reading a French book or playing the flute, rather than to take part in the chase or in military exercises. What good would it do if I should tickle your fancy and have a maitre de flute come from Paris with a dozen pipes and music books and a whole band of comedians and a great orchestra; if I should send for a company of Frenchmen and Frenchwomen and a couple of dancing masters and should build a big theatre for them? This would please you much more than a company of grenadiers, for grenadiers are in your opinion canailles. But a petite-maitre, a French girl, un bon mot with music and comedians—that seems to you nobler and more royal, that seems to you worthy of the dignity of a prince."

Less than a year after his visit to Dresden, Frederick's father forbade his playing the flute altogether. "I am the most miserable of human beings," he wrote to his sister Wilhelmina. "Surrounded by spies from morning until evening, my father forbids me the most innocent recreations; I dare not even read. Music is wholly forbidden me and I can only enjoy these things in secret and in fear and trembling."

After the attempted flight of the two, the King had Katte beheaded and he would even have taken the life of his own son but for the opposition of his ministers.

In 1732 began the happiest period of Frederick's life. From this time on, until he ascended the throne in 1740, he lived in his own palace at Rheinsberg, and here, free both from the tyranny of his father and from the responsibilities of the government, he enjoyed to his content music and poetry. Here he gathered about him a circle of congenial friends, founded a small orchestra and devoted several hours each day to flute practice. It was during these years that Frederick developed into a real flute virtuoso.

During all these years at Rheinsberg, the Crown Prince diligently studied the flute and composition under the guidance of Quantz and Graun. At the concerts Frederick played to the accompaniments of his orchestra flute solos either by himself or his teacher, Quantz.

In 1733, when Frederick was twenty-one years old, he was married to the Princess Elizabeth Christine. This marriage was arranged entirely by Frederick's father; the wishes of the young couple were not in the least considered, and later developments proved that the union was a great mistake. Frederick had always called the flute his *"principessa"* and had often declared to his sister Wilhelmina, who had accompanied him on the lute, that he would never have any other princess. And so it proved to be, for no woman ever succeeded in winning the permanent affection of Frederick-the-Great.

The ascension of Frederick-the-Great to the throne in 1740 marked the beginning of the musical life of the capital of Prussia. Frederick not only founded a royal opera, but he took care that an excellent orchestra composed of thoroughly capable musicians was provided and among the singers was the best available talent of the day.

A wonderful and versatile man he was, one of the most extraordinary personalities in the annals of history. The librettos of two of the most successful operas produced at Berlin during this period, *Sulla*, given in 1753, and *Montezuma*, given in 1755, were written in their entirety by the King himself. It has also been proved that Frederick wrote in part the text of numerous other operas, as *Cleopatra*, in 1742; *Fetonte (Phaeton)*, in 1750; *Coriolan*, in 1749; *Fratelli Nemici*, in 1756, and others. Frederick's favorite operas were *Coriolan*, *Sulla*, and *Montezuma*.

As a patron and performer of chamber music, Frederick-the-Great's achievements interest us no less than in the field of opera, and in this branch of art, as I have already said, he retained a keen interest to the very last. The philosopher of Sans Souci loved his flute above all things, and the fact that he composed no less than 121 sonatas for the instrument speaks for his passion for it, as well as for his industry. The manuscripts of the greater number of these compositions can still be seen here in the Royal Library. Considering the numerous demands made on his time in so many different directions, it is a matter of astonishment that the King found time to conceive and write out so many musical works. He composed nine operatic arias which were always sung in the various operas of Graun; three cantatas; two overtures in D and G; four concertos for flute, and thirty-four army marches, and Frederick was something more than a royal amateur trying his hand at composition; he had ideas in abundance and a thorough knowledge of the technic of the art. He always made a comprehensive study of every score penned by Graun, Agricola and the others, and his suggestions for changes and additions were always found to be valuable.

As a performer on the flute, Frederick was a veritable virtuoso, who won the unstinted praise of Quantz, the greatest flutist of the eighteenth century. Originality of invention the King did not reveal. For that reason his compositions have not survived, but they are of great historical interest and are invaluable in revealing to us, even to this date, the soul life of the famous monarch. For Frederick music was more than a pastime; it was a ruling passion, and if fate had not put him upon a throne and compelled him to become the greatest warrior of his time, he would undoubtedly have been one of the leading professional musicians of his day.

During the most brilliant musical period of Frederick's reign, 1741-56, Frederick devoted the hours from six to nine several evenings a week to chamber music; that is, he or Quantz played flute solos to the accompaniment of the small orchestra. Occasionally, by way of contrast, some of the leading artists of the Royal Opera would sing arias between the instrumental numbers. Karl Philipp Emanuel, the son of Johann Sebastian Bach, regularly played the harpsichord at these concerts. He was in the service of Frederick-the-Great from 1740 to 1767. Franz Benda was Frederick's concertmaster throughout his entire reign, from 1740-1786. Frederick's repertory was limited to compositions by Quantz and himself and the few pieces written for flute by Graun. The monarch has often been reproached for his onesidedness in this respect, but it must be remembered that very little had been written for flute solo at that time.

Quantz was equally honest and courageous in praising or censuring Frederick's compositions. Once when the orchestra was trying a new sonata by the King, the attention of all the musicians was attracted to an ill-sounding progression in open fifths. Karl Philipp Emanuel Bach gave emphasis to the forbidden fifths, but he said nothing and the other musicians also kept their counsel. Quantz cleared his throat, but he, too, said nothing, as he, of course, could not compromise the King before the others. A few days later Frederick conferred secretly with Franz Benda, his concertmaster, and under his direction changed the passage, saying jokingly, "We must not let this place cause Quantz a sore throat."

Quantz died while at work upon his three hundredth concerto for flute. The finale was finished by Frederick himself, and while performing it shortly afterwards at a concert at Sans Souci, the King remarked, after finishing the last movement, which he himself had written, "You see, gentlemen, that Quantz left this world with very good ideas." Frederick caused a beautiful monument to be erected in honor of his beloved flutist, which still stands in the old cemetery at Potsdam. The figure of Euterpe is seated with her head leaning on her right hand; her expression is inexpressibly sad; the flute has slipped out of her hand and her left arm encircles a sleeping boy who is holding in his hands a burnt out torch. Below the figure is engraved in marble a sheet of music, at the top of which is a flute with a laurel wreath entwined about it.

Let us now consider this remarkable potentate in that branch of the musical art in which he became most celebrated—as a performer on the flute. Before the outbreak of the Seven Years' War the King was wont to take up his flute four and five times daily. He always practiced for half an hour immediately after breakfast and then again during the forenoon, after the noonday meal and at the evening concerts he played for two and sometimes three hours. Night and morning he practiced regularly and diligently scales and arpeggios that Quantz had written out. During the Rheinsberg days, while he was still Crown Prince, Frederick frequently played six concertos for flute in succession, a circumstance that testified to his remarkable powers of endurance. There is no lack of testimony written down by the best connoisseurs of the period concerning the monarch's ability and proficiency as a performer on the flute. Some of these opinions are extravagant in their praise. Algarotti, for instance, writes in such superlatives that we are justified in supposing that he intentionally flattered the King. But in accordance with the consensus of opinion of the best judges, Frederick was a real virtuoso and far removed from the plane of the amateur. Mara said of him, "He does not play like a king, but like a real artist." Burney, another authority, who heard Frederick as late as 1772, when he was sixty years old, wrote, "The king's flute playing surpasses anything I ever heard among amateurs and in many respects even among professional flutists." In his younger years his execution of quick and difficult passages was very brilliant, but as he grew older, because of lack of breath and loss of teeth, his playing deteriorated in this respect. It then became a habit with him to cover up his lack of breath by taking liberties with the tempo.

All authorities agree as to his adagio playing. Quantz, Reichardt, Benda and even Johann Sebastian Bach himself admired the refined, artistic taste evident in Frederick's playing. Reichardt, himself a very critical professional musician, once wrote, "The King played an adagio with such depth of feeling and with such noble simplicity and truth that one could seldom listen to it without weeping."

Frederick himself always declared that he had a passion for the adagio, and whereas in all other things he generally wore a mask and seldom revealed his inner life to the world at large, he was wont to pour his whole soul into his beloved flute when playing an adagio. Many of the King's contemporaries, who were otherwise little given to associating sentimentality with their monarch, have testified that his playing of a slow movement frequently brought tears to their eyes. His flute playing served to relieve the terrible inner tension during his military campaigns. His soldiers in camp became so accustomed to his moods that they could tell the mental state of their beloved leader by the manner in which he played a slow movement. Quantz declared that even Frederick's allegro playing proclaimed to him whether the King's soul was troubled or at rest.

A number of flutes and a little traveling clavichord accompanied the great general on all of his military campaigns during the two Silesian wars. He played the flute daily. It afforded him great pleasure and he wrote jokingly of how the Austrians had stolen both his flute and his little portable spinet and he requested his friend Fredersdorf to send him a new one, as he

84

could not do without it. "The Austrians," he wrote, "have taken not only my equipage, but also my instruments." During the Seven Years' War, when the hand of fate rested so heavily on Frederick, the flute was a great solace to him. Weighed down with cares, he would improvise the most sad and melancholy tunes, which would conjure up to him mental pictures of his beloved Sans Souci of which he sometimes said, "I can hardly realize that such a place still exists"; and when the memory of happy days at Rheinsberg came over him and he fancied he heard the murmuring of the old lindens, "like the Jews at the waters of Babylon when they thought of Zion," as he expressed it, then he would seek consolation with his faithful little companion and forget the desperate present. No one will ever know what the music of his flute meant to Frederick-the-Great during the seven years of that fearful war. When in winter quarters Frederick would have a piano player and occasionally a quartet come from his capital to accompany him.

Fasch, who in the seventies was director of the Royal Opera, visited the monarch at his headquarters during the winter of 1760-61. The ravages of four years' hard campaigning had left their imprint. "I found," wrote Fasch to a friend, "an old and broken man. The five years of warfare and the hard fighting had filled him with care and sorrow. There had come over him an atmosphere of melancholy and weariness that was unnatural for a man of his age and quite in contrast to his former nature. It seemed to be a great effort for him even to play the flute."

The King's love of his chosen instrument and his interest in music, however, never waned, and during his last campaign he summoned a quartet of accompanists to Breslau. Scarcely had they reached camp when he called upon them to accompany him in a flute concerto. The King seemed greatly to enjoy the music. After the first solo he shouted, "Ach, das schmeckt wie Zucker!" (Ah, that tastes like sugar!) But the musicians noticed a great difference in his playing; his fingers had become stiff, he was short of breath, and his technic was very rusty. When he returned to Potsdam in 1779 the gout in his fingers had become so bad that he could no longer manage the instrument. It was a sad day for the great monarch when he laid away his flutes forever, saying to his faithful concertmaster, "My dear Benda, I have lost my best friend."

Frederick-the-Great's compositions were never intended by him for publication and it was without his knowledge that one of his compositions was published in Nuremberg in 1743. We have Quantz's testimony that all the parts of this composition were written by Frederick himself and Quantz had nothing to correct in it. Even Spitta, one of the greatest authorities of the nineteenth century, who made a thorough study of Frederick's compositions, declared this overture to be of "*tadelloser Sauberkeit.*" The work consists of three movements, an allegro, an andante and a finale. The first and last movements are written for string quartet, two oboes and two horns, the andante for two flutes and two violins. In speaking of Frederick's compositions, Nicolai once declared, "Whoever has seen solos by the king must admit that the harmonies of this amateur are more correct than those of many a professional musician." Spitta also claimed that this praise was just. After making a thorough study of Frederick's sonatas, Spitta wrote, "Although there are some amateurish peculiarities and even mistakes, there are many movements in which even the most exacting eye can detect nothing to criticize." At another time, Nicolai wrote, "In each solo it was the intention of the king to illustrate in a practical manner some difficulty or something pertaining to delivery. If we take these solos collectively, they form a musical curiosity, for they contain for the connoisseur nothing less than a practical course in flute playing." And to quote Spitta again, "In quick movements Frederick worked out very cleverly figures that interested him technically." The academic studies which often follow a deep, poetic and genuinely artistic thought, correspond to that combination of genuine feeling and dry, calculating coldness that one so frequently noticed in Frederick's actions and which formed such a mysterious part of his nature.

In 1886 the four concertos and twenty-five of the most interesting of the 121 sonatas composed by Frederick-the-Great were published. Spitta made the selections. The collection was published by Breitkopf and Härtel under the title "Musical

Works by Frederick-the-Great." Their appearance caused a sensation.

His compositions have recently been performed by Paul Wetzger, who also lectured on them. (R.S.R.)

DOTHEL, NICHOLAS: a noted German flute-player and composer of the 18th century. About the year 1750 he was connected with the chapel of the Grand Duke of Tuscany. Dothel is stated by Mendel and Reissmann, and by other writers, to have advocated a system of playing the flute, in opposition to that taught by Quantz, without the use of the tongue. This statement seems to have been founded on a criticism of Dothel's performance contributed to *Cramer's Magazine* by Dr. Ribock in 1783. The paper certainly affords no warrant for supposing that Dothel taught or advocated the avoidance of the employment of the tongue in flute-playing, but it seems rather to point to the fact that he did not articulate with sufficient force to satisfy his critic. He is also censured by Ribock for his monotony of style; his manner of taking breath, and his too frequent use of the tempo rubato, but, as Ribock's criticisms of all the flute-players whom he notices may be fairly summed up as a general condemnation of everything they did, his opinions are not entitled to such consideration.

Dothel's compositions were very numerous, and are said by Fétis to have been much prized in Germany. They include: Nine Concertos for the flute.—Seven Quartets for various instruments.—*Studi per il flauto, in tutti tuoni e Modi, 1763*. These were reprinted in London under the title: Twenty-one Capriccios or Preludes for the German Flute in All the Keys. The work was recommended by John Gunn as a supplement to his Art of Playing the German-Flute (1793). The following compositions of Dothel were also printed in London and may be seen in the Library of the British Museum: Six Duos for two German-flutes, or Violins.—Six Sonatas for the German-flute or Violin, with a figured bass for the Harpsichord or Violoncello.—Six Sonatas for two Flutes, or two Violins. Op. 3.—XII. *Sonatine Notturne per due Flautitraversi, o due Violini.*—Six Trios for two German-flutes, or two Violins, with a Violoncello obbligato figured for the Harpsichord. (R.S.R.)

JOHANN GEORGE TROMLITZ: was born at Gera in Saxony on February 9, 1726 and was well known as a flutist-composer-author, and especially flute-maker. In 1760 he settled in Leipzig, and there resided until his death. It does not appear that he ever occupied any orchestral post of importance, and although he frequently played solos in public he achieved but moderate success, as he always played at a disadvantage owing to his excessive nervousness. On this point he was evidently keenly sensitive, for he writes (1786):

"Flute players should not be judged by one performance, as it is impossible for a man to be always at his best. He may be unwell or otherwise temporarily unfitted for playing. If it is wished to hear a man play well he should be heard at home, for it is not every one who can play in public. Of all instruments the flute shows most plainly when one is out of condition, for a bad *embouchure* spoils the performance completely. It is all very well for people to say that he who understands his work thoroughly has nothing to fear; such is not the case. Nervousness is not always the result of incompetence; with ambitious persons it is often caused by the desire for success. Some there are who care equally little for praise or blame: that may be taken as a sign of incompetence. I have always observed that the more knowledge one gains, and the more skill one acquires, the more timid one is likely to become."

Before Tromlitz attained the age of fifty he relinquished public performance, devoting the remainder of his life to teaching and to the improvement of his instrument. In the latter occupation he was eminently successful, and we are perhaps more deeply indebted to him than to any other flute-constructor for the excellent system of open keys now in vogue, as it was he who first conceived the idea of extending the application of the open finger-holes of the primitive diatonic flute to the chromatic one of more recent times.

For many years Tromlitz held constant and friendly intercourse with his pupil, Dr. J. J. H. Ribock, but a feud occurred between them which was carried on by Tromlitz with most unjustifiable rancour. Although, as it appears, Ribock paid no fees for the lessons that he received, he was certainly charged heavily for the numerous flutes and extra joints that were constructed, and continually altered for him, by Tromlitz. It is, however, only fair to add that Ribock must have been an excessively trying customer, not only difficult to please, but prone to attribute the failure of his schemes to the manner in which they were carried out by his constructor. He published (1783) some disparaging remarks on the work and the charges of Tromlitz; he also, in an interesting though prolix article on music, particularly addressed to lovers of the flute, which was published in *Cramer's Magazine* (1783), further raised the ire of Tromlitz by omitting to mention his name either as a player, as a composer, or as a manufacturer. Considering himself slighted as well as traduced, Tromlitz entertained the most bitter animosity against his former friend and patron, which he did not scruple to display, in language decidedly venomous, even after Ribock's lips were sealed by death.

Besides his three important treatises on the flute (1786, 1791, 1800), Tromlitz wrote an often quoted article on tone-production (Ueber den schonen Ton auf der Flote) which was published in the *Allgemeine Musikalische Zeitung* for the year 1800. This essay, which contains much useful information, is disfigured by some severe but unjust strictures on the excellent Quantz and his admirable work on the flute. In its turn it was rather savagely criticized by Heinrich Grenser (1800), a noted flute-maker of Dresden, who seems to have lost no opportunity of attacking his rivals.

His compositions do not appear to have been held in very high repute, and they have been long since forgotten. Amongst those published were three concertos for flute and orchestra, two sets of sonatas for flute and harpsichord, and six solos for the flute.

Tromlitz died at Leipsig on February 4, 1805. (R.S.R.)

RAULT, FÉLIX: born at Bordeaux in 1736, the son of Charles Rault, Ordinaire de la Musique du Roi and principal bassoonist

89

at the Paris Opéra. While very young, Félix received lessons from the famous Blavet, and when only seventeen years of age was engaged in the orchestra of the Opéra, where he eventually succeeded his master as principal flutist. In 1768, the year of Blavet's death, Rault received an appointment in the Musique du Roi. He obtained his pension de rétraite from the Opéra in 1776, at which time he was a member of the Concert Spirituel. Amongst his pupils was Wunderlich, the instructor of Tulou.

In the *Essai sur la Musique* (1780) it is written of Félix Rault:

"His talents are so well known that they are beyond all praise. Since the death of Blavet no one has carried the art of flute-playing to such perfection, particularly in accompanying the voice, an art much more difficult than that of playing concertos, which are generally well studied before being played in public. Such study is, however, unnecessary for Rault who is unrivalled in the facility with which he reads music, as well as in style and expression. The beauty of the tone that he produces from the flute; the precision with which he plays, and his command of embouchure, extraordinary as they are, yet merit less praise than his personal qualities, which have endeared him to all who know him."

During the "reign of terror" Rault lost his pension and his appointments; he was then obliged to enter the orchestra of the Théâtre de la Cité. By the closing of this theatre, in 1800, he was reduced to extreme poverty, and died shortly afterwards.

Amongst the numerous compositions of Rault are mentioned: Trois Duos pour deux flutes. Op. 1—Idem. Op. 2.—Deux Concertos pour la flute avec orchestre, (No. 1 in D, No. 2 in G). Six Duos faciles pour deux flutes. Op. 5.—Six Duos pour deux flutes. Op. 6.—Six ditto, Op. 7.—Six Duos concertants pour deux flutes. Op. 8.—Six trios pour deux flutes et Bassoon. Op. 25-26—Recueil d'Airs pour deux flutes.—Six Trios pour flute, violon et alto.—Sonates pour flute avec basse. (R.S.R.)

WUNDERLICH, JOHANN GEORG: The son of an oboe player was born at Bayreuth in 1755. He received his first lessons on the flute from his father, but when he was twenty-one years old he went to Paris where he studied with Rault, who was at that time the most famous performer in France. Wunderlich became professor of the second class in the Paris Conservatoire de Musique when it was formed in 1795. Two years later he became the teacher of Tulou who was then only eleven years old. He became the only professor of flute at the Conservatory in 1803 and received Berbiguier as a pupil in 1805. He retired from the opera in 1813 and was succeeded by Tulou but he remained as professor at the Conservatory until his death in 1819. He is chiefly remembered as the editor of the "Methode de Flute" (1801) which had been prepared by Hugot. Wunderlich collected and arranged the manuscript when Hugot's intellect failed. It was published in the joint names of the author and editor and was at once accepted by the Conservatory. (R.S.R.)

DEVIENNE, FRANÇOIS: was born at Joinville in France on 31st January, 1759. While yet a child he played the flute in a regimental band, and at ten years of age he composed a mass with accompaniments for wind instruments, which was performed by his comrades. After having been for a short time in the service of Cardinal de Rohan, he joined the band of the Gardes Suisses, in which he remained until he entered the orchestra of the Théâtre de Monsieur as bassoonist in 1788. When, by the decree of the Convention Nationale in 1795, the Conservatoire National de Musique was formed by the amalgamation of the Ecole de Chant et de déclamation with the Institut National de Musique, Devienne was appointed professor of the flute in the first class, at that establishment, and there he received Guillou as a pupil. Equally skillful in his performance on the flute and the bassoon, he was engaged as principal bassoonist in the orchestra of the Paris Opéra in 1796. On the reform of the Conservatoire in 1802 his professorship ceased.

As a flute-player Devienne must be pronounced decidedly old-fashioned, even for the time at which he lived; he evidently made little use of the extra keys, although he recommended them to his pupils. Double-tonguing of all kinds he unreservedly condemned, designating it "bredouillage" (stuttering).

Notwithstanding his other professional avocations, and the

horrible turmoil of the Revolution, he composed in ten years sixty-two works, including six operas, several symphonies and some overtures, and he undertook, besides, the editorship of the *Journal d'Harmonie*, which was issued in monthly parts. At the age of forty-four he fell a martyr to his intense industry, and died insane at Charenton Lunatic Asylum on September 5, 1803.

Devienne's music was at one time held in great repute; his opera, *Les Visitandines*, was performed two hundred times, and his symphonies for wind instruments were particularly esteemed. The work by which this indefatigable composer is now best known is his *Méthode pour la Flute* (1795). Amongst his compositions for the flute are: thirteen concertos, in D, D, G, G, G, D, E minor, G, E minor, A and G (posthumous) respectively; several sinfonies concertantes for wind instruments; numerous quartets and trios for various instruments, including six trios for three flutes; sonatas for flute and 'cello, and flute and piano; twenty-four solos for the flute, and no less than eighty-four original duets for two flutes (Opp. 1, 2, 5, 6, 7, 8, 15, 18, 20, 53, 63, 64, 65 and 68), besides a large number of smaller works. (R.S.R.)

DULON, FRIEDRICH LUDWIG: a celebrated flute-player, blind from early infancy was born August 14th, 1769, at Oranienburg, in the province of Brandenburg. His father, a government official (*Stadt-Inspektor*), was a fairly good flute-player, having taken lessons from Neuff, a distinguished pupil of Quantz.

While very young, Dulon showed signs of great musical ability, and this was fostered by an old nurse, who, possessing a very good voice, was in the habit of singing all sorts of little songs, which the child soon learned. When scarcely eight years of age he could sing, or play on a comb with a piece of paper placed round it, two of Quantz's Allegros which he had heard his father play on the flute. On March 16th, 1778, a blind flute-player named Joseph Winter, visited Oranienburg, and little Ludwig on hearing him perform, evinced such a strong desire to learn to play the flute that his father undertook to teach him; but his fingers being too small to stop the holes, he had to content himself with the head-joint only, and to practice the production of tone. Having mastered this in a few days, he begged for the whole flute, and by dint of much perseverance succeeded in covering the holes.

At the age of nine he composed a minuet, and as he had little knowledge of time-signatures or the value of notes, he played it to his father who wrote it down for him. In 1777 he performed for the first time in public at Stendal, his tone and execution exciting universal admiration. His memory was marvelous; he could learn a Hoffmeister concerto by heart in three hours, and one by Quantz in an hour. About this time he commenced the study of harmony and the pianoforte, under Angelstein but although he made good progress in the former, he never was able to play the most simple pianoforte accompaniment.

On October 9, 1781, Dulon gave his first concert in Berlin, and during his journey to that city in the company of his father he made the acquaintance of Neuff at Potsdam, from whom he received some valuable advice. Kirnberger, a celebrated musician who had studied under Sebastian Bach, also took great interest in the young flute-player, although, as Dulon laments in his autobiography he never had an opportunity of playing before Bach's eminent pupil. In 1782 and 1783 Dulon again visited Berlin, and, when passing through Hamburg on the latter occasion, was fortunate enough to get an introduction to Kapellmeister Karl Philipp Emanuel Bach, who, on hearing him play, expressed great approval and encouraged him to persevere in composition. Dulon also visited Luchow, where he became acquainted with Dr. Ribock, with whom he played duets, and whom he describes as a "most engaging and intellectual man, whose well-contrived flutes were far superior to many manufactured by so-called masters." He also mentions Ribock's fancy with regard to "an excavation he was in the habit of making in that part of the head-joint of a flute which rests on the chin, thinking by this means to bring the flute nearer the mouth, so as to prevent any slipping in the event of the chin perspiring," adding: "I would not recommend any flute-player to adopt this plan, as the embouchure is thereby destroyed for any other flute." During the year 1783 Dulon formed a friendship with Karl Benda, the ballet-master at the Berlin Opera, and this excellent musician took great pains in teaching him the true style of playing an Adagio.

At Rheinsberg the kindly interest of Capellmeister Schultz enabled him to perform before Prince Heinrich, who, as a mark of approbation, made him a handsome present. Leaving Rheinsberg for Oranienburg, Dulon was introduced by Capellmeister Zeller to the Grand Duke of Mecklenburg Strelitz, whose sister played the flute, and after he had performed before these illustrious personages, the Princess requested that Dulon's father might be presented to her. To him she expressed a desire to become the possessor of the flute upon which his son had played, offering him six louis d'or and a Quantz flute in exchange. Her wish being gratified, she desired that Ludwig should give her lessons, and this he did.

In 1784 Dulon met Tromlitz at Leipsig and they played duets together. A year later he became associated with Forkel, the director of the music at the University of Gottingen, and with Weiss, a well-known flute-player of Mulhausen, the father of C. N. Weiss, who was long popular in London. Dulon speaks highly of the beauty and purity of tone, as well as of the rapid execution of Weiss.

In 1786 young Dulon was joined by his sister, who, for seventeen years, was his constant and devoted companion, never wearying of reading to him hour after hour, and to whom he was indebted for the large store of knowledge he possessed. During this year he paid a visit to England, and thanks to a letter of introduction to Queen Charlotte from the Duke of Mecklenburg Strelitz, he had the honor of playing at the court on several occasions.

During a visit to St. Petersburg, in 1792, Dulon was engaged as royal musician to the Russian Emperor, at a yearly salary of a thousand roubles, but in 1798 the Emperor granted him a pension, and he returned to Germany, where he gave many most successful concerts. From the year 1800 he resided for some time at Stendal in Marienburg, and there he composed his autobiography (1808), by means of a raised alphabet which had been invented for him by Wolke, the principal of a Dresden college.

In 1823 Dulon established himself at Wurzburg in Bavaria,

and not long afterwards he purchased an estate in Waldenburg, intending to spend the remainder of his days there in rest. His desire, however, was not fulfilled for he died at Wurzburg, on July 7th, 1826.

Dulon composed numerous works for his instrument, which were dictated by him with such care that not a single rest was wanting; they comprise the following pieces, all of which were printed at Leipsig: Concerto, Op. 8, in G; Duets for flute and piano—Six, Op. 1; Six, Op. 2; Twelve Variations, Op. 3; For two flutes—Three Duets, Op. 5; For flute and tenor—Three duets, Op. 6; For one or two flutes—Caprices, Op. 4. (R.S.R.)

BAYR, GEORG: born of poor parents in 1773 at Bomischkrud in Lower Austria. He was one of the numerous celebrated continental flute-players whose fame has scarcely reached this country. After having received his first music lessons at a Cistertian monastery near Vienna, Bayr manifested an extraordinary talent for flute playing, which he cultivated with assiduity. We have no further tidings of him until 1803, when he was playing the flute in the orchestra of one of the Viennese theatres. Subsequently he made a professional tour, which extended as far as St. Petersburg, and at last settled for a time at Krzemeniek in Podolia. In 1810 he returned to Vienna, and then for the first time, his great merits received the recognition they deserved.

Bayr seems to have been the discoverer of an ingenious artifice, now perhaps too commonly employed, namely, causing one flute to produce an effect similar to that of two. This pleasing novelty so astounded the musical public of Vienna that a commission was appointed to enquire as to the means by which the deception was produced, and whether all the sounds that were heard were really obtained from a single instrument. The report left no doubt that the means employed were perfectly legitimate, and that the apparently simultaneous sounds were veritably produced from one flute. In the meantime certain wild reports had been circulated, which eventually found their way into some of the standard musical dictionaries, so that one still meets with a statement that Bayr played double notes on the flute.

It will hardly be necessary to inform the flute-playing reader that the effect which created so much surprise was simply the result of playing a moderately soft "running" or arpeggio accompaniment between strong detached notes at some distance either above or below the accompaniment. The deception was, of course, partly due to the peculiar faculty of the ear for the retention of vivid impressions, in consequence of which the detached notes appeared to be prolonged and therefore to sound at the same time as the accompanying passage. Drouet created a similar feeling of astonishment, on the occasion of his first performance in London, by his skillful employment of the same artifice.

Bayr died in Vienna in 1833.

The following list of Bayr's works for the flute were all published in Vienna. Premier Concerto, Op. 3; Quartette, Op. 4; Six Variations, Op. 5; Second Concerto, avec quatuor, Op. 6; Variations avec quatuor, Op. 7; Deux Caprices pour flûte, Op. 8; Solos mit quart. oder P.F., No. 1-6; Praktische Flotenschule; 12 Landler und 4 Polonaisen; 7 Variationen, and Favorit Polonaise für 2 Floten. (R.S.R.)

WEISS, CHARLES N.: was born in 1777, probably in England. The father of this well-known flute-player and composer was Carl Weiss, a native of Mulhausen, who, in the year 1760, accompanied an English nobleman to Rome, in the capacity of music-master, and soon afterwards came to England. Through the interest of his pupil he obtained an appointment as principal flutist in the private band of George the Third. He is said to have been an excellent flute-player, and to have composed some good music for his instrument. He died in London in 1795.

Charles N. Weiss, though not intended to follow the musical profession, received lessons on the flute from his father at a very early age, and when only nine years old he played a concerto in public. While a lad, he was placed, much against his inclinations, in a counting-house, but he soon left his situation and was then sent to Paris, and afterward to Italy. In Bergamo he took lessons in composition from Simon Mayer, the Maître de Chapelle in the Church of Santa Maria Maggiore, but he still followed, in desultory fashion, his mercantile pursuits, until a dispute with his employer at length brought matters to a crisis, and young Weiss determined to gratify his own inclinations by adopting music as a profession.

He first started on his new career at Naples, where he gave lessons on the flute; he then went to Rome, and there he gave his first concert, which was highly successful. Traveling through Italy, he went to Geneva, and was there presented to Madame de Stael, who promised him good letters of introduction for England, but her death, in 1817, prevented the fulfillment of her promise. Soon after this event C. N. Weiss settled in London and became both popular and prosperous.

The termination of his career has been variously reported, and as I have no grounds for forming an opinion as to which is the correct account, I leave the question, perforce, an open one.

C. N. Weiss composed a great quantity of music, most of which is now forgotten. His published works for the flute include: Concerto in D, Op. 1; Studies on Modulation for two flutes, Op. 2; Two Hundred Studies, Op. 3; Seven Trios for three flutes; numerous Fantasias and Airs Variés for flute and piano; duets for two flutes; *Methodical Instruction* (book), Op. 50, an excellent work of its kind. (R.S.R.)

CAPELLER, JOHANN NEPOMUK: German flutist and guitarist who was a member of the court orchestra of the King of Bavaria in the early part of the last century. He was a good performer on both his instruments, particularly on the flute, but he did not acquire much celebrity. He was the instructor of Boehm, who played "second flute" to him in the King's band. Capeller is chiefly remembered as the inventor of certain contrivances for the improvement of the flute. A rather highly coloured account of these was written by the illustrious C. M. von Weber, and published in the *Allgemeine Muskalische Zeitung* in 1811. Weber says that it has an important bearing on the history of the flute, as will hereafter be seen. "Herr J. Nepomuk Capeller, a member of the Court-orchestra of Munich, has perfected the flute by a most ingenious invention which leaves scarcely anything to be desired. The advantages gained by his improvements are facility in altering the pitch without deterioration of the intonation, and great improvement in the shakes: thus the principal defects of the flute are removed.

"Herr Capeller took his first idea from an earlier invention, the tuning slide in the head-joint, to which Tromlitz has already drawn attention, and with which this invention must not be confused, for although the instrument could be altered in pitch by means of the slide, it lost its pure intonation. Herr Capeller's new flute consists of three pieces only. The two ordinary middle pieces are combined, and, in order that this middle joint may not be too long in proportion to the others, the length of the latter is somewhat increased while the middle is shortened, so that the entire length of the flute is the same as that of the ordinary flutes which are provided with the low c key.

"This flute has nine keys. The G-sharp key can be opened from both sides, the lower lever being governed either by the first or the second finger of the right hand, which gives great facility in making the shake F-sharp and G-sharp. The newly invented D-natural key, used by the first finger of the right hand, is intended for the shakes on C-sharp with D, but it serves also for the shakes on B with C-sharp and on d″′ with e″′. The low C key is so arranged that one can slur easily from C′♯ to C″, which was not possible with the ordinary C key. The other keys are as generally constructed, and with them all the notes and shakes can be produced in tune and with facility.

"The most important and interesting part of this flute is the mechanism for tuning. In order that this might be as perfect as possible, Herr Capeller has adopted a movable mouth-hole. This is placed in an oval plate of gold which is arranged in an elegant manner on the head of the flute. Not only the mouthpiece, but also the cork, can be moved at will by means of a screw. By this arrangement the pitch of the whole instrument can be rapidly altered, without any detriment, on the whole, to the general intonation.

"The great advantages of these improvements are so plain that it is unnecessary to say anything further in their praise, and the writer only has to remark that these flutes are made, not by a musical instrument maker, but by an artistic turner named

98

Fiegel, with such good results that the flute is on a par with those of the best instrument makers, as regards the neatness and the beauty of the workmanship.

"The price is not higher than that of an ordinary good flute, and Herr Capeller will be good enough to obtain one of the new flutes for anyone who desires to have one."

The following list contains the titles of all the known compositions of Capeller: Six Quartets for flute, violin, tenor and violoncello; Variations on a popular Swiss air, for the same instruments; a set of quartets for two flutes, guitar and violoncello; serenade for flute, tenor and guitar; twelve easy pieces for the same instruments. (R.S.R.)

BERBIGUIER, TRANQUILLE (Antoine, or Benoit): was born on December 21st, 1782, at Caderousse in France. He was destined by his family for the bar, but his attention seems to have been chiefly occupied by music, as he learned, without any instruction, to play the flute, the violin and the violoncello. At the age of twenty-three he left his native town, entered the Paris Conservatoire, and began to study the flute under Wunderlich and harmony under Berton. He followed the musical profession in Paris until 1823, when he left that city to avoid the conscription, a decree having been passed authorizing the raising of a levy of three hundred thousand men. In 1815 he joined the gardes de corps, in which he obtained the rank of lieutenant. He left the service in 1819, reestablished himself in Paris, and devoted the remainder of his life to music, but in 1830 he became involved in political troubles and was forced to quit the capital.

Berbiguier does not appear to have held any orchestral post of importance, but he was renowned as a solo-player, and as a composer for his instrument he still ranks high. The late Frederick Hill, who was his pupil for some years, used to say that he was an exceedingly fine player and that his style was particularly grand, but that his tone was not altogether free from coarseness, and that in artistic finish his performance was far superior to Tulou's. Berbiguier's views on the subject of tone, and his efforts to induce his compatriots to strive to obtain a larger volume of

99

sound than it was their wont to produce, were well known at that time, and it is not altogether improbable that the tone which was pronounced coarse, by many others besides Frederick Hill, was only thought so by those who had been accustomed to hear and to admire the "joueurs de flageolet" so contemptuously mentioned in Berbiguier's letter. Frederick Hill, who had long resided in Paris, could not endure a tone of any power or brilliancy in the lowest octave of the flute, and he accused Cornelius Ward of making flutes which had a "roaring tone in the lower notes," the fact being that the tone of Ward's flutes was rather weak than otherwise. Like many other flute-players of his time, Berbiguier played left-handed.

As regards the music of this celebrated composer for the flute, the usual variety of opinions prevails, the only point on which his critics agree being the inequality of his composition, as if any one ever did, or ever will, write a number of works verging on two hundred, of equal merit. As might have been expected, some of his compositions are poor in comparison with the best, but, on the other hand, some of them are simply delightful, and although none, that I have seen, can be fairly pronounced music of the higher class, yet the melodies, with which all his works are replete, occasionally savor of positive inspiration. Unfortunately most of Berbiguier's compositions are out of print, but some of them are still popular. His *Eighteen Grand Studies* have passed through at least six editions, and perhaps had a larger sale than any flute music ever printed. Schilling says: "It seems a strange thing that the Germans, who condemned his compositions, should have printed only the worst of them. His best works were printed in Paris."

Berbiguier lived eight years in retirement at Pont le Voye in Blois. Fétis thus describes the last scenes of his life: "The sorrow caused by the death of his friend Hugues Desforges proved fatal to him. After following the remains of his friend to the grave, he remarked to his companions: '*dans huit jours vous viendrez ici pour moi!*'" This prediction was verified. Berbiguier died on January 20, 1838.

A complete list of the works of this prolific composer would occupy more space than can well be afforded. The following are characteristic of his style and are among the best of them:

Concertos for flute and orchestra: No. 1, in D; No. 2, Op. 12, in A; No. 3, Op. 18, in B minor; No. 4, Op. 26, in E minor; No. 5, Op. 27, in E minor; No. 6, Op. 29, in G minor; No. 7, Op. 30, in E flat; No. 8, Op. 44, in D; No. 9, Op. 54, in D; No. 10, Op. 64, in A minor; No. 11, Op. 74, in D.

First Symphonie pour deux flutes, avec Orchestra, Op. 5; Second Symphonie pour deux flutes, avec Orchestra, Op. 154.

Trios for flute, violin and alto: Trois Grands, Op. 37.

Trios for three flutes: Op. 13, 33, 40, 51, 62, 70 and 110 (this is a delightful little work, an original cavatina, dedicated to his pupil, Frederick Hill).

For flute and pianoforte: Sonata in C, Op. 43; Sonata in F, Op. 79; 9 Themes variés; numerous melodies du salon; fantasias on operas; airs with variations.

Duets for two flutes: Three Duets, Op. 2, dedies a M. Colcough; three, Op. 4; three, Op. 15, a M. Chaix; three, Op. 22; six duets, Op. 28, a M. Bonecorse; three, Op. 35, a M. de Froment; three, Op. 38, a M. Camus (a remarkably fine set); three, Op. 45, a M. Bisetsky; three, Op. 46, a M. Rebsomen (the one-handed flute player); three, Op. 47, a M. du Medic; three, Op. 57, a M. de Rochefoucauld; three, Op. 58; six, Op. 59; three, Op. 61, a M. du Lac (the composer's favorite set); six (operatic), Op. 66; three, Op. 71 a M. Dubusc; three, Op. 85, a M. de Ste. Hilaire; six (operatic), Op. 93; three, Op. 99, to George Rudall (first printed in London); 36 petits dues, Op. 72 (invaluable for beginners); six, Op. 83; 48 preparatory duets, in 12 books.

Duets for flute and violin: three, Op. 32; three, Op. 76.

Numerous studies and solos, including the celebrated eighteen Grand Studies, originally forming part of the Méthode (1820 circa), and Thirty Grand Preludes or Cadences, Op. 140. (R.S.R.)

RUDALL, GEORGE: born in 1781 at Crediton in Devonshire, was the son of Samuel Rudall, a solicitor of that town. During his early childhood he evinced extraordinary fondness for the instrument with which his name probably always will be associated, and amused himself by making flutes of reeds, on which he taught himself to play tunes. It is a tradition in his family that he and his little flutes were such inseparable companions that he always took one of them to bed with him. He was apprenticed by his father to a serge-maker, but that calling was utterly distasteful to him, and he soon relinquished it. Shortly afterwards he received a commission in the South Devon Militia; flute-playing was, however, his ruling passion, and he practiced assiduously, unaided by any instruction. While quartered with his regiment at Liverpool he became acquainted with the Nicholsons, father and son, and from the latter he received a few lessons, but he really was almost self-taught.

In 1820, or shortly before, he left his regiment, and thenceforth resided in London, where he soon acquired an extensive connection as a teacher of the flute. According to the custom of the time, he supplied his pupils with flutes stamped with his name. These were made for him by a man of some repute named Willis, who resided in Clement's Inn, and they were the first instruments which bore the name that was destined to become so famous.

About the year 1821 a Scotch gentleman named James McWhirter, mentioned to Rudall, in terms of high commendation, a young flute-maker of Edinburgh who had served an apprenticeship at the organ manufactory of Messrs. Wood and Company in that city, and who had recently started in business on his own account. This was none other than John Mitchell Rose, who having long been an amateur flute-player, and possessing some knowledge of flute-construction, as well as great mechanical skill, was able to make a good flute from beginning to end with his own hands. Rudall undertook a journey to Edinburgh on purpose to see the young man who had been so warmly recommended, and the result of their meeting was a partnership of fifty years' duration. The firm, Rudall and Rose, first began business about the year 1821, at 11 Tavistock Street, Covent Garden; shortly afterwards they removed to number 7 in the same street; in 1827 they wee established at 15 piazza, Covent Garden; in 1847 at 38 Southampton Street, where Mr. Carte joined them in 1850; in 1852 they were at 100 New Bond

Street; in 1856 at 20 Charing Cross, having taken over the well-known military musical instrument factory of Key and Company. They carried on the two houses until 1857, when they removed entirely to 20 Charing Cross, and Rudall ceased to take an active part in the business. After the death of Rose the title of the firm was changed to Rudall, Carte and Company, and Mr. Carte shortly afterwards became the sole proprietor of the business. In 1878, the establishment was removed to 23 Berners Street.

For many years Rudall played on an eight-keyed boxwood flute, with what were then considered large holes; at the age of sixty-two he successfully adopted the so-called Boehm-flute, with the open g♯ key, and four years later he made a further change to the "cylinder flute." His nephew, Mr. Frank Rudall, informs me that the old gentleman "always felt a lingering fondness for the box-wood eight-keyed instrument on which his early triumphs in the musical world had been achieved." One can scarcely wonder at this, considering his advanced age when he changed his fingering.

It was always a source of regret to his friends that Rudall could never be induced to play in public; he even declined an invitation to play before George the Third, but as a drawing-room player he was immensely popular. I well remember my delight on first hearing him play; I thought he produced the most charming music that I had ever heard. Though his tone was not powerful, it was so clear, so sweet, and so indescribably sympathetic, that once heard it was not likely to be forgotten. His expression was absolutely enchanting, and his execution, as far as it went, perfect. He continued to teach the flute long after he had entered into business; one of his pupils was his future partner, Mr. Carte, who took lessons from him in 1822-23, and who still speaks in the warmest terms of the benefit that he derived from those lessons.

George Rudall was, in every sense of the word, a gentleman, his polished manners and his genial disposition causing him to be a favourite with all who knew him. For many years I enjoyed his friendship, and I retain the most vivid impression of his invariable kindness and urbanity. He played the flute until a very short time before his death, which occurred in 1871. In six weeks he would have completed his ninetieth year.

Many of the foregoing particulars have been kindly furnished by Mr. Frank Rudall and Mr. Carte. (R.S.R.)

TULOU, JEAN LOUIS. This eminent musician was born in Paris, on September 12, 1786. His father, Jean Pierre, played the bassoon in the orchestra of the Paris Opéra, and was one of the original staff of professors at the Conservatoire. At ten years of age Jean Louis entered the Conservatoire, and the following year he became a pupil of Wunderlich. In 1799 he gained the second prize for flute-playing, and the first prize was only withheld from him the next year on account of his youth, and because the authorities wished him to continue his studies, but he received an extra prize in recognition of his assiduity. At the succeeding examination, in 1801, the superiority of Tulou over the other competitors was so manifest that it was considered impossible to withhold the first prize from him any longer, for even at that early age he was regarded by many as the finest flute-player in France. He is reported to have played perfectly in tune, notwithstanding the imperfections of the flutes of that period; his tone, according to French ideas, was perfect; his execution was remarkable for its precision and brilliancy, but the greatest charm in the performance of this gifted youth was due to the inimitable grace and refinement of his expression. At eighteen years of age he was appointed principal flutist at the Opéra Italien, where he remained until the year 1813; he then succeeded to the position of his master Wunderlich at the Grand Opéra.

About the year 1814 Tulou was obliged to look to his laurels, for a most formidable rival had appeared in the field. This was none other than the redoubtable Drouet, then about twenty-two years of age, who was beginning to charm the fancy of the Parisians by his marvellous execution and the novel effects that he produced. The disputes between the respective partisans of the two champions waxed warm, and for about two years the question of supremacy was undecided, but on the occasion of the first performance of Lebrun's opera Le Rossignol, in 1816, Tulou played the important solo flute-part with such ineffable grace and tenderness of expression that all Paris hailed him as the victor.

Unfortunately for his own interests, Tulou was an ardent republican, and being in the habit of making use of intemperate language concerning the restoration of Louis the Eighteenth to the throne of France in 1815, he at last fell into disgrace, consequently he was not offered an appointment in the Royal Chapel. Soon after his immense success at the Opéra, he seems to have become rather unsteady, being much too fond of enjoying himself in society, not always of the most intellectual order, and being, besides, passionately addicted to "la chasse." In addition to these distractions, he became seized with an unfounded notion that he was destined to become a great painter, and he neglected his flute practice to such an extent that it was feared he would lose his supremacy over his rivals. He became at last so careless of his professional duties that frequently, when he was required to play in public, he had to borrow a flute, having mislaid his own. The following amusing anecdote, illustrative of his extraordinary carelessness, nerve and readiness of resource, is related by Fétis. At a concert given by Madame Catalani at the Théâtre Royal Italien, Tulou, being about to play a difficult solo before a crowded audience, discovered that a joint of his flute was cracked from one end to the other. Nothing daunted, he produced a piece of wax and some thread from his pocket; on the platform, before the audience, he proceeded to mend his flute, and while his friends were trembling in anticipation of a disaster, he, as confident as if his instrument had been in perfect condition, played his solo with so much taste and brilliancy that his hearers were transported with enthusiasm.

Tulou first visited England about the year 1817, but he did not there meet with the success which he anticipated and which he richly deserved. It must, I fear, be recorded that the average Englishman of the period was not gifted with very refined musical taste; he could enjoy a popular tune, played with a style of expression to which he was accustomed, and lavishly decorated with "embellishments"; he could admire the astonishing rapidity of execution and the *ad captandum* music of Drouet, but the artistic elegance and delicacy of the highest school of French flute-playing were utterly beyond his sense of appreciation. Tulou's performances were therefore coldly received, the English critics accorded to him only faint praise, and he soon returned to Paris much disappointed. The following criticism, which appeared in the *Quarterly Musical Magazine,* may be found interesting: "The reputation which Tulou had obtained in his own country was rather injurious to his success in this. The expectation which it raised in a public already accustomed to the brilliancy and clear articulation of Drouet, and the masculine power and expression of Nicholson, was not easily satisfied, and Tulou, although a very elegant and finished performer, was treated with an indifference which his talents by no means deserved. His compositions are greatly superior to those of Drouet, evincing much more science, taste and feeling."

On the death of Wunderlich in 1819, Tulou, being still under a cloud, was not elected to fill the vacant professorship at the Conservatoire, but Guillou, an artist of far inferior merit, received the appointment. Tulou was much irritated at what he deemed unjust treatment, perhaps none the less so because it was evidently the result of his own indiscretion. In 1822 he resigned his position at the Opéra, and this appointment also was conferred upon Guillou.

Having in the meantime re-visited London, and played a solo at one of the Philharmonic concerts, Tulou was induced in 1826, to return to his former position at the Opéra, and on January 1, 1829, he received the long coveted professorship at the Conservatoire. During a third visit which he paid to this country in 1829, he gave a concert in conjunction with a noted violoncellist named Bohrer. He played on that occasion a fantasia, an obbligato with Madame Malibran, and two duets with Bohrer. His performance, however, only seems to have confirmed the impressions previously formed.

The compositions of Tulou are exceedingly numerous, and most of them are excellent. Those amongst them which are the best suited for public performance, at the present time, are the fifteen Grand Solos for the flute with accompaniments for orchestra, quartet or piano. Thirty of his duets for two flutes have been arranged progressively and published in an excellent uniform edition at Leipsig.

Amongst the numerous pupils of Tulou were Captain Gordon, Walckiers, Coche, Brunot, Remusat, Demersseman and Dorus.

The well-known and successful flute manufactory, carried on in Paris by Tulou and Nonon, was established in 1831. Nonon separated from his partner in 1853, and then adopted as his trademark a treble clef; Tulou took for his a nightingale, no doubt, as Chouquet (1884) has suggested, in memory of his triumphant success in Lebrun's opera. The ideas of Tulou on the respective merits of the old and the new flutes are quoted in *The Flute* [a treatise by Rockstro]. To the end of his career he maintained the same opinions, and his especial pride seems to have been "stare super vias antiquas." The flutes which he made and used only differed from the ordinary old-fashioned French flutes, with the smallest holes and twelve keys, in respect of the f-sharp key. He retired from his profession in 1856, and died at Nantes on July 23, 1865. (R.S.R.)

KUHLAU, FRIEDRICH: was born on September 11, 1786, at Uelzen in Hanover. While quite a child, he showed such great musical talent that his parents, though poor, obtained pianoforte lessons for him. When seven years old, he had the misfortune to lose the sight of one eye through a fall when fetching water from a well on a dark winter's evening; but this loss did not seem to have arrested his musical studies, for his parents, still further taking their slender resources, soon afterwards sent him to Brunswick, where he entered a choir and received, besides the usual instruction in singing, good lessons on the piano, the flute, and the violin. He then went to Hamburg and studied composition under Christian Friedrich Schwencke, who had been a pupil of the celebrated Kirnberger. He pursued his studies with zeal and success, eventually gaining well-merited distinction, not only as a performer on the flute and the piano, but also as a composer, and especially as a contrapuntist.

In 1810 Kuhlau went to Copenhagen, in order to avoid the

conscription, and was appointed first flutist in the orchestra of the Royal Chapel and the Opera, receiving the title of "Chamber-Musician to the King of Denmark." At that time the national opera house was not in a flourishing condition, but the clever young musician succeeded in restoring its fortunes, and at the same time in establishing his own reputation by producing an opera of his composition entitled *Roeverborgen*. This work met with unequivocal success, and created so much enthusiasm amongst the good people of Copenhagen that Kuhlau's nationality was forgotten and he was hailed as "the great Danish composer." After the performance of his second opera, *Elisa*, which was almost as successful as the first, the King bestowed upon him the title of "Composer to the Court"; he then ceased to play in the orchestra.

Being naturally elated with his success and grateful for the favor that had been accorded to him, he determined to make his home in Denmark; he therefore purchased a house at Lyndbye, a small town near Copenhagen, where he resided with his parents, to whom he was most devoted and for whose sake he remained unmarried.

In 1825, Kuhlau visited Vienna and became intimate with Beethoven, who, indulging his well-known propensity for punning, wrote a round or canon on the words *Kuhl nicht lau* (which, but for the omission of the diaeresis on the first *u*, would mean "Cool, not luke-warm"). The canon begins with the notes in B-flat major, B-flat, A, C, and B-natural, which, according to the German nomenclature, spell the name B-A-C-H. This may have been intended as an allusion to the fact that Kuhlau was, in a musical sense, a descendant of the mighty master who had been the instructor to Kirnberger. (Note: See below for further comment on the Canon.)

The greater part of Kuhlau's works were composed in his abode at Lyndbye, where he wrote four more operas: *Lulu, Die Zauberharfe, Hugo og Adelheide,* and *Elvershojen.* the last of these was performed in 1828, and was enthusiastically received, but the reputation of the composer rests chiefly upon his splendid chamber music, in most of which the flute plays a leading part.

Friedrich Kuhlau has certainly done more than any other composer to raise the standard of flute music. For many generations to come, if not for all time, his name will be honored, and his music loved, by every admirer of the flute who has a soul above fantasias and variations on Scottish and Irish airs. The ever-increasing popularity of his works, and the numerous editions through which most of them have passed, may be regarded as a most hopeful sign that the taste for really classical flute music is extending. It was not to be expected that so great a man would escape calumny: he has been accused of all kinds of musical vices, including mannerisms, but it is somewhat reassuring to find his compositions are best appreciated by those who are the best qualified to judge of their merits. Kuhlau's greatest detractors have never dared to question his originality, and, as regards his so-called mannerism, it would be more just to describe it as a strong individuality, a quality common to all artists of mark, and from which neither Bach, Handel, Haydn, Mozart, Weber, nor Spohr was exempt. There is one supreme virtue in the music of Kuhlau, it never palls; on the contrary, one may play it every day, year after year, without its losing its freshness, and the more intimately one becomes acquainted with it, the more strongly one becomes impressed with the genius of its illustrious composer, to whom might indeed have been said: "*Semper honor, nomenque tuum, laudesque manebunt.*"

The good fortune which had been Kuhlau's constant attendant for twenty years was brought to a sad and abrupt termination by a series of terrible calamities which happened to him in 1830. His house was burned down; all his manuscripts, including a large number of unpublished compositions, were destroyed, and very shortly afterwards he lost both his parents. Under this accumulation of disaster he broke down completely, his health becoming seriously and permanently affected. He died on March 12, 1832, his obsequies being performed with great pomp, and his memory honored by various solemnities at the theatre as well as at the meetings of numerous private societies.

The world of flute-players declares him as "The Beethoven of the Flute," a sobriquet he deserves as a result of his achievements.

The following list includes all the compositions of Kuhlau, for the flute, that have escaped destruction:

Three Quintets for flute, violin, two tenors and violoncello, Op. 51; No. 1 in D, No. 2 in E minor, No. 3 in A. Grand Quartet for four flutes, Op. 103, in E minor, dedicated to Gabrielski. Grand Trio for two flutes and pianoforte, Op. 119, in G.

Trios for three flutes: No. 1, Op. 13, in D, dedicated to A. E. Muller; No. 2, Op. 13, in G minor to G. Kummer; No. 3, Op. 13, in F to G. Klingenbrunner; No. 1, Op. 86, in E minor to C. Keller; No. 2, Op. 86, in D to B. Romberg; No. 3, Op. 86, in E-flat, to L. Drouet; No. 7, Op. 90, in B minor to T. Berbiguier.

Sonatas for flute and pianoforte concertante: No. 1, Op. 64, in E-flat, dedicated to M. deKaas; No. 2, Op. 69, in G, to C. Keller; No. 3, Op. 71, in E minor, to J. Sellner; No. 4, Op. 83, in G; No. 5, Op. 83, in C; No. 6, Op. 93, in G minor (this set is dedicated to George Onslow); No. 7, Op. 85, in A minor, to L. Maurer; No. 8, Op. 110, in B-flat; No. 9, Op. 110, in E minor; No. 10, Op. 110, in D (this set is dedicated to Mme. La Baronne de Schwerin); No. 11, Op. 51, in D, to Franz Schubert; No. 12, Op. 51, in E minor, to J. W. Kalliwoda; No. 13, Op. 51, in A (these three are the composer's arrangements of the quintets); No. 14, Op. 33, in F minor, to L. Spohr (this is an arrangement by Louis Drouet, of a sonata for violin and piano); Four Sonatinas for flute and piano; "Recollections of Copenhagen" (the flute part adapted by Sedlatzek), Op. 6, in D; Op. 79, in F, A minor, and C.

Fantasias, etc., for flute and Piano concertante: Introduction and Variations on a romance from Weber's *Euryanthe*, Op. 63; Variations on *Le Colporteur*, Op. 94; Introduction and Rondo on *Le Colporteur*, Op. 98; Variations on *Le Colporteur*, Op. 99; Introduction and Variations on the duet ("Fairest Maiden") from Spohr's *Jessonda*, Op. 101.

Duets for two flutes concertante: First Set, Op. 10, in E minor, D and G (1, 2, 3), dedicated to G. D. deLorichs; Second Set, Op. 39, in E minor, B-flat and D (4, 5, 6), to A. B. Furstenau; Third Set, Op. 80, in G, C, and E minor (7, 8, 9), to Gabrielski; Fourth Set, Op. 81, in D, F, and G minor (10, 11, 12), to Tulou; Fifth Set, Op. 87, in A, G minor and D (13, 14,

15), to Counsellor Thornam; Sixth Set, Op. 102, in D, E minor and A (16, 17, 18), to C. Scholl, Op. 103, No. 2, Op. 119, No. 3.

Solos without accompaniments: First Set, Op. 54, in D, G minor and C (1, 2, 3), dedicated to G. A. Schneider; Second Set, Op. 57, in F, A minor and G (4, 5, 6), to Tulou; Third Set, Op. 68, in G, D and B (7, 8, 9), to P. N. Petersen; Fourth Set, Op. 68, in E-flat G and C-sharp minor (10, 11, 12), to M. Parish; Fifth Set, Op. 95, in G, E minor and D (13, 14, 15), to C. H. Wiehe; twelve small solos, published in London as Passetemps; Fantasia on "Durandarte and Balerma"; Fantasia on "Groves of Blarney" ("The Last Rose of Summer"). Pianoforte accompaniments have been added to the last-mentioned fantasias, as well as to the second set of grand solos, by Frederick Hill. To Nos. 1 and 2 of Op. 68, and Nos. 1 and 2 of Op. 95, accompaniments have been added by Franz Doppler. (R.S.R.)

A word of blame is due to all the editors for omitting the names, in modern editions, of those artists to whom the author dedicated his works, as this is always of interest.

Many years ago, to be exact in 1903, I first read that Beethoven, on an outing where much eating and much more drinking took place, wrote, or attempted to write, a Canon in honor of Kuhlau's name. Kuhlau was greatly admired by Beethoven whose friendship on this particular occasion became more cordial. Since 1903 I have repeatedly tried to procure details about the Canon with no result. In 1935 a Milano musical paper reported that the whole story about the Canon and the outing at which Beethoven had composed on Kuhlau's name was published in Die Musik, a Berlin music magazine. In vain I tried to secure a copy through German friends and even wrote to Germany. At last I said: "I have asked numerous people except a friend of mine, Dr. Gustav Arlt, who is a musicologist at the University of California." And, indeed, through him I obtained Die Musik for 1935 bound in one book.

At last I was able to find out that the man who wrote the much sought after article knew Kuhlau only as the composer of the piano sonatinas and a few operas amongst which was one

—*The Robber's Castle*—which had met with fine success at Copenhagen. In a footnote he says that Kuhlau wrote three flute quartets! We flutists know how erroneous this statement is. Kuhlau wrote three quintets for flute, violin, two violas and 'cello, Op. 51, but only one flute quartet, not counting the one in manuscript destroyed by fire.

I was glad to learn, though, that the Canon in question was written, or attempted to be, in the names of Kuhlau and Bach and that there is a whole book on Kuhlau by Karl Thrane which I am going to include in my library one day if possible.

The article, written by Walther Nohl (Berlin) has three sketches. The first is clear enough except the letters on the second, third, and fourth notes.

The second sketch is evidently, a puzzle. It more than resembles the one on Kuhlau's lithograph in my possession and of which I have written and illustrated before. The slight difference will be found in the numbers which will not produce the same chords. Nohl, the writer, thinks it might have been written by Tobias Haslinger, also of the party, but I am inclined to think it was written by Kuhlau.

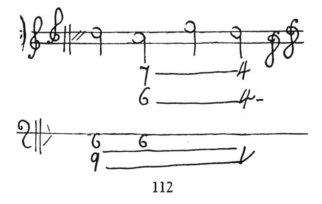

The third sketch, written by Beethoven, is in five staves, and even more illegible than the second, a veritable Egyptian hiero-glyphics.

The outing, or picnic, on which Beethoven, Kuhlau, and several of their friends took part, occurred at the beginning of August 1825. There was plenty of hilarity and genuine fun, but at no time was there the least sign of triviality or vulgarity. In a letter to Kuhlau, the next day, Beethoven apologizes that on account of too much champagne the Canon was not what it was meant to be. Kuhlau, writing to a friend, says that Bee-thoven, a few days later, did send him a magnificent Canon on his name. This Canon was never found and, evidently, never seen by any of their friends. It might have been in the box of Kuhlau's manuscripts which was destroyed by fire.

DROUET, LOUIS FRANCOIS PHILIPPE, the famous flute virtuoso, was born in Amsterdam in 1792. His father, a refugee, left France, of which country he was native, because of the turmoil occasioned by the Revolution. As a child Drouet was regarded as a flute-playing prodigy. He appears to have been self-taught. It is stated that his serious study of the flute began in 1807 after a great success at a concert of Rode's in Amsterdam. As early as 1808, when only sixteen years of age, he received an appoint-ment as solo flutist to the King of Holland; three years later he accepted an invitation from Napoleon I to become Imperial Court Flutist at Paris.

He soon acquired continental celebrity and made many suc-cessful concert journeys through Europe. Although the tone he produced was not large, his general technic was excellent and his double-tonguing remarkably brilliant and characteristic.

In 1815 he came to London and established a flute-making

113

business. This he carried on until 1819 when it was given up owing, it has been stated, to the number of bogus "Drouet" flutes put upon the market by trade rivals.

Drouet made his first appearance at the famous Philharmonic, London, on March 25, 1816. He played at other places in the British capital in 1817, 1829, 1830 and 1832. The 1829 visit was made in company with Mendelssohn who joined the flutist in the concert venture. The first appearance of this celebrity in London was made in 1841-42, at Buckingham Palace, on which occasion he played before Queen Victoria and Prince Albert.

During his active career as a flute virtuoso Drouet was responsible for a vast amount of flute music—concertos, fantasias, studies, duets, trios, etc., etc. His *Robin Adair, God Save the Queen,* and *Rule Britannia* enjoyed wide popularity. It is stated that he assisted Queen Hortense in composing the music to the song *Partant pour la Syrie.* Captain Gordon (he of the Boehm-Gordon controversy) and the King of Holland were two of his pupils.

In 1836 in succession to Gaspard Kummer, he became Chapel Master to the Duke of Saxe-Coburg-Gotha and thenceforth his wandering about Europe was restricted. For years little was heard of him outside of Germany. He did not adopt the Boehm flute, indeed, it has often been said that he was opposed to its use, but no evidence has yet been adduced to prove this. On the contrary, as may be seen hereunder, when he became acquainted with the Boehm he was most favorably impressed with its value as a musical instrument.

In 1854 Drouet ceased to be Chapel Master and during that year he visited America. In New York he found himself in the congenial society of Philip Ernst, at that date probably the most eminent flute-player in America. Ernst lent him a Boehm flute. This was returned with a letter the full text of which is here given:

To Messrs. Philip Ernst & Son
   New York.   June 6th, 1854.
Gentlemen:
   With many thanks I would return the instrument which you have had the politeness to lend me. Although I have known for some time

114

of Mr. Boehm's new flute, it was not until now, owing to my arduous duties as Chapel Master, that I was induced to make a thorough trial of its superior merits.

I find its mechanism by far less complicated than I had imagined and the fingering remarkably simple. But what pleases me more is the great ease with which each note can be produced and the perfectness of tune and tone of the whole scale. It offers also to the tasteful player the possibility of blowing loud and soft without getting out of tune. These have appeared to me the most prominent features of Mr. Boehm's valuable invention and they will no doubt insure its general adoption by our rising flutists, and especially those who would secure a good degree of execution at the expense of as little time and labour as possible.

Yours respectfully,

L. DROUET

The above letter was published together with a number of flute studies especially written for the Boehm flute by Drouet. These flute studies were issued by Ernst to subscribers whose names are detailed in a list within the volume. In this list the names of the most prominent American flute-players of that date may be found. The copy of this work which I have used was formerly the property of W. N. Habersham, of Savannah, Georgia, U.S.A.

After his return from America to Europe, Drouet lived in Gotha and Frankfort. He died in Berne, Switzerland, September 30, 1873. (John Finn.)

FUERSTENAU, ANTON BERNHARD: was born at Munster in Hanover on October 20, 1792. At six years of age he received his first lessons on the flute from his father, Caspar Fuerstenau, an artist of some repute, and his precocity seems to have been extraordinary, for after one year's training he was sufficiently advanced to play a solo in public before the Duke of Oldenburg, who presented him with a new flute. After that time the child frequently played at public concerts in Bremen and Oldenburg. At the age of nine he began a concert tour which extended to Copenhagen. In 1805, the father and son, who were inseparable companions, traveled through Germany and to St. Petersburg.

They undertook long journeys almost every year, and one of these, in 1811, extended through the greater part of Europe. At every place they visited, young Fuerstenau gained fresh laurels, being always received with the greatest enthusiasm.

In 1817, Anton, being tired of his peregrinations, accepted an engagement in an orchestra at Frankfort-on-Main, and settled there with his family. In that town he formed a friendship with a good musician named Volweiler, from whom he received further instruction in harmony, and by whose aid he became an adept in the art of composition.

In the following year the elder Fuerstenau began to grow weary of leading a life of inactivity, therefore Anton, who was always most devoted to his father, gave up his appointment, and once more the two set out on a concert tour. This journey, their longest and last, proved a great success, and not until 1819 were the family re-united at Oldenburg. Soon afterwards the father died, and Anton was attacked by a long and serious illness. Having at length regained his health, he accepted, in 1820, an appointment as first flutist at the Royal Chapel in Dresden, under the directorship of Carl Maria von Weber, with whom he formed a close friendship. Fuerstenau made his home in Dresden for more than thirty years, enjoying great popularity and consideration, but he did not altogether relinquish his concert tours. In 1823 he went to Denmark; in 1824 to Bavaria; in 1826 to Paris, and, with his friend Weber, to London, where he met with but indifferent success. In 1828 he gave concerts in Vienna and Prague.

A. B. Fuerstenau was not only the most finished flute-player that Germany ever produced, but he was one of the most skillful artists in all Europe. That his playing was no better appreciated in England than that of Tulou had been, can only be set down to the prevailing uncultured taste of the British people. The following extract from *The Quarterly Musical Magazine*, 1826, the best English musical periodical of the time, will serve to show how little Fuerstenau's refined style was understood in England. *The Oratorios*—Mr. Fuerstenau, first flute at the Chapel Royal, Dresden, played a fantasia. His execution is brilliant, but his tone is thin; he falls infinitely short

116

of Nicholson, a celebrated English flutist (1795-1837). We believe this quality, or rather defect of tone, appertains to the instrument now generally in use throughout Germany; it resembles the flageolet. Mr. Fuerstenau has been heard at several other concerts, but this defective tone always operates as a drawback from his general ability." The opinions of the editor of *The Flutist's Magazine* (1827) are couched in a similar strain: "The name of Fuerstenau was well known in England, before he himself arrived in London, for the beauty of his music had long ago made every amateur well acquainted with it. That his introduction to the London musical world, therefore, should have created a sensation, was a circumstance naturally to be expected and, like most other things of high expectations, was, we might say, as naturally doomed to cause disappointment. Mr. Fuerstenau, too, was disappointed as well as his audience . . . the cause of this may be stated very shortly and simply . . . It is solely and entirely to be attributed to his deficiency in tone, for in execution he was scarcely inferior to any performer who had previously appeared; his expression, likewise, was of a high character, tender, soothing and appropriate; his articulation perfect and finely softened, and his feelings those of the true musician. But with all these requisites he produced little or no effect in the performance of a concerto. His tone was thin and meagre, and this . . . was completely felt and acknowledged."

The cause of Fuerstenau's want of success in England lay probably in the fact that he did not strive to make his flute sound like a trumpet, a hautboy, or a clarinet. His notes were no doubt somewhat wanting in strength, but R. S. Rockstro states that he has been informed by those who had often heard him play, that his tone was so sweet, so flexible and so absolutely flute-like throughout the whole compass of the instrument, as to make ample amends for its deficiency in the matter of mere power. The following remarks of Fétis on the performance of Fuerstenau (1865) seem to be more worthy of consideration than those of the English critics: "Fuerstenau has justly been esteemed in Germany as one of the first, if not quite the most accomplished of European flutists. His performance was remarkable for purity and volume of tone; subtle gradations of light and shade; promptness and clearness of articulation; elegance of style and loftiness of expression. . . . In 1849 I met Fuerstenau in Dresden; he was still full of enthusiasm for his art."

This able artist did not approve of double-tonguing, and like Tulou, whom he resembled in many points, he was a strong opponent of the open-keyed system and the altered fingering. He continued to play on an old-fashioned flute with only nine keys, including that for the low B-natural, until his death, which occurred at Dresden on November 18th, 1852.

The following list includes his principal compositions:

Concertos, etc., for Flute with Orchestra or Pianoforte accompaniments: Op. 12, in E minor; Op. 31, in F; Op. 33, in A; Op. 35, in C-sharp minor; Op. 40, in E minor; Op. 52, in A-flat; Op. 58, in G minor; Op. 77, in E minor; Op. 84, in D; Op. 100, in B minor; Op. 104, in A; Op. 119, in G; Rondo brilliant, Op. 38, in E; Polonaise (two), Op. 3 and 31; Concerto pour deux flutes, Op. 41 (in F).

Quartets for Flute, Violin, Viola and 'Cello: Op. 39, in E; Op. 60, in A-flat; Op. 62, in F; Op. 74, in G minor.

Quartet for Four Flutes: Op. 88 (introducing the Austrian National Anthem), in F.

Trio for Three Flutes: Two, Op. 14; Trios, avec des Fugues, Op. 22 and 66; Trio, Op. 118.

Duets for Two Flutes with Pianoforte accompaniment Adagio et Variations, Op. 55; Concertino, Op. 87; Introduction et Variations, Op. 102; L'Union, Op. 115; La Ravalite, Op. 116; Deux Rondolettos, Op. 124; Introduction et Rondeau, Op. 132.

Solos for Flute with Piano Accompaniment: Trois grands Solos, Op. 37; Numerous Fantasies, Nocturnes, Caprices, Airs varies, Divertissements, etc.

Duets for Two Flutes: Three each, Op. 13, 36, 39, 56, 59, 61, 75, 83, 85, 89, 112 and 114; Six, Op. 137.

Songs with Flute Obbligato: Romance in E, "Lovely Flute"; "Le jour ou je te vis" (in F); "Stille der Nacht" (Grateful Silence); "Le Chant d'Amour" (Oh sing forever), in C.

118

Studies, etc.: Exercises, Op. 15; Etudes, Op. 26; Grandes Etudes, Op. 29; Flotenschule, Op. 42; Uebungen (Studies) Liv. 1-2, Op. 107; Tagliche Studien, Op. 125; Die Kunst des Flotenspiels, Op. 138 (1834, post). Numerous flute solos. (R.S.R.)

WALCKIERS, EUGENE: This highly distinguished composer of music for the flute was born in the year 1793 (not in 1789, as generally stated) at Avesnes in French Flanders. He received his first lessons from Marchand, but he afterwards studied composition under Reicha, with whom his talent and assiduity caused him to be a great favourite, and he was fortunate enough to obtain flute lessons from Tulou. Walckiers played the old-fashioned French flute throughout his life, and his well-known excellent instruction book (*circa* 1829) is written for that instrument, but, in common with many French and German players he trifled with the new flute for a short time, when it was first gaining public favour, without seriously adopting it or discarding the old one. It does not appear that he ever acquired great distinction as a flute-player, and all my researches for particulars of his career in that capacity have proved nearly fruitless. As a composer of chamber music for the flute his memory will long be revered by all true lovers of the instrument, indeed he can scarcely be said to have a superior in composition of this class, for although it must be conceded that his music is less scientific than that of Kuhlau and Kummer, yet it abounds in such delightful freshness and such impulsive variety of sentiment that in its own peculiar style it is absolutely unrivalled. The duets, trios and quartets of Walckiers belong to the highest school of French art, and prove their composer to have been a man of real genius. They are exceedingly imaginative, occasionally rather eccentric, yet always elegant, charming, and scholarly. As a writer of flute-solos, however, he was generally inferior to Tulou. Walckiers died in Paris on September 1, 1866.

The most important of his compositions are included in the following list: Quintette pour flûte, deux violons, alto et violoncelle; contra-basse ad lib. Op. 49 (in A); Idem pour flûte, violon, alto, violoncelle et contrabasse (in A minor), Op. 90;

Quartets for Flute, Violin, Alto and Violoncello: Three, Op. 5, in A, G and D minor; One, Op. 50, in D; Quartets for Flute, Clarinet, Horn and Bassoon: Three, Op. 7, in B♭, A and F; One, Op. 48, in B♭. Trois Trios pour flûte, clarinette et basson (in B♭, F and C minor), Op. 12; Premier Trio pour flûte, violon et violoncelle, Op. 35; Trois Trios pour flûte, violon et violoncelle, ou pour trois flûtes (in E♭, A, and C) Op. 93; Trio pour flûte, violon (ou alto, ou clarinette) et piano (in G minor), Op. 95; Trio pour flûte, piano et violoncelle (in D minor), Op. 97; Quartets for four flutes: Op. 46, in F♯ minor; Op. 70, in F. (London); Trios for Three Flutes: Op. 2, in F; Op. 3, in D; Op. 29, in D; Op. 37, in B♭; Three, Op. 93, No. 1 in E♭, No. 2 in A, No. 3 in C; Duets for Two Flutes: Three, Op. 1; Three, Op. 11; Three (à son frère), Op. 16; Three, Op. 19; Three, Op. 23; Three, Op. 27; Twelve ("faciles"), Op. 55; Six ("moins faciles"), Op. 56; Six ("brillants"), Op. 57; Six ("difficiles"), Op. 58; Duets for Flute and Violin: Six, Op. 6; Three, Op. 8; Three, Op. 10; Three, Op. 14; Grand Duo pour flûte et piano concertantes, Op. 24; Sonatas for Flute and Piano: Op. 89, in D; Op. 92, in A minor; Op. 98, in F; Op. 109, in E♭; Solos for Flute with Piano or Quartet Accompaniment: Premier Concertino, Op. 28; Rondo Savoyard, Op. 20; Fantaisie, Op. 21; Rondo espagnol, Op. 31; a large number of operatic fantasias and airs with variations; Grand duo pour flûte et piano sur des motifs de *Robert le Diable* (Kalkbrenner et Walckiers; Idem sur des melodies styriennes (Thalberg et Walckiers); Méthode de Flûte, Op. 30, in deux parties. (R.S.R.)

BOEHM, THEOBALD: At various times in this series mention has been made of the Boehm flute as the new flute, the new system flute, and so forth; its merits, advantages, and superiority were also cited without having ever more than merely touched on the life and career of its inventor. Yet the story of the personality, trials, successes, travels, experiences and work of this great man fill many pages of the flute's history. His renown shall always be remembered as long as the flute shall remain an instrument of musical expression.

Theobald Boehm was born in Munich, Bavaria, on April

9th, 1794, the son of Karl Frederick Boehm, a celebrated gold-smith and jeweler.

Young Boehm was apprentice to him in his workshop and was, of course, intended to carry on his father's business. He attended the drawing school of the famous Professor Mitterer and very soon reached first place amongst the pupils. Already in his fourteenth year, Boehm was a goldsmith of consummate skill and left the beaten track in all he did.

While still a child, Boehm was exceedingly fond of music, and his first instrument was a flageolet, which, however, he soon abandoned in favor of the flute. In 1810, he constructed his own flute after a model of an instrument with four keys from the workshop of Karl August Grenser, of Dresden. His enthu-siasm aroused the attention of Johann Nepomuck Capeller, a member of the court orchestra, who said to him one day, "You young flute player, I can no longer stand your noise; come to me; I will show you how to set about it." Thereafter, he became for two years the most painstaking pupil and constructed flutes for himself and his teacher—both working at the improvement of the faulty old flute.

After less than two years' practice, young Boehm's command of the flute had become the topic of the day in Munich, and he was accordingly appointed first flute in the orchestra of the new theatre at the Isargate, when he was eighteen years old. During the day he worked as a goldsmith and jeweller in his shop; in the evening he sat in the orchestra as a flutist.

In 1816 Boehm made his first tour to Switzerland as "gold-smith and musician." There he took considerable interest in the manufacture of music boxes and it was not very long before he invented and constructed a small machine to supersede the tedious process of driving the pins into the cylinders by hand.

Boehm was appointed court flutist in the place vacated by the deceased Becke in 1818. He now began to study composition under the celebrated Joseph Graz. His first composition was published in 1822.

By that time Boehm ranked amongst the favorite virtuosi of Munich and an increase of salary having been granted, he gave up working as a goldsmith and devoted himself entirely to music. His playing and compositions received unstinted applause whether at home or on the various concert tours he undertook.

The sale of flutes made under his superintendence by the instrument makers of Munich had helped to increase his income, although the latter was hardly large enough for the support of his family. However, the shortcomings of the flute in those days and the unsatisfactory, inaccurate methods of manufacture prompted Boehm to found a factory of his own. His chief object henceforth was the production of a musically perfect flute. In his capacity as an artist he had had plenty of opportunities of discovering the imperfections of an instrument otherwise so charming, and he set about to remedy the defects one by one.

The first flute manufactured in the workshop of Boehm had the improved key mechanism characteristic of the instrument which bears his name. This was in 1828. Orders for these flutes soon exceeded the capacity of the factory.

In January 1831, Boehm went to Paris, where he caused the greatest sensation by his playing and his flute. From there he left for London, at the end of March. Everyone was struck with the purity of tone possessed by Boehm's flute. Here he made the acquaintance of the great English flute player, Charles Nicholson. The extraordinary and previously unheard of volume of tone of this tall and vigorous Englishman set Boehm athinking on the nature of the musical tone. The flute played by Nicholson was the ordinary one, but the holes had been so increased in size as to suit the large and powerful fingers of the player; consequently, his tone surpassed in fullness and force that of all flutists of his time.

Boehm returned to Munich in 1832 and immediately proceeded to execute his plan, which was the total reconstruction of the flute and its key system, his chief aim being to place the fingerholes exactly as required by theory. Another improvement of the flute of 1832 was the ring key system. That the necessity of covering fourteen holes with nine fingers required this complicated mechanism stands as a matter of course.

The bore of the instrument was changed from conical to cylindrical in 1847.

This flute received the first prize at the Industrial Exhibition of All Nations in London, 1851, the great memorial medal at the General German Industrial Exhibition at Munich, 1855, and the first prize, the first great gold medal, at the Industrial Exhibition in Paris; at the same time evoking from Prince Napoleon flattering comment.

The efforts of his rivals to despoil Boehm of the credit of all these improvements casts a dark shadow over the history of the flute. His name in connection with the instrument might have gradually passed into oblivion, for not only was the credit for these improvements severely contested, but the superiority over the old system is even denied by some today. The greatest opposition his flute has met with was in his own fatherland, Germany.

The severity with which his title as inventor of these improvements was contested serves only to bear witness to the importance of the claims. To the fine sense of justice enjoyed by Mr. Christopher Welch we owe recognition of the true state of affairs. To his everlasting credit, the masterful work, *History of the Boehm Flute,* sealed the controversy once and for all.

In addition to the inventions for the improvement of the flute, he deserves mention for the following: his alto flute, invention of a method for making steel, the overstrung pianoforte and the above-mentioned machine for driving pins in music boxes.

Of his compositions there are forty-seven and twelve arrangements of compositions by celebrated masters for flute and piano.

His last years were entirely devoted to instruction and of his pupils that have achieved fame may be mentioned Hans Heindl, Moritz Fuerstenau, Karl Krueger, Carl Wehner, and Rudolpf Tillmetz.

Theobald Boehm was survived by seven sons and a daughter, none of whom, however, became musicians. He breathed his last in the same house in which he was born on November 25, 1881.

He was a great thinker, a clever, ingenious, indefatigable worker, a man of lofty character and a virtuoso and creative artist. Such a man alone was able to combine the results of theory and practice in such a manner as to answer the highest purposes of art. (R.S.R. and L.D.)

KUMMER, KASPER: an excellent flute-player and fine composer, was born at Erlan, Germany in 1795. He studied flute with a musician named Neumeister and harmony with a cantor named Staps. In 1835 he became flutist in the orchestra of the Ducal chapel at Coburg and twenty years later became music director upon the retirement of Drouet. He was held in high esteem as a flute player and composer. He wrote some excellent etudes for the flute and very fine chamber music and even his lightest and easiest fantasias are always well written. He played only on the old-fashioned small-holed flute of the ordinary German model. He died at Coburg in 1870. (R.S.R.)

NICHOLSON, CHARLES: this eminently popular performer was born at Liverpool in 1795. His father was a successful flutist, who, according to the son, "devoted the greater part of his life to the acquirement of that peculiarity of tone which led to his acknowledged preeminence amongst the professors of the German flute." This peculiarity was due, in some degree, to the sacrifice of the soft dulcet sounds of the early flute, and the substitution of a powerful and brilliant, though rather hard, quality of tone, which was not exactly flute-like. In the opinion of the younger Nicholson "the tone ought to be as reedy as possible; as much like the hautboy as you can get it, but embodying the round mellowness of the clarionet." Nicholson the elder greatly increased the tone of the flute by the enlargement of the finger-holes and the mouth-hole, and his son still further improved the instrument, but the hard tone that the Nicholsons brought into fashion was not by any means a necessary consequence of the increase in the size of the holes, as the continental flute players supposed it to have been. Charles Nicholson preferred Potter's flutes to those of Monzani or Milhouse, but he afterwards used one by Astor who was the favourite maker of his father.

While quite a young man, the younger Nicholson, who was even then an accomplished performer, sought distinction in London, and he soon obtained a higher position as a soloist than was ever accorded to any other flute player in England. On the establishment of the Royal Academy of Music, in 1822, he was appointed a professor of that institution, and not long afterwards he became principal at the Italian Opera, then styled the King's Theatre. In short, every engagement that he thought fit to accept fell to his share, and he received many more applications for lessons, at a guinea an hour, then he cared to entertain. He also added greatly to his income by the sale of the large-holed flutes made by Clementi and Company, on which he received a handsome royalty. The following notice, extracted from the *Quarterly Musical Magazine* of 1823, conveys, notwithstanding its evident exaggerations, some idea of the estimation in which Nicholson was held at that time: "Mr. Nicholson's father was an admirable performer on the flute, who dedicated much time to the improvement of the instrument. In this he was eminently successful, and at his death he left his son in possession of a knowledge of the principles on which he proceeded, and a genius highly capable of carrying those principles into execution. The rich, mellow, and finely graduated quality of tone which he now produces throughout the whole compass of the instrument, sufficiently evinces the success which has attended his exertions. It would be superfluous to enter into an elaborate examination of Mr. Nicholson's unrivalled excellence as a performer, since all our readers must have, in common with ourselves, frequently felt and witnessed the delight and admiration which always accompany his performances. His purity of intonation, his perfection of double-tonguing, and the rich contrast and variety of which he is enabled to avail himself, from the great power as well as delicacy and sweetness of his tone, are sufficiently known; his whirlwind rush from the bottom to the top of the instrument, in the chromatic scale, is also too striking a characteristic of his style to need comment; but we must not

125

pass over two new effects on the instrument, which he was the first to introduce: we mean that species of vibration which is particularly observable in the musical glasses, and which, judiciously used, has a very beautiful effect, and the still more important accomplishment of gliding, which, on the violin and other stringed instruments, is productive of so much expression, and which has hitherto been deemed unattainable on the flute. The opinion, long entertained, that this is an imperfect instrument, must now be considered as no longer just, since by the rules reduced to practice in Mr. Nicholson's *Preceptive Lessons* every note may be produced by more than one mode of fingering, and even should that be found insufficient, the end may be obtained by the modification of the embouchure; so that the flute may now be said to approximate as nearly as possible to the human voice. . . . Nothing can more clearly show the mastery this artist has obtained over the grand impediments of the instrument than his performance last year at Covent Garden, where he executed an adagio (that test of tone, taste and expression), without the accompaniment of a single instrument, and such was his complete success, that an encore was demanded by the whole house with acclamation. In pathetic movements he has no rival."

There were, however, certain critics who did not entertain so high an opinion of Nicholson's performance as did the reviewer for the *Quarterly*, and there were some who objected to his style as being decidedly old-fashioned and not altogether free from vulgarity. The much vaunted glide, too, was severely and justly condemned by many. It was even said that Nicholson often disfigured a simple air by the introduction of a cadenza as long as the tune, with a shake at the end nearly as long as the cadenza. His double-tonguing, in which he used the syllables *too-tle* now happily discarded, was also mentioned in very disparaging terms, and comparisons were made between the articulation of Drouet and that of Nicholson, which were much to the disadvantage of the latter.

With regard to the tone produced by Nicholson, there can be no doubt that it was exceedingly grand. Many of my old friends who remembered it, have told me that although it might have been occasionally hard in quality, yet it was really noble in its general character; and I have been informed, moreover, that this popular artist had such consummate mastery over his instrument, that the effects of light and shade which he was thereby able to produce were truly marvellous. Some idea of his style of performance may be formed by an inspection of his fantasias, and it is easy to trace therein the immense improvement that he made during his sixteen years' residence in London.

Nicholson had many pupils who reflected great credit on their master; amongst these were Richardson and Saynor. Samuel Thornton Saynor, though possessing less rapidity of execution than his fellow-pupil, was certainly a better artist; in fact, there were few better orchestral or solo flute players than Saynor. His intonation was almost irreproachable; his style admirable; his articulation both neat and vigorous, and his tone really splendid. Unfortunately, his habits and his manners prevented his attaining the high position for which he would otherwise have been qualified. The eight-keyed flute on which Saynor played, had been the favourite instrument of his master.

Nicholson had a decided talent for composition, and some of his passages are most pleasing as well as brilliant, but unhappily he was not an educated musician, consequently he was obliged to obtain assistance from those who were better versed in the art. The introductions of his twelfth and thirteenth fantasias were written by Bochsa, the celebrated harpist; that of his fourteenth fantasia, an excellent work of its kind, by E. J. Loder. In his earlier efforts, he was generally aided by Burrowes. His best original composition is the Polonaise with "Kitty Tyrrell," now out of print.

Nicholson appears to have been a singularly improvident man, for after a career of almost unexampled prosperity as a flute player, he became reduced to absolute poverty. He died in London, on March 26, 1837, having been supported in his last illness by Messrs. Clementi and Collard. (R.S.R.)

SOUSSMANN, HEINRICH: born in Berlin on January 23, 1796, was the son of a musician. At the age of six he began to receive lessons on the violin from his father, and his talent for music was so great that in an incredibly short time he was sufficiently advanced to take part in a duet. Through the kindness of Kammermusikus Wendtrodt, he was enabled to attend concerts, and at one of these he heard Schroeck, the instructor of Gabrielski and Belcke, play a solo on the flute. Recognizing the superiority of the tone of that instrument over that of the violin, he resolved to be a flute player, and procuring a flute without keys, soon learned to play upon it. Gottlieb Kruger, first flutist to the King of Wurtemburg, rendered him great assistance, and the boy was soon able to play well enough to appear in public. As his parents were too poor to procure for him a first-rate master, he did his best to imitate the fine players he had heard, always taking Schroeck as his chief model. Having entered his sixteenth year, however, he summoned up courage enough to beg a few lessons from Schroeck, and that generous musician gave him the much coveted instruction, refusing to accept any payment. In 1812, Soussmann entered the band of an infantry regiment, and during 1812 and 1814 served through the campaigns against France. Receiving a wound in the chest at La Belle Alliance, he was obliged to return home and passed an examination fitting him for a civil post. There was, however, no vacancy, and as he could not support himself and his parents on the slender pay that he received from the government, and his wound prevented his playing the flute, he resorted once more to the violin and earned a living by performing in the Thiergarten. After a year had elapsed, Soussmann, having recovered sufficiently to resume his flute playing, offered his services to the Chapel Royal, and was retained as a supernumerary. He now devoted himself to his art, and studied harmony under Zelter, but he soon left this master on account of his rude manners; started on a concert tour, and visited St. Petersburg. His success in that city was so great that he remained there for sixteen years, playing first flute at the Grand Opera, and obtaining an appointment at the Chapel Royal. In 1836 he was made musical director at the Royal Theatre, and was considered one of the first flutists of his time. In 1837 he revisited Germany and played at a concert in Breslau, receiving a most enthusiastic welcome. A notice of this concert, in the *Allgemeine Zeitung*, comments upon the improvement Soussmann had made during his sixteen years' residence in Russia, and praises his powerful, full tone, his excellent embouchure, the tenderness of his expression, his extraordinary facility of execution, both in slurred and staccato passages, his rapid shakes and double-tonguing, and his faultless intonation. Soussmann appeared also at concerts in Berlin, his success being complete. He died at St. Petersburg in May 1848.

Among the great number of works which he composed for his instrument, the following may be mentioned:

Concertino pour flûte, avec orchestre ou piano, Op. 19; Theme varié pour flûte avec quatuor, Op. 3; Potpourri pour violon et flûte, avec violon, alto et violoncelle.

Quartets for Four Flutes: Op. 5, in D; Two, Op. 27, in G and C.

Trio concertante, pour deux flûtes et piano; Duo pour deux flûtes, avec piano, Op. 30; Serenade für Guitarre und Flote ,Op. 6; Serenade für Piano-forte und Flote, Op. 12; Grosse Fantasia für Flote und Piano-forte, Op. 28; Souvenir de Paganini, Fantaisie pour flûte avec piano, Op. 56; Introduction et Variations pour flûte avec piano, Op. 57.

Duets for Two Flutes: three, concertante, Op. 2; three, brilliant and easy, Op. 4; three, Op. 24; three, Op. 36; Trois Grands Exercises en forme de Duos (in E, A and E-flat). These fine studies are unfortunately out of print.

Solos and Studies: Sechs Solos für die Flote, Op. 25; Trente grands exercises, ou Etudes, dans tous les Tons, livres, I. et II. (known all over the world); 24 Tagliche Studien für die Flote (24 daily studies); Praktische, Flotenschule, Op. 53. (R.S.R.)

RIBAS, JOSE MARIA DEL CARMEN: was born on July 16, 1796, at Burgos, a town of Old Castile. He was the son of a bandmaster in a Spanish infantry regiment, and under his father's tuition he learned at a very early age to play the flute, the oboe and the clarinet. He served for some years as a clarinet player in the band of the regiment, and during the Peninsular War, having been taken prisoner by the French, he was conveyed to

129

the island of Funen, whence he was rescued by the British. He afterwards served under Wellington, and was present at the battle of Toulouse. On the termination of the war, Ribas left the army and settled in Oporto, where his father then resided. At that time he began to study under Parado, a Portuguese flute player of great merit, and he soon became celebrated both in Spain and Portugal, as a performer on the flute and the clarinet. He was at one time first flutist at the Opera in Lisbon, and besides many other important positions that he occupied while a young man, he was first clarinetist in the orchestra of the Philharmonic Society of Oporto, the members of which presented him with a diamond scarf-pin.

Towards the close of 1825, or at the beginning of the following year, he incurred the displeasure of certain priests of Oporto, who posted his name, as that of a recalcitrant, on the church doors. Not choosing to submit to this indignity, he left the country and came to England. In a sketch of the state of music in London, published in the *Quarterly Musical Magazine* of 1826, appears the following notice: "Mr. Ribas, of Lisbon, was introduced, and took the station of first clarinet during the season." As a matter of fact, he never was the leading clarinet player in London, but he soon gained a good position as a performer on that instrument, as well as on the flute, and he was one of the very few who ever played solos in public on the flute and the clarinet during the same evening. In 1835 he was engaged as "second flute" at the King's Theatre, then under the management of Laporte. On the death of Charles Nicholson, in 1837, Ribas was appointed principal. Not long after this he became the leading orchestral flute player in London, and that position he retained until 1851, when, after an extremely successful "farewell concert," on August 7th in that year, he finally left England.

His intention, on quitting this country, was never to allow himself to be heard again in public, wishing, as he said, to retire before the slightest falling off should be perceptible in his performance. He did not, however, immediately carry out that intention, for he made a tour through Spain and Portugal, giving concerts in some of the principal towns, as he had been accustomed to do at intervals during his twenty-five years' residence in London. It should be mentioned that during one of these visits, Queen Isabella of Spain presented to him a diamond brooch. In 1853 he once more settled in Oporto and occupied his time in giving lessons on the flute and the concertina.

If Ribas was less celebrated as a soloist than as an orchestral player, it was not owing to any deficiency of talent manifested by him in the former capacity, but because his orchestral playing was so superlatively fine that it eclipsed his performance as a solo player. In his time the work of the principal instrumentalist in the opera orchestra was much more arduous than at present, for that was the epoch when the ballet was in its zenith, and the charming dancers Taglioni, Cerito, Carlotta Grisi, and Duvernay, were as highly esteemed as the illustrious singers Giulia Grisi, Persiani, Rubini and Lablache. The ballet music of those days abounded in long and important solos for the principal instruments, and artistic interpretation as necessary for the music to the elegant *pas seul* as for the delicate *obbligato* accompaniment to the voice. It need hardly be said that Ribas, finished musician as he was, never failed to make the most of his opportunities. I have often heard him at Her Majesty's Theatre, playing the most difficult passages with consummate ease, and with such a clear, full tone that not a note was lost. In the matter of fullness and power of tone throughout the compass of his instrument, Ribas was perhaps unequalled. He was one of the first in England to play the celebrated staccato solo in the Scherzo of Mendelssohn's *Midsummer Night's Dream* music. The composer, who conducted, was so pleased with the performance of Ribas that he asked him to play the passage three times, at the rehearsal, saying that he had no idea it could be made so effective.

Ribas played the old-fashioned large-holed flute, not because he failed to recognize the advantages of the new system, but because he saw plainly that he was too old, as well as too busy, to be able to change his fingering with any prospect of success. He made several modifications in his instrument, with a view to improving its intonation and its power of tone. For the sake of

131

the latter he greatly enlarged the upper part of the bore; he also added to the thickness of the wood, thus enabling the tone to be increased in power with less risk of the loss of its full character. Throughout his long and successful career, Ribas was highly respected, as well as admired, by all who knew him; he had, indeed a most happy talent for making friends. He died at Oporto in July 1861.

I am much indebted to the kindness of Madame Ribas (née Scott) and of my friend Mr. James Ramsay Dow, for most of the foregoing particulars. It is not a little surprising that the name of José Maria Ribas is not so much as mentioned in any Dictionary of Musicians, and I am, on that account, especially pleased to have an opportunity of paying a tribute to the memory of this worthy gentleman and excellent artist. (R.S.R.)

MARINI, LUIGI, COUNT PORTI, was born at Gubbio, Umbria, in 1803, of a noble family. He was a member of the Academy of Santa Cecilia and many other institutes.

He counted the first people of his time as his friends, amongst whom was Rossini. He is never known to have performed in any orchestra and very few have had the opportunity to hear him as a soloist, as it was thought his appearance on a stage would cause his social standing to suffer. He was nevertheless of a most congenial nature and only observed an appearance of exclusiveness in deference to his wife's opinion.

His last concert was given in Palermo when Marini was 79 years of age. It is written: "Nobody believed to be listening to an old flute player. He was always the great master, the king of his instrument." Many flutists considered him the greatest flute virtuoso of Italy, an opinion also shared by Briccialdi and Ciardi.

Marini wrote about fifty melodious and artistic compositions. He died on December 9, 1886, in Palermo, Sicily.

FAHRBACH, JOSEF: a famous flute virtuoso and guitar player, was born in Vienna, August 25, 1804, and died there on June 7, 1883.

He was exceedingly successful as a concert player and was

finally appointed first flute of the Royal Opera House Orchestra in Vienna. He was a self-taught player and composer, and after appearing as soloist for many years, he established an orchestra and achieved additional successes as a conductor. As a composer he gave evidence of varied talents, and produced many creditable works for the flute. Among these were a large number of fantasias and transcriptions, dance music for orchestra, a method for the flute and another one for the oboe.

Another member of the Fahrbach family who also made a reputation as a fine flute player was Philipp Fahrbach, Sr., born in Vienna on October 25, 1815, and died there on March 31, 1885. He was a military bandmaster and was the first one to introduce string instruments into a military band. In his concerts he was frequently heard in flute solos as well as in flute duets with his son, the music for which he had specially composed. In addition to his duties as a bandmaster, he was also a teacher at the Royal Institute for the Blind in Vienna.

FRISCH, ROBERT: This highly distinguished German flute player was born in or about 1804. While quite a young man he was engaged as solo flutist in the orchestra of the celebrated Johann Strauss I of Vienna, and in that capacity he traveled much on the Continent. In the year 1838, he accompanied Strauss to England; here he soon became so popular as a solo player that he decided to remain, and therefore resigned his position in Strauss's band. At the first promenade concerts given in London, by Eliason, Musard and Jullien, successively, Frisch was a great attraction, especially to the flute players, his style of performance being entirely novel, and his music much more interesting than that of Drouet, Nicholson or Richardson. His solos are by far the most difficult that have ever been written for the flute, yet the brilliant passages with which they abound are generally elegant, sometimes extremely so.

Frisch had such complete mastery over his instrument, and executed the greatest difficulties with such graceful ease, that anyone unacquainted with the technicalities of the flute might have believed that he was playing the very simplest music, had it not been for his singular habit of practising the coming solo, in dumb motion, during the preceding *tutti,* and his appearing to read every note of his music, which he invariably had before him. His facility in playing the highest notes was simply marvellous; the last few staves of his *Réminiscences à Herold,* the first piece that I heard him play, may be cited as an example of the difficulties that he was accustomed to execute. He employed the old-fashioned method of double-tonguing (too-tle), his articulation being the least satisfactory feature in his performance; his tone also left much to be desired, for though in the upper notes it was fairly good and clear, in the middle and lower registers it was of the character technically called "fluffy," besides being decidedly weak. As a player on the piccolo he was perfect, and although superior to anyone I ever heard.

Frisch played on an old-fashioned flute of German make, with numerous keys, including one for b and an extra c'♯ lever for the little finger of the left hand. In 1840 he began to practice on a flute, made on the new system, by Buffet of Paris, but as might have been expected, he soon found that the change in the fingering would have caused the sacrifice of the dexterity which he had acquired on the German model, and he must have been aware that execution was the only point in which he was pre-eminent; he therefore gave up all idea of conquering the new fingering, and sold his French flute.

In or about 1842 he obtained an appointment as bandmaster in an English cavalry regiment, and Joseph Richardson succeeded him as soloist at the Promenade concerts. On the expiration of his term of office, Frisch became so reduced in circumstances that he was glad to accept an engagement to play as second to myself at the concerts of the late Mr. John Hullah in St. Martin's Hall. When I last saw him, I think in 1859, he was still using the same old flute on which he had played twenty years previously, but he felt that he was left completely behind, and he expressed his regret that he had not persevered with the new fingering, though, as he said, it was too late to think of it then. Soon afterwards he took another engagement as bandmaster; went with his regiment to India, and died there.

As in the case of Ribas, Frisch's name is not mentioned in any

134

dictionary of musicians. I have made the most persevering enquiries for further particulars of his career, but having been entirely unsuccessful I have been obliged to depend upon my almost unaided memory for the facts above related.

Frisch's compositions are generally so difficult that few would care to attempt to play them before an audience; they are, however, so interesting as studies, and they are replete with such elegant and charming passages, that every ambitious flute player should practice some of them. (R.S.R.)

DORUS, VINCENT JOSEPH, flute virtuoso and exponent of the French school of flutists, was born at Valenciennes in 1812. He studied at the Paris Conservatory and was one of the first to adopt the Boehm system for which he devised the change from the original open G-sharp to the closed G-sharp. He became first flute of the Paris Grand Opéra about 1835. In 1858 he succeeded Tulou as professor at the Conservatory of Paris. He was made a Knight of the Legion of Honor in 1866. He composed several works for the flute and died in 1896 near Paris.

BRICCIALDI, GIULIO. This famous flutist, who may justly be claimed as having been one of the greatest players of his country, was born at Terni, Papal States, Italy, on March 1, 1818. He received his first instruction from his father. Upon the death of the latter in 1829, his relatives wished him to enter the Church, but in order to avoid the career which had been marked out for him, he ran away from home, with only three bajocchi (papal money amounting to about four and one-half cents in United States money) in his pocket, and tramped to Rome, a distance of forty miles, where he lived a life of wretched poverty until a charitable singer of the Pope's Chapel, named Ravagli, rescued him from his miserable condition, placed him under good masters, and supported him until he was able to earn his own living.

At an early age Briccialdi obtained the diploma of the Academy of Saint Cecilia in Rome; in 1836 he went to Naples and gave lessons to the Count of Syracuse, brother to the King; in 1839 he set out for the north of Italy, staying fifteen months in Milan and in 1841 he visited Vienna. Afterwards he traveled over the greater part of Europe, meeting with signal success as a soloist wherever he appeared. In 1847 he went to Munich. Briccialdi at once adopted the Boehm flute, and soon afterwards came to England. He made his first appearance in that country when Boehm had just completed his new head-joint, May 3, 1848, at a concert given by Mr. Carte in the Greenwich Lecture Hall, where his performance was received with acclamation. After this he became exceedingly popular in London and in the provinces. Soon after his first public performance in England, Mr. Richard Shepherd Rockstro, the author of the famous *Treatise on the Flute,* was introduced to him by George Rudall and at the request of the latter, Briccialdi was kind enough to play a solo for the author's special benefit.

In speaking of the artist's playing Mr. Rockstro remarked in the above mentioned *Treatise:*

"I have no hesitation in saying that Briccialdi was one of the finest performers that I ever heard on any instrument. His perfect intonation, carried style, and consummate mastery over his instrument are to be remembered but not described, and his tone made such an impression upon me that I immediately set it up as a model to be imitated if possible, and I therefore seized every opportunity of hearing him play."

Briccialdi made several improvements on the flute which were of lasting benefit. The most notable was the introduction of the "double B-flat key," which is used on most all of the Boehm system flutes.

After his departure from England it is thought that he settled for some time at Milan, but he subsequently became professor of the flute at the Medici Institute in Florence. He died in that city on December 17, 1881.

Briccialdi was a very talented and most prolific composer for his instrument and the following list contains the greater part of his original works for the flute:

For Flute and Pianoforte: Three concertos, Op. 19, Op. 61, and Op. 65; Concertino, Op. 104; Scherzo, Op. 16; Il primo Amore, Fantasia, Op. 21; Notturno, Op. 32; Andante et Polonaise, Op. 62; Deux Fleurs, Morceaux de Salon: No. 1, La

Pensee, No. 2, La Rose, Op. 63; Capriccio, Op. 46; Allegro alla Spagnola, Op. 69; Cavatina originale, Op. 70; Capriccio originale, Op. 71; Solo romantico, Op. 72; L'Inglesina, Rondo brillante, Op. 74; Pezzo originale a guisa di Scena melo-drammatica, Op. 77; Solo Brillante, Op. 80; Secondo Notturno, Op. 87; Romanza e Polonaise; Capriccio, Op. 105; Il Vento, Capriccio, Op. 112; La Romanzesca, Capriccio, Op. 113; Solo, La Primavera, Op. 117; numerous Operatic Fantasias and Airs with Variations, including an excellent Carnevale di Venezia.

For Two Flutes with Piano: Soiree musicale de Rossini, Op. 49; Portafogli per i Diletantti, Op. 67.

Duets for Two Flutes: Duetto, Op. 36; Duo sur des motifs du ballet *Caterina*, Op. 45; Duo sur des motifs de l'opera *I Vespri Siciliani*, Op. 88; Duo Concertant, Op. 100 and Op. 118; 16 Duos dialogues, Op. 132.

Exercises and Studies for the Flute: Exercises indispensables et journaliers; Quatre grandes Etudes. (R.S.R.)

CIARDI, CESARE: was born in the same year as Briccialdi, June 29, 1818, at Prato, Tuscany.

John Finn of London wrote about Ciardi:

"There can be no doubt whatever as to the capacity and skill of Cesare Ciardi as flutist and as composer. Many of the writer's friends have described the surpassing talent of this remarkable performer. A good many years ago he came to this country and when brought before Rudall he produced a cracked old boxwood instrument upon which he commenced to play with such clear, beautiful tone, faultless elegance and taste that Rudall—himself an accomplished flutist—who had been listening like one hypnotized, declared to that ardent amateur, Walter Stewart Broadwood, that 'he is fit to play before a chorus of angels!' Ciardi at once secured an engagement to play at a concert at the Opera House and was encored while Grisi, Mario and Tamburini (the greatest vocalist of their day) were waiting to be heard. He also played at the Philharmonic; but the *genie* of the cracked boxwood flute did not stay long enough in this country to materially influence the style of playing then in vogue here."

Ciardi, after a deal of traveling, ultimately settled in St.

Petersburg, where he was solo flute at the Imperial Opera for many years, having as colleagues in the orchestra, Carl Wehner and Ernesto Koehler.

Ciardi was a flutist of the old school. That he sent the aristocratic applicants for instruction on the new flute to Wehner has been told in Wehner's biography. Ciardi thereby displayed real generosity and the assistance to the struggling young artist resultant therefrom was gratefully remembered by Wehner to the last. The writer is in possession of some sketches showing Ciardi to have been a caricaturist of considerable merit. He was also a sculptor. It is recalled that on the occasion of Rubinstein's birthday, Rubinstein was presented with his bust, the work of Ciardi. This serves to illustrate the many-sidedness of this artist.

The memory of his charming personality is fondly cherished by all who were fortunate enough to have made his acquaintance.

Ciardi left upwards of 212 compositions; the fame of which may be readily exemplified by his *Carneval Russe*. He was also the author of *A Method for the Flute* and *An Album for Singing*. He died at Strelva, St. Petersburg, on June 13, 1877.

DOPPLER, ALBERT FRANZ: noted flutist and composer, was born October 16, 1821 at Lemberg, Austria. He studied flute with his father who was first oboe at the theatre in Warsaw. Together with his brother Karl, he concertized all over Europe, creating quite a sensation. They played the most rapid passages absolutely together and with every shading of expression. He settled for a time in Budapest, composing and playing, and in 1858 was named conductor for the Royal Theatre at Vienna, and in 1865 teacher of flute at the Conservatory. He composed many works for one and two flutes; also several overtures, ballets and operas. He died in Baden, near Vienna, on July 27, 1883.

DOPPLER, KARL: born at Lemberg on September 12, 1825. He was a pupil of his father and his brother, Franz, but was not so fine a performer as his brother. He composed two operas and collaborated with his brother in several ballets and concert pieces for two flutes. He settled in Stuttgart and died there on March 10, 1900.

PRATTEN, ROBERT SIDNEY: one of the most distinguished amongst flute players, was born at Bristol on January 23, 1824. Brought up, as he was, in a thoroughly musical family, he became a musician almost from infancy, without receiving any regular instruction, and it is related that his first and only lesson on the flute was given to him, when he was but seven years old, by his elder brother Frederick, afterwards a celebrated double-bass player. Chiefly by his own unaided exertions Robert Sidney not only acquired some knowledge of harmony, and of singing, but also became skilled in the practice of the flute, the pianoforte and the tenor. The last-named instrument he played left-handed; he held the flute in the usual manner. In his twelfth year he began to play solos on the flute at concerts in Bath and Bristol; while still a boy he obtained a place in the orchestra of the Theatre Royal, Dublin, and, after travelling over a great part of the United Kingdom, in January 1845, he settled in London, where he was engaged as "first flute" at the Theatre Royal, Covent Garden, two years before the Italian Opera was located there.

In the following month Pratten made his first appearance in London as a solo player, at a "Monster Concert" given by All-croft at Covent Garden Theatre. The piece he selected was Charles Nicholson's Twelfth Fantasia (Air from *Nina*). His performance created a most favorable impression, and the critics of the musical press bestowed high encomiums on the young artist, commenting especially on his full tone and expressive style. The mantle of Nicholson was said to have fallen on his shoulders; Richardson was mentioned in terms of unfavorable comparison, and the *Pictorial Times* even went so far as to say that Pratten's style "fortunately" differed from that of the established favorite. From this time he was a celebrity, being not only famous as a flute player, but popular as a man.

Not content with being merely a practical musician, and feeling that he possessed talent for composition, Pratten wisely began, shortly after his arrival in London, to take regular les-

139

sons in harmony and counterpoint from Charles Lucas, the noted violoncellist. He mastered these difficult branches of musical knowledge in so short a time, that he fairly astonished his instructor, but, as a matter of fact, a naturally quick perception, combined with an exceptionally true ear, always rendered everything connected with music easier to him than to most persons.

During his provincial tours, he had been fortunate enough to gain the friendship of Sir Warwick Hele Tonkin: that general Baronet and his Lady, being about to travel on the Continent, proposed to take the young musician with them, in order to give him an opportunity of seeing the world, and at the same time extending his reputation by playing solos in some of the principal cities of Europe. The tour was begun early in August, 1846, and was not ended until June in the following year. Unvarying success attended Pratten throughout; he received complimentary letters from a host of distinguished musicians, and the continental journals overwhelmed him with praise. Many of these letters and newspaper criticisms, kindly entrusted to me by his widow, Madame Sydney Pratten, are lying before me as I write; they all breathe the same spirit of admiration for the talent of the English flute player, and almost at random I select the following notice from *Galignani's Messenger:*

"Paris, May 10, 1847. Mr. Pratten has arrived in Paris on his return to London from Vienna, where he had the honor of performing before the Emperor. At one of the concerts at the Imperial Theatre his success was so great that he was called for three times to receive the plaudits of the audience. All the Vienna journals speak of him as superior to any flutist hitherto heard in Germany."

Soon after his return to England, Pratten, who had until then played on an eight-keyed flute by Rudall and Rose, adopted Siccama's flute. It really mattered little what flute he used, for such was his amazing command of the instrument, and so accurate was his ear, that he could have played with perfect intonation and a fine tone on almost any kind of flute. On the retirement of Richardson from Jullien's orchestra, Pratten took his place, and was long one of the chief attractions of the Promenade Concerts; in 1851 he succeeded Ribas at the Italian opera, and soon afterwards he was engaged at the concerts of the Philharmonic and Sacred Harmonic Societies, becoming in fact the leading flute player of England.

I find an entry in my diary March 29, 1852, stating that he showed me an eight-keyed flute made under his direction, and exceedingly good of its kind though it had the usual unequal finger-holes. I think this was his earliest effort at improvement, and I know that he did not use Siccama's flute after that time.

Owing to a deeply rooted aversion to extra keys, Pratten would not allow the shake-key for $C''\sharp$-$d''\sharp$ to be placed on his flute, though he eventually adopted that for $c''\sharp$-d''. This objection of his gave rise to an amusing incident: at a rehearsal for a concert, in St. James' Hall, an overture of the late Sir Julius Benedict, containing the shake $c''\sharp$-$d''\sharp$ in a prominent position, was conducted by the composer. I pointed out the shake to Pratten asking him chaffingly, what he was going to do? He only replied by a sly wink, and when the time came he shook his $c''\sharp$-d'' key very quickly, looking at me with a most comical expression. Benedict, who, it is almost needless to say, had not a quick ear, was delighted, and exclaimed: "Mr. Bratten, dat is de feerst dime I hafe heerd dat shague made broberly." It was too much for the equanimity of the orchestra; their respect for the conductor's position gave way in a peal of Homeric laughter. It should be observed that the shake in question was very rarely written at that time, and was generally regarded as being impossible to perform neatly.

On July 10, 1853, a society, which at my suggestion was called The Orchestral Union, was started by Alfred Mellon, afterwards celebrated as a conductor, and my valued friend Alfred Nicholson, the noted oboe-player. As a matter of course Pratten was invited to join this society, and I, only too glad to be in such good company, undertook the parts of piccolo and second flute. Then began the close friendship between Pratten and myself which lasted uninterruptedly until his death. The Orchestral Union was exceedingly successful in procuring positions for its members, especially for its conductor, though in a pecuniary sense it was a very decided failure. At one of the concerts of this society, held at the Hanover Square Rooms on May 13, 1854, I heard, for the first time, Pratten play his *Concertstuck* with the orchestra. His performance of this fine composition was simply superb. It was about this time that he began to discontinue writing variations, and unless specially requested to do so, he did not even play them. In his later compositions, as well as in the above-mentioned Concertstuck, he adopted, with the happiest results, the device of employing passages in florid counterpoint, in lieu of the variations which had become nauseous to him, for the display of his great execution. His still popular fantasia on an air from Niedermayer's *Marie Stuart* is, however, a splendid example of variations, and the introduction to this piece is exceedingly fine, but the Concertstuck is by far the best of his works. (R.S.R.)

BUCHNER, FERDINAND: was born at Pyrmont, Waldeck (Germany), in 1825. He commenced to play the flute at a very early age under the guidance of his father, who was also a flute player of splendid ability. Later on he was placed with the famous C. Heinemeyer, for advanced instruction. An account which mentions Mr. Buchner's successful appearances in London as long ago as 1838, when the artist was about 13 years of age, sustains our belief that at even such an early age he gave evidence of those prodigious abilities which characterized his later activities.

For some time Buchner remained at Hanover under Heinemeyer perfecting his technical equipment and as opportunity offered itself, studying harmony, orchestration and other musical subjects in general.

He terminated his studies in 1847 and accepted an engagement in Berlin. He stayed there over three years, steadily rising in the estimation of concert audiences and leading professionals. In 1850 he went to Russia and took an active part in the musical life in St. Petersburg for the next six years. St. Petersburg at that time was a convenient art center from which innumerable concert tours were arranged and carried through. In 1856 the position of soloist at the Imperial Theatre in Moscow was offered to him. The advantages and opportunities offered by this position prompted him to accept and he kept this position with ever increasing success until a short time before his death. Buchner established an enviable reputation in Russia through his solo playing and successful teaching. When Rubinstein established the Conservatory of Music in Moscow, Buchner was selected as teacher of the flute classes. Later on, he occupied a leading position in the Moscow Philharmonic Society as soloist.

Buchner always played an old-style flute and preferred one of Vienna manufacture for his own particular uses. His performance of a solo is said to have been very fine and artistic, combining a round, noble tone production with correct technic and elegant, refined interpretation.

As a composer, this artist has long commanded the opinion of all those interested in the literature of the flute. As may be imagined, his long residence in Russia, as well as his association with the musicians of that country, had a decided effect upon his style of composition. This is particularly noticeable in his Nocturne, Op. 20; his Serenade, Op. 31, and his Mazurka Fantasie, Op. 32. Always well written, his works in the main are charmingly melodious and bear the unmistakable stamp of individuality.

His Grand Russian Fantasie, Op. 22, with its noble opening, is an admirable specimen of this style of writing; the Andante with the grand cadence, Op. 28, dedicated to Ernesto Kohler, contains an interesting example of a complicated cadence with harmonic passages; the Concertino, Andante and Polonaise and Concertos are works cast in larger mould and specially designed for advanced flutists. His First Concerto in F minor, Op. 38, in the opinion of the writer, is one of the greatest and most beautiful concertos ever written for the flute, and the Concertino, Op. 40, is also an exceedingly fine composition.

Some of his last works are remarkable for their vigor, individuality and beauty. The character and style of his compositions, such as Op. 45, 50, 51, 52, 54, 55, 59, 63 and 64 would lead one to believe that they had been written by a young man instead of an octogenarian.

Many of Buchner's earlier works were not written for the flute but for piano and various other instruments. The musical world at large and the flute-playing fraternity in general lost one of its most prominent representatives of the art of flute playing through the death of Buchner, an artist who was active for over three-quarters of a century.

In conclusion, a list of compositions by Ferdinand Buchner is added: Le Rossignol, Fantaisie; arrangements of Six Etudes by F. Chopin; Nocturne, Op. 20; Concert Waltz, Op. 21; Grand Russian Fantasie, Op. 22; Concert Waltz, Op. 27; Andante with great Cadence, Op. 28; Idylle, Op. 29; Kosak, Op. 30; Serenade, Op. 31; Mazurka, Fantaisie, Op. 32; Hungarian Fantasie, Op. 33; Auf dem Lande, Op. 34; Gipsy Dance, Op. 35; Mascha und Pascha, Op. 36; First Concerto in F major, Op. 38; Concert Waltz, Op. 39; Concertino, Op. 40; Andante and Polonaise, Op. 41; Six Duets(two flutes), Op. 42; Sophien Waltzer (two flutes and piano), Op. 43; Hungarian Dance (two flutes and piano), Op. 44; Second Concerto in A minor, Op. 45; Romance, Op. 46; Romance (for 'cello and piano), Op. 47; Prelude (flute solo), Op. 48; Spring (two flutes and piano), Op. 49; Third Concerto in D major, Op. 50; Fourth Concerto in E major, Op. 51; Fifth Concerto in E major, Op. 52; Sixth Concerto in E minor, Op. 55; Lebens Pulse, Op. 56; Bella Donna, Op. 57; Grille und Libelle, Op. 58; Fourth Concert Waltz, Op. 59; Freut euch des Lebens, Op. 60; Erinnerung. Op. 61; Espagnole, Op. 62; Seventh Concerto in G major, Op. 63; Eighth Concerto in C major, Op. 64; Sixteen Characteristic Pieces for two flutes and piano, Op. 65, and Daily Etudes for the Flute, Op. 66.

TERSCHAK, ADOLF: was born at Hermannstadt, Hungary, in 1832, and is known as a great musician as well as a flute virtuoso. The article from the *Musical Opinion* of London entitled "The Last Years of Terschak," by John Finn, whose contributions to musical periodicals are well known to flute players, being so well suited to the needs of this biography, is here quoted verbatim:

It is a common mistake of many who ought to know better to

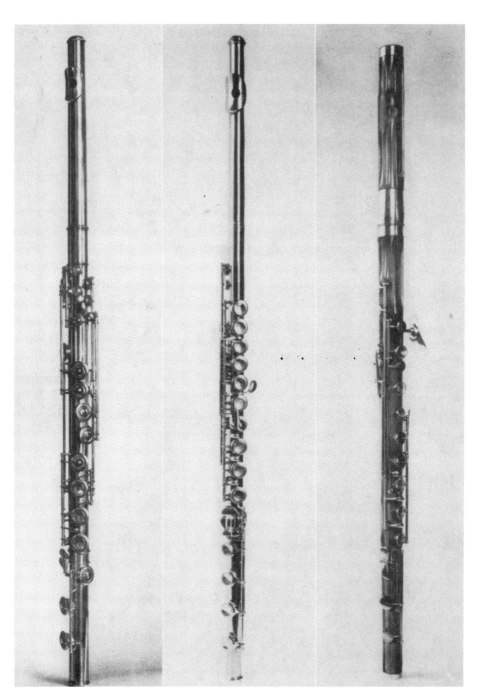

Silver Flute in G; Flute in Solid Gold; Flute in Uranium, Green
Glass, Silver Keys

DR. DAYTON C. MILLER'S GREAT FLUTE COLLECTION

Now in the Library of Congress in Washington, D. C.

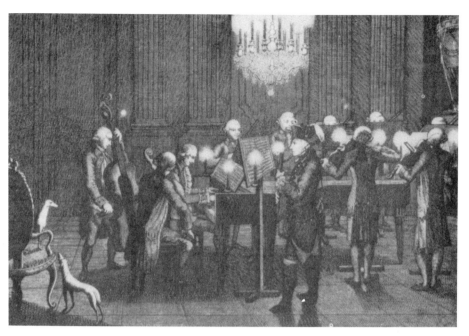

Frederick-the-Great Trying out his Flute Symphony at his Sans-Souci Palace at Potsdam

GEORGE LAURENT

JOHN WUMMER

GARETH MORRIS

WILLIAM KINCAID

LOS ANGELES FLUTE CLUB

Top Row: I. Miccoli, B. T. Sweney, A. Frazer, F. Le Baron, M. Henthorne, M. L. White, E. Ziegler, W. Tafel, F. Badollet, Norma Beauchamp, H. T. Staats, W. Bassett

2nd Row: L. B. Moore, M. Jeanette Rogers, T. S. Ogilvie, C. G. Cambern, L. Dowling, J. J. Gilbert, Dr. L. Weber, E. Gertrude Jones, A. Borsum

3rd Row: Geo. Mulford, Helen M. Little, W. C. McQuillen, S. T. Exley, W. E. Hullinger, H. V. Baxter, A. Maquarre, Jay Plowe, H. C. Knox.

ARY VAN LEEUWEN

GEORGE BARRÈRE

LUIGI HUGUES

LEONARDO DE LORENZO

ROBERT N. CAVALLY AND HIS PUPILS
(*Cincinnati College of Music, 1946-47*)

JOHN FINN

VICTOR SAFRONOFF

EMIL MEDICUS

ALFRED E. FENBOQUE

ARTHUR BROOKE AND HIS PUPILS
(San Diego and Chula Vista Flute Club, 1946)

ERNESTO KOEHLER

FERDINAND BUCHNER

RUDOLF TILLMETZ

THEOBALD BOEHM

CARL WEHNER

ABELARDO ALBISI

JOHN LEMMONÉ

W. LEWIS BARRETT

INDIAN FLUTE BAND

GLINSKY SAFRONOFF AND HIS PUPILS

(*Moscow, September 1929*)

JOHN AMADIO

JOHN AMANS

GEORGE DREXLER

ERNEST LIEGL

LEONARDO DE LORENZO AND HIS PUPILS
(*Eastman School of Music, 1932*)

PHILIPPE GAUBERT

CLAUDE-PAUL TAFFANEL

LOUIS FLEURY
Playing a Flute Quartet

JEAN LOUIS TULOU

suppose that Adolf Terschak wrote only for the flute. To say nothing of the Concerto for Pianoforte and Orchestra, there is much vocal, piano, and orchestral music to his credit. Besides the *Unser Vater* for soprano solo and chorus, an *Ave Maria* and an ambitious opera *Thais* (in four acts, published by Bote & Bock of Berlin in 1876), are worthy of note in this connection.

But as a traveler and flute pioneer Terschak has a unique record. Almost from that day in the autumn of 1852 when he left the Vienna Conservatorium the "pilgrim's staff" was in his hand. In the fifties and sixties long tours were made through France, Switzerland, Holland, and Belgium in company with some very renowned artists. The famous *Concertstuck* (Op. 51), which so strongly reflects the influence of Mendelssohn was generally his *cheval de bataille*; the well-known *Le Babillard* (Op. 23) and *La Sirène* (Op. 12) are also frequently found in the programs of this period. Most of 1876 was occupied touring through Norway. After a concert in Christiania, the King presented the order of St. Andrew as a mark of the royal appreciation of the *Nordlands* Bilder (Op. 164) which he then heard for the first time. The fine Sonatas Op. 168, 174, 175 were composed about this period. It has often been contended that these are the best of Terschak's flute works. It may be conceded that they present fully his power and capacity as a flute composer.

England was visited in 1878, but the stay was short and left no happy memories. Gratified by the results of the 1876 journey to Norway, another and more extended tour (which included Sweden) was planned and carried out in 1881. This project finished, there was commenced a series of concert journeys, broken only by lengthy sojourns at Constantinople and Munich, which lasted nearly twenty years. Bohemia, Hungary, Roumania, and the Orient were traversed in the early eighties.

Leaving Munich in 1885, Terschak went to Russia for the second time as a flute artist. Thirty years before (in 1856), the "tall, handsome young flutist" was in Moscow during the coronation festivities. Enormous success attended his appearances at numerous concerts in the old capital, and everywhere else in Russia his flute performance was regarded as phenomenal. After an interval of thirty years, there had been much change

145

even in slow going Russia; the artist had changed also, but his powers were undiminished and he was warmly received and many of the former triumphs were repeated. Flute recitals and traveling in South Russia, Caucasia, and Daghestan took up the whole of 1887. The late summer of 1888 found our artist in West Siberia organizing orchestral concerts and conducting Beethoven's symphonies in Tomsk, the university state of West Siberia. This venture over fresh fields was mapped out, and a long journey to Irkutsk (the east capital of Siberia) undertaken. Immediately on arrival more orchestral concerts were given. The remarkable tour was then continued to Vladivostock, and thence to Japan and China. Altogether eighteen months were passed in these countries, and many highly profitable flute recitals were given before the European populations of Nagasaki, Tokio, Yokohama, Shanghai, Nanking, Pekin, and other towns of Japan and North and South China. November, 1900, found Terschak back again in Vladivostock, whence he shortly afterwards started for the Amur country, visiting and giving recitals in Blagovestchensk, Stretjensk, Nertschinsk, and Werchne-Udinsk. Returning across Lake Baikal to the capital of East Siberia, symphony concerts were organized at Irkusk and other towns on the three thousand miles journey back to Moscow, which place was reached in May 1893.

The inexorable hand of time cannot be stayed, and now at the age of sixty-one years Terschak began to suffer much from his eyes. As a consequence of this, the whole of the year 1894 was spent at Dorpat, Livonia, upon the advice of a physician and oculist, who urged rest as an aid to cure. Here at Dorpat were composed or prepared for publication the last of Terschak's works for flute and piano. Commencing with the *Russische Rhapsodie* (Op. 176), *Die Flammen* (Op. 181), *Rhapsodie Orientale* (Op. 185), the series runs to about twenty numbers, nearly all of which are published by J. H. Zimmerman of Leipzig and London. These works are very interesting and well worth the attention of flute players.

Although Terschak's letters of this date contain an occasional outburst of cheery optimism, there is frequently a very mournful note in them. It was becoming painfully evident that the once robust health of the distinguished virtuoso and composer was fast failing. He too recognized this, and when the eye trouble was ameliorated longed for change of scene. In the hope of restoring that health which had long been a priceless possession, he once more picked up the "pilgrim's staff" and sped away, as a flute recitalist, through South Russia, Caucasia, Daghestan, then across the Caspian Sea, continuing the remarkable journey through Samarkand and Bokhara to Tashkend! All was going well, and the writer can vividly recall a letter received on Christmas morning, 1895, in which, together with the usual greetings, was a graphic account of the bestowal by the Emir of Bokhara of the order of the Golden Star following a performance of the Fourth Concert Allegro (Op. 190). Shortly after reaching Tashkend, Terschak had a severe attack of influenza. For awhile he was near death's door, and it was only with great difficulty that he got back to St. Petersburg. After many months' nursing in the Russian capital, he struggled on to Breslau, where a long painful illness terminated his career on October 3, 1901.

Terschak's adherence to the old flute has been the subject of comment not always overwise or kind. He played on a sixteen-keyed flute by Ziegler of Vienna, which was made for him in 1850.

During his fifty years of public life Terschak was the recipient of numerous decorations. The royal order "Jesu Christi" was conferred by the King of Portugal for an "Ave Maria." The late Shah of Persia so appreciated some articles on "Oriental Poetry" written by Terschak that he sent him the order of "The Lion and Sun." The Sultan of Turkey, greatly impressed by the "Selamik" for orchestral and military band, presented the "Mejidie"; the King of Norway, the "St. Andrew"; and the Emir of Bokhara, the "Golden Star."

Terschak's eccentricities and adherence to the old system flute are well illustrated by the two following anecdotes:

The writer was told by the late Carl Wehner, whom it was related to in turn by Theobald Boehm, that the latter was once visited by Terschak during a stop in Munich on one of his concert tours. The new flute was played to his seemingly entire satisfaction and after having expressed his admiration, took the instrument with the intention of playing on it himself. On perceiving his inability to do so, he left the house greatly irritated, telling the inventor that a flute which could not be played by him could not be of any value.

Another time, years later, on Terschak's last visit to London, as the writer was informed at the firm of Rudall, Carte and Company, Terschak maintained in a discussion on the new and old system that several of his latest compositions could not possibly be played on the Boehm flute. Subsequently, it was arranged to have Mr. John Radcliff, one of England's greatest flutists, play the pieces designated by Terschak. Radcliff, whose sight reading was phenomenal, notwithstanding Terschak's indistinct writing, played these pieces with such mastery, exceeding all expectations, that Terschak left in an angry, confused, not to mention disappointed, state of mind.

Terschak is also cited in Welch's book as follows:

In the present day the outpourings of the believers in the old system, whom like the battalions of Kosciusko, are

". . . few, but undismay'd"

breathe a spirit of pious resignation. "Lord, forgive them, for they know not what they do" is the prayer of the sorrowful, but not too reverent Terschak.

In citing these peculiarities, it is not the intention to cast a shade on the lustre of this great artist's renown; on the contrary, Terschak must be placed among the greatest flute composers and performers the world ever knew.

HUGUES, LUIGI: professor of geography at the University of Turin, Italy, and a remarkable flutist-composer, was born in 1836 at Casale Monferrato, near Alessandria, Piemonte.

From his youth he evinced a passionate love for the flute and although he remained an amateur, yet he surpassed the best virtuosos and composers of his time. He even found time in his leisure hours to write a *School of Flute Duets* in four books which, with his "three grand duets," have long been considered some of the finest music in the literature of the flute. Hugues composed many pieces for flute and piano, a concerto dedicated to Briccialdi, etudes, chamber music and numerous religious compositions including a "Requiem."

His brother, Felice, also played flute and for him he composed an interesting *Carnevale di Venezia* for two flutes and piano. Hugues earned and enjoyed the universal esteem of his music loving countrymen. He died in 1913.

POPP, WILHELM: one of the best and most widely known flutists and composers of flute literature, was born in Coburg, Germany, April 29, 1828. In his home city he was court pianist and in 1867 was appointed solo flutist of the Philharmonic Orchestra in Hamburg. He was a pupil of Kaspar Kummer and Louis Drouet.

He was very successful as a writer for his instrument and his solo works are known throughout the world. He wrote innumerable instructive works and over five hundred solo compositions for flute with piano accompaniment. He died at Hamburg, Germany, June 25, 1903.

WEHNER, CARL: dean of the flutists of America, was born in Mannheim, Germany, on February 27, 1838. Descended from a musical family, his grandfather had been a flute player of some prominence as had been his father, who was young Carl's first instructor. His father having died very young, Wehner continued his studies in Wuerzburg under Caspar Roeder, professor at the royal music school. This professor had been a pupil of Carl Wehner's father and mixed corporal punishment with flute instruction. After having imparted to him all he knew about flute playing, Roeder frankly admitted this by saying: "Now I have nothing more to teach you" Wehner went to Theobald Boehm, the inventor of the new system flute, with whom he finished his education. Wehner had been sent to Boehm for further instruction by an archduke who had been informed of his remarkable talents. The necessary payment for this instruction, however, was never made by the duke. On account of the attachment Boehm had conceived for him, he received not only the instruction gratis, but on parting was told that he owed him absolutely nothing.

149

Wehner then went to Russia, where, at first, he did not get along flourishingly; in fact, he was compelled to play for occasional dances from early evening to daybreak for a few kopeks. Frequently, after returning from such engagements, during Russia's coldest season, he was compelled to sleep in a room without fire, and in the absence of a bed, in his overcoat upon the top of a box. However, a change for the better occurred after he became acquainted with Cesare Ciardi, who, recognizing his ability, assisted him in establishing his reputation. Ciardi, a great master of the old flute, sent all the aristocratic applicants who desired instruction in the new system as a novelty to Wehner, as having come fresh from the tutelage of the inventor. To the last he remained Ciardi's grateful friend and enthusiastic admirer.

He eventually became first flute of the ballet of the Imperial Opera at St. Petersburg, which post was subsequently occupied by the late Ernesto Koehler.

After seventeen years' stay in Russia, during which time he also traveled in Siberia, he accepted the position as first flute at the Royal Theatre in Hanover, but after a short engagement came to New York at the request of Theodore Thomas. As first flute of the New York Philharmonic and Metropolitan Opera House orchestras he confirmed the worldwide reputation he had gained in Europe.

His career was as remarkable as it was long and brilliant and of the greatest interest, he having played under the direction of Wagner, Brahms, Verdi, Berlioz, Rubinstein, Liszt, Johann Strauss, Tchaikowsky, Mancinelli, Arditi, Theodore Thomas, Seidl, Damrosch and other foremost men of his time. Adelina Patti also had kind words of praise and admiration for him.

All who heard him in the prime of his life are unanimous in saying that his clearness of tone and interpretation were unique and unsurpassed.

In 1898, he published *Twelve Grand Technical Exercises for the Flute* and in later years devoted himself to instruction only. He was a fervid partisan of the wooden open G-sharp flute and would easily become excited when the metal instrument came under discussion.

The autographed portraits of the above mentioned musical

celebrities in time became a valuable collection and nothing grieved him more than the loss of Richard Wagner's autographed photo which several individuals under pretext of looking over his rare collection had appropriated at one time.

In conclusion, it may be fitting to observe that when the writer requested the particulars of his life in order to write his biography, Wehner protested by saying: "But, please, Mr. de Lorenzo, not yet; wait until I am dead, then it will be complete. You will not have to wait long." He died on March 27, 1912.

RADCLIFF, JOHN (1842-1916?): the paper from which I gather the following writing calls Radcliff "the most famous of flutists." He was undoubtedly the most famous and also the most popular of English flutists of his time, but more than that is rather doubtful as he was a contemporary of Doppler, Andersen, Briccialdi and Taffanel. However, let us not disturb this famous flutist's eternal peace!

It seems that flute playing in the Radcliff family must have been an indispensable habit for, "long before it was thought necessary to procure any instrument for young John, he had provided himself with a penny whistle, and by stopping up the end with a cork and improvising a mouth-hole at the side, he converted it into a flute, upon which he sedulously practiced for a full year! So much progress did he make that at length he was permitted to practice with his father and three elder brothers, who were all proficient amateur players upon the flute!" Imagine four flute players already in one family and a fifth on the way. This is, I think, very close to a record. But let us proceed. Realizing the lad's bent, his father placed him under proper tuition, and at twelve years of age the lad made his first appearance at a concert in Birkenhead. In 1857 Radcliff went to London and became acquainted with the new cylinder or Boehm flute with its new method of fingering and at once adopted it. He was admitted to the Royal Academy of Music and a year later the new pupil was elected an associate. Almost as soon as he graduated from the Academy he leaped at once into popular favor, and the record of his life from 1858 to 1868 is that of a professional musician whose services were in constant demand.

In 1868 he accepted an engagement from Sir (then Mr.) Michael Costa as principal flutist of the Covent Garden Italian Opera, and for the following fifteen years he never missed a single performance. The story of the musician's abrupt withdrawal from his lucrative sphere of action in London is tinged with romance. When Pauline Rita was the reigning cantatrice in comic opera, the Orpheus of the flute fell over head and ears in love with her. This passion proved to be reciprocated, and an engagement followed. Unfortunately, the vocalist had to pay the penalty of popularity. Her voice suffered from overwork, and her medical advisers recommended a warmer climate. She had a brother in Melbourne, Australia, and went out to him for a short holiday. Six months grew into a year, and still Pauline Rita remained in seclusion. A year and a half passed, and still she was unable to name the date of intended departure. Then Mr. Radcliff resolved to go to find his Eurydice. He left London on the day after fulfilling his engagement at the Leeds Festival of 1883 and set foot in Melbourne in December of that year. In January, 1884, Orpheus and Eurydice were married.

In a letter from John Finn in London in 1912, he mentions an incident that occurred during the visit there of the great flutist composer Terschak, who was an inveterate hater of the Boehm flute. At a meeting, after he arrived in London, Terschak produced four manuscripts of his own compositions and said to Radcliff, who was present, "Which shall I dedicate to you?" Radcliff played over, in his unsurpassed manner, several of these and selected *Hommage à Venice*. No doubt Terschak was astonished at finding such reading and such skill. Mr. Finn continues: "Terschak was too clever a man not to know that there was much in the new flute. He was anxious to possess the instrument and wrote me to send him one!" However, it is a known fact that no one ever heard Terschak play a single note on the new flute."

Radcliff was the possessor of a unique collection of reed instruments of all kinds, from the crudest and most bizarre of ancient and modern times up to the most finished and approved types. At one time he gave a lecture under the title, "From Pan to pinafore," in which he illustrated his remarks by performing

152

on the different instruments he exhibited. This collection included the Pandean pipes; the arghool, an Egyptian pipe of two reeds which has been used by the Nile boatmen from pre-historic times; a broken remnant of a Roman Tibia carved out of a bone dredged up from the bottom of the Thames; New Guinea Indian snake-charmer's bowl-shaped flute; a Chinese flute, like our six-keyed instrument, but with another hole covered with tissue paper so as to produce the peculiar strident intonation so grateful to Mongolian ears; the Zulu pipe, held closely under the nose in order that the native performer's protrusive underlip may not unduly interfere with the hole.

TAFFANEL, CLAUDE-PAUL: This remarkable musician and great flutist was born in Bordeaux, France, on September 16, 1844. When seven years old, his father started to give him his first lessons in flute-playing, while other teachers started him on the violin and piano at the same time.

Of these various instruments, the flute became his favorite and he progressed so rapidly that when only ten years old (1854), he appeared as a soloist in La Rochelle, where his father was bandmaster. This first appearance took place in one of the *Concerts du Mail*, and was attended with considerable success. After studying for several years, Taffanel concertized in Bordeaux (1857) and one of his appearances at the Franklin Hall was criticized by one of the leading papers at the time as follows:

"At the benefit concert recently given at the Franklin Hall, we had occasion to hear a young boy, son of the well-known music teacher Taffanel, who although only twelve years old, gave evidence of unusual talent and ability as a flute virtuoso. It was a genuine delight to listen to his beautiful tone and admire his remarkable technical surety and facility. There can be little doubt that he will follow in the footsteps of Remusat."

About this time an accomplished amateur flutist and music lover, Paul Quercy, commenced to take an interest in the boy and assisted him in many ways. Quercy was a pupil of Guillon and a friend of Dorus. In 1858 he recommended his young protege to Dorus and after only two years with this master, young Taffanel had arrived at the utmost perfection of his art.

When Dorus had succeeded Tulou at the Conservatory in 1860, Taffanel joined his class and captured first prize in the same year of his entrance.

The appointment of Dorus as teacher at the Conservatory in Paris marked an important turning point in the history of the flute in France, as up to his time only the old style flute had been taught. Dorus introduced the Boehm flute which has been taught and played in France ever since.

Filled with enthusiasm and a desire to widen his musical knowledge, Taffanel joined the class of Reber and gained first prize for harmony in 1863, and first prize for counterpoint and fugue in 1865. One of his fellow students at the time was Jules Massenet. After a short engagement at the Palais Royal, Taffanel was appointed first flute at the Opéra Comique (1862-1864) and after this at the Grand Opéra. In 1871 he was appointed solo flutist and in 1890 he was elected as conductor, holding this position until 1906. We will refer to this position again later on.

Pasdeloup, the founder of the famous popular Paris concerts bearing his name, counted Taffanel among the foremost of his orchestral players, and presented him as his flute soloist in 1864, Taffanel playing Pratten's *Marie Stuart Fantasia* on this occasion. In the following year, Taffanel was admitted into the *Konzertgesellschaft* of the Conservatory. The extraordinary experience which Taffanel gained in this orchestra, the advantages of becoming intimately acquainted with the greatest classic and modern masterpieces, all proved of greatest benefit to him and influenced his entire future career in the most advantageous manner.

Taffanel concertized in France, Germany, England, Russia, etc., for more than thirty years with the most gratifying and extraordinary success. Hughes Imbert, a well-known music critic, expressed the following opinion of Taffanel at one time:

"Taffanel's virtuosity on the flute is distinguished through his unusual pure, soulful and sweet tone, as well as through his immaculate understanding and interpretation of the classic works. His technical facility and surety are astonishing and without exaggeration it might be claimed that his playing is absolutely perfect."

As the classic literature of flute solos is rather a limited one, Taffanel always endeavored, ever since the beginning of his career, to find artistic satisfaction in the presentation of chamber music. In 1872, together with Arming, Ed. Lalo and Jacquard, he founded the so-called *Société Classique*, which consisted of a string and wind quintet. This organization gave very interesting concerts at the Salle Erard for three years. The experiences gained in these years induced Taffanel, in 1879, to found another organization made up of artists who played only wind instruments—flutes, oboes, clarinets, horns and bassoons.

However, Taffanel, was not mainly concerned about his own instrument. He was very anxious to advance and raise the standards of all the other wind instruments. His ideas in this respect were well considered and he always claimed that advancement in correct playing, combination of the various tonal qualities, as well as surety and precise attack in the playing of these instruments would only be possible in the orchestra if these instruments constituted a complete and perfect ensemble among themselves. For fifteen years he devoted his entire time and attention to this organization. The performances he gave with his artists became famous and were attended with the most gratifying success, not only in Paris, but also in Germany, Switzerland, Belgium and wherever they appeared. There is little doubt that the standard and quality of wind instrument playing was raised to an extraordinary degree of excellence both in France and other countries through this organization, as many similar ones were formed in other countries and beneficial influences were scattered broadcast through efficient players needed for the various ensembles.

When the position of conductor at the Grand Opéra became vacant in 1887, Taffanel was recommended by Gailhard, the managing director of the National Academy, to fill the vacancy. He had followed Taffanel's career up to this time and believed that he would be the best and most capable conductor the institution could find.

Taffanel was peculiarly fitted to fill this position owing to his musical ability and his experience as conductor of chamber music organizations for over fifteen years, and the very first performance given under his direction at the Opéra proved the wisdom of Gailhard's choice. His appointment as conductor introduced a new era at the Opéra and all modern works heard in Paris from this time forth were produced under his personal direction. It might be mentioned that among the most important works produced by him were Wagner's *Tristan und Isolde, Tannhäuser, Siegfried,* and *Die Meistersinger.*

When Henry Altes, the successor of Dorus, resigned his position in 1893, Taffanel was appointed flute teacher at the Conservatory. He was quickly surrounded by many talented pupils who spread his system of teaching and playing in France and other countries.

After 1897, Taffanel was also appointed leader of the orchestral classes at the Conservatory. When, in 1892, J. Garcius retired as conductor of the *Konzertgesellschaft* of the Conservatory, Taffanel was appointed his successor, and thanks to his experience and thorough knowledge of the entire literature of music, he achieved the greatest success with this admirable body of artists.

In 1900, Taffanel was appointed conductor of the official exhibition concerts of the French government. The exertions in this connection with this appointment were so extraordinary and fatiguing that Taffanel was forced to resign his position as conductor of the Conservatory concerts.

As a composer, Taffanel proved himself possessed of exceptional talents. He wrote a fine quintet for flute, oboe, clarinet, horn, and bassoon, and has left many transpositions for flute and piano.

Taffanel was an officer of the Legion of Honor as well as of *L'Instruction publique.* Furthermore, he was decorated with the Swedish Polar Star Order, the Italian Crown Order, the Russian St. Anne Order, and the Persian Order of the Lions and

156

the Sun. In addition to this, Taffanel was also a member of the Royal Swedish Academy of Music.

Taffanel died in Paris on November 22, 1908.

TILLMETZ, RUDOLF: This prominent artist ranks as one of the very foremost flute players of modern times. In a like manner as Gantenberg of Berlin, he combines the rare qualities of an active virtuoso with the more important ones of a pedagogue, and it may justly be stated that the development of our modern interpretative ideas in flute playing is mostly due to Tillmetz's achievements as a teacher and to his literary achievements along technical lines.

Rudolf Tillmetz was a native of Munich, Germany, where he was born on April 1, 1847. His father, Franz Paul Tillmetz, noticed his son's musical talents when the latter was still very young, and decided to give him every possible advantage in the way of a thorough musical education. In the course of time, the boy received piano instruction from Franz Barraga, and instruction in musical theory from Kapellmeister Otto Muller, but his greatest benefits were derived from the famous Munich flute virtuoso, Theobald Boehm. Through close association with this master, young Tillmetz's attention was directed towards the instrument with which he in turn achieved such astonishing success in the course of his brilliant career.

His artistic activities commenced at a very early age. His first appearance occurred in 1858 in Munich, when he was eleven years old. This first concert was quickly followed by others, together with successful concert tours, given as frequently as his attendance at school would permit. As soon as his studies at school and those for the flute were at an end, he was immediately appointed first flute at the Royal Bavarian Opera Orchestra under Franz Lachner in 1864. During this time he profited greatly through association with Richard Wagner, who at that time conducted at the Munich Hoftheater.

In 1869 Tillmetz was appointed teacher for the Royal Bavarian Cadetcorps. He remained in this position for twelve years, during which time his pedagogic talents developed to such an

157

extent that in 1883 he was appointed teacher of the flute at the Royal Music School of the Bavarian capital. Some of his greatest successes were gained with his ensemble concerts for wind instruments. He founded a chamber music organization together with his colleagues, Franz Strauss and E. Reichenbacher, which is firmly established in the musical life of Munich and the performances of which are looked upon in every art centre of Northern Germany as models of their kind.

Tillmetz was a player of exceptional ability and his tone both in quality and volume earned for him a most enviable reputation. His style was specially adapted for interpretation of classic works and he was particularly successful in his interpretation of the works of Bach, Handel and Mozart.

He died in Munich on January 25, 1915.

It should also be mentioned that Rudolf Tillmetz was an excellent pianist.

His literary works include a very important technical treatise entitled *Method for Learning the Boehm Flute With Conical Bore*. It is a remarkable work, although not as yet translated into the English language.

Tillmetz was the recipient of many personal honors and decorations bestowed upon him by royalty and private organizations.

Tillmetz also achieved noteworthy successes as a composer for his instrument. Some of his best known works include: Twenty-four Studies for flute, Op. 12, introduced at the Academy of Tonal Art in Munich and at the Royal Musical School in Wurzburg. Twenty-six Studies in all Keys. Melodic Studies, Op. 29. Among his solos with piano accompaniment the best known are: Album Leaf, Op. 8; Fantasiestuck, Op. 9; Six Easy Solos, Op. 10; Andante and Polonaise, Op. 15; Nocturno, Alpine Round and Rondoletta pastorale, Op. 17; Concert Study for flute and orchestra, Op. 22; a Grand Konzertstuck, Op. 23; Hungarian Fantasia, Op. 25; Six Solos, Op. 28; Nocturne for flute, French horn and piano, Op. 31; Six Characteristic Solos, Op. 32; Lyric Pieces, Op. 33; Fantasie Pastorale roumaine, Op. 34, and one of his best and most recent works, a Notturno, Op. 50, dedicated to this writer, Leonardo De Lorenzo. His latest works include Op. 52, Thirty Studies in duet form, and Op. 54,

Twelve Rhythmic exercises in form of duets. It should also be mentioned that Tillmetz issued a newly revised edition of the well-known method for flute by Soussmann, Part I. This work alone proved his ability as a pedagogue and his new exercising material as well as additions to suit modern demands are admirable.

ANDERSEN, CARL JOACHIM: was born in Copenhagen, Denmark, on April 29, 1847. He was one of the most accomplished musicians of his time as flutist (old system), composer and conductor. He studied flute with his father, Christian Joachim Andersen, and when only thirteen years old made public appearance as a flute soloist. He began his career as first flutist in the orchestra under Niels Gade. In 1869 he became a member of the Royal Court Chapel. During these years he made concert tours in the Scandinavian countries and Finland, and in 1877 went to St. Petersburg, leaving there for Berlin in 1881. Early in this century he was in this country for a short visit. As solo flutist and conductor he enjoyed the esteem of von Bülow, Joachim, Grieg, Klindworth and Moszkowski.

Andersen composed many beautiful concert pieces for the flute and his Etudes are held in highest regard. He died in Copenhagen on May 7, 1909.

BARRETT, W. LEWIS: Among the prominent modern flute-players who have in a great measure helped to regain an ascending popularity for their instrument should be mentioned W. Lewis Barrett, recognized throughout the flute-playing world as a player of extraordinary and unusual abilities.

When considering the enormous difficulties which players such as Barrett, Krakamp, Taffanel, Wehner, and Radcliff, had to battle against in the face of never-ending discussion about an old system on the one hand and the new with its open G-sharp and closed G-sharp partisans on the other, when the strife was being championed to the dismay of all flutists, when every discoverer of this or that real or imaginary improvement advocated his invention to the exclusion of every other, when every claimant for this or that system open G-sharp or closed

G-sharp key, wood or metal instrument, brought the flute into disrepute—it is when considering such unfavorable conditions that the true artistic ability and ceaseless endeavors of such artists as the above are fully appreciated.

In discussing the achievements of Barrett and in consideration of his subtle mastery of the flute and his assiduous efforts to impart his art to others, it may be claimed without exaggeration that he has been a prominent factor in bringing about the recognition of the flute as a principal orchestra and solo instrument.

W. Lewis Barrett was born in London in 1848. His father, Thomas Barrett, was a violinist and came from a well-known professional family. He intended his son for a commercial career and to this end placed him in a wholesale mercantile house, where he served for a period of six years. During this period, all Barrett's spare time was devoted to music. At first he studied the violin, but one day a friend of his father's lent him a B-flat boxwood fife and he took such an immediate liking to this instrument that he determined to master it. To quote his own words in speaking of this period of his life, he said: "I stuck to it for hours at a time and, at last, after some splitting headaches, I managed to get the right tone and after this progressed so rapidly that a relative of mine presented me with an eight-keyed flute."

This should be encouraging to embryo flutists, since Barrett was famous for the purity and quality of his tone. He took lessons from R. S. Rockstro, the famous author of *A Treatise on the Flute*, and when his father died he took up flute playing as a profession, having never had any real taste or desire for a mercantile career.

In addition to his studies on the flute, he now took up harmony, studying with W. Castell, a double bass player. One of his earliest important engagements was a tour with an English opera company. This was probably about the year 1868, since he succeeded John Radcliff, who left the company to take R. S. Pratten's place in the Royal Opera.

Barrett was an especial favorite with Sir Michael Costa who, after a severe test, engaged him for the Sacred Harmony Society

160

in the opera orchestra and elsewhere. He played under this eminent conductor for a period of twelve years.

When Olaf Svendsen died in 1888, Barrett succeeded him as principal flute in the orchestras of the Philharmonic Society, Bach Choir, Birmingham Festival, Richter's and Henschel's concerts, etc. He was also for several seasons solo flutist at the Promenade Concerts, Covent Garden, where his reputation for artistic rendering and execution was established.

In 1883, at the opening of the Royal College of Music, Barrett was appointed professor of the flute, and he held this important post a long time, having turned out many excellent pupils well known in England. Among these may be named Laubach, W. Carrodus, Ingham, D. S. Wood and Eli Hudson. At the turn of the century he made an extensive tour with Mme. Albani, visiting all the chief cities in the United States and Canada, sharing the successes in every place with the prima donna. In various places the effect of the instrument in the hands of Barrett was the subject of special comment.

On several occasions Barrett played before Queen Victoria, both at Windsor and at Balmoral, having been personally presented and complimented on each occasion.

Barrett composed several pieces for flute and piano and gathered an important collection of orchestral passages for the benefit of students.

In conclusion, it should be stated that Barrett's unusual practical experience in every branch of the profession and the thoroughly artistic results which he had to his credit, place him at the very head of modern flute players, and his achievements as a soloist, a teacher and orchestral performer at classical concerts, in oratorio or opera, have been the means of establishing him among the representatives in the musical history of his time. Barrett died in 1928.

KÖHLER, ERNESTO: was prominent among those who gained favor and popularity in flute-playing circles in Europe and America by their labors in the field of flute composition. The "neglected wind" has always been a trite and rather worn theme, and many interested in the "little bit of wood" of romantic story, the inherent musical power and tone beauty of which Ernesto Köhler was such an able exponent, do not usually regard the period of his special activity as a composer (1875-1890) as of any particular moment in the annals of their instrument. The writer ventures to say that these views are not well founded; and, further, that if it were possible to forget the brightest epoch in the history of the flute, those palmy years of the last century (1820-1850), when Kuhlau, Kummer, Berbiguier, Gabrielsky, Walckiers, and a long roll of virtuosi were dignifying the instrument by their compositions and performances, and Boehm was laboring to perfect its tones and intonation, it is open to doubt whether the intervening period has produced anything like the numerous really good works put forth in the last decade.

Ernesto Köhler was born at Modena, Italy, on December 4, 1849. Like many other famous flutists, he came of a musical stock and was reared in a musical atmosphere. While a child he commenced to play the flute under the gentle, affectionate tuition of his father, *Venceslau* Joseph Köhler, who was first flute in the orchestra of the Duke of Modena. Quantz, Nicholson, Boehm and Briccialdi alike have insisted that there is no "royal road" to success in flute playing. Natural aptitude, hard work and good teaching have ever been considered the most useful aids to proficiency on what is really a difficult instrument.* Young Köhler, besides a natural aptitude for the instrument of his choice, had a good instructor in the father, whose heart was gladdened by the eager willingness and receptive nature of the bright pupil who made such rapid progress. Ernesto pursued his flute and musical studies with such ardor that at an early age he became a first rate performer; and, long before boyhood was over, in company with his brother Ferdinando, a pianist of repute, numerous concert tours were made in Italy with unvarying success. The critics were unanimous in commending the brilliant execution, fine tone, chaste style and general elegance of delivery of the young flute artist; they also remarked the frequent ap-

---

* My own answer as to how easy or how difficult it is to master the flute has invariably been: "The flute is the easiest instrument to play badly."

proval of an exacting public. On attaining twenty years of age, in the year 1869, Köhler was desirous of seeing more of the world, and, as might be expected, of obtaining fame and fortune; or, failing that, to at least secure a comfortable musical appointment. At this juncture in the young artist's career the seat of first flute in the orchestra of the Karl Theatre, Vienna, happened to be unfilled, and the young flutist was urged to take the position. He decided to do so, and held the place for about two years; during which time, as opportunity served, he gave flute concerts at various towns in Austria. He also devoted some of his leisure to composition, and published several pieces for flute and piano, the freshness and merit of which at once attracted the attention of continental flute players.

A couple of years in the Austrian capital enabled Köhler to look well around him and to consider duly the prospects before the would-be flute soloist. In 1871, he decided to act on the advice of the famous veteran, Cesare Ciardi, who had urged him to leave Vienna and take up his residence in St. Petersburg. The journey to the Russian capital was made, and, supported by the strong recommendation of his renowned *confrère* who held an important position as flutist, Köhler at once obtained an appointment in the orchestra of the Imperial Ballet.

In the closing decades of the 19th century, Cesare Ciardi had great renown as a flutist. In the early years of his life, when the flute solo was an important item on the concert program, he made long journeys, played and traveled all over Europe. He had considerable fame also as a composer, and is well remembered as the writer of fantasias. *Le Carneval Russe* is still popular.

In some interesting but all too short flute gossip prefaced to the English edition of *Boehm On The Flute*, the late Walter Stewart Broadwood of London gives us an idea of the talent of this flutist. It appears that many years ago Ciardi was on a musical mission in London. As an incidental necessity he had his flute with him. Describing the artist, his instrument and performance, Broadwood said: "He played on an old wooden instrument by Koch (I think) of Vienna, with a crack down the head joint which, as I remember, much exercised Mr. Rose; yet I have heard him sustain a crescendo for four consecutive bars of an adagio—after which I took him (he had only just arrived) to Mr. Rudall, who, not speaking Italian, begged me to explain that he, Ciardi, 'was fit to play before a chorus of angels.' Ciardi was encored (his entire piece) in a concert of the Opera House, where Grisi, Mario, and Tamburini were waiting to be heard; and in consequence was engaged to play a solo at the classically exclusive Philharmonic, whose members he shocked prodigiously by playing a fantasia on airs from *Lucia*. His tone, coloring, and facile execution, always faultless in their elegance, carried all before them.''

Ciardi died in St. Petersburg in 1877, and was succeeded as soloist by the friend he had induced to settle in the city of Neva. In 1900 Köhler was appointed first flute in the orchestra of the Imperial Russian Opera, thereby holding the premier flute position in the Empire of the Czar.

The prominent appointments held for so many years by Köhler undoubtedly restricted his fame as a soloist; but any loss in this respect was more than made good by the promises of enduring popularity as a composer. Köhler wrote a number of excellent flute works well planned for educational purposes, and many solos decidedly pleasant to play, which have met the approbation alike of flutists and of the musical public. As a composer, his strong points are melody—genuine and spontaneous—a good knowledge of the technique of the flute, together with the art of adding appropriate, tasteful accompaniments to all his pieces. In composing for the flute, Köhler, who had many pupils, was mindful of the need of meeting the requirements of medium performers; numbers of his pieces being written for this class of flutists. The concert solos are, of course, composed to exhibit the power of the virtuoso, and will, generally, be found difficult enough. Köhler's enthusiasm and industry were apparently ceaseless. The list of his works passed the hundred mark. This includes a theoretical and practical flute school (which had been adopted at several Continental conservatories of music), numerous flute studies, duets for two flutes, pieces for two flutes and piano, and some scores of bright, melodious and often charming salon pieces with piano; besides larger works, notably *Schwalbenflug, Hirten Idylle, La Romantique, Papillon*, Concerto Op. 97, etc. which have been frequently played by the leading soloists of Europe, America and Australia.

In addition to the works detailed in the list appended to this notice, Köhler wrote an opera, *Ben Achmed,* which had a successful run in St. Petersburg (1893), and some ballets—one entitled *Clorinda,* being very popular at the Imperial Theatre, St. Petersburg.

List of Ernesto Köhler's compositions up to Op. 98:

Il Tramonto del Sole, Idillio, Op. 2; Reminiscenze Belliniane, Fantasie, Op. 3; Danse Savoyarde, Morceau de Salon, Op. 8; Chagrin, Morceau de Salon, Op. 9; Fantaisie Romantique, Op. 13; Valse Caprice, Op. 14; Polka du Rossignol; Souvenir de St. Petersbourg; Nocturne; Regrets, Melodie; Saltarello, Scherzo; Danse Champetre, Morceau de Concert, Op. 43; Tarantelle Napolitaine, Morceau de Concert, Op. 42; Fleurs d'Italie, Fantaisie de Concert; Twenty-four Characteristic Etudes; Reverie Russe, Caprice Brillant; Mathilde, Mazourka de Concert; Caprice Original; Fantaisie Brillante sur des Motifs Italiens; Theoretical and Practical Flute School; Bon Soir Romance, Op. 27; Six Brilliant Pieces, Op. 30: No. 1—Chant du Soir, No. 2—Berceuse, No. 3 —Barcarolle, No. 4—Papillon Etude, No. 5—Au Bord du Volga, No. 6—Valse des Roses; Der Fortschritt im Flotenspiel, Op. 33: Book I—15 Easy Exercises, Book II—12 Medium Difficult Exercises, Book III—8 Difficult Exercises; Amorettenstandchen, Op. 36; Marsch der Aengstlichen, Op. 37; Spring Song, Op. 38; Alla Mazurka, Op. 39; Echo, for flute, cornet and piano, Op. 40; Reverie Poetique, Op. 40; On the Alps, Op. 51; Forty Progressive Duets for Two Flutes, Op. 55; Dance Album (three books), Op. 53; Marches and Gavottes (Book 4), Op. 53; Opera Album (Book 5), Op. 53; Song Album (Book 6), Op. 53; Gipsy Songs and Romances (Book 7), Op. 53; Valse Espagnole, Op. 57; Shepherd Idylle, Op. 58; Serenade, Op. 59; Six Salon Pieces, Op. 60: No. 1—Romance, No. 2—Gavotte, No. 3—Souvenir, No. 4—Rejouissance, No. 5—Meditation, No. 6—Danse des Marionettes: Six Easy Fantasias on Russian Folk-Songs, Op. 61; Concert Fantasia on a Russian Folk-Song, Moskwa, Op. 62; Six Easy Fantasias on German Folk-Songs, Op. 63; Concert Fantasia from the Opera, *Der Gouverneur von Tours,* by C. Reinecke,

Op. 64; Twenty-five Romantic Etudes, Op. 66; First Concert Duet on a Melody by Schubert, for two flutes and piano, Op. 67; Second Concert Duet on a Melody by Chopin, for two flutes and piano, Op. 68; Echo, Concert Aria for Soprano, flute and piano, Op. 69 (German and Italian text); Oriental Serenade, Op. 70; Valse Mignon, Op. 71; Flight of the Swallows, Concert Etude, Op. 72; Concert Fantasia on a Theme by Donizetti, Op. 73; Italian Serenade, Op. 74; Thirty Virtuoso Etudes in all Major and Minor Keys, Op. 75 (known all over the world); At the Sea Shore, Concert piece, Op. 76; School of Velocity, Daily Studies, Op. 77; Three Characteristic Pieces, Op. 78; No. 1—Morgengrüss, No. 2—Vergissmeinnicht, No. 3—Landlicher Tänze; Dream of the Future, Op. 70; La Romantique, Concert Fantasie, Op. 80; Zephyr Concert Waltz, Op. 81; Ten Concert Etudes, Op. 82: No. 1—Am Bache, No. 2—Spruhende Funken, No. 3—Hasche Mich, No. 4—Schneeflocken, No. 5—Hammer und Ambross, No. 6—Sturm, No. 7—Die Eigensinnige, No. 8—Reverie, No. 9—Ersehntes Glück, No. 10—Im Schlitten; Six Solo Pieces, Op. 84: No. 1—Gondoliera, No. 2—Solitude, No. 3—Arlequin et Colombine, No. 4—Declaration, No. 5—Souvenir de Gaibola, No. 6—Feu Follet; Carlton Mazurka, Op. 85; La Perle du Nord, Concert Piece, Op. 86; Flower Waltz, for two flutes and pianoforte, Op. 87; Four Morceaux Caracteristiques, Op. 88: No. 1—Souvenir de Spala (Nocturne), No. 2—Grace et Coquetrie (Impromptu), No. 3—Dans le bois (Scherzino), No. 4—Danse des Pirrots; 22 Exercises for Technique and Interpretation, Op. 89; Fantasia (transcription) Love in Idleness, Op. 90; Fantasia (Concert Piece), Op. 91; Grand Quartet for Four Flutes, Op. 92; 20 Easy Melodic Progressive Lessons, Op. 93; La Capriccieuse, Concert Piece, Op. 94; Ruslan and Ludmilla, Concert Fantasie, Op. 95; Life of the Czar, Concert Fantasie, Op. 96; Concerto, Op. 97; Au vol d'Oiseau, Scènes pittoresques (cello ad lib.), Op. 98; Op. 99, II Concerto, unfinished.

The concert pieces enumerated in the foregoing list have been scored for orchestra as well as piano.

The writer is in possession of a clipping from the *St. Petersburg Herald* of November 25, 1906, which gives a brief descrip-

166

tion of his career on the occasion of the thirty-fifth anniversary of his being flutist of the Imperial Opera and towards the end of that year received a letter from him making an appointment to meet in Milan in the following spring, saying that he had given up the active life of the profession and that he hoped after thirty-five years of hard work to enjoy his remaining days in peace and quiet. Upon arrival in Italy six months later, the writer was astonished and grieved to receive the news of his demise. Ernesto Köhler died in St. Petersburg on May 17, 1907.

LEMMONÉ, JOHN: If enthusiasm is requisite for success in any field of endeavor, the amount of enthusiasm Lemmoné displayed in his efforts to restore the flute as a solo instrument should bring him to as great a prominence as those whose names are associated with the highest achievements on that instrument.

The confidence Lemmoné had in the possibilities of the instrument is evident from the following observation: "There is," he said, "a great deal of classical musical literature for the flute —sonatas written by Bach, Handel and Beethoven, and concerti by Mozart. Had the Boehm instrument been invented in their day, however, musical literature for the flute would have been enriched greatly." A point of view shared by all flutists of prominence.

As an artist he ranked with the greatest that any country has produced and what Lemmoné did on the platform and as manager in his own country forms part of the musical history of Australia.

The esteem as a flutist in which Lemmoné is held is especially remarkable on account of the insufficient opportunities for instruction at his disposal during his youth; instruction being entirely dependent upon his own capabilities and talents and upon itinerant musicians that visited the country from time to time. Lemmoné was born at Ballarat, Victoria, Australia, on June 22, 1862, at a time when that country was in its earliest stages of development.

Lemmoné made his first appearance as a virtuoso at twenty-two years of age with great success. As it happened, it was also the occasion of Mme. Melba's debut as a singer. After that, he made a tour of the East with Mme. Amy Sherwin, which was repeated two years later with the famous contralto, Mme. Patey.

Lemmoné went to London and made his debut by giving a flute recital at the Salle Erard on October 25, 1894. When in London, he was strictly a soloist, although during a special engagement, he played in three orchestral concerts at the Queen's Hall, Artur Nikisch conducting. During the English period of his career—from 1894 to 1897—he performed at concerts in most of the cities of Great Britain. He made many tours with Mme. Melba and five tours with Mme. Adelina Patti.

In 1895 the artist was associated with Paderewski, at the Nikisch concerts. He was in South Africa as a soloist with Mme. Amy Sherwin in 1895 to 1896, the success of which left such a deep impression that it was vividly remembered by those who had been present and lauded upon the writer's arrival there three years later. The rendering of the celebrated caprice, *Il Vento*, by Briccialdi, was especially praised.

In 1910 he visited the United States and Canada with Mme. Melba on a concert tour.

As concert director he managed the Australasian tours of Paderewski, Mark Hambourg, Mme. Alda and Adela Verne. He piloted Mme. Melba on every tour through Australia. In spite of these activities, he never neglected his favorite instrument, which he invariably played at the concerts.

Lemmoné wrote many solos for the flute with piano accompaniment. He was better known, however, on account of having made several good gramophone records. He died in 1950.

FRANSELLA, ALBERT, born in or about 1866 in Amsterdam. Although of Dutch parentage, he was of Italian extraction, as his name indicates. His father (an excellent flutist and a professor of music in Amsterdam) gave him his first musical instruction. This was followed by a course of study under the late Jacques de Jong, solo flutist to the late King of Holland.

His progress was rapid, and at the age of fifteen the youthful musician had the honor of appearing at the concert of the Grand Duke Friedrich Franz II of Mecklenburg. A year later, while playing at one of the Classical concerts in Amsterdam, he was greatly encouraged by Brahms, who had come to Amsterdam on one of his yearly visits, and who complimented the youthful flutist, predicting for him a brilliant future. The permanent conductor of these concerts at the time (Johann Verhulst) was so conservative in his musical ideas that rather than conduct any of Wagner's compositions he resigned his post.

After many successful appearances in Holland and elsewhere, Fransella came to England, refusing a tempting offer from France. Playing on a sweet-toned conical bore flute, he, on his arrival in London, appeared at the Promenade concerts under Riviere. But on going further afield he soon found that a more sonorous and richer-toned instrument was required, and he adopted the cylinder bore flute now universally used, thereby gaining two points—a bigger and more sonorous tone and better intonation. It was his opinion though that the old conical eight-keyed flute is very sweet in timbre and that the tone which he in his youth heard Dahmen (the principal flutist in Amsterdam at the time) produce is never to be forgotten.

Fransella's stay in England, intended to be a short one, lasted, almost unbrokenly, until he died in 1934. He successively held the principal positions to be had, such as in the Scottish Orchestra at Glasgow, Sir August Mann's Crystal Palace Orchestra, the Royal Opera of Covent Garden, the Queen's Hall Orchestra and the Royal Philharmonic; further, he held the appointments of solo professor at the Guildhall School of Music and Trinity College of Music, at which he attracted pupils from all parts of the world.

At numerous chamber concerts in combination with string and wind instruments his appearance was as much welcomed as on the concert platform. Last but not least, he was mostly in request when such great artists as Albani, Melba, Tetrazzini, etc., wanted to sing their celebrated arias with flute obbligati. So it is not to be wondered at when we echo the opinion that his position in Great Britain was a unique one, for in that teeming city of London with its seven millions of people, his name amongst the musical portion was a household word.

We conclude by culling an extract from the *Times* which, in speaking of this Dutch flutist, says:

"Fransella held a very high position among flute players, and deservedly so, for he was not merely an accomplished player who fully understood the technic of his instrument; he was a musician to whom phrasing, tone, and expression came naturally as a method of interpretation and his playing always commanded admiration by the skillful gradation of tone."

Fransella died in 1934.

PRILL, EMIL: This eminent flute player was born in Stettin, Germany, on May 10, 1867. His first lessons, as well as the greater part of his musical education, were derived by him from his father, a man of very uncommon musical knowledge and ability. Later on he was put into the care of the chamber virtuoso Gantenberg who developed the young artist's talents in a most remarkable manner. At a very early age, Emil Prill toured Germany, Sweden, Denmark and Russia with his brothers Paul and Carl (the former a splendid conductor, the latter a solo violinist of considerable fame), and earned a considerable share of the artistic successes gained. From 1881-1883, he attended the high schools at Berlin and completed his studies with the best and most satisfactory results.

After prominent engagements in St. Petersburg and Moscow, Emil Prill was engaged as teacher at the Royal Music School at Kharkov. Later on (1889-1892), he changed his sphere of activity to Hamburg, where he became first flutist of the Philharmonic Orchestra.

It is related that Felix Weingartner was conductor of this orchestra at the time when Prill applied for the position of first soloist. It is said that after hearing him play, Weingartner became unusually excited and remarked that never in his life had he listened to such perfection in flute playing and from that time forth he was untiring in his efforts to have Prill installed as solo flutist in the Royal Opera House Orchestra. When this was finally accomplished, the great conductor considered the engagement as a personal gain.

The admiration for Prill as voiced by Weingartner (one of the most particular of conductors) placed this artist in a most enviable position, and was the means of giving him every opportunity to unfold his remarkable talents and accomplishments as a solo flutist.

As a writer for his instrument, Emil Prill distinguished himself in a very prominent way. He was very successful in arranging classic and modern compositions for flute solo and edited a guide through the literature of the flute which was published by a European firm with very considerable success. Some of his best known arrangements include Waltzes, Mazurkas and the Impromptu, Op. 29, by Chopin. He also edited an attractive Schumann Album. He died in Berlin in 1940.

WETZGER, PAUL: This prominent flutist was born in Dahme, a small town in Germany, on December 26, 1870. His father, a gardener, was very musical and when Paul had reached his ninth year, he took him to the local musical director to have him instructed in violin playing. This teacher, besides being a good violinist, was also a very capable flutist and when Paul had reached his twelfth year, his teacher induced him to take up the flute as his principal instrument. In a short time Paul became an enthusiast for the new instrument and studied it with ever-increasing zeal and ambition.

His first public appearance took place when he was fourteen years old, the occasion being an important concert given at the principal church of his home town. Shortly after his confirmation, Wetzger procured a steady position as second flutist in the city orchestra. After one year's service he was advanced to the first choir. His studies in harmony and piano were taken up with Cantor Lucke and in less than two years many of his compositions for band and orchestra were heard in public. Other teachers with whom he pursued his studies were Karl Thorbratz, musical director in Berlin, and Hugo Ikker, a very prominent flutist and teacher.

After considerable experience in theatre, opera and symphony orchestras, Wetzger was finally appointed first flutist in the well-known Stadt Orchester of Essen, Germany, an admirable organization. At the same time he was appointed teacher of his instrument at the principal Conservatory of this city, and these duties, together with his considerable activities as a writer, arranger and composer, gave him every opportunity for the development of his numerous talents.

He was invited by the well-known collector, Goldberg of Berlin, to contribute a sketch of his career for his collection of celebrities and in return was presented with a valuable silver flute.

Wetzger distinguished himself in a marked manner as a writer for his instrument. He edited the flute works of Demersseman for a European publisher and in addition to many ambitious orchestral works, he wrote a very large number of original flute solos, many of which are still in manuscript. He is also well-known as a lecturer and has been particularly successful in Essen and Dortmund with his lectures on Frederick-the-Great and his solo recitals of some of the flute compositions of this monarch.

Among the best known published flute compositions of Paul Wetzger are the following:

(1) Fantasia on a German Folk-song, "Verlassen bin i'," with piano or orchestra; (2) Birdie's Morning Greeting for flute or piccolo with piano or orchestra; (3) From the Highlands with piano or orchestra; (4) Sakadas for flute or piccolo with piano or orchestra; (5) Sounds from the East with piano or orchestra; (6) Forget-me-not, solo for flute with piano; (7) Whispering Zephyrs with piano or orchestra; (8) The Fairies, Fantasia-Caprice with piano or orchestra; (9) At the Forest Brook, Idylle, with piano or orchestra; (10) Immortal Sparks for flute or piccolo with piano or orchestra; (11) Santa Notte with piano or orchestra; (12) Reminiscences of Jos. Haydn, Fantasia with piano or orchestra; (13) Christmas Joys for flute and piano; (14) Joyful Feelings for flute and piano; (15) Auf Wiedersehen, Fantasia with piano or orchestra (manuscript); (16) Fantasia on a German song with piano or orchestra (manuscript); (17) Four solos in brilliant style for two flutes; (18) a Collection of Flute Cadenzas; (19) Systematic Scales and Chord Studies for Flute; (20) Avant e retour (Forward and Backward), two musical jokes for flute and violin.

ROBLES, DANIEL ALOMIAS: Peruvian archaeologist, composer, compiler of folk music, and flutist, who was born in Huanuco, Peru, on January 3, 1871. When very young he began to study folk music and started a crusade which carried him all over Peru and into Bolivia and Equador. On foot, at one time, he journeyed from Lima to Iquitos seeking the origins of musical folklore.

Robles collected over 1,200 Indian, Colonial and Republican melodies. Through concert and lecture tours he carried Peruvian music to the rest of this hemisphere. In 1919 he came to the United States and spent fourteen years here, leaving in 1933. His great interest in folk music led him to compose the "Ballet Inca"; an opera "Illa Cori" which was selected by the President of the United States to be presented at the Panama Canal inauguration festivities in 1914, which were never held because of World War I. He composed also two symphonic poems, *El Indio* and *El Resurgimiento de los Andes; Himno al Sol* and a number of other compositions. Robles died in Lima on July 17, 1942.

MANIGOLD, JULIUS: a native of Nasmunster, in Upper Elsass, where he was born on November 23, 1873. He received his first musical instruction at a very early age from his father. From 1888 to 1892 he attended the Conservatory in Strassburg, where he was fortunate enough to be instructed by the famous Frederic Rucquoy. Through his enthusiastic ambition and unceasing endeavors he advanced so rapidly that he received an appointment as first flute-player and soloist with the Royal Orchestra in Kissingen in 1892. After several important engagements in a number of the art centers of Europe, Manigold was appointed first flute player and soloist in the Ducal Hofkapelle at Meiningen. His unusual artistic qualifications were appreciated so highly that in 1897 he was appointed ducal chamber musician, and in 1901 he was the recipient of the gold medal for art and learning, while in 1908 he received the title of Chamber Musician of the Duke of Sachse-Meiningen.

In Europe, Manigold established a most enviable reputation as one of the very best living soloists and symphony players. He traveled through Europe as a soloist and in connection with the

famous Meininger Hofkapelle, under direction of Fritz Stein-
bach, his performances in the art centers of Germany, Holland,
England, Denmark and Switzerland always were attended with
the greatest possible success. He always associated with the foremost artists, among whom may be mentioned Joseph Joachim,
Henri Marteau, Georg Schumann, Ernst Dohnanyi, as well as
many others.

After 1902 he played for many years at Bayreuth and in this
way had the honor and experience of personal acquaintance with
such prominent musical personalities as Hans Richter, Felix
Mottl, Karl Muck and Siegfried Wagner.

In 1911 he was honored by a call as first flute teacher at the
Royal Music School in Wurzburg, which position he accepted.

In addition to a beautiful Concerto for flute and orchestra,
Op. 6, published in 1911 and dedicated to Professor Rudolf
Tillmetz, Manigold wrote extensively for the flute, and many
of his smaller compositions have achieved a great measure of
success.

DE LORENZO, LEONARDO: was born August 29, 1875 in the
musical town of Viggiano, Potenza, Italy. He began the study
of solfeggio and flute at the age of eight years, with Giacomo
Nigro. The daily lessons continued under him for two years and
lasted one and a half to two hours, a pretty strenuous regime
for a small lad. Other teachers followed and then two years more
were spent on the flute under Alfonso Pagnotti, a pupil of
Krakamp. It was a bitter disappointment when necessity discontinued these lessons but he determined at that time that
some day he would be graduated from the Conservatory of
Naples in spite of the great odds against him. Shortly thereafter
he was thrown upon his own resources and at the age of sixteen
he landed in America at the beginning of 1892. Four strenuous
years followed trying to make a living at any sort of a job he
could get and every penny possible was saved and sent home
to help provide for the younger children.

He had been advised not to remain in New York because
there were too many musicians, so his first engagement was
with an ensemble of four musicians at Cerulean Springs, Ken-

174

tucky. The pay was, also for the violinist leader, $30.00 per month. The duties were: playing one hour each time for breakfast at 5:30 A.M., 12:00 noon and 6:00 for dinner, also playing for dancing three nights a week from 9 to 12. The third and last month of that memorable first summer engagement they received no pay because, the manager said, business had been bad, and they were forced to pay their own fares from New York and back.

He was then called to serve in the Italian army, and since he realized he must return if he ever wished to see his family again, he set sail on March 1, 1896. He arrived in Genoa three days late and his first summons was to appear in court-martial on a charge of tardiness. His defender's plea that a young man who had come all the way from America deserved more praise than blame was of no avail and he was given a fifty-day sentence. A general amnesty for small offenders in celebration of the King's marriage saved him from this punishment.

He was assigned to duty in a military band at Alessandria under the direction of Giovanni Moranzoni, father of former Conductor Moranzoni, of the Metropolitan Opera House, New York. He finally secured special privilege from the colonel to play for the local opera season, which relieved the tedium of military drill and furnished much needed spending money. He seldom had over three hours' rest nightly, and several times was reprimanded because he had failed to hear the bugle and arise at five A.M.

The junior Moranzoni, who played violin, was studying at Pesaro with Mascagni and occasionally came home on a vacation. In the band was a graduate of the Conservatory at Palermo, an accomplished pianist and composer by the name of Cambria, and, as opportunity afforded, trios for violin, flute and piano were studied, and played at musicales in the Moranzoni home. These were great treats for the ambitious young flutist.

It was during this period that De Lorenzo's first serious attempt at composition was made. Being frequently excused from section rehearsals to teach beginners to keep time, he found some opportunity for retiring to the attic for practice, and here began what are now known as his *Nine Grand Studies*. His much cherished acquaintance with Ernesto Köhler was formed at this time.

Köhler had just published his *Thirty Studies of Virtuosity*, Op. 75, and sent a copy to his nephew, Captain Palmieri, an officer in the regiment, who sought out De Lorenzo to show him the new work. The studies were so interesting that De Lorenzo memorized several and performed them for Moranzoni. When Köhler heard of this he wrote to Moranzoni, thanking him for his interest in the "new studies."

After his discharge from the army he spent one year at his home and then set out for Johannesburg, South Africa. Because of the Boer war he was refused passports and was compelled to stay in Cape Town, where he shortly secured a class of pupils and positions in a theatre and the Symphony Orchestra under Dr. Dowling.

It was in Cape Town that he formed the friendship of the late Edward de Jong, celebrated Dutch flutist, who, in 1904, made a concert tour with Ben Davies, the tenor. Having heard that de Jong was somewhat of an egotist, it was with a certain timorousness that De Lorenzo decided to send him a copy of his studies, and, to his surprise, he received in return a personal call from the artist, who proved to be a most affable gentleman. De Jong was then sixty-nine years old, hale, hearty, and recently married for the third time. He took a keen delight in playing Briccialdi and Kuhlau duets and was as great a lover of the outdoors as a truant schoolboy. He enjoyed relating his experiences, and told with great interest of having heard the famous Doppler brothers in concert. When they parted he urged De Lorenzo to come to England and join his orchestra.

In the spring of 1907 De Lorenzo decided to leave South Africa. His mother having died, he was in no hurry to reach his home and took a rather circuitous journey via Southampton, London, Paris and Milan, where he enjoyed a "ravioli dinner" with the distinguished Albisi, and the perusal of many unpublished manuscripts by this well-known composer. Through Albisi an introduction to Italy's greatest veteran flutist, Zamperoni, was secured, which was followed by an invitation to his home. Italo Piazza has called Zamperoni Italy's most perfect and accomplished flutist. In his home was a beautiful oil painting of his illustrious teacher, Rabboni (the only one in existence), and

176

many other interesting flute mementos, the treasuring of which seemed his greatest delight. Maestro Moranzoni, the friend of military days, lived in Varese, a short distance from Milan, and De Lorenzo could not pass on without accepting the oft-repeated invitation to call again on his former army chief. The old gentleman was quite poor, but took De Lorenzo on a beautiful sightseeing trip and insisted on the host's privilege at every turn, a touching tribute which was highly appreciated by the rising artist.

The next stop was at Rome and the first thought was to look up Professor Franceschini. He was a handsome elderly gentleman, with white moustache and hair; very modest, with little to say of himself but full of praise for others. It was very interesting to hear him tell of his friendships with Ciardi, Briccialdi, De Michelis, and Count Luigi Marini. De Lorenzo accepted an invitation to remain for luncheon, and found it was a birthday anniversary, which they proceeded to celebrate by "doing Rome" with Franceschini as guide, and a wonderful guide he made, being thoroughly posted on all the points of interest in the historical city.

A week was then spent in Naples before setting out for his visit in his native town. It was a sad homecoming when his father greeted him in Viggiano. The sire had grown a beard, an Italian custom while in mourning for the dead, and there were constant reminders of the one who had departed which made the time drag heavily. After two months he could stand it no longer and left for Naples to resume the study of his profession.

Martucci, with whom it was De Lorenzo's ambition to study, was so busy with his duties as Director of the Conservatory that he could not accept the ambitious student but recommended De Nardis, which advice was followed. Like all who have gone so far as to merit a diploma, De Lorenzo realized that it means but little if one has not the ability to back it up, and that, with such ability, it is not a necessity. However, it had served as a goal for his ambition and after one year of study De Nardis was eager for him to take the examinations, which he passed successfully on the first attempt. These dealt with literature, harmony, piano and flute. One had to play a concerto, a solo on which only two

177

hours of preparation were allowed, and pass a rigid test on transposition, the basis of which would be a melody written by the professor of composition immediately before the examination and on which no preparation was allowed. All the teachers of wind instruments were present and one flutist from outside the Conservatory. Each had the privilege of calling for the interval to which he wished the transposition to be made and the candidate was required to comply immediately. He succeeded in capturing all the highest points except on piano, having used an instrument for practice with a very light action, so that with several of Italy's greatest pianists on the committee and a strange piano with heavy action for his instrument he was "routed." After he struggled partly through a Czerny etude the judges said, "enough" and graciously passed him.

After two more years of study in Naples he left for America arriving in New York November 3, 1909. He soon met Carl Wehner and a close friendship developed between the two. Through Wehner's influence he was engaged as first flute with the New York Philharmonic Orchestra. He later joined the New York Symphony Orchestra under Damrosch, substituting for Barrère when he was on tour with his ensemble or other engagements.

In 1914 De Lorenzo left New York to join the Minneapolis Symphony Orchestra where he held the chair of solo flutist for five years and it was here he met and married a talented pianist, Maude Peterson.

While on tour with the Minneapolis Orchestra, De Lorenzo became inoculated with the "California fever" and when a very flattering offer came to him from Mr. Adolph Tandler, conductor of the Los Angeles Symphony orchestra, he succumbed and played solo flute with that organization during the season of 1919-20. The orchestra, unfortunately collapsed one week before the opening of the second season and a contract became a mere scrap of paper. The following year he became first flute of the Los Angeles Philharmonic Orchestra and in 1923 he left for Rochester, New York, to become solo flutist of the Rochester Philharmonic and teacher of flute at the Eastman School of Music. Here he remained for twelve harmonious years and in 1935 he resigned to retire to California where he hopes to spend

178

the remainder of his life. He is now living in an idyllic spot —overlooking the blue Pacific—Palos Verdes Estates. De Lorenzo's published works, solos, pedagogical and chamber music, are known all over the world. To these he has added a few others.

Works for flute, and for flute and other wind instruments.

Published:

"Nine etudes"; "I due virtuosi" for two flutes; numerous easy, medium and difficult solos for flute and piano.

"L'Indispensabile" published in New York in 1911 has gone through many editions and it is used all over the world.

"L'Arte moderna del Preludio" for flute alone. "Two Divertimenti" for flute, clarinet and bassoon. "Il non plus ultra" for flute alone. "I tre virtuosi" for three flutes. "I seguaci di pan" for four flutes.

Unpublished:

"The Flutist in the Modern Orchestra" a pedagogical work of nearly one thousand pages. "L'Arte di ben suonare il flauto" (The art of good flute playing, in two books). Many easy, medium and difficult solos for flute and piano. "Suite moderna" for two flutes. "Fantasietta eccentrica" for flute, clarinet and bassoon. "Divertimento quasi moderno" for flute, oboe and clarinet. "Divertimento fantastico" for flute, oboe, clarinet and bassoon. "Divertimento flautistico" for five flutes (with flute in G and piccolo). 18 "Preludi" and "Preludietti" for flute alone.

De Lorenzo's hobby is playing billiards for hours without tiring.

VAN LEEUWEN, ARY: "I was born in Arnhem, Holland, where my father was one of the foremost musical directors, and where I, at the age of five, commenced with the study of piano playing; I was, as I can remember myself, so small that in playing scales I had to walk to reach the octaves of the compass. Some years later I became interested in percussion instruments, which enabled me to render my services in my father's orchestra as tympany, big and snare-drum and xylophone player.

"At the age of ten I received my first lesson on the flute from Fransella, who was at that time first flute with my father's orchestra in Utrecht. Shortly after, when Fransella left for London,

179

I continued with Jacques De Jong, in Amsterdam. At the same time I received my tuition at the Music School in Leiden (together with Conrad Bos, the piano soloist and eminent accompanist, at present also in New York), studying piano, organ, harmony and counterpoint.

"The summer seasons of the Berlin Philharmonic in Scheveningen, Holland, enabled me to study with Joachim Andersen, the solo flute and second conductor of the orchestra, who, in his enthusiasm for me, got my father's permission to take me to Berlin to complete my studies with him.

"From this period started my nomadic life. Season engagements were filled as solo flutist in Amsterdam, Warsaw, Vienna, Cochin (China), Germany, Russia, Finland, France, Belgium, Helsingfors, till after a successful competitive examination I was chosen as first and solo flutist with the Berlin Philharmonic. This orchestra usually played seven months in Berlin, four months in Scheveningen, and each year one-month trips through Italy, France, Spain, Portugal, Switzerland, Sweden, Norway and Russia, under the direction of Nikisch, Weingartner and others.

"The season 1901-1902 brought me to the Philadelphia Symphony Orchestra, of which Fritz Scheel was conductor. Although I liked the engagement very much, family affairs called me back to Europe. The season 1902-1903 found me in Warsaw as soloist and second conductor. Gustav Mahler, who as guest conductor came to perform his three symphonies, offered me the engagement at the Hof-Opera in Vienna as first flute and professor at the Academy of Music, which engagement I filled till 1920.

"This period was for me the most idealistic one of my life, alas! that belongs to the past and may never return again. I was instrumental in making the silver flute preferred to the wood in Vienna, and was also the creator of a chamber music society for wind instruments, in Vienna.

"In 1920 I was engaged as solo flute and second conductor with the Bucharest Philharmonic, and in 1921 went back to Vienna to resume flute teaching.

"Deeply filled with the sorrows of the World War catastrophe,

I left Europe for America; I hope to win the friendship of musical America."

This interesting autobiography of Ary van Leeuwen would be incomplete without a list of his published and unpublished compositions. Among the former we find the following:

Perlen alter Meister, for flute and piano, 40 numbers.

Melody and Capriccietta, Op. 12, for flute and piano.

Bohemian Folk Songs, Fantasia, for flute and piano.

Chopin's Minute Waltz, for two flutes and piano.

L. Drouet, selected and revised, 62 Etudes for flute alone.

Polka Characteristic, for piccolo and piano or orchestra.

All of the foregoing are published by Jul. Heinr. Zimmermann, Leipzig, which firm will also publish in the near future his arrangements for flute and piano of Johannes Mattheson's, 12 Sonatas, and one Sonata by Carl Phillip Emanuel Bach, all originally for flute with figured bass.

Still in manuscript are three books of Etudes for flute; Scales and Daily Exercises; two Polkas for piccolo and orchestra; three Suites for flute and piano; Paraphrase on Greek Folk Hymns; Sonata for two flutes and piano, by Wilhelm Friedman Bach; three Concertos by Carl Phillip Emanuel Bach, with cadenzas, accompaniment of piano or orchestra; four Concertos by Carl Hasse, with cadenzas, accompaniment of piano or orchestra; Duets by Zielcke; Arias by Grétry, Scarlatti and Filke, for soprano, flute and piano; and Sonata for flute alone by Karl Phillip Emanuel Bach.

In addition to the above and still in manuscript are the following operas, musical plays, burlesques and ballets:

The Fountain Nymph, rococo play in one act.

The Latest Fashion, a musical satire in one act.

Border Adventure, one-act play, performed for two months in Zurich (1922).

Lysa, the Extravagant Princess, Ballet Pantomime in one act.

A musical comedy in two acts.

The Cheoppyranise, operetta burlesque.

The Fairy of Fortune, operetta in three acts.

The one-act operas, specially arranged for strings and piano, based on music by Mozart, Frederick the Great and Lorzing,

Mozart enroute to Prague, Fredericus Rex, and *Autocracy in the Kitchen,* text by A. Friedmann (the first and last published by Herzmansky, Doblinger, in Vienna). Each of these was performed for one month in Vienna, van Leeuwen taking the part of king. In passing it should be noted that these three operas were well received.

From all accounts at hand, fortune has been kind, indeed, to Ary van Leeuwen, his first flute-playing activities, his tasks as second conductor of the Warsaw Philharmonic Orchestra and the Bucharest Philharmonic Society, and his achievements as composer have received enthusiastic praise from both public and press. He has lived in Los Angeles for a number of years.

BARRÈRE, GEORGES: To find Georges Barrère in a reminiscent mood is a delightful experience as the following will attest:

"It is hard for me to believe that I was born in Bordeaux, France, because when visiting that fair city, one May, I found there no sign of the important event. Not the smallest statue, not the narrowest boulevard, not the humblest triumphal arch would tell the visitor it was here on October 31, 1876, I bought my season ticket to life. I still hold it very tightly too, you may well believe. To tell you the truth, I was so stupid when it was given me that even six months after, I did not know what to do with it.

"When I was about three years of age, my dear parents moved away from this hopelessly wet city to quieter surroundings and a few days before 1880, I landed in Paris, a city very accessible to every one but the German Army. I was then walking nicely, a fact which made father, mother and the janitor very proud of me.

"To make this a genuine musician's autobiography, I must of course say that I sang delightfully even when a very young child. As that was long before the advent of the talking machine (Happy Days!), no one took any notice of the flagrant inaccuracy of pitch floating from 440-A to 495 and perhaps descending dolefully to 327 or thereabouts. Dear father and mother could never detect it as they were prominently non-musicians although mother had a really lovely voice. The memory of it is still sweet to my heart. Father was firmly convinced that he should have been a tenor singer rather than a maker of furniture but I feel no shame in declaring with the neighbors that he made *no* mistake in sticking to his own trade.

"Brother had ambition and a cheap (oh, how very cheap!) violin. This piece of furniture decided his musical career. He discarded the tin whistle upon which he had been playing a few popular tunes and seized Kubelik's weapon. At that time we were living about twenty miles from Paris in a little town called Epernon. The leading violinist was an old man, a retired captain of Gendarmery who might properly be called a Minstrel Musician. My brother, burning with ambition, applied to him for instruction. While he was working hard on his fiddle in an attempt to master the scales of C major and A minor at the first position, I got hold of the discarded tin whistle and tried it. With some hints from brother who was then the musical (White Hope) of the Barrère family, I found my way through all the scales on my six-holed flute (without a thumb crutch, please notice).

"At recess, all the boys neglected marbles for lessons from Georges Barrère on the tin whistle. The toy shops of Epernon could not supply these vehicles for virtuosity fast enough. This was between the years 1886 and 1888 when I was between ten and twelve years of age.

"The director of the school was also conductor of the local brass band. I well remember following this body on Sunday parade, playing upon my primitive flute and receiving encouragement from every member of the band. Whether that proves my puerile ability or their lack of musical judgment, I hesitate to say, as I dislike to be either conceited or unkind.

"In August, 1888, my father was again called to Paris and with him went the entire family. The schoolmaster of Epernon recommended my father to look after the furtherance of my musical instruction. The night schools of Paris maintained what was then called Bataillons Scholaires which are something like Scholars Battalions. These gave military training to the boys and furnished them with uniforms, bugles, drums and fifes. Of course I entered the fife corps. The teacher was a flute pupil of the Paris Conservatoire and was most encouraging to the youthful Georges Barrère.

"On Bastile Day, July 14, 1889, centenary of the French Revolution, the Ninth Bataillon Scholaire was parading before the grand reviewing stand of Paris City Hall, headed by the bugle, drum, and fife corps of which Georges Barrère was the leading sergeant. This did not make a militarist of me although I was very proud of my position and uniform.

"I was at this time studying the Boehm flute (silver, too, mind you) with the private teacher of my own fife teacher, Leon Richaud, who had previously taken a first prize at the Paris Conservatory and was a member of the celebrated Lamoureux Orchestra.

"In October, 1889, my teacher took me to Henry Altès who was then the teacher at the Paris Conservatory. I played for him a melodic exercise in C major from the middle of the first part of his *Method for Flute.*

"I was not sufficiently advanced to be admitted as a student of this famous and justly celebrated institution but Altès permitted me the privilege of attending all the classes where I had an opportunity to hear the work of his pupils and listen to his instructions. In other words, I was what is called in France an "auditor." About once a week, Altès would spare a few minutes to supervise my work. With his help and that of my private teacher, I was advanced enough to play the first two pages of the Kuhlau First Solo (Op. 57) for the examination of October 1890, at which time I was enrolled as regular member of Altès' class. I was at this time the chum of many of the older flute players who were as stars in my musical firmament. I was the Benjamin of the class, all the other boys being between seventeen and twenty-five years of age, some of them in military uniform. They looked upon the small fourteen year old boy as a little more than a baby in their midst. What happy, happy times those were! I went along pleasantly learning something about flute playing and many things about billiards, even swimming at a nearby school for the latter sport. How many times did I ask the venerable Altès to excuse me from class for some reason or other in order that I might join André Maquarre or other boys in a billiards tournament around the corner. In spite of this mischief, I was studying seriously and am proud to say that billiards playing did not take so well with me as flute playing.

My progress was slow and not altogether encouraging. After two years in class, I passed the yearly public examination, playing the Seventh solo of Tulou, and was granted only a second *Accessit* which is the smallest award given. This was in the year 1892. My work was worse the next year as flute player but I became an expert swimmer in the company of Henri and Robert Casadesus. I did not show enough improvement over the preceding year, however, and at the 1893 examination I was not graduated though I struggled hard with the Eighth Solo of Altès.

"Henri Altès was a great teacher but I did not progress as well as I should under his tutorship. I still believe his very systematic teaching gave me no chance to develop my own. This was his last year in the Conservatory. He was then very old and wished to be retired.

"In October, 1893, all the flute students of the Conservatory were called to the director's office and I still remember dear old Ambroise Thomas presenting to us our new master, Paul Taffanel. I always considered that day as the turning point of my life. While I have a reverent memory of Altès' strictness and severe training, I must avow if it were not for all Paul Taffanel did for me, I should not, today, be tooting upon what the wood flute-players so irreverently call the "Gas-pipe."

"While I did not entirely drop my mischief, I now studied diligently and more seriously than ever before.

"Among my new colleagues in class during the year 1894 were Daniel Maquarre and Philippe Gaubert who is at the present time [c. 1925] teacher of the same class at the Conservatoire. I was then nearly eighteen years of age, and right here, should like to make a little parenthesis in the story of my musical career to talk about my family life. Did you note, reader, how softly I dropped brother? Let us now pick him up again. Whether or not it was because I had begun to take my study music seriously, I do not know but at all events, he dropped his study of the violin, being firmly convinced he was not called of the Muses. As far as that conviction was concerned, "I beat him to it," as some of my American friends would say. Brother now went into business with father and did not talk violin any longer. With the money I had earned as a professional player, I bought a piano on which I struggled with scales and exercises. I considered this piece of property sacred to my own use and when, one afternoon, I heard brother playing a profane tune on it, I decided to shut down the cover and fasten it with the right key. There was a scene, needless to state. Mother did not want me to take such an attitude with my brother and I did not want to retract anything I had said but as I had to obey father and mother, I surrendered the key with the threat that I would no longer live at home, if I must do so. This decision was met with a smile from father who believed I wouldn't do such a thing, by mother who believed I couldn't, and by triumphant brother who didn't care much so long as he was the proud possessor of the key to the "Thirds Box."

"At eight P.M. I left the house to play my engagement at the Folies Bergère and did not return home that night. With the assistance of some friends, I arranged my Bohemian existence which did not last long. Taffanel knew about it and realizing he was "wise" I redoubled my efforts as a student, making it a point of pride to excel in my studies as I had not done previous to this time. I can see that infinitesimal hotel room where I practiced, using my bed for a music stand and having actually to open the window in order to secure the correct position of a flute player.

"July came anon with its examinations. André Maquarre and Philippe Gaubert (fifteen year old flutists) received the First Prize. I do not remember who had second. (I know perfectly well it was not Georges Barrère, who won only a First *Accessit*, July 1, 1894, with F. Langer's Concerto, thus saving himself from being expelled from the Institution, it being the second year after his first graduation. He knew it and was ready to quit as it was impossible for him to swallow his pride sufficiently to go on in his flute playing career without a First Prize.) I was at this time negotiating with a vaudeville act at the Folies Bergère and had it not been for that First *Accessit*, I might be at this moment on Keith's Circuit or with Barnum and Bailey.

186

"A peace treaty was entered upon with my family about this time which happily put an end to my Bohemian life.

"In 1895 while I was playing at the Concert de l'Opéra with Paul Vidal and G. Marty as conductors, I worked my way to a good finish and on July 29, 1895, Theodore Dubois, President of the Jury, proclaimed me First Prize with Andersen's First Concerto. I had jumped at last above one graduation, the Second Prize. The First Prize is the end of the studies. However, I did not quit the Conservatory for that. I was still studying harmony with Raoul Pugno and later with Xavier Leroux. Knowing what Taffanel was to me, I asked as a special favor that I might continue to come to the class one more year. My request was granted and this was without doubt the most inspirational period of my studies. Taffanel was teaching me, at that time, the repertoire of a flute virtuoso—Mozart's Concertos, Bach's and Handel's Sonatas, Schubert's Variations, compositions of Widor, Godard's Suite, Reinecke's Sonata and so forth. Being nineteen years of age, I was in a position to look upon the new pupils as novices though some of them were older than I in years. At this time, I frequently told them how wrong they were not to use every opportunity to hear Taffanel whether he was playing or teaching.

"Taffanel was the leader of the Society of the Conservatory, made up of all the teachers of the institution. He was also first conductor of the Grand Opéra orchestra and played as virtuoso quite often. Needless to say I never missed an opportunity of hearing him. Since I have been living in America, the use of superlatives does not mean much to me as we so often hear them abused. But right here, I should like to say with a *European's meaning* that Taffanel was not only the best flutist in the world but I doubt if any one can ever fill his place. Quality as well as quantity of tone and fine technique were only a small part of his splendid characteristics as a flute player.

"His musicianship, his style particularly, was highly inspirational. He loathed cheap sentimentality, excessive expression, endless vibrato or shaking of tone, in a word, all the cheap tricks which are as undignified as they are unmusical.

He was very careful to assign to his pupils such work as would

187

enable them to progress surely and rapidly. Unlike Altès, he did not pay such strict attention to school routine. Many times we would stay after class to listen to solos which he would play for us in his own inimitable style. While he was teaching one pupil the remainder of the class would listen attentively to every observation or suggestion made to improve our friend's work. Scales and exercises were assigned but when Taffanel knew the pupil was conscientious, he did not use the recitation period in which to listen to technical works but would spend the entire time teaching an Andersen study in which he led us to find many beautiful things which would otherwise have passed unnoticed, even though we thoroughly mastered the technical difficulties of the study. Each pupil was a musical son and I doubt if there is in the whole world one flute player who has sat at the feet of Taffanel who does not bear in his heart the loveliest memories of that great master and who does not entertain the greatest veneration and respect for him both as a man and a musician.

"Previous to July, 1895, I had planned to revive in Paris, the Society of Wind Instruments, founded by Taffanel in 1876. This organization had dropped out of existence in 1893. I was always dreaming of the day when I should found a similar society of my own, so as soon as I was no longer a pupil, a few of my associates responded to my earnest appeal and we gave three concerts during the musical season of 1895-1896, calling ourselves the Society, Modern, of Wind instruments. This was the first group of the kind to meet in Paris after the disbanding of the Taffanel Society. I am pleased to say the society is still in existence and has, this year, celebrated its twenty-fifth anniversary. The organization is growing old but alas, the founder is still older!

"Taffanel helped me greatly in the formation as well as the maintenance and perpetuation of such a venture. It showed real fearlessness and nerve on the part of a young lad to ring the door bells of noted composers and ask them for compositions if they had any ready; if not, to go a step farther and persuade them to write something for our benefit. This sort of canvassing had some practical results. In 1905, celebrating our tenth anniversary, we could clearly show we were responsible for eighty-one compositions written specially for our group. The French Ministry of Fine Arts encouraged our Society by an annual subvention. I had stationed myself for hours in the corridors of the Administration Building to secure an audience with the Secretary of Fine Arts that I might plead for his interest in our venture. I finally succeeded in my purpose.

In the Spring of 1898, I was engaged as first flute at the orchestra of the Exposition of Geneva, Switzerland. This was my first engagement as soloist of a symphony orchestra and I greatly enjoyed the work. The regular conductor, G. Doret, very often lent his baton to some great visiting conductor so we had the pleasure of playing there under the leadership of Saint-Saëns, Chausson, Stavehagen, Dalcroze and at the afternoon concerts of the Exposition, I very often played flute solos with the organ accompaniment of Gustave Ferrari, the well-known composer, now in this country.

This lasted six months. I had a nice salary there and my room and board cost me scarcely one-third of it.

The fact that I was obliged to send my excess baggage home C.O.D. for the express charges, does not argue well in favor of my behavior during this engagement. Needless to say, father was the consignee of my goods and the payee of the express charges.

During the 1896-1897 season, I was substituting at the Opéra and was quite busy with my Wind Instrument Society.

In the Spring of 1897, I passed an examination and became third flute of the Colonne Orchestra over twenty other competitors. The orchestra toured Switzerland and Alsace, the first city visited being Geneva. When I knew it, I decided not to accept a seashore summer engagement but instead to return to Geneva when the Colonne Orchestra season was ended that I might tour Switzerland hotels with some musical friends whom I had met in Geneva.

The orchestra left Paris one May evening. There were many friends assembled at the railway station to see us off. Jacques Thibaud asked me as a joke if I had forgotten my flute. "By Jove," said I (or its equivalent, as I knew no English then), "I have forgotten it." No one believed me until I opened my valise and showed them my startling statement was true. One of my good friends ran to father's house and woke him up at midnight so my flute could be packed and shipped special delivery to Geneva. Happily we stopped there three days and as I knew every flute player in town, it was an easy matter to borrow an instrument for the first concert I had ever played with Colonne. The second morning in the midst of rehearsal a special delivery messenger entered hastily and noisily, bringing the orchestra to a full stop while he delivered a package addressed to "The New Third Flute Player." Colonne did not allow the interruption to pass without making a speech in which he asked us to be kind enough to receive our mail and parcels elsewhere than at rehearsals. It is easy to imagine the silent laughter of Jacques Thibaud and the others, and the burning confusion of the "green man" in the orchestra.

We finished the first week's tour in Mulhouse. This is the proper French spelling of the name of this Alsatian city which some people still insist upon calling the less euphonious and less sympathetic name of Mulhausen. This was the place where I had arranged to leave the orchestra in order to return to Geneva to organize the tour I had in mind.

Here should begin the first chapter of a book which I shall some day write. It will be called—"My Tour of Switzerland." From the day I said "good-bye" to my Colonne friends until my return to Paris, adventures crowded fast upon one another's heels.

For the present, know that I left Mulhouse, which was then German, with only German money and a railway ticket to Bienne, Switzerland, where I stopped to dine. In order to pay for my dinner, I was obliged to purchase a necktie at the only shop which could be induced to give me Swiss change for German money. I had enough to settle for the dinner, but when I was ready to pass through the gate to my train, I discovered my ticket was gone—completely—so another necktie, for enough change to send a telegram to Geneva asking for money and informing my friends I had lost my railroad connection.

Being, as I thought, obliged to spend the night in this small town, I went back to the inn where I had dined. As I was walking into the cafe can you guess what I saw on the floor? My ticket, of course! This lucky find enabled me to arrange to take a late train to Geneva. Wishing to wire to that city a cancellation of my request for money (I am still wondering if a favorable answer would have been received anyway), I was once more compelled to buy a necktie. I kept the three of them a long time as souvenirs but they were never worn as they were inexpensive.

As mentioned before, this is only one of the many adventures I could narrate of my first experience as a tour manager. The remainder must be told in the book which I have promised.

It would be interesting to read of speeches made; piano movings; running for trains and just barely catching them after concerts in order to save hotel bills; taking collections after each number, sometimes gathering one penny per capita; announcements of concerts by the local drummer barker, gaining permits to give concerts, thus associating ourselves with bear tamers and onion peddlers; my singing as encore to flute numbers with my flute under my arm and climbing to the tip top of Mt. St. Bernard where we were hospitably entertained by the monks.

In September, I returned to Paris with a friend who had sung through this wonderful tour with me. We stayed in Paris long enough to borrow a few francs from dear father again!!! We then went to Liége, Belgium, where my friend was engaged to sing in the Opéra Comique. As I had taught him many of his parts with my flute, unaccompanied, we decided it was eminently fitting that I should accompany him to Liége in order to attend his debut.

On November first, I entered the Army. Having won first prize at the Conservatory, it was not compulsory for me to serve longer than one year. The ordinary period of service is three years. Curiously enough, the same thing which gave me exemption from two years of service prevented me from joining the regiment band so for ten months I served as a dignified second-class private, doing my best at all times not to serve my country but to secure leave of absence. This year was spent in Rheims, two hours from Paris. How many times did I make the trip! Only two hours from Paris but the Germans could not make the trip after six years hard work and preparation. No wonder Pershing is not popular "Unter den Linden."

191

We made maneuvers through the Ardennes and the Argonne so I can truthfully state I was eighteen years ahead of the Americans.

It was a happy day for me when I again found myself in civilian clothes. I do not doubt that I glanced into every available mirror.

You will not discredit the statement, when I say my hour for retiring was not 8:30 on the evening of the first day of my return to Paris.

I again took up my work with the Colonne Orchestra, substituting at the Opéra and doing some interesting things with the Wood Wind Society, growing a little more serious in my work but perhaps not quite so much as I should.

On St. George's Day, 1899, I knew my first great sorrow. My dear, good mother passed into the Great Beyond and for the first time in my career, I realized no matter how carefree or optimistic one may be, Fate can strike such a blow at the heart of one's most reverent love and affection as to banish light, happy thoughts, displacing them with sober, serious ones. For the first time in my life I realized the inexorability of death, less vicious but as insouciant as Don Giovanni. How often previous to this time, I had smiled at the mere suggestion of unhappiness. It was in the zenith of my carefree existence that the cruel blow fell. Though twenty-one years have elapsed, my sorrow is still deep. Many times when visiting friends I have envied them the presence of a sweet, old mother in the family circle. How proud I should have been to have given my mother every care but to my deep regret that happy privilege was denied me. Without doubt this accounts for my respectful fondness for aged people whenever and wherever I have the pleasure of meeting them.

At the Paris Exposition in 1900, I again played in Colonne's Orchestra at a series of concerts given in the "Old Paris Exhibition."

Business was poor and the great conductor failed to finish his contract. It was rather pitiless, I fear, as I sued him for my money for the concerts and won, thus losing for the time being, the affection of our conductor. He could not expel me from the Winter Concerts as we were an Association and I was a member in good standing. However, the fact that Colonne no longer felt friendly toward me made the members of the Orchestra committee rather cold toward me. Consequently, when the second flute chair was vacant, the fourth flute player was given the position instead of myself, who was then playing third flute. My friends were sorry and some of the members of the Committee came to apologize. I think I was the only one who saw anything at all humorous in the situation. I realized the trick had been played in the hope that I would withdraw my membership from the Association, but trick for trick, I kept it and wise was I as two years later I was given first position, being promoted over the head of the same flute player who had jumped over mine, leaving him second flute once more. He (an excellent friend of mine by the way) did not again occupy the first chair until 1905 when I left for America.

About this time I was unsuccessfully competing for the 2nd chair in the Colonne Orchestra, an examination was announced at the Opéra for the fourth flute position. The colleague who had occupied the fourth chair had died of a form of apoplexy brought about by disappointment because an invention of his failed to interest flute-makers. If I recall rightly, he had tried to have flutes made with a bell attachment such as are used on brass instruments. I am sorry for the death of my colleague but am rather happy over the non-success of his invention. Most of us are agreed that the better the flute, the fewer the attachments and ornaments, such as the thumb rest and other inconveniences. It would have been a hard blow at the pride of many of us had we been obliged to carry a sort of baby phonograph under our arms.

Thirty applicants presented themselves at the examination. The jury was composed of the two directors of the house, the three conductors and of every first soloist of the wood wind section. I like to remember this examination as we were all obliged to play.

1st. A flute concerto.

2nd. Sight reading of difficult music for flute.

3rd. Sight reading of difficult music for piccolo.

When I came to this country it amused me greatly to learn

that musicians for a renowned opera house in New York were chosen by the tympani player unaided. I was awarded the position which was not particularly a remunerative one but through association with this famous orchestra I became somewhat like a government official. At that time honors were much more important than money. My colleagues at the Opéra were Hennebains, La Fleurance and Gaubert.

I was still busy with my Society of Wind Instruments and had many pupils. I also held a position with Colonne and the Opera and was instructor at the new Schola Cantorum founded at that time by Vincent d'Indy, A. Guilmant and Charles Bordes.

In 1903, I became first flute of the Colonne Orchestra, and in 1904 was elected a member of the Committee of the Association. These nominations effaced all dissension with Colonne with whom I was then on the best of terms.

Though a busy man, I found time to organize concerts which kept me in touch with the whole pleiad of composers and artists.

Charles M. Widor, the great organist and celebrated composer, asked me to write a flute chapter for his orchestration book. Many new compositions were sent to me for performance and it certainly was inspiring to play for and with d'Indy, Widor, Pierné, Catherine, Vidal, Thome, R. Hahn, X. Leroux, Cortot, Mme. Delcourt, C. de Boisdeffre, G. Huë, Caplet, Monteux, Leitz, Larcroix, Dubois, Charpentier, Bruneau, Chausson and many others.

About this time I received an offer to come to America. To many of my conservative colleagues my acceptance seemed utter folly. I was then twenty-nine years of age and had been the recipient of many honors such as the Academic Palms given by the Ministry of Fine Arts making me an Academic Officer.

The Adventures of Columbus had always stirred my blood and tickled my curiosity so I decided to take the trip. I asked a year's leave of absence both at the Opéra and Colonne's Orchestra. At the former I had a hard time but again Taffanel helped me by interceding in my behalf with Gailhard and Capone, then directors, who seemed to think that the absence of their regular piccolo player would cause a drop in the receipts of the house. However, with Taffanel's assistance I secured a temporary release. It was somewhat easier to arrange matters at the Colonne Orchestra, being a member of the Committee I voted "Yes," to my own request.

One May day in 1905, I left Paris at midnight. Many, many dear friends were assembled at the station and when the train pulled out I could hear the Marseillaise being played by more than a dozen flutes. What an ensemble! The next day, I sailed on the Savoie from le Havre, landing in New York, May 30, 1905.

Before docking, I saw the great downtown sky scrapers on that grey, cloudy morning and watched the busy traffic of the harbor with its noisy ferry boats and important little tugs snorting about, and suddenly, I began to feel myself very small and distressingly unknown in all the pandemonium.

I began to regret leaving Paris and all the dear friends there, to say nothing of my work. I felt they would be utterly withdrawn from my life and I must now deal with strange people, new customs, wrestle with the English language and in short enter into an entirely new element.

This state of mind did not last long. The very next day I walked about New York as in my own home town. I must confess I walked all the time being afraid to use street cars whose strange signs meant nothing to me. I knew New York topography, however, having studied the map assiduously while crossing, so was quite sure when I was on 23rd Street, I was between 22nd and 24th, thus showing my great intelligence. I began to study English at once and would not go to bed without having learned the names of the days of the week, months of the year, numbers, or any other lesson which I had set myself to master.

In June 1905, Walter Damrosch asked me to play as soloist at the Spring Concerts of the New York Theatre Roof Garden. I began work in America very low; playing first the *Madrigal* by André Wormser which begins with a low C-sharp. Since then I have played many high B-naturals, three octaves higher but as little as possible of the high C-sharps which may show the cleverness of the player but which, because of their shrieking, piercing tone are certainly stones thrown against any possible popularity of the instrument. Now, dear colleagues, do not think I mean that only the low C-sharp is to be played. There are many other lovely and agreeable notes on the flute but do please let us make it our motto to play all things for beauty, and nothing which is ugly and ear splitting for the mere purpose of "showing off."

If any of my pupils and associates chance to read this exposition I am sure they are saying, "This from Georges Barrère who does not believe in teaching by correspondence!"

Now that I am established in America, my country through adoption and naturalization, here shall close the story of my life as it is my firm intention to die on American soil but so many years hence that only our grandsons will be able to tell of the many more glorious years, which I hope to round out. I cannot die yet because of many things—first I must have time to pay all my debts, second I must make my own fortune, third I want to be present at the weddings of my three sons so I may become acquainted with their children, thus making of the old French Barrère family a one hundred per cent American New Touche.

Fifteen years spent in America will not take up much space. Those fifteen years with the New York Symphony Orchestra made me consider its conductor my dear friend rather than "My Boss." Because of that feeling, I have always enjoyed my work under his leadership in spite of hard traveling and long rehearsals. If each musician in our orchestras highly respected his conductor, looking upon him as a guiding friend, rehearsals would become enjoyable affairs and work would not be punishment, as I have known it to be with some of our good colleagues. It would certainly be helpful to the conductor as he would feel the sympathetic response of his men and could therefore allow his interpretative powers free rein. But this, alas, seems to be a Utopian dream!

In 1910, The Barrère Ensemble of Wind Instruments was founded. This society is the ten-year-old sister of my similar society in France. I used the same policy toward Americans which was used toward French composers. I am proud to say that, outside its own repertoire, the ensemble played works by

196

Victor Herbert, Seth Bingham, Howard Brockway, Charles T. Griffes, John Beach, Ward Stephens, Christian Kriens, A. Walter Kramer, Archer Gibson, George Chadwick, Edward MacDowell, Ethelbert Nevin, F. T. Hill and Harriett Ware.

In 1914, with Paul Kefer, 'cellist, and Carlos Salzedo, harpist, I founded the Trio de Lutèce. In 1915, the Little Symphony began its career. It is a small orchestra, almost a chamber-music organization. Each time I play a solo, I make it a point to do something useful, either playing some good music to elevate the standards of our instrument or by playing some new worthy compositions which will help furnish an incentive for present-day composers to write for our beloved instrument.

At a sonata recital in New York with Ernesto Consolo, I played a Sonata by Bach, Variations by Schubert, and a Sonata by Pierné. Such programs help to elevate the standards of flute playing instead of encouraging easy success by playing compositions cleverly written for flute by flute players who are more interested in pyrotechnical display than in real musical worth.

I know well that soloists on other instruments indulge in such false demonstrations but we must not follow their bad example. Our mission is to serve Music—not ourselves. We must always avoid sugarly sentimentality, rough exaggeration of style, futile exhibition of technique and bear in mind nobility and dignity of expression and right sense of proportion.

(*Editor's Note:* Thus ends this article, which was quoted by Mrs. William S. Haynes, permeated with the whimsy of Barrère. Flutists are familiar, I am sure, with the remainder of his musical life: his resignation from and then his return to the New York Symphony Society. He also continued his work with his own organizations, and this lasted until he suffered a stroke. On June 14, 1944, this great artist passed on in Kingston, New York.)

LAURENT, GEORGES: was born in Paris, France, on June 7, 1886. He began his musical studies at eleven years of age under the direction of his uncle, Louis Bas, the celebrated French oboe player. For twenty-five years Monsieur Bas was solo oboist at the Paris Opéra and at the Société des Concerts du Conservatoire de Paris.

197

It is always somewhat fascinating to know the particular incident that determines one's choice of an instrument. The French Government renders military service compulsory and therefore every French boy knows that his country will demand his services in some capacity for at least a period of two years. In view of the musical traditions in his family, it is not surprising that Georges should have been attracted to the music section of the army. So with all the sagacity of a small boy, he decided that he would play flute in the Military Band. Christmas was drawing near . . . Uncle Louis Bas asked him to choose his Christmas present. To the uncle's delight, the little boy whispered, "Une flute."

This first instrument was of wood and had seven keys. It was comparatively simple to "produce a tune" out of it, but an entirely different proposition to manipulate one's fingers. However, the boy was far from discouraged. He secured a copy of a *Méthode de Flûte* and in that way obtained an idea of fingering. For the first year it was impossible to practice more than a few hours a week on account of school studies. Meanwhile, Uncle Louis continued to keep an eye on the small boy and was tremendously surprised and pleased with the child's efforts. He proposed that Georges study music seriously with the idea of playing flute professionally.

So it happened that an eleven-year-old boy with a song in his heart and a wooden flute under his arm presented himself to Philippe Gaubert for his first flute instruction. The boy was Georges Laurent.

Gaubert laughed gaily at the small boy and his seven-keyed wooden flute, and suggested that to study seriously, he must have a modern instrument and advised his uncle to secure one. One evening at the Opera House during intermission, the musicians were assembled as usual in the tuning room to smoke and chat. Monsieur Bas was with his friend the harpist, who was bewailing his luck at the horse races that afternoon. He was indebted to one of his colleagues and was absolutely obliged to raise the money that same evening.

"I am without cash—I must find a buyer for that French silver flute that I bought a few years ago." Monsieur asked quietly to see the instrument. He took it at once to Gaubert who advised him to buy it and he returned to his bewildered but grateful friend with the money for the flute. In this way, Georges received his first silver flute and his serious study commenced.

After three years of hard practice, Gaubert decided that the boy was prepared to study with Paul Taffanel at the Conservatoire de Paris.

It is with charming simplicity and amusement that Georges Laurent recalls his first public appearance. It was while he was still a pupil of Gaubert's. He was engaged to play second flute in a theatre orchestra. At rehearsal the conductor discovered that he played better than the first flutist, so he was moved up to the first chair. Incidentally the play was not a success but nevertheless the orchestra members applied for their salaries. Georges lagged behind, confused and embarrassed on account of receiving money for the fun and experience of playing in public, until his more practical and enterprising companions urged him somewhat forcibly to apply for his share of the "booty."

At the time that Gaubert suggested that Georges enter the Conservatory, the flute class consisted of ten regular students and two auditors. This particular year there were only two vacancies and twenty-five applicants for these coveted places! The majority of these young men had already received first prize for flute in their respective towns. Each applicant was required to play a concerto of his own choice and one composition at sight before a jury composed of the Director and the Faculty. Everyone was nervous, which is a universal characteristic of students in general. Several hours later the announcement was made:

"The jury has admitted as pupils to the class of Monsieur Taffanel, Messrs. Joffroy and Laurent." (The former valiantly gave his life in the World War.)

How very easy to imagine the boy's joy and happiness! He must have been a serious-minded little chap either by nature of necessity because he realized fully that with this privilege to study with Taffanel came also the absolute need to sacrifice all outside interests and concentrate his entire energy on his studies. Dating from this period, his life was dominated by one thought, one motive, one ambition and that was summed up in the single phrase, "Get the first prize in flute!" At the same time, he followed supplementary courses in solfeggio with M. Schwartz and harmony under the instruction of M. Xavier Leroux.

The first year at the Conservatory, he did not enter the final contest. The second year he competed in the contest held in the Salle des Concerts du Conservatoire and was awarded a second *accessit*. He was now utilizing every odd moment in preparation for the third year exams. Often if the compartment of the suburban train in which he rode for about twenty minutes, was empty, he used to take out his flute and study. This third year, he was awarded by unanimous vote the first prize for flute in the contest held in the Théâtre de L'Opéra Comique. The composition offered was the Andante and Scherzo by Louis Ganne and one other for sight reading.

Thus ended the school days of the boy, Georges. Life so far had been uneventful. The future awaited to be explored. The first reward for faithful study came in the form of an offer to play for a time in the Colonne Orchestra in Paris with G. Pierné, Conductor. That lead to the position of first flute at the Théâtre de la Gaîté Lyrique, playing operas. We find him next with the Monte Carlo Symphony Orchestra under Louis Ganne, Conductor. He passed "several wonderful winters in this ideal place." In the summer, he played first flute under Georges Marty and later, A. Amalon, at Vichy, the famous French summer resort. Here the orchestra gave classical symphonic concerts and also played all the French, Italian and German operas.

The World War intervened. Mobilization began and Georges Laurent was ordered to report at a military hospital and placed in charge of typhoid patients.

After the signing of the Armistice, life resumed more normal tendencies. Many changes had occurred at the Conservatoire de Paris. The renowned teacher Paul Taffanel had died; so also had Adolphe Hennebains in whom Georges Laurent had found a good friend and who had succeeded Taffanel as teacher at the Conservatoire and as first flute in the Societe des Concerts du Conservatoire de Paris. This chair was offered to M. Laurent by André Messager, at that time conductor of the orchestra. Speaking of that occasion, M. Laurent says, "It was truly a great honor to occupy the place held by such talented men as Dorus, Taffanel, Hennebains and Gaubert." He remained with this splendid orchestra for two years and was sent with it on an American concert tour. It was at the close of that tour that Mr. Rabaud, conductor of the Boston Symphony Orchestra, asked him to come to Boston. Since that time, he has continued to play first flute under the direction of Pierre Monteux who succeeded Rabaud and who in turn has been replaced by Serge Koussevitsky and Charles Muench. (Berthe Kennarie)

Being devoted particularly to solos and chamber-music works, and in order to afford a wider opportunity of hearing modern American and European composers, Laurent founded in 1921 a chamber music organization called "The Boston Flute Players' Club." This is the most unique organization in America in the way of instrumental combinations represented, from a single instrument to a double-quintet, strings, woodwinds and piano with artists selected from among the Boston Symphony Orchestra. Six concerts are given every winter in the Boston Art Club Galleries by this self-supporting organization and are attended by the musical intelligentsia of New England.

Besides this Chamber Music Club, Laurent started a new group called the Boston Society of Ancient Instrments, composed of flute, viola d'amore, viola da gamba, and harpsichord, which appeared in Boston at different clubs. It proved a success. This society was founded for the purpose of recalling the old masters and reviving the old favorite groups of chamber music of Louis XIV and Louis XV.

Those who have had the rare good fortune of hearing a program by Georges Laurent will understand and appreciate my few simple words of appreciation to this artist and to his skill which he insists has been attained only by constant, intelligent, and assiduous study. I speak merely of his tone because we all know that he knows well what to do with it. His is a tone that expresses infinite delicacy and decision, pathos and strength, intense ardor and repose, and purity of intonation. His is a tone that is dominated by a masculine tenderness and beauty that are at no time feminine in quality.

201

Georges Laurent is also a teacher at the New England Conservatory.

AMADIO, JOHN: the world-famous Australasian flutist, was born in Wellington, New Zealand on November 15, 1887, and at a very early age gave signs of great musical talent. At the age of twelve, he played a flute concerto with the Wellington Orchestral Society, conducted by Alfred Hill, composer of the celebrated Maori Poi Song. The people of New Zealand were quick to recognize the astonishing talent of the young prodigy and a year later he was sent to Australia for further study.

At the age of fifteen he was engaged as principal flutist to a famous Italian Opera Company which toured Australia, and the prima donna of the company (Madame De Vere Sapio) was so delighted with his playing of the obbligato to the "Mad Scene" from *Lucia,* that on the final performance she came forward to the footlights and handed a bouquet of flowers and a beautiful ruby ring to the youthful flutist.

After a few more years of assiduous study, practicing on an average of five hours daily, Amadio's great chance came. He was engaged as principal flutist to the first Melba Opera Company (which included John McCormack). His success was so great that engagements as solo flutist to all the visiting celebrities quickly ensued. Tour followed tour with such great artists as Calve, Melba, Parkina, De Vere Sapio, etc.

Over 2,000 people assembled at the Melbourne Town Hall at his farewell concert to wish him "bon voyage" prior to departure for Europe.

Amadio made his first appearance in England as solo flutist to Madame Tetrazzini, and scored an instantaneous success. A tour two years later with Madame Frieda Hempel further enhanced his great reputation.

His appearances as solo artist in Rome, Paris, Berlin and New York have been a sensational success—in every town he has been accorded a personal triumph.

John Amadio had the honor of being specially presented to Her Majesty the Queen and Princess Mary by Dame Nellie Melba.

KINCAID, WILLIAM M.: "I was born April 26, 1897, in Minneapolis, Minnesota. At the age of six months I did not show any aptitude for music beyond a pair of good lungs. When I was three years old my parents moved to Honolulu and I went with them to bring them up in the way all good parents should be brought up. My father, being a Presbyterian minister, thought his guiding hand would be needed. We lived there for about eight years, during which time I began to take lessons on the piano and the flute.

"My father's health failing him, due to the tropical climate, we returned to the States and made our home in Charlotte, North Carolina, where my father bacame pastor of the First Presbyterian Church, and I continued to study the flute in a more serious manner.

"After the death of my father in 1911, I went to New York City and entered the Institute of Musical Art in order that I might have the privilege of studying under the great artist and teacher of the flute, George Barrère. My teacher in theory and counterpoint was Dr. Goetschius, and in ear training, Franklin Robinson. I graduated from the regular course at the Institute in 1914, and from the Artist's Course with highest honors in 1918, winning the medal.

"In 1914 I was engaged as assistant first flute by the New York Symphony Orchestra, playing with that organization until the spring of 1918 when I enlisted in the U. S. Navy at Pelham Naval Station. After spending nearly a year in the service I was released and in the fall of 1919 was engaged by the New York Chamber Music Society with which I played for two years, touring the entire United States and a part of Canada.

"I have been first flute with the Philadelphia Orchestra, appearing as soloist upon many occasions. At present I am instructor of flute at the Curtis Institute and the Swarthmore School of Music. In addition to my pupils in these institutions, I have a large private class.

"During the summer months I go to Little Sebago Lake in Maine and spend most of my time fishing, swimming and sailing. This sort of recreation enables me to go through a very strenuous season.

"During this past season I have taken part in some 200 performances which range from symphony concerts, opera performances and chamber music concerts to playing solos in recitals."

LE ROY, RENÉ: graduate of Paris' historic Conservatory of Music, founder and leader of the internationally known Paris Instrumental Quintet as well as of the Le Roy Trio.

René Le Roy was born in Maisons-Laffitte, a suburb of Paris, on March 4, 1898. His father was an excellent amateur flutist and his mother played the piano quite well. At an early age, René played the piano and, when he was eight years old, he began the study of the flute, under his father's tutelage. After six months, the boy was so proficient that the flute instructor at the Paris Conservatory urged the elder Le Roy to enroll René in his classes. Mr. Le Roy, however, felt it would be better for the boy to complete his academic course at the Lycée Condorcet before concentrating on a musical career. He did not consider it wise to allow his son to embark, prematurely, on a professional career as a child prodigy.

So it was not until he was eighteen that René entered the Conservatory. At the end of his second year, he was awarded the Premier Prix and shortly after, he succeeded his distinguished teacher, Phillipe Gaubert, as head of the Paris Society of Wind Instruments—a post which he held for ten years. His first real professional engagements were on a tour of twenty cities in Switzerland with the Society in 1919, the year after he became its leader. He followed this with many seasons of successful tours of Europe, both with the Society and in concerts of his own, which helped immeasurably to establish the position of flute as a solo instrument.

In 1922, Le Roy founded the Paris Instrumental Quintet which, in a very short time, became internationally known and renowned. This ensemble played more than 800 concerts in Europe and America, coming to the United States for the first time during the season of 1934-35. It was not Le Roy's first American visit, however, for 1929 marked his debut in this country and in that year he made his first American concert tour as a solo artist.

Since the year which marked his first apearance here, René Le Roy has been a favorite in this country. He has appeared many times as soloist with leading European and American Symphony Orchestras in addition to being celebrated as a recitalist and chamber musician. He has made recordings for Victor and Musicraft, and has been heard as guest artist on outstanding coast-to-coast radio programs. Several composers, inspired by his playing, have written music especially for him and his chamber music groups. Among them have been Vincent d'Indy, Albert Roussel, Joseph Jongen and Cyril Scott.

Now that he makes the United States his home, Mr. Le Roy divides his concert activities between solo work, both with and without orchestra, and essemble music. Currently, in addition to his solo activities, he is performing in ensemble with Janos Scholz, world-renowned 'cellist, and Sidney Foster, outstanding young American pianist.

Hobbies of a famous musician: Photography and collecting rare flutes are the chief hobbies of René Le Roy, flutist extraordinaire. His photography is an outgrowth of his love for the country and nature and he's particularly interested in wildlife pictures. He finds his flute very useful in the latter instance. He imitates the calls of various birds with it and it's possible to do this so accurately that "the birds will be charmed and come almost to one's hand." Then, of course, photographing them is easy.

As for his collection of flutes, he has two which he plays in concert. One is the work of the French master craftsman, Louis Lot, which Le Roy's father gave him when he was eight years old, and the other is a silver instrument made by an American firm. Many of his flutes are rare old items—museum pieces. He has an exquisite crystal instrument with silver rings, made by a Persian artisan in 1815; severwl Oriental flutes of bamboo, silk, and jade; and a sacred flute from the ancient Aztec pyramids of Mexico, made of a human shin bone. Among the most interesting of his many old and beautiful instruments is an elaborately carved ivory flute which once belonged to Frederick-the-Great. It was sent to Le Roy, in its original sumptuous case with the royal arms of Prussia on the cover, by a friend who enclosed a note: "This belonged to the flutist King; now I give it to the King of Flutists."

In addition to his collecting, and his photography, Le Roy likes good movies, good music and good theatre of any sort. He enjoys bridge, fishing and spectator sports, though he's not particularly athletic. And, until rationing made it such a serious matter, he found great pleasure in dabbling in cookery.

WOEMPNER, HENRY: At the tender age of fourteen Henry Woempner was already a valued member of the Minneapolis Symphony Orchestra, playing next to his father, an excellent solo flutist and fine musician, who had been his only teacher. After the untimely passing of his father, Henry continued with the Minneapolis Symphony and, at the age of twenty-three, after an absence from that orchestra of only one year, was called back as solo flutist of that famous Symphony, being one of the youngest to occupy such a responsible position in America. Its conductor, Emil Oberhoffer, who had been the founder, resigned and other conductors followed while young Woempner continued with ever-growing success.

A few years after, he began to conduct a radio station in St. Paul, Minnesota, and also conducted the summer concerts at Lake Harriet for a number of years. Suddenly, in 1934, he resigned the position which he had held for so long a time, and a year or so later became first flute of the San Francisco Symphony where he enjoyed great popularity and success for nearly ten years. Since 1945, Woempner has been with one of Hollywood's most important motion picture studios but . . . he really belongs in a major symphony orchestra where he is happiest.

WUMMER, JOHN: While still a lad of ten, John Wummer was still in a fair way to master the violin. The violin might still have been his chosen instrument if he had not chanced to find an old

206

six-keyed piccolo of his father's that had lain away forgotten in a drawer.

Right from the start, the boy evinced an unbounded enthusiasm in his find. His father, pleased with such an ardor, and who had some knowledge of the instrument, gave the youngster his first instruction.

John was so infatuated with his piccolo that he used to take it to school where, at recess, he would indulge in its delight. Even during lessons he could not resist the temptation of taking it from his pocket to do some silent practice. On one of these occasions the teacher discovered his lack of attention to the lesson and forthwith commanded him to come before the class.

As a punishment he was to demonstrate his musical ability. To many a boy this would have been a real predicament, a position of overwhelming embarrassment. To Johnny, however, it was a golden opportunity. The call had come; he was prepared. His solo was such a success that thereafter his playing was a feature of the regular Friday afternoon leisure hour. Incidentally this was his first public appearance in the capacity of a piccolo virtuoso.

At thirteen he was to be found in the band of his home town, Reading, Pennsylvania, and being featured as soloist. By this time he was the proud possessor of a wooden Boehm C flute and a Fred Lax tutor, working hard and teaching himself.

At fifteen he had graduated from the local band and was enjoying life in a theatre pit in Trenton, New Jersey. He now commenced studying with Julius Spindler, in New York. Ambition is a hard taskmaster! John worked harder than ever, practicing whenever he could be at it, even after getting home from the theatre at night.

It was while in Trenton that he changed to a silver flute. It happened thus: one cold winter day the temperature of the theatre nearly matched that outside, and while John was practicing before the show the body of his flute cracked. Fortunately he was able to borrow another flute in time, a silver one, however, being the only one available. It was so much to his liking that he has played a silver flute ever since.

207

After one and a half years at Trenton, he studied with André Maquarre, in Philadelphia, spending nearly three years with this famous flutist and taking up harmony and theory with him in addition to flute.

During this time he gained his first symphony orchestra experience at a Bach Festival under Dr. Wolle, at Bethlehem in the company of members from the Philadelphia orchestra.

A little later on he made his debut as an artist with Pryor's band at Asbury Park. Playing with Pryor at this particular time demonstrated musical ability and self-confidence remarkable for one so young. He was the ninth flute player to try out with this organization in a period of six weeks. This cheerful news was imparted to him just before his first concert, by a fellow musician. John admits that it did not tend toward calmness. He played the parts from scores written for band flute and piccolo on his C flute and piccolo, having come direct from the theatre to the band, so acceptably that he continued with Pryor for several seasons.

After Maquarre left Philadelphia, John Wummer went to New York to study with Georges Barrère. His stay in New York lasted several years, during which time he played with numerous organizations, including the Capitol Theatre, and at the Chamber Music Society concerts, also doing some solo work.

The latter years of his New York stay were devoted to Metropolitan engagements and with Simone Mantia's symphony orchestra at Asbury Park, with which he appeared as soloist.

The musical season of 1923-24 found him as associate first flute of the Detroit Symphony Orchestra, under Ossip Gabrilowitsch. After a year's absence he returned to the Detroit orchestra, this time as the only first flutist and remained until it disbanded. He then went to New York where he became first flute of the N.B.C. Orchestra and later accepted the position as solo flute with the New York Philharmonic Orchestra.

"After hearing him play one ceases to wonder why he is such a prime favorite with the musical public. Possessing a beautiful tone of rare purity and sweetness, a brilliant technique, and greatest of all, a wonderful gift of interpretation by which he is able to reach the hearts of his listeners, he is an artist of exceptional merit.

"Of a genial nature and modest disposition, John Wummer is one of the finest fellows one could ever wish to know and treasure as a friend." (Norman J. Holloway)

LORA, ARTHUR: was born on March 11, 1903, in Novale, Province of Vicenza, Italy. His family came to the United States in 1907, settling in Woonsocket, Rhode Island. When eight years old, he began the study of solfeggio and flute, but preferred drawing and oil painting to music. In 1916, his family moved to New York. He decided to make flute playing his career during his high school days, and in 1919 he was enrolled at the Institute of Musical Art, studying flute with Georges Barrère; ear-training, harmony and counterpoint with Franklin Robinson, Dr. Madeley Richardson and Percy Goetschius. In 1922 he received a diploma in flute from the Institute of Musical Art.

He was flutist with the Chamber Music Art Society of New York during 1921-22. In the late summer of 1922, Lora played at the Berkshire Festival of Chamber Music. Other members of the woodwind quintette, all solo members of the Philadelphia Orchestra, New York Philharmonic, or Boston Symphony, were Marcel Tabuteau, oboe, Georges Grisez, clarinet, Auguste Mesnard, bassoon and Arthur Wendler, French-horn. In the autumn of 1922, after a competitive examination, he was chosen as first flutist of the City Symphony of New York. Continuing his studies, he was awarded the Post-graduate "Artist Diploma" by the Institute of Musical Art in 1924, and was appointed to the faculty of the school.

He was first flutist of the State Symphony of New York in 1925 and was a member of the Chamber Music Society of New York (Carolyn Beebe, Founder) from 1926 to 1936. Other members of the woodwind quintette were Bruno Labate, oboe, Gustave Langemis, clarinet, Benjamin Kohon, bassoon, and Bruno Jaenicke, French-horn.

From 1928 to 1936, he was first flutist with the National Broadcasting Company and from 1937 to 1944 first flutist with the Metropolitan Opera Company, playing with conductors Arthur Bodanzky, Gennario Papi, Wilfred Pelletier, Maurice Abravanel, Pietro Cimara, Fausto Cleva, Erich Leinsdorf, Ettore Panizza, Paul Breisach, Bruno Walter, George Szell, and Sir Thomas Beecham.

In 1939, he became a member of the faculty of the Manhattan School of Music and in 1943 he was appointed "Foreign Professor" of flute at the Conservatoire de Musique et d'Arte Dramatique of Montreal, Canada. In 1944, following the death of Georges Barrère, he was appointed to succeed his teacher on the faculty of the Juilliard School of Music, and, resigning from his position as first flutist of the Metropolitan, devoted his time to teaching, solo and ensemble work.

Some of his prominent pupils are Leonard Posella, first flutist of the Los Angeles Philharmonic; Lambros D. Callimahos, who has toured Europe many times as a flute recitalist; Carmine Coppola, first flutist of the National Broadcasting Symphony, and members of the New York City Symphony, Minneapolis, Cleveland, Chautauqua Symphonies and other orchestras. Since 1948, Lora has been with the N.B.C. Orchestra.

COPPOLA, CARMINE, was born in New York City, June 11, 1910, of Italian parents. He started studying the flute at nine years of age, had a scholarship with the now defunct B. F. Keith's Boy Band, studied with Alfred Goebel, and later won a scholarship with Georges Barrère through the high schools of New York City. He continued studying with Barrère after winning a scholarship from the Institute of Musical Art. He graduated in 1929 and obtained a position as flute and piccolo soloist with Creatore's Band in Atlantic City. He gave a Carnegie Hall recital in September 19, 1929 and the critics were very enthusiastic in their praise. He went to Hartford, Conn., to Radio Station WTIC with Christian Krein (conductor) and later became chief arranger and house conductor, specializing in concert programs.

Coppola came to New York City as flute soloist with Erno Rapée at the Music Hall (1935) and stayed for two years; he also studied composition during this time with the famous Joseph Schillinger. He obtained the first flutist position with the

Detroit Symphony Orchestra in 1937, replacing John Wummer and held that position for four years, until returning to New York City again. While in Detroit, he wrote several orchestral compositions, chamber music, etc. When Wummer left to replace John Amans, the opening at the N.B.C. Symphony was filled by Carmine Coppola, after many flutists had auditioned for Stokowski and Toscanini. Coppola resigned from the N.B.C. Symphony in 1948.

II | Thumb-Nail Biographies

(The following capsule biographies are of eminent flutists and distinguished dillettanti who contributed to the furtherance of the art of flute playing, and of a number of the most promising young flutists whose worth has already been proved.)

ABBAS, MAX: (1844- ?) This excellent flutist was Ducal Court musician at Weimar in the court orchestra at Coburg-Gotha.

ACKROYD, A.: (contemporary) English. "An excellent flutist who is invariably found partnering Arthur Gleghorn, for whom he is regularly deputising as first flute with the London International orchestra."

ACQUAVELLA, MARIO: (contemporary) Italian businessman and enthusiastic flute dilettante of distinction now residing in Los Angeles, California.

ADAMS, BELA: (circa 1880-) Austrian flutist, at one time a member of the Los Angeles Symphony and Los Angeles Philharmonic. He lives in Los Angeles.

AERTS, EGIDE: (1822-1853) In 1837 had the honor of playing before King Louis Philippe in a court concert. Was against the Boehm flute. He composed piano pieces, songs and a few operas.

ALARY, JULES: (1827- ?) Was born in Italy and was flutist with La Scala Orchestra. From 1833 he lived in Paris as piano and voice teacher and composed

213

piano pieces, songs and a few operas.

ALBERGHINI, LOUIS: (c.1890-1950) At one time solo flutist of the St. Paul (Minnesota) Symphony and also of Creatore's band. He died in New York.

ALBISI, ABELARDO: (1872-1939) Solo flutist of the La Scala; composer and inventor of the Albisiphone. He died in Switzerland.

ALMBAGERC, AUTUMN: (contemporary) Solo flutist with the Erie, Pennsylvania Philharmonic.

ALRIT, ANTOINE NOEL: (1822-1879) Was solo flutist at Théâtre Lyrique in Paris and at Grand Théâtre in Lyon. Played the old system flute.

ALTES, HENRY: (1826-1899) In 1868 he succeeded Dorus as teacher at the Paris Conservatory and wrote an excellent method for the Boehm system flute known throughout the world. Also many solos.

AMADIO, JOHN: (contemporary) New Zealander flute virtuoso of fine reputation. (See biography.)

AMANS, JOHN: (contemporary) For many years solo flutist with the New York Philharmonic. Amans was born in Holland and is now living in Europe.

AMERENA, PASQUALE A.: (1891-c.1930) Born in Brighton, England, of Italian parents from Viggiano, Potenza. He made his home in Boston, Massachusetts

and was member of both the St. Louis and Boston Symphony orchestras. Amarena died in Boston.

ANDERSEN, CHRISTIAN: (1816- ?) Self-taught from early youth, he enlisted as a young man in a Danish military band and served until the termination of the War in 1864. Under his tutelage came forth his two famous sons, Joachim and Vigo.

ANDERSEN, JOACHIM: (1847-1909) Began his career as first flutist of the Music Association under Niels W. Gade and resigned in 1868 to become a member of the Royal Court Orchestra. He also lived in Russia and in Germany. In latter years he turned his attention towards the field of conducting. His fine compositions are widely known.

ANDERSEN, VIGO: (1852-1895) Was solo flutist with the Thomas orchestra in Chicago and was considered one of the foremost virtuosos of his instrument.

ANTHONY, THEOPHILE: (1850- ?) Professor at the Royal Conservatories of Brussels and Antwerp, as well as solo flutist at the Theatre Royal de la Monnaie in Antwerp.

ANTHONY, DORIOT: (contemporary) She studied first with Ernest Liegl in Chicago and then at the Eastman School of Music and made her California debut at the Bach Festival in Carmel-by-the-Sea, playing the B minor suite and other compositions and, soon after, August 5, 1946, in Los Angeles at a Hancock Concert, played Griffes' *Poem* for flute and orchestra. She is a member of the Los Angeles Philharmonic.

ARCARO, JAMES: (c.1885-) Flutist member of the National Symphony, Washington, D. C. He was born in Viggiano, Potenza, Italy.

ARGENTIERI, BALILLA: (c.1885-) Studied first with Giacomo Nigro and then with Franceschini in Rome, Italy. He has been in America since the beginning of this century. Now living in New York.

ARLOM, ALBERT WM.: (1860-) Solo flutist of the municipal orchestra at Harrogate, as well as in many concerts in North England.

ARMER, ROBERT: (contemporary) Young American flutist living in Los Angeles. He studied at the University of California and on November 21, 1947, performed Mozart's flute Concerto in D major at Royce Hall Auditorium. In 1946, Armer performed Chaminade's Concertino for Flute and Orchestra in Japan.

ARMFIELD, GLADYS: (contemporary) American woman flutist of talent from Kansas City, Missouri.

ARRIVABENE, FERRUCCIO: (c.1880-) One of the most cultured flute virtuosi and famous teachers of South America, where he was born. He lives in Sao Paulo.

ARZ, VON DIETLAND: (1849-) Director of the Music School in Winterthur and also solo flutist in the Zurich Tonhallen orchestra and, later, many years a member of the Gewandhaus orchestra at Leipzig. Wrote a school for the flute.

ASHE, ANDREW: (1759-1841) Irish composer-flutist.

ATKINSON, BURNETT: (contemporary) American flutist member of the Philadelphia Symphony. Graduate of Eastman School of Music and Curtis Institute.

AUBERTY, DU BOULLEY PRUDENCE LOUIS: (1796-1870) Child prodigy. Extremely prolific chamber music composer, played flute since he was ten years of age. He was born and died in Verneuil, France.

AZEVEDO, ALEXIS JACQUES: (1813-1875) Music critic of great culture and violinist. He was also an excellent flutist, having studied with Tulou at the Paris Conservatory. He was born in Bordeaux and died in Paris.

AZZANO, GIUSEPPE: (c.1870-) Italian flutist, member of the La Scala opera orchestra and teacher at the "Scuola Popolare di Musica" in Milan.

BACKOFEN, JOHANN HEINRICH: (1768-1839) Musician to the

Court of Gotha, was a virtuoso on the harp, clarinet, horn and bassoon, and was especially admired for his virtuosity in performing concerti on the flute. He was born in Durlach and died in Darmstadt.

BADAL: (contemporary) Hindu left-handed flutist of remarkable skill. An interesting article on Badal, written by Joseph Marx, was published in *Woodwind* Magazine, February 1950.

BADES, PAUL: (1873-) Solo flutist of the Nice Opera House and court conductor of the Casino Concerts of Calais. He is also known as a music critic and composer.

BADOLLET, FRANK: (1870-) American flutist who was connected with the Cincinnati Symphony for a number of years.

BAJER, ANTOINE: (1785-1860?) Studied music with two celebrated personalities, the Abbé Vogler and Carl Maria von Weber. Joseph Rossler was his flute teacher for three years, from 1802 to 1805, in Prague. He traveled through Germany, France and Italy with fine success as flute and piano virtuoso and, from 1807 to 1823, was secretary to the music teacher of Count Gallas in Prague. He was also, in the same city, solo flutist at the opera theatre and flute teacher at the Conservatory. Bajer composed several successful comic operas and was the first music teacher of the famous opera soprano, Enrichetta Sontag.

BAKER, JULIUS: (contemporary) A talented flutist of the younger American generation. He is solo flutist with the CBS in New York City. Baker gave the first performance in America of Ibert Concerto for flute and orchestra in 1948.

BALDINI, GIROLAMO: (1560?-1620) Excellent flutist and composer for his instrument. His sonatas for flute alone, well and beautifully constructed in their classical style, were published in one book by Attaignant, Paris. Baldini was born in Verona, Italy and died in Paris.

BALLERON, LOUIS: (1871-) Member of the orchestra of the Opera Comique in Paris and also instructor at the College Sainte Barbe.

BARGE, WILHELM: (1836- ?) First flutist in the court orchestra at Detmold and from 1867 to 1895 first flutist in Gewandhaus orchestra at Leipzig. Was instructor at the Royal Conservatory at Leipzig since 1862. Barge wrote a school for the flute and some orchestral studies.

BARON, SAMUEL: (contemporary) One of New York's most active flutists. He, with Charles Ehrenberg, played a number of times, Bach's Sonata in G major for two

216

flutes and figured bass, worked out by Baron.

BARONE, CLEMENTE: (1876-1934) Was born in Marsico Nuovo, Potenza, Italy. He came to America at the age of three years and was with the Philadelphia Symphony first as a piccolo player and later as solo flutist for about four years. In 1910 was engaged by the Victor Recording Company, with whom he was connected as solo flutist for many years, making records with many famous singers.

BARRÈRE, GEORGES: (1876-1944) Most popular and beloved French flute virtuoso. Lived in America nearly forty years. (See biography.)

BARRETT, WILLIAM LEWIS: (1852-1927) Professor at the Royal College of Music in London, where he was born. Was solo flutist in Her Majesty's Opera, later in the Royal Italian Opera. (See biography.)

BARSANTI, FRANCESCO: (1690-1760) When very young, on company of the violinist and composer, Francesco Geminiani, went to London where soon after was given the flute position at the Italian Theatre. Later, he went to Scotland as teacher of flute, oboe and viola and, in 1750, returned once more to London, this time as violinist in the same theatre mentioned above and also in the orchestra of Vauxhall. His published compositions in London were: 12 Soli for flute and numbered bass, six sonatas for two violins and numbered bass from Geminiani's music. Also an album of folk songs of Scotland and many concerti, overtures for four instruments, etc., all published by Walsh, London. However, in spite of his admirable and artistic activity, the last years of his life were spent in the most abject poverty. Barsanti was born in Lucca and died in London.

BARTON, GILBERT S.: (contemporary) English flute virtuoso residing in London.

BARRY, ELIZABETH: (contemporary) In a vaudeville act in which I saw her many years ago in New York, she played flute, trombone, piano and sang. She specialized, however, in trombone playing, in which she excelled.

BARTUSCHAT, CARL: (1882-) Member of the Gewandhaus orchestra in Leipzig.

BAUDIN, URBAIN: (1882-) Member of the Colonne orchestra in Paris.

BAUER, PAUL: (1864-) Royal chamber music virtuoso, solo flutist of the Royal Court orchestra and teacher in the Royal Conservatory at Dresden.

BAXTER, HARRY V.: (contemporary) Founder of the Los Angeles Flute Club and head of the Baxter-Northup firm of Los Angeles, California. His daughter, Elise,

217

is also an enthusiastic flutist and teacher, and his son-in-law, Horth Moennig, maker and repairer of woodwind *par excellence*, plays flute too. Mrs. Harry Baxter, to complete the family name, is so well acquainted with everything pertaining to the woodwind literature and that of the flute in particular that she knows who composed this or that piece in an uncanny manner.

BAYR, GEORGE: (1773-1833) Austrian flute virtuoso and composer. He was the first to discover an ingenious artifice, now commonly employed, causing one flute to produce an effect similar to that **of two.**

BECKE, JOHANN BAPTISTE: (1743- ?) From his father, who was his first teacher, he learned the clavicembalo, singing, bassoon and flute. In 1763, under military service in Stockholm, he perfected himself further in studying flute with Steinhard. In 1766, having been discharged from the army, he went to Munich as flutist of the Bavarian Chapel. There, he studied flute with Wendling and composition with Joseph Michel and, by 1780, he was hailed as one of the great flutists. He composed some good flute music which, at that time, became very popular with flutists and one or two of these concerti may be had even now in the Meyer edition, Brunswick.

Becke was born in Nuremberg, Germany.

BECQUIE, A.: (1800-1825) French flutist at the Opéra Comique. Wrote *Grande fantasie et fugue* for flute and piano, etc. Died at 25.

BEHM, EMIL: (c. 1835- ?) German flute virtuoso and composer of a few pieces for flute and piano on operatic themes. One of these is for three flutes and piano on *Ti prego o madre*. Behm lived in Russia for many years. In 1871 he met Carl Wehner and gave him a small autographed picture of himself which was presented to me by Wehner in 1910. Behm died in St. Petersburg.

BELCKE, CHRISTIAN GOTTFRIED: (1796-1875) Solo flutist and composer, Dresden, Germany.

BELLERMANN, CONSTANTIN: (1696-1758) Poet, attorney-at-law and composer. Played flute well and composed three concerti for that instrument and also six sonatas for flute, viola da gamba and clavicembalo. Was born at Munden, Germany.

BENIAMINO, VITTORIO: (1833-1906) Solo flutist at the Royal Theatre in Torino, Italy, for 50 years and teacher at the Liceo Musicale. Was famous for his beautiful tone.

BENNET, HAROLD: (contemporary) Flutist with the Metropolitan Opera. He claims to have invented an apparatus to protect the tone of the flute and other wind instruments from change of temperature.

BENTON, THOMAS P.: (contemporary) Talented young American flutist of Boston who studied with Georges Laurent. In a recital sponsored by W. S. Haynes Company on May 12, 1949, Benton performed admirably works of Bach, Mozart and other composers.

BERBIGUIER, BENOIT TRANQUILLE: (1782-1838) Left his law studies for music. Flute soloist and composer of merit. Wrote a valuable flute school, many solos, chamber music and operas. Berbiguier was a left-handed flute player. (See biography.)

BERENGUER, MANUEL: (c. 1870-1930?) Spanish flutist who, having been with the famous singer, Galli-Curci, for many years, was presented with an excellent gold flute by that artist in appreciation of his work.

BERGH, HAAKOM: (contemporary) Los Angeles flutist. He was chosen as the flutist for the first performance of Krenek's *Concertino* for solo flute, solo violin (Ralph Shaffer) and piano (the composer), with string orchestra, November 17, 1948.

BERGSETH, PAULINE: (contemporary) Solo flutist of the New Orleans Symphony orchestra succeeding Julius Gelfius who died in 1948. Her husband, Boris Leventon, attorney, whose name was legally changed to Michael Lewton, is the son of Alexander Leventon, the excellent Russian violinist, since 1922 with the Rochester Philharmonic and Civic orchestras. Pauline first studied flute in Seattle with Frederick Wing who told her she had great talent. After she graduated from the University of Washington in Seattle she studied for three years at the Juilliard School of Music with Arthur Lora. In 1948, while a member of the Washington, D. C. National Symphony, she took some lessons from William Kincaid. Now I hope I will be pardoned if I tell briefly of the unusual and uncanny precocity (in sociological matters) little Boris showed at the tender age of three in Rochester, New York, where he was born. One day his mother, a very beautiful Russian lady whose friendship with my wife was of long standing, telephoned that she was ill in bed. My wife rushed to her home and while she was giving the boy a bath she said, "What a nice boy you are, Boris. I wish I had one like you." Boris, looking at her, answered, "Why don't you?" "Well," said my wife, "babies cost so much money in our days, you know." Boris, again surprised at such ignorance, said, "Babies don't cost

219

anything; babies grow in your stomach."

BERTONE, GIULIO: (1858-) Born in Italy. Was solo flutist at Dieppe, France and also at the Opéra Khediviale at Cairo, Egypt.

BEVILACQUA, MATHIEU: (1772-1849) Flutist, guitarist and tenor. Composed duets for two flutes; trios for two clarinets and bassoon; quartets for guitar, violin, flute and 'cello; sonatas for flute and piano and many other compositions including *Principes ou Methode nouvelle pour pincer la guitarre.*

BEYNON, CHARLES O.: (contemporary) Flutist, teacher and singer residing in Los Angeles. Beynor plays flute in the writer's *flute ensemble* which meets monthly in Palos Verdes Estates and sings in one of Los Angeles' churches every Sunday morning.

BIANCHINI, MARIA: (c.1835-1910?) Italian woman flutist of talent; pupil of Giulio Briccialdi.

BILLORO, LUIGI: (1875-) Italian flute virtuoso, writer, poet, journalist, painter and the founder of a flute factory in Milano. He was born at Monselice, a suburb of Venezia, and lived for a number of years in Rio de Janeiro. There he made a great number of friends and admirers, one of whom was the flutist and pedagogue, Pedro De Assisi, who wrote an interesting sketch of Billoro's life in his *Manual do Flautista.*

BIMBONI, GIOVACCHINO: (1810-1895) Professor of trumpet and trombone at the Royal Institute of Music in Florence, Italy, gave successful concerts as a flute-virtuoso. He was born and died in Firenze.

—BLADET, ROBERT: (contemporary) French flutist; for a number of years with the Minneapolis Symphony. Now with one of the motion picture studios in Hollywood.

BLAISDELL, FRANCES: (contemporary) One of the finest women flutists of the younger generation in America. Now living in New York City. Her manager since the 1947-8 season has been Claude Barrère.

BLODECK, WILHELM: (1834-1874) Bohemian flutist and composer of overtures, choirs and an opera.

BOCKSA, KARL: (? -1821) Flute and clarinet virtuoso and composer of flute pieces.

BOEHM, ALFRED AUGUST: (c.1880-) Flutist and honorary conductor of the South Australian Flute Club, Adelaide.

BOEHM, THEOBALD: (1794-1881) Flute virtuoso, composer, inventor and writer. (See biography.)

BOECKELMAN, JOHN SEBASTIAN: (1848- ?) Dutch flute virtuoso.

220

BOOM, JOHANNES, E. G.: (1890-1883) Dutch flutist and composer.

BOONE, ABRAM: (contemporary) An excellent student in the 1930's of the Eastman School of Music on both the violin and the flute. He is the assistant concertmaster of the Rochester Philharmonic Symphony and now, 1947, also on the faculty of the Eastman School of Music. He is of Dutch extraction.

BORNE, FRANCOIS: (contemporary) French flutist of Toulouse.

BOTELHO, MANUEL GIOACHIN PEDRO: (1795-1873) Portuguese flutist and teacher of fine reputation. For forty years, from 1825 to 1865, was principal of the San Carlo in Lisbon and also of the court orchestra. He was born and died in Lisbon.

BOTGORSCHK, FRANZ: (1812-1863) Austrian flute virtuoso.

BOVE, J. HENRY: (contemporary) American flutist of Italian extraction. Was on tour with Mme. Tetrazzini.

BRICCIALDI, GIULIO: (1818-1881) Flute virtuoso, composer and inventor. (See biography.)

BRODSKY: (contemporary) Russian flute virtuoso; Riga.

BROOKE, ARTHUR: (c.1864-1950) English flutist and composer. Has written also a school for the flute and was member of the Boston Symphony for nearly thirty years. At one time Brooke was conductor of the Honolulu Symphony. He died in San Diego, California.

BROSSA, FIRMIN: (1839- ?) Belgian flutist; Manchester, England.

BRUCKNER, SAMUEL: (c.1900-) American flutist and teacher of Salt Lake City, Utah, who advocates the standardization of the flute, as many others did, into the original open G-sharp key because of many advantages.

BRUNOT, LOUIS: (1820-1850) French flutist and composer.

BUCHEIM, ADOLPH: (1864-) German flutist of Düsseldorf.

BUCHNER, FERDINAND: (1825-1912) German flute virtuoso, composer and teacher who resided most of his life in Russia. (See biography.)

BUDDENHAGEN, FRITZ: (1858-) German flutist residing in Switzerland.

BUFFARDIN, PIERRE GABRIEL: (1670-1739) French pioneer who raised standard of teaching method for the flute. Quantz was his pupil; was pensioned by his government in 1749 and died in Dresden, Germany.

BUKOVSKY, WENZEL: (1845-) Bohemian flute virtuoso of Troja.

BURGER, FRITZ: (1866-) Flutist and composer of Crivitz-Mecklenburg, Schwerin, Germany.

BURGESS, CHARLOTTE JUNE STE-VENSON: (contemporary) American woman flutist of talent. She is a member of a trio for flute, 'cello (Walter Coleman) and harpsichord (Louis Gardner).

BURGESS, JOHN: (contemporary) Flutist with the Baltimore Symphony.

BUROSE, ADOLPH: (1858-) Flute virtuoso and composer of Budapest, Hungary.

BUSH, VANNEVAR: (1890-) One of the greatest and most eminent scientists of present-day America is Dr. Vannevar Bush. We, the disciples of Pan, are just as proud of the fact that this eminent man plays flute as violinists are because Albert Einstein makes his hobby violin playing. However, upon my inquiring, Dr. Bush said: "My flute playing has been only to amuse myself and some of my friends but surely not well enough to be included in your book!" I should have told the good doctor that it is not how much or how well a distinguished dilettante plays. It is enough that at one time or another he has made flute playing his hobby. Dr. Bush is Director, U. S. Office of Scientific Research and Development, Chairman of the Joint Committee on New Weapons, President and Dean of Engineering and is also a writer and inventor. His office is in the White House with the President of the United States— see *World Biographies of 1948*, p. 911.

BUYSSENS, PAUL: (1871-) Belgian flutist of Tournal.

BUZZOLA, ANTONIO: (1815-1871) Dramatic composer, pupil of Donizetti and Mercadante at the Naples Conservatory. He studied also violin and flute and, for some time was solo flutist at the Fenice Theatre of Venezia and later first violinist in the same orchestra. Buzzola was born at Adria and died in Venezia.

CAFARO, RODOLFO: (c.1880-) Semi-professional flutist from Roma, Italy. He had great enthusiasm for everything pertaining to that instrument and its literature. Whenever a new composition came out in any country he was not only one of the first to know about it but would inform a number of his friends, accompanying the note with his personal comment in regard to the new piece.

CALL, LEONARD de: (1779-1815) German flute and guitar virtuoso and composer. Wrote pieces and duets for the two instruments and trios for three flutes.

CALLIMAHOS, LAMBROS: (contemporary) Flute virtuoso and teacher of the younger generation residing in New York; of Greek ancestry.

CAMBINI, GIOVANNI GIUSEPPE:

222

(1746-1825) Italian flutist and composer.

CAMUS, PAUL HIPPOLYTE: (1796-?) French flutist and composer.

CANTHAL, AUGUST: (1804-1881) German flutist and composer.

CANTIE, AUGUSTE: (1844-) French flutist and composer.

CAPELLER, JOHANN NEPOMUK: (1776- ?) German flutist, composer, inventor and teacher of Th. Boehm. Composed quartets for flute, violin, viola and 'cello.

CAPUTO, AUGUST: (contemporary) Italo-American flutist and band leader. Has written a series of Etudes for the flute.

CARATELLI, SEBASTIAN: (contemporary) Italian flutist. He was born in Rome and came to America in 1929. Studied flute with John Wummer in Detroit and harmony and composition with Bernard Heidn and Franklin Robinson, all under scholarships. He was a member of the National Orchestra Association and also the NBC under Toscanini. In 1943 Fritz Reiner engaged Caratelli as solo flutist with the Pittsburgh Symphony Orchestra. His wife, Ann Sacchi, is the harpist in the same symphony. In the summer they stay on Long Island, New York. The season of 1947-8 finds him solo flutist with the Detroit Symphony.

CARDIGAN, CORA: (Mrs. Louis Honig, 1840- ?) English woman flute virtuosa.

CARL, THEADOR: (1724-1799) German cellist, flutist and noted teacher.

CARLO, SALVATORE de: (1838?-1897) Italian piccolo virtuoso with Gilmore's band. Died in New York.

CARRANO, ALBINIO: (c.1870-) Italian semi-professional flutist and composer of a grand opera.

CARTE, RICHARD: (1808-1891) English flutist and composer and one of the founders of the firm of Rudall-Carte & Co., London.

CASO, PIETRO: (contemporary) Italian flutist living in New York since the beginning of this century. At one time toured with the singer Tetrazzini and also member of the Metropolitan Opera and solo flutist with the Russian Ballet.

CASOLI, ALFREDO: (1864-) Solo flutist of the La Scala Opera of Milan and one of the first to manufacture Boehm flutes there.

CASTELLINI, FILIPPO: (1870?-) An excellent artist and professor of flute at the Instituto Musicale Giuseppe Verdi of Ravenna, Italy. A friend of Abelardo Albisi who dedicated his Suite Miniature No. 1 for three flutes to him.

CAVALLY, ROBERT: (contemporary) American flutist member of the Cincinnati Symphony and

223

teacher at the College of Music, Cincinnati, Ohio.

CECH, FRANK: (contemporary) Solo flutist with the Czech Philharmonic Orchestra, Prague, Czechoslovakia.

CERNY, RUDOLF: (1878-) Bohemian flute virtuoso and teacher at the Konservatorium in Prague.

CHARLES, AUGUST: (1833-1896) Dutch flutist and composer. Died in Belgium.

CHRISTMANN, JOHANN FRIEDRICH: (1752-1817) German flutist and composer of Ludwigsburg (Swabia).

CIARDI, CESARE: (1818-1877) Italian solo flutist of the Imperial Opera of St. Petersburg, and composer of much fine flute music. He died in St. Petersburg. (See biography.)

CIGARINI, FERRANTE: (1833-) Flute soloist at the *Accademia Musicale* of Ravenna, Italy.

CIGARINI, EDMONDO: (1882-) Solo flutist of the Municipal Theatre of Modena.

CLARK, ELAINE H.: (contemporary) Miss Clark from Rochester, New York, besides being a graduate from two universities, is an enthusiastic flute dilettante and a very busy lady with many civic activities. The interesting specimen of the nose bamboo flute, which I own, was graciously presented to me by Miss Clark who acquired it—not an easy job—from a chief in the mountains of the Philippines.

CLAYTON, JOHN BOYES: (1870-) English flutist of Rock-Ferry.

CLINTON, JOHN: (1810-1864) Irish flutist and composer. Wrote one of the first methods for the Boehm flute. Also duets, trios, etc.

COCHE, VICTOR JEAN BAPTISTE: (1806-1881) French flute virtuoso and composer. At one time he was a devoted admirer of Boehm but, later, turned against him. Coche wrote a school for the Boehm flute and also pamphlets widely read by most artists.

COLBIG, DAVIA: (contemporary) Flutist with the Houston, Texas, Symphony.

COLLARD, A.: (c.1850- ?) English flutist, author of *Method of Practising the Flute*. London, 1875.

CONOVER, MARY CHASE: (contemporary) An enthusiastic flute dilettante and traveler whose husband, Townsend Conover, also plays flute.

COOK, SAMUEL E.: (contemporary) Australian flute amateur of great enthusiasm who resides in Sydney.

COPPOLA, CARMINE: (contemporary) Solo flutist of the NBC orchestra. He is one of the younger generation of Italian ancestry. Has composed some orchestral pieces. In 1949 he became associated with the radio station WOR.

COPPOLA, RAFFAELE: (1841-1910) Flutist, composer and director of the municipal band of Cremona, succeeding Ponchielli. A symphonic poem of his was rewarded with a prize by the Academy of Brussels. He composed also operas and religious music. Coppola played flute very well and at one time was solo flutist in a military band. He was born at Capua, near Napoli, and died in Torino.

CORREGGIO, HEINRICH: (1843-) Austrian flutist of Linz-Donau.

COX, JOHN S.: (1834-1902) Irish flutist and composer. Lived in America many years and died in New York.

CRAMER, JACOB B.: (1705-1770) German flutist and composer. Lived in Sachau and Mannheim where he died.

CRISTOFORETTI, PAOLO: (1857-1933?) Italian flute virtuoso and teacher at the Parma Conservatory. He was one of Adelina Patti's favored flutists and enjoyed the friendship of Giuseppe Verdi who held him in high esteem.

DAHMEN, ARNOLD: (1765-1829) Dutch flute virtuoso of Harlingen.

DAHMEN, PETER WILHELM: (1808-1886) Dutch flutist of Amsterdam.

DAHMEN, J. F. A. T.: (1837- ?) Dutch flutist of Amsterdam.

DAMM, AUGUST: (1848-1925?) German flutist and composer of popular piccolo solos. Resided and died in Boston.

DANICAN, PETER: (1681-1731) He belonged to a family of musicians and was an extremely fine flutist and the composer of Suites for two transverse flutes and a number of trios for three flutes, published by Ballard, Paris. Danican was born and died in Paris.

DANNEBERG, FRANZ: (1876-) German flutist and teacher at the Conservatory of Wiesbaden.

DAUSCHER, ANDREAS: (c.1800- ?) German flutist and composer.

DAY, GORDON: (contemporary) Solo flutist with the Toronto Symphony.

DE ASSISI, PEDRO: (c.1870- ?) South American flutist, teacher and pedagogue. He is the author of Manual do Flautista—commentarios sobre diversos conservatorios da Europa—and professor of flute at the Institute National de Musica, Rio de Janeiro, Brazil.

DE GIOSA, NICOLA: (1820-1885) Prolific operatic composer of the Neapolitan school, having studied with Ruggi, Zingarelli and Donizetti, played flute so well that at one time at the Naples Conservatory was appointed *maestrino di flauto*, assistant flute teacher. De Giosa was born and died in Bari.

DE JONG, EDWARD: (1837-1920) Dutch flutist, composer and conductor in England where he died.

DE JONG, JACQUES: (?) Brother of Edward; was solo flutist to the King of Holland.

DE LA BARRE, MICHAEL: (1675-1744) French flute virtuoso of great merit and composer of pieces for flute and basso (?); two flutes; and flute, violin and basso. These compositions were published by De La Barre in Paris and Schott in Germany. He was also the composer, in 1700, of an opera-ballet *Le triomphe des Arts* and in 1705, a comedy-ballet *La Venitienne*. De La Barre was born and died in Paris.

DE LORENZO, JOSEPH: (1891-) A flutist of fine talent, good tone and an unusual facile technique. Peppino—his pet name—is the youngest of nine children. Strange to say that none of his father's three older children, two girls and a boy by his first wife, who died very young, became musicians, while the six—five boys and a girl from his second wife—turned out to be all professional musicians. Peppino first studied the violin with his brother Nicola and the old system flute with Giacomo Nigro.

However, when in 1907 he heard his other brother, Leonardo, who had just returned home from South Africa, perform on the modern flute, he abandoned both the violin and the old flute for the modern one.

At first he had a long lesson every day and later every other day, making astonishing progress and leaving for California after eighteen months of intensive flute study. With a little more ambition and sound musicianship he could have become one of the finest of flutists. Peppino enlisted in the American Army in World War I and in World War II worked in an airplane defense job. At one time he was solo flutist with the Seattle Symphony and played also with several of Hollywood's motion picture studios. His talent in playing billiards almost equals that of the flute.

DE LORENZO, LEONARDO: (1875-) Italian flutist, pedagogue and composer of numerous works, including woodwind chamber music. "Known in Europe since 1897 as a superior flutist." (*Grove's Dictionary of Music and Musicians*)

DE LA PENA, ENRICQUE: (c.1890-) Mexican flute and piccolo soloist.

DELUSSE, CHARLES: (1731-1798) French solo flutist of the Opera Comique of Paris and composer of sonatinas for flute with figured bass, *Six Divertissements* for two flutes, etc. He was also a famous instrument maker and invented the "flute harmonique," a sort of double-flageolet. Delusse was an author and the composer of a successful comic opera.

DEL VECCHIO, ANDREA: (contemporary) American flutist of Italian ancestry and a teacher at the University of Miami, Florida.

DE MAILLY, CHARLES: (1893-1920) Studied first with L. Blanquart and later, at the Paris Conservatory, with A. Hennebains. He won second prize in 1911 and first prize in 1912. Was a member of the *Concert Colonne* and solo flute of the Paris band. In 1915 De Mailly joined the Boston Symphony in which city he died July 26, 1920, at the untimely age of 27.

DEMERSSEMAN, JULES: (1833-1866) Flute virtuoso—old system —and composer born at Hondschoote, Holland. When only twelve years of age, he received a first prize for flute playing. His stubbornness and his antipathy for the Boehm flute, aping his illustrious teacher, Tulou, deprived Demersseman of being appointed instructor at the Paris Conservatory for which position he had all the necessary qualifications. He lived most of his 33 years in Paris.

DEMEURS, JULES ANTONIO: (1814-

1880?) Belgian flutist and composer.

DE MICHELIS, VINCENZO: (1825-1891) Italian flutist, composer and inventor.

DE MILITA, VINCENZO: (1881-) Semi-professional Italian flutist of talent and literary gifts. Had he pursued a writing career or become a university professor, he might have become another Luigi Hugues. De Milita was born in Viggiano, Potenza, and the writer has known him for over half a century.

DE NARDIS, CAMILLO: (1852- ?) This famous teacher of composition, for nearly half a century at the Naples Conservatory, was a flute prodigy when very young and composed a fine *Tarantella* for flute and piano at the age of thirteen. He was one of the notable counterpuntists of his time. His many operas were not successful but his compositions for orchestra and in particular those for symphonic band are considered of high artistic value. De Nardis was born in Abruzzi, Italy.

DENNER, JOHANN CHRISTOPHER: (1655-1707) German flutist and inventor of the clarinet was born in Leipzig and died in Nurnberg.

–DENECKE, JULIA: (contemporary) American woman flutist with the Minneapolis Symphony.

–DENNING, ARTHUR: (contemporary) American flutist with the Indianapolis Symphony.

DENNY, PHILIPPE LEON: (1844-) French flutist and conductor of the 61st infantry regiment band.

DE PAULI, GIUSEPPE: (c.1825- ?) Italian flute virtuoso and composer.

DE RUBERTIS, JULIUS: (1916-) American flutist of Italian extraction. He was born in Kansas City, Missouri, and comes from a family of distinguished musicians. His father was an excellent violinist and composer and his mother a concert pianist. Julius has lived many years in Los Angeles, California, and is now with one of the major motion picture studios. He is also a member of the Santa Monica Symphony.

DESCHAMPS, PIERRE: (1874-) Solo flutist with the Lamoureux orchestra in Paris.

DEVIENNE, FRANCOIS: (1759-1803) French flute and bassoon virtuoso and composer of much music for the two instruments. At ten years of age he was quite a flutist. In 1788 was first bassoon of the Théâtre de Monsieur and later of the Grand Opéra in Paris. In 1795 he was given the flute professorship at the Conservatory. Devienne died at the Charimont Asylum. (See biography.)

DE VRIES, ENDRIK: (contemporary) Dutch flute virtuoso, at one time soloist with the Capitol Theatre orchestra, New York. Now with the Metropolitan Opera.

DI BIANCA, NATALE: (c.1875-) Italian flutist of San Francisco, California, where he has resided for several years.

DI LASCIA, ANTHONY: (contemporary) Graduated from New England Conservatory with honors in 1913. He studied also with Charles North, Arthur Brooke and Georges Barrère. Di Lascia was appointed teacher of flute and piccolo for the Music School for the Navy, Newport, Rhode Island.

– DI SEVO, ORESTE: (c.1890-) At one time solo piccolo with the Toscanini orchestra. He studied with Professor Cristoforetti in Parma, Italy, and has been in America many years.

DOBBERT, CHRISTIAN FRIEDRICH: (1700-1770) One of the greatest oboe players of the 18th century. In Berlin he eventually changed to the flute and in 1763 entered the orchestra of the Baron von Ansbach-Bayreuth as a chamber music virtuoso.

DOBIGNY, A.: (c.1890-) Author of Self Instructor for the Flute, London.

–DOLING, JAMES H.: (1885-) Former flutist with the Cleveland "Pop" Symphony, the Cleveland Municipal Symphony, the Cleveland Symphony and

228

Radio Station WHK-WTAM. Now, 1947, teaching exclusively at the Baldwin Wallace Conservatory of Music, Cleveland, Ohio. Doling has been teaching flute in Cleveland for thirty years.

DOM, JEAN: (1825- ?) Belgian flute and piccolo soloist with the Grenadier regiment band in Brussels. Was decorated with the Leopold-Order.

DONJON, JOHANNES: (1839-1912?) French flute virtuoso and composer of many *Etudes* and solos for flute and piano. Was also solo flutist with the Paris Grand Opéra and Société des Concerts du Conservatoire of Paris.

DOPPLER, FRANZ: (1821-1883) Austrian flute virtuoso, composer and conductor. He composed a number of operas; two of the most successful are W*enjowski* and *Ilka*. With his brother Karl, also an eminent flutist, he toured with great success France, England, Germany, South Russia, Rumania, etc. Franz also wrote many ballets, overtures and other orchestral compositions.

DOPPLER, KARL: (1825-1900) In 1865 was made court conductor in Stuttgart, Germany and retired in 1898. Karl also composed operas and in some of these was associated with Franz Liszt.

DORMIEUL, H. F. L.: (c.1785-) French flutist and composer.

DORUS, VINCENT JOSEPH VAN STEENKISTE: (1812-1896) French flutist, teacher and composer. Dorus devised the change on the Boehm flute from the original open G-sharp to the closed G-sharp. He was instructor at the Paris Conservatory.

DOTHEL, NICHOLAS: (1750- ?) German flutist and composer of nine concertos, seven quartets for various instruments, studies, capriccios, preludes, etc. He was connected with the Chapel of the Grand Duke of Tuscany.

DOTZEL, JOHN: (1893?-) At one time flutist with the Minneapolis Symphony. Now living in Sacramento, California.

DRESSLER, RAPHAEL: (1784-1835) Austrian flutist and composer.

DREXLER, GEORGE: (1906-) Born in Rochester, New York. This talented flutist studied at the Eastman School of Music and joined the Rochester Philharmonic when he was eighteen. After a number of years he went to the Cleveland Symphony and there played with Alfred Wallenstein's Symphonietta at the Station WOR, New York. Since 1947 he has been solo flutist with the Los Angeles Philharmonic. In 1948 Drexler performed the Ibert Concerto with excellent success.

DROUET, LOUIS: (1792-1873) Dutch flute virtuoso and composer; was born in Amsterdam,

229

lived many years in France and died in Bern, Switzerland.

DUBUSC, GUSTAV: (contemporary) French flute virtuoso of Normandie.

DULON, LUDWIG: (1769-1826) German blind flutist and composer. When scarcely eight years of age he could sing, or play on a comb with a piece of paper placed around it, two of Quantz' Allegros which he had heard his father play on the flute. His memory was marvellous; he could memorize a concerto by Quantz in one hour. Dulon gave many concerts and composed much music including duets, caprices and a concerto, all dictated to his sister who was his inseparable companion.

DUMON, JEAN: (1829-1889) Belgian flutist and teacher at the Conservatory of Brussels.

DUNCAN, CHARLES: (c.1890-) Author of *Popular Instruction Book for the Flute-Flageolet*, London.

DUNNING, RUTH: (contemporary) American flutist; member of the Cincinnati Symphony.

DUVERGES, MARIE JOSEPH: (1838-1877) French flutist and composer and soloist with the Regiment de Guides de la Garde Imperiale.

DYSON, H.: (contemporary) English. "Principal flutist with the Scottish Reginal (BBC) orchestra. A fine player with great experience."

ECK, EMIL: (contemporary) Flutist and solo piccolo with the Chicago Symphony.

EGNER, FRIEDRICH: (1842-1878) German flutist with the Hoftheater in Karlsruhe as principal.

EHRENBERG, CHARLES: (contemporary) An extremely active New York flutist in solo and ensemble playing. He, with Samuel Baron, often performs compositions for two flutes and piano and also Hindemith's *Canonic Sonatina* for two flutes.

ELIE, JEAN BAPTISTE: (1830-1895) French flutist with the Republican Guard.

ELINESCU, P.: (contemporary) Rumanian flutist and composer residing in Bucharest.

ELKIN, FLORENCE: (contemporary) An Australian woman flute virtuosa and member of the Sydney Flute Club.

ELTON, HARRY: (contemporary) Flutist and orchestra manager of the Toronto (Canada) Symphony.

ERLICH, D.: (c.1850-1925?) Photographer by profession, taught and traded in flutes for many years in New York, where he died. He wrote *The History of the Flute From Ancient Times to Boehm's Invention* (New York, 1920).

230

ESPOSITO, RAFFAELE: (c.1873-)
He graduated from the Naples
Conservatory at the beginning of
this century; settled in New
York soon after and has been
there ever since occupying different positions in theatres, etc.
He has two sons who are excellent musicians and a brother,
Pasquale, a fine bassoon player.

FABRIZIO, JOHN: (c.1875-1945)
Italian flutist, for a number of
years member of the New York
Philharmonic.

FAGA, VINCENT: (c.1890) Italian
flutist and bandmaster, at one
time member of the Rochester
Philharmonic Symphony. Now
he is trying his hand at being an
Italian opera impresario in Rochester, New York.

FAHRBACH, JOSEPH: (1804-1883)
Austrian flutist and composer.

FAHRBACH, PHILLIP: (1815-1885)
Flutist and composer, brother of
Joseph.

—FAIR, REX ELTON: (contemporary)
Flutist and teacher at the University of Lincoln, Nebraska.

— FARGASON, NILES: (contemporary)
American flutist, teacher and
solo flute of the "Prudential
Family Hour" and "Borden's
Wednesday Night" program,
New York.

FARRENC, JACQUES HIPPOLYTE
ARISTIDE: (1794-1865) French
flutist and composer.

FARRIS, MAUD PRICE: (contemporary) Enthusiastic woman flutist
residing in Osborn, Kansas.

FAYER, ANTON: (1872-1935) Bohemian flutist. For several years
solo flutist of the New York Philharmonic.

FEDERHAUS, JULIUS: (1862- ?)
Bohemian flutist residing in Russia. Was also soloist with the
Warsaw Opera and teacher at
the Conservatory.

—FENBOQUE, ALFRED E.: (contemporary) Canadian; solo flutist
with the Cincinnati Symphony.
He was chosen by Eugene Goossens to succeed Ary van Leeuwen.

FENTUM, JONATHAN: (c.1784)
Flute virtuoso. Lived many years
in England.

FERRANTINI, GIOVANNI: (1733?-
1794) Italian flutist and composer; was born in Venice and
died in Munich, Germany.

FERRARI, ANGELO: (1884-) Italian flutist and clarinetist. In 1900
he came to America and resided
both in Washington and Philadelphia. In 1903 he returned to
Italy. Ferrari is the composer of
several pieces for piano, for voice
and piano, as well as for plectrum (mandoline, mandola, guitarre, etc.) and also compositions
for band.

FERRER, MATEO: (1788-1864)
Composer and noted orchestral
conductor, was also an excellent
flute, double bass, piano and organ player. He was born and died
in Barcelona, Spain.

231

FERRONI, VINCENZO: (1858-1925?) Like De Nardis, this eminent contrapuntist started his career as a flutist. When very young he entered the Paris Conservatory in the class of Massenet. He was professor of composition at the Conservatorio di Milano from 1886 and published a book of fugues, a *Corale e Fuga* for organ and two operas (or melodrammi), *Rudello* and *Ettore Fieramosca*. Ferroni was born in Tramutola, Potenza, and died in Milano.

FERSTL, JACOB: (1884- ?) German Catholic priest and excellent flute dilettante.

FESTING, MICHAEL CHRISTIAN: (c.1720) Flute virtuoso; lived in England.

FEWKES, JESSE WALTER: (c.1870) Author of *Tusayan Flute and Snake Ceremonies* (Washington, D. C., 1900).

⁻FIELDER, A.: (contemporary) Solo flutist of the Dallas Symphony.

FINN, JOHN: (1862- ?) English semi-professional flute virtuoso and eminent flute historian. Many compositions were dedicated to John Finn.

FIORE, FAUST D.: (contemporary) American flutist of talent of the younger generation. He resides in Boston, Massachusetts.

⁻FIORE, NICHOLAS: (contemporary) With the Vancouver, B.C. Symphony.

⁻FISCHER, JOHN: (contemporary) Flutist and solo piccolo with the Philadelphia Symphony for many years.

FISCHER, OSKAR: (1870-) Flute virtuoso born in Grosnaja, Russia, and resided in Leipzig, Germany, as soloist of the Gewandhaus orchestra.

⁻ FITZGERALD, FRANCIS: (contemporary) Flutist with Indianapolis Symphony.

FITZGIBBON, HENRY MACAULAY: (1855- ?) Irish attorney, enthusiastic flute dilettante and author of *The Story of the Flute*.

FLACK, LAMBERT C.: (contemporary) English. "Began to play flute at nine years of age. Flute and piccolo first class military band at eleven years. Member of four or five military bands at the age of twelve. Toured the Continent at thirteen as soloist. Wrote for the church choir whilst still at school. Did opera, ballet, etc. at the Theatre Royal, Newcastle on Tyne, from the age of fourteen for nine years, three of these in the first World War. Flack is an author and the composer of many solos, librettos, poems, etc. Exponent of the full flute family, including the Bass Flute in C made by Rudall-Carte. Came to London as principal flute to Gaumont British in 1928. Rejoined the BBC as principal flute in the theatre orchestra in 1930. In 1932 was transferred to sym-

232

phony orchestra as fourth player. Since 1946 he has been principal flute of the BBC symphony orchestra. Intensely interested in schools where I have talked to over 30,000 children in recent months, illustrating with ancient instruments, including one which is a copy at least of the first flute ever made, played obliquely. I play on Rudal-Carte flutes!" The above was written and signed by Lambert C. Flack.

FLADD, FREDERICH: (1855-1924) Noted mechanical engineer and an enthusiastic and able flute dilettante. He died in New Canaan, Connecticut.

FLEURY, LOUIS: (1878-1928) Very popular and cultured flute virtuoso. Well known also in England and in America for his masterly playing. Fleury was a member of the Société Moderne d'Instruments à Vent in Paris.

FLORIO, PIETRO GRASSI: (?c.1795) Italian flutist, composer and inventor. Lived also in Germany, France and in England. Florio was one of the first to play on a flute with the F-natural, G-sharp and B-flat keys. His son also was a famous flutist and a protege of Madame Mara, a famous singer. Florio Senior died in London in extreme poverty.

FOLZ, MICHEL: (c.1820- ?) Very little is known of this flute virtuoso and composer who was born in Naples, Italy, and played on a Boehm flute.

FONTAINE, CAMILLE: (1858-) Belgian flutist and composer. Solo flutist of the Theatre Royal de la Monnaie in Brussels.

FONTANA, N. J.: (contemporary) Flutist and solo piccolo with the Toronto Symphony.

FONTBONNE, LEON: (1859- ?) French flutist and composer. Was soloist with Garde Republicaine and conductor of the Casino de St. Germain and member of the Association Artistique in Paris.

FOREST, MARGUERITE ANDERSON de: (1882-1925) This American lady flutist traveled extensively. At the New England Conservatory in Boston she studied voice, violin, piano and flute, majoring on the last instrument. She died in Los Angeles.

FORMAN, EDMUND: (c.1870) Author of *Self Instructor for the Piccolo or Flageolet*, London.

FRANCESCHINI, FILIPPO: (1841-1915) Italian flute teacher and pedagogue was for many years instructor at the Santa Cecilia of Rome. He wrote two books of daily studies for the flute and died in Sao Paulo, Brazil, while on a visit to his son.

FRANCIS, JOHN: (contemporary) English. "Perhaps best known as the flutist in the 'Sylvan Trio.' A popular soloist."

FRANSELLA, ALBERT: (1865-1934) Dutch flute virtuoso and teacher. Lived most of his life in London where he was connected with the Queen's Hall orchestra, London Academy of Music and the Hapstead Conservatory. (See biography.)

FREDERSDORF, MICHAEL GABRIEL: (c.1750) Flute virtuoso and Frederick II's personal attendant and favorite.

FREEMAN, RUTH: (contemporary) One of America's finest flutists. Studied at Oberlin Conservatory, also at Juilliard Graduate School in New York with Georges Barrère. Has made several tours throughout the United States and Canada. Frequent soloist in New York's Carnegie and Town Hall concerts with outstanding success.

FREEMAN, TELEJOE: (contemporary) Flutist with the MGM motion picture studio in Los Angeles and member of the *Villa Pan Flute Ensemble* which meets every first Saturday of the month at Palos Verdes Estates, California. He is also an excellent mechanic and now (1949) is building a bass flute in C.

FREITAG, AUGUST: (1820-1905) German flutist and pupil of Boehm. He was soloist with the Munchener Hoforchesters.

FREUDENTHAL, JULIUS: (1805- ?) German violinist, flutist and conductor. Composed pieces for flute and piano.

FRIDZERI, ALESSANDRO MARIA ANTONIO: (1741-1825) Composer, violinist, mandolin virtuoso, dealer of music and instruments, played flute very well, being passionately fond of that instrument. He was born in Verona and died in Anversa, Italy.

FRIEDRICH der GROSSE—Frederick II, King of Prussia: (1712-1786) Eminent flute dilettante, composer and pupil of Quantz. (See biography.)

FRIEDRICH, Margrave of Brandenburg-Culbach-Bayreuth: (1711-1763) A great lover of music, a composer and flute virtuoso in his own right. Was taught by the famous Dobbert. Some years before his death he dedicated an Academy of Music to Bayreuth.

FRISCH, ROBERT: (1805-1865) German flutist and composer of great skill. Changed to the Boehm flute but went back to the old one. Frisch died in British India.

FRITSCHE, FRANZ: (1833-1896) Violinist, flutist, teacher and musical director.

FRITZE, LOUIS: (contemporary) American solo flutist with Sousa's band and also toured Europe with the singer Frieda Hempel.

FRITSCHE, REINHARD: (contemporary) Professor Fritzsche is one of the finest flutists and teachers of contemporary Germany.

234

FUMAGALLI, POLIBIO: (c.1835-)
Italian flutist and composer. He
studied with Giuseppe Rabboni
to whom he dedicated his original piece, *Il Pollo* (The Chicken).

FURSTENAU, ANTON BERNHARD:
(1792-1852) The son of Caspar
became much more famous than
his father both as composer and
player. (See biography.)

FURSTENAU, CASPAR: (1772-1819)
German flutist, bassoonist and
composer of about 60 flute works.

FURSTENAU, MORITZ: (1824-1889)
The son of Anton Bernhard was
sent to Boehm to change from
the old to the new flute. However, when Moritz returned to
Dresden after much success
abroad with the Boehm flute,
the old members and directors
of the Saxon Court band were so
much opposed to the new flute
that he, for fear of losing his
appointment, was obliged to return to the old flute.

FVEROF, JOSEPH: (contemporary)
Flutist with the Columbus, Ohio,
Philharmonic Orchestra.

GABRIELSKI, JOHANN WILHELM:
(1795-1846) German flutist and
composer.

GABRIELSKI, JULIUS: (1806-1878)
At eleven years of age was already
a good player. In 1825 he left
military service and later received a life position as chamber
music player in Berlin. Wrote

many compositions including
quartets with flute.

GABRIELSKI, ADOLPH: (1830-1899)
Son of Julius and flutist with the
court orchestra in Berlin.

GABUS, EDOUARD: (1859-) Solo
flutist of the Casino Orchestra of
Monte Carlo.

GAGLIARDI, AMERICO: (c.1885-)
Italian flutist of talent born in
Viggiano, Potenza. He has lived
in Melbourne, Australia, for
many years and at one time was
solo flutist with the Melba Opera
Company.

GALLA RINI, ANTHONY: (c.1905-
) Is of Italian extraction and
from a family of talented vaudeville musicians. He is not only an
able flutist, a virtuoso *par excellence* on the accordion, on which
he often gives successful concerts, but plays with equal facility many other instruments, in
particular the *euphonium*, a
large brass instrument. Galla
Rini also composes and arranges
pieces for the accordion in a masterly fashion.

GALLI, RAFFAELLO: (1824-1889)
Italian flutist, composer of about
200 works for the flute, including
a method. He was a banker in
Florence where he was born and
died.

GALPIN, FRANCIS W.: (c.1860- ?)
Author of *Whistles and Reed
Instruments of American Indians
of the Northwest Coast* (London, 1902-3).

GANDOLFI, RICCARDO: (c.1850) Author of *Appunti Intorno al Flauto* (Firenze, 1887).

GANTENBERG, HEINRICH: (1823-1906) Chamber music flute virtuoso and teacher at the Royal Conservatory in Berlin.

GARIBOLDI, GIUSEPPE: (1833-1905) Italian flutist and composer. Wrote also a school for the Boehm flute. Was born and died in Italy but lived in France for many years.

GARSIDE, E. W.: (contemporary) Flutist and honorary secretary of the Sydney Flute Club, Australia, with a membership of over sixty.

GASKELL, WINIFRED: (contemporary) English, principal flutist with the Liverpool Philharmonic orchestra. Fine technician with a somewhat light sound. She is well known as a soloist.

GASKINS, BENJAMIN: (contemporary) Flutist with the NBC orchestra, New York.

GATTERMAN, PH.: (c.1860) German flutist and composer.

GAUBERT, PHILIPPE: (1879-1941) French flutist, composer of many works for the flute and also of symphonic music and operas. Was flute instructor at the Paris Conservatory and conductor for the Paris Grand Opéra.

GAUTHAL, AUGUST M.: (1775?-) Solo flutist at the Opera of Hamburg, to whom Soussman dedi-cated his two flute quartets Op. 27 No. 1 and 2.

GELFIUS, JUSTUS: (contemporary) German flutist with the San Antonio Symphony orchestra, San Antonio, Texas. He died in New Orleans in 1948.

GENENNICHEN, RICHARD: (1857-) German chamber music flutist.

GENIN, PAUL AGRICOL: (1832-1903) French, solo flutist of Théâtre Italien and the Colonne Orchestra, Paris. Composed pieces for flute and piano.

GHIGNATTI, AMEDEO: (contemporary) Flutist with the New York Philharmonic.

GERSDORF, RICHARD: (1873-) Flutist of the Royal Chapel of Dresden.

GHISAS, EURYSTHENES: (1875-1900) Greek flute virtuoso of great talent. Studied in Vienna with Kukula and died there at 25 years of age.

GIALDINI, LUIGI: (1762-1817) As some of the ancient Greek flute-players who could play with equal facility the vertical flute and the reed flute, Gialdini, who studied in Firenze with Michele Sozzi, became a virtuoso on the flute, oboe, bassoon and English horn. In Livorno he was oboist with that orchestra and com-posed a concerto for flute and orchestra, duets and trios for flutes and duets for flute and

236

violin. He was born in Pescia and died in Livorno.

GIANELLA, L.: (c.1850-) Italian flutist and composer who lived in England. He wrote pieces for flute and piano, two flutes and piano and a quartet for four flutes. He died in London.

GIANNINI, PROSPERO: (contemporary) Flutist of talent and of Italian extraction residing in New York.

GIBSON, JAMES S.: (1862-1928) A successful business man born in Rockford, Illinois. He was an ardent lover of the flute which he played so well as to appear as soloist on many occasions. Mr. Gibson was secretary and treasurer of the Denver Symphony Association in which he was one of the flute players. He was also a collector of books and flute music. He died in Santa Barbara, California, on July 31.

GILBERT, J. J.: (contemporary) An excellent American flutist, teacher, composer and poet. He has written an *Andante con moto* for four flutes and other pieces. Played obbligatos to Madame Melba in Seattle, Washington. His daughter, Jeanne, is also a professional flutist of talent. Gilbert was a member of the Los Angeles Philharmonic for a number of years in the nineteen twenties.

― GILLAM, JOHN B., JR.: (1919-) American flutist and veteran of World War II. Studied with Joseph Mariano at the Eastman School of Music and in 1939 worked for Verne Powell in Boston. During his military service he was trained as an airplane mechanic and later was placed in Air Corps Supply. Since 1947, he has had his own repair shop for flute and piccolo exclusively that he calls "Gillam's Shop— Fine repairing for the flutist." In 1946 he was engaged as a member of the flute section of the Kansas City Philharmonic Orchestra.

GILLONE, EMILIO: (1852-1925?) Was born at Casalmonferrato (Piemonte), Italy, November 28. He was a favored pupil of Zamperoni at the Royal Conservatory of Music in Milan. For many years he was one of the highly esteemed and beloved flute soloists of the lyrica theatres and symphony concerts at Bologna. Gillone was a member of the Royal Academy of Music and a teacher of high reputation.

GILSON, PAUL: (-1930?) French flutist and composer of orchestral works and a Septette for flutes. He died in Los Angeles, California.

GIROUD, AUGUSTE: (1874-) Solo flutist of the Orchestre Symphonique and teacher at the Conservatory of Lausanne, Switzerland.

― GLEGHORN, A.: (contemporary) English. Principal flute with the

237

Philharmonia Orchestra. Possessed of a brilliant and impeccable technique coupled with a sweet, sympathetic tone and splendid intonation. Undoubtedly our finest player." Also, S. Foster writes to me in his letter of February, 1947, "Mr. Arthur Gleghorn is, without a doubt, the finest player we have at the moment in England. He is a real wizard Artiste, and plays the most difficult compositions with great ease." Since 1949 Gleghorn has made his home in Los Angeles, California.

GOEPFART, KARL: (1859- ?) German flutist, composer and conductor. At one time was member of the Baltimore Symphony. Besides solos for flute and piano, he wrote trios and quartets for woodwind.

GOLDBERG, ADOLPH: (?c.1920) Enthusiastic and wealthy flute dilettante of Berlin, Germany. Presented several gold flutes to his friends and made a valuable biographical collection of famous flutists with a separate album of large photographs, both of which he distributed gratis to all the noted flutists of his day.

— GOLDBERG, BERNARD: (contemporary) American flutist with the Pittsburgh Chamber of the International Society for Contemporary Music. He played Varese's *Density 21.05* in April, 1948.

— GOLDING, V.: (contemporary)

Flutist, at one time member of the Cleveland Symphony.

GOLDSMITH, DR. OLIVER: (1729-1774) Irish novelist, traveler and flute dilettante.

GOLTERMANN, HEINRICH LUDOLF: (1821-1894) Royal chamber music flutist and soloist with the Hoftheater in Hanover, Germany.

GONZALES-VAL, EUSEBIO: (1826-1887) Spanish, solo flutist of the Royal Theatre and teacher at the Madrid Conservatory.

GONZALES-MAESTRE, FRANCISCO: (1862-) Son of Eusebio. Solo flutist of the Royal Chapel and Symphony orchestra and teacher at the National Conservatory of Music in Madrid and president of the symphony orchestra.

— GOODE, B.: (contemporary) American flutist with the Dallas Symphony.

GRANOM, LEW C. A.: (c.1700) Author of *Plain and Easy Instructions for Playing on the German Flute* (London, 1766).

GORDON, WILHELM: (?c.1840) Swiss by birth and a captain in one of the regiments of the Swiss Guards of Charles the Tenth. A distinguished amateur flutist who studied with Drouet and Tulou. His experiments with a "new flute" led to the famous controversy as to who was the real inventor of the Boehm flute. Christopher Welch later clarified and settled the issue.

238

GRAF, FRIEDRICH HARTMANN: (1727-1795) German flutist, composer and conductor to whom, 1789, was given the title of Doctor of Music.

~ GRAITZER, MURRAY: (contemporary) Solo flutist with the San Francisco Symphony replacing Paul Renzi who is now with the NBC Symphony, New York.

GRAVINA-COUNT-GILBERTO: (1890-) Grandson of Cosima Wagner and von Bulow and great-grandson of Franz Liszt, is an excellent flutist, composer and conductor. He has honored our instrument by writing a *Preludio e Fuga in Do* for twelve flutes and wishes to be addressed as Maestro Gravina.

GRENIER, ALBERT: (1870-) French flutist with Lamoreux Orchestra of Paris.

GRENSER, KARL AUGUST: (1794-1864) German flutist and composer of duets for *Two Flutes à bec*, vertical flutes. Also compositions for the transverse flute.

GRIFFITH, FREDERICK; (c.1860) English flutist, writer and teacher at the Royal Academy of Music in London and solo flutist at the Royal Italian Opera, London. Griffith has also composed some flute pieces with piano.

~ GROTH, DANIEL: (contemporary) Flutist and solo piccolo with the Rochester Philharmonic.

GRUTZMACHER, CARL: (? -1883) Royal chamber music flutist and member of the Royal Chapel in Berlin.

GUNN, JOHN: (c.1765-1824) Scotch flutist and violincellist and author of *The Theory of the Violoncello; The School of the German Flute*, etc. Also *Essay on Harmony* and *An Historical Inquiry Respecting the Performance on the Harp in the Highlands of Scotland*, from the earliest times until it was discontinued about the year 1734. He died in Edinburgh where he was born.

GUNTHER, KARL: (1858-) German flutist and member of the Opera House orchestra in Frankfurt-on-Main.

GUNTHER, RICHARD: (1870-) German flutist and court musician to the Grand Duke.

GUILLOU, JOSEPH: (1787-1853) French flutist and composer. Died in Russia.

GUSIKOW, MICHEL JOSEPH: (1790-1837) One of the greatest xylophone virtuosos of all time and greatly admired all over Europe, he was also an expert flutist. Due to a serious chest malady he was reluctantly forced to abandon the flute and died when only 28 years old. Gusikow was born at Schklow and died in Aquisgrana, Russia.

HAAKE, WILHELM: (1804-1875) Solo flutist of the Stadttheater

239

and Gewandhaus orchestra in Leipzig. Composed a concerto for flute and orchestra.

HABERSHAM, WILLIAM NEYLE: (1807- ?) American enthusiastic flute dilettante from Savannah, Georgia.

HACKMEISTER, THEODOR: (1868-) German flutist, pedagogue and court musician.

HACK, JOHN W.: (1920-) American veteran of World War II. An extremely talented performer on the flute, clarinet, bassoon and the saxophones which he plays successfully at the MGM studios in Hollywood.

HALBERSTADT, JOSEPH: (1813-1881) Flute virtuoso. Died in London.

HALL, BLANCHE: (contemporary) American woman professional flutist. Resides near New York.

HALSTEAD, ALFRED: (1864-) Solo flutist of the Scottish orchestra in Glasgow.

HANLON, B. R.: (contemporary) English. "Third flute and piccolo in the R.P.O. A brilliant piccolo player who has only temporarily laid aside the flute which he plays equally well."

HAMMERLA, JOSEPH: (1841-1889) Bohemian flutist. Died in Germany, where he had been a member of the Duke's Chamber orchestra.

HARRISON, JOAN: (contemporary) American flutist of talent and a star pupil of Robert Cavally at the College of Music, Cincinnati, Ohio.

HARSCH, FERDINAND von: (? - 1785) Imperial ordnance master for Austria. Passionate music lover, good flutist and music promoter.

HARTMANN, CHRISTIAN KARL: (1750-1804) German flutist from Altenburg; died in Paris, France.

HARZER, ALBERT: (1880- ?) German solo flutist of the Berlin Philharmonic and for a number of years solo flutist with the Detroit Symphony under Gabrilowitsch. When Harzer returned to Germany in 1925 he played with excellent success, in one of the Berlin Philharmonic concerts, Saint-Saens' *Romanza* and De Lorenzo's *Tarantella Napolitana* Op. 8 with Harzer's own orchestration.

HASLAM, E.: (c.1820) Author of *New Method for the Boehm Flute* (Boston, 1868).

HAUG, JULIA: (contemporary) San Francisco woman flutist of merit. Her father, Julius Haug, is a composer and Julia interprets his *Barcarolle* magnificently.

HAYNES, GEORGE W.: (1865-1947) American flutist and "Master Flute-maker," originally from Boston, later located in Los Angeles, California. Died in 1947.

HAYNES, WILLIAM S.: (c.1870-

1938) The founder and head of the famous flute firm which is known throughout the world was only an amateur on the flute, but, like his brother George, he was a master flute maker and, because of his delightful personality, was loved by all who knew him.

HECHT, ELIAS: (c.1875-1934) Semiprofessional, wealthy flutist and a *sponsor maecenas* of chamber music. With a quintet of four distinguished stringed instrumentalists and himself as flutist he traveled in many states giving many successful concerts. He resided in San Francisco where he died.

— HEDGES, A.: (contemporary) English. "A well known flutist doing important orchestral work in London."

— HEIM, WILLIAM: (contemporary) Flutist with the New York Philharmonic.

HEIDELBERG, H.: (c.1870-) American flutist of German ancestry. He was connected with the New York Philharmonic and the New York Symphony early in this century.

HEINDL, EDWARD: (c.1860-) A pupil of Boehm and solo flutist of the Boston Symphony orchestra and the Mendelssohn Quintet Club.

HEINDL, HANS: (1828-1849) German flutist of remarkable talent.

Also a pupil of Boehm; died at 21 years of age, killed in accident.

HEINDL, MARTIN: (1837-1896) Brother of Hans and pupil of Boehm. Died in Boston.

HEINEMEYER, CHRISTIAN: (1796-1873) German flutist and composer.

HEINEMEYER, ERNEST WILHELM: (1827-1869) German flutist and composer. Died in Vienna, Austria.

HELSTED, KARL ADOLF: (1818-1904) Musical director of the Royal Theatre in Copenhagen, teacher in that conservatory, composer of symphonies, quartets and vocal music. He also appeared in concerts as flute soloist. Helsted was born and died in Copenhagen.

HENNEBAINS, ADOLPHE: (1862-1915) Solo flutist of the Grant Opéra and of the Société des Concerts du Conservatoire. Member of the Double Quintette and teacher at the Paris Conservatory. Traveled with great success in Germany.

HENRY VIII, KING OF GREAT BRITAIN AND IRELAND: (1491-1547) Played flute, recorder and composed.

HERBERT, PAUL: (1880-) Flutist and court musician to the Grand Duke of Altenburg, Germany.

HERMAN, JULES ARTHUR: (1830-?) French flutist and teacher at the Royal Conservatory in Brussels, Belgium. Was also flutist for

Adelina Patti, Peneo, Frezzolini, and Mme. Laborde.

HERON, LUKE: (c.1700) Author of A Treatise on the German Flute (London, 1771).

— HEYLMAN, MARTIN: (contemporary) Flutist with the Cleveland Symphony.

HEYWOOD, JOHN: (contemporary) English amateur flutist who, from the age of sixteen to fifty, claims to have developed a peculiar kind of sex appeal flute for rats. Heywood also claims that in one night he caught 1,147 rodents.

HIERHOLZER, DR. JOHN M.: (contemporary) Flute dilettante, poet and member of the Pittsburg Flute Club.

HIRT, ALBERT: (1853-) Royal chamber music flutist and teacher of the Conservatory of Cassel, Germany.

— HIRSH, H.: (contemporary) American flutist, member of the Metropolitan Opera, New York.

— HOCKSTAD, PAUL: (contemporary) Flutist with the Denver Symphony.

HOLLIS, HARRY WARNER: (c.1870-) Musician in Ordinary to His Majesty King Edward of England. Solo flutist of the Private Royal Chapel and member of the Symphony orchestra and of the Royal Opera Covent Garden in London.

HONDIUS, HEINRICH: (16th century) Flute blower of the 16th century in Germany.

— HOPKINSON, L.: (contemporary) English. "Principal flute of the BBC Theatre orchestra. He is the father of James Hopkinson, flutist of the BBC orchestra and of Cecelia Hopkinson, second flute of the Johannesburg (South Africa) Symphony orchestra, late L.S.O. and Covent Garden Opera House."

— HORSFALL, FRANK: (contemporary) Solo flutist with the Pacific Northwest Symphony.

— HOSMER, JAMES: (contemporary) Flutist with the Metropolitan Opera, New York.

HOTTETERRE, LOUIS: (1645-1740) French flutist, composer, inventor and member of a family of famous musicians and instrument makers.

HOWARD, ALBERT A.: (c.1860) American flutist and author of The Aulos or Tibia (Boston, 1893).

— HOWARD, LUELLA: (contemporary) Studied at the Eastman School of Music. Was solo flutist with the Hollywood Bowl Orchestra for two seasons under Stokowski and after that with one of the major motion picture studios in Hollywood.

HOWE, CHARLES: (c.1850) American flutist and teacher by correspondence. He was the author of *All About the Flute* (Columbus, Ohio, 1898).

HUDSON, ELI: (1877-1923) Member of the Royal College of Music and soloist of the London Symphony orchestra. Also teacher at the Royal Military School of Music in London; was badly wounded in World War I.

HUGOT, A.: (1761-1803) French flutist and composer of some fine etudes. (See biography.)

HUGUES, LUIGI: (1836-1913) Professor of geography at the University of Torino, Italy. Was an excellent flutist and composed about 200 works for the flute and chamber music. Wrote much religious music also.

—HULLINGER, WILLIAM E.: (1898-) Los Angeles flutist and teacher and at one time member of the Los Angeles Symphony, Los Angeles Philharmonic and the Hollywood Bowl orchestra.

—HUSTANA, LUIS: (contemporary) Hollywood flutist of Spanish extraction.

—HUSTED, ARTHUR: (contemporary) American flutist from Toledo, Ohio.

IMMYNS, JOHN: (c.1764) English attorney-at-law, born in London. Was an expert collector of ancient music and lutist of the Royal chapter in London and played exceptionally well flute, violin, viola di gamba and cembalo.

—IULA, ROBERT PAUL: (c.1915-) Young American flutist and permanent conductor of the Baltimore "pop" concerts of sixty-piece orchestra. He was playing solo flute in the Peabody Institute Symphony orchestra at twelve years of age and at sixteen was conducting the Park Little Symphony orchestra. In 1932 Iula was director of the Civic Summer Symphony at Carlins Park and in 1939 organized the Stadium Civic Summer Symphony.

—JACKSON, G.: (contemporary) English. Principal flute of the Royal Philharmonic orchestra and pupil of the late Albert Fransella. Experienced Player with wide knowledge of the symphonic repertoire. He was, originally, principal flute of the L.P.O. and eight years with the BBC Symphony orchestra.

JAMES, VICTOR S.: (c.1890-) Flutist, teacher and dealer in flutes, and flute music in Wellington, New Zealand.

JACQUES, GEORGE AUGUSTUS: (1868-) Flutist member of the Society of Musicians, London, England.

JAURRET, ANDRÉ: (contemporary) First-prize winner at the National Conservatory of Paris in 1931. He is a flute instructor at the Zurich Conservatory.

JENSEN, NIELS PETER: (1802-1846) Blind from infancy he

243

studied with Kuhlau and became an excellent flutist, organist and composer. From 1828 he was organist at the Saint Peter church and composed sonatas, variazioni, fantasie, studies, duetti, etc., for flute and music for piano and for the theatre, published by Ricordi, Milano. Jenson was born and died in Copenhagen.

JENZSCH, ERNEST: (1829- ?) Flute virtuoso and teacher of great reputation. He was born in Dresden, Germany, but taught in Paris, Breslau, Colmari and 25 years at the Prague Conservatory of Music.

JESPERSEN-HOLGOR, GILBERT: (c. 1900-) Flute virtuoso and teacher residing in Copenhagen, Denmark. He played the solo part in the first performance in Paris, with the composer conducting, of Carl Nielson's Flute Concerto in 1928.

JOHNSON, BRITTON: (contemporary) Solo flutist with the Baltimore Symphony.

JONES, C. L.: (contemporary) English. "With the BBC Theatre orchestra. A most versatile player who successfully combines flute, piccolo, bass clarinet and the saxophone."

JORDAN, MERRILL: (contemporary) Flutist with the San Francisco Symphony.

JOSEPH I, Emperor of Germany and King of Hungary: (1678-1711) Was passionately fond of the flute and played it well.

JUBAL: (?) According to legend, was the inventor of the "reed pipe."

JUNG, HERMANN: (1872-) German flutist and teacher at the "Kaiserlichen Musikschule" in Riga, Russia.

JUST, VICTOR: (contemporary) American flutist of younger generation residing in New York.

KAPLAN, PHILIP: (contemporary) American flutist from Brookline, Massachusetts. An unusual record for solo violin, solo flute and orchestra was issued in 1947. The composition is by Alan Hovhaness, a young American composer of Persian and Armenian ancestry, with the title *Tzaikerk* (Evening Song) in which Anahid Ajeman is the violinist, Kaplan the able flutist and the composer conducting.

KAUER, FERDINAND: (1751-1830) Bohemian flutist and composer.

KEETBAAS, DIRK: (contemporary) Solo flutist with the Toronto Symphony Orchestra. Toronto, Canada.

KELLER, KARL: (1784-1855) German flutist and composer.

KELLOGG, OAKLEY H.: (contemporary) Flute dilettante, member of the Cincinnati Flute Club.

KEPPEL, PERCY: (contemporary) English flutist of the Royal Italian Opera, London.

244

KIBURZ, JOHN: (contemporary) American flutist member of the St. Louis Symphony.

KINCAID, WILLIAM M.: (1897-) For more than one reason many of the talented young flutists are graduated from the Curtis Institute of Music. The first, and very important one, is that only talented players are admitted; the second reason, almost as important as the first, is that the tuition is gratis; and the last, but not the least, is the eminence and reputation of its flute teacher. Kincaid, comparatively young, has been with that famous institution, as well as solo flute with the Philadelphia Symphony, since 1921, more than twenty-five years at this writing! It will be interesting to know that another of Kincaid's hobbies is collecting flutes. The Glendale News Press of July 29, 1947, published the following:

> FLUTE COLLECTION Philadelphia—Flutes played by George Washington, Lord Byron and Dr. Johnson's Boswell are in the collection of William Kincaid, flutist of the Philadelphia Orchestra. Other notables of history who played the flute included Robert Louis Stevenson, Rousseau, Schopenhauer, Casanova, Cellini and Leonardo da Vinci.

KINDLER, C. CHRISTOPHER: (1830-1889) Danish flutist and composer.

KLEINSTUBER, CARL: (1816-1879) German solo flutist of the Royal Chapel, Dessau.

KLICPERA, EMANUEL: (1860-) Bohemian solo flutist of the Koniglich Deutschen Landestheater in Prague.

KLINGENBRUNNER, WILHELM: (c.1790) German flutist and composer.

KNORR, FREIHERR von: (c.1800) Baron Knorr was court secretary in Vienna and an unusually fine flute dilettante. Composed several variations for two flutes and other pieces.

KNOSING, GUSTAV: (1855-1889) German solo flutist of the court orchestra in Karlsruhe.

KNOWLAND, LILBURN M.: (1900-) American flutist. At the age of eight, sang in a professional quartet. At twelve, his father presented him with an old system flute with ivory head; and at sixteen he started playing professionally at a motion picture theatre. He played for two years before he could read music! Since 1947, he has taught flute and has held the position of second flute, piccolo, tenor saxophone and alto flute in the Kansas City Philharmonic orchestra.

KNOX, HARRY: (c.1875-1942) One of the most enthusiastic semi-

245

professional flutists anywhere. He was one of the founders, with Harry Baxter and William Hullinger, of the Los Angeles Flute Club. Also one of the founders and first president of the Flutists' Guild of Los Angeles. His daughter Edyth is one of the noted pianists and teachers in Los Angeles.

KOCH, CARL: (1854-) German solo flutist and chamber virtuoso of the Koniglichen Hoforchester in Stuttgart.

KOCK, RICHARD: (contemporary) Flutist and solo piccolo with the Indianapolis Symphony.

KOHLER, ERNESTO: (1849-1907) Flutist and composer of numerous works for the flute as well as an opera and several successful ballets given in St. Petersburg where he died. Was the son of Giuseppe Wenceslau. (See biography.)

KÖHLER, GIUSEPPE WENCESLAU: (1809-1878) Bohemian solo flutist, composer and teacher at the Collegio dei Nobili in Modena, Italy.

KÖHLER, HANS: (c.1860) German flutist and composer.

KOHLAR, OSKAR: (1861-) Solo flutist of the Tonhallen-Orchesters and teacher at the Musik-Akademie in Zurich, Switzerland.

KOHLERT, JULIUS: (1849-1894) Bohemian flutist. Resided and died in Budapest, Hungary.

KOHOUT, IGNATZ: (1855-) Bohemian flutist from Prague.

KONIG, PAUL VALENTIN: (1866-) German flutist, teacher, pedagogue and royal chamber musician in Dresden.

KONITZ, AUGUST: (1870-) German solo flutist of the opera orchestra and teacher at the Conservatory in Frankfort-on-the-Main.

KONY, C.: (c.1890-) English flute virtuoso and teacher residing in London.

KORAL, JOSEPH: (1859-1902) Bohemian solo flutist of the Royal Theatre and teacher at the Conservatory of Prague.

KOULOUKIS, NICHOLAS: (c.1880-) Greek flutist and composer of several orchestral works. Was solo flutist of the Cincinnati and New York Philharmonic Symphony orchestras for many years. Now living in New York.

KRAKAMP, EMANUELE: (1813-1883) Noted flutist, composer and pedagogue, was born in Palermo, Sicily, February 3. He studied with his father who was a band master and was able to play with great virtuosity. Concert tours followed through Messina, Catania, Malta, the United States, Mexico, Canada, and the Antilles. Later he became conductor of the 92nd band at Corfu, Greece; and in 1841, returned to Naples to devote his

246

life to teaching and composing. Krakamp was the first in Italy to adopt the Boehm flute for which he wrote numerous compositions, including a grand Méthode. Later he adopted the Boehm system also for other woodwind instruments and wrote excellent instruction books for clarinet, oboe and bassoon. He died in Naples.

KRAMER, AUGUST: (1858-) German solo flutist and teacher at the Conservatory in Hamburg.

KRANTZ, LOUIS ADOLPH: (1846-1903) German flutist and composer. Was teacher at the Conservatory in Ghent, Belgium, where he died.

KRASSNOKUTZKY, N.: (18?-) Russian flutist from St. Petersburg.

KREITH, CARL: (? -1890) Austrian flutist and composer from Vienna.

KRELL, JOHN: (contemporary) Flutist with the Washington, D. C., Symphony.

KRETSCHMANN, WILHELM: (1848-1923) German solo flutist of the Imperial Theatre in Moskau, Russia, and teacher in that Conservatory.

KRETZCHMAR, MAX: (1852-1898) German solo flutist of the Opera Orchestra and teacher at the Conservatory of Frankfurt-Main.

KRUEGER, OTTO E.: (contemporary) At one time solo flutist of the Detroit Symphony and conductor and soloist for many years of the The News radio orchestra. He studied first with Hean Van Der Velpen of Detroit and Alfred Quensel in Chicago.

KRUGER, GOTTLIEB: (1790-1868) German solo flutist of the Royal Chapel, composer and chamber musician in Stuttgart.

KRUGER, KARL: (1831- ?) Solo flutist, chamber musician, composer and professor at the conservatory in Stuttgart. Was the son of Gottlieb.

KUERSTEINER, W. B.: (contemporary) Flute virtuoso and member of the Louisville Flute Club, Louisville, Kentucky.

KUHLAU, FRIEDRICK: (1786-1832) German flutist, composer of numerous flute works as well as many operas, and musical director in Kopenhagen, Denmark. Kuhlau is called the Beethoven of the flute. (See biography.)

KUHLAU, GUSTAV ALBERT: (1854-1903) Swedish flutist from Uddvalla. Lived for many years in New York and died there.

KUHN, LOUIS: (1819-1883) German flutist and royal chamber musician in Hanover.

KUKULA, ROMAN: (1851-1908) Austrian solo flutist of the Royal orchestra, the Royal Chapel and teacher at the Conservatory in Vienna.

KUMMER, KASPAR: (1795-1870) Austrian flutist and composer. Was also in the orchestra of the Ducal Chapel at Coburg, Germany, and twenty years later, on the retirement of Drouet, he was raised to the position of Kapellmeister.

KUPETZKY (or KUPEZKY) JOHANN: (1667-1740) Noted painter and enthusiastic flute dilettante was born at Posing, near Pressburg. He studied painting with Klaus for three years, after which he went to Italy where he resided for 22 years. Returning to Germany he was made painter to the Emperor Joseph I. At one time, in spite of the Emperor's protection, he was accused of heresy and to escape the Inquisition he withdrew secretly from Vienna and settled at Nurnberg where he died after a few years of peace, painting and flute playing.

KURTH, ALBERT: (1857-) German flutist from Niellebenhalle, who resided in Berlin and composed a few pieces for flute and piano.

KYLE, JOHN A.: (c.1860) American flute virtuoso.

LA BARRE, MICHEL DE: (1675-1743) French flutist and composer.

LA FALCE, PHILLIP: (contemporary) New York flutist of Italian extraction and member of the New York Flute Club.

LAFLEURANCE, EDOUARD: (1836-1897) French solo flutist of the Grand Opéra and the Concerts du Conservatoire.

LAFLEURANCE, LEOPOLD: (1865-) Like his uncle Edouard, he was solo flute with the Société des Concerts du Conservatoire and the Grand Opéra. Also teacher at the Paris Music School.

LAHOU, JEAN FRANCOIS JOSEPH: (1789-1847) French flutist and composer who resided and died in Brussels, Belgium.

LAMBERT, JEAN HENRY: (c.1700-1777) A distinguished French mathematician, philosopher and enthusiastic flute dilettante. He lived in Berlin for a number of years and is the author of *Observations sur les Flutes* and other interesting writings pertaining to the flute.

LA MONACA, JOSEPH: (1873-) Italian flutist, composer and conductor. Was for nearly thirty years member of the Philadelphia Symphony and appointed permanent conductor of the Ocean City's Municipal Orchestra in April, 1946. He was born in Noicattaro (Bari) Italy.

LANIER, SIDNEY: (1842-1881) American poet and solo flutist of the Peabody Symphony orchestra in Baltimore. (See biography.)

LAUBENDER, JOSEPH: (1869-) German solo flutist of the Royal

Chamber music and Royal Theatre in Hanover, Riga and Hamburg.

LAUCELLA, NICOLA: (1877-) Italian flutist and composer of some orchestral works, an opera and wood-wind chamber music. Was for many years a member of the New York Philharmonic and also solo flutist of the Metropolitan Opera. Has resided in New York since the beginning of this century.

LAURENT, GEORGES: (1886-) French solo flutist of the Boston Symphony for nearly twenty-five years and teacher at the New England Conservatory of Music, Boston. He is also the founder and director of the Boston Flute Club.

LAURET, SIMON: (1808-1890) French flutist born in Orleans and died in Marseilles.

LAX, FREDERICK: (1858-1920?) English flutist and composer of a flute school. Was solo flute with many prominent bands in America.

LEATHER, FITZHERBERT: (contemporary) American flutist member of the Seattle Flute Club.

LEDUC, ALPHONSE: (1804-1868) Prolific French composer of over 1300 pieces for piano and other instruments and the founder of the noted music publishing firm of that name; was also an expert player of bassoon, guitar, violin and flute. He composed no less than 38 pieces for the flute. Leduc was born at Nantes and died in Paris.

LEMAIRE, ALFRED: (1842-) French flutist and composer. Was director of a military band of the Shah of Persia for many years.

LEMATTE, EUGENE FERDINAND: (1856-) French "Officier de l'Instruction Publique" and member of the Opéra Comique orchestra in Paris. Also flute instructor of the Lycée Louis Legrand and Lycée Montaigne in Paris.

LEMMONÉ, JOHN: (1862-1949) Australian flutist, composer and impresario. One of the most beloved artists ever produced by that country, he made his debut on the same concert with Madame Nellie Melba with whom he was associated ever after. Lemmoné was held in such esteem by her that she bequeathed him a trust fund when she passed on a few years ago. His father was of Greek ancestry and his mother English. (See biography.)

LEMOU, GUSTAV: (1828-1877) French solo flutist for a long time with the Théâtre Dejazet in Paris.

LENNIG, EDWIN: (contemporary) Flutist with the Detroit Symphony.

LEONOFF: (contemporary) Russian flutist residing in Moscow.

249

— LE ROY, RENÉ: (1898-) French flutist. Succeeded Philippe Gaubert who was one of his flute teachers, as soloist of the Société des Instruments à Vent. Le Roy founded the Quintette Instrumentale de Paris. After residing a few years in America, Le Roy decided to return to France in 1950.

— LEVY, HERBERT: (contemporary) Flutist and solo piccolo with the Pittsburgh Symphony.

LEVY, JOSIAH: (contemporary) Australian semi-professional flutist, member of the Glendale Symphony of which Scipione Guidi is conductor. Levy's wife is concert master and her sister, Mabel Crowell is in the flute section. Levy died suddenly in his office on June 14, 1950.

LEWIN, M.: (contemporary) Russian flutist also residing in Moscow.

LEWIS, HAROLD: (contemporary) Young American flutist located in Hollywood, California.

LEWIS, LOUIS: (contemporary) Another young American flutist located in Glendale, California, and member of the Symphony of Dallas, Texas. He is also an enthusiastic student of chemistry and a medical student.

LICHTENSTEIN, ALFRED: (c.1890-) German flute virtuoso whose recitals with the assistance of Dr. Felix Gunther and Alfred Wilde proved of unusual artistic interest.

LIEBESKIND, GEORGE GOTTHELF: (1732-1800) German flutist from Allenburg; died in Anspach, Franconia.

LIEBIG, GUSTAV: (1843-) German solo flutist of the Royal Chamber Music and Royal Chapel in Berlin.

— LIEGL, ERNEST: (1899-) American flutist of great talent. For a number of years a member of the Minneapolis Symphony and solo flutist with the Chicago Symphony. He is now with a Chicago radio station.

— LINDEN, ANTHONY: (contemporary) American solo flutist. At various times associated with the Minneapolis, San Francisco and Los Angeles Philharmonic Symphony orchestras. Now with a Hollywood motion picture studio.

LITTLE, HELEN MEAD: (contemporary) Popular American flutist of Los Angeles, California. She was also a member of the Los Angeles Philharmonic and the Hancock Ensemble.

LOBE, JOHANN CHRISTIAN: (1797-1881) German flutist, composer and writer.

LOEILLET, JEAN BAPTISTE: (1680-1728) French flutist and harpsichordist of eminence and excellent composer for both instruments.

250

LOEWE, GABRIEL HEINRICH: (?-1864) German solo flutist of the Royal Chapel in Dresden.

LOGIER, JOHANN BERNARD: (1777-1848) This famous organist, pianist, composer, conductor and inventor of the *chiroplast*, a mechanism to train the hands for piano playing, made his debut as a precocious flutist at the age of ten. He was also the inventor of a new system of teaching. He was born in Kassel, Germany, and died in Dublin where he lived for many years.

— LONGHI, LUIGI: (1872-) Italian solo flutist of La Scala Theatre, Milano, and teacher at the Conservatory.

LONGO, FRANCESCO: (1884-1932) One of Italo Piazza's finest flute students at the Naples Conservatory. He was also an excellent pianist. Longo was born in Rutino, Salerno, and died in New York.

LOOTS, JEAN: (1875-) Belgian solo flutist at the Theatre de la Monnaie in Brussels.

— LORA, ARTHUR: (1903-) Formerly solo flutist of the Metropolitan Opera House, New York. Succeeded Georges Barrère as teacher at the Juilliard School of Music, New York. Also solo and ensemble work.

LORENTZ, ALFRED: (1872-1931) Flutist, conductor and composer. Studied flute with Rucquoy and Taffanel and at one time was flutist with the Baden Baden orchestra. From 1899 to 1925 was court director at Karlsruhe and composed the operas *Der Monch von Sendomir*, *Die Beiden Automaten*, *Liebesmacht* and the operetta *Die Mondscheindame*. Lorentz was born in Strassburg, Alsace, and died in Karlsruhe, Germany.

LORENZONI, DR. ANTONIO: (c.1700-?) A flute virtuoso and composer of great merit. Several of his works on the flute and also a *History of Music* may be found in the library of the Liceo Musicale di Bologna, State Library of Berlin and Museo Storico Musicale of Trieste. Lorenzoni was born in Montecchio Maggiore and in 1779 was living in Vicenza.

LOVREGLIO, DONATO: (1845?-1907) Italian flutist and composer of orchestral and band works.

LOWECKE, RICHARD: (1862-) German flutist and Grand-Ducal court musician; also member of the Imperial Theatre.

LUENING, OTTO: (1900-) American composer, flutist, teacher, and conductor. His numerous works are for orchestra, chamber music, choral and a concertino for flute with harp, celesta and strings. Also an opera, *Evangeline*, in four acts.

251

LUFSKY, MARSHALL P.: (contemporary) Was flute soloist with Sousa's band for a number of years and also connected with some record-making companies.

LUTHER, DR. MARTIN: (1483-1546) German religious reformer and translator of the Bible. Composed numerous hymns and played flute assiduously.

→ MCLAY, B.: (contemporary) English. "A natural flutist. Principal with the BBC Variety orchestra."

→ MADSEN, G.: (contemporary) American flutist with the Boston Symphony.

MAGANINI, QUINTO: (1897-) American flutist and composer of Italian extraction. Among his numerous compositions are pieces for flute, chamber music for wind instruments, also for strings, and orchestral works and operas.

MAHAUT, ANTON: (c.1700) Author of *Nouvelle Méthode pour Apprendre en Peu de Temps à Jouer de la Flute Traversière* (Amsterdam, 1759).

MANCINELLI, ANDREA: (c.1740-1802) He lived for a few years in Paris then went to London the last few years of his life. In both cities he was considered a first class flutist and the five books of duets for two flutes were published in Paris by Sieber and in London by Longmann. He was born in Italy and died in England.

MANIGOLD, JULIUS: (1873-) German Ducal chamber musician, teacher and composer of many flute pieces including a concerto with orchestra.

→ MANN, WALLACE W.: (contemporary) American solo flutist of the National Symphony, Washington, D. C.

MAQUARRE, ANDRÉ: (1875-1936?) French flutist and composer of wood-wind chamber music, etc. At various times solo flutist for the Boston Symphony, Philadelphia Symphony and Los Angeles Philharmonic Symphony orchestras. Was also member of the Société des Auteurs Compositeurs in Paris. He died in France.

MAQUARRE, DANIEL: (1881-) Brother of André and at various times flute teacher at the New England Conservatory, Boston, and member of the Boston Symphony, New York Philharmonic and solo flutist for the Philadelphia Symphony. He returned to France many years ago.

→ MARIANO, JOSEPH: (1911-) American flutist of Italian extraction. He is flute teacher at the Eastman School of Music and soloist of the Rochester Philharmonic Symphony. He was born in Pittsburgh, Pennsylvania.

MARINI-PORTI COUNT LUIGI: (1803-1886) Italian dilettante of great virtuosity and composer of many flute works.

252

MARKL, ALOIS: (1856-) Austrian solo flutist of the Royal Chapel, Vienna.

MARSCHALL, HERMAN: (1839-1888) German solo flutist of the State Theatre in Frankfurt. Also violinist, pianist, choral director and composer of songs, etc.

MARSYAS: (B.C.) A Phrygian mythologic satyr who found Athena's discarded flute, challenged Apollo to a musical contest and was flayed alive. From his blood sprang the river Marsyas.

— MARTIN, MARILYN: (contemporary) Flutist with Spitalney's all-girl orchestra.

MARTIN, THEODOR: (1842-1868) French solo flutist of the Military Chapel of "Garde" in Paris.

MASCRET, JULES LOUIS: (1843-1895) French flutist, director of the State Chapel and teacher at the Music school in Cambrai-Nord.

MASI, COUNT COSIMO: (c.1850) A great patron of the arts, Count Masi was mayor of the city of Ferrara and a flute dilettante of note. It was he who initiated Gatti-Casazza at the age of 24 as the impresario or general manager of the Teatro Communale at Ferrara in 1893, a position which he occupied later at the Metropolitan Opera of New York for 27 years.

MASINI, GAETANO: (?c.1880) Ital-ian flutist and composer from Bologna.

MASUTTO, GIOVANNI: (1830-1894) Founder of the Instituto Musicale Trevigiano, Director of the Scuola Popolare di Musica a Venezia, conductor of the Concerto Instrumentale nell' Instituto Coletti, teacher and director of the Concerto dell' Orfanotrofio dei Gesuiti, noted musicologist and professor of the advanced flute class at the Convitto Nazionale Marco Foscarini. Masutto was born at Treviso and died in Venezia.

MATHEWS, JAMES: (1828-1901) English flutist, composer and president of the Birmingham Flute Society.

MATTAVELLI, S. B.: (?c.1870) Italian flutist and composer.

— MCKENNA, DANIEL J.: (contemporary) American flutist from Toledo, Ohio.

MCQUILLEN, W. C.: (1864-1948) A retired banker and an enthusiastic and able flute dilettante. The numerous readers of *The Flutist* some twenty years ago remember him well for the interesting articles he wrote from so many foreign countries in which he mingled the pleasure of traveling and attending interesting concerts wherever possible. McQuillen was the proud possessor of a wooden flute made for him by his friend George Haynes in 1900. The workman-

253

ship is remarkable and there isn't a sign of a crack anywhere. McQuillen lived in a hotel but he also maintained an office where he kept the mementoes of flutes and flutists and his travel experiences and where he played his flute every day. Here, too, his friends came to visit, reminisce, play duets, etc. McQuillen was born in Cleveland, Ohio; lived sixty-three years in Los Angeles, and was also one of the first presidents of the Los Angeles Flute Club. He died in Los Angeles in 1948.

MECHLER, STEPHAN: (1867-) German royal court flutist and member of the Royal Court Chapel in Stuttgart.

MEDICUS, EMIL: (1881-) American flutist, teacher, writer and editor for many years of *The Flutist*, a magazine devoted entirely to the flute. Author of "Systematic Flute Instruction."

MEINEL, FRIEDRICH AUGUST: (1827-1902) Studied violin, piano and flute in his youth and later perfected himself under the world famous A. B. Furstenau, becoming a great performer and teacher on the flute.

MENDOZA, AUGUSTINE: (contemporary) Mexican flutist; at one time member of the Cincinnati Symphony.

MERCY, LOUIS: (c.1735) English flutist and composer, died in London.

MEYER, AUGUSTO PAULO DUQUE ESTRADA: (1846- ?) Eminent Brazilian flutist and teacher who, in 1888, "O governo do Imperio agaciou-o com a fita de cavalleirio do Ordem Rosa" and who in 1902 became director of the Conservatory introducing important changes. He studied flute with the Dutch flutist-composer Reichert for whom Pedro De Assisi in his *Manual do Flautista* exhausts all his superlatives by calling him "divine Belgian Flutist," "incomparable flute virtuoso who never had a rival in the whole world," etc. De Assisi assures us that Duque Estrada Meyer is undoubtedly the most glorious pupil of Reichert and furnishes us with a list of the most extraordinary gold medal pupils who graduated from the Instituto Nacional de Musica where Estrada Meyer was the flute professor; here it is: "Sao os seguintes flautistas brasileiros que fizeran o curso do Instituto, sob a mossa direccao, alcancando o primeiro premio medalha de ouro em concurse:"

Em 1911, *Agenor da Bens;*
Em 1912, *Antenor Guimaraes;*
Em 1913, *Jose Joaquim de Andrade Neves,* professor do Conservatorio, de Porto Alegre, capital do Estado do Rio Grande do Sul;
Em 1916, *Enclydes da Silva Novo,* professor do Conserva-

254

torio de Fortaleza, capital do Estado do Ceara;

Em 1917, *Pedro Vieira Goncalves*, professor da Escola Arcangelo Corelli;

Em 1918, *Indalicio Franca da Fonseca*;

Em 1919, Capitao da Policia Milita do Estado do Rio de Janeiro, *Antonio Teixeira da Costa Guedes*;

Em 1920, *Jose Passidomo*;

Em 1921, *Joao Cesario Camargo*, sargento-mestre da banda de policia desta Capital;

Em 1922, *Fausto Assumpcao*;

Em 1923, *Maocyr Goncalves Liserra*.

In order to illustrate that South America is not a bit behind our North America, flutistically speaking, I will include another list of excellent flute virtuosos and what De Assisi calls *eminent dilettanti*, mostly graduated from the same Instituto Nacional de Musica of Rio de Janeiro and to each of whom he devotes a short biography:

ABDON, JULIEN BOURGEOIS: Enthusiastic dilettante of French ancestry.

ADALBERTO DE ASSISSIS ROSELIER: Talented dilettante who also studied with Philippe Gaubert.

DR. ADRIANO CARLOS HENRIQUES DIAS BROCOS: Enthusiastic flute dilettante of merit.

AGENOR BENS: Noted Brazilian flutist and composer for his instrument.

ALBERTO GUARISCHI: Young flutist of merit graduated from the Institute National.

ALCIDES FLORES LEGEY: Enthusiastic flute dilettante of merit.

ALFREDO AMARAL: Semi-professional flutist of considerable merit.

DR. ALFREDO LOUREIRO BERNARDES: Scientist, attorney-at-law and enthusiastic flute dilettante.

ALFREDO MANOEL DE AZEVEDO: Secretary in the military school and a good flutist.

DR. ALLYRIO LOPES: Flute dilettante of talent and great enthusiasm.

ATHOS DUQUE ESTRADA MEYER: Flutist of great merit and son of professor Duque Estrada.

ALVARO DO AMARAL BRITTO SANCHES: Banker and flute dilettante of great merit.

DR. ALVARO DE CASTRO: Physician of note and enthusiastic flute dilettante.

ALVARO MONTEIRO LAZARO: Wealthy business man and flute dilettante of great merit.

ALVARO TAVARES DE LACERDA: Brazilian flutist, composer and conductor of fame.

AMERICO MARTINS COELHO DA SILVA: Business man and enthusiastic flute dilettante.

255

ANTONIO BRANCO DE MIRANDA FILHO: Very able flutist of note, born in Sao Paulo.

CAPTAIN ANTONIO DA COSTA GUEDES: Chief of military police, flute virtuoso and composer of band music.

ANTONIO JOSE RODRIGUES DE MORAES: Official of the post office and flute dilettante of merit.

DR. ANTONIO LOPES DE AZEVEDO: Civil engineer, excellent musician and flutist of great ability.

ANTONIO MARTINS VIANNA: Well known and able clarinetist, flutist and composer.

ANTONIO MOREIRA: Flutist of wide orchestral experience.

ANTONIO DE OLIVEIRA PORTO JUNIOR: Flutist of great ability whose many tours are still remembered.

ANTONIO SALITURO: Flutist of great and unusual talent who died in 1923 at 19 years of age.

ANTONIO DOS SANTOS VIERIRA: An excellent orchestral flutist who is now in the asylum "Joao Alfredo."

DR. ANTONIO DO AMARAL VIERIRA: An illustrious flute dilettante of note of Sao Paulo.

ARMANDO DE KERGAZ MARQUES OLIVEIRA: Flutist of note from the conservatory of Porto Alegro.

DR. ARTHUR TOLENTINO DA COSTA: Illustrious flute dilettante, pupil of Duque Estrada Meyer.

ARLINDO SODOMA DA FONSECA: Professor at the "Escola Normal" and flute dilettante of note.

AUBIERGIO MOREIRA DA COSTA: Brazilian flutist of note from Pernambuco.

AURELIANO DE AZEVEDA: Dealer in pianos and an enthusiastic flute dilettante.

(For 19 pages of the *Manual do Flautista*, every first name of each flutist begins with an A—Antonio in the majority. It includes also the author's great and venerated friend, Augusto Duque Estrada Meyer. Now we proceed.)

BERNARDINO PEREIRA: Flute dilettante and business man residing in Bello Horisonte.

CANDIDO FILHO: Noted flutist and composer from Pernambuco.

BERTINO MORALES DE MELLO: Famous business man and flute dilettante from Boa Esperanza.

CARLOS DINIZ: Young and talented flutist from Pernambuco.

CARLOS JATAHY: Proprietor of a typographical establishment and flute dilettante.

CLOVIS MARTINS: The son of one of the most prominent families of Sao Paulo; is a flute dilettante.

COARACYARA PEREIRA: Student at a military school and enthusiastic flute dilettante.

DR. DAVID GUEDES: Well known dentist and excellent flute dilettante.

DEOCLECIANO PEREIRA DE GOES: Young flute dilettante pupil of the Instituto Nacional de Musica.

DOMINGOS RAIMUNDO: Young flutist, pianist and well versed in theory.

DR. DOMINGOS VALENTINO: Well known dentist and enthusiastic flute dilettante.

DORGIVAL FALLETTI: Banker and flute dilettante of ability.

DOURIVAL GOMES: Young public official and flute amateur.

EUCLIDES DA SILVA NOVO: Well known Brazilian flute virtuoso and composer of sacred music.

EDGARD PEREIRA DOS SANTOS: Student of the classes of solfeggio and flute, with considerable talent.

EMILIO BRAGA: Public official and amateur flutist from Cachoeiras de Itapemirim (Esperito Santo).

CAPTAIN FAUSTO CONZAGA: Poet, chemist, composer and enthusiastic amateur flutist from Parahyba.

FRITZ SCHOTT: Official of a German electrical company and an excellent flute amateur.

FREDERICO MAURY: Director and proprietor of the Almanack Commercial and talented flute amateur.

FAUSTO ASSUMPCAO: Talented gold medal flute student from the Instituto Nacional.

FRANCISCO MANOEL DE CASTRO: Extremely talented flutist also from the Instituto Nacional.

GERVASIO DE CASTRO: Noted flutist and director of several motion picture theatres.

GUILHERME AGOSTINHO PEREIRA: Noted flutist, public official and director of Centro Musical.

GUIOMAR DE OLIVEIRA: Extremely fine young woman flutist who has performed in many concerts.

HENRIQUE SANCHES: Noted Spanish flutist who made his home in Rio de Janeiro.

HERACLITO CARDOZO: An ambitious student of flute, solfeggio, theory and voice (baritone).

IGNACIO MORAES DE MELLO: Excellent flute amateur from Rio Bonito, suburb of Rio de Janeiro.

INDALICIO FRANCA FONSECA: Talented gold medal flute student of the 1917 class.

DR. IVO PAGANI: Attorney, scientist

257

and an excellent flutist from a family of famous musicians.

JOAO JUPYACARA XAVIER: Captain of defense and an extremely fine flute composer.

JOAQUIM ANTONIO DOS PASSOS BARROSO: Famous Brazilian flute virtuoso and composer.

JOAQUIM ARISTOTELES: Young Brazilian flutist and composer.

DR. JOSE ALBERTO PIRES: Public official and flute dilettante.

DR. ANTONIO DA SILVA CALLADO: Flute professor at the Imperial Conservatorio of Rio de Janeiro.

JOSE PASSIDOMO: Noted Italian flutist student of the Institute National de Rio de Janeiro.

DR. JEFFERSON VALENTE: Well known dentist and enthusiastic flute amateur.

JOAO CESARIO DE MARAGO: First sergeant in the military band and gold medal flute student of 1919.

JOAO DAMASCENO CALLADO RODRIGUES: Brazilian flute virtuoso of the first order.

JOAO DOLABELLA DA SILVA: Agricultural banker and an excellent flute dilettante.

DR. JOSE PACHECO DE MADEIROS: Distinguished flute amateur from Sao Pedro de Muriahe.

DR. JOSE FELICIANO DE ARAUJO: Illustrious doctor and flute dilettante of unusual merit.

DR. JOSE HENRIQUE MARTINS DE OLIVEIRA: Official in the Treasury Department and flute amateur.

JOVENTINO DA SILVA BORGES: Official of the Central Railroad of Brazil and flute amateur.

JULIO HORTA BARBOSA: Public official and flute dilettante of much ability.

JULIO O. GRAO: Gold medal flutist from the Conservatorio de Porto Alegro.

LAFAYETTE PALMEIRA: Amateur flutist from Bella Venez Americana: now residing in Rio de Janeiro.

LOURIVAL RIBEIRO COELHO: Flute dilettante from Victoria, Espirito Santo, now in Rio de Janeiro.

LYDIO PURPURARIO SANTIAGO DE OLIVEIRA: Flutist and orchestra director from Pernambuco.

MARIA JOSE DE BRITO BECKER: Gold medal woman flutist (class of 1899) of great talent.

MANOEL DE OLIVEIRA BARBOSA: Highly esteemed in the Federal district and flute amateur.

MANOEL MARCELLINO DO VALLE: Flute virtuoso born in 1839. Studied with Reichert and loved Kuhlau's compositions in particular.

MARIO CAPELLO BARROSO: In the Federal Tribunal; an enthusiastic flute amateur.

258

MANOEL DO CARMO: Flute virtuoso and public official in Ruy Barbosa.

DR. MARIO VASCONCELLOS: Well known doctor and flute dilettante of fine talent.

MANOEL DE OLIVEIRA BIENTENDODOS: Silversmith and flute virtuoso; born in 1804—and highly esteemed in the Federal District.

MANOEL RODRIGUES: Talented flute student of the Institute National.

MARIO CARDOSO DE OLIVEIRA: Journalist with a great flutistic talent; died suddenly in 1921.

MARIO NOGUEIRA DA GAMA: Commercial traveler and talented flute amateur.

MOACYR GONCALVES LISERRA: The son of a high government official and a flutist of great talent.

MANOEL TARGINO LEOPOLDINO DOS SANTOS: Distinguished flutist from Nazareth, near Pernambuco.

MANOEL PORCIUNCULA: One of the most illustrious flutists of Brazil from Venezia Americana.

MOYSES BRANDAO MARTINS: Young Brazilian flutist of fine talent.

NELSON DIAS DE AGUIAR: Young and intelligent flute student of the Instituto Nacional.

NELSON SILVERIO DE SOUZA: Fourteen year old flute student of much promise.

MERIGGIOLI, GLAUCO: (1872-1941) Italian band master and solo flutist of the St. Paul and Seattle Symphony orchestras. Died in Italy.

MERTZ, JOHANN GASPAR: (1806-1856) Extremely popular teacher and famed guitar virtuoso; was also a fine performer on the mandoline, cello and flute. He was born in Pressburg-Bratislavia and died in Vienna, Austria.

MESSINA, JOSEPH: (1873-1942) Italian flutist and splendid musician; self-taught. He was a chum of mine in my early youth and inspired me to study seriously. Messina abandoned the flute professionally because of other business, but continued to play his much beloved flute until he died, in Vicksburg, Mississippi, where he was held in great esteem.

MICHAILOFSKY, IVAN DMITREWITSCH: (c.1880-) Russian solo flutist to whom Ernesto Koehler's Concerto Op. 97 is dedicated.

MICHEL, GEORG: (1775-1835) German flutist and composer; died in Russia.

MIGNOLET, JEAN: (c.1880-) Belgian Consul and an excellent flute dilettante.

MIGNONE, ALFERIO: (c.1870-) Italian flutist and teacher at the Conservatory of Sao Paulo, Brazil, where he resided the greater part of his life, is highly esteemed

259

in that capital. He is the father of the famous Brazilian composer, Francisco Mignone (1897-) whose opera *Contractador does Diamantes* is well known in Europe and in South America. This composer, who also plays flute, is well known here, having conducted several of his orchestral works with different symphony orchestras all over this country. Alferio Mignone was born in Southern Italy.

MILLARD, ROBERT E.: (1882-) American flutist born in Milwaukee where he studied with Carl Woempner who, later, became solo flutist of the Minneapolis Symphony. He has been connected with several artistic institutions in Portland, Oregon.

MILLER, ALBERT E.: (contemporary) American flutist from Toledo, Ohio.

MILLER, DR. DAYTON C.: (1872-1942) American physicist, inventor, writer, flute dilettante and flute collector of over 1400 specimens. Besides a valuable book on acoustics, Dr. Miller has written *The Science of Musical Sound* and *List of Works Relating to the Flute.*

MILLER, EDWARD: (1731-1807) English flute and piano virtuoso and composer.

—MILLER, PAUL: (1900-) Pupil of Arthur Deming and Georges Barrère. Was with the El Paso Symphony, 1940-42; had a short tour

with Lily Pons in 1942. Since 1943, Miller has resided in Los Angeles.

—MILLION, ERNEST: (1871-) French solo flutist of the Colonne Orchestra in Paris.

MILLOCHER, KARL: (1842-1899) This talented operetta composer studied flute at the Conservatory of Vienna and at one time in his youth gave several flute recitals. He was born in Baden and died in Vienna.

MILLS, FREDERICK H.: (1857-1924) Enthusiastic flute amateur and member of the Boston Flute Club.

MEUNIER, ANDRÉ: (contemporary) Belgian flute virtuoso and teacher at the Conservatory of Vervière.

MINASI, NICOLA: (?c.1870) Italian flutist and composer. Wrote also a quartet for four flutes. Lived in England many years and died in London.

MITCHELL, ELEANORE: (contemporary) American flutist of considerable talent from Tulsa, Oklahoma. She studied at the Eastman School of Music and the Curtis Institute.

MOLE, CHARLES: (1857-1905) French flutist and composer of great reputation with the Boston Symphony. Died in New York.

MONONE, F.: (contemporary) Flutist of Italian ancestry and member of the Metropolitan Opera orchestra, New York.

260

MONTEUX, CLAUDE: (contemporary) Son of the eminent French conductor Pierre Monteux, has been engaged as solo flutist with the Kansas City Philharmonic by Efrem Kurtz, conductor of the Kansas City orchestra, for the 1946-1947 season.

MONZANI, TEOBALDO: (1762-1839) Italian flutist, oboist, composer, inventor and manufacturer of musical instruments. Was born in Modena and died in London, in which city he lived many years.

MOOR, WEYERT: (contemporary) Dutch solo flutist and orchestra manager of the Cleveland Symphony for many years. Now lives in Tujunga, California.

MOORE, GEORGE: (1870-1938) American flutist and active member of the Los Angeles Flute Club.

MOORE, LINTON B.: (c.1865-1929) Enthusiastic flute amateur who, when not in his prime, changed from the old flute to the Boehm system with considerable success. He was also president of the Los Angeles Flute Club.

MORALT, CARL: (1836-1901) German royal court musician and solo flutist of the Royal Court orchestra. Also teacher at the Royal Cadette-Corps in Munich.

MOREY, CAROLYN GRANT: (contemporary) at one time solo flutist with the New Orleans Symphony.

MORRIS, GARRET: (1920-) English. "Born at Cleverson, Somerset and first studied with Robert Murchie, later winning a scholarship to the Royal Academy of Music. Debut at Wigmore Hall, London, in 1940; since then has appeared regularly as a soloist, and in chamber music, both in public concerts and for the BBC. Appointed Professor of the Flute at the Royal Academy of Music in 1945." Mr. Foster considers Garret Morris "undoubtedly the next on the Roll after Arthur Gleghorn."

MORRIS, ROBERT: (contemporary) Flutist with the Cleveland Symphony.

MOSELL, EGISTO: (c.1800- ?) Flute and oboe virtuoso. His compositions for both instruments are good and beautifully written and his dramatic symphony *Ultima Battaglia* played in Florence in 1841, was considered an excellent orchestral work. It is not known where Mosell was born, but he was living in Florence in 1820.

MOYSE, MARCEL: (1889-) One of the most distinguished artists of France. Moyse was born May 17, 1889. He is professor of the flute at the Paris Conservatory, succeeding the brilliant Philippe Gaubert, who died in 1941, and also gives special courses at the Conservatories of Zurich, Geneva, and Lucerne. He is the author of 21 Studies for the flute

261

and is a Chevalier de la Legion d'Honneur. In 1932 he founded the famous Moyse Trio which is well-known in Europe through its concert tours. His daughter-in-law, Madame Blanche Honegger, a cousin of the famous composer, Arthur Honegger, is the violinist of the trio; and his son, Louis, who is also an excellent flutist and composer, is the pianist. Louis Moyse has recently (1947) written a *Suite of seven Caprices* for flute and piano, two of which have been recorded in London by the Phonograph Company.

Marcel Moyse won the grand prize for records in 1932 with the concerto in D by Mozart and the Moyse Trio, the grand prize with Trio, Sonata by Bach in G Major. Since 1937, because of his many activities, he no longer plays in an orchestra.

On one occasion, when Joachim Andersen was in Paris on a short visit and paying his respects to Taffanell at the Conservatory, it happened that young Marcel was taking his lesson and playing an Etude by Andersen. The famous flutist and composer said "Bravo! I didn't know that that Etude of mine could sound so beautiful."

The Moyse Trio at the end of 1947 completed a new and interesting series of records in London.

Marcel Moyse is known in this country not only through his records in solo and ensemble playing, but also because a number of excellent flutists have studied with him in Paris. In 1950 the Moyse Trio visited New York.

MULLER, AUGUST EBERHARD: (1767 1817) German solo flutist of the Concert Orchestra in Leipzig and composer. He died at Weimar.

MULLER, LOUIS: (1832-1889) German solo flutist of the Royal court Chapel in Stockholm, Sweden, where he died.

MULLER, WENZEL: (1802-1883) Bohemian flutist and teacher at the Conservatory of Prague.

MURCHIE, ROBERT: (1884-) Scotch solo flutist of the Queen's Hall Orchestra. Albert Fransella wrote a beautiful sketch on Murchie published in *The Flutist* of February, 1925.

NAZZI, CHRISTINE: (contemporary) American woman flutist with Michel Nazzi's *Chamber Music Concertante*, a group consisting of flute, oboe, violin, viola, cello and piano. She resides in New York.

NEEDHAM, VINCENT: (1856-1930?) English solo flutist of the Hans Richter Concerts of Manchester, Philharmonic Orchestra of Liverpool and teacher at the College of Music in Liverpool.

NESPORY, GUSTAV: (1875-) Bohemian solo flutist of the Philharmonic in Prague.

NEUHOFER, FRANZ: (1832-1887) German solo flutist of the Court Orchestra in Mannheim.

NEUHOFER, GEORGE: (1833-1898) German solo flutist of the Allgemeinen Musikgesellschaft in Basle, Switzerland, where he died. Was one of Boehm's numerous pupils.

NICHOLSON, CHARLES: (1795-1837) English flutist and composer of great prominence. Was professor of the Royal Academy of Music and principal at the Italian Opera in London. His father was also a successful flutist. (See biography.)

NIEHOFF, ANDREAS: (1856-) Russian solo flutist of the Imperial Opera Orchestra in St. Petersburg (now Leningrad). Studied there with Carl Wehner.

NIGRO, GIACOMO: (1848-1918) Italian flutist and teacher of most of the flute players of Viggiano-Potenza, including Leonardo and Joseph De Lorenzo, Joseph Messina, Amerigo Gagliardi, and many others.

NILLSON, CHRISTINE: (1843-1921) Famous Swedish operatic soprano, surnamed the "Swedish Nightingale" was an enthusiastic flute dilettante. She was born in Wexio and died in Stockholm.

— NIOSO, EMIL: (contemporary) American flutist, member of Minneapolis Symphony.

— NOACK, HARVEY: (contemporary) American solo flutist with the Chicago Symphony.

NORSTRAND, RAGNA: (contemporary) A Danish flute virtuoso and teacher from Copenhagen.

— NORTH, CHARLES: (?-1935?) American flutist member of several symphony orchestras.

OESTERLE, OTTO: (1861-1895) American flutist born in St. Louis and died in New York. Was solo flutist of the North American orchestra and teacher at the National Conservatory in New York.

OESTMAN, CARL ORIAN: (1866-) Swedish solo flutist of the Royal Opera and teacher at the Conservatory in Stockholm.

OLDS, REGINALD: (contemporary) President and owner of one of the world's finest band instrument factories, specializing in trombones. Olds is a patron of the arts and has been an amateur flutist for years. The famous factory which bears his name is located in Los Angeles where Olds was born.

OLSCHOWSKY, KARL: (1875-) Russian solo flutist of the State Theatre orchestra in Rostock.

OSTREICHER, WALTER: (c.1870-1941) Flutist and orchestra manager of the San Francisco Symphony for many years. He died in San Francisco.

OTT, SEBASTIAN: (1836-1870) German solo flutist of the Royal Court Theatre in Hanover.

263

Studied with Boehm at the same time as Rudolph Tillmetz and Carl Wehner. In 1906 in Cape Town, South Africa, I met the widow of Ott who had remarried and their daughter, Mrs. Hartman. From her I received a photograph of her father, five original letters of Boehm and other old documents.

OROPEZA, AUGUSTIN: (contemporary) Professor Oropeza is a flute virtuoso and teacher at the National Conservatory of Music, Mexico City, Mexico.

PAGANI, LUIGI: (c.1850) Italian flutist and composer who devised a flute on which he produced as low a note as F below the staff, that is, a full tone below the lowest G on the violin or our flute in G. His excellent *Quattro grandi studi di bravura*, long out of print, were published by Ricordi and had extra lines so they could be also played with the ordinary flute.

PAGANO, EMIL: (contemporary) Flutist with the New York Philharmonic.

PAGGI, ANITA: (contemporary) English flute virtuosa of Italian extraction and member of the London Flute Society.

PAGGI, G.: (c.1865) Italian flutist and composer. Died in London.

PAGNOTTI, ALFONSO (?-1930) Italian flutist and oboist pupil of Krakamp who resided many years in Sydney, Australia, where he died.

PAISIBLE: (c.1695) Nationality unknown. Flutist and composer. Died in London.

PAN: In Greek mythology, the god of shepherds and protector of flocks of herds, wild beasts and bees. Chief of the Satyrs and inventor of Syrinx or Pan's pipes; hence the word panic. He is represented as having two small horns and the lower limbs of a goat.

PANE, EFFISIO: (c.1800) We learn from Giulio Roberti's *La Cappella Regia di Torino*, 1515-1870, that the first time a flute was used in the Royal Chapel of Turin, Italy, was in 1814 and the flutist was Giovanni Grancesco Deponte. I am indebted to that very fine and cultured Brazilian flutist and teacher, Ferruccio Arrivabene, for the following pamphlets and books. Some are devoted entirely to the flute, its history, etc., and others give considerable space to our instrument: *La Cappella Regia di Torino*, 1515-1870, *O Materialism e a arte musical* by Th. Ortolan, *Appunti intorno al Flauto* by Cav. Prof. Riccardo Gandolfi, *Notizie intorno alla storia degli strumenti a fiarto in legno* by Giuseppe Prestini (Professore di oboe nel R. Instituto Musicale di Firenze), *Il Flauto*—cenno storico—by Francesco Squarzoni,

Manual do Flautista—Comentarios sobre diversos Conservatorios da Europa—by Pedro De Assis. This book, in Spanish, contains 326 pages. It is curious that the *organaro* and *cimbalaro*—old Italian for organist and cymbalist —Gioachino Concone, received the same stipend as the flutist Pane, 420 lire, for performing on two instruments. In 1824 two flutes were introduced for the first time. They were Effisio Pane and Camillo Romanino. Deponte's yearly salary was 420 lire or $84.00. Pane and Romanino's yearly salary was 1200 lire for the two of them or $240.00.

PANITZ, MURRAY W.: (contemporary) American flutist from Mount Rainier, Md. He studied at the Eastman School of Music and claims to have given the first performance of Norman Dello-Joio's Concertino for flute and orchestra with the Eastman Rochester Symphony Orchestra in 1945. However, Milton Wittgenstein of New York disclaims that statement. He says that the first performance of the Concertino was given by him with the WQXR orchestra in 1943.

PANORMO, FRANCESCO: (1764-1844) Italian flutist and composer. Died in London.

PANZINI, ANGELO: (1820-1886) Professor of harmony, counterpoint, and fugue at the conservatory of Milano, from which he graduated in piano and flute, having studied under Rabboni in the last-named instrument. Panzini was born at Lodi and died in Milano.

PAPPOITSAKIS, J.: (contemporary) Greek flutist; member of the Boston Symphony.

PARKER, EVALYN G.: (contemporary) A fine flutist and active member of the Columbus, Ohio, Flute Club.

PARKER, JOHN: (1848-1905) English flutist from Sunderland. Principal of the Concert Orchestra of North England.

PATHAK, VINOD: (contemporary) Hindu flutist, student at the University of Southern California. Pathak plays on a one-reed brass flute.

PATRONE, JAMES: (contemporary) Hollywood flutist of Italian extraction.

PAULI, G. de: (c.1865) Italian flutist and composer.

PAULMANN, KONRAD: (?-1473) Bavarian flute, violin and organ virtuoso at the service of the Royal Albert III of Munich.

PEACOCK, HARRIET WEST: (contemporary) Solo flutist of the Indianapolis Symphony since 1942. Studied first with George Madsen and Georges Laurent. Her formal education has included the New England Conservatory of Music, Butler University and two summers a member of the Institute of Tanglewood in the Berkshire Music Center. She belongs to the Zeta chapter of Sigma Alpha Iota and has played under the direction of Arthur Fiedler, Serge Koussevitzsky, Fabien Sevitzky and others. When not occupied with the Symphony, she does radio work in Boston and Springfield, Massachusetts.

PEICHLER, ANTONIO CLEMENTE: (c.1820) Spanish flutist and composer. His *Forty Etudes* are among the finest in the flute literature.

PENAS, JEAN BAPTISTE: (1828-1888) Although having a Spanish name, he was born in Metz, Germany, and died at Neuilly near Paris. Penas was flutist and director of a regiment band in Lyon, France.

PENVILLE, EDITH: (contemporary) English woman flutist of merit.

PERRAULT: (c.1670) Flutist and composer of unknown nationality.

PERCIVAL, SAMUEL: (1824-1876) English flutist and composer born in London and died in Liverpool.

PESCHEK, FRANZ: (1870-) German solo flutist of the Royal Chapel in Dresden and teacher in that Music School.

PESSARD, EMIL: (1843-1917) Played flute, double bass and timpani in various orchestras at the beginning of his career. Then became professor of harmony at the Paris Conservatory. Composed some flute pieces and a number of successful operas.

PETERSEN, JORGEN: (1827-1899) Danish solo flutist of the Royal Court Chapel in Copenhagen.

PETERSEN, PETER NICHOLAS: (1761-1830) German flutist and composer from Bederkesa-Hanover. Died in Hamburg.

PHARES, HALE: (contemporary) Flutist with the Detroit Symphony.

PHILBERT OR PHILIBERT: (c. 1650) French flutist, singer, mimic and gardener of great skill. Was favorite of Louis the Fourteenth.

PIACENZA, PASQUALE: (1816-1888) Composer of operas and operettas and author of musical subjects. He played bassoon and flute very well. Piacenza was born at Casale Monferrato and died in Pistoia.

PIATTI, BORTOLO: (c. 1820-1897) Opera impresario, correspondent of the *Gazzetta Musicale* of Milano, *maecenas* of Amilcare Ponchielli and solo flutist in the city orchestra of Cremona. He was born and died in that city.

PIAZZA, ITALO: (1860-) Italian flutist, composer, writer and teacher at the Naples Conservatory.

PICTON, ALFRED: (1870-) English solo flutist of the Scottish

266

orchestra in Glasgow and teacher at the Glasgow College of Music.

PIERONI, LEOPOLDO: (1847-1920?) Italian flutist, composer of numerous flute pieces and much music for small orchestra, and teacher at the Instituto Vittorio Emanuele in Florence.

PIZZO, VINCENZO: (c.1885-) Was born in Viggiano, Italy, and has been residing in New York for many years. He studied with several teachers including Professor Franceschini in Rome. His brother, Joseph, was for several years solo harpist with the New York Symphony.

PLOW, JAY: (1870-1943) American solo flutist of the Los Angeles Symphony and Los Angeles Philharmonic and prominent teacher. Studied with Joachim Andersen and Emil Prill.

PLUNDER, ANTON: (1829-1893) Bohemian flute virtuoso. Died in Dresden, Germany.

POPP, WILHELM: (1828-1903) German solo flutist of the Philharmonic Orchestra in Hamburg, court pianist in Coburg and composer of more than 500 flute compositions.

PORTRE, EUGENE: (contemporary) French solo flutist of the Garde Republicaine in Paris.

POSELLA, LEONARD: (c.1910-) Italian solo flutist of the Los Angeles Philharmonic. Of the many excellent solo flutists the

Los Angeles Philharmonic has had during the quarter-century of its existence, Posella is one of the finest. Now, 1947-8, he is back in the motion picture studios.

POSSELL, GEORGE L.: (contemporary) American flutist, at one time member of the New York Symphony.

POSSELL, SARAH L.: (Mrs. George L., contemporary) One of America's finest women flutists. Both she and her husband reside in New York City.

POTT, ERNST: (1849-) German Royal music director, flutist and conductor of the Royal Matrosen Division band in Berlin.

POWELL, VERNE Q.: (contemporary) American flutist who for a number of years has been devoting all his time to the making of flutes in Boston, Mass.

PRATTEN, ROBERT SIDNEY: (1824-1868) English flute virtuoso, composer, pianist and singer. His only flute lesson was given to him when he was seven years old by his brother Frederick, afterwards a celebrated double-bass player. Robert Sidney's first appearance in London as a solo player was at Covent Garden Theatre in a monster concert in Nicholson's *Twelfth Fantasia*.

PRENDIVILLE, HARRY: (c.1850) American, author of *Excelsior Method for the Flute* (Philadelphia, 1881).

PRETZ, GODFREY: (contemporary) American flutist and composer. His *Humoresque* for four flutes is well known.

PRILL, EMIL: (1867-1940) German solo flutist of the Royal Opera, composer and teacher at the Royal Court School of Music in Berlin. (See biography.)

PRITCHARD, BENSON: (contemporary) Solo flute with the South Side Symphony (Chicago) with which he performed A. B. Furstenau's Concertino.

PROBOST, FRANZ: (1870-   ) Austrian flutist of the Court Opera Orchestra and teacher at the Music and Opera School in Vienna.

PTOLOMAEUS, CLAUDIUS: (c.139 A.D.) Egyptian astronomer and geographer, was a flute dilettante.

PUCCI, SAVERIO: (c.1845-c.1895) Italian flutist and composer from Catanzaro. Died in Venice.

PUTNAM, BARBARA: (contemporary) Flutist with the Janssen Symphony of Los Angeles.

PUYANS, EMILIO: (1883-1930?) Cuban flutist and Consul from Puerto Plata. Was member of the New York Symphony and solo flutist of the San Francisco Symphony.

QUALEN, JOHN: (c.1900-   ) A motion picture artist with various studios in Hollywood, who is also a flute dilettante. At one time he toured in vaudeville in an act in which he played a flute solo written by himself.

QUANTZ, JOHANN JOACHIM: (1697- 1773) German flutist, inventor and composer of 300 concerti and 200 sonatas all written for his royal pupil Frederich II, King of Prussia. (See biography.)

QUENSEL, ALFRED: (1869-1947) Solo flutist of the Berlin Philharmonic and the Chicago Symphony for many years, also teacher and composer. Upon his retirement, he returned to Germany where he died.

QUESNAY, ALFRED: (1867-   ) Belgian solo flutist of the Concerts Populaire, teacher in the Conservatory in Lille and Director of Cercle Musical, le Club des Vingt.

RABBONI, GIUSEPPE: (1800-1856) One of the most outstanding and beloved of Italian flutists, composers and teachers was born at Cremona. He was solo flutist at La Scala Opera for thirty years and teacher at the Conservatory of Milan. He wrote numerous solos, duets, trios, as well as well as several books of beautiful studies. He died at Ravenna, near Milan.

RADCLIFF, JOHN: (1842-1918) English flutist, composer and inventor. Was solo flute of the Royal Italian Opera and professor at the Royal Academy of Music and Trinity College at London. Was born in Liverpool and died in London.

RADOUX, NICOLAS LIBERT: (1877-) Belgian flutist and teacher at the Conservatory of Ghent.

RAIMONDO, EMANUELE: (c.1870) Italian flutist and composer.

RALLO, ANGELO: (c.1920-) Studied flute at the Eastman School of Music, Rochester, New York, and at one time it appeared he would have a brilliant career. However, suddenly it was discovered that he was almost a genius in mathematics. Now, married, with children, he still enjoys playing flute very much, but . . . is professor of mathematics in one of the high schools there. Angelo once told me that, contrary to the majority of other students, he enjoys playing etudes on the flute more than solos.

··· RATEAU, RENÉ: (contemporary) American solo flutist of the Minneapolis Symphony of French ancestry.

RAUCH, ALFRED: (1840-) At first solo flutist and then conductor of the Garde Republicaine in Paris. Was born in Strassburg, Alsace-Lorraine.

RAULT, FELIX: (1736-1800) French flutist, bassoonist and composer.

RAVEL, ALFREDO: (c.1880-) In spite of his French name he is a southern Italian and a very able flutist on the old system flute. He was one of Creatore's most favorite flutists and has lived in America many years.

REBSOMEN, COLONEL: (c.1830) Was an accomplished French flute dilettante who, to replace the left arm that he lost in battle, constructed special instruments by means of which he produced his admirable flute. No one would have discovered, from his performance, that he had less than the usual number of fingers.

REDFERN, EDWARD BEEDON: (1837-1893) English solo flutist of the Philharmonic orchestra in Liverpool. He had his own flute school.

REDFERN, EDWARD STANLEY: (1866-) The son of Edward Beedon; solo flutist of the Royal Italian Opera Covent Garden in London.

REICHA, ANTON: (1770-1836) Bohemian prolific composer of symphonies, operas, oratorios, theoretical works and numerous chamber music compositions for strings, wood-wind and a quartet for four flutes. Reicha played second flute in the same orchestra where Beethoven played viola. Was also professor of counterpoint and fugue at the Paris Conservatory and enjoyed the friendship of Haydn, Albrechtsberger, Salieri, Beethoven and many others.

REICHERT, MATTHIEU ANDRÉ: (1830-1870?) Dutch flutist and composer. Born at Maastricht,

269

studied at the Brussels Conservatory and died in Brazil.

REMUSAT, JEAN: (1815-1880) French flutist and composer. Born in Bordeaux and died in Shanghai, China.

REINICKE, MAX: (1878-) German solo flutist of the Berlin Philharmonic.

RENZI, PAUL: (contemporary) Solo flutist with the San Francisco Symphony. Now (1949) with the NBC, New York.

RIBAS, JOSÉ MARIA DEL CARMINE: (1796-1861) Spanish artist of great merit on the flute, oboe, clarinet and concertina. He was at one time first flutist at the Opera in Lisbon and first clarinetist of the Philharmonic of Oporto where he was born. Lived many years in England and served under Wellington, and was present at the battle of Toulouse. Ribas pleased Mendelssohn very much with his masterly performance of the famous "Scherzo" of *Midsummer Night's Dream* music. Ribas composed many pieces for flute and piano, numerous duets for two flutes, some for flute and clarinet, a concerto for flute and orchestra and much other music. (See biography.)

RIBITSCH, FRANK: (c.1885-) Austrian flutist, at one time member of the Rochester Philharmonic Symphony and Eastman Theatre orchestra.

RIBOCK, J. J. H.: (1745?-1810?) German flute dilettante who attempted many improvements on the old flute. Was born and died in Luchow, Hanover.

RICHARDSON, JOSEPH: (1814-1862) Became professor of the flute at the Royal Academy of Music, London, after the death of his teacher, Nicholson, in 1837. Was one of the chief attractions at the Jullien Promenade Concerts in London. Played on a Siccama flute and composed some pieces for flute and piano.

RICHAUD, LEON HIPPOLYTE: (1861-) French solo flutist of the Lamoureux orchestra in Paris and teacher at the Conservatory in Avignon.

RICHTER, FRANCIS: (contemporary) American flutist and composer of *Scherzino* for four flutes.

RICHTER, MICHAEL A.: (contemporary) Flutist with the Baltimore Symphony.

RICHTER, OSKAR: (1852-) German solo flutist of the State Theatre in Mainz.

RIEDT, FRIEDRICH WILHELM: (1710-1783) German flutist and composer from Berlin.

RITTER, EMILE: (1842-) French solo flutist of the Grand Opera and professor at the Conservatory of Lyon.

ROBBILARD, WILFRID: (contemporary) Flutist with the Baltimore Symphony.

270

ROBLES, DANIEL ALOMIA: (1871-1942) Peruvian archaeologist, composer, compiler of folk music and flutist. When very young he began to study folk music and started a crusade which carried him all over Peru and into Bolivia and Equador. On foot, at one time, he journeyed from Lima to Iquitos seeking the origins of musical folklore.

Robles collected over 1,200 Indian, Colonial and Republican melodies. Through concert and lecture tours carried Peruvian music to the rest of this hemisphere. In 1919 he came to the United States and spent fourteen years here, leaving in 1933. His great interest in folk music led him to compose the *Ballet Inca*; an opera, *Illa Cori*, which was selected by the President of the United States to be presented at the Panama Canal inauguration festivities in 1914, which were never held because of World War I. He composed also two symphonic poems, *El Indio* and *El Resurgimiento de los Andes*; *Himno al Sol* and a number of other compositions. Robles died in Lima on July 17, 1942.

ROBERTI, ALBERTO: (1833- ?) Italian solo flutist to the Sultan in Constantinople and teacher at the Royal Harem and at the Palace School. Has composed some flute Etudes.

ROCKSTRO, RICHARD SHEPHERD: (1826-1906) English flutist, inventor, writer of A *Treatise*, the construction, history and practice of the flute, including a sketch of the elements of acoustics. Was also teacher at the Guildhall School of Music, London.

ROE, GEORGE: (contemporary) English flutist and composer residing in London.

ROGERS, JEANETTE M.: (contemporary) American woman flutist of Hollywood, California.

ROGOWOI, F.: (contemporary) Russian flutist residing in Odessa.

ROMANINO, CAMILLO: (1805-1868) Born in Verdun, France, of Italian parents. Was solo flutist of the Royal Chapel in Turin, Italy, and composed pieces for flute and piano, two flutes and three flutes. Died in Turin.

ROOSE, CONRAT VAN DER: (c.1482) Court flutist and jester to Maximilian I.

ROSE, JOHN MITCHEL: (c.1790) An amateur flutist and flute-maker of great mechanical skill, from Edinburgh, Scotland, who, in 1821, entered into partnership with George Rudall. Thus the Rudall and Rose firm was formed and never restricted their efforts by constructing only one pattern of flute. Rose made several improvements in the old system flute.

ROSSI, MICHELANGELO: (1850-

271

1917) Born in Marsicovetere, Potenza, Italy. An excellent veteran flute player and teacher of the old flute, he had come to America while quite young, establishing himself in Philadelphia where he was highly esteemed. His wife died in that city at the age of 92 in July, 1946. There is no relation whatsoever with the 17th century composer of the same name. The Roman Michelangelo Rossi was the composer of *Toccate* and *Correnti* for organ or clavicembalo, and the opera *Erminia sul Giordano* performed in 1736, published in 1737 and dedicated to Signora Anna Colonna Barberini, Princess of Palestrina. I met the flutist Michelangelo Rossi in Philadelphia in 1893 and he advised me not to settle in that city, "because," he said, "there are too many flutists here already."

ROSSLER, OTTO: (1869-) German flutist residing in Berlin. Solo flutist of the Royal Chapel and teacher at the Stern'schen Conservatory.

RUBSAMEN, WALTER H.: (1911-) Flutist, musicologist and teacher. He received his Ph.D. from the University of Munich in 1937. Rubsamen is instructor in musical history at the University of California, Los Angeles.

RUCQUOY, FREDERICSEN: (1829-1910) Solo flutist of the State Orchestra and teacher at the State Conservatory in Strassburg, Alsace. Composed some pieces for flute and piano.

RUCQUOY, FREDERIC JUN: (1852-) Solo flutist of the National Theatre, New York. Was born in Brussels, Belgium.

RUDALL, GEORGE: (1781-1871) The founder of the firm of Rudall-Carte Company of London, was an extremely fine player; when he was a child he was always making flutes of reeds on which he taught himself to play tunes and took one of them always to bed with him. Was ninety when he died and played flute until two days before.

RUDEMAN, MARTIN: (contemporary) Solo flutist of the Janssen Symphony of Los Angeles and made records in solo and ensemble compositions with the Delco Recording Company of Los Angeles, California. He is the owner of a bass flute in C.

RUDEMAN, SYLVIA: (contemporary) Flutist member of the Janssen Symphony of Los Angeles and sister of Martin.

SAAL, WILHELM: (contemporary) Chamber musician to the Grand Duke and solo flutist of the Royal Chapel in Weimar, Germany.

SABATHIL, FERDINAND: (1856-) Solo flutist, composer and chamber musician to the Grand Duke of Schweriner, Germany. Studied at the Prague Conservatory.

272

SACCHETTI, ANTOINE: (c.1850) Italian flutist and composer who lived many years in Russia. Friend of Boehm, Ciardi and Carl Wehner. Died in St. Petersburg.

SAFRONOFF, VICTOR: (1875?-) Russian flute virtuoso and teacher residing in Moscow. Studied with Ferdinand Buchner. Has composed some etudes.

SAGUL, EDITH: (contemporary) An American woman flutist of merit who is the founder of the Sagul Trio (flute, cello and piano). She gave the first performance of Marion Bauer's *Prelude and Fugue* for flute and piano in New York in February, 1948 with Geraldine Winnet at the piano. Miss Sagul resides in New York.

SAMUELS, BERNARD EDWARD: (1872-) German inventor of the *Aerophor* and solo flutist of the State Orchestra in Essen A. D. Ruhr.

SANDRINI, PAOLO: (1782-1813) Oboist of the court chapel in Dresden, Germany, was also an excellent guitarist, flutist and composer for these instruments. Sandrini was born in Gorizia and died in Dresden.

SAUDEK, VICTOR: (contemporary) Flutist, teacher and conductor from Pittsburgh, Pennsylvania.

SAUST, CARL: (1773-1845?) German flutist and composer. Died in London.

SAUVLET, FRANCOIS: (c.1840) Solo flutist of the Imperial Theatre in St. Petersburg. Brother of Antoine Baptiste. Died in St. Petersburg.

SAUVLET, ANTOINE BAPTISTE: (1845- ?) Dutch solo flutist of the Bilse'schen Concert Orchestra in Berlin.

SAX, ADOLPHE ANTOINE JOSEPH: (1814-1894) A clever and capable wind-instrument maker and inventor of the saxophone, was professor of that instrument at the Paris Conservatory and studied both flute and clarinet at the Brussels Conservatory. Sax was born at Dinant-on-the-Meuse, Belgium, and died in Paris.

SAYNOR, SAMUEL THORNTON: (c.1800) An excellent English flutist whose "intonation was almost irreproachable; his style admirable; his articulation both neat and vigorous, and his tone really splendid. The eight-keyed flute, on which Saynor played, had been the favorite instrument of his master, Nicholson." (R. S. Rockstro)

SCHACHTZABEL, ROBERT: (1838-1904) Solo flutist of the Royal Theatre and Royal Chamber musician in Wiesbaden, Germany.

SCHADE, WILLIAM: (1850?-1920?) German flutist and composer. Died in New York.

SCHEERS, GEORGES: (1875-) Belgian solo flutist of the Concert-

273

gebouw Orchestra in Amsterdam and teacher in that Conservatory.

SCHERRER, HEINRICH: (1865-) Solo flutist of the Royal Court Orchestra in Munich.

SCHERZER, JOSEPH: (1854-1900) Solo flutist of the Royal Court Orchestra and also at the festivals of Bayreuth.

SCHICKHARD, JOHANN CHRISTIAN: (c.1720) German flutist and composer.

SCHINDLER, FRITZ: (1871-) Flutist and composer of many works. Born in Biel, Switzerland.

SCHLEGEL, FRIEDRICH ANTON: (c.1780) Flutist and composer.

SCHLEVOGT, LEOPOLD: (1860-) German solo flutist of the Grand Duke's Royal Chapel and teacher at the Grand Duke's Music School in Weimar.

SCHMIEDEL, MAX: (1873-) Solo flutist of the State Orchestra in Heidelberg.

SCHMIT, GUSTAVE: (1870-) Belgian solo flutist of the Grand Opera and Concert du Conservatoire. Also teacher at the Conservatory in Luttich.

SCHMOLZER, JACOB EDWARD: (1812- ?) German flutist and composer.

SCHNEITZAEFFER, JEAN MADELINE: (1785-1852) Noted composer of ballets, was timpanist at the opera and of the King's Chapel,

chorus-master of the opera and professor at the Conservatory; was passionately fond of the flute which he played masterfully. He was born and died in Paris.

SCHOEMAN, GEORG HUBERT: (1832- ?) Dutch solo flutist at the Crystal-Palace Orchestra in London and also Paleis voor Volksvly orchestra in Amsterdam.

SCHONFELD, FREDERICK: (1895-) Austrian flutist who studied with Ary van Leeuwen in Vienna.

SCHONICKE, WILHELM: (1850-) Royal chamber musician and flutist member of the Royal Chapel in Berlin. Composed pieces for flute and piano and for flute and harp.

SCHRADER, FRANK W.: (c.1875-1938?) German flutist and popular and beloved teacher of our instrument in Rochester, New York, for many years. He was also the founder of a very successful Flute Club in that city.

SCHROECK, AUGUST: (1779-1854) German flute virtuoso and teacher. He was chamber-musician at the Prussian Court and first flutist at the Royal Opera in Berlin. He was distinguished especially for his correct intonation and his clear, full tone. Among his many pupils were Gabrielski, Belcke and Soussman. Schroeck was born and died in Berlin.

SCHUTTER, LEOPOLD: (1858-) Grand Ducal Court musician

and member of the Grand Ducal Royal Theatre Orchestra in Darmstadt, Germany.

SCHUTZE, ARTUR: (contemporary) An excellent flutist who studied with Schwedler. He was killed by a bomb in World War II.

SCHWAB, CARL: (1873-) German flutist, member of the Imperial Ballet Orchestra in St. Petersburg, Russia.

SCHWEDLER, MAXIMILIAN: (1853- ?) Solo flutist of the Theatre and Gewandhaus Orchestras in Leipzig. Writer of *Katechismus of the Flute and Flutists* and played on a flute devised by himself which he called "Reform Flute." Made also many transcriptions for flute and piano.

SCHWINDEL, FRIEDRICH: (c.1720-1786) Was a skillful player on the violin, flute, and piano. He was at the Hague in 1770 and in Geneva and Mulhausen; he brought out several operettas and finally settled at Carlsruhe where he died.

SCONZO, FORTUNATO: (1903-) Italian flutist, composer and writer from Palermo. He is the author of *Il Flauto e i Flautisti* published in Milano in 1930 and of *L'Auletica, sagio critico sulla moderna scuola flautistica*.

SEDLATZEK, JOHANN: (1789-1855?) Noted German flutist who used a flute which descended as low as the G of the violin. The flute was made by Trexler and by Koch in Vienna and by Laurent (1834) in Paris. The low G very seldom came out successfully and when it did, Sedlatzek "would stand the flute up in a corner and salute it with a profound obeisance!" (Rockstro in *The Flute.*)

SEDLOCK: (c.1800) Austrian flutist.

SEFFERN, FERDINAND: (1839-1880) Solo flutist of the State Theatre in Aachen and also in the Bilse-'schen Concert orchestra, Berlin, as well as with the Thomas orchestra, Chicago.

SEGA, ANTOINE: (1858-) French officer of the Academy, flutist and conductor of the 96th Infantry Regiment in Lyon.

SELMER, CHARLES: (1860-1921?) French solo flutist of the Opéra Comique and of the Colonne Orchestra in Paris. Born in Algiers, died in Paris.

—SEMPLE, ARTHUR E.: (contemporary) Canadian flutist who attaches the following to his name: Mus. Bac. L.R.A.M. Is also director of the Harmony Symphony Orchestra.

—SHAFFER, ELAINE: (contemporary) American woman flutist of talent. She was solo flutist at the Hollywood Bowl's concerts under the stars, 1948 season. Soon after, she was engaged as solo flutist with the Dallas Symphony.

275

SHANIS, RALPH: (contemporary) American flutist, member of the San Francisco Symphony.

SICCAMA, ABEL: (c.1810-1865?) A teacher of languages in London and a flute dilettante; claimed that all flutes, including the Boehm flute, were imperfect. He, then, in 1842 conceived an instrument and after repeated experiments succeeded in producing a flute equal in correctness of tune to the . . . violin! It was called the "Siccama flute."

SIEBRECHT, HERMANN: (1873-) Solo flutist of the Opera House Orchestra in Frankfurt-Main, Germany.

SIEBURG, PHILIP: (1919-) Hungarian flutist. Started studying the piano at nine, but in 1934, studied flute with much enthusiasm, first with David Van Vactor, four years, and then six years with Ernest Liegl in Chicago. He played first with the Chicago Civic Orchestra, then four years with the Indianapolis Symphony. Now, 1947, is with the Pittsburgh Symphony Orchestra.

SIEDLER, CHARLES: (c.1820?) When Jenny Lind, the great Swedish singer, came to this country in 1850, the flutist chosen to play her flute obbligati was Charles Siedler. A program of that time is owned by Leonard Hyams who resides in Denville, New Jersey.

SILVA, ANGELO: (1901-) An enthusiastic and able flutist. He was born in New York, lived for a number of years in South America, then settled in Birmingham, Alabama, where he was one of the founders, program annotator and solo flutist of that symphony. Silva's knowledge of flutes, flutists and its literature is admirable. Besides a number of arrangements from the classics for wood wind and for flute and strings, Silva has written three interesting cadenzas for Mozart's Flute Concerto in D. He now lives in Los Angeles.

SILVA, CARMEN—QUEEN OF RUMANIA: (1843-1916) This charming and noble lady was a great patron and lover of music. She it was who helped Georges Enesco, the greatest of all Rumanian composers, who contributed to flute literature, when he was hardly twenty years of age, one of the finest compositions for our instrument, *Andante et Presto*, written for the Conservatory of Paris in 1904 and dedicated to Paul Taffanel. The Queen was not, technically speaking, a *flute virtuosa*, but was a great lover of the instrument and played it with much charm and gusto.

SKEFFINGTON, T. C.: (c.1850) English, author of *The Flute in Its Transition State*.

SLATER, J.: (contemporary) English. "Well-known solo flutist,

276

in 1947 with the BBC Symphony Orchestra."

SMITH, ALBERT: (c.1870-1915?) Accomplished Negro flutist. A native of Jamaica, B.W.I., he gained a scholarship to Kneller Hall, England, where he studied with Henry Chapman. Subsequently flutist with various musical organizations in British Guiana. He was a man of unusual culture and an able musician. Possessed a beautiful tone; his playing generally evinced much refinement.

SMITH, CARLETON SPRAGUE: (contemporary) Dr. Smith, chief of the music division of the New York Public Library, although a dilettante, should be classified as the equal of the best professional flutists. The new Sonatina for flute and piano by the Brazilian composer, Camargo Guarnieri, is dedicated to Dr. Smith who played its first performance with excellent success in New York in 1948.

SMITH, E. T.: (contemporary) Flutist with the Toronto Symphony.

SMITH, MAY LYLE: (1873-) Flute virtuosa born in Hudson, New York.

SMITH, LEO J.: (contemporary) An enthusiastic amateur flutist of considerable ability who founded, in 1926, in a suburb west of Chicago, a Pipes of Pan Club with the motto: "We would rather play the flute than to play cards and so we have a flute club instead of a card club." The following are the charter members, mostly non-professionals: W. B. Kirby, L. J. Smith, A. L. Zilmer, A. J. Allison, T. A. McGill, J. H. Beckerman, A. R. Rifflind, E. Kuttig, C. Kelley, E. F. Gielow, G. Zenker, W. Wood, E. Sims, H. Granzow. The invitation says: "Come with your friends and enjoy this delightful hour of music."

SMITH, STERLING D.: (1913-) Says: "I have been playing the flute for nearly 22 years and my life is wrapped up in the flute." He was graduated from the Eastman School of Music in 1939 and studied also with George C. Moore, William Hullinger, Julius Furman and Leonard Posella in Los Angeles. Smith teaches in schools and now is also with Hancock Ensemble in which he does splendid work. As Captain Hancock is one of America's most beloved maecenas, not only of music (he is an enthusiastic and able amateur cellist) but of scientific expeditions as well, Sterling Smith was for two summers a member and assistant of the Galapagos Islands expeditions. He resides in Long Beach, California.

SOELLER, GEORGE: (contemporary) American flutist member of the Chicago Symphony.

277

SOLA, CARLO MICHELE ALESSIO: (1786-1845) This Italian left-handed flute player and composer studied violin at first with the celebrated Gaetano Pugnani. Later he abandoned the violin for the flute. Sola was also a guitar virtuoso, singing teacher and contrapuntist. His opera *Le Tribunal d'Amille* was given at Geneva, Switzerland, with great success.

—SOLFRONK, CAROLINE: (contemporary) American of Bohemian ancestry. She is an able flutist who, at one time, toured with Alberto Salvi's quintet with fine success.

SOLOMON, L.: (contemporary) English. "A splendid all-round player who has 'free-lanced' since leaving the BBC Revue Orchestra."

SOLLER, WILHELM: (1852-1891) Royal Court musician, solo flutist in the orchestra in Zurich Town Hall and teacher at the Royal Cadet Corps in Munich.

SONNEBERG, WILHELM: (1877-) German flutist member of the court orchestra in Vienna, Austria.

SOUPER, CHARLES ALEXANDER: (1879-) Irish solo flutist of several London orchestras and teacher at the London Academy of Music, London College of Music and Metropolitan College.

SOUSSMAN, HEINRICH: (1796-1848) Like Sola, Soussman studied violin first and abandoned it for the flute. Lived many years in St. Petersburg and in 1812, entered the band of an infantry regiment and was wounded in the campaigns of 1813 and 1814. His excellent compositions, including some fine Etudes, are enjoyed by most flutists. Was born in Germany and died in Russia. (See biography.)

SPIELER, HUGO: (1858-) Royal Court musician and member of the Royal Court Orchestra in Hanover.

SPURT, J. van der: (c.1850) Noted Dutch flute virtuoso.

SQUARZONI, FRANCESCO: (c.1875) Italian, author of *Il Flauto, cenno storico* (Ferrara, 1917).

SSEMENOFF, ALEXANDER: (1862-) Imperial chamber music virtuoso, solo flutist of the Imperial Court Orchestra and teacher in the Choir School in St. Petersburg (now Leningrad).

STANELLE, EMIL: (1855-) Grand Ducal Court musician, solo flutist of the Court Chapel and teacher at the Allgemeinen Musikbildungsangstalt in Karlsruhe-Baden.

STANZIONE, CARMINE: (c.1870-) Well-known Italian flutist and at one time a member of the New York Symphony. He has lived in America for more than half a century. His home is in New York.

STEPANOFF, TEODOR: (1866-)

278

Solo flutist of the Imperial Ballet Orchestra and professor at the Imperial Conservatory in St. Petersburg, Russia.

STETTMEYER, LUDWIG: (1814-1877) Solo flutist of the Chapel of the Fursten von Hohenzollern-Hechingen and also member of the Royal Orchestra in Munich. Has composed some pieces for flute and piano.

— STEVENS, ROGER: (contemporary) Talented flutist, teacher, and solo piccolo with the Los Angeles Philharmonic.

STICHNOTH, LUDWIG: (1847- ?) Ducal chamber musician and solo flutist of the Braunschweiger Hofkapelle in Hanover, Germany.

STOEKERT, OTTO: (1860?-1913) German solo flutist of the Metropolitan Opera House in New York. Composed a flute quartet, unpublished.

STORM, FREDERIK: (1867-) Danish solo flutist of the Royal Chapel and teacher at the Royal Conservatory in Copenhagen.

STRAUSS, ROBERT: (1851-) German solo flutist of the Furstlichen Royal Chapel and teacher at the Royal Conservatory in Sondershausen.

STRAUWEN, AUGUSTE: (1874-) Belgian solo flutist of the Orchestra of the Elector and teacher at the Scola Musical Schaerbeek in Brussels.

STRINGFIELD, LAMAR: (1897-) American flutist, conductor and composer of "symphonic ballads" and "poems," orchestra suites, chamber music and an opera.

STRUNZ, GIACOMO: (1783-1852) Flute virtuoso and composer of fine reputation. His concerts were a great success in Germany, Holland, England, Spain, Greece and Egypt. He was also journalist and critic and wrote four operas, two ballets, overtures, intermezzi, quartets, songs and the famous Cantata Eroica, dedicated to Napoleon I, who valued it very much. Strunz was born in Poppenheim, Germany, and died in Monaco.

STURGES, RICHARD JATES: (1843-1911) English poet, Dante scholar, and enthusiastic flute dilettante. Some of his lyrics were put to music by the famous flutist, Adolf Terschak.

SUDA, STANISLAV: (1865-) Bohemian flute virtuoso, composer of some pieces for flute and piano, the opera Bei den Gottesqualen and other music.

SUPPÉ, FRANZ de: (1814-1895) This world famous operetta composer, when a young man, studied and played flute with much delight. One of his first compositions was Il Primo Amore (First Love) for flute and piano. Suppé was born in Spalato and died in Vienna.

SVENDSEN, OLUF: (1832-1888) Danish solo flutist of the Royal

279

Chapel and also of several orchestras in London and professor at the Royal Academy of Music. Died in London.

TABORDA, JULIO THEODORO da CUNHA: (1852- ?) Portuguese solo flutist of the Theatro da Trinidade and teacher at the Royal Conservatory in Lisbon.

TACET, JOSEPH: (1770- ?) English flutist and composer of solos, sonatas, concerti and much other flute music. It was claimed at one time that Tacet was the inventor of several keys for the improvement of the old flute but this proved to be erroneous. (See biography.)

TAFFANEL, PAUL: (1844-1908) One of the most eminent French flutists, teacher at the Paris Conservatory and conductor at the Grand Opera House. Taffanel wrote an excellent quintet for flute, oboe, clarinet, bassoon, and horn, besides many arrangements for flute and piano.

TAILLARD, ANTOINE: (c.1780) French flutist and composer of whom little is known.

TAMPLINI, GIUSEPPE: (c.1850) Italian, author of *Brevi cenni sul sistema Boehm e della sua applicazione al Fagotto* (Bologna, 1888).

TAMBORINI, ODOARDO: (1843-1882) Italian flutist and composer. Was teacher at the Civiche Scuole Populari di Musica and director of the State Chapel in Milano.

TASSINARI, ARRIGO: (1889-) A graduate of the Bologna Conservatory, he is one of the most distinguished of the present-day flute virtuosi.

His flute teacher was Emilio Gillone. For many years, he was solo flutist of La Scala of Milano and has played in numerous concerts as soloist and ensemble. On May 24, 1947, he played Jacques Ibert's Concerto for Flute and Orchestra at Naples which was repeated later in Rome. The following are some of the ensembles with which he has played with great success all over Europe: *Trio* — Arnaldi (piano), Bagni (singer), Tassinari (flute). *Trio "Artis" di Roma* — Ada Ruata Sassoli (harp), Arrigo Tassinari (flute), Renzo Sabatini (viola and viola d'amore). *Quintetto strumentale di Roma*—Arrigo Tassinari (flute), Pina Carminelli (violin), Renzo Sabatini (viola and viola d'Amore), Arturo Bonucci (violoncello), Alberta Suriani (harp).

Tassinari has taught at the Licei Musicali "Tartini" e "Verdi" at Trieste, at the Royal Conservatories of Parma and Naples and is now at the Santa Cecilia of Rome.

TAUBERT, J. F.: (1750-1803) German flutist and composer of several concerti and other works for the flute.

280

TAYLOR, LAWRENCE: (contemporary) Solo piccolo and third flute of the San Antonio (Texas) Symphony Orchestra. Taylor is also a writer on flute matters and has arranged many compositions for wood-wind ensemble. Since 1944 Taylor has been a member of the committee in Instrumental Ensembles for the Music Educators' National Conference.

TERADA, T.: (c.1870) Author of *Acoustical Investigation of the Japanese Bamboo Pipe, Syakuhati)* Tokyo, 1907).

— TERRY, KENTON: (contemporary) American flutist member of the Philadelphia Symphony.

TERSCHAK, ADOLF: (1832-1901) Austrian flute virtuoso, composer of much fine flute music including chamber music and opera *Thaïs.* Terschak's concert tours included many countries with the Orient, Russia, China and Japan in predominance. He was born in Hermannstadt-Siebenburgen and died in Breslau, capital of Silesia. (See complete biography.)

THOMAS, JOSIAH: (contemporary) American flutist of talent from Scranton, Pennsylvania.

THYROLF, CARL: (1864-) German solo flutist of the Kaim orchestra in Munich.

TIEFTRUNK, WILHELM: (1846- ?) Solo flutist of the Philharmonic Orchestra in Hamburg and teacher at the Royal School of Music of both Wurzburg and Hamburg.

TILLMETZ, RUDOLF: (1847-1915) German flutist, composer and teacher. A pupil of Boehm, Tillmetz was born and died in Munich. (See biography.)

— TIPTON, ALBERT: (1920?-) American talented flutist from Tulsa, Oklahoma, whose mother is also flutist and teacher. Young Tipton has been assistant solo flutist in the Philadelphia Symphony. In 1948 he was solo flutist with the St. Louis Symphony.

TIPTON, VENA: (contemporary) An able flutist and teacher of Tulsa, Oklahoma. She is the mother of Albert Tipton, the talented solo flutist of the St. Louis Symphony, and also the founder of "Pipes of Pan" Wind Instrument Studio of that city.

— TORNO, LAURENCE: (c.1900) He studied with Georges Laurent in Boston and at one time was solo flutist with the Cleveland Symphony, now member of the St. Louis Symphony.

TOUNSEND, RICHARD: (contemporary) Flutist and Chief Warrant Officer and assistant band leader of the U. S. Navy Band, Washington, D. C.

TOVAGLIARI, FLAMINIO: (c.1860) Italian flutist and composer from Parma.

TRICOT, EDUARD: (1832-1894) Solo flutist of the Royal Theatre and teacher at the Royal Conservatory in Luttich, Germany.

TROMLITZ, JOHANN GEORG: (1726-1805) German flutist, composer, author and flute-maker. Tromlitz was very nervous when he played in public and confessed that he was a much better performer in private. In improving the old flute, he was eminently successful. Tromlitz was born in Gera, Saxony, and died in Leipzig. (See biography.)

TROUGHTON, ELLA D.: (contemporary) Flutist, poet and active member of the Rochester (New York) Flute Club.

TROUSSEAU, CHARLES CYPRIEN: (1840-1897) French flutist pupil of Tulou and Dorus. Was director of the "Elysée-Menilmontant" in Paris.

TSCHAIKOVSKY, PETER ILICH: (1840-1893) This world famous Russian composer was very fond of the flute and played it beautifully, having studied it with the noted Italian flutist, Cesare Ciardi, in St. Petersburg.

TULOU, JEAN LOUIS: (1786-1865) French flutist, composer and teacher. Tulou was highly temperamental and also an ardent republican which brought him much sorrow and disappointment as he was arrested more than once. He was considered a flutistic genius and was also passionately fond of hunting. At one period of his brilliant career he became so careless that when he was called to perform he had no instrument and his friends had to borrow one for him. Tulou was born in Paris and died at Nantes. (See biography.)

TURPE, CARL: (1832-1903) Flutist member of the State Orchestra in Königsberg, Prussia.

UNGER, ADOLPH: (1851- ?) Ducal chamber musician and solo flutist of the Dessauer Hofkapelle, Germany.

VACHA, CAROLINE: (contemporary) American flutist member of the Chicago Symphony.

VAILLANT, P.: (c.1780) French flutist and composer.

VALDOVINOS, TEODORO JUAN Y PUYOL: (1883-) Spanish solo flutist of the Teatro Principal in Zaragoza.

VALENTIN, ROBERT: (c.1700) Wrote many works for flute, two flutes and bass and a *Chaccoon* for two flutes. His nationality is unknown.

VALERIO, NICHOLAS: (c.1885-1933) American flutist of Italian extraction and member of the Rochester Philharmonic for several years.

VAN BOOM, JOHANN: (1783- ?) An extremely fine flutist and composer from Rotterdam, Holland. His excessively modest and retiring nature made it so he was almost entirely ignored. He was happiest when playing his flute and composing. His son Herman —Utrecht 1809-1883—who went to Paris to study with Tulou, was a different kind of character. He became one of Holland's most famous flutists and resided in Amsterdam.

VAN DEEVEN, WILLIAM: (c.1880-) Dutch flutist, at one time member of the St. Paul, Minnesota, Symphony and Los Angeles Symphony. He lives in Los Angeles.

VANDERHAGEN, ARMAND: (c.1725) Author of *Méthode claire et facile pour apprendre à jouer en tres peu de temps de la Flute* (Paris, 1798).

VANHAL: (c. 1725) Professional flutist, brother of Jan Baptist Vanhall or Wanhall (1739-1813) prolific Dutch composer of 100 symphonies, 100 string quartets, 25 masses, numerous piano pieces, etc. The flutist was, at one time, on friendly terms and had business dealings in *flute matter* with the noted Irish flutist, Andrew Ashe.

VAN LEEUWEN, ARY: (1875-) Dutch flutist, composer, teacher, pianist and singer. At one time instructor at the Vienna Conservatory. Also solo flutist with the Cincinnati Symphony. Now living in Hollywood, California.

— VAN VACTOR, DAVID: (1906-) American flutist, teacher and composer of a number of orchestral works. He also wrote many flute compositions. In 1947 Van Vactor was appointed the new conductor of the Knoxville, Tennessee, Symphony Orchestra and also the head of the University's new Department of Fine Arts.

VAS, SANDOR: (1885-) Distinguished Hungarian pianist and teacher at the Eastman School of Music for many years; plays also cello, studied conducting with Nikisch and is an enthusiastic lover of the flute which he studied and plays creditably.

VEGGETTI, ALBERTO: (1874-1948) Italian flutist, writer and teacher at the Santa Cecilia in Rome, where he died.

VENDEUR, FELIZ: (1856- ?) French solo flutist of the Grande Theatre, teaching at the Conservatory and Officer of the Public Instruction in Dijon.

VICARIO, FRANCESCO: (c.1700) In May and June of 1795 he appeared at La Scala of Milano playing on wind-instruments made of a single reed tube and a small pumpkin from which a little flute was made and played on.

VIGGIANO, VINCENT: (1887-1928) Flutist with the Detroit Symphony Orchestra, died of pneumonia April 3 after a short illness.

— JOHN VINCENT: (contemporary) Played with the Peoples Symphony Orchestra at Boston and also on occasion with the Boston Symphony under Koussevitsky (1926-27). His teacher was Georges Laurent, first flutist with the Boston Symphony.

Dr. Vincent qualifies as composer, educator and conductor. He was graduated from the New England Conservatory, studied at Harvard and in Paris, took his Ph.D. at Cornell University, headed the Music Department at Western Kentucky State before coming to U.C.L.A. Is now Chairman of the Music Department at U.C.L.A.

His compositions are String Quartet in G, Three Grecian Songs, Cindy Gal, O Shenando'h, Miracle of the Cherry Tree; publisher Mills Music, Inc. His publications are *Music for Sight Reading, More Music for Sight Reading,* and the *Diatonic Modes in Modern Music.*

In a personal letter to the writer, Dr. Vincent says: "I am afraid my flute-playing days are somewhat behind me although I keep my flute (an 1892 silver French model Louis-Lot with low B joint) in good order. I enjoy playing for myself and while I find my technique, except tonguing, is still in fair shape, my tone has suffered badly. I have not played professionally in 15 years but would not take anything for the experience and enjoyment I gained through playing the flute.

"Dr. Arlt has often spoken of you and I hope sometime to meet you.

"With my cordial greetings, I am, Sincerely yours, Dr. John Vincent, Chairman, Dept. of Music." University of California, Los Angeles, Nov. 18, 1949.

VITA, MICHELE: (1895-1913) Flutist of exceptional talent. Was born in Viggiano, Italy, and died in New York at eighteen years of age.

VIVIAN, A. P.: (1855-1903) English solo flutist of the "Richter Concerts," Royal Choral Society and teacher at the Royal Academy of Music in London. He composed some pieces for flute and piano. Vivian was born in Devonshire and died in London.

VOIGT, MAX: (1861-   ) German flutist member of the Opera House Orchestra in Frankfurt-Main. He was born in Stettin.

VOIGT, OTTO: (1858-   ) Royal Chamber musician, solo flutist of the Royal Court Theatre and teacher at the Conservatory in Hanover, Germany.

VON BEUST, DR. THEODORE: (contemporary) Dilettante of distinction and president of the Louisville Flute Club, Louisville, Kentucky.

VROYE, A. DE: (1835-1890) Belgian solo flutist of the Theatre Lyrique and Musique de la Garde. Toured all over England

and Germany. Saint-Saens' *Romanze* for flute and orchestra is dedicated to De Vroye who was also Officer d'Academie and of l'Instruction Publique. He died in Paris.

~ WAGNER, ERNEST: (c.1875-) For over forty years flutist and solo piccolo player with the New York Philharmonic. He has written an instruction book for the flute.

WAHLS, H.: (c.1880) German flutist and composer.

WALKER, E.: (contemporary) English. "In 1946, succeeded his father, Gordon Walker, as principal flute of L.S.O. Worthy son of an outstanding father."

~ WALKER, GORDON: (1885?-) English solo flutist of the Royal Opera, Covent Garden. He has the reputation of being one of England's finest performers.

WALKIERS, EUGENE: (1793-1866) French flutist and prolific composer of much fine chamber music. He studied composition with Reicha, with whom he was a great favorite, and flute with Tulou. Walkiers was born in Avexnes, Flanders, and died in Paris. (See biography.)

WALLENSTEIN, FRITZ: (c.1865?) The father of the eminent conductor of the Los Angeles Symphony, Alfred Wallenstein, was a sculptor and an enthusiastic flute dilettante.

WATERSTRAAT, THEODOR: (1835-1896) German solo flutist of the "Imperial Opera" and teacher at the Conservatory in St. Petersburg. He wrote some etudes for the flute. Waterstraat was born in Pomerania and died in St. Petersburg.

WATSON, LLOYD R.: (c.1870-) Dr. Watson, a most gentle soul and passionately fond of the flute, used to drive 85 miles each way, in good or stormy weather, for a flute lesson with the writer, from Alfred University, Alfred, New York, to the Eastman School of Music, in 1934 and 1935. He was teacher of chemistry and specialized in bee culture in which he excelled, eliminating the sting and developing mating on the ground instead of in flight, thus producing larger bees and a better quality of honey. Dr. Watson won the Guggenheim award for this.

WEBER, GOTTFRIED: (1779-1839) Attorney-at-law, writer, composer, theoretic and critic, played flute and cello with much gusto and virtuosity. He was born in Freinsheim and died in Kreuznach, Germany.

WEHNER, CARL: (1838-1912) German flutist at the service of the Czar in St. Petersburg when a young man and solo flutist of the New York Philharmonic for many years. He wrote some Etudes. (See biography.)

285

WEHNER, RUTH: (contemporary) Flutist and geologist. She studied flute five years with A. C. Petersen of Milwaukee, Wisconsin, from the age of nine. Went to the University of Michigan where she received a B.S. in geology. She also took a few music courses there and played in the University band and orchestra. Later she received a scholarship to the Curtis School of Music, studying with Kincaid only one winter. Was in Texas two years as a geologist. Now, 1949, she is in Iowa City, Iowa, working in geology in the mornings and teaching flute at the University in the afternoon, also playing in the orchestra. Ruth Wehner is not related to the famous Carl Wehner, although her father came from Germany when a little boy and died when Ruth was two years old.

WEHRLE, FERDINAND: (1815-1889) Solo flutist of the Court Theatre in Mannheim and thirty years in Karlsruhe, Germany.

WEHSENER, EMIL: (1859-) Solo flutist of the State Theatre, the Gurzeich-Konzerte and teacher at the Conservatory in Cologne, Germany.

— WETHERLY, ALBERT: (contemporary) American flutist member of the National Symphony, Washington, D. C.

WEIMERSHAUS, EMIL THEODOR: (1847- ?) Another pupil of Boehm who was solo flutist of the State Orchestra and the Gurzenich-Konzerte in Cologne, Germany. He was born in Penig and resided in Cologne.

WEINER, EUGENE: (1847-1903) Hungarian flutist member of the Bilse-Orchestra in Berlin and also with the Theodor Thomas orchestra in Chicago. He was born in Breslau and died in New York.

WEINERT, J.: (contemporary) Russian flutist residing in Rostow a Don.

WEISS, CARL: (1735?-1795) German flutist, composer and principal in the private band of George the Third of England. He was born in Mulhausen-Alsace, and died in London.

WEISS, CHARLES N.: (1777-1845?) Studied flute with his father Carl and when only nine years old played a concerto in public. While in Bergamo, Italy, studied composition with Simon Mayer, director of Santa Maria Maggiore. Charles wrote many flute compositions, two hundred studies, many duets for two flutes and a *Methodical Instruction* book. He was born and died in London. (See biography.)

WELCH, CHRISTOPHER: (1832-1916) English flute dilettante and eminent flute historian. His two major books are: *History of the Boehm Flute* and *Six Lectures on the Recorder*. Welch

286

studied flute with Richardson, Pratten, Radcliff and Rockstro.

WELLS, BENJAMIN: (1826?-1899) English flutist and teacher at the Royal Academy of Music, London. He composed some pieces for flute and piano.

WENCK, HEINRICH MORITZ: (1813-1879) Flutist and director of the "Communalgarde" in Leipzig, Germany.

WENDLING, JOHANN BAPTISTE: (?1800) An excellent flutist and composer whose manuscripts are in the Royal Conservatory of Music in Brussels. He was for forty-six years much loved and admired solo flutist in the chapel of Mannheim.

WENDLING: (c.1730- ?) In an interesting old book, *The Life of Mozart* by Edward Holmes, published in 1845 and which I bought a few years ago in a second-hand bookstore, Leopold Mozart says: "I had the pleasure to hear, besides good singers of both sexes, the admirable flauto traverso, Wendling." Then on a footnote it says: "Wendling afterward became one of the most generous and enthusiastic friends of young Mozart, who took an opportunity of bringing his talents, and those of his daughters, conspicuously before the public, in the opera 'Idomeneo.' The German flute, now in the infancy of its mechanism, was called the *flauto traverso* to distinguish it from the *flute à bec* which was held longitudinally." We also learn from the same old book that Leopold Mozart, besides his famous *Violin School*, had composed six violin trios, twelve pieces for piano, twelve oratorios, numerous pieces for the church and the theatre, several pantomimes, more than thirty grand serenades, many symphonies, concertos for wind instruments, trios, etc. However, as soon as he was convinced of the great superiority of the genius of his son, he stopped composing and devoted all his attention to him.

WERNICKE, ALFRED: (1856-) Solo flutist of the Court Theatre orchestra and teacher at the High School of Music at Mannheim, Germany. He has composed a number of pieces for flute and piano.

WESTERDAL, OLOF: (1807-1891) Swedish solo flutist of the Second Regiment of Grenadiers in Stockholm. He was born and died in Kikils Kirchenspiel bei Kinkeping.

WETZGER, PAUL: (1870-) Flutist, composer and writer of *Die Flöte*. Wetzger made many transcriptions and new editions of Demersseman's compositions, etc., besides original works of his own. (See biography.)

WHITELOCK, LUPTON: (1878-) English flutist who studied at

287

the Guildhall School in London, with Rockstro, DeJong, and Brossa.

WIELAND, C. W.: (c.1840) German, author of *Die Ergindung der flöte und die Bestrafung des Marsyas* (Leipzig).

WIGENT, MARY: (contemporary) Solo flutist of the Corpus Christi Symphony. In a recital in April, 1948, she played the Hindemith Sonata, an Andante by Mozart, and Ibert's *Little White Donkey*, with Irene Strune at the piano.

WILCOCKE, JAMES: (1853- ?) English flutist with many London orchestras and teacher at the Kneller Hall Royal Military School of Music as well as at the Guildhall School in London.

WILDER, GEORGE HUBBART: (1870?-1925?) American flutist and teacher. He was born in Montpelier, Vermont, and died in Burlington.

WILKINS, FREDERICK: (contemporary) Flutist of merit and teacher at Juilliard School of Music, Manhattan School of Music, and Chautauqua School of Music. Wilkins, with John Wummer and Arthur Lora, were judges in the first contest of one hundred dollar prize for the flute and piano composition sponsored by the New York Flute Club. The composition selected was a Sonatina by Eldin Burton, published by Carl Fischer, New York.

WILKINS, JAMES S., JR.: (c.1850) American, author of *Theobald Boehm—Musician, Scientist, Mechanic.* (MSS Life of Boehm by a pupil.) (Philadelphia, 1900.)

WILLOUGHBY, ROBERT: (contemporary) Flutist with the Cleveland Symphony.

WILMS, JAN WILLEM: (1771- ?) Dutch flute and piano virtuoso. He was also musical director in Amsterdam and composed pieces for flute and piano.

WILSCHAUER, ADALBERT: (1843-1888) Solo flutist of the Bilse-'schen Konsert-orchesters in Berlin.

WILT, THOMAS: (contemporary) Flutist with the Rochester Philharmonic.

WINCKLER, CARL: (1814-1868) Solo flutist of the Royal Chapel in Stockholm. He was born in Berlin and died in Stockholm.

WINKLER, ANTON: (contemporary) Flutist with the Minneapolis Symphony.

WINKLER, THEODOR: (1834-1905) Grand Ducal flute chamber virtuoso and member of the Royal Chamber in Weimar. He was also a prominent teacher and composer. Winkler was born in Eilenburg and died in Weimar.

WITTEBORG, AUGUST: (contemporary) Flutist with the Detroit Symphony.

WITTGENSTEIN, HUGO: (c.1850)

288

Solo flutist of the Metropolitan Opera, New York.

WITTGENSTEIN, MILTON: (1898-) A notable and well-known New York flutist. He is the organizer and director of the Oxford Ensemble (chamber music group) of flute and strings which broadcasts from coast to coast on Columbia and NBC. Wittgenstein is also president of the New York Flute Club and director of the musical programs since its inception.

WOEMPNER, CARL: (1866-1915) Excellent German solo flutist of the Minneapolis Symphony until his untimely passing. He was a fine musician and highly respected by all. Woempner taught two of his three sons, Henry and Carl, the art of fine flute-playing.

WOEMPNER, HENRY: (1898-) Is one of the finest flutists of our time. He was for a number of years solo flutist with the Minneapolis Symphony and also with the San Francisco Symphony. He was born in Milwaukee, Wisconsin, and now resides in Hollywood, California.

WOLFRAM, JOSEPH: (1789- ?) Grand Ducal flutist and court musician. Wolfram was born in Mahrisch, Neustadt, and toured Russia, Germany, Hungary, Italy, France, Belgium, and Holland with fine success. His wife was a fine pianist.

WOOD, BETTY: (contemporary) American woman flutist of merit. She has made a number of records in solo and ensemble.

WOOD, DANIEL S.: (1872-1930?) Solo flutist of the London Symphony orchestra and also with the Philharmonic orchestra and King's Private Band in London. He was born in Yorkshire and died in London.

WRAGG, J.: (c.1750) English, author of The Flute Preceptor; or the Whole Art of Playing the German Flute. Rendered easy to all Capacities, etc. (London, 13th edition, 1795. 1st edition, 1792.)

WUMMER, JOHN: (1900-) One of America's finest flutists. He was solo flutist with the Detroit Symphony for a number of years and also with the NBC. Now Wummer is principal flutist with the New York Philharmonic Society.

WUMMER, MILDRED HUNT: (contemporary) Pianist and flutist, wife of John Wummer. Official accompanist of the New York Flute Club, is often featured as soloist and co-artist with her husband in the Bach Circle of New York, Adolph Busch Chamber Players, and New Friends of Music. Gives joint recitals with her husband as accompanist and flutist. Also on the faculties of the Mannes Music School and the Dalcroze School of Music, and is, besides, director of woodwind

289

ensemble classes at the latter. Was music critic of a prominent mid-western paper for several years. She studied flute with John Wummer and Georges Barrère and piano with her mother, a very good musician. Her father was an able cellist.

WUNDERLICH, JOHANN GEORGE: (1755-1819) German flutist and composer. He was born in Bayreuth and died in Paris.

WUNDERLICH, JOHANN: (1833-1896) Flute virtuoso and conductor of the Stuttgarter Private Orchestra. He studied with Boehm, was born in Neustadt-Bayern, and died in Stuttgart. He was the father of Phillipp.

WUNDERLICH, PHILLIPP: (1868-) Solo flutist of the Royal Opera in Dresden and Royal Chamber musician. He was born in Stuttgart.

WYSHAM, HENRY CLAY: (1828-1902) American solo flutist of the Baltimore and Boston Symphony orchestras. He was also a composer, writer and pedagogue. Wysham wrote *The Evolution of the Boehm Flute;* an essay on the *Development of the Reed Primeval to the Perfect System of Theobald Boehm* (Elkhart, Indiana). He was born in Baltimore and died in San Francisco.

YOUNG, JOHN HARRINGTON: (c.1895) English flutist and composer. He died in London.

ZADUCK, SIGMUND: (1804-1887) Solo flutist of the Court Orchestra and Royal Court musician in Munich where he studied with Boehm. He was born in Munich and died there.

ZAMPERONI, ANTONIO: (1844-1909) Italian solo flutist of the La Scala Opera House and teacher at the Conservatory in Milano. Zamperoni studied with Rabboni and was vice-president of the Società di Mutuo Soccorso Italiano. He was born in Milano and died in Varese, near Milano.

ZENTNER, FRANZ: (1856-) Solo flutist of the Bohemian Royal Chapel in Prague and at the Court Theatre in Mannheim, Germany. He was born in Prague.

ZERRAHN, CARL: (1826-1906?) German flute virtuoso and teacher.

ZESEWITZ, MORITZ: (1837-1886) Solo flutist of the State Theatre and of the Museume-Konzerta and teacher at Dr. Hoch'schen Konservatorium in Frankfurt-Main. He was born in Podelwitz-Saxony and died in Frankfurt.

—ZIEGLER, ROY: (contemporary) American solo flutist with the Joliet Symphony of Joliet, Illinois.

ZIELCHE, JOHANN HEINRICH: (1730-1790) Noted flutist, was also organist to the Danish court, chamber musician and flutist to the King. He published six soli

290

for the flute, six quartets for flute, viola, cello and basso and many other soli for the flute in 1787. Zielche was born and died in Copenhagen.

ZIERER, FRANZ: (c.1850) As a child he was a left-handed flute player and, as he could not read the notes, played by ear. Later he became a valued member of the Court Theatre in Vienna, although he still played flute left-handed.

ZINCK, HARTNACK OTTO CONRAD: (1746-1832) From 1768 to 1777 he worked as chorister for Carl Ph. Emanuel Bach, then became first flute in the Chapel of the Duke of Mecklinburg-Schwerin. He was also an organist and singing teacher.

ZINK, WILHELM: (1805-1895) Royal court musician and solo flutist of the Munich Royal Orchestra. He studied with Boehm, was born in Eichstadt and died in Munich.

ZIZOLD, AUGUST JUN: (1825-1880) Solo flutist and chamber musician of the Royal Chapel in Dresden. He was born in Weimar and died in Dresden.

ZIZOLD, WILHELM: (1837- ?) Solo flutist of the Municipal Theatre in Frankfurt-am-Main and director of the Court Orchestra in Neustrelitz. He was the son of August jun.

ZLOTNIK, HENRY: (contemporary) American flutist and teacher residing in New York.

ZUCCHI, G.: (c.1875) Italian flutist and composer.

ZYBIN, WLADIMIRE: (c.1880) Russian flute virtuoso residing in Leningrad.

(NOTE: It will be noted that I have included many flutists in my "Thumbnail Biographies" who never became solo flutists of a great orchestra. Any player of wind instruments in an important orchestra has big responsibilities, whether he be second flute, second trumpet or third bassoon. Many of the finest solo flutists acquired invaluable experience as second flutist or piccolo at the start of their careers and there have been unusual men who occupied that position for many long years. To mention only three: Arthur Brooke was second flute in the Boston Symphony for about thirty years. Joseph La Monaca occupied the same position for just as long a time in the Philadelphia Symphony and Paul Wetzger in Germany played second flute all his life. Apart from the fact that these splendid colleagues of ours have filled the first chair many times without notice when an emergency arose, their wonderful musicianship would have made them eligible to any honorable and artistic niche. Mr. Brooke has recorded many solos and has done much conducting. Mr. La Monaca's compositions and also his activities as conductor I have dwelt with at length in a special article. Mr. Paul Wetzger is well-known for his compositions, his arrangements, and as a pedagogue.

To the numerous living and worthy flutists of this and other countries missing in my "Thumbnail Biographies," I wish to express my humble apologies. It has been difficult during the war to trace many of them. However, I sincerely hope to add an *addenda* in a future edition of this work. Also, it is unavoidable that many whom I have listed as occupying this and that position will be found in other places by the time this book is issued, as changes occur oftener than many realize.

In compiling the "Thumbnail Biographies," I have discovered with considerable fun that a great number of colleagues of the stronger sex are as jealous in divulging their age as the fair and gentle sex. Then it must be true, what *The Real McCoy* said in the Sunday Examiner, Los Angeles, a little while ago: "The weaker sex is the stronger sex, because of the weakness of the stronger sex for the weaker sex.")

III The Amateur Flutist

The following is a list of distinguished amateurs of the flute:

Nicholas II, Czar of Russia (1868-1918).

Raffaello Galli, the Florentine banker, was also an excellent player, and composed a fine method and over 300 other compositions.

Other flute amateurs were:

Sten. Stenson Blicher (1782-1848), poet and novelist.
Carl Theodor (1724-1799), Crown Prince of Bavaria.
Johann Friedrich Christmann (1752-1817), clergyman.
Jacob Ferstl (1844), Roman Catholic priest.
Frederick (1711-1763), Margrave of Brandenburg—Culmach —Bayreuth.
Dr. Oliver Goldsmith (1729-1788), poet, author, traveler.
Ferdinand Von Harsch (-1785), Imperial Master of Ordnance.
Joseph I (1678- ?), Roman-German King.
Baron von Knorr (?   ), court secretary in Vienna.
Luigi Hugues (1836-1913), Professor of geography, University of Turin, and prolific composer.
Count Rebsomen (19th century), the one-armed general who

contrived an ingenious mechanism in order to play the flute with only his right hand.

Sidney Lanier (1842-1881), American poet.

Richard Jates Sturges (1843-1914), poet and translator of Dante.

Christopher Welch (1832-1916), M.A. and voluminous writings on flute history.

George Eastman (1854-1932), inventor and maecenas, flute dilettante as a young man.

John Finn (1853- ?), M.A. and flute historian.

Barezzi, a wealthy merchant of Busseto who, to a great extent, was responsible for Verdi's education and who afterwards became the great musician's father-in-law, was passionately fond of music. He not only played the flute well but had a working acquaintance with the clarinet, the horn and the ophicleid (brass instrument).

Henry Macaulay Fitzgibbon (1855-   ), barrister at law and writer on flutes.

Libero Stradivarius (1845- ?), barrister at law and direct descendant of the great Stradivarius of Cremona.

Enrico Caruso (1873-1921), famous tenor. On one occasion after complying with the request to make a flute record he was asked if he did not intend to purchase it. After hearing himself he concluded instead that it were better to sell the flute.

Charles W. Cadman, American composer of California, played on an original Indian flute which he obtained when living with the aborigines to study their music.

The American, Dr. H. G. Wetherill, besides being an enthusiastic flute amateur, devised what he calls a slide flute. It consists of a tube held vertically and produces a glissando effect. It has no finger holes or keys. Professor Giorgi of Florence, Italy, anticipated Dr. Wetherill by a number of years and justly called it a "toy flute." I heard him play upon it a few years ago.

Pablo Casals (1875-   ), famous cellist, conductor and composer.

Gebuehr, the German dramatic artist who plays in *Frederick the Great* and who resembles that monarch, is an accomplished flute player.

294

Daniel Beamer (1796-1838), civil engineer. His one-keyed flute of boxwood with ivory trimming is in perfect condition and is in the possession of his great-granddaughter, Miss Elaine Clark of Rochester, New York, who is also an enthusiastic dilettante. During her travels in the Far East she found, on the Philippine Islands in the Province of Kalinga, north of Manila, a settlement where "Pans Pipes" were played exclusively by women and they made their own instruments. The men played a "nose flute." Miss Clark succeeded in obtaining one each of these quaint instruments after great difficulty because the natives were suspicious and could not understand why the white foreigner would be interested in their instruments. Through her graciousness I also have a nose flute but, as yet, have not succeeded in producing a sound!

*   *   *   *

The following is an additional list of names of noted people who played the flute:

The brother of the King of Naples studied flute with Briccialdi.

Blunt King Hal of England not only played the flute but was the owner of 72 varieties of flutes, including gold and glass. Though the King of Holland did not play the flute, he loved the instrument so much that he presented Drouet, one of the world's greatest performers and composers, with a rare glass flute studded with precious stones. It is well known that Schopenhauer played the flute but it is not so well known that he had all the operas of Rossini arranged for flute and piano, and was accustomed to playing every day after dinner. This, incidentally, is against the advice of all eminent flute teachers, as it may sometimes cause hiccoughs. Major General Ethan Allen Hitchcock, noted veteran of Indian and Mexican campaigns and personal advisor of Abraham Lincoln during the Civil War, played flute. Victor Herbert played third flute and piccolo in the school orchestra but his mother insisted he play cello because Alfredo Piatti, the great cellist, had been a very good friend of his grandfather.

Carmen Silva, Queen of Roumania, played flute with much grace, and Albert, the Prince Consort of England, handled the flute in a masterly fashion. It was also the favored instrument of Joseph I of Hungary. The father of Spohr was a flute dilettante. Webster and his son were also enthusiastic dilettanti. (The famous Monk Savonarola played on the Pipes of Pan when a boy, taught by his grandfather, Dr. Michele Savonarola.) Heine's father, also, loved to play flute. There may be flute dilettanti who have never heard of Spohr, and there may be others who do not know who Savonarola and Heine were. It is highly improbable that there is anyone who wouldn't know who Webster was, unless he belonged to the non-English speaking race. However, it is not the intention of the writer to put in doubt the historical knowledge of the lover of the flute, if I say that : Ludwig Spohr (1784-1859), famous violinist, was the composer of nearly two hundred works. His *Violin School* still is a standard work for that instrument. He composed ten operas, five oratorios, nine symphonies, twelve concertos for violin, and a great quantity of chamber music. Girolamo Savonarola (1452-1498), one of the most famous names in the history of Florence, Italy, who was burned at the stake, played on the Pipes of Pan. Heinrich Heine (1797-1856) was one of the greatest German-Jewish lyric poets who, in June 1825, had himself baptized a Christian. Noah Webster (1758-1843) was an American lexicographer. His reputation rests upon his dictionary of the English language. Both he and his son were enthusiastic flute dilettanti. The flutist has always boasted of the eminent men who played flute. However, of Nero who, besides playing the violin,* played also the flute, and Henry the VIII, who played flute, the recorder, clavichord and composed—silence is golden!

* * * *

Everyone knows that Leonardo da Vinci, that universal genius, was supreme as a painter, sculptor, musician, scholar, engineer, architect, anatomist, alchemist, astronomer, geologist,

---

* The violin at the time of Nero (37-68 A.D.) was not known. The first violin of which there is any record was made in Brescia, Italy, in 1540 by Gaspar da Salo. Following him came Giovanni Paolo Maggini, his pupil, and Andrea Amati, who, at almost the same time, founded violin-making at Cremona, about sixty miles from Brescia. Thus, Nero may have played the lyre instead of the violin.

physicist, etc., etc., but it is not generally known that he was proficient not only on all musical instruments, including both the Pandean pipes and the transverse flute, but that he invented a number of musical instruments upon some of which he himself, alone, could produce exquisite music. His musicianship was recognized by the court of Milano where he was invited to play the harp and sing his own compositions. A strict vegetarian, Da Vinci was the illegitimate son of a peasant girl and a Florentine attorney.

Da Vinci, incidentally, never played on any musical instrument which was not made by himself, including harp and a silver flute. When he played it was in tones that moved the heart. With his music he could bring tears to eyes that had never shed them.

*　　*　　*　　*

The following is taken from Elbert Hubbard's *Little Journeys* (Vol. VI):

"The father of Benvenuto Cellini was a designer, a goldsmith, and an engineer, and he might have succeeded in a masterly way in these sublime arts had he not early in life acquired the habit of the flute. He played the flute all day long, and often played the flute in the morning and the fife at night. As it was the flute that had won him his gracious wife, he thanked God for the gift and continued to play as long as he had breath. Now, it was his ambition that his son should play the flute, too, as all fond fathers regard themselves as a worthy pattern on which their children should model their manners and morals. But Benvenuto despised the damnable invention of a flute—it was only blowing one's breath through a horn and making a noise—yet to please his father he mastered the instrument, and actuated by filial piety he occasionally played in a way that caused his father and mother to weep with joy."

Benvenuto, who later was entangled in a terrific fight with some rogues who had nearly killed his younger brother, was banished, with all the gang, from Florence. "Shortly after this Benvenuto found himself at Pisa on the road to Rome. He was footsore, penniless, and as he stood gazing into the window of a goldsmith the proprietor came out and asked him his business.

He replied, 'Sir, I am a designer and goldsmith of no mean ability.' Straightway the man, seeing the lad was likely and honest, set him to work. The motto of the boy at this time was supplied by his father. It ran thus: 'In whatsoever house you be, steal not and live honestlee." Seeing this motto, the proprietor straightway trusted him with all the precious jewels in the store. He remained a year at Pisa, and was very happy and contented in his work, for never once did he have to play the flute, nor did he hear one played. Nearly every week came loving letters from his father begging him to come home, and admonishing him not to omit practice of the flute. At the end of a year he got a touch of fever and decided to go home, as Florence was much more healthful than Pisa. Arriving home his father embraced him with tears of unfeigned joy. His changed and manly appearance pleased his family greatly, and straightway when their tears were dried and welcomes said, his father placed a flute in his hands and begged him to play in order that he might see if his playing had kept pace with his growth and skill in other ways. The young man set the instrument to his lips and played an original selection in a way that made his father shout with joy, 'Genius is indispensable, but practice alone makes perfect!' "

*   *   *   *

George Washington never played the flute. . . .

In the Mt. Vernon collection is a flute said to have belonged to George Washington, and from this has arisen the natural supposition that Washington played the flute. Familiar to many is the delightful picture of Washington playing the flute in his home, with Nellie Custis at the piano and Martha Washington listening intently. The flute has an ivory head. Then I have, also in my album, a small picture of Washington crossing the Delaware, in 1776, and standing in his boat playing the flute! In February 22, 1919 there was published in *Musical America* a letter written by George Washington to Francis Hopkinson which disproves all these surmises and in which Washington admits he cannot play a note on any instrument. This letter was written to Hopkinson, one of America's first composers, upon the receipt of some compositions—and I should like to reproduce it here in full, for its historical significance, musically:

"Mount Vernon, Feb. 15, 1789

"Dear Sir:

We are told of the amazing powers of Musick in ancient times; but the stories of its effects are so surprising that we are not obliged to believe them unless they have been found upon better authority than poetic assertion—for the poets of old (whatever they may do in these days) were strangely addicted to the marvelous—and if I before *doubted* the truth of their relation with respect to the power of musick, I am now fully convinced of their falsity—because I would not for the honor of my country, avow that we are left by the ancients at an immeasurable distance in everything, and if they could sooth the ferocity of wild beasts; could draw the trees and the stones after them, and could even charm the powers of hate by their musick, I am sure that your productions would have had at least virtue enough in them (without the aid of voice or instrument) to soften the ice of the Delaware and Potomack—and in that case you would have had an earlier acknowledgement of your favor of that of December which came to hand but last Saturday.

I readily admit the force of your distinction between a thing done and a thing to be done; and as I do not believe that you would do 'a very bad thing indeed', I must ever make a virtue of necessity and defend your performance to the last effort of my musical ability. But, my dear sir, if you had any doubts about the reception which your work would meet with—or had the smallest reason to think that you should need any assistance to defend it—you have not acted with your usual judgment in the choice of a coadjustor—for should the tide of prejudice flow in favor of it (and so various are the tastes, opinions and whims of men that even the sanction of Diversity does not ensure universal concurrence) what, alas! can I do to support it?

I can neither sing nor raise a single note on any instrument to convince the unbelieveing; but I have, however, one argument which will prevail with persons of true taste (at least in America—I can tell them it is the production of Mr. Hopkinson).

With the compliments of Mrs. Washington added to mine, for you and yours, I am, dear sir,

Your most obedient and very humble servant,

George Washington."

299

Of course there is the possibility that Washington might have acquired the art of playing the flute after he wrote that letter to Hopkinson, when he was fifty-seven. Why, someone may say, if it was possible for the artist Louis Maurer to change from the old flute to the Boehm at seventy-nine wouldn't it be reasonable that Washington could master the playing of a few melodies at around sixty? The answer is that Louis Maurer had played the old flute 65 years and, therefore, it is not quite the same thing.

George Washington's Flute

"George Washington's hatchet has had a world-wide reputation, but his flute has known only the most meager fame. Fame is generally like that, paying more attention to works of destruction than to the forces which lift up the heart. Washington himself was more widely known as a soldier than as a farmer, though his farming doubtless better expressed his tastes.

"Washington's flute playing, too, certainly expressed his tastes. It is a sweet and human picture; the soldier, statesman and President, the father of his country, retired to his beautiful farm, singing to his flute through sunny afternoons of well-earned respite from care. The hatchet has disappeared. Even the story about it is denied. But the flute is no myth. There it is still to be seen in the Mount Vernon collection.

"The flute itself is an excellent specimen of the Meyer model, with the so-called ivory head, popular in those days, and still widely used. I am positive that if it were cleaned and repadded it would be easily playable today, and one would gladly predict that it would show a mellow, tender voice.

"There is little difficulty in surmising what tunes Washington played on his flute. The flute music of those times is still extant.

"There were old English, Irish and Scottish airs, such as 'McPherson's Lament,' 'Rothemurche's Rant,' 'Auld Robin Gray,' 'The Charming Fair Elly,' and the 'Post Horn Waltz with Variations.' There were also a few French and German tunes, but not many. Excerpts from the Italian operas, from Verdi, Rossini, and Donizetti and even from Mozart, were frequently played. Then there were endless 'variations,' very fashionable for

300

the flute. Some were built upon popular songs; others were written to trifling, stupid themes invented by would-be composers who could not compose music. It was all the vogue in those times to play the flute with elaborate trills and turns upon every second note.

"But it is hard to imagine the retired President and quiet farmer wasting his time with trills and 'variations.' Rather, we believe he loved the good old English and Scottish folk songs and the tuneful arias of Mozart and Donizetti. Washington loved his flute and played it often; he owned a good instrument and he doubtless played it reasonably well. Unquestionably he had plenty of good music, and there need be no doubt, in view of the noble simplicity that was so large an element in his great character, that he had the taste to prefer what was simple and good.

"Suppose we could replace the symbolic hatchet with a better symbol, one authentically associated with George Washington's best days and expressive of his better qualities? Let the hatchet make way for the flute, or at least make room beside itself for this more worthy symbol."

The above beautiful article on "Washington's Flute" is interesting in spite of its shortcomings historically: How could Washington have played airs by Verdi when this composer was born fourteen years after Washington's death? He is said to have loved Rossini's music . . . but Rossini was only seven years old when Washington died, and Donizetti was only two years of age. There remains only Mozart, who was born twenty-six years after Washington and died eight years before.

*   *   *   *

There is no doubt that John Quincy Adams, the sixth president of the United States, played the flute, as he himself said, in a paper also from my album: "I am extremely fond of music, and by dint of great pains have learnt to blow very badly the flute, but could never learn to perform upon the violin, because I could never acquire the art of putting the instrument in tune. I console myself with the idea of being an American, and therefore not susceptible of great musical powers. Many of my coun-

301

trymen, though, have a musical ear, and can tune an instrument with little or no instruction at all."

Traveling in Germany in 1797-1798, while representing the United States at the Court of Berlin, Adams seemed particularly struck by the fact that "in almost every house we found works of music and reading." In one "miserable village, we could find scarce anything. We saw, however, at the post-house, a small library, a forte-piano, and music."

In England, during March 1816, the only mention of Beethoven in all his writings appears. The music played at a special concert in celebration of the victory over Napoleon included, *Israel in Egypt*, and a "grand battle symphony, composed by Beethoven to show the triumph of *Rule Britannia*, and *God Save The King*, over Marlbrook. Bad music, but patriotic. The entertainment like that of all English oratorios, dull."

Later in the same month he heard the *Messiah*, and *Acis and Galatea*, and an Italian air by Mozart.

His own fondness for the flute evidently still persisted for he adds, "Mr. Drouet, first flute player to the King of France's chapel, performed a concerto on the flute and surpassed everything that I have ever heard upon that instrument."

In the early days of the Republic, serenading the ladies was a great pastime. Adams found particular pleasure in it and made many entries in the Northampton diaries such as this of May 21, 1788: "Went with my flute to Storey's lodging. About a quarter before twelve sallied forth upon a scheme of serenading. We paraded around the town till about four in the morning." And the next day he laments, "Felt stiff and unfit for almost everything."

The violin and the flute indifferently played were the only common instruments in rural New England. The fortepiano and the harpsichord were luxuries, practically unknown in the frugal northern states. There is not a single mention of either of them in the Adams diaries.

*　　*　　*　　*

Stephen Grover Cleveland, Mayor of Buffalo in 1881, Governor of New York in 1882, and President of the United States of America from 1885 to 1889; owned a very beautiful flute made of glass with gold keys. The instrument was presented to him by a distinguished admirer and friend. However, there is no record that Cleveland ever played or could play on that elegant instrument which, years later, became the property of Dr. Dayton C. Miller and is now in the great flute collection in the Library of Congress at Washington, D. C.

* * * *

Dr. Dayton C. Miller (1868-1942), famous scientist, inventor and authority on acoustics; translated Boehm's *The Flute and Flute Playing*, and he owned the greatest flute collection in the world, comprising over 1400 flutes made of all varieties of material, including gold, glass, ram's horn and one made from a human shin bone. He also had the most complete library in the world on the flute. The oldest of the volumes was printed in Latin in 1488. Collecting flutes and literature on the flute was not a hobby for Dr. Miller. In an interview he said: "My motives are far deeper than one supposes. The flute is man's first sound instrument. It follows that a study of the flute is really a study of man. No, my flute collection is no mere incident. Some day I shall publish a series of books about my research." Among his inventions an instrument which photographs sound waves is of particular interest. In 1927, when at the invitation of the University of Rochester, Dr. Miller lectured and demonstrated his machine, the writer played an unaccompanied melody with the corresponding wave sounds clearly shown on the screen. It was extremely interesting. Dr. Miller took the first surgical X-ray photograph in the United States and during World War I was also the first to photograph the speed of a cannon ball. No wonder, then, that the flutistic world loves and speaks of him as one of the greatest minds of all times who has honored the flute and its long history. Both the great flute collection and books and music on the flute he willed to the Library of Congress in Washington, D. C.

* * * *

George III of England played the violin and flute. Joseph I, King of Hungary, played the flute. Prince of Siracusa, brother to the King of Naples, studied with Briccialdi. Count Luigi

303

Marini, one of the finest players of his century and held in great esteem by Briccialdi, Ciardi and other famous contemporary players, composed many works for the flute.

* * * *

Mozart, in one of his letters to his father dated 14th May, 1778, said: "The Duke de Guines, whose daughter is my pupil in composition, plays the flute *incomparably* and she plays the harp *magnifique*. She has much talent and genius and in particular an incomparable memory so that she can play all her pieces, actually some two hundred, by heart." The beautiful double concerto in C major for flute and harp was composed for the Duke de Guines and his daughter by Mozart about 1778.

* * * *

The Frenchman, Jean Henry Lambert, was a distinguished mathematician, philosopher—and flute dilettante.

* * * *

Carlo Michele Alessio Sola, the left-handed flutist and composer, was engaged by Madame de Staël—famous writer, conversationalist and social queen—as professor of singing for her daughter, and professor of the flute for her son.

* * * *

Dr. Florient Corneille Kist, born at Arnhem, Holland, on January 28, 1796, was an enthusiastic dilettante of great ability on the flute and cornet, and composed many excellent works for these two instruments.

* * * *

Joseph Bonaparte, King of Spain and brother of the great Napoleon, who fled to the United States after the battle of Waterloo under the name of Count de Survilliers, played on a flute of glass with pearls and silver keys.

Count Gilberto Gravina, grandson of Cosima Wagner and Hans von Bulow, and great-grandson of Liszt, is a flute virtuoso, composer, and an excellent symphony conductor.

THE ROCHESTER PHILHARMONIC WOODWIND QUINTET
Standing left to right: Frederick Lockhart, Richard Swingley, Rufus
Arey; *Seated left to right:* Joseph Mariano, Vincent Pezzi

RENÉ LE ROY

HENRY C. WOEMPNER

ARTHUR LORA

JOSEPH MARIANO

FRIEDRICH KUHLAU

GIULIO BRICCIALDI

EMIL PRILL

FRIEDRICH DULON

EXPRESSIONLESS GROUP OF 1886

The reason why there wasn't a smile in this group is Leonardo, then about ten, who wanted mezza lira (ten cents) to pose for the picture. He wanted very much, he said, to buy a beautiful bouquet of flowers for a . . . friend! Result: a good, sound spanking from his mother. The others in the picture are three sisters and a brother: Marietta Russo (now living with her daughter, Anna Salvi, wife of the famous harpist Alberto Salvi, in Wilmette, Ill.) holding her baby girl; Caterina Coccaro, living in Vicksburg, Miss. since 1909; Teresa Pugliese, who died in Italy in July 1950; Vincenzina, living in California since 1905; and Paolo, who died in New Haven, Conn. in 1946. Father and two elder sons were then abroad. Later, two other younger sons arrived, Gerardo and Peppino, both of whom settled in California after the beginning of this century.

THE AMERICAN COMPOSERS WOODWIND QUINTET
Left to right: David Van Vactor, Adolph Weiss, John Barrows,
Robert McBride, and Alvin Etler

MARCEL MOYSE

ARRIGO TASSINARI

JACQUES IBERT

LAMBERT C. FLECK

Three excerpts from
"Density 21.05" ①
for flute solo   Edgard Varèse

N.B. Used by permission of the composer and New Music Edition.

① written in Jan. 1936 at the request of Georges Barrère for the inauguration of his platinum flute. Revised April 1946. 21.05 is the density of platinum.

② always strictly in time – no rubato.
③ notes marked ⊥ to be played very softly, hitting the keys at the same time to produce a percussive effect.

Flauto solo — Leonardo De Lorenzo
"Il Velivolo (The Airplane) Preludietto volante in La minore
Presto (♩)

(1) To be played in one and one half minutes.

NOTE: The above piece is from a set of "19 Preludi e Preludietti."

RUTH FREEMAN

HARRIET PEACOCK

FRANCES BLAISDELL

MILDRED HUNT WUMMER

VINCENZO DEMICHELIS

FERRUCCIO ARRIVABENE

JOSEPH LA MONACA

FRANZ DOPPLER

PAUL WETZGER

JULIUS MANIGOLD

MICHELE VITA

LOUIS MAURER

PAN PLAYING THE TRANSVERSE FLUTE
This beautiful piece of sculpture was presented to the author on his
70th birthday by the artist Edgardo Simone

SYDNEY FLUTE CLUB

DR. JOSEPH G. BRECO

LEONARDO DE LORENZO
In 1950 at the age of 75

General Charles Dawes must have played a fine flute in his youth according to an article in the *American Magazine* which stated: "Charley did some surveying on a branch railroad near Marietta, Ohio, his hometown, and he won renown for his virtuosity in playing the flute."

*   *   *   *

Dr. Leonard Corning, discoverer of spinal anesthenia, played flute—while walking up and down his studio.

*   *   *   *

Christina Nillson, the great Swedish singer, played the flute.

*   *   *   *

Audubon, famous ornithologist, and painter of birds, played both the violin and the flute.

*   *   *   *

Lord Byron, one of England's great poets, and Schopenhauer, one of the most pessimistic of philosophers, played the flute assiduously, after dinner.

*   *   *   *

Gladstone, English statesman and writer, and John Jacob Astor, financier, both were excellent amateur flutists. When Astor arrived from Germany in 1784, he brought with him $25, a spare suit of clothes, and seven flutes. With one of these flutes he ventured into the forest among the Indians. He was not long discovering that musical sounds had the power of soothing many a savage Seneca breast. It is not often in history that the foundation of a huge fortune was laid with the aid of a flute.

*   *   *   *

The late William J. Guard, for many years the press representative of the Metropolitan Opera House, was an inveterate lover of the flute. He kept it always near him in his workroom and then when time permitted he would play upon it his favorite bits from the operas heard the previous night. He was sojourning in Sorrento at the time of the 1929 earthquake, and calmed many a panic-stricken inhabitant by playing his flute on the terrace of his hotel.

* * * *

The Berlin millionaire, Adolph Goldberg, wrote a huge *Biographical Sketches and Portraits of Famous Flutists* which he forwarded gratis to all living flutists included in his work. He also presented many a worthy artist of his acquaintance with a gold flute.

* * * *

Henry David Thoreau, the author of *Walden*, enjoyed playing the flute.

* * * *

Carlo Levi, author of the fascinating novel, *Christ Stopped at Eboli* (1947), considered the greatest post-war literary contribution from Italy, is an excellent painter, a fine doctor, writer, essayist, and newspaper man. He is also a political leader, and was sentenced to exile for his anti-fascist activities in a forsaken town not far from my native Viggiano. Among the remarkable portraits in his book are "a barber and a flute-player whose dream is to follow the author to the ends of the earth as his private secretary, and a Homeric pig-doctor."

* * * *

A few years ago, an amateur flutist successfully tried an interesting experiment on the outskirts of New York City. In the early evening when the frogs began to croak, he posted himself nearby and began to play. The frogs, evidently appreciative of finer music than they could make, not only ceased their noise but hopped out of the water and surrounded the charmer. They were then ungratefully scooped up like potatoes and carried off to the man who paid for their legs!

* * * *

A small book entitled *A Little Night-Music* by Gerald W. Johnson, which is quite humorous because it concerns music made by amateurs, has the following dedication: "To John C. Bohl, teacher of many fine flute players and one of the world's worst, yet who has remained through it all, a patient and amiable gentleman, this book is inscribed with admiration." And the first chapter is: "On Playing the Flute Badly."

* * * *

A Letter to G.B.S.

"Villa Pan By the Sea"
Palos Verdes Estates, Calif.
December 10, 1949

My dear, honored Sir,
The other day an English musician of many years in America, who had read the advance announcement of my forthcoming book remarked: "I see that your book will include many prominent men whose hobby was playing the flute; however, you have missed one who is just as famous, probably more, than your George Eastman or even Frederick-the-Great, namely, G.B.S."

"If G.B.S. had played flute in his younger days," I answered, "I would have known it." "Probably you are confusing the fact that G.B.S. many years ago became also famous as a distinguished music critic."

"I do not confuse anything," the Englishman answered, "and I will bet a good sum of money that G.B.S. played the flute in his youth."

Now, as betting or gambling of any sort has been against my principle—or shall I say my religion?—I have decided to write direct to you, G.B.S., in regard to this matter.

With the good wishes on my part, that you did not play the flute and that you will live to be not more than 125 years in good health, I am

Sincerely,
Leonardo De Lorenzo

On December 29, the following card reached me:

(printed)   From
                                      Bernard Shaw

Phone & Wire: AYOT SAINT LAWRENCE,
CODICOTE 218.   WELWYN, HERTS.
    13/12/1949.

(manuscript, presumably in his own clear hand writing)

307

"I have never in my life owned, played, or touched a flute.

But I am old enough to have heard it played by pre-Boehm Nicholson, who could make it sound like an organ pipe.

He cut the holes large, and corrected the pitch by his blowing.

The only instrument I ever learnt was the cornet, formerly called the cornopean and substituted for the trumpet in the orchestra.

I took it up because my uncle gave me an old and very bad one. I gave it up because I was told that it would spoil my singing voice.

G.B.S."

I wish to call attention to the fact that my airmail letter had no other address than: "To G.B.S., London, England." I wrote it on December 10, 1949; the answer from the famous 93 years (young) writer and philosopher, was penned on the 13th, three days afterward.

(However grateful I am to G.B.S. for answering my request promptly and interestingly, it would be unfair not to call attention to the fact that he must have had another flutist in mind for the one he had heard many years ago, because Nicholson died in 1837 and G.B.S. was born in 1856!)

IV ⎮ A Thing or Two
About Flutists

In his *Moralia*, Plutarch cites a musicologist, Alexander Pollis-
tor, living at the beginning of the first century B.C., who reports
(in his collection of Phrygian information) that flute-players
first put in an appearance in Phrygia; also that the father of all
flutists was called Hyagnis, and that Marsyas was his son. This
brings us to the mythological age, when the flute was invented,
a time of which Pliny says: "The transverse flute was invented
by Midas in Phrygia; the double-flute by Marsyas, in the same
land; the Lydian by Amphion, and the Dorian by Thamaris the
Thracian." It is with Marsyas in particular that the tradition
of the invention of the flute is connected. Apuleius says: "Hyagnis was the father of the fluteplayer Marsyas, who was the first
to make use of both hands in playing. He was the first to blow
two flutes with one breath, and the first to secure a musical
consonance by the simultaneous sounding of the various holes
of the left and right flute, a high tone, and a lower, more solemn
one." Didorus, the Sicilian, said that "Marsyas of Phrygia, friend
and companion of Cibele, a serious man and most intelligent,
imitated the tones of the many-reeded Pan pipes of the flute."

309

The *Musical Quarterly* of April 1923 reported the following: "The fluteplayers of Greek days were attractive young ladies of uncertain moral standing; those of today are old gentlemen of irreproachable character. The former played nude in the theatre; the latter, never do."

*   *   *   *

The flutist Ismenias played so well it was said he cured Boetians of pains in the thighs; and before him Gellius claimed that the music of the flute soothed bodily suffering and was especially good in case of snake-bite; and Maritanus wrote: "Who does not know that ischialgia may be cured by flute music?"

*   *   *   *

When the Attic philosopher Antisthenes heard the famous fluteplayer, Ismenias of Thebes, called a worthy man he said: "Pah, the fellow must be a miserable wretch, else he would not be such an excellent flutist!"

*   *   *   *

Ancient poet-flutists. . . .

Lasos, born in or about 545 B.C., and who lived in Athens, was an orator and philosopher besides being a fluteplayer and poet.

Simonides, born on the Island of Chios in 559 B.C., lived many years at the court of Hipparchos and enjoyed the friendship of Psaos and Anacreon; Simonides died in Syracuse at the age of ninety.

Bacchylides, Simonides' nephew, was born at Chios in or about 472 B.C., and was at the court of Hieron with Aeschylus and his uncle Pindar.

Thaletas, the great poet and fluteplayer, appeared in Sparta about 670 B.C., from the town of Gortyn in Crete, an island in which the flute was extensively cultivated. His songs are said to have brought peace and contentment back to the city terrorized by the plague.

Timotheos, fluteplayer, writer, and composer, was born in 447 B.C. and died in 357 B.C. He lived in Miletus.

Midas, King of Phrygia, was decorated with asses' ears because he decided in favor of Marsyas and his flute in the contest with Apollo and the lyre.

* * * *

Greek flute virtuosi were highly paid everywhere. The well-known Lama, attached to the court of Ptolemy Soter, King of Egypt, and born in Athens, fell into the hands of Ptolemy when he defeated Demetrius Poliocertes at sea in 306 B.C., and her beauty and musical gifts so enraptured that monarch that he neglected to follow up his victory and made her his mistress. The Athenians even built a temple in which her statue was rendered divine honors.

* * * *

The fluteplayer, Pindar, wrote the twelfth ode in praise of "Midas the Glorious," a Sicilian, twice winner of the prize for fluteplaying at the Phrygian games.

* * * *

Terpander (in or about 680 B.C.) once quelled a tumult by his flute; he is also credited with having invented notation.

* * * *

The Thebans were esteemed the greatest performers on the flute, and when their city was destroyed their chief anxiety was to recover from the ruins a statue of Mercury with this inscription: "Greece has declared that Thebes wins the prize upon the flute."

* * * *

Pronomus of Thebes (in or about 440 B.C.), who taught Alcibiades, could play in three modes on his flute.

* * * *

The fluteplayer Antigenidas (in or about 380 B.C.), who increased the number of holes on the flute, so transported the King by his playing of a national air at a banquet that the monarch seized his weapons and almost attacked his guests.

311

The famous fluteplayer, Philoxenes, was a notorious glutton, and wished that he were all neck, so that he could enjoy food more!

*　　*　　*　　*

Xenophon said that if a bad player on the flute wished to appear to be a good player, he must imitate their example and expend large sums on rich furniture and keep many servants. In fact, the expression "to live the life of a fluteplayer" became proverbial as typifying luxury.

*　　*　　*　　*

Aristophanes' *The Birds, The Peace,* and flute obbligati. . . .
"The performance of the flute player Chaeris (c.450 B.C.) in his flute obbligati in the two plays of Aristophanes, the Greek dramatist, was, evidently, as offensive to the eye as it was to the ear. He is represented as *puffing* and *laboring.* His struggles in forcing out the upper register of his instrument seem to have been painful to witness. These unseemly motions of the body appear to have been not uncommon amongst ancient flute players as Saint Epiphanus, in an attack on the flute, says that the movements of the player as 'he bends to the right and bends to the left' resemble the gestures of the Devil when engaged in blaspheming!"

"In discussing the question, which was sweeter, the voice or the flute, it was admitted that the voice was sweeter than the flute; yet they were of the opinion that if the singer sang notes without words, it was not sweeter. They thought the flute sweeter than the lyre and a most delightful accompaniment to the voice. 'Why,' says Aristotle, 'do we listen to a vocal solo with greater pleasure when it is sung to the flute than when it is sung to the lyre? It is because anything which is sweet, when it is mingled with that which is more sweet, becomes sweeter?' "

*　　*　　*　　*

If the following tragi-comic story had not been told by that noted, reliable and erudite Christopher Welch, one would be inclined to be skeptical of the authenticity of it.

How can a player on the flute blow so hard that he would drop dead, because of it, on the platform? Had he played a tuba, a sarrusophone or any of the other mastodontic instruments that would have been credible but . . . a flute! However, the flutist was one Harmonides (c.440 B.C.) much too musical a name for an unmusical fellow who confessed to his teacher, Timotheus, that his only motive in becoming a flute player was to gratify his vanity. Timotheus said the most certain way to acquire fame was to pay little heed to the many who know how to clap and to hiss, and to endeavor to gain the approval of the few who know how to judge. His words, however, fell on deaf ears. Harmonides, on his first competition, destined to be also his last, played with so many contortions and blew so eagerly and so hard in his yearning for popularity, that he fell dead on the platform!

*　　*　　*　　*

The sacrificial flute player was also called "Temple Flute Player" and, at other times, "Tomb Piper." In ancient times, at a sacrificial ceremony, the most important personage next to the High Priest, was the flute player. The priest, in this imposing ceremony had to be a man whose qualifications for his sacred office were an unblemished body and a blameless life. The sacerdotal apparel with which he was arrayed was of spotless purity, and sometimes of such magnificence that it could scarcely be distinguished from the dress worn by kings on state occasions. Second in importance to the priest, crowned like him with a chaplet of leaves, and robed in a flowing vestment, was the fluteplayer who with his instrument (often a double flute of exceptional length, sometimes made of ivory) took his station near the altar. For special occasions medals were issued representing a Roman emperor, a priest, a fluteplayer, an attendant youth, often of the noble class, with portions of the victim, usually a bullock, on spits. On the altar could be discerned a token that the sacrifice had been accepted, the tail of the victim standing erect in the fire, signifying victory!

*　　*　　*　　*

The noted ancient flute teacher *Caphisias* once said to a pupil who was playing too loud: "The good is not always contained in the great; but the great is always contained in the good."

Among the statues of the Muses in the Vatican at Rome we find Euterpe seated upon a fragment of rock, a shepherd's pipe held idly in her hand, and her gaze fixed in the distance as though lost in recollection of some sweet old melody.

* * * *

An epoch in the history of the flute was marked by the advent of the fluteplayer Sacades of Argos. His elegies were heard at the Parthenian festivals, flute and cithara sounding together, so that it was said of him that he had reconciled the god Apollo with the flute. This reconciliation between flute and lyre was made evident at various religious festivities, in musical contests of which Sacades was a three-times victor, though some authorities object that it was not until some years later that the Epigonian school used the cithara in company with the flute. Although Sacades wrote elegies, he was more famed as a fluteplayer, composer and inventor of flute solos. He lived in the fifth century B.C.

* * * *

About three thousand years ago, the body of a woman was placed in a tomb in Egypt. The tomb was opened close to half a century ago by W. Flinders Petrie, noted English scientist, and he found many interesting objects. The mummy was not well preserved but near it was an ancient chair; and there were earrings, beads, combs, pomade jars, and a bronze mirror as well. Most important, there were two pipes or flutes—"Lady Maket's flutes," as they came to be called. Lady Maket's flutes were taken to a museum at Oxford, England, and placed on public view. They really formed two parts of the same instrument—a double-flute. The length of each was found to be not quite one and a half feet. One had four holes in the side, while the other had three holes.

* * * *

A short story of an immortal Chinese flutist-poet, written by Herbert P. Whitlock in *Junior Natural History Magazine*. He says in part: "Han Hsiang-tzu was said to have been a great musician; and his playing upon his favorite instrument—a flute carved entirely of jade by a Chinese artist, was so marvelous that

314

it caused flowers to spring up out of the earth and blossom as he played. As if that were not enough, the leaves of the flowers were found to be inscribed in gold with delightful poems! Han Hsiang-tzu was a grand nephew of one of China's great statesmen; and he lived in China at about the time that Charlemagne (A.D. 744-814) was emperor of France.

* * * *

So numerous were the ancient female fluteplayers that a general in the army of Alexander the Great wrote that he had captured 329 ladies of the Persian monarch harem, all of whom were skilled flutists.

* * * *

A book of biographies of no fewer than 535 women flutists was destroyed in the burning of the Alexandrian Library at Athens.

* * * *

Plutarch says that a beautiful girl named Nanna was so fine a flutist that Mimnermus, himself a good player on that instrument, composed an elegiac poem in her honor.

* * * *

For centuries many of the Ladies in Waiting to the Empress of China, as a sign of culture and distinction, played the bamboo flute, ornamented at the tail end with a silk parcel.

* * * *

For a long time I had heard about a book written over a thousand years ago by a grand court lady in Japan and in which many of the characters played the flute. The title is "Tale of Genji" by Lady Murasaki, translated by Arthur Waley—and it is considered a classic. After a long search I was able to obtain the book. The principal character is Prince Genji, a son of the Emperor. This young man played the flute proficiently. Handsome as Apollo he was married at seventeen and in our time would be considered the worst of libertines as his amours seem to have been his chief occupation.

One of his guards, a nobleman named Chūjo, also played

the flute and it was his duty to look after the Prince and protect him from his numerous nocturnal escapades. The Prince went out alone on his adventures only suspecting at times that his guard was watching him. They were both in disguise. One night, or rather early one morning, upon returning from one of these excursions in a carriage, the Prince, seeing him, asked his noble guard to enter his own carriage. There, to vary the monotony of the journey, both took their flutes from their pockets and . . . played duets! The concert was continued when they reached the palace and Chūjo's father, whose favorite instrument was the flageolet, joined in the performance. It was said to have been "very agreeable!" Upon another occasion on one of his adventures, Prince Genji saw a very beautiful little girl who resembled greatly one of the women he had loved most ardently and who had died at the early age of nineteen years. He had the child kidnapped—in spite of the fact that she was also the daughter of a nobleman—and brought to his palace. She became his wife at the age of twelve. Although he was irresistible to all women, young, old, handsome, ugly, plebeian, or aristocratic, he was hated by his extremely beautiful first wife who was four years older than he.

The Prince played the zithern also fairly well, was proficient on the lute and danced so well that all the admiring ladies shed tears! He was said to have been taught the zithern by an old lover twice his age and because he felt sorry for her he continued to visit her now and then.

This noble and aristocratic lady played the zithern so well that she often appeared as soloist with the all-men Imperial orchestra.

The Emperor had many children, but Prince Genji, although he could not be heir to the throne, was his favorite. At one time a son was said to have been born to the Emperor who was so handsome and bore so marked a resemblance to Prince Genji that the Emperor was happy beyond words and told his son that when he was a baby he was exactly like the new-born child. He did not know that the child was in reality the son of Prince Genji! (and one of the Emperor's younger wives).

Because of his unusual mastery of the flute, Prince Genji was

316

often commanded by the Emperor, his father, to perform and many times he would play the flute while walking! During some of the festivities, the author tells us, "the recorder and the big flute were all the while in full blast," and even the big drum was rolled out on the verandah, the younger princes meanwhile amusing themselves "by experimenting upon it," and further: "When, at last, under the leafage of tall autumn trees forty men stood circle-wise with their flutes, and to the music that they made, a strong wind from the hills, sweeping the pinewoods, added its fierce harmonies, while from amid a wreckage of whirling and scattered leaves, the Dance of the Blue Waves suddenly broke out in all its glittering splendour—a rapture seized the onlookers that was akin to fear!" *

*   *   *   *

The flutist's urn—a picture postal card which I bought in Perugia, the beautiful Etruscan city north of Rome, in 1926—depicting a boy in a position of playing the transverse flute. He had no instrument in his hands except a small portion of the mouthpiece. My friend, Professor Alberto Veggetti, teacher at the Santa Cecilia in Rome, found out for me that the rest of the flute had been lost or destroyed during the many centuries in the cemetery of the so-called "Palazzone" near Ponte San Giovanni. The urn had the boy flutist's family name on it thus: INANA. However, as the Etruscans wrote and read from right to left, the name was, in reality, ANANI!

*   *   *   *

Louis Hotteterre, surnamed "The Roman" was the third son and the most famous of a family of celebrated musicians and wood-wind instrument makers. He was the first who had the honor of playing the flute transversely in the orchestra of the Paris Opéra in 1697. He was court musician to Louis the Fourteenth and died when near the century mark.

---

* By kind permission of the publishers, George Allen and Unwin Ltd., London, England. The translation, from the original Chinese is by Arthur Waley. Published in America by Houghton Mifflin Co.

317

"A Phantom Procession" is the title of an interesting and amusing article in the issue of *Musical America* of February 1950, by the noted British authority on orchestration, Adam Carse. The collection of nearly 350 wind instruments, belonging at one time to various personages of all ranks and nationalities, which Adam Carse presented to the Horniman Museum, London, is the subject of this spooky phantasy. He pictures the ghost of each original owner of these instruments in a procession to the museum to claim his flute, piccolo, army fife, oboe, clarinet, bassoon, French horn, trombone, tuba, keyed-bugle, serpent, etc., etc. Adam Carse himself, whose first wind instrument of his collection was an ivory flute made by Cahusac, given to him by his barber at Blackheath in 1895 in exchange for an old bicycle, does not appear in the procession for the simple reason that he was still alive!

To be brief, I will mention only fluteplayers in this Phantom Procession. The first to appear is a courtier with powdered wig, sword, silk stockings and long embroidered coat, proclaim him a man who moved in the most exalted circles; it was Johann Joachim Quantz, the famous flute-master of Frederick the Great who, with a smile, picks out his boxwood flute. The next flutist, an august personage, attended by a retinue of fawning courtiers and magnificently dressed, goes up to a case, where lies a flute, with a gold key on which are engraved a royal crown and cipher. The important personage was Louis XV of France and the flute was made by Thomas Lot of Paris in 1750. Next came several English gentlemen, all amateurs, busy with the one-keyed flute. Other Englishmen followed, who were interested in the eight-keyed flutes. Next came a grave-looking German, Th. Boehm, who was carefully examining two flutes made in his own workshop at Munich. The volcanic Drouet carries away the ivory and silver flute that bears his name. A Frenchman who selected a French flageolet was next. Next came an elegant and handsome Englishman with side whiskers, the great flutist, Charles Nicholson, who was followed by another of his nationality and almost equally famous, Joseph Richardson, with his Siccama flute. However, an original character made his appearance; a young man with a virgin beard, an Italian mountaineer with sheep-skin

318

jacket, breeches and a hat with feathers. He feels his way along slowly as he is totally blind! He is a Sardinian shepherd, Picco, of the Picco pipe, who was brought to London in 1856. He created such a sensation by his marvellous performance of the most elaborate and florid variations covering a chromatic compass of three octaves on a little pipe barely three inches long and equipped with only two finger-holes and a thumb hole!

*　　*　　*　　*

The flute in Beethoven's life. . . .

Beethoven's father was a tenor singer by profession but he had some knowledge of violin and clavier, which he taught his son. At eight, Beethoven already knew all he could give him. His father is also said to have played oboe and flute and sometimes during the day when sober, as he was an inveterate drunkard, he would play upon these instruments, accompanied by his son. It must have sounded very nice because passersby stopped to listen to the delightful music.

All this helped to give Beethoven a familiarity with various instruments so that as a growing boy he was already writing trios for piano, flute and bassoon, duets for two flutes, an octet for wood wind and other music, now mostly lost or destroyed. Strange to say, Beethoven was never able to dance as a youth because he could not keep step with the music.

When Beethoven was around thirty, there were wild rumors that he was actually an illegitimate son of Frederick-the-Great. He resembled him, and Beethoven never bothered to refute the story. It may even have pleased him to look like an Emperor—for he was, indeed, himself king of all. However, a number of Beethoven's devoted and faithful friends were indignant, because these stories were published in several newspapers throughout Europe and nothing was done to contradict them. "The absurdity of the whole affair," they used to say, "don't they know that, unlike Beethoven's real father, whose wife religiously delivered a child every year, Frederick-the-Great has been impotent all his life and that when Beethoven was born he was close to sixty?"

Beethoven experienced his first real knowledge of his deafness one morning, when walking with his friend and pupil Ries, in the country outside Vienna. Ries asked him to stop and listen to the beautiful sound of a lilac-wood flute made and played by a shepherd, not very far from where they were. Beethoven, to his horror, had heard not a single sound and he was only a little over thirty!

*   *   *   *

The flutist's ten commandments. . . .

The original title of the following is: "The Instrumentalist's Ten Commandments" and it concerns students. It was taken from the *Etude* years ago and is as good today as it will be many years hence.

1. Keep your instrument clean.

2. Remember that slow practice is the study of the gods.

3. Honor your teacher—even if you do believe that you know more than he does.

4. Less practice on your instrument—but more thinking and studying away from it will be conducive to greater results and higher development.

5. Embrace every opportunity to play concerted music. If there are no opportunities, create them.

6. Keep your ears and eyes open to everything and everybody; in other words, study carefully the method of every artist.

7. Be a musician as well as an executant.

8. Remember that though you may be able to play everything from A to Z it does not mean that you are a musician.

9. Remember that an ounce of tonal quality is worth a ton of technique.

10. Work for your health, while working to achieve artistic ambitions; for fresh air, deep breathing and long walks mean renewed vigor and mental activity.

*   *   *   *

Famous flutists who changed from the old to the Boehm flute. . . .

Altès, Briccialdi, Carte, Dorus, Radcliff, Rockstro, Taffanel, Krakamp, Barrett, Clinton, Coché. A number of the above famous flutists who had played the old system made the change

320

readily to the Boehm flute and some tried to improve it. Dorus thought the change to the new flute with the open G-sharp was much too difficult and contrived the closed G-sharp key which made it easier. Flutists in general, particularly those that had played the old flute, called it "an improvement on the Boehm flute." Briccialdi, whose enthusiasm for the new flute was so great that he mastered it and appeared in concert after only two weeks—a feat unequalled by any other flutist—devised, besides the useful B-flat lever, the Briccialdi flute. It was a combination of the two and retained many positions of the old flute. Because of Briccialdi's great reputation it lasted longer than its merits warranted. Many others, especially the English flutists, Carte, Radcliff, Siccama, Barrett, Rockstro, etc., thought they could improve the Boehm flute. However, it remains today, with the exception of the Briccialdi B-flat lever and the Dorus closed G-sharp key, just as Boehm made it.

To Krakamp goes the credit for devising and applying the Boehm system to the other wood-wind instruments, particularly the clarinet, oboe and bassoon, and for which he wrote valuable methods. Tulou, who was as obstinate in his opposition to the new flute as Terschak was later, adapted the foot joint of the Boehm flute to the old, and called it the "Tulou flute."

The Schwedler "Reform flute" which was no reform at all, being simply the old flute polished up, has passed into oblivion.

Coché, another supposed innovator, whose admiration for Boehm was later changed into hostility, has been called a sort of a traitor by Christopher Welch, who did not hold the integrity of this otherwise fine artist's character in high esteem. Professor Piazza, and a few others, claimed that the best flute of them all was devised by Vincenzo De Michelis of Rome. He was at one time so famous a flutist in the eternal city that in order to have him play a solo, wealthy people used to send their luxurious four-horse carriages for him. I have never even heard of a De Michelis flute being played by anybody. The flute was exclusively made of a very special kind of wood, never of metal!

Now that flutists, and others, have nearly given up improving the Boehm flute, what should concern them most is the new material of which the flute should be made. Platinum, on ac-

321

count of its prohibitive price has not been and could not be popular. There remain the plastics. What we really need is a material that will combine the beautiful, true flute tone that wood imparts with the freedom from care and ease of tone production to be found in the metal flute. In Munich, in 1926, I met a prominent flutist and composer who had been a pupil of Professor Tillmetz. He played on a conical Boehm flute because, he told me, he considered its tone much more satisfactory and *flute-like* than the cylindrical Boehm flute. And this in the City of Boehm and long after its acceptance by all!

*　*　*　*

Famous flutists who declined to change from the old to the Boehm flute. . . .

Among these were: Andersen, Ciardi, Demersseman, Drouet, De Michelis, Galli, Hugues, Marini, Franceschini, Piazza, Terschak, Tulou, Franz and Karl Doppler, Rabboni, Furstenau, Buchner, Zamperoni, and Koehler.

Some thought that by changing, it would jeopardize the mastery and virtuosity for which they had worked so hard and so long. Others, holding important and responsible positions were afraid of the transition and, others still, were naturally against innovations and refused emphatically to make the change.

Andersen who, by the way, was as much against double tonguing as he was antagonistic to the Boehm flute, said that the real staccato on the flute should be single tonguing. He, therefore, while his contemporaries were discussing or studying the possibilities of the new flute, practiced so much single tonguing staccato, to prove his theory that it could be done, that he injured the tip of his tongue and, in the last years of his life, could not play at all!

Ciardi was not against the new flute. He simply had neither the patience nor the time to master it. In St. Petersburg, where he enjoyed a great reputation as solo flutist to the Czar, he composed a great deal, had numerous pupils, mostly among the aristocracy and, besides, he devoted much time to his avocation, sculpture. When some of his pupils wanted to learn the new flute he good-naturedly sent them to Carl Wehner who had arrived from Munich and had studied with Boehm himself. The same may be said of Professor Franceschini of Rome who took enough interest in the new flute to write a valuable work on it and also adopted it at Santa Cecilia Conservatory. It was different with Tulou, Drouet, Piazza, Demersseman, the last of whom was refused the professorship at the Paris Conservatory because of it, Terschak, and many others. These were ferocious and real detractors of the Boehm flute and held back its adoption for a long time.

*   *   *   *

The sad fate of some talented flutists. . . .

(Note: The following list—fortunately not a long one—comprises some eminent names. I would like to reverse the chronological order and begin with comparatively recent events while going gradually backwards in time.)

ALBERT FRANSELLA: World-famous Dutch flute virtuoso and teacher, took his own life in London in 1934 at the age of 69.

FRANCESCO LONGO: An excellent Italian flutist and pianist, took his own life in New York in 1932 at 46 years of age.

MICHELE VITA: A flutist of unusual talent, died of appendicitis in Jersey City, New Jersey, in 1912 at the age of 18.

RICHARD SHEPHERD ROCKSTRO: This world-famous flutist, teacher and author of *The Flute* while taking his usual morning walk dropped dead on the sidewalk in London in 1906. His body lay for many hours in the morgue, unknown, before his family claimed it. He was 81 years of age.

EURYSTHENES GHISAS: A Greek flutist of great talent who studied at Vienna Conservatory with Roman Kukula, died of tuberculosis in Vienna in 1900 at the age of 25.

VIGO ANDERSEN: Solo flutist of the Chicago Symphony, of great talent and a brother to Joachim Andersen, took his own life in Chicago in 1895 at the age of 43.

EMANUELE KRAKAMP: Famous flutist, teacher, composer and pedagogue, died blind in Naples in 1883 at 70 years of age.

SIDNEY LANIER: American flutist and poet of distinction died of consumption in 1881 in Baltimore at 39 years of age.

SEBASTIAN OTT: German flutist who studied with Boehm at the same time as Carl Wehner, died of consumption in Hanover in 1870 at the age of 34.

AGIDE AERTS: Eminent Belgian flutist and composer also of orchestral works, died of consumption in 1853 in Antwerp at 31 years of age.

JULES DEMERSSEMAN: Eminent Dutch flute virtuoso and prolific composer also of orchestral works, died of tuberculosis in France in 1866 at 33 years of age.

HANS HEINDL: German flutist of rare talent was killed by accident in Germany in 1849 at 21 years of age.

LUDWIG DULON: German flutist and composer who had a marvelous memory, was born blind. He died in Germany in 1826 at 57 years of age.

A. BECQUIE: French flutist and composer of talent, died of consumption in Paris in 1825 at the age of 25.

A. HUGOT: Famous French flutist, composer and teacher at the Paris Conservatory, because of a nervous fever, took his own life in Paris in 1803 at 42 years of age.

FRANCOIS DEVIENNE: French flutist and composer of operas of great distinction died insane in Paris in 1803 at 44 years of age.

*　　*　　*　　*

Flutists innovators. . . .

Quantz, Capeller, Boehm, Monzani, Hotteterre, Rudall, Tromlitz, Siccama, Radcliff, Briccialdi, Dorus, Logier, Rockstro, Albisi, Schwedler, De Michelis, Ribock, Giorgi, Barrett.

*　　*　　*　　*

One-armed flutists. . . .

Several one-armed persons have played the flute with special mechanical aids, the lower end being supported by a pillar attached to a table. The most famous of these was Count Rebsomen who had lost his left arm and his right leg in Napoleon's

324

campaigns. The Count was an excellent performer, possessing considerable execution, and it is said that the audience would not have discovered from his playing that he had only one hand. The keys were opened by the second joints of the right hand fingers and all his flutes were made either by him or under his personal supervision. He was a pupil of Berbiguier and Coché held him in high esteem for his ingenuity and skill.

*   *   *   *

Berbiguier, Blavet and Sola were left-handed flutists.

*   *   *   *

Famous flutists and noted dilettanti who attained old age. . . .

Krakamp, 70; Wysham, 70; Farrenc, 71; Hugues, 71; Giulius Gabrielsky, 72; Franceschini, 73; Radcliff, 74; Tillmetz, 74; Dr. Dayton C. Miller, 74; Wehner, 74; Frederick II, King of Prussia, 74; Coché, 75; Karl Doppler, 76; Heinemayer, 76; Quantz, 76; Belcke, 79; Tromlitz, 79; Rockstro, 81; Drouet, 82; Gariboldi, 82; Richard Carte, 83; Count Marini, 83; Lobe, 84; Barge, 85; Edward De Jong, 85; John Lemmoné, 87; Boehm, 88; Büchner, 88; Rudall, 90; Schroeck, 96; L. Hotteterre, 99; Maurer, 101.

*   *   *   *

Famous flutists who died young. . . .

Duverges, 39; Lanier, 39; Egner, 36; Knosing, 34; Sagras, 31; Becquié, 25; Heindl, 21; Vita, 18.

*   *   *   *

Famous detractors of the flute. . . .

It is not known definitely whether Mozart or Cherubini originated the well-known quip, "What is worse than one flute?" the answer to which was, "two flutes." This always reminds me of an incident many years ago while on tour with a symphony orchestra. We played Mozart's Concerto for flute, harp and orchestra almost every afternoon, and upon one occasion just before going on stage, the harpist turned to me and said, "De Lorenzo, what is worse than one flute?" My snappy retort was,

325

"two harps." (After the concert, Emil Oberhoffer, the conductor, told Williams, the harpist, and myself that this was a remarkable performance. However, I called my colleague's attention to what Berlioz once said: "A harpist is a person who spends half of his life tuning the harp, and the other half playing out-of-tune.") Among the famous personalities who have expressed a dislike for the flute were Goethe, Dickens, Bulwer-Lytton, Browning, Charlotte Bronte, Ernest Newman and Antonio Ghislanzoni. I presume there are many others but these illustrate that it is not all praise and a "bed of roses" for flutists in this world. However, it will not harm us to see ourselves as others see us and therefore let us know the worst. Since it is not too long, I should like to quote here entirely an article which originated, it seems, in the *Philadelphia Inquirer*. It bears the caption, "Flute Players Never Popular as Neighbors."

"Flute playing appears to have gone out of fashion and it has been suggested that this is because of the denunciation that the instrument has received from the pen of eminent writers. Violinists and pianists sometimes figure in fiction as heroes and heroines, but performers upon the flute are generally introduced into novels only as comic or unpleasant characters. At least three comic characters of Dickens were flute players: Dick Swiveller, who took to it as a 'good, sound, dismal occupation' and was consequently requested to remove himself to another lodging; Mr. Mell, the schoolmaster, who 'made the most dismal sounds I ever heard produced by any means, natural or artificial,' and the young gentleman at Mrs. Todger's musical party who 'blew his melancholy into the flute.' Bulwer-Lytton wrote of a clever school boy who, 'unluckily took to the flute and unfitted himself for the present century,' and Charlotte Bronte represents 'inept curates' as performing upon it. Then there was also Goethe, who summed up the case against the flute thus: 'There is scarcely a more melancholy suffering to be undergone that what is forced upon us by the neighborhood of an incipient player on the flute.' In his *A Musical Motley* Ernest Newman, the distinguished English musical critic and writer, becomes almost eloquent in his denunciations of the flute. He calls it a

326

'rather lymphatic instrument'—'the pale flute of the modern orchestra'—'the flaxen-haired high school Miss among orchestral instruments.' He goes on further to say, 'of all instruments the flute is intellectually the feeblest—it should be played by young men in spectacles, rejoicing in some gravely comical name, as Tootal—The very manner of playing it, sideways from the face, is an incitement to hilarity; no artist would dare to depict an angel playing the transverse flute!' "

It was because of his love for the flute that Benvenuto Cellini's father was called a failure and this has also been said of Thoreau. However, certainly Schopenhauer was not a failure. Yet he, who was most happy when unhappy, played the flute every day of his life. The most sympathetic and amusing satire on the flute, however, comes from the pen of Antonio Ghislanzoni, the librettist of Verdi's *Aida*. In writing of musical instruments he said of the flute: "The unhappy man who succumbs to the fascinations of this instrument is never one who has attained the full development of his intellectual faculties. He always has a pointed nose, marries a short-sighted woman, and dies run over by an omnibus." "The flute is the most deadly of all instruments. It requires a peculiar conformation and special culture of the thumb-nail, with a view to those holes which have to be only half closed. The man who plays the flute frequently adds to his other infirmities a mania for keeping weasels, turtle doves or guinea pigs." Finally, in the book of Revelations the author cites flutists and other musicians as among the factors responsible for the downfall of Babylon!

All the above insidious propaganda against our beautiful instrument and its performers is, needless to say, ill grounded and stupid. The flutist will continue to play and enjoy his favorite instrument to the chagrin of sour-faced people by ignoring them. He knows, too, that in his preference for the flute he is in the company of many famous men and rulers among whom—to name but a few—have been Frederick-the-Great, Francis I of Austria, those two noble souls, Henry David Thoreau and Sidney Lanier, and, to come down to recent times, the world-renowned physicist, Dr. Dayton C. Miller.

Flutists who earned distinction in fields other than flute-playing. . . .

Boehm, who, besides inventing the modern flute which bears his name, was the first to suggest the overstringing of the piano. He also invented a "device for transmitting rotatory motion" and was an expert goldsmith.

Ciardi, who, it was said, was fit to play with angels, was also a fine sculptor, a bust by him (of Anton Rubinstein) existing in one of the Russian theatres.

The prolific William Popp, who composed over 500 works for the flute, was also an excellent piano virtuoso, and appeared as soloist on that instrument with well-known orchestras.

Denner, the German flutist and instrument maker (1655-1707) was the inventor of the clarinet.

Briccialdi, called by many the Paganini of the flute, invented the B-flat thumb key (or lever) for the Boehm flute and later devised a flute of his own which was not a success.

Albisi (1873-1939), for many years solo flutist at La Scala in Milan, was the inventor of the "Albisiphone," a flute an octave lower, played vertically.

*   *   *   *

Krakamp, the great flute teacher, composer, and pedagogue, was wont to tell his pupils the old Italian proverb: "Chi più sa, meno sa" (He who knows more, knows less); and reminded them frequently that "per sonar bene, bisogna sonar molto" (to play well, one must play much), and also "l'esperienza è il miglior maestro" (experience is the best teacher).

*   *   *   *

Emil Medicus,* enthusiastic flute virtuoso, teacher, writer, idealist, philosopher, and one of the finest of men, telephoned me a couple of years ago that he was in Los Angeles. I immediately asked him to come up to Summit Ridge to our "Villa Pan" in Beverly Hills. We had been corresponding for about a

---

* I wish to express here my gratitude to Emil Medicus for allowing me many quotations from *The Flutist* and also supplying a number of "cuts" or "half-tones." His cooperation has been most admirable.

quarter of a century but had never met personally; so it was a pleasure to have him spend an afternoon with us. He visited us many times thereafter for dinner, flute ensemble and musicales. Medicus does not drink even the lightest kind of wines nor anything that could be called intoxicants; of course, he does not smoke. He is an ardent devotee of the wood flute, and believes it is the only real flute and that it will come back—but he generously agrees others should choose for themselves.

Medicus is such a fine gentleman and so gentle in character, one is inclined to think of him as a clergyman more than a musician and . . . a flute player! When, about twenty-five years ago, Medicus had the beautiful thought of publishing and editing a magazine entirely devoted to the flute, the response from all over, not only from the English-speaking countries but from practically all the countries of the civilized world, was amazing! Thus the flutists were, for the first time, given the pleasure of reading articles, programs, pictures, jokes, etc., etc., all concerning their favorite instrument! Flutists, too, began to contribute interesting material from South America, Australia, New Zealand, South Africa, the Scandinavian countries, Russia, the Orient, and of course, France, England, Germany, Italy, Austria, Spain, Honolulu, and, I am quite certain that not a single state of these United States of America and Canada was missing!

Now, how can one explain that a magazine which in a few years had won the hearts of so many lovers of the flute as to be thought almost indispensable, had to be given up and ceased to exist. It is unbelievable, especially in a country like America where newspapers, whether daily, weekly or monthly, have often grown and reached gigantic size? The answer is that Medicus was all alone in the great task and, consequently, it could not be done!

The Flutist, in order to survive and flourish should have been in the hands and management of a Colonel McCormick, a Pulitzer, or a Hearst.

Poor Medicus, when he was questioned about *The Flutist* answered as if he had lost a favourite child and, when "Villa Pan" changed its residence, in March of 1944, from Beverly

329

Hills to "Palos Verdes" (only about 45 minutes from Los Angeles), we for a time lost trace of him! I wrote to his Asheville address but several months elapsed before a letter reached me dated July 15, 1945. They had sold their farm and were building a new home on a beautiful place in the mountains of Western North Carolina, surrounded by beautiful scenery and with the most invigorating air one could desire and, last but not least, in a land of *sunshine!*

*   *   *   *

Hollywood flutists. . . .

California and the motion-picture studios have attracted numerous musicians of all sorts, from the lowest jazz players to the greatest virtuosi and composers. Some of the flutists who occupied prominent positions in symphony orchestras and who were lured by the more handsome salaries are: Ary Van Leeuwen, Henry Woempner, Anthony Linden, Julius Furman, J. J. Gilbert, Robert Bladet, Archie Wade, Leonard Posella, and Arthur Gleghorn.

Often an inferior violinist is concertmaster in the same orchestra in which a famous one sits on the last stand. If a studio wants an instrumentalist badly and desires to keep him, he is offered double pay! In this category I know of a cellist and a bassoonist. The same applies to players of other instruments; they include eminent violinists, cellists, oboists, bassoonists, etc. However, I have yet to hear one of these fine artists who is happy in this environment. Financially they have no complaint, but artistically . . . they are starved! Some of the more ambitious ones find comfort in ensemble playing of string quartets once a week in their homes. It is much more difficult for wind players. The long hours in the studios, often playing till 5 A.M., takes all the artistic feeling and ambition out of them.

Aside from these players, are other good flutists each in his own niche, such as: Helen Little, Janet Rogers, Luella Howard, Icilio Miccoli, Weyert Moor, William Hullinger, Harold Lewis, Louis Lewis, Martin Rudeman, and that prince of a fellow, the genial Harry Baxter.

330

The famous English flutist John Radcliff was at one time on a weekly salary of about $50.00 just to play duets for an hour or so with a lord who loved especially flute duet playing. One of the finest English flutists of today is indubitably Gordon Walker who, having not been in America, is known to but few here. Another notable flutist of theirs is John Amadio (Australasian), who is known here, having toured in concerts with more than one singer.

*   *   *   *

Carl Wehner had two sons and a daughter. Of these only the youngest, Anthony, is now living and I was most interested to hear from John Wummer, the noted flutist, that he is now caretaker for his summer home. He played flute at one time but gave it up several years ago. Carl Wehner told me that none of his children and least of all his wife, were musical.

*   *   *   *

Diego Rivera's *Creation* is a great mural painting in the National Preparatory School in Mexico. In modern idiom, it depicts Science, Earth, Woman Virtue, Charity, Hope, Faith, Prayer, Infinity, etc. Music is illustrated by an Indian playing on a double-flute of gold.

*   *   *   *

Daniel Alomia Robles, flutist and historian of Inca civilization, has devoted a great part of his life to archaeological and ethnological investigations in Peru tracing the "Lost Continent." Professor Robles exhibited in New York a group of ancient instruments of the Incan and earlier civilization including a set of Pan Pipes and flutes collected in his explorations in Andean tombs.

*   *   *   *

I had never heard the designation of "champion" applied to anybody except in boxing, prizefighting, wrestling, etc., until a friend of mine (a distinguished Doctor of Science, but, I am afraid, not a very distinguished flute dilettante) introduced a country boy of about fifteen to me as a "champion flute player."

The good doctor, who also lived in a small town in the State of New York, told me that he had promised the boy to secure for him an audition with me. The young man had brought two pieces with which he had always captured great applause and prizes. In placing Kranz's "Whirlwind" on the music stand without losing time, he attacked a veritable whirlwind by playing all the high notes with the positions of the lower ones and playing every A-sharp with the thumb on the B-flat. At long last, when the end came, both the doctor and the boy, I could see, were anxiously awaiting my verdict. "With whom did you study? He was not a flute player, was he?" I asked. "No, sir," the boy answered, "my flute teacher was a violinist" and immediately took out of his portfolio, to my horror, Briccialdi's "Il Vento." However, as soon as he played the first measure

fortissimo and struggling the best he could by shifting the thumb up and down from B-flat to B-natural, I stopped him. "My boy," I said, "that poor violinist didn't know a thing about the flute, and of course, you know just as little, you have been wasting precious time." I was very sorry to have disconcerted the boy. The doctor in private told me that in spite of the technical prowess which he admired, he had suspected that there might be something wrong with the instruction the boy had had. However, as the above tragi-comic story about the "champion flutist" took place at our country summer home near Naples, New York, in 1933, my wife treated our guests, these included also the doctor's wife and their two sons, one of whom was also interested in flute playing, with an excellent spaghetti dinner. After pitching horseshoes in many games, our guests departed happy and thankful for the wonderful day spent with us.

*   *   *   *

With a few strokes of his pen a few years ago, that amiable and distinguished French flutist, Louis Fleury, sought to bring down from their pedestals several famous and much-loved pioneers of the flute.

Fleury, unlike his illustrious schoolmate, Philippe Gaubert, who composed much and well, had not himself the gift of creating. Probably that was one of the reasons why he stated that flutists should not compose. Flutists, he said, compose trash because they lack musicianship!

And why, one likes to ask, should flutists lack musicianship? Quantz, one of his victims, was an honored pupil of the great Johann Sebastian Bach and his numerous and beautiful compositions reveal at a glance that his musicianship was of the highest level!

Kuhlau, another of our most beloved, he dismisses by saying that he is a "second rate composer." It has been stated numerous times by competent musicians that Kuhlau's trios for three flutes, the quartet for four flutes, and his three quintets for flute and strings can stand comparison with the best of Beethoven's chamber music for any combination of instruments. Their melodic invention, perfect form and contrapuntil inspiration are that of a genius, not less.

Fleury, then, goes on to say that Drouet, Demerssemann, Tulou and Berbiguier—all Frenchmen according to him, ignoring the fact that Drouet and Demerssemann were born in Holland—did a great deal of harm to good flute playing with their shallow compositions. I regret that Fleury held flute players in such low esteem that he evidently thought they could not distinguish good compositions from bad ones.

To these unjust remarks an excellent and scholarly answer was written by that fine and cultured gentleman and great lover of the flute, Mr. John Finn, in *The Flutist* of November 1924. Fleury, in quite different tone, but briefly, answers thus in *The Flutist* of February 1925:

"My article, 'The Flute and its Powers of Expression' was, above all, an explanation of my musical tastes and preferences. I do not like what Mr. Finn admires and he dislikes what I love. That is all. Indeed, I owe an apology to the glorious memory of Kuhlau, fine musician, who, without the slightest doubt was for

333

us flutists, a great master, though belonging to the Nineteenth Century."

Of course, Fleury eulogizes the sonatas of Bach and Handel, which we all possess and admire, though, of the six Bach sonatas we also know that the master had the flute in mind in only a couple of them because the others were written for violin instead of flute. In many editions one finds: "Six sonatas for violin (or flute) and piano." Fleury also informs us that he has unearthed worthy sonatas for flute and piano by little-known but excellent composers. These are by John Stanley, Daniel Purcell, Leonardo Vinci, Michel La Barre, General Reid, and a few others. Well, after perusing some of them, one is inclined to think that it was a mistake to disturb their long slumber. How infinitely superior to these are those unearthed, and rescued from eternal oblivion by Ary Van Leeuwen. I have in mind in particular a great sonata for two flutes and piano by Wilhelm Friedemann Bach, one for flute and piano in C major by Karl Philipp Emanuel Bach, a concerto by Boccherini and a concerto by Grétry for flute and strings, and numerous others, published abroad and in America some years ago. Also, unpublished because of the war, two sonatas by Domenico Scarlatti, one in E minor and one in G minor, a sonata for two flutes and piano by Karl Heinrich Graun (1701-1759), a trio for flute, viola d' Amore and piano by Johann Joachim Quantz. Six quintets for flute and strings by Boccherini, six for flute, and strings by Johann Christian Bach and a concerto for flute and strings by Karl Philipp Emanuel Bach, etc., etc. The flutistic world really owes a debt of gratitude to Ary Van Leeuwen, a great artist and an accomplished musician, second to none of the past and present.

Now, as for other giants unceremoniously pulled down from the niches, the following will amply illustrate. A friend of mine, an excellent violinist-composer, who studied violin with Sarasate and Auer and composition with Rimsky-Korsakov, Glazunov and Liadov, told me the following almost incredible story. At a "soirée" which he had arranged for a number of his friends, the majority of whom were ultra-modern composers, several of them made the request that there should be no mention of Beethoven's name the whole evening. One of them, however, went a little further. "When I answered the bell myself," said my friend, "this particular gentleman, who is in his early fifties and who has a considerable reputation internationally, acquired in the last twenty years, said to me: 'I hope you haven't a picture of Beethoven in your studio.' I said: 'I have a large portrait and a bust of Beethoven in my studio.' The modern composer announced that unless both were removed he would not enter but would return home at once!" Beethoven was hated the most, but Brahms and Wagner were treated with the same contempt. Not a word was said, however, against papa Bach, but Mozart, Gluck and Schubert were entirely ignored.

For Shostakovich they had great admiration and permitted no word to be said against him, though most of them were of the opinion that some of his symphonies were not very inspired.

*   *   *   *

In 1901 there came to Cape Town, South Africa, an American concert party in which there was a young lady flutist of considerable prominence and reputation. In an interview she stated that in order to keep in top shape, flute players should and must taboo . . . kissing! Of course, most of the flutists did not agree with the statement at all.

However, a week later, a young man, in coming for his lesson, told me that he regretted very much to have to give up flute playing because, he said, it is too difficult and it required more time in practicing than he could spare. He was advised, he said, to play, instead, a new instrument invented in Hawaii! When I saw him a few months later he confessed that it was the statement of the young American flutist that had caused him to give up his flute for the Ukulele—but, he continued, I hate the instrument and I want to go back to the flute—you see, he said with a smile, at that time I was engaged and now I am married!

*   *   *   *

Almost every music teacher is familiar with the type of student who changes from one teacher to another. Always on the search for the wonder teacher who can make artists of them in short order, not realizing that the fault lies in themselves. Unstable in

335

character, possibly unmusical and unable to learn as rapidly as they think they should, they invariably believe their lack of progress is all the teacher's fault. These students abound in all cities but especially so in New York City.

Then there are the students who disappear after a few lessons without paying for them, and those who borrow instruments and never return them. It has been my sad experience to know them both. I arrived in New York with an abiding faith in all mankind—and with a total lack of business experience. Among my first pupils was one who took a whole month's lessons and then vanished, without paying for them. Another, an Italian, who had been in America a number of years and spoke poor English and abominable Italian, never returned an instrument I had lent him. This young man of about 35 said he was working in a sweater shop in Brooklyn. He had only a six-keyed flute— and he spoke disparagingly of an old man to whom he had gone to inquire about lessons, saying he had shut the door in his face when he saw his miserable flute. A little careful questioning revealed that it was Carl Wehner. Poor old man, he was reduced to teaching for only one dollar per lesson. I made it very clear to the young man that he was a "grand old man" and worthy of great respect.

It was, of course, necessary for this would-be student to have a fairly satisfactory flute, and when I advised him to buy an inexpensive Boehm flute, possibly on easy terms, he said he had tried but that it was necessary for someone to guarantee the payments. He then told me that I, as a compatriot, should help him either as a guarantor or, better still, lend him one if I had an extra one to spare.

I had a cheap metal flute for emergencies, which had cost me about $40.00 including the change from closed to open G-sharp; I lent that to him. He, unfortunately, showed little aptitude for music and I was on the point of telling him to give up flute playing and stick to sweater making when he disappeared—flute and all!

But I still have my faith and I have continued to lend my extra flutes to my pupils and friends.

Also in New York, at that time, another young man came.

336

He said: "I should very much like to become a professional musician, and as I am particularly fond of the flute, I came to you to inquire about preliminary arrangements. "However," he said, "before anything else I wish to know *how soon I would be ready for a good job.*" My answer was: "How long have you played the flute, with whom have you studied previously and what kind of a flute have you?" He answered that he had never played on any musical instrument before and had never taken a music lesson in his life, but thought he could do as well as anyone else with his *above the average* intelligence and desire to be a musician!

* * * *

A young woman of unusual intelligence and culture decided to study flute with me at the Eastman School of Music in Rochester, New York, a few years ago because, she said, her great uncle, a colonel, had played flute and she inherited the relic, a six-keyed flute made at least 150 years ago. The other reason was because of all the instruments in the Rochester Philharmonic, the flute appealed to her more than any other. She was, incidentally, captain of the Girl Scouts and visited Europe nearly every summer. On the ship back home the third year of her flute studies she met two other young women, also flute students. Upon asking one of them where she was from and who was her teacher, she said: "I am from Cincinnati and my teacher is the greatest flute player and teacher in the world—Ary Van Leeuwen. He has taught at the Vienna Conservatory and played under Gustave Mahler, Nikish and Richard Strauss!" The other young lady was from New York. She said: "I am quite sure that I am the privileged one because everybody knows that Georges Barrère, and no other, is the greatest player and teacher of the flute in the world!" When the Rochester young lady, finally, had to say whom was she studying with, she answered: "As the two of you have exhausted all the superlatives, I might as well tell you that that is exactly the way I feel about my teacher." Incidentally, the three veteran flutists, a Dutchman, a Frenchman and an Italian, born within a few months of each other—Barrère being the junior—were on good terms and the admiration was mutual!

337

The above authentic little story reminds me that, way back in 1893, when only about 17 years old, in a little town in Arkansas while waiting for a winter job which never materialized, I was having a grand time one day practicing some beautiful etudes of Soussman, Drouet, Furstenau and also Briccialdi's excellent Op. 31 book II, when suddenly the door of my modest little room was opened and an old farmer entered and, without as much as introducing himself, said to me: "Young man, I thought I was the greatest flute player in the world, now I know that I was wrong," and left without another word!

A few days later, also while practicing, there was a knock on the door and a man of about 35 came in. He said: "Well, I thought it was a man who was playing. I see you are only a boy, where did you learn? You are an extraordinary player and should be in a large town. I am a flutist, myself, traveling with a show and leaving tomorrow." I played for him some Drouet etudes which I had memorized and invited him to play some duets by Kuhlau with me. He said he had no time because he had a show to play in the afternoon and one at night and was leaving in the morning for New York where he lived with his wife and children. I did not know of what nationality he might be but he spoke with almost as strong an accent as I. He suggested that if I would give him the etudes of Drouet he would forward, in exchange, some marvellous studies which he knew I did not have. I did what he suggested and lost the Drouet book. I never have remembered his name and could never understand his behavior, as he was apparently a fine person. Possibly he lost my name and address; this would be the kindest thing to say of him.

*   *   *   *

Women flutists. . . .

Four of the finest women flutists in New York City are: Frances Blaisdell, Ruth Freeman, Sarah Possell, and Mildred Hunt Wummer.

Four of the finest women flutists in Los Angeles are: Luella Howard, Helen Mead Little, Jeanette M. Rogers, and Doriot Anthony.

The solo flutist of the Indianapolis Symphony is Harriet Peacock.

* * * *

An interesting book was published by Theodor Presser Company, of Philadelphia, and edited by Guy McCoy in 1946, entitled *Portraits of the World's Best Known Musicians* and subtitled "Nearly 5000 portraits each accompanied by a short biographical note. In the grand procession of those foremost throughout five centuries of musical progress" the following flutists are included: Barrère, Boehm, De Lorenzo, Devienne, Frederick-the-Great, Gaubert, Henry VIII, Kincaid, Kuhlau, Lanier, Le Roy, Lobe, Luening, Maganini, Nicholson, Popp, Prill, Quantz, Richardson, Sabathil, Schwedler, Strinfield, Taffanel, Van Vactor and Meredith Willson.

Many flutists will ask: "How about the other great followers of Pan: Amadio, Andersen, Briccialdi, De Assis, Doppler, Fleury, Kohler, Lemmoné, Moyse, Radcliff, Reichert, Ribas, Terschak, Van Leeuwen, Wehner and numerous others of equal importance?" The answer is that only those few came to the notice of the editor and, besides, it is not a *book on flutists!*

* * * *

Carlo Tommaso Giorgi, of the famous Keyless "Flauto Giorgi"—see the Encyclopedia Britannica—whom I met at Viareggio, near Florence, Italy, in 1926, was one of the youngest men of 72 I had ever met. As I suggested that I would compose a piece for flute on his hundredth birthday, he said: "Fine, but be sure to avoid double sharps and double flats, which I hate!" Giorgi broke another flutistic rule, he was a . . . millionaire.

* * * *

A flutist's peculiar hobby. . . .

A boy, fourteen years of age, and extremely talented on the flute, had a hobby rare in a boy of that age, namely hunting *palindromes*, that is, words or sentences which can be read the same forward and backward. He would peruse books of all sorts, dictionaries, magazines, newspapers, etc., and whenever he found

339

a word that could be read both ways he was happy beyond words and immediately would write it in his album. The following are a few of them: "aa," river in Livonia; "Aa," a Hawaiian brittle substance; "aiaia," word composed entirely of vowels. "Now, Ned, I am a maiden won." "Aekkea," airplane factory in Athens, Greece. "Eye," name of pharaoh who succeeded Tutenkhamon. "En af dem der med fane," it means: one of those who rode with a banner. "Anna Reber, 404 Renner," name and address of a lady in Cincinnati, Ohio. "Naian," Chinese general. "Iki," island in Japan. "Serres," a Macedonian city. "Aya," Spanish for governess. "Xolox," town in Mexico. "Seres," community of the far East. "Edde," president of Republic of Lebanon. "Name no one man." "Kayak," Eskimo canoe for one person. "Kazak," Republic of soviet Russia in Central Asia. "Oro," Italian for gold. "Kanatanak," in Alaska. "Akka," a wandering tribe of dwarfs in central Africa in 1874. "Ofo," family god of Nigeria, West Africa. "Ala," name of Iranian Ambassador and also Italian for *wing*. "Nonon," name of Tulou's partner in a flute manufactory (1831). "Sas," Peruvian living composer. "Utu," a religious Sumarian name. "Solos." "A man, a plan, a canal, Panama." "Reher," solo cellist Los Angeles Philharmonic. "Reger," German composer. "Reyer," French composer. "Repper," American composer. "Nin," Spanish composer. "Isasi," Basque composer. "Mem," Egyptian flute. "Kodok," region in Central Africa. "Nun." "Sees." "Radar." "Sinis," a river in Lucania, Italy.

The boy's album contains numerous others, some in Latin, Hebrew, and other languages. Also several "canons" to be played with one or two flutes forward and backward at the same time and one, almost a full page, for flute and bassoon, and his initials, also read the same backward, A.B.A.

The boy told me he had another hobby, started only a few weeks ago, but much more important and useful to the general public than *palindromes*. Easy automobile numbers for everyone to remember. Instead of say: 5917, or 4086, or 2819 and so forth, why not: 1122, 1112-1222-2221-1221-2211-2121-1212-2222-1111, etc., etc., *ad infinitum?* As you see, by using only two figures I have already easy numbers for ten cars. "This way,"

340

he said, "I could furnish an easy number for every automobile in Los Angeles, or Detroit, New York, London and all the other great cities in the world. Do you see," he continued, "the advantage of having easy numbers?" Not only at a distance and at full speed a person could instantly see and memorize the four or five numbers of a car but one's own number would also be easy to remember.

* * * *

Apparently, nothing is impossible to a flute-player. However, to most people it is difficult to reconcile the fact that a sober and serious musician who composes symphonies can at the same time be a professional comedian! It is a paradox, no doubt, but that is the case and the man is right here in Beverly Hills. Of course, we have flutist jesters in olden times but, as far as is known, they couldn't compose a symphony. But let us proceed.

Some time ago, to be exact on Friday the 13th of September 1946, the stenographer, Mrs. Clara Meyer of Redondo Beach, California, who worked on my book intelligently and efficiently and now claims vast knowledge of the history of the flute and flutists, called me on the telephone and told me that an interesting illustrated article about a flutist composer who was also a comedian had appeared in *Radio Life* that week.

The article, written by Coy Williams, tells of Meredith Willson's experience during twenty years with radio and contains several pictures of Willson, etc., some playing the flute. It speaks of him as a noted conductor-composer and a comedian and emcee of growing importance who has seen radio expand from an "awkward stepchild of the entertainment field into the world's most powerful medium of information."

Willson, who, besides some popular music has composed two symphonies, performed several times in San Francisco and other places, was solo flutist with the famous Sousa band, with which he traveled all over Europe, and for several seasons was a member of the flute section of the New York Philharmonic.

* * * *

W. S. Haynes said a few years ago that there were 20,000 flutists, including the amateurs in America. Other authorities state

341

that the professional alone approximates 30,000. Therefore, with an incredible number of dilettanti, the stupendous figure of 100,000 will be reached! It is one of the healthiest of instruments to play upon and one of the most beloved.

* * * *

While most of the numerous "Flute Clubs" in America and other countries discontinued their activities during the war, the San Diego and Chula Vista Flute Club, with that excellent artist, Arthur Brooke, at the head as teacher and advisor, flourished and is flourishing now as much as ever. A picture of a group of fifteen handsome flute players, eleven girls and four boys, with Brooke in the center, has just reached me (June 1946). There are a number of others in the Club who could not be present at the time the picture was taken. They meet once a month at one of their homes to play solos and ensemble music. Each member has the privilege to bring two guests and there are no dues or other expenses at any time.

* * * *

An attractive, young and very able colleague visited me one afternoon. On my writing desk were numerous papers concerning "Famous Flutes and Flutists." In scanning several pages at random in *Thumbnail Biographies*, the young man remarked: "Very interesting, it must have taken you an awfully long time of research; my goodness, you have hundreds and hundreds of our colleagues here." Suddenly he stopped and, pointing to one place, said: "I envy that man more than any other. For a position of that sort, I would sign a *life contract* for just board and lodging." He was pointing to the name of the man who was flute instructor at the *Harem of Constantinople!*

* * * *

The American Woodwind-Composer Quintet——
A group of five young American Instrumentalist Composers:
Flute, David Van Vactor (Chicago, Ill.), born in Plymouth, Indiana, 1906.

342

Oboe, Alvin Etler (Indianapolis, Ind.), born in Battle Creek, Iowa, 1913.

Clarinet, Robert McBride (Bennington, Vt.), born in Tucson, Arizona, 1911.

Bassoon, Adolph Weiss (Los Angeles, Calif.), born in Baltimore, Maryland, 1891.

French Horn, John Barrows (Minneapolis, Minn.), born in Glendale, California, 1913.

The fact that each of the five is a virtuoso of his instrument as well as a composer, makes this particular group almost a unique one. It was carefully chosen to represent, in an artistic way, this country's good will toward South America. The itinerary, always by air, was as follows:

August	8, 1941	Mexico City, D.F.
August	16	Guatemala City, Guatemala
August	17	San Jose, Costa Rica
August	19	Panama City, Panama
August	24	Medellin, Colombia
August	25	Bogota, Colombia
August	27	Cali, Colombia
August	29	Quito, Ecuador
August	31	Lima, Peru
September	6	Santiago, Chile
September	9	Buenos Aires, Argentina
September	11	Rosario, Argentina
September	12	Rio de Janeiro, Brazil
September	17	Recife, Pernambuco, Brazil
September	26	Port of Spain, Trinidad
October	1	San Juan, Porto Rico
October	3	Trujillo, San Domingo
October	5	Port au Prince, Haiti
October	6, 1941	Back to U.S. via Cuba to Miami, Fla.

The programs included classics as well as modern compositions by Walter Piston, Villa Lobos, Leo Sowerby, O. L. Fernandez and a *Divertimento* in five movements, each composed by one of the group:

343

Allegro by Alvin Etler
Andante by John Barrows
Rondo by Adolph Weiss
Gavotta by David Van Vactor
Jam Session by Robert McBride

The dean of the five is Adolph Weiss for two reasons: he is a few years older than the rest and also because of his unusual number of compositions to his credit which includes sonatas, quartets (for both wind and strings), quintets, sextets, orchestral works, songs with string quartet, a concerto for bassoon with string quartet (recorded with the composer playing the solo part and Scipione Guidi's Quartet), etc. Weiss is one of Arnold Schoenberg's most faithful disciples. The other member of equal eminence in composition is the flutist, David Van Vactor.

Besides compositions for the quintet, they also played duets, trios and quartets.

*   *   *   *

The flute sections of major American orchestras. . . .

New York Philharmonic—John Wummer, Amedeo Ghignatti, William Heim, Emil Pagano.

Philadelphia Orchestra—William Kincaid, Kenton Terry, Burnett Atkinson, John Fischer.

Boston Symphony—Georges Laurent, J. Pappoutsakis, P. Kaplan, G. Madsen.

Cincinnati Symphony—Alfred E. Fenboque, Robert Cavally, Ruth Dunning.

Chicago Symphony—Harvey Noack, George Soeller, Emil Eck, Caroline Vacha.

Cleveland Symphony—Maurice Sharp, Martin Heylman, Robert Willoughby, Robert Morris.

Baltimore Symphony—Britton Johnson, Wilfrid Robbilard, Michael A. Richter.

Los Angeles Philharmonic—George Drexler, Doriot Anthony, Roger Stevens.

Janssen Symphony of Los Angeles—Harold Lewis, Barbara Putnam, Telejoe Freeman.

San Francisco Symphony—Paul Renzi, Ralph Shanis, Herbert Benkman.
Pittsburgh Symphony—Sebastian Caratelli, Philip Sieburg, Herbert Levy.
Indianapolis Symphony—Harriet Peacock, Francis Fitzgerald, Richard Koch, Artur Denning.
Washington National Symphony—Wallace W. Mann, Albert Wetherly, James Arcaro.
Rochester Philharmonic—Joseph Mariano, Thomas Wilt, Daniel Groth.
Kansas City Symphony—Claude Monteux, Lilburn Knowland, John B. Gillam.
Saint Louis Symphony—Albert N. Tipton, Laurent Torno, John F. Kiburz.
Minneapolis Symphony—René Rateau, Julia Denecke, Emil Niosi.
Metropolitan Opera Orchestra, New York—H. Bennett, H. de Vries, H. Hirsh, F. Monone.

*   *   *   *

A modern Pied Piper. . . .
John Heywood, of England, has been using a flute of his own construction to exterminate pests. A query which I sent him about his endeavors elicited the following reply:

164 Stephensons Way
Corby, Northants, England
21—3—50

Dear Mr. DeLorenzo:
Received your letter of the 15th inst. for which I thank you. Well, my flute is made of wood with metal end and fitted with a reed something after the style of a mouth organ but with only two reeds. It is made to imitate the call of a Rat, the Mating Call, both Male and Female. I have made a few cases of Ebonite with metal ends and Brass Reeds, a better job altogether and would last for years made like this. Well, I am the only man in the world to my knowledge that can flute Rats from their nests. This flute will not be much use commercially as it would take people so long to get the right

notes. By the way, it took me four years to get the right notes after laying amongst rats for weeks on end, also keeping them in captivity. I do use this flute in my work on Pest Destruction, as I am a professional in this class of work.

Do you write stories for books? Well, I have just finished my life story of Rats and other vermin which a gentleman asked for in New York, but I have not heard from him since. I have had letters from all over the world asking for my services, hundreds of them. Do you think my story as the Pied Piper would have a great sale in America? The gentleman who asked for it said that it would be easy to get rid of a million copies. Please drop me a line what you think about it. I have scores of press-cuttings and photos, which would all help to make it popular. Thanking you once again.

Yours sincerely,

J. Heywood (signed)

P.S. My age is 50 years. Married with one daughter aged 14 years.

On the very day I received Heywood's letter, there appeared an Associated Press story in the newspapers calling for a new Pied Piper for the town of Hamelin, Germany, which appeared once again to be infested with rats. The story ran as follows:

"The city fathers of Hamelin are looking for another Pied Piper.

"The town, site of many grain mills, is infested with rats and mice. Some officials claim Hamelin has more rats per capita than any other city in Germany. . . .

"According to an ancient legend, a Pied Piper appeared in Hamelin one day in the year 1284 and offered to rid the city of its then current rat plague. He was hired and walked through Hamelin tootling on his flute. All the rats and mice followed him and drowned in the River Weser.

"But, the legend says, the town refused to pay the piper his agreed reward, so he piped all Hamelin's children—numbering 130—out of the city in the same way and all were lost except two—one blind, and the other lame. Every summer the fairy tale is reenacted here down to the last detail.

"Now, if you think you can rid Hamelin of its rodent population, with a pipe or by any other means, you will be accepted with open arms in Hamelin—if your scheme works. You will be expected, however, to leave the children. There are more of them now."

John Heywood, please take note!

Part Three

THE MUSIC

A Thing or Two
About Flute Music

Folia is an old 14th century Spanish dance to the accompaniment of several flutes and castanets. It suggests the "madness" of pleasure rather than of insanity.

*   *   *   *

In Rome, Italy, in 1714, there lived a man by the name of Roberto Valentini, or Valentin (of uncertain nationality) who published numerous solos and sonatas for the flute with the Wash Company of London. He also published sonatas for two flutes, and two flutes and bass, and some *Sets of Airs* and a *Chaconne* for two flutes.

*   *   *   *

Three old Italian composers were among the first to introduce the flute in an opera orchestra: Striggio (1535-1587), Corteccia (?-1571), and Cavaliere (c.1550-1602).

*   *   *   *

In December 1600, Jacopo Peri (1561-1633), of noble parentage, produced the first opera-seria, *Euridice*, at Florence. This opera was accompanied by an orchestra consisting of harpsi-

349

chord, a large guitar, a great lyre (viola da gamba), a large lute (theorbo). These instruments were hidden from the proscenium as were, in all probability, three flutes used in a certain scene in which the shepherd, Tirsi, pretends to play upon a triple pipe (Triflauto) which he holds in his hands.

* * * *

A manuscript of Girolamo Frescobaldi (1583-1643), famous Italian organist and composer, was discovered in Rome in 1943. It contains twenty-seven fugues in three and four parts, an "elevation," nineteen songs—and a sonata for flute.

* * * *

Other Italian composers of the past wrote fine works for the flute. . . .

Pietro Locatelli (1693-1764), famous violinist and composer, wrote several sonatas for two flutes.

Francesco Maria Veracini (1690-1750) published a set of sonatas for violin and flute in Venice in 1716.

Antonio Vivaldi (1675-1741) wrote a concerto for flute and orchestra, in the key of D major, which he subtitled "Il Cardellino."

* * * *

Two famous themes and three historical personalities. . . .

The first of the two themes is the one given to J. S. Bach on the latter's visit to San Souci in 1740 by Frederick-the-Great; the other was supplied to Domenico Scarlatti by his pet cat while the master was at the instrument, probably putting down one of his famous 500 piano sonatas.

Frederick-the-Great's theme is the following:

This is called "Soggetto Reale" in the Sonata in C minor for flute, violin and basso continuo which Bach developed into a veritable masterpiece of counterpoint. The theme is heard in-

350

termittingly by the three instruments. When the theme is played by the flute, the violin plays thus:

to which the flute answers:

On that occasion Bach, besides visiting his son, Karl Philipp Emanuel, who was the harpsichordist in Frederick-the-Great's orchestra, paid homage to the King who had invited him and who was a great admirer of the master, and also was happy to greet Joachim Quantz, who had been one of Bach's most eminent pupils in composition.

The second theme, Scarlatti's *Cat Fugue*, is the following:

A part of this sonata the writer has transcribed for two flutes and may be found at the end of volume II in his *The Flutist's Vademecum* (Aug. Cranz, Leipzig).

*   *   *   *

The Flute Sonatas of Bach and Handel. . . .

The flute sonatas of Bach and Handel occupy a preeminent place in the literature of the flute.

In the Peter's edition of the flute sonatas the first three were edited by Ferd. David, the famous violinist, because it was believed that Bach wrote them for either violin or flute. However, they are listed as *Three Sonatas for Clavier and Flute* in the Bach Gesellshalft edition, brought out in 1859.

The Handel sonatas, on the other hand, in the Peter's edition were edited by the flutist Maximilian Schwedler. Handel was very fond of the oboe and very possibly had the oboe also in mind when composing these sonatas as, with the exception of a short passage here and there which must be played an octave lower, they fit the oboe admirably and are much enjoyed by oboists.

THE SIX SONATAS OF BACH

I B minor-Andante (Allegro Moderato); Largo, Presto, Allegro (moderato).

II E-flat major-Allegro Moderato, Siciliano, Allegro.

III A minor-Largo e dolce, Allegro, (Vivace).

IV C major-Andante, Presto, Allegro, Adagio, Minuetto I, Minuetto II.

V E minor-Adagio ma non tanto, Allegro, Andante, Allegro.

VI E major-Adagio ma non tanto, Allegro, Siciliano, Allegro Assai.

THE SEVEN SONATAS OF HANDEL

I E minor-Grave, Allegro, Adagio, Allegro.

II G minor-Adagio, Andante, Adagio, Presto.

III G major-Adagio, Allegro, Andante, Bourrée, Menuett.

IV C major-Larghetto, Allegro, Larghetto, Allegro, Tempo di Gavotta.

V F major-Larghetto, Allegro, Siciliana, Giga.

VI B minor-Largo, Vivace, Presto, Adagio, Minuetto.

VII A minor-Grave, Allegro, Adagio, Allegro appassionato.

* * * *

The flute played a prominent role as solo instrument in two of Bach's famous Brandenburg Concertos: the 2nd in F major, which calls for one solo flute, and the 4th in G major, enlisting two solo flutes.

Flute compositions by the Bach family. . . .

Bach, Karl Ph. Em., Sonata for flute alone (ed. Zimmermann).

Bach, Wilhelm Fr., Sonata for two flutes (ed. Adolph Nagel, Hanover).

Bach, Wilhelm Fr., Six duets for two flutes (ed. Breitkopf and Härtel). '

Bach, K. Ph. E., Trio in E major for two flutes and piano (ed. Zimmermann).

Bach, K. Ph. E., Sonata for flute, violin and piano (ed. Zimmermann).

Bach, Johann, Ch. Fr., Six Sonatas for flute and piano (ed. Zimmermann).

Bach, Wilhelm Fr., Sonata in D major for flute and piano (ed. Zimmermann).

Bach, K. Ph. E., Sonata in C major (ed. Zimmermann).

Bach, Wilhelm Fr., Sinfonia in D major, for two flutes and strings.

*　　*　　*　　*

Flute compositions by other of the great classical composers. . . .

Joseph Haydn (1732-1890) wrote a Sonata for flute and harpsichord, and several trios in which the flute was one of the three instruments.

Wolfgang Amadeus Mozart (1765-1791) loved the flute. He used it with extraordinary effect in his symphonies and divertimenti; and besides wrote several major works for it. Two concertos for flute and orchestra are particularly famous, one in G major (K.313), and another in D major (K.314); there is a third Mozart concerto, for flute and harp and orchestra, in C major (K.299). Besides these works, Mozart wrote three quartets for flute and strings, and an Andante in C major, for flute and orchestra. It is interesting to note that all of these flute compositions were written by Mozart in a single period: 1777-78.

Ludwig van Beethoven (1770-1827)—in or about his twentieth year—wrote an Allegro and Menuetto, for two flutes, for his friend Degenrath, a flute dilettante. Two other Beethoven works are: the Serenade for flute, violin and viola, and the Trio for flute, bassoon, and piano—both early works.

*   *   *   *

More than one eminent musicologist apparently knows Kuhlau only as the composer of piano sonatinas and some successful operas. They do not mention in their writings that 46 years of his life were devoted mostly to creating so much beautiful flute music that he was called "the Beethoven of the flute."

*   *   *   *

At the University of California, Los Angeles, on October 29, 1946, Kuhlau's famous quartet for four flutes, op. 103, was performed during a noon recital by Elizabeth Burr, Violet Rockney, Roma Sarno and Ernest Trumble. It was acclaimed and considered a novelty of the first order.

*   *   *   *

Dedications by Kummer and Kuhlau. . . .

I wish to call attention to some of the interesting dedications made by Kummer and Kuhlau to personalities of distinction and famous composers and flutists.

The titles of Mons., Captain, Madame, Baronne, etc., are used only for dilettanti but are omitted for illustrious composers like Spohr, Schubert and others.

KUMMER: *Trios for three flutes;* No. 1 in G Op. 24, to Capt. Hempel. No. 2 in D Op. 30, to Mons. Constantin Loeffler. No. 3 in E minor Op. 52, to J. W. Gabrielsky. No. 4 in C Op. 53, to Mons. H. Fischer. No. 5 in D Op. 58, to Karl Keller. No. 6 in A Op. 59, to F. Kuhlau. No. 7 in D minor Op. 65, to A. B. Furstenau. No. 8 in G Op. 72 to Eug. Walkiers. No. 9 in A Op. 77, to Mons. Schwarz.

KUHLAU: *Sonatas* or *Grand Concertante Duets* for pianoforte and flute; 1st, in E Flat Op. 64, to le Chamberlain de Kaas. 2nd, in G Op. 69, to Karl Keller. 3rd, in E minor Op. 71, to J. Sellner of Vienna. 4th, in G Op. 83 No. 1; 5th, in C Op. 83 No. 2; 6th, in G minor Op. 83 No. 3, to George Onslow.* 7th,

---

* A wealthy and prolific French composer of noble birth (1784-1853).

in A minor Op. 85, to Louis Maurer.* 8th, in B flat Op. 110 No. 1; 9th, in E minor Op. 110, No. 2; 10th in D major No. 3 to Madame la Baronne M. de Schwerin; 11th in D major Op. 51 No. 1 to Franz Schubert; 12th in E minor Op. 51 No. 2 to J. Kalliwoda; 13th in A major Op. 51 No. 3; no dedication; 14th in F minor to Louis Spohr.

Kuhlau's *six famous sets of duets for two flutes* are dedicated as follows: First set, Op. 10, to G. D. de Lorichs. Second set, Op. 39 (the greatest of all), to A. B. Furstenau. Third set, Op. 80, to J. W. Gabrielski, to whom also the grand quartet for four flutes, Op. 103 is dedicated. Fourth set, Op. 81, to Tulou. Fifth set, Op. 87, to Counsellor Thorman. Sixth set, Op. 102, to C. Scholl.

Kuhlau's *trios for three flutes*: No. 1, Op. 13, to G. Kummer. No. 3, Op. 13, to G. Klingenbrunner. No. 4, Op. 86, to Karl Keller. No. 5, Op. 86, to B. Romberg. No. 6, Op. 86, to L. Drouet. No. 7, Op. 90, to T. Berbiguier.

Kuhlau's *Unaccompanied Solos*: First set, Op. 54, to G. A. Schneider (the only flutist who composed *eight quartets for four flutes*, besides numerous other chamber music for flute and other instruments). Second set, Op. 57, to Tulou. Third set, Op. 68, to P. N. Petersen. Fourth set, Op. 68(?), to M. Parish. Fifth set, Op. 95, to C. H. Wiehe.

* * * *

Mendelssohn and the flute. . . .

Mendelssohn knew exactly what he could demand from each instrument. When he rehearsed his famous Scherzo in the *Midsummer Night's Dream* for the first time, the first flutist failed in the difficult passage, and declared impatiently that it could not be played. The composer immediately said to the second

---

* This is not the noted artist and flute dilettante of New York City who was born the year of Kuhlau's death and who played flute at the age of one hundred years, but the violinist and composer who is chiefly known as a concertmaster for Frederick-the-Great and also for his *Symphonie Concertante* for four violins and orchestra which was first performed in Paris by himself, Spohr, Muller and Wich in 1838. He is also the composer of some string quartets and two operas. He was born in Potsdam in 1789 and died at St. Petersburg in 1878.

flutist: "Then, please, Mr. Haacke, will you play it?" and Haacke did so successfully.

* * * *

When the famous Italian flute virtuoso, Giulio Briccialdi, lived for several months in Leipzig he was much sought after and very often heard in musical circles. On one occasion Briccialdi was invited to play the Rondo of one of his own compositions, but feared he would have to decline because he had not brought the music. Mendelssohn, who had once accompanied him several weeks before, said: "Oh, I beg of you to play it because I know it by heart," thus displaying an exceptional and very remarkable memory.

* * * *

It is interesting and not generally known that Stephen Collins Foster, the creator of about 175 songs, amongst which are many famous ones, taught himself to play on the flageolet when only seven years of age. A few years later he acquired a cheap flute, the only instrument within his scanty financial means and which was his inseparable companion, until he was twenty-two. He also taught himself French and German with the same facility and at thirteen he composed a waltz which he called *Tioga*, for four flutes.

* * * *

Among the numerous compositions by Ferruccio Busoni (1866-1924) there is one *Canonic Variations and Fugue* on a theme of Frederick-the-Great (published in 1916). Also two Cadenzas for slow movements of Mozart's flute concertos in D major and G major (published in 1919).

* * * *

Eugène D'Albert (1864-1932) composed a beautiful opera called *Flauto solo*. Louis Ganne (1862-1923) was the composer of a charming operetta, *Hans the Fluteplayer*.

* * * *

The delicate and sensitive style of Claude Debussy (1862-1918) seems to lend itself so naturally to the flute that it is a wonder he did not produce many major works for that instrument. Famous, of course, is the exquisite opening of Debussy's tone-poem *The Afternoon of a Faun*, for the flute, in which the atmosphere for the entire work is immediately established. Debussy wrote two works for the flute, *Syrinx*, for unaccompanied solo flute, and the Sonata for flute, viola, and harp.

* * * *

Max Reger (1873-1916), that splendid German theoretician and composer, wrote two fine trios for flute, viola, and violin.

Another great theoretician-composer, the English Daniel Francis Tovey (1875-1940) wrote a set of *Variations on a Theme of Gluck*, for flute and string quartet.

* * * *

Two fine 20th century French composers—one a woman—made contributions to the flute repertoire. Cecil Chaminade (1857-1944), who is perhaps most famous for her little piece *Scarf Dance*, wrote a charming Concertino for flute and orchestra. The famous French modernist, Darius Milhaud (1892-   ) composed a delightful Sonatina for Flute and Piano.

* * * *

Three living South American composers have also written fine flute works: Heitor Villa-Lobos (1881-   ), a Quintet for flute, oboe, English horn, clarinet, and bassoon; Jacobo Ficher (1896-   ), a Sonatina for Flute and Piano; and Camargo Guarnieri (1907-   ), a Sonatina for Flute and Piano.

* * * *

In 1931 I wrote a letter to the well-known Belgian organist and composer Adolphe F. Wouters telling him that his *Adagio et Scherzando* Op. 77 for four flutes was greatly enjoyed at the Eastman School of Music each time it was performed. An answer came from Madame Wouters informing me that Monsieur Wouters had passed on only a few months before! Wouters was born in 1849 and had been organist of Notre-Dame di Finisterre,

357

Brussels, from 1868. He was the composer of symphonies, overtures, and much religious music.

*   *   *   *

Soon after the publication of my *Nine Etudes* in 1903 I received two pieces, Op. 53 and 54, published by Zimmermann of Leipzig, and dedicated to me by that grand old man and famous flutist, composer and teacher, Ferdinand Büchner. He was then at the end of his long career as far as playing was concerned but yet active in teaching. I was at the beginning of my career and therefore I was thrilled to have been thus honored by so famous an artist a half century my senior. Other dedications followed. Ernesto Koehler with his Op. 92 *La Capriceuse* for flute and orchestra. Paul Wetzger forwarded a manuscript which was lost in the disaster of the Titanic in 1912. Rudolph Tillmetz, a year or two after, dedicated a composition for flute, violin, cello, harp and harmonium. Then Eugenio Pirani, three pieces for flute and orchestra and next was the famous Australian flutist John Lemmoné with his *Winds Amongst the Trees*. After that a few others followed but the most important dedication in these last dozen years was the Sonata in G for three flutes, two piccolos and flute in G (four players) by Joseph La Monaca and *Preludio e Fuga in Do* for twelve flutes by Gilberto Gravina.

*   *   *   *

One of the most colossal orchestral scores, if not the most colossal, written in modern times, is Arnold Schoenberg's *Gurrelieder*. It was called a "musical skyscraper." It has five solo voices, three four-part male choirs, and one eight-part mixed choir; the orchestra demanded is as follows: 4 piccolos, 4 flutes, 3 oboes, 2 English horns, 2 E-flat clarinets, 3 B-flat clarinets, 2 bass clarinets, 3 bassoons, 2 contra-bassoons, 10 horns, 6 trumpets, 1 bass trumpet, 1 alto trombone, 4 tenor trombones, 1 bass trombone, 1 contrabass trombone, 1 contrabass tuba, kettle drums, tenor drums, side drum, bass drum, cymbals, triangle, gong, glockenspiel, xylophone, rattle, some large iron chains, celesta, 4 harps, and a great number of strings.

358

The ultra-modern Dutch composer and pianist Willem Pijer (1894-1946) entitled his first symphony *Pan*. He has composed much chamber music and also a Sonata for flute and piano.

* * * *

Mario Castelnuovo Tedesco, eminent Italian composer and Adolph Weiss, the noted modernist, have each composed a composition for bassoon and piano. They were performed in Los Angeles for the first time with great success on March 1947. We were unable to be present and, learning of our regret, they most graciously later played them for us in our home. It was indeed a privilege.

The Sonatina by Castelnuovo-Tedesco and the *Ten Choral Pieces* by Adolph Weiss are both rich in melodic and harmonic invention and each a masterpiece. Those who are convinced that Weiss takes pleasure in writing only dissonant and complex pieces will now have to revise their opinions. When published, no bassoon player, whether dilettante or professional, can well afford not to include these compositions in their libraries, as the literature of the bassoon has been enriched as never before at one time.

* * * *

One of the most important as well as one of the most difficult additions to the literature of the flute in recent years is the concerto for flute and orchestra by the famous French composer Jacques Ibert, who was born in Paris in 1900 (Prix de Rome 1919). Ibert has been the director of the French Academy in Villa Medici in Rome since 1938. The concerto was composed in 1933 and published the following year. It is dedicated to Marcel Moyse, the brilliant French flute virtuoso who is teacher at the National Conservatory, succeeding Philippe Gaubert who died in 1941. Moyse played the first performance in Paris in 1933 with the conservatory orchestra.

It took a dozen or more years before some other first rate flutists decided to show that they, too, had both enough courage and ability to play it before the public and on the radio. The year 1948 was, so far, the most successful. The first performance in

America, though with piano accompaniment instead of orchestra, was given by John Wummer, solo flutist of the New York Philharmonic, in the winter season of 1947 at the New York Flute Club. Arrigo Tassinari, though little known in America, is one of the most eminent flutists of the day. He is flute instructor at the Santa Cecilia in Rome and his Quintetto Strumentale di Roma is known all over Europe. The personnel of the Quintetto, all of equal virtuosity, is the following: Arrigo Tassinari, flute; Pina Carminelli, violin; Renzo Sabatini, viola e viola d'Amore; Arturo Bonucci, violoncello; Alberta Suriani, harp. In Spain and Portugal in particular they play every season not less than thirty concerts always with triumphal success. Tassinari first played Ibert's concerto at the Naples Conservatory, with the San Carlo orchestra directed by Nino Sonzogno, on May 24, 1947. The success was such that Tassinari was requested to play it in Rome the following season.

The performance in Rome took place on June 30, 1948 at the historical Basilica di Massenzio with the Augusteo orchestra conducted by Giulio Gedda. All the local newspapers exhausted their superlatives for both the concerto and the superb performance. The composer, who was present, was equally delighted and shook the hands of Tassinari and the conductor with warmth and gratitude. The concerto was later played on the radio.

The first performance in America with orchestra took place on June 13, 1948. The orchestra was that of CBS (Columbia Broadcasting System) with Julius Baker as the soloist and Alfredo Antonini conducting. This splendid performance was enjoyed by millions of people. The first to play it on the West Coast was George Drexler, another talented flutist of the new generation, with Alfred Wallenstein conducting the Los Angeles Philharmonic Orchestra on January 20, 1949 and January 21, 1949. In England the Ibert concerto was first performed on June 17, 1948 by Geoffry Gilbert, solo flutist of the BBC (British Broadcasting Company) Orchestra, conducted by Georges Enesco.

* * * *

One of the finest works for flute by an American composer is the Poem for flute and orchestra by Charles T. Griffes (1884-

1920). Griffes wrote his Poem for the celebrated flutist, Georges Barrère, and it was Barrère who introduced it with the New York Symphony Society on November 16, 1919.

* * * *

A composition for platinum flute. . . .
Density 21.05 is the name of a composition for the platinum flute composed at the request of Georges Barrère by Edgar Varèse.

Edgar Varèse has been variously called: "A futuristic composer," "An eccentric composer," "The composer of monstrosities," and "A composer who, instead of applause, encourages a deluge of protests."

Among Varèse's many compositions are *Amerique* for orchestra, in which he portrays the noise of the airplanes; *Intégrales* for chamber orchestra; *Arcano*, chamber orchestra; *Hyperprism*, chamber orchestra; and *Offrandes* for chamber orchestra and soprano.

Varèse is a gentleman of high culture but his music, like that of Schoenberg, is difficult for the general public to understand, therefore these eminent and erudite musicians not only do not enjoy popularity (which usually goes hand in hand with prosperity) but often suffer being ridiculed! This is to be regretted, but nothing can be done about it. Georges Barrère, who loved novelties and modernism, requested Varèse to compose the first piece for his platinum flute, the only one in existence then. The composition, with chamber orchestra, was first performed by Georges Barrère at a gala concert for the benefit of "Lycée François" of New York, given at Carnegie Hall February 16, 1936.

Edgar Varèse gives a few hints as to how it should be played. "Do not treat it charmingly," he says, "as it calls for dynamic, tense rendition—strictly adhering to indications." As some of the ultramodern composers are fond of percussion instruments, Varèse applied it also to the flute in the lower register; he also suggests: "The notes marked with an X are to be played very softly, hitting the keys at the same time to produce a percussion effect." The piece, interesting and extremely original, was requested by an unusual flutist and written by an unusual com-

361

poser. I do think that when the flutist has played the *first four* of the last sixteen measures by blowing alternatingly and insistingly two notes, D and B, in the *altissimo*—or better still in the stratosphere of the flute—for about fifteen times, he will be convinced that the composer has succeeded in transferring 21.05, which is the density of platinum, from the instrument to the player! After that, the flutist will be ready for the process of Franz Werfel's *retrovolution* in his "Astromental World!"

*　　*　　*　　*

The American composer of Italian descent Walter Piston (1894-　　), whose orchestral work *The Incredible Flutist* won much acclaim, has written considerable chamber music including three pieces for flute, clarinet and bassoon and a Sonata for flute and piano.

*　　*　　*　　*

Louis Gesenway, the composer of a flute concerto in color harmony, has been a member of the Philadelphia Orchestra for many years. He claims to have developed new tonal theories by expanding the diatonic scale to 40 tones and consequently, for example, recognizing the separate identity of F double sharp and G.

The concerto was written for William Kincaid who performed it in New York with the Philadelphia Orchestra on November 19, 1946. *Musical America* of December 10, 1946, had the following criticism in regard to the composer's own tonal theories:

"Whatever merits these theories may possess was not self-evident in the concerto. In spite of a wealth of harmonic color, either by chance or design, the musical ideas were faintly suggested in pale tints. For those then who shun clearly etched lines in music, here is an ideal piece."

*　　*　　*　　*

Charles Ives (1874-　　) is an American prophet of modernism. Among his numerous compositions, which include symphonies, much excellent chamber music and songs, are two tone pictures *The Unanswered Question* and *Central Park in the Dark*

362

for four flutes to be played at the front of the stage with an off-stage chamber orchestra. The first, *The Unanswered Question*, raises pessimistically The Perennial Question of Existence, answered only by the "Silences." The second, *Central Park in the Dark*, in the author's words, purports to be a picture in sound of the sounds of nature and of the happenings that men could have heard over thirty years ago while seated on a bench in Central Park on a hot summer night.

*   *   *   *

Santa Cruz is a Chilean modernist composer who has written a *Simfonia Concertante* for flute and orchestra. The work is dedicated to David Van Vactor, the American composer-flutist.

*   *   *   *

Prophecies are absurd, but in this case, nevertheless, I should like to predict that David Van Vactor may be our "new Kuhlau!" This young flutist-composer-conductor has already produced an enviable number of serious works for small and large orchestras including a Concerto Grosso for three flutes and harp, with orchestra; a ballet, a symphony, choral works, a quintet for flute and strings, pieces for voice and string quartet, ten variations and fugue on a theme by Beethoven for flute and piano, and for flute alone, 24 preludes. Some of the above compositions were written before his twentieth year. However, Van Vactor will be a different Kuhlau. A modern, twentieth century Kuhlau, sparkling with melody and enough modernism to be interesting and up-to-date but . . . not beyond that, I sincerely hope!

*   *   *   *

For nearly thirty years a member of the Philadelphia Orchestra, Joseph La Monaca is known to flutists chiefly for his two splendid and unusual flute quartets. The first is *Scherzo Capriccioso*. The dedication reads: "To my friend and colleague, William M. Kincaid, first flutist in our Philadelphia Orchestra." It is for three flutes and flute in G (alto flute). The second quartet is Sonata in G. The dedication reads: "To my dear friend,

363

Leonardo DeLorenzo, flutist, composer, teacher." It is scored for three flutes—second and third flutes interchanging with piccolos—and flute in G (alto flute). Both these quartets were played at concerts of the Philadelphia Orchestra.

As La Monaca graduated, many years ago in Italy both as flutist and bandmaster, it is natural that he has composed numerous pieces for band and at one time in Philadelphia was the conductor of a "plectrum orchestra" composed of mandolines, mandolas, guitars, etc., with wood wind and horns from the Philadelphia Orchestra. However, La Monaca's love has been for the symphony orchestra for which he has composed several tone poems, the two outstanding of which are *Caius Graccus*, Roman history; and *The Earth*, his greatest.

A *Saltarello* for the solo piccolo and orchestra by La Monaca was performed by the orchestra's piccolo player, John Fischer, at the Pension Fund Benefit Concert on October 27, 1935 conducted by Leopold Stokowski.

Since his retirement La Monaca has added to his long list of compositions a Concerto for bassoon and orchestra (1945) which will be published by a Philadelphia firm in the near future.

La Monaca's *opus magnum* is a grand opera in three acts on a Hindu subject *La Festa di Gauri*. The piano score, a copy of which was sent to me by the composer, covers 265 large pages. This opera has not yet been produced in full but excerpts were played by Stokowski and the Philadelphia Orchestra with considerable success.

* * * *

I presume because a flutist (Joseph La Monaca) has written a Concerto for bassoon and orchestra (mentioned above), a bassoon player meant to exchange the compliment by giving to flutists a composition called *Pictures*, for flute and orchestra. The composer, Louis Palange, who resides in Hollywood, has, besides a number of other pieces, a symphony for large orchestra to his credit. His parents are Italians from Abbruzzi, and live in San Francisco where Louis was born in 1917. The score of this unusual composition, which might have been inspired by the Ibert Flute Concerto, is now in the hands of Professor Arrigo Tassinari of Rome, Italy.

The erudite composer and contrapuntist, Wesley LaViolette, has contributed to the flute literature an excellent Sonata for flute and piano which was composed at the suggestion of Henry Woempner to whom it is dedicated. Woempner was for many years solo flutist of the Minneapolis and San Francisco Symphonies. He now resides in Hollywood.

LaViolette has also composed two very charming pieces for four flutes, *Filigree* and *Charade*, a quintet (1944) for flute and strings and a *Serenade* (1945) for flute in G and orchestra. In larger form LaViolette has to his credit several symphonies, one opera and much chamber music. He is also distinguished as a writer; one of his books *Music and Its Makers* (the story of Musical Expression) is widely known. He is also a poet and is deeply interested in metaphysics, philosophy, Indian lore, and psychology. A recent book is entitled *The Creative Light* (David McKay Company).

* * * *

At the elegant and spacious apartment of Wesley LaViolette, in Los Angeles, the evening of January 26, 1946, there was given a program which, for novelty and artistic performance will long be remembered by those privileged to be present. LaViolette's Sonata for violin and piano and his new quintet for flute and strings and De Lorenzo's new woodwind quartet was originally scheduled for performance. Due to unavoidable circumstances some of the string players were not able to come and so, less than two days before, Henry Woempner, with incredible energy and good will, succeeded in gathering together other musicians. The program as finally given was as follows:

Divertimento flautistico by Leonardo De Lorenzo for five flutes, with flute in G and piccolo, masterly performed by Henry Woempner, 1st flute; Luis Hustana, 2nd flute; Jimmy Welton, 3rd flute and piccolo; James Patrone, 4th flute and Robert Bladet, flute in G, whose many important solos in the composition were played in a masterly fashion. Next came a beautiful piano piece *Caprice* composed and played impeccably by the charming seventeen year old Dorothy Wright. Miss Wright is also a poet and writes philosophic essays.

Number three on the program was the first performance of

365

De Lorenzo's *Divertimento fantastico* (quasi moderno) for flute, oboe, clarinet in B-flat and bassoon. This piece, which is very difficult, was played magnificently, with only two rushed rehearsals, by the following virtuosi who manifestly enjoyed its intricacies: Henry Woempner, flute; Philip Memoli, oboe; Alfred Peterson, clarinet; and Adolph Weiss, bassoon.

Number four was a charming trio *Ricercare* for flute, clarinet in B-flat and bassoon by Adolph Weiss, played by Woempner, Peterson and the composer.

Number five was *Charade* for four flutes by the distinguished host Wesley LaViolette and beautifully played by Woempner, Bladet, Hustana and Patrone.

Number six was a group of songs sung by Stephen Considine with a superb basso voice which reminded us of Ezio Pinza.

Number seven a trio for three flutes by Henry Woempner which I requested him to perform. It had so much beauty in it and sparkled with so many happy thoughts that it was a pleasure to listen to it. The players were the composer, Bladet and Hustana.

Number eight was another group of songs by a tenor, Roy Jarman, and number nine, the last in the program, was by Wesley LaViolette, his ever magnificent Sonata for flute and piano superbly played by Woempner and the composer!

Thus ended an evening of beautiful music that will long be remembered and in which the flute predominated.

*   *   *   *

Five pieces for flute and clarinet, three pieces for flute and piano, and three pieces for flute and clarinet are comparatively new works composed by the ultra-modern Canadian composer Gerald Strang (1908-   ), who is director and managing editor of the New Music Society of California and, at one time, assistant to Arnold Schoenberg in the Department of Music at the University of California.

*   *   *   *

A Suite for flute solo, three canons for flute, oboe, clarinet and bassoon and a Divertissement for harp, flute and cello are other works recently published by that excellent modern American composer Wallingford Riegger (1885-   ).

*   *   *   *

Other interesting works by modern composers are the following: Sonata for two flutes and viola by J. Ardevol (c.1910-   ). Sonata for flute alone by Virgil Thomson (1896-   ). Three pieces—Phrygian mode, Dorian mode, Lydian mode—for three flutes by Charles Haubiel (1894-   ). Theme and Variations for flute, clarinet, violin and cello by Joseph Wagner (1900-   ). And, in 1946, an interesting composition, Serenade, for flute, harp and strings, was given its first performance by the Boston Symphony with Georges Laurent as soloist. The composer was none other than Dr. Howard Hanson, the director of the Eastman School of Music.

*   *   *   *

Some other contemporary American composers who have written major works for the flute:

Paul Bowles (1911): Sonata for Flute and Piano, recorded by Concert Hall Society.

Henry Brant (1913): *All Day*, for flute family.

Mario Castelnuovo-Tedesco (1895): Divertimento, for two flutes.

Norman Cazden (1914): Sonata for Flute and Piano.

Norman Dello Joio (1913): Trio for Flute, 'Cello and Piano; and Concertino for Flute and Orchestra.

David Diamond (1915): Quintet for Flute, String Trio, and Piano.

Vladimir Dukelsky (1903): Trio for Flute, Bassoon, and Piano.

Arthur Foote (1853-1937): *Night Piece*, for flute and orchestra.

Isadore Freed (1900): Trio for Flute, Harp, and Viola.

Anis Fuleihan (1900): Sonata for Flute and Piano.

Vittorio Giannini (1903): Quintet for Flute, Oboe, Clarinet, Bassoon, and Horn.

Miriam Gideon (1906): Sonata for Flute and Piano.

367

Herbert Haufrecht (1909): *Bitter Suite*, for flute, violin, and piano.

E. Burlingame Hill (1872-   ): Sonata for Flute and Piano.

Paul Hindemith (1895-   ): Canonic Suite for two solo flutes; Concerto for Two Flutes and Small Orchestra; *Echo*, for flute and piano.

Boris Koutzen (1901): Trio for Flute, 'Cello and Harp.

Ernst Krenek (1900): Sonatina for Flute and Clarinet.

Felix R. Labunski (1892): Divertimento, for flute and strings.

Otto Luening (1900): Trio for flute, violin and soprano.

Quinto Maganini (1897): *Realm of Dolls*, for four flutes; *Sonata Gauloise*, for flute and piano; *Gaeta*, for flute, English horn and tambourine.

Bohuslav Martinu (1890): Trio for Flute, 'Cello and Piano; Sonata for Flute and Piano; Concerto for Flute, Violin and Orchestra; *Madrigal Sonata*, for flute, violin and piano.

Peter Mennin (1923): Concertino for Flute, Strings and Percussion.

Harold Morris (1890): Suite for Flute, Violin, 'Cello and Piano.

Quincy Porter (1897): Little Trio for Flute, Violin, and Viola.

Gardner Read (1913): *Threnody*, for flute and strings.

Bernard Rogers (1893): Fantasy for Flute, Viola, and Orchestras; Soliloquy for Flute and Orchestra.

Charles Sanford Skilton (1868-1941): *Sioux Flute Serenade*.

David Stanley Smith (1877-1950): *Fetes galantes*, for flute and orchestra.

Leo Sowerby (1895): Trio for Flute, Violin and Piano.

Lamar Stringfield (1897): *Mountain Sketches*, for flute, 'cello and piano; *Indian Sketches*, for flute and string quartet; *Mountain Dawn*, for flute solo and strings.

Virgil Thomson (1896): Serenade for Flute and Violin.

Burnet Tuthill (1888): Sonatina for Flute and Clarinet; *Nocturne*, for flute and strings.

Frederick Woltmann (1908): *Poem*, for flute and orchestra.

368

Some interesting flute music was written in recent years by composers living in Los Angeles and its vicinity:
Wesley LaViolette: *Canticle*, for flute alone.
Radie Britain (Mrs. Edgardo Simone): Sonata for oboe or flute and piano.
Joseph Piastro: *Trio classique* in E-flat major for flute, violin, and piano.

*   *   *   *

Works with flutistic titles. . . .

Mozart, *The Magic Flute* (opera).

Kempff, *The Flute of Sans Souci* (opera).

Bryson, *The Leper's Flute* (opera).

Closkey, *Pied Piper* (opera).

Freer, *Legend of the Piper*.

Maude, Col. Raymond, *The Last Faun* (opera).

Converse, *Pipes of Desire* (opera).

Venth, *Pan in America* (operatic pageant).

Ganne, *Hans the Flute Player* (operetta).

D'Albert, *Il Suonatore di Flauto* (operetta).

Bach, *Phoebus and Pan* (cantata).

Debussy, *L'apres midi d'un Faune* (symphonic poem).

Pierne, *Entrance of the Little Fauns* (from a symphonic poem).

Klyng, *The Flautist* (opera).

Ravel, *La Flute Enchante* (flute, voice and orchestra).

Hanson, *Pan and the Priest* (symphonic poem).

Hadley, *The Atonement of Pan* (orchestra).

Thompson, *The Piper at the Gates of Dawn* (symphonic poem).

? *Mademoiselle Flute*, comedie bouffe (nonmusical).

Mouquet, *La Flute de Pan*, (1) *Pan and the Shepherd*, (2) *Pan and the Birds*, (3) *Pan and the Nymphes* (flute and orchestra).

Bantock, (a) *Pan's Piping*, (b) *The Garden of Pan* (flute and voice unaccompanied).

Mortimer Wilson, *Pipes and Reeds* (two flutes, two clarinets, oboe and bassoon).

Ciardi, *Il Pifferaro* (harp and flute).

Pearl G. Curran, *Ho! Mr. Piper* (voice and piano or four-part chorus).

Strickland, *I Have Heard a Flute* (voice and piano).

Densmore, *The Voice and the Flute*.

Maganini, *A Flute in the Garden of Allah* (flute and piano).

369

Moore, *Song of the Faun* (voice, flute and piano).

Sauvrezis, *La Flute* (voice, flute and harp).

Saint-Saens, *Une Flute Invisible* (voice, flute and piano).

Breville-De, *Une Flute Dans Les Verges* (flute and piano).

Wachs, *La Flute de Pan* (flute and piano).

William McFee, *The Reflections of Marsyas* (book).

Logan, *The Pipes of Pan* (No. 5 Nymphs and Fauns).

Skilton, *Sioux Flute Serenade* (flute and orchestra, also piano solo).

Henry Harold, *While the Piper Played* (piano solo).

Debussy, *Syrinx* (Pan Pipes) (flute solo unaccompanied).

Debussy, *Le Petit Berger* (The Little Shepherd) (flute and piano).

Donjon, *Pan* (flute and piano).

H. Waldo Warner, *The Sound o' Pipes* (voice and piano).

Roussel, *Pan* from *Joueurs de Flute* (flute and piano).

Van Leeuwen, *The Lament of Pan* (flute solo unaccompanied).

Moreau, *Girls Playing the Flute* (flute and piano).

DeLorenzo, *I Seguaci di Pan* (four flutes).

DeLorenzo, *Divertimento Flautistico* (five flutes with flute in G and piccolo; II. Serenata breve a Pan).

De Lorenzo, *Il Pifferaro* (solo unaccompanied: from L'Arte Moderna del Pruldio, Op. 25).

DeLorenzo, *Pan, Marsyas* (solos unaccompanied; from Suite Mythologique Op. 38).

DeLorenzo, *The Modern Art of Flute Playing* (pedagogical work).

Gillmor Frances, *Flute of the Smoking Mirrow* (1949 book).

Debussy, *Por Invoquer Pan, Dieu du Vent d'Ete*.

Piston, *The Incredible Flutist* (ballet).

Rouault, *La Flute de Pan* (modernistic oil painting).

Angelo Silva, *The Terz Flute*— Terzino di flauto in Mib. (*The Flutist*, December 1923).

George Kleinsinger, *Pan the Piper* (orchestra, flute, and narrator).

Frederick Cramer, *The Mysterious Flute* (voice, flute, and piano).

Grampion Norval, *Lost Pan* (sonnet).

Louisa May Alcott, *The Flute of Thoreau* (poem).

G. L. Joerissen (Li-Tai-Po-702-763), *The Two Flutes* (from *The Lost Flute*, book).

Franz Toussaint-G. L. Joerissen, *The Lost Flute* (book), published by Brentano, N. Y.

Frank Dempster, *Come, Pan and Pipe* (poem).

Muriel Percy Brown, *Echoes of Himalayan Flutes* (from International Studio, May 1924); *The Jeweled Flute* (picture in

370

the International Studio, November 1922).
D. C. Bhattacharia, *Sonthali Flute Player* (picture, International Studio, January 1922).
L. Adams Beck, *The Flute of Krishna* (International Studio, January 1922).
V. Sackville West, *The Persian Flute* (poem); *His Majesty's Flute* (picture of Frederick's flute); *As Pipers, The Older Shepherds Excel* (color plate picture); *Flute: From Reeds to Platinum* (Literary Digest, November 30, 1935).
Gabrielle Roy, *The Tin Flute* (book).
Frederick-the-Great, *The Flute Symphony* (orchestra).
Zandonai, *Il Flauto Notturno* (flute and orchestra; poem by Arturo Graf).
Julian Ritter, *The Girl and the Flute Player* (painting of 1947).
Anonymous, *The Pied Piper of Cali 4 nia; New York Flute Club* (founded by Georges Barrère in 1910).
Nicolar Poussin, *Pan and Syrinx* (painting).
Meissonier, *The Flute Player* (painting).
Elizabeth Westermain, *The Flute Girl to Terpander* (poem).
S. E. Kiser, *The Old Flute* (poem).
Le-Tai-Pe, *The Mysterious Flute* (Chinese poem).

Li-po, *The Flute of Marvel* (Chinese poem).
Emil Ludwig, *The Fatal Flute*, title on page 59 of *Beethoven* (book).
Hokusai, *Apsara Playing the Flute* (an oil painting of the goddess of ancient Hindu Mythology).
Tschaikovski, *Dance of the Reed-Pipes* (three flutes and orchestra).
Stringfield, *The Piping Shepherd* (flute, cello and piano).
DeBreville, *Une Flute dans les Verges* (flute and piano).
DeLorenzo, *Baby Pan* (flute alone, to be played also backwards).
Gosse, *On Viol and Flute* (book of 1888).
Claudel, *Pan et la Syrinx* (baritone, soprano and orchestra. Lyrics by de Piis).
Donjon, *Pipeaux* (flute and piano).
Mahler, *The Chinese Flute* (Das Lied von der Erde, Tragic Symphony).
Granville Bantock, *The Great God Pan* (orchestra).
Graener, *Die Flute von Sans Souci* (flute and piano).
Spencer, *Chinese Boy and Bamboo Flute* (organ).
Boehm-Miller, *The Flute and Flute Playing* (book).
Adelaide Love, *The Crystal Flute* (book).
Deledda, *Il Flauto nel Bosco* (book).

Hoffenbach, *La Flute Enchante* (operetta).

Marah Ellis Ryan, *The Flute of the Gods* (book).

Barry, *Peter Pan* (book).

W. Bowen, *Pan in California; Philip and the Faun* (book).

Hawthorne, *The Marble Faun* (poem).

Hamelin, *Pied Piper* (book).

Mabel Wood Martin, *The Lingering Faun* (book).

Graham, *The Piper at the Gates of Dawn* (book).

Lally Reinhardt, *Magic Flute* (oil painting, 1947).

Jean Bothwell, *Little Flute Player* (illustrated book of 1949 on northern India).

Gaston La Touche, *Le Faune* (water-colour).

R. Hinton Perry, *Pan the Piperess* (sculpture-double flute).

Woodward Boyd, *The Unpaid Piper* (book).

Ivonne French, *Pan* (poem).

Mrs. Browning, *Pan* (poem).

Virgil, *Pan Cajoled the Moon* from *Georgie* (poem).

Sydney Lanier, *Velvet Flute Note* (poem from *Symphony*).

Sir George Frampton, R. A., *Peter Pan* (statue).

Edgardo Simone, *Study of Pan* (in terracotta).

Longfellow, *Flutes of Chibiabos* (from *Hiawatha*).

Elizabeth Keith, *A Korean Flutist* (etching).

Violet Alleyn Storey, *Peter Pan in London* (poem).

Vena C. Tipton, *Pipes of Pan* (wind instrument studio, Tulsa, Oklahoma).

Pierre Lavalley, *Apollo Kills Marsyas* (statue).

Michelangelo, *Apollo e Marsyas* (statue).

Los Angeles Flute Club (founded by Baxter, Hullinger and Knox).

Radcliff, *Pan and His Pipes* (lecture).

Sconzo, *Il Flauto e i Flautisti* (book).

Fitzgibbon, *The Story of the Flute* (book).

John Finn, *The Recorder, Flute, Fife, and Piccolo* (book from the music story series).

Rockstro, *The Flute* (book).

Welch, *History of the Boehm Flute* (book).

Welch, *Six Lectures on the Recorder* (book).

Marion Bauer, *Pan and Syrinx* (choreographic sketch for ballet and eight instruments).

J. C. Abbott, *The Flute in Oriental Funeral* (The Flutist, May 1926).

Ada S. Garding, *The Unknown Flutist* (poem).

Curtiss, *The Left-Handed Piccolo Player* (poem).

Louis Fleury, *Song and the Flute* (The Flutist).

Westminster Bank Review, *Female Flutists of Ancient Greece.*

Park, *O, Lovely Flute* (poem from Australia, The Flutist).

372

R. E. Key, *Peter Pan Statue* (poem).
C. M. Cellars, *A Flute* (poem, dedicated to Ary Van Leeuwen).
M. Willson, *And there I stood with my Piccolo* (book).

Max Weber, *The Flute Soloist* (painting).
Frans Hals, *Singing Boy With a Flute* (painting).
DeLorenzo, *Villa Pan by the Sea* (residence of writer at Palos Verdes Estates, California).

(N.B. Although many more titles could be added, this amply illustrates the world's interest in the flute.)

* * * *

Flutists who composed operas and symphonies. . . .

Kuhlau, Belcke, Berbiguier, Mahault, Lobe, Briccialdi, Koehler, Lovreglio, Terschak, Gaubert, Sola, Franz and Karl Doppler, Laucella, Van Leeuwen, Maganini, Stringfield, Kouloukis, La Monaca, Willson and Van Vactor.

Kuhlau wrote six operas—not counting two others destroyed by fire—one of which was on William Shakespeare. Like most of the others, it was given with success at Copenhagen.

Briccialdi wrote the opera *Leonora de Medici*. Lobe, Johann Christian (1797-1881) wrote operas, symphonies, oratorios and pedagogical books on music. Terschak wrote the opera *Thaïs*, sonatas, and violin and piano concerti. Ernesto Köhler wrote to me in 1906 that on a visit to Italy from St. Petersburg he officiated in three capacities in a concert at Modena; soloist, composer and conductor. He gave excerpts from his opera *Ben Achmed* and one of his ballets *Clorinda* both of which had a successful run in St. Petersburg in 1903.

Donato Lovreglio wrote an opera, overtures and some chamber music. Carlo Michele Sola wrote several orchestral pieces and chamber music. Both Franz and Karl Doppler composed operas.

Of Philippe Gaubert I wrote in chapter II.

Nicola Laucella, a member of the New York Philharmonic and, later, of the Metropolitan Opera House for many years, wrote an opera and orchestral compositions performed under Stransky with the New York Philharmonic.

373

Ary Van Leeuwen, composed chamber music and orchestral pieces and operettas.

Nicholas Kouloukis, for many years with the Cincinnati Symphony and the New York Philharmonic orchestras, composed several symphonic poems for orchestra.

Of Joseph La Monaca and David Van Vactor I have written in other chapters. Quinto Maganini, for a number of years a member of the New York Symphony orchestra, conducted by Walter Damrosch, composed orchestral works, choral numbers, wind instrument chamber music and four operas.

Lamar Stringfield composed five symphonic ballads and poems, three orchestral suites, chamber music and an opera.

Meredith Willson, at one time associated with the New York Chamber Music Society and New York Philharmonic Symphony orchestra, composed two symphonies and many other orchestral pieces.

* * * *

Flutists who became orchestral conductors. . . .

Andersen, Barrère, Gaubert, Guthrie, Koehler, Maquarre, Taffanel, Stringfield, Van Vactor, Willson and Woempner.

The most prominent flutist conductor was Paul Taffanel who, besides being a flute virtuoso of rare attainments, was teacher at the Paris Conservatory and conductor for the Paris Grand Opéra. Taffanel produced two famous pupils who also became conductors, Barrère and Gaubert. Barrère's Little Symphony Orchestra and other musical ensemble of his founding gave him great prominence, especially in America. Philippe Gaubert, his friend and schoolmate, composed some beautiful and highly artistic sonatas for flute and piano and also operas and symphonies. He, like his illustrious teacher, became conductor for the Paris Grand Opéra.

Joachim Andersen, famous for his flute compositions and particularly his *Etudes* conducted at the well-known Tivoli theatre in Copenhagen.

Henry Woempner, for many years solo flutist of the Minneapolis Symphony orchestra and San Francisco Symphony orchestra, conducted the summer concerts at Lake Harriet, at a radio station in Minneapolis and Saint Paul and also in Chicago and

San Francisco. André Maquarre, solo flutist with the Boston Symphony orchestra and the Los Angeles Philharmonic orchestra for a number of years, conducted the "Pop concerts" in Boston. Meredith Willson has been for many years general musical director of NBC, Western Division, San Francisco and member of the San Francisco Art Commission. Willson has conducted with fine success for several radio stations and during World War II was bandmaster with the rank of major. At present he is in Los Angeles.

Lamar Stringfield, as a flutist was a member of several symphony orchestras and chamber music ensemble in New York until 1930. He organized the Institute of Folk Music at the University of North Carolina and the North Carolina Symphony Society, of which he has been musical director since 1932. He was organizer and conductor of the North Carolina Symphony orchestra; guest conductor of the National Symphony orchestra in Washington; the Baltimore Symphony orchestra, New York Civic Orchestra, New York Festival Orchestra, Philadelphia City Symphony, Miami Symphony, Nashville Symphony, Virginia Symphony, and others. He also conducted NBC network in 1935 and a U. S. Navy Band.

David Van Vactor as flutist was a member of the Chicago Symphony orchestra under Frederick Stock, who conducted several of his compositions, notably and with fine success the Concerto Grosso for three flutes and harp with orchestra. He was also solo flutist and associate conductor with the Kansas City Symphony Orchestra. Since 1947 Van Vactor is the new conductor of the Knoxville, Tennessee Symphony Orchestra and also the head of the University's new Department of Fine Arts.

James K. Guthrie studied flute with the late Jay Plow and Julius Furman, both of Los Angeles. He conducts the Redlands Symphony.

*   *   *   *

An unusual and unique flute program (?) . . .

I   *Scherzo Capriccioso* for four flutes ....   Robert Russell
     Georges Barrère (platinum flute)   Bennett

375

Ary Van Leeuwen (gold flute)
Arthur Brooke (silver flute)
Leonardo DeLorenzo (cocus wood
   flute)

II Sonata for two flutes and piano .... Bach-Van
Ary Van Leeuwen   Leeuwen
Leonardo De Lorenzo
Modina De Lorenzo at the piano

III *Burlesca* for three flutes and piano ..... Carl Rorich
Georges Barrère
Ary Van Leeuwen
Leonardo De Lorenzo
Adolph Weiss at the piano

IV Two short pieces for flute, clarinet and
bassoon
(a) *Ricercare* .... Adolph Weiss
(b) *Capriccetto eccentrico* .... Leonardo De
Leonardo De Lorenzo   Lorenzo
Alfred Peterson
Adolph Weiss

V Sonata in Sol for three flutes, two pic- Joseph La Monaca
colos and flute in G ....
Arthur Brooke (flute and piccolo)
Helen M. Little
Harry V. Baxter (flute and piccolo)
Leonardo De Lorenzo (flute in G)

VI Two pieces
(a) flute and piano; (b) flute alone
(a) *Nocturn* .... Georges Barrère
(b) *Density 21.05* .... Edgar Varèse
Georges Barrère
Edgar Varèse at the piano

VII Quartet on Roumanian themes for three
flutes and flute in B-flat .... Ary Van Leeuwen
Ary Van Leeuwen
Arthur Brooke
Brown Schoenheit
Leonardo De Lorenzo (flute in B-flat)

VIII Solo for Albisiphone and piano .... Ary Van Leeuwen
      Ary Van Leeuwen
      Modina De Lorenzo at the piano

IX *Serenata a Pan* from *Divertimento Flau-*
    tistico for four flutes and flute in G .. Leonardo De
    Leonardo De Lorenzo   Lorenzo
    Helen M. Little
    Brown Schoenheit
    Harry V. Baxter
    Ary Van Leeuwen (flute in G)

X *Preludio e Fuga in Do* for twelve flutes Gilberto (conte)
   (with flute in G, bass flute in C and   Gravina
   Albisiphone) ....
   Georges Barrère, Arthur Brooke,
   Joseph De Lorenzo, Harry Baxter,
   William Hullinger, Helen M. Little,
   Louis Lewis, Luis Hustana,
   Vincenzo De Milita, Julius De Rubertis,
   Elise B. Moenning, Joseph Messina,
   Brown Schoenheit (flute in B-flat),
   Leonardo De Lorenzo (flute in G),
   Dr. Dayton C. Miller (bass flute in C),
   Ary Van Leeuwen (Albisiphone)

When word reached me that both Georges Barrère and Dr.
Dayton C. Miller were coming to Los Angeles, within a few
weeks of each other, in the summer of 1939, I decided to arrange
a flutistic program to honor Barrère and, later, Dr. Miller by
repeating it, that would be superlative in every way. Both answered enthusiastically, although Barrère wrote that he might
have to disappoint us because of his Little Symphony engagements. However, we went ahead and had some rehearsals; particularly with compositions which required special attention.
As the first number on the program was to be played by four
great virtuosi, all with years of chamber music experience, it did
not need rehearsals. The quartet, a very fine one, was composed
by an American. Each player was of international reputation,
one a Frenchman, one Dutch, one English and the other Italian,

377

and the diversity of the instruments played—platinum, gold, silver and wood—had never before been thus employed in a flute quartet.

The originality and importance of the rest of the program can readily be seen at a glance. The sad part of it is the real meaning of the question mark in the title of this article. In spite of the titanic efforts to see it through, it had to be postponed from one time to another, and before it could be given, the two principal figures whom this unique program was to honor, passed on!

A few words now about Mr. Arthur Brooke, who has not been spoken of yet in this work. Brooke was born in England and was, until a few years ago, a valued member of the Boston Symphony with which he played for nearly thirty years. He has written a school for the flute, has edited a collection of flute passages encountered in symphonic and operatic works. He has made a number of arrangements for the flute and has also flute records to his credit. Mr. Brooke was also conductor of the Honolulu symphony, a position he regretfully had to relinquish because of his wife's health.

As I have emphasized, the composition and players of the first number on the program *Scherzo Capriccioso* for four flutes, I now wish to say a word or two about the last number, *Preludio e Fuga* for twelve flutes:

It so happened that a charming lady from Rochester who was studying flute with me was the friend of Countess Gravina, who was English. Count Gravina was an excellent musician, played flute very well and, besides, was a symphony conductor. It was only natural and logical that he should have all these requisites. He was the grandson of Cosima Wagner and Von Buelow and the great-grandson of Franz Liszt. His father was the Italian nobleman Count Gravina, who married the eldest daughter of Buelow and Cosima.

This student sent her friend the picture of my 1932 flute class and as soon as her husband saw it he went to his desk and composed the *Preludio e Fuga* for twelve flutes. In his letter to me he said that he knew me through my *Nine Etudes*. He had added a piano part to Number 3 Andante and has played it in concert many times with fine success. He wished to be addressed simply as Maestro Gravina. His family's name is mentioned in that splendid book *Immortal Franz*—the life and love affairs of Franz Liszt—by Zsolt Harsayi, p. 472.

Part Four

~~~~~~

REMINISCENCES
OF A FLUTIST

I 〉 Notes for a Personal History

There were no progressive educational methods in my youth and music for me began the hard way. For months I had tedious and interminable daily lessons in *solfeggio*, which sometimes lasted as long as two hours. I had to keep accurate time with my right hand on the palm of the left hand, beating at the same time with the right foot, and my teacher, who was a nice man and a great friend of the family, demonstrated his special attention for me by stamping on my foot at every mistake. Never will I forget the morning when I arrived at Giacomo Nigro's house and was told there could be no lesson that day as he had gone to the country on urgent business. So great was my delight that in running as fast as I could, I fell, bruising my knees and face, and all the papers in the *teoria musicale* in my hand were scattered all over that narrow street.

How I yearned for some kind of a musical instrument upon which I could produce a sound and when, at last, a six-keyed flute arrived for me from Milano my happiness knew no bounds. I was nine years old when my elder sister Marietta married and could already play some nice tunes on the flute in the higher register which I preferred, as the notes were easier to produce and, then too, the neighbors could enjoy them—or so I thought.

383

There came a little girl of my age to the wedding, my mother had told me we were born within a few days of each other—a girl so beautiful and so attractively dressed, that she looked like a miniature *signorina*, a veritable fairy tale angel! She was the daughter of Don Domenico, the notary public, who had married the girl's beautiful mother when she was barely fifteen years and he long past fifty.

Much dancing of the *polca* and *tarantella* took place on these festive occasions, usually three polcas to one tarantella in which three or four young couples displayed their prowess. The little fairy tale angel seemed happy to dance with me until she discovered that I wanted to dance with no one else and that as soon as the first strains of a polca began I made a rush for her. After the wedding I found myself thinking continuously of the adorable signorina and when it didn't interfere with my school and music lessons I would walk to one of the highest points of our hill town—my home was about three minutes from the cathedral or *Chiesa della Madonna*—hoping I could get a glimpse of Carmelina. I thrilled to the sound of her voice; I found myself getting up in the morning at daylight around five o'clock, practicing my flute pieces on the high notes. For this almost miraculous change, I suddenly became famous! My parents and the neighbors as well as the *carabinieri*, who at that time were quartered only one block from our house, marvelled at my practicing at that early hour. Little did they guess that it was *love* that inspired me and that I had made a vow to become a great man, a great artist and rich so that I could offer my beloved a marvellous palace of marble and furnished with the most luxurious things imaginable.

Sadly though, I suspected that my love for Carmelina was not reciprocated. Either she did not like me at all or else considered herself superior because she was as proud and snobbish as a princess could have been and whenever I met her and greeted her with an emphatic "buon giorno" accompanied by a deep bow, she seldom answered. Probably it was because I had been such a clumsy dancer at that memorable wedding, I thought, and I shuddered to think of the many times I had stepped on her cute little feet. If only she could hear me play the flute prob-

384

ably she would change her mind, I said to myself, and practiced more diligently than ever.

So unusual was my progress—although my teacher never praised me nor said *bravo*, as that spoils young students, he said —that my parents rewarded me with an excellent and handsome thirteen-keyed flute with a beautiful ivory headjoint and made in Milano at a cost of 125 lire. My old six-keyed flute, which I had outgrown, as some of the trills could not be produced on it, had cost 20 lire ($4.00) and was sold when my new one arrived to a new pupil for 12 lire.

The opportunity to impress my signorina now came sooner than I had dared to dream. The grand festa of the Madonna occurs the First Sunday of September in my native town and for this great feast the town engages one of the well-known bands from many miles away. This particular year the community also hired the small local orchestra to alternate with the band. My teacher recommended me to be the flutist, as he was out of practice, and on the third and last day it was suggested that I play Titl's *Serenade*, from a second floor balcony, to be accompanied by the orchestra in the piazza below. "What luck," I now thought, "I will show Carmelina what I can do."

Titl's *Serenade* was a big success. The applause was huge, long and enthusiastic. Even the bandsmen from the bandstand joined in fervently and Titl's *Serenade* had to be repeated. I was positively intoxicated with my success and I thanked the Madonna to have made me a flute player. I must admit, though, that even had I played badly I would have been successful. The setting itself, the incomparable scenery must have made an inspiring and beautiful picture for the multitude of people, many of whom had come from far away towns. Some had trudged barefoot all the way to fulfill their vow to the Madonna and two or three among these had been ordered by their confessors to *strisciare la lingua sul pavimento della chiesa* (to creep from the door to the altar of the church with their tongues to the floor) as a penance for their sins—surely a medieval and barbarous punishment. The floor, it is true, was of marble and very smooth and the ordeal did not take long, but as the penance had to be done when at least one half of the huge crowd had left

385

and before the religious ceremonies were over and the church swept, one can imagine how dirty the floor must have been!

I looked forward to my next meeting with Carmelina—confident that now she would smile graciously upon me, but I was disappointed. When I again saw her, my heart beating hard, she ignored me as usual and I realized that she did not understand nor appreciate music.

Carmelina was always accompanied by her half-sister Filomena, a natural daughter of her distinguished father, who had had many affairs before his marriage. She was nineteen years of age and very beautiful with a wonderful complexion and healthy and strong. She dressed in the ordinary style but that was very becoming to her. On different occasions, when I could successfuly invent a pretext to go to their home, Filomena was always to be seen first because she did all the house work. She would greet me with a hug and inquire about the welfare of all my family, praising me for getting up so early to practice and adding that she too got up at that hour, not to study, she said, but to work. Before I knew it I found myself in love also with Filomena! That, however, did not last long. She treated me like a sweet little boy which I resented and told her I now was a man and put my chest way up. She laughed and was going to hug me again when, insulted and indignant, I ran away without even seeing the angelic Carmelina! A few days later I heard my mother saying that a young man was expected to arrive soon from America who was coming to marry Filomena and take her back with him. My disillusionment was now complete but it increased, if it were possible, my great love and admiration for Carmelina.

At the mature age of fifteen and playing, as many people said, very fine flute, I was asked to go to America and I left Italy soon after with the treasured flute on which I had played Titl's *Serenade* on the balcony. It is curious that the ivory headjoint of this flute, contrary to all others and in particular the one on my teacher's flute, which was always splitting, never cracked in all the years I used it in America in all sorts of climates, in the Italian army band, in Northern Italy, and South Africa, until I changed to the Boehm flute in 1903.

386

About a year after my arrival, the news reached me that on account of financial difficulties and the death of her father, Carmelina had married a cousin of hers who was twenty-eight years her senior. He was an excellent and intelligent man, with two fine qualifications, he played flute and was a clever business man. The terrible news almost crushed me! How ungrateful and black the world then looked to me. The ambition of becoming a great artist and a wealthy man for Carmelina's sake was now gone! My studies were abandoned, although I continued to play flute in the miserable job I had in a hotel at Columbus, Georgia. This melancholic spell, however, did not last long. With the buoyancy of youth I was amazed at how quickly I began to recover. Carmelina, I knew, could not be blamed as I had never had the courage nor the chance to tell her of my feelings. So time marched on. Filomena I saw again many years after, when on tour with the Walter Damrosch's New York Symphony in 1913, we played in Columbus, Ohio. Her good looks and wonderful complexion were gone, but her hospitality and warm manners were still there. Carmelina and her husband lived in America for many years, prosperous and happy. They had no children and finally returned to Italy. In 1918 her husband passed on, a victim of the Spanish Influenza which raged all over the world. My wife and I visited Italy in 1926, and in my native town we lived with my brother Francescantonio's charming family, of three children, the one born in Italy was in America, and of the two then in Italy, the boy was born in Vicksburg, Mississippi and the girl, the youngest, in Minneapolis, Minnesota. They didn't remember a thing of America, except, the boy said, Charlie Chaplin!

A few days after our arrival we were told that Carmelina and her American sister-in-law were to pay us a visit. It was an interesting and unforgettable one. I hadn't seen her for over forty years and now the adorable, angelic and divine Carmelina was . . . old, short, fat and had grown whiskers!!! Ah! could we but look ahead! Her sister-in-law, the "Americana," as she was affectionately called, had become a master of the local dialect. She spoke it as fluently as any native, but with a strong American accent. It sounded extremely funny and we all had a grand time, including my wife because the "Americana" shifted from the dialect to English with an ease that was truly admirable.

In regard to sentimental precocity, history repeated itself in the opposite sex nearly half a century later. Just prior to my retirement, and when I was close to sixty, a darling and vivacious little girl of about ten years of age, who was studying flute with me at the Eastman School of Music, said one day: "Mr. De Lorenzo, please let us omit the scales today! You know, I really don't like them!"

"I know you don't," I answered, "but scales, arpeggi and long notes teach one to play well with a beautiful tone. They are like spinach for your health!"

On another occasion, her mother had telephoned to me the previous day that this girl had told her there was only one reason why she was practicing regularly without being told to do so and that was that she was fond of her teacher. One day, at the start of the lesson, she said: "I am tired today, let us visit a little before the lesson; you know, I don't think that there is in the whole world another man like you. Don't you think it would be marvellous if both of us could tour the world, first in the Orient, China, Japan, India, and then in Italy, France, England, Germany and South America!"

"My dear child," I answered, but she interrupted me with: "I am *not* a child. I am nearly eleven, you know!"

"If you don't bring me a good lesson next time," I said as firmly as I could, "I will eat you alive."

She snapped back: "You will find me tough, Mr. De Lorenzo."

Adjusting the music stand for her to begin playing, I said: "Don't you know that these lessons are costing your dear parents good money, and losing precious time with nonsense means cheating them?"

*   *   *   *

When I was about twelve years of age my teacher acquainted me with the 25 *Etudes* by A. Hugot. He told me that I would enjoy them because they were written by a great artist.

I did enjoy them so much that for a number of years, every few months, I went back to them always with increasing pleasure

388

because, naturally, as I was progressing I played them better and better.

Many years after, upon learning the sad fate of the creator of those etudes, I was wondering what would have been my reaction at that tender age had I known that Professor Hugot, the admired and respected virtuoso and teacher at the Paris Conservatory, attacked by a nervous fever which drove him insane, stabbed himself in several places and threw himself from a window four stories high, dying a few moments afterwards, at the age of 44 years. That dreadful event occurred on the 18th of September, 1803.

Now I wish to go back to other etudes, this time without the tragic story. In 1942 in Beverly Hills I was talking over the telephone with a talented young flutist to whom I promised a set of new etudes, many of which were veritable unaccompanied modern solos. The young man, upon hearing the word etudes said, "No thank you, I hate etudes of all sorts no matter who wrote them."

"Are you acquainted with the piano etudes of Chopin?" I asked, "each one a masterpiece?" to which he answered: "No, I do not know them, but I am certain I wouldn't like them!" "Poor boy," I said to myself.

*   *   *   *

From my album comes a cutting with the following title: "A Recipe for a Man With a Swelled-Head." As this work deals exclusively about flutes and flutists, I hope I will be pardoned a slight digression, for one can easily see that it can be applied to any person, any profession, and any age.

When a boy of about sixteen I was told by two old flute players, for whom I had played some etudes by Soussman, Briccialdi and Drouet, that I was so exceptional in my flute playing, that they were sure there was not another to equal me! That was just too bad, because although I was warned by some wise relative "never to over-estimate yourself" the nasty germ of being a "genius of superior ability" got hold of me. One day, several months after, I invited a middle-aged man, whom I was told was a very fine flutist, to play duets with me. We played a long time and apparently were having a grand time, when suddenly he stopped playing and began what I thought was an unwarranted lecture. He began by saying thus: "Listen, young man, when persons exaggerate in their praise, before you accept it you must first of all analyze their intelligence, their experience on the subject and their sincerity. Some people, in order to secure other people's friendship, go to extremes in their expression of adulation. My advice to you is: continue to work hard, keep aloof from shallow people and always have in mind that it is not what we think we are but what we really are that counts. Players like you, but with more culture and more experience, are to be found everywhere by the dozens."

After these severe words he left, telling me that he rather enjoyed playing with me. My first reaction was that he was jealous and wanted to discourage me. At any rate, having in mind that better and more cultured players than I could be found by the dozens on every corner, I did not touch my flute for two days. Suddenly the thought came to me that he was probably not only sincere but he meant well in advising me as he did. Now for the article which not only fitted me marvellously when I was sixteen but looking around me in later years I saw many others, flutists, violinists, oboists, etc., etc., as guilty and more than I when sixteen!

"The man who tells this story about himself doesn't say what really ailed, so let's say it.

"He had a bad case of swelled head. A terrible but very common disease. He got to making money fast, and then he 'blew it in' right and left for the purpose of showing off. He felt that he was invincible. He allowed his feet to get off the ground, and he became a victim of self-flattery—the worst flattery that can attack anybody. So he 'blew up with a loud report,' and now he is getting back on his feet.

"It takes a man with a lot of sense to keep level-headed in the presence of sudden success. Still it can be done. The way to do it is to keep saying to yourself: 'Now, young fellow, don't fool yourself. Remember that millions before you, for untold generations, have shot up like rockets and then shot down. There is nothing remarkable about you yet. You are still about as rare as a garden snake—there have been so many like you in the past. You haven't even begun to distinguish yourself, and you won't distinguish yourself except by doing a good job well, for a long time. Now, the surest way for you to interrupt that good work is for you to develop a swelled head. Don't do it. You need your head for thinking purposes, and a swelled head can't think straight.'—*The Editor.*"

*   *   *   *

Just prior to my coming to America the first time in 1892, when I was about fifteen years of age, I was asked to take part in a grand benefit concert for the betterment of the town. Such an occasion, which seems so momentous at the time, remains very vivid in one's memory. The artistic leader of the event was a young man, Amedeo, who put his soul and all his artistic knowledge into the affair.

The son of poor peasants, he had gone to Naples on a scholarship and had recently been graduated from the Naples Conservatory. He had there studied violin with Professor Ferni, piano with Professor Beniamino Cesi and harmony, first with Primo Bandini, and a little later with Camillo De Nardis, to whom he had asked to be transferred because he was out of sympathy with Bandini's outspoken socialistic and atheistic views. Amedeo returned a fullfledged and cultured artist, and with his polished manners and lovable personality, he became my model.

Since the concert was to be an important one I thought I should play a Concerto by either Mozart or Molique but Amedeo objected, saying that "more than one-half of the large audience will be farmers and it would be unwise to impose concerti or sonatas on such simple country folk. So play, instead," he continued, "a popular piece with plenty of good melody and not too long." So, acting upon his advice, I chose a fantasia by Krakamp called *Luisella*. It was in E minor with an interesting introduction, a beautiful Neapolitan theme and three or four excellent and effective but difficult variations and with an interesting piano part. I felt flattered when Amedeo offered to play the accompaniment for me, since I was aware of the fact that pieces with variations were not considered artistic, especially pieces made up from operatic motives, but there was nothing cheap about *Luisella*.

The following was the program; there were no printed ones. Amedeo announced each number to the packed theatre:

I	Piano solo—Paraphrase on *Rigoletto* . . .	Verdi-Liszt
II	Mandoline solo—Fantasia on *Traviata* .	Verdi
III	Tenor solo—*La Donna è Mobile*.	Verdi
IV	Violin solo—(a) *Gypsy Dance*	Sarasate
	(b) *Le Streghe*	Paganini
V	Soprano solo—Aria from *Norma*	Bellini
VI	Flute solo—Fantasia Luisella	Krakamp
VII	Soprano and tenor—duet from *Semi-* *ramide*	Rossini

As soon as the concert was over we found ourselves surrounded by numerous admirers, some of whom were of the so-called *aristocrati* who posed as real *conoscenti* and whose judgment was pronounced in a low, serious and . . . careful tone of voice. Of course those that were loudest in their praise were the farmers, rich and poor alike. One of these said: "It was worth coming just to hear that wonderful mandoline playing and, best of all, the singing of *La Donna è Mobile*. Another thought the best number was the song on *La Traviata* and the wife of one of the prosperous farmers said: "Well, I heard much singing in Naples when I went to the *bagni* of *Castellammare* but never in my life have I heard anything that could approach the duet by Rossini. By the way," she added, "I even saw Rossini himself on one occasion at Naples a few years ago." Her husband interrupted her and said: "You must have Rossini confused with someone else because that great composer died over one hundred years ago."

Amedeo was, of course, the admiration of all and they were unanimous in predicting that he would soon be considered one of "Italy's new glories." He was called another Liszt on the piano and a second Paganini on the violin, no less.* Besides these rare

---

* Paganini and Liszt in one man is, to say the least, a bit exaggerated. However, to mention only two of our famous contemporaries, Kreisler and Enesco both play the piano like veritable virtuosi.

attainments he had already composed two string quartets, a quintet for piano and strings and, three or four years previously while at the Conservatory had composed a *Farsa in Musica* (Musical Comedy), which had been judged by most of the faculty and the director Platania, a *little masterpiece.* However, Amedeo did not favor the theatre. Now he was carefully working on a symphony, although he thought himself too young but, he added, Mozart and Schubert composed beautiful symphonies when very young, too.

As my solo was next to the last number, the long wait made me a little nervous. There was really no reason, not only because I had played solos before, although never before so large an audience but, I had memorized my piece well and thoroughly, including every bit of the piano part. I called myself a coward! However, the closer the program came to my solo the worse I felt and I found myself praying that something would happen before my turn came—a fire, a hurricane, an earthquake—but, nothing occurred and it was getting closer and closer! I looked around for a door, yet at the same time I thought of the shame and the ridicule if I did not appear. I tried to tell myself that the best way was to boost all my courage and play as well as I knew how. Then I thought of making a fine, dashing opening but . . . horrors, I had forgotten how to begin! Just then Amedeo said: "Leonardo, you are next, let us go." "Oh yes, you go first," I said. "No, you are the soloist," he snapped, then added graciously as if he sensed my misgivings, "I know how beautiful your flute is going to sound." Well, it must have sounded as Amedeo predicted because the applause was so insistent I had to play a short unaccompanied piece as an encore. The first number on the program, masterly performed by Amedeo, drew enormous applause, especially by the *aristocrati* who said he had no rival. The mandoline solo was so successful with the country people, it was repeated. The next number *La Donna è Mobile* brought down the house and I, in my misery, was thinking that by the time my turn came there would be no applause left. The violin soli showed what a master of that instrument Amedeo was. He was called the *Paganini redivivo* and although the country folk didn't know what it was all about, they applauded frantically. The aria from *Norma*, sung by the soprano, proved to be one of the most successful on the program, and the flute solo, to my great surprise, and relief, went beautifully and without a slip. I, then and there, made a vow *never* to be so stupidly scared again.

The final number by Rossini brought the concert to a very successful end with a deluge of applause and it was repeated.

A young and handsome couple came to me and told me that my solo was masterly played and they had enjoyed it very much. "Now I understand," the young man said, "why one of the aristocrati was positive, in spite of your youth, that you could be favorably compared with the best flute virtuosi in Europe." My answer was: "I will have to do a lot of intelligent and serious studying for many years before I will be worthy of such extravagant praise." Then the young woman said that a farmer inquired of another about the difference between the instrument I played, sideways, and the one played this way (meaning vertically). The other farmer answered that the one I played was a "fraulo" which takes real skill and lots of schooling and learning to play with notes, while the one we hear on our mountains by our *pastori*, usually accompanied by the *zambogna* (bagpipe), is, as you know a *ciaramella* (a flageolet kind of flute with a large opening at the end, like a clarinet). The farmer was not convinced because he shook his head and said: "This young man played just like our shepherds and he did not have any notes in front of him."

Soon after the concert Amedeo decided to emigrate to either North or South America. His wish was to establish himself in one of these two great lands and send for his beloved parents and the three brothers and the sister, Filomena, who was very musical. They, the brothers and sister, were all younger than himself and looked upon their brother as their little god, just as his name, which meant *Love God*. Some of Amedeo's dearest friends convinced him that South America would be better because the language was easier and could be mastered within a few months. Also, they had dear and influential friends to whom he could be recommended. So, after a couple of months, when the passport arrived, Amedeo was given a sumptuous farewell dinner with the sincerest best wishes of his admirers and off he went.

At the pier of Rio De Janeiro some dear persons, unknown to him because they had left Italy long before Amedeo was born, were looking for him and told him he was to be their guest. A wonderful start to be sure. Within a few weeks a successful concert was arranged and a tour of the interior of the country was to follow.

Just before beginning this tour Amedeo was preparing plans to form a string quartet, his great artistic love and, eventually, open a "school of music" with an excellent faculty.

Also, besides these excellent thoughts of the near future, there was another very dear person far away of whom he could not help thinking constantly. Signorina Elvira, the beautiful eighteen-year-old daughter of the attorney (whose full name on a metal slab on the front door of his gorgeous home read: Avv. Luigi cav. Pennacchia, the two abbreviated words meaning Avvocato and Cavaliere) was one of his piano pupils. Prior to becoming his pupil she had never shown much inclination for music and her former lady teacher said there wasn't much music in the signorina. However, as soon as Amedeo was graduated her parents said to her, "we will give you the last chance at the piano." And what a change that proved to be! She practiced hours and hours every day and she seemed never to be tired. One day her mother, Donna Amalia, smilingly whispered in her husband's ears that Elvira's enthusiasm and love for the piano was because of her fondness for her new teacher Amedeo! To this startling news the Avvocato Cavaliere was disturbed to such an extent that he in a violent scene had ordered the lessons stopped immediately. "Has she forgotten," he said, "that he is the son of cafoni?" "I have been wishing for a long time that she would show a little more common sense by being more courteous to the son of my illustrious friend the Commendatore (Dottor Francesco Comm. Polledro)* who, I have been told, is desperately

---

* The so-called aristocrati who are not Cavalieri or Commendatori are addressed either by their professional titles as Avvocato, Ingegnere, Dottore, etc., or by their first names with the Don before it: Don Pasquale, Don Paolo, Don Vincenzo. All priests are similarly addressed. There is

in love with her!" However, when the outburst of the Avvocato Cavaliere was over, due to Donna Amalia's gentle and charming persuasion, the piano lessons were continued.

Amedeo was thinking that although there was a thorough understanding between Elvira and himself and, he was almost certain of her favor as well as of Donna Amalia's, how would the news of his wanting to become the son-in-law of the aristocratic and autocratic Avvocato Cavaliere be taken?

I well remember, he thought, that he greeted me only when I came face to face with him in his gorgeous home when I went to give lessons to his daughter; otherwise he always pretended not to see me. Amedeo hadn't ever forgotten that when he first entered the Conservatory many of his fellow students used to whisper, sometimes loud enough so he could hear, that he was the son of very humble *contadini*. That, though, did not last long because his progress was so startling and his manners so beautiful that he was soon admired and loved by everyone. The professors alone still called him *Il Montagnaro* (the mountain boy) in an affectionate way.

However, things went differently. The tour was hardly a week old when, in a remote town, he was attacked by a pernicious and malignant fever and in less than three days this wonderful young man, barely twenty-six years old, died!

Even persons in the same profession who at first thought that Amedeo was, after all, born with a golden spoon in his mouth, wept bitter tears at the unexpected and untimely tragedy of his passing!

*　　*　　*　　*

In 1926, my wife and I made a journey through Europe which was the fruition of many years' planning. I had expected to cast aside all thoughts of my work, but how was it possible? I happen to be a disciple of Pan and I have given a lifetime of energetic devotion to my beloved art. Everywhere my wife and I went we stumbled upon a work of art in which the flute was vividly represented. So, I accepted the inevitable joyfully and

---

also another familiar expression used in many towns south of Naples and in particular in my native town: *Galantuomo*, which does not mean, as it sounds, a gallant man, but that he belongs to the upper class.

decided then and there to try and pass a few of my experiences on to my friends.

On our first day in Naples we strolled into the Giardini Pubblici and I remembered that among the many statues before the entrance there used to be one of a youth playing the transverse flute. There it was, but it seemed that seventeen years before the foot joint of the marble instrument and two fingers of the player's right hand were not missing. Inside the gardens many bas-reliefs on different monuments had either a flute or a figure playing upon it.

The great Naples museum possesses an interesting collection of flutes excavated from Pompeii some years ago and others brought to light only recently. One sees, besides the real flutes, which once upon a time had produced music, numerous pictures of them everywhere. In the ruins of Pompeii though, the only reminders were to be seen on old frescoes, some of which lay underneath frescoes of a later date. On these, too, we could detect symbols of flutes and flute players. The Museo San Martino, on the heights of Naples, which was formerly an old monastery with a great historical fortress nearby, was the only museum in which I could not find traces of either flutes or flute playing.

We spent seventeen wonderful days, much too brief a visit, in my native town of Viggiano. I neither saw nor heard a flute, yet the archeologists might uncover much, for there are the ruins of three large castles here connected by means of an underground passage which was used by the prince of Viggiano in time of trouble. This little town, which has a most healthful and picturesque location on a mountain 3000 feet above sea level, has sent many strolling musicians to the four corners of the world. Its chief music teacher for over half a century was Giacomo Nigro (1848-1919) and he not only taught the flute but imparted the rudiments of music to all whether would-be violinist, harpist or flutist. At the beginning of his teaching career—he was only about twenty when he returned from New York—his price for tuition was but a few carlini, equivalent to about three lire or sixty cents for one month's lessons, which included a lesson every day in the week but Sunday. Years after, when I came to him as a pupil, he had raised his price to five lire and as a result had immediately lost, for a while, one half of his pupils. My lessons came at the unearthly hour of 6:30 A.M. lasting from one to two hours, and, mind, every day in the week. The first six months, which Giacomo Nigro invariably devoted to solfeggio only, were most tedious for a little boy of eight. I remember well the joyful day when at last a six-keyed flute arrived from Milano and in a short time I was able to play some tunes from Berbiguier's old method. The first melody that appealed to me strongly was, I recall, from Mozart's *Marriage of Figaro*, in duet form.

How I loved those duets. The beautiful harmony of two flutes made a most agreeable impression on my youthful ear. Strange to say, in some of the duets, for reasons unknown to me to this day, the second flute part was written in the bass clef. These recollections rushed through my mind as I passed under the window where had lived the good old Giacomo Nigro. He had asked me, a few days before I left for America in 1909, how long before I would return and I had replied, "Who knows, possibly twenty years." "Ah, if you remain away twenty years, it will be my cicunala (slang for old bones) you will visit," and it proved too true.

But I have digressed long enough. Returning to Naples I proceeded to call upon Professor Italo Piazza, who had been a teacher of the flute at that Conservatory for thirty-seven years. He was as difficult of approach as twenty years ago. I found him collarless and in shirt sleeves and he reluctantly allowed the "intruder" to enter. Finally, having assured himself who I was he unbent a little. He said "Did I not see some studies of yours and were you not graduated from our Conservatory? Then you must know I have nothing to do with my colleagues and that they call me l'orso (bear)." He continued: "I have been obliged to do without the services of the woman who came every other week to clean my apartment. My pay is so miserable that it would take one-half of my salary to pay her, as servants now make a better living than professors. The Flutist of the municipal band has a much larger salary than I after thirty-seven years teaching, nor do I give a lesson outside the Conservatory." Then I asked, "What about the students who in some way cannot comply with the entrance requirements of the school?" "Oh, they don't interest me," and he went into the other room. He soon returned with some papers, saying that if I were interested I could have them. Among them was his *Adagio Mistico* for strings, harmonium and harp, which he informed me had been performed in Naples with splendid success, also a piece for string quartet, two wood-wind and horn quintets in manuscript which he forgot to include when he wrapped up the package and a treatise, published years ago, on musical matters in which he makes the novel suggestion that the woodwind choir be reproduced with a keyboard.

I found myself beginning to like "the bear" and now that I have read his book and learned that he has an unusual, original and highly intellectual mind, I respect and admire him more and wish that fate had been kinder to him. He tragically lost his beautiful young wife years ago and was with difficulty dissuaded from entering a monastic order of the strictest form.

For the benefit, not only of the flutistic world, but of all music lovers, I wish someone with sufficient leisure would translate some of Italo Piazza's original writings. Of general interest, I think, would be *Un documento strano* (A Strange Document), which was published in Ricordi's *Gazzetta Musicale di Milano* some twenty years back, and *Proemio ad una storia della musica ed altri scritti d'interesse musicale. Un progetto*, in the latter, I know would be enjoyed by wood-wind players.

I have forgotten to mention that on our way back to Naples we stopped for a few days each at Amalfi, Ravello, Capri and Sorrento. At Amalfi my wife accused me of being very much of a materialist as I insisted on lingering because the food at Hotel Luna was so delicious. That chef was surely a great artist.

What a paradise on earth is Ravello! One thousand feet higher than Amalfi, it has surely one of the greatest views of mountain and sea that any place in this beautiful world can have. Here are the enchanted Rufoli palace and gardens. In an old cathedral is to be seen a famous pulpit made entirely of mosaic. On one of the highest points facing Ravello is a monastery to which the devout make a pillgrimage twice a year. They come on donkey, mule or horse-back and some who have made special vows, climb wearily to the top barefooted, their pifferi and zampogne making music on the way. Because of tradition, they eat no flesh food while on that place of holy prayers but later, descending to an inn below, indulge to their heart's content.

Capri and Sorrento are, of course, very beautiful but the flutist must be on his way to Rome.

Roma! the eternal city which has the unique and astounding power of growing younger and more beautiful with age, is yet so colossal and contains so many of the world's masterpieces that we were obliged to rest now and then that we might digest what we had seen. The Italian often reverses the word Roma, which gives him "amor," love.

It is in Rome that our beloved flute tells many a story. One sees it on cinerary urns, sarcophagi, and vases; in pictures of battlefields, dancing scenes; the lone faun in a field with his pan-flute, the satyr joyfully playing on a vertical flute or a charming young lady playing a double flute to the delight of her audience. Then again one sees a whole troupe of flute players supplying the music in a funeral procession. I wonder how many more I must have missed, for the guides (with but few exceptions quite unsympathetic creatures) were always in a hurry. One day upon passing a statue of Marsyas, who was posed with his back to a tree, his hands tied with a rope above his head and Apollo in the attitude of skinning him, I thought to have some fun and asked, "Who is this poor creature and what can he have done that he is so cruelly punished?" "Oh," he replied (this guide had been to America), "you see he did not learn his instrument, some kind of a ukulele, well enough to suit his teacher. So one day in a rage he skinned him alive." "But when could such a thing have happened?" "Two or three hundred years ago," he answered confidently. So then I proceeded to tell him the story of Marsyas and Apollo as I had read it when a boy. It was a story of a challenge between Marsyas playing the flute

400

and Apollo the lyre—the loser to be at the mercy of the winner. Apollo was almost defeated when the inspiration came to him to sing while he played his lyre, and thereby he won the contest. He then skinned alive his unfortunate victim. But, my story was treated with skepticism by my guide; he was sure that had nothing to do with it and besides, why should I care?

The prehistoric museum is wonderful and unique. It illustrates vividly the evolution and different ages of man, but is no place for an impressionable person to visit. There are enough gruesome sights to make shivers run up and down the spine of almost anyone and I readily forgave my wife for wanting to run away. Among other things we saw flutes of human bones made by cannibals who also used skins of humans to embellish their canoes.

When we descended into the catacombs I thought this would be one place where the flute would not haunt me, but I was mistaken. They were the catacombs of St. Calixtus on the Appian Way and we were conducted through these underground labyrinths by one of the Trappist fathers, who are monks dedicated to silence which can only be broken when assigned as a guide. We were given a little candle and cautioned to remain with the party; there were many narrow turns and one could soon be lost in that dark underground cryptic old Christian burial and meeting place. We did not go lower than the second floor but our guide said there were four more and that they were continually excavating and finding new labyrinths where the early Christians buried their dead and valuables. At one place he pointed out to us a large marble slab which had recently been found. I was amazed to see on it a wonderfully well done Pan's flute. Although I was at the tag-end I could not refrain from stopping and with the aid of my feeble candle, was intently studying the details when I noticed that I was alone. I rushed madly and luckily arrived just in time to catch a glance of the last man rounding another turn. I confess my weakness but in those few seconds I became so frightened that from then on I remained in the closest proximity to the good monk. But I had seen the flute in the catacombs, and, of course, I would have died for a good cause. But who would have told the story?

401

I must not forget to mention the effect that was produced upon the entire party as we came unexpectedly upon the recumbent statue of Santa Cecilia, the patron saint of music, who some claim was the inventor of the organ. The white marble, the lighted candles, the flowers around her in that dark underground, produced an atmosphere that was most holy.

It contributed a great deal of pleasure to our sojourn in Rome to meet there Professor Alberto Veggetti, who placed himself at our entire disposal. He was the successor of Franceschini at the Royal Liceo Santa Cecilia and was a most amiable gentleman and an enthusiastic lover of flutes and flute playing.

Our next stop, much too brief I regret to say, was Perugia, loveliest of hill cities. Beautiful scenery, architecturally interesting buildings, fine art in the churches, all this it has, and nearby too is Assisi, which that year celebrated the seventh centenary of the birth of St. Francis.

There are numerous signs of Etruscan flutes and flute players in Perugia. They have only recently excavated nearby many sarcophagi, vases and queer dishes on which were depicted strange instruments. Of the utmost importance was a small terra cotta dish on which was an extremely long flute played by a person in a unique costume and who had on his mouth a special strap to facilitate the emission of the sound. From his belt were suspended a number of small wind instruments. The long flute had at the extreme end a kind of baglike extension for sonority and was played like a piffero, being held with one hand. It is certain that the instrument was indigenous.

From the window of our pensione on Lungarno (along the Arno) in Florence we had a fine view of the Ponte Vecchio with its old jewelry shops, the dome of the cathedral, the lovely campanile and the picturesque tower of the Palazzo Vecchio. We daily crossed the self-same bridge that Dante trod and on which, it is believed, he saw Beatrice the first time. But what great art Florence has in its churches, museums and galleries! There is so much to see and so rich is the feast that we could only hope to absorb a fraction in the short time we had at our disposal. I remember vividly, though, two large statues of Marsyas which were prominently displayed facing each other in, if I

402

remember correctly, the Uffizi gallery, and in the National Museum, Donatello's Marble Faun, the hero of Hawthorne's story. I have a haunting impression of the Faun from Praxiteles but cannot recall where I saw it.

I called one afternoon at the address of Tommaso Giorgi, because I wished to meet the man who, a number of years ago, in the nineties, had made quite a stir in the flutistic world with his vertical and keyless flute. I did not find Mr. Giorgi in but was told by his sister, who was herself upon the point of departure, that he was spending the summer in Viareggio, which is the popular seashore resort of Tuscany. It so happened that we had planned to take a much needed rest at the same place. In a few days I found myself talking flute with a most charming, cultured, elegant, and last but not least, the youngest man of past seventy summers I had ever met and who spoke English beautifully. I was naturally anxious to see the discussed Giorgi flute and learn how it was conceived. But I am sorry to say, Mr. Giorgi had left it in Florence. He said he had with him another little invention, which he called the "Toy flute," and for which he had obtained a patent in Italy. In a jiffy he took down from a shelf a tiny thing the length and thickness of a head joint and began to play upon it. I had laughed upon seeing it thinking it a facsimile of that unsympathetic whistle (flageolet-like) used in jazz bands, but to my surprise it had a flute tone of pleasing quality with a compass from G second line to incredible heights. It is holeless and keyless and has a rod on the outside which is moved up and down like a trombone and this catches in notches placed every fourth or fifth interval, just which I do not recall exactly. It is not unchromatic as might be supposed and is so simple that Mr. Giorgi asserts it can be mastered in an hour. Of course, it has the same embouchure, the one undisputed valuable feature of the Giorgi flute and which Professor Veggetti told me was adopted by Albisi on his Albisiphone. Altogether it is a most ingenious little instrument.

Giorgi and I soon became friends and spent most of the days together walking in the wonderful "pineti" or in bathing attire on the beach and I gradually learned from him the details of his flute, about which I had heard so much against and so little in

403

its favor years ago and that suddenly was plunged into obscurity. Here is the story of the man and the flute.

Giorgi's father was a wealthy gentleman, a friend and a great admirer of Cesare Ciardi, of whose wonderful flute playing he enthused continuously. He decided that his boy Tommasino should become as fine an artist, for he often said to the boy, "If you can learn to play the flute as my friend Cesare, you will not only be held in esteem, but it is a profession, which in case of need—God forbid—will make a good livelihood, besides pleasing me very much." Tommasino was willing but not very enthusiastic and arrangements were made to begin lessons with Ciardi. However, news suddenly came that Ciardi had been offered a wonderful position in the Czar's service in Russia and Briccialdi was induced to replace him at the Conservatory and Tommasino began his lessons, using the so-called Briccialdi flute. Briccialdi showed his interest in his pupil by giving him an extra lesson every week at his home. After considerable study, some old fogy musicians began to whisper in the youth's ear that he was playing on the wrong instrument, that it was neither new nor old. Nevertheless he made such fine progress that Briccialdi took him as second flute when he was called to Perugia to play in *Aida*, then the greatest operatic novelty, the first performance of which had only recently taken place in Cairo, Egypt. Mr. Giorgi related that when there Briccialdi composed a charming flute solo *I giardini di Perugia*. His numerous solos on operatic airs were all composed at a commission of between two and three hundred lire. But he was at his best in his original creations, as is proved by his beautiful exercises, studies, duets and original solos, all replete with very charming melodies. Briccialdi, according to Mr. Giorgi, especially in his later years, was extremely careless with his financial affairs, and when he died in 1881 he left his widow, a frail little woman, in such dire straits that she was forced to become a professional medium, a power she had until then used only to entertain friends.

Meanwhile young Giorgi, who had never been serious about the flute as a career, became discouraged and tired of the continuous discussions about the different flutes—flutes with six keys—flutes with twelve keys and others all keys, etc. One bright day a brilliant idea came to him to make a flute himself entirely without keys, to be played vertically as in the days of old. So with lots of enthusiasm and the scientific knowledge which a fine university education had given him, he set to work to make this flute, which was to have all the good qualities of the other flutes and none of the bad. The instrument was finally completed and Mr. Giorgi said he was able to perform anything written on it and all trills were possible because the necessity of cross-fingering had been eliminated. It was, besides, built of a material which was wonderfully adapted to the tone of the flute and which could not crack. This material was ebonite. He had been told that Ciardi had seldom been seen playing on a flute without a crack. One of its greatest advantages he had thought, but which proved one of the main causes of failure, was its small cost, which would have brought it within the reach of everyone.

The instrument being ready and satisfactory beyond his expectations, he set out on a lecture tour to demonstrate its merits. At Bologna, after he had played, the commission suggested that someone else try it and Alberto Veggetti volunteered and played it without much difficulty. Most people, especially the flutists, smiled skeptically upon seeing the instrument but he was soon able to convince them of its merits. Mr. Giorgi related gleefully that upon one occasion an old famous German flute professor had laughed heartily at the mere idea of playing duets with him, but consented to do so as a joke. To his astonishment and delight the duets went famously and he entertained Giorgi for many hours thereafter. I asked him if he had read Italo Piazza's pamphlet on the subject, to which he replied "Yes, he was certainly ferocious." However, he played the instrument for many famous musicians, who evinced much interest as the numerous testimonials he has in his possession testify.

Giorgi gave lecture recitals in England also and sold for a good sum of money the right of his flute in the British Empire to a musical instrument firm. The manager died soon after, plans were changed and the flute put aside.

Yet, it was through this same flute that indirectly Giorgi

405

amassed a fortune. While lecturing in New York City he forwarded newspaper cuttings to his brother, who was in business in Genoa. His brother replied that the advertisement on the back of the newspaper cutting interested him much more than the concert and advised him to get in touch at once with the great American firm that had a capital of five million dollars in pipes. If he could obtain the agency for Italy, that would be something worth while. What a strange coincidence! The manager of the company was interested in flute playing and had attended his recital. He invited Giorgi to his home several times, but would discuss nothing but flute pipes and how to play them. "Plumbing pipes," he said "we shall discuss sometime at my office." Matters were eventually arranged to Giorgi's satisfaction and he became the head of a great firm with branches in most of the important cities of Italy, selling American pipes to all the kingdom. His business prospered mightily, as prior to that time only pipes of inferior quality could be obtained in Italy. He made many visits to New York thereafter but as a business man and not as a flute lecturer.

Upon one of these visits he succeeded in interesting the manager of a brass instrument factory in his instrument. This factory was at that time beginning to build flutes also and although they told him no money could be made on his flute, as it was too simple in construction and would have to be sold for two small a price, yet they nevertheless bought his instrument and the rights to it. That was the last the inventor heard of it. Then came the great war. Everything, of course, that did not feed the colossal wheel of the mighty Mars was crushed and his fine business came to a sudden end.

Giorgi related his story with much good nature and added that the failure of his flute had not broken his heart as some might have thought. Music was for him a fine pastime and nothing more—but indeed a very good pastime I may add, for Mr. Giorgi has written a learned little book on music, which treats of acoustics, sound vibration, the defects of music and its future. It is entitled *La nostra musica*.

We talked also of various Florentine flutists and I was surprised to learn that Raffaello Galli, who is so well known for

406

his exercises, duets and solos—mostly all on operatic themes—and a voluminous school, Op. 100, was not a professional musician. He was a wealthy banker with an enthusiastic love for the flute, a fine musicianship and a fondness for composing. Signora Galli, on the other hand, was not interested in the artistic pursuits of her husband. Her one great passion was cats, for they had no children. She had no less than twenty-five of these "pest cats," as their friends called them, and although she was a painstaking housewife and kept a maid, whose sole work—the fate of life!—was the care of that prolific family, the odor in their beautiful home was awful but the Gallis were apparently not disturbed. In some respects the peaceful banker-flutist resembled Count Luigi Marini, minus the noble title, plus the numerous cats!

Giorgi has promised to send me, upon his return to Florence, as a memento of our meeting, some music which he was sure I did not have, amongst which was an unpublished concerto by Briccialdi in his original handwriting.

The citizens of Viareggio are justly proud of their little city. It has not the picturesqueness, perhaps, of the old Italian towns, it is too new and modern for that, but it is very comfortable and very clean and, like all European resorts, has no stupid merry-go-rounds and hot dog stands to disturb one's peace of mind. It has set aside one fine avenue entirely for pedestrians and here young and old promenade in the evening or sit at one of the numerous outdoor cafes, enjoying the music and gelati. Its streets have been named in honor of Italy's great men and we were quite thrilled on our first walk to discover—to mention a few—Viale Dante, Petrarca, Carducci, d'Annunzio, Michelangelo, Raffaello, Da Vinci, Colombo, Volta, Galvani, Galileo, Palestrina, Scarlatti, Verdi, Puccini. In fact, there is also a Piazza Puccini. The composer was very fond of Viareggio, spending the summers in his villa, which we visited. I have forgotten to tell you that on our way to Viareggio we stopped for a day at Pisa, and what a worthwhile day it was! The famous leaning tower is in the beautiful Piazza del Duomo at a quiet end of the city and here, grouped together, is also the cathedral, the Baptistry, and the Campo Santo, presenting a strikingly harmonious picture.

The restored pulpit, Pisano's great masterpiece, in the cathedral had but recently been dedicated by Mussolini. It is truly a marvel of art.

Our next stop was Milano, a very beautiful city and the wealthiest manufacturing town in Italy. But that which gives it a unique distinction is its marvelous cathedral, one of the largest in the world, "A poem in marble" Mark Twain called it. Its roof is adorned with ninety-eight turrets and there are about 2,000 statues in marble on the exterior! We held our breaths spellbound when we first beheld it, for the effect of the whole is fairylike. Among the different statues in the impressive interior we noted that of a man who had been flayed and his skin draped in folds on his arm, a rare masterpiece, the cognoscenti tell us. However, he was not Marsyas and had been thus punished for political or religious reasons—I do not remember—and not for playing the flute! Many years ago when in Italy I often met Zamperoni and Albisi in the famous Galleria Vittorio Emanuele II. This time, as it was July, most musical activities were at an end and Professor Longhi, of the Conservatory, whom I would have enjoyed meeting, was on his vacation.

The lure of the Italian Lakes! Who has not read of their charms? We saw only Lago Maggiore and Lago di Como, but the luxuriant vegetation of their wooded slopes and the view of the Alps made us realize why they have enchanted travelers from time immemorial. At Lago Maggiore, which is but a two-hour journey from Milano, we stopped at Baveno and one of the first things we did was to hire a boatman to take us to the beautiful Borromean Islands, the most famous of which is Isola Bella. This was once a barren rock and was transformed into a princely domain by Count Borromeo. The huge unfinished palace has a series of gorgeous reception rooms which contain rare works of art and I saw several reminders of the flute.

Venice was a new, a delightful experience. We spent many happy hours in a gondola gliding in and out through the canals just nowhere in particular. That was heaven! We would question our gondoliere about the various palaces and old buildings and he proudly related to us many old traditions. "There," he pointed out, "is the palace in which Robert Browning died, and the tablet on the palace reads: 'Open my heart and you will find graved on it, Italy.' And yes, there is where Wagner died and the tablet below was composed by D'Annunzio. See that palace with the blue and white striped posts in front? That was where Byron lived in state. Then in the next palace with the dark blue post, Giordano Bruno was betrayed!" And so he chatted on at length in his Venetian dialect, which was most difficult for me to understand, thereby losing many little details of his conversation. I remember, though, one story he told of a very wealthy Venetian who, to impress his richness upon his guests, insisted that they throw the silver service of each course in the canal. This was repeated at each banquet he gave and when it reached the ear of the populace they succeeded in putting nets in the water to gather the valuable silver without his knowledge. The vanity of man!

In the famous Piazza of San Marco we were brought face to face with the ancient glory of Venice and, of course, we fed the pigeons. Flutist, poet or carpenter, they know no distinction. And when we desired a change of scene it was but a short ride across the lagoon to the famous Lido, where we would lie on the wonderful sands and forget for a while the tourist crowds.

What Ruskin considered one of the very greatest paintings in the world is in the church of the Frari. It is the Madonna of Giovanni Bellini, and what more fitting, to the mind of a flutist, at least, that therein one of the angel-musicians should be pictured playing the flute! In the same church is also the Pesaro Madonna of Tiziano and the two impressive tombs, facing each other, of Canova and Tiziano whose last painting, begun at 99, is at the Accademia.

We were very glad to be able to hear an unusually fine performance of *Paganini*, operetta by Franz Lehár, based on the life of Paganini.

But our great disappointment in Venice was that we could not get good spaghetti, and incidentally, my wife is as fond of that unsurpassable dish as the most rabid Italian. And that is saying a great deal! No, Venetian cookery is sadly lacking; it is

409

neither Italian, Austrian nor German, as we learned to our sorrow after moving three times the first three days we spent in Venice.

We went from Venice to Munich through the beautiful Tyrol country and got into a real tourist jam. We were compelled to stand five hours in a crowded corridor on that train and, to add insult to injury, the conductor endeavored to make us pay an extra fare because we had stood in the wrong corridor. We thought longingly of our good, incomparable American service as a wave of homesickness swept over us.

Munich is a lovely, lovable city, very interesting, clean, happy and prosperous and—the München beer! A jugful, I am quite sure it was a quart, for twenty pfennig. When we got to Berlin and had to pay fifty-five pfennig for an ordinary glass of inferior beer, I thought of the advantages of Munich. To add to the pleasure of our stay an old pupil of mine, who was sojourning at the moment in Munich, took us in hand and proved a most delightful guide. Together, after much difficulty, we found the house of Boehm. "Theobald Boehm." "Who was he?" They replied to our inquiries at the music store. "What instrument did he play?" "Oh, wait a minute, we have it," and handed us a book which contained a short biography. We were entertained by Boehm's daughter-in-law and grand-daughter, the former of whom was the widow of Boehm's youngest son Otto. They indicated to us the two windows of the rooms in which the artist-inventor had worked for so long a time and which were then occupied by a family who had no conception of their history.

With the aid of my friend I managed to have a lengthy conversation with Professor Gustav Kaleve, a charming gentleman and the successor of the late Rudolph Tillmetz. I was greatly surprised to learn that he, and in fact, most of the flute players in Munich, use the conical flute. They considered it more suitable and better adapted to chamber music, as it more nearly approached the flute for which the music was written. To which statement I could not agree. The old masters, I rejoined, knew no better instruments and therefore had to content themselves with what they had. Professor Kaleve is the possessor of an excellent Albisiphone for which, he told me, he had paid only

410

1,000 gold marks and was offered, soon after, 2000. It was entirely of sterling silver! He regretted that he could not play it well but intended to devote considerable attention to it as soon as time would permit. He said he had played the solo part which Pfitzner had written expressly for that grandfather of the flute in his opera *Palestrina*. Kaleve was then playing at the Wagner-Mozart Festival which we reluctantly had to forego as the series had been sold out long before we reached Munich. I called also at the address of Tillmetz as I wanted to learn from his relatives the correct date of the Professor's demise, as some have said it was in 1919, others 1915, but found that Dr. Oskar Tillmetz, his son, was in Italy on his vacation. The maid, however, said she positively knew that the Professor had died January 25, 1915.

Everyone who comes to Munich must, of course, go to the Marienplatz to see and hear the famous glockenspiel. It has an interesting old-country flavor but the effect is rather ruined by the continual tooting of the automobile horns. Those horns—by the way—were a veritable pest everywhere we went in Europe. Munich has the finest picture gallery in Germany and there I saw our flute in many interesting canvases by Rubens, De Marees, Poussin and Guido Reni, in the latter of which is again depicted Apollo skinning Marsyas.

Four o'clock coffee is almost an institution in Germany and all cafés in Munich were crowded at that hour. It was really delightful to go, for instance, to the *Englischer Garten*, formerly a great private royal park, and after a long stroll to sit down at a little table in the open and partake of some refreshments while listening to good music. We regretfully bade goodbye to Munich. Its architectural monuments, the picturesque vista, the atmosphere of *"gemutlichkeit"* will linger long in our memory.

The old Saxon city of Leipzig unites in a wonderful way the old and the new, the practical and the artistic. It is the greatest book mart and music publishing center in the world; it has the largest railway station in Europe and it is the seat of the great Leipzig fair, which has been repeated for over seven hundred years. Yet it was the musical and artistic atmosphere—that much abused expression—of the city which we sensed the most.

411

Possibly this may have been due in great measure to our contact with Messrs. Zimmermann, of the firm of Jules Heinrich Zimmermann, who treated us with a beautiful courtesy and hospitality. Europeans always seem to have time for the niceties of life. With young Mr. Zimmermann, Jr., who, like his father and uncle, spoke fine English, we went to the quaint little restaurant where Schumann was accustomed to come and gazed reverently at the very table at which he used to sit. Then, of course, St. Thomas Kirche, hallowed through its association with Johann Sebastian Bach, and the Gewandhaus with its great musical tradition and history.

The Gewandhaus had an ideal setting in the finest section of Leipzig, with the Conservatory just around the corner and the University buildings nearby. The townspeople call this the *Musikant* quarter and have appropriately designated the surrounding streets Beethoven Strasse, Mozart Strasse, Haydn Strasse, etc. In front of the Gewandhaus is a fine statue of Mendelssohn and we chortled with glee when we discovered that one of the cherubs at his feet played the transverse flute.

As there are no concerts in the Gewandhaus during the summer, we had to be content to just go through the building, but even that was very worthwhile.

The German is never wholly without music and so we heard a splendid performance of Weber's *Oberon*. There were no great stars in the cast but the ensemble, the orchestra, and the spirit in general were excellent and the stage-technique masterly, utilizing in a novel way the moving picture camera which made possible a rapid change of scene and added much to the realistic effect.

The German audiences were a revelation. Not a whisper and no applause until the end of the act—not scene, mind—and then not until the last note of the orchestra had died away. That is genuine musical appreciation!

The Leipzig picture gallery was housed in a beautiful building facing a huge square at the other extremity of which was the Opera House, and in the heart of the downtown district. The gallery is not great (in the sense of Munich and the wonderful Italian museums) but it is very interesting and had a very

412

fine modern collection. I was happy to see the original of *The Isle of Death* by Boecklin, which was the inspiration of Rachmaninoff's symphonic poem by the same name. Max Klinger was very well represented, including both painting and sculpture, among which was his much disputed *Beethoven*. And again the flute! There was a beautiful relief in white marble by Joseph Kopf called *Die Musik*, showing a little boy playing Pan's flute to his mother, also a very original conception of Hugo Kaufman's entitled: *Koketterie*. It is a statuette in bronze of a nude woman seated, holding on the palm of her left hand a tiny baby Faun playing Pan's pipes. I was guilty of wanting to steal that! Among the paintings I remember only one with the flute, a picture called *Apollo* by Joseph Koch, in which were two figures playing the flute of Pan.

I called on Professor Maximilian Schwedler (of the Schwedler *Reformflöte*), Germany's veteran flutist, who lived almost next door to the Gewandhaus, on Mozart Strasse. He was solo flutist of the Gewandhaus orchestra for many years but was then on a pension. However, he had taught in the Conservatory for over thirty-five years, I was told, and was still very active. It gave me great pleasure to see in what elegant and prosperous quarters he lived. His apartments were luxuriously furnished and the atmosphere was that of a contented and successful artistic life. Our conversation was carried on with great difficulty as he could speak neither English nor Italian and I knew no German to boast of. I shall leave the result to your imagination! So, finally, in despair we made an appointment to meet the next day at Zimmermann's, and there with William Zimmermann as our interpreter, we got along famously.

One of Leipzig's finest flutists of that generation was Karl Bartuzat, whom I shall remember as a polished and elegant gentleman. To this artist we owe indirectly the majority of Karg-Elert's wonderful modern compositions for flute and flute in conjunction with other instruments. Bartuzat and Karg-Elert served in the same regiment during World War I. The flutist had his instrument always with him and urged the famous composer to write for the flute. Many of Karg-Elert's flute compositions were written, therefore, to relieve the monotony of that

413

most uncomfortable trench life and make his flutist friend the happier.

I must not forget to tell you that one of the finest, neatest and most elegant hotels in the city, the Sedan Hotel, was owned by an enthusiastic flute amateur. It was almost next door to the great railway station. The proprietor, Herr Vogd, knew most of the prominent followers of Pan and was so interested in flutes and flute playing that I felt instantly at ease in his company. It was a rare delight to meet him. We bade an affectionate farewell to the beautiful city of Leipzig for I had reason to be very fond of it. It was here that through the encouragement of that big soul, Ernesto Köhler, my first work, *Nove Studi Artistici*, was published by Jules Heinrich Zimmermann. I learned with regret, while in Leipzig, that Köhler's widow, who still lived in Russia, was having a difficult time to make ends meet as the Soviet government had deprived her of her pension. The Zimmermanns were helping her all they could, sending her, now and then, money and even packages of food, but these sometimes did not reach her.

Berlin is a great modern city and we decided to just enjoy it; no more museums and picture galleries for us, we were weary of them. So with an old pupil* who was in the city we spent the greater part of the first day on the upper deck of the big bus just enjoying the sights. We were even guilty of going to Luna Park, a small edition of Coney Island. In the evening we attended the opera and heard a creditable performance of Carmen, the ballet, especially, being very well done. Mozart's *The Magic Flute* had been given the night before our arrival. I was very sorry to have missed it. The next day we went to Potsdam and roamed to our hearts' content through the grounds of the lovely park and the rooms of Sans Souci, still today haunted by the shadows of Frederick-the-Great, Quantz and their flutes. This little palace—little, compared with the

---

* Julius Modesti of New York, a fine and likeable fellow, acted as interpreter between Prill and myself. As a young man, around 1912, Modesti, being quite ambitious, studied flute with several well-known flute virtuosi including Georges Barrère. Somehow, however, as a flutist he seemed to have always "missed the bus!"

great, matchless royal palace at Naples—is beautifully situated on a high elevation and has a truly marvelous approach. The terraces, tier upon tier, to the top and the great stairway, make a wonderful picture. This erstwhile abode of Frederick-the-Great had a homelike atmosphere, a very unusual attribute of a palace, and due, I think, in great measure to the rather small rooms. The flute was the motif for the decorations in most of these rooms and I remember particularly the little round library, which is panelled entirely of wood embellished on walls and ceiling with gilded flutes of Pan and simple flutes. In the music room we saw the flute of the King reposing in a glass case on a beautiful spinet. It had the two Quantz keys, D-sharp and E-flat and was of ivory and wood. On the exquisite old music stand was a manuscript and on the cover was inscribed: "*Sonata per il flauto transverso solo e basso di Quantz.*" There was, of course, much else to see in Potsdam but to have gone through all the palaces would have made too fatiguing a day. We were content to have seen Sans Souci, although we also visited the former summer palace of the Kaiser in which we saw some very fine and well preserved harpsichords.

Professor Emil Prill, Germany's foremost exponent of the flute, invited us to his home but I was unable to come at the hour mentioned, much to my regret. However, that evening by a lucky coincidence, Prill played the Frederick-the-Great Concerto in C with the Berlin Philharmonic over the radio and I felt very happy to be able to hear him. It was a beautiful performance and he seemed in excellent form, although he had just returned from his vacation.

As we were leaving the next day we arranged to meet after the radio concert and spend a most memorable evening together. We had corresponded on and off for over twenty years and had much to talk about. He told me that his five sisters and some brothers were all artists and began their concert tours in 1875 when he was a little fellow. He had two daughters, one of whom was a doctor and the other a student and an enthusiastic amateur flute player.

Prill used a gold flute which was given to him by the late Adolph Goldberg who was, it will be remembered, the Berlin

415

silk hose millionaire. His name, Prill said, should have been Gold Flute, because he had presented one to almost every artist he met. Goldberg was such a lover of the flute that he spent 300,000 gold marks on a collection of pictures and biographies of noted flutists which was published in a private edition in 1907. This huge collection was distributed gratis to all prominent flutists throughout the world.

I promised Prill, upon parting with him, that should I ever return to Berlin I would remain longer. Flutes and flutists are a wonderful subject for a friendly discussion.

I regretted that I did not again see Harzer, who is an excellent flutist of Berlin. I had met him in America in 1925. I was told he was on his vacation.

Our travels were now approaching an end, we had become homesick, and tired of the eternal sameness of the restaurant food, and so decided to hurry on to Gothenburg, Sweden, thinking, perchance, we could get an earlier sailing. There are usually cancellations at the last moment, and so it proved. We had to give up our visit to Stockholm, thereby, but America was beckoning too strongly and we yielded to the call.

We visited one museum in Gothenberg, against my wishes I confess, but I was happy my wife persuaded me to go because I saw there a fine portrait by Franz Hals of a flute player playing the transverse flute.

And so our European trip began and ended with the flute!

*   *   *   *

In most Latin countries, if a man is able to but play the mandoline a little he very often is addressed as a Maestro. In announcing a short opera season in almost any town where opera is usually given, the large placards in the piazza will announce a second-rate singer as a famous prima donna who has sung with *strepitoso successo* or tumultuous success in every great theatre of importance in the world, including La Scala of Milano, Cairo in Egypt, San Petersburg, Rio de Janeiro and, most important of all, "The Metropolitan Opera House" of New York! Of course, the other singers, in particular the tenor (with his thrilling and very long high notes which he is extremely nervous about, because if he cracks, besides the fact that ripe tomatoes, stale eggs, and even pillows for which the spectator paid two cents to be in comfort, will rain upon him, he is finished) gets more than his share of bombastic publicity. Then it announces, in larger types, the greatest star of them all, the one whom every artist must obey and take orders from according to this *master* and *lord's* wishes; he is the Maestro Commendatore e gr. uff. (*grande ufficiale*) Pasquale Scozzamosca, Direttore e Concertatore D'Orchestra. This great man, who may be kind and amiable when in company of his intimate friends, becomes, the moment he steps on the podium, the most autocratic and vicious of tyrants, abusing even the artists selected by himself, with violent and abominably profane language! A conductor of this type who insulted a singer of repute in one of the famous opera houses in Europe, was found murdered one early morning in the alley of the theatre. However, fortunately, this type of conductor is becoming more scarce every day and the reason, I think, is because America has taught us a valuable lesson. This country has some of the world's greatest conductors who are also fine gentlemen.

Now let us proceed about the honorary titles. Each professor of a Royal Conservatory of music, after a few years of good service is honored by the government with the title of Cavaliere della Corona D'Italia, in the case of the now defunct Italian Royal House. This same Cavaliere, after another number of years of teaching becomes, *ipso facto*, Commendatore. If one is a Cavaliere or Commendatore, he is no longer addressed, except by his immediate relatives, by his name. He is now called by the title. In Naples, during my student days, one of the professors had just received his "crocetta" and, on his way one morning to the Conservatory a friend of his in a loud voice called, "Cavaliere, Cavaliere." The professor, recognizing his friend's voice, stopped and said, "pst . . . *sotto voce*, my friend, otherwise all the shoemakers in this neighborhood will turn their heads, because they too, you know, are all Cavalieri!"

When my wife and I visited Italy in 1926 I found several new Cavalieri in my native town. One was called "Il Cavaliere Cafone" (peasant), and another "Il Cavaliere Porcaro" (mer-

417

chant in pigs). Upon inquiring what they had done of value for the government to be so honored, I was told that they hadn't done anything for the government but had supplied "Sua Eccellenza il Sig. Ministro with ample and the best of wines, meats and other good things indispensable to the welfare and happiness of His Excellency!"

However, talking about these government honors given also to some schoolmates of mine, one day a dear lady of around three score and ten, whom I had known for years as *zia Caterina*, came to visit us. I saw that she was very interested in my wife, the "Americana." Finally she came and sat next to me and said: "Leonardo, your wife seems charming, gentle, and very kind and, I was told, sings and plays the harp beautifully." I said, "No, she does not sing or play harp, but she is an excellent pianist, is a good cook and an incomparable housekeeper." "Housekeeper," she repeated in surprise, "don't you have servants?" The dear lady who, many years before, had been told that I was desperately in love with her beautiful daughter, said: "Don't you think that if you had remained in our beautiful Italy and secured a professorship in one of the noted conservatories, Naples or Milan, by now you too would enjoy a life of leisure with a pension and honored by all as a loved Commendatore?"

*   *   *   *

A tall, erect and majestically handsome lady who, in spite of her seventy-five years of age, and with an irresistible and almost overpowering personality, visited us for the third time on the New Year Day of 1947. She came from Chicago on a visit to her brother, a retired attorney, philosopher and scholar, of Glendale, California, who incidentally, was one of our most delightful and devoted friends.

The handsome lady was an accomplished musician, a composer of a number of songs and was also a painter. This last accomplishment she acquired when past fifty and her canvases were selling for a good price. She seldom mentioned that she was the mother of a famous writer, a wealthy and much married man, his latest, not last, divorced wife was the fifth, and—con-

418

trary to his mother—was not a bit religiously disposed. However, his books have been best-sellers and made into motion pictures from which he received astronomical sums of money.

The lady's brother, Leicester, who was a great lover of music and played piano creditably enough to attempt playing Chopin, never missed a prize fight or a wrestling match when within reach, and was also a chess and billiard enthusiast, although the last named game he played atrociously. He had told his sister that my wife and I might play for her, which we did.

A Handel Sonata and Rieti's Sonatina were greatly enjoyed by our guests and particularly by our guest of honor. She appreciated the unusual contrast between the somber and serious Handel and the almost sarcastic wit and humor of the modern Rieti Sonatina. The following is the letter written to my wife:

May 23rd, 1947

My Dear Maud De Lorenzo:

I have thought of you so many times since returning from California. We never did have that nice chat we were going to have because you were always so busy taking care of our hungry needs. When Gertrude told me that you had a lady friend (I think it was the wife of Mr. De Lorenzo's publisher) who was anxious to talk to me about mysticism, I felt I must write out just what I really do believe, I try to make clear to anyone desiring to know more about the subject.

When I was young I was not particularly interested in the Bible. I thought reincarnation meant that we returned to this world, in the body of some animal. No wonder the whole subject was obnoxious. I had always prayed that I might live a pure life, obeying God's will, and helping others do the same. I never doubted for a moment that Jesus Christ was God's only begotten Son, and that He had died for me, and for every sinner. I had a half hearted belief in prayer, but practiced it always. "Lord, I believe: Help thou mine unbelief." I experienced no sudden conversion but just gradually grew more interested in Heavenly things. I found that I could talk to my Heavenly Father, about everything, and quietly wait for His answers. I am never disappointed when I ask for His guidance, for He has said, "Be still, and know that I am God." I have wonderful friends among the Christian Mystics of the present day. They are simple hearted capable guides in this present world.

419

Dr. Frank C. Laubach is one of them. He and his wife were missionaries in the Philippine Islands for 25 years. He has written many religious books, the latest one, just out, is called *Prayer: The Mightiest Force in the World*. Don't fail to read it. *Letters by a Modern Mystic* is another. Another great mystic friend is Edgar Cayce of Virginia Beach, Virginia. I never met him face to face, but corresponded with him, the last few years of his life, and sent many of my friends to him, who were suffering mentally or physically. *There Is a River* is the story of his life, written by Thomas Sugrace, the college roommate of his son, Hugh Cayce; Edgar Cayce died a year ago last January, at sixty-seven years, just two months after sending me the history of my soul's previous incarnations: in Egypt, in the Holy Land, at the time of Christ! Then, the end of the 14th century and the first of the 15th—painting with Raphael. The present is my fifth life experience in this world.

Sincerely yours, G. H. H.

P.S. *God Calling* is a most helpful book. It is an English publication. Hope you can see a movie called *A Stairway to Heaven*. Perhaps your friend would like to read this letter. Do as you like about it.

*　　*　　*　　*

In 1922, William E. Hullinger, well-known flutist and teacher of Los Angeles, wrote a short biography of the writer which was published in *The Flutist*. This biography highlights an interesting and instructive controversy. The following is taken from the August 1922 issue of that magazine:

"In 1904 De Lorenzo had a very interesting controversy with a fine gentleman, whom we will call Smith, of between 50 and 60, and an excellent flute-player. Smith had studied the old system flute all his life and, having recently unsuccessfully tried to change to the Boehm flute, had become its most stubborn enemy, whereas De Lorenzo who had made the change only a year or so before, was tremendously enthusiastic about it. Smith, who was twice De Lorenzo's age, was a bit over-confident of his knowledge of both systems, forgetting that his younger colleague had also extensive knowledge of the possibilities and shortcomings of the Ziegler flute, as the old player used to call his Meyer system. The following conversation took place:

"Smith: 'This cannot be done

without that ridiculous shifting of the thumb.'

"De Lorenzo: 'What difference can that make as long as one is able to play it fine and clean?' (And he played it with considerable ease.)

" 'You must confess that the arpeggio in the dominant seventh in E-flat, which is so simple on the new flute, is almost impossible except for a virtuoso who is equipped with an instrument like yours, with an extra G-sharp key.'

"Smith: 'It makes no difference how many keys one may have, but it can be done beautifully (playing it really fine and clean). That high F-sharp on the Boehm flute is enough to discourage anyone with a good ear, especially so if one uses the middle finger for an easy change of fingering.'

"De Lorenzo: 'Not necessarily. All F-sharps with the middle finger must be avoided except in very rapid passages when it is followed or preceded by an E. The high F-sharp, when written *pp.*, can be produced with great ease and beautifully in tune if one places his right hand little finger on the C-sharp key.'

"Smith: 'But you cannot shift the little finger on each high F-sharp in the noted passage from *William Tell.'*

"De Lorenzo: 'Play the whole passage with the right hand little finger on the C-sharp key. (Passage played.) Besides, the Brossa F-sharp lever, which can be placed just near the fourth finger of the right hand without shifting the trill keys, is very valuable if one desires it on his flute.'

"Smith: 'You are a hard worker and a very ambitious young

man, but I am more than convinced that the old Ziegler flute is superior to the new, as I have here (producing from his pocket) a phenomenal passage for you which I know is a stumbling block for the Boehm flute.'

"De Lorenzo (who at a glance saw what he was up against): 'Yes, that passage is tremendously difficult, but with patience and hard work the intelligent player will be able to master it by using the harmonic position on the high G-flat and shifting the thumb when necessary. I see that you are well acquainted with the Boehm flute and it really surprises me that you did not stick to it.'

"Smith: 'The high B-flat on the Boehm flute is flat when played *pp* in the original position and sharp if one uses the first trill key (D-sharp).'

"De Lorenzo: 'The master of his instrument will always find means of adjusting those little inevitable defects which are a characteristic of all wind instruments. The following position for high B-flat may be used only in the *p* and sustained note: left hand, first and third finger closed, upper trill key open.

" 'In regard to trills, the Boehm flute is simply wonderful when one thinks that the following, which are

impossible on the old flute are, comparatively speaking, easy on the Boehm flute.'

"In spite of the animated argument, Smith and De Lorenzo parted the best of friends."

*　　*　　*　　*

A flute student's "sad comedy." . . .
Walter Kirk ascended the five flights of stairs in an old apart-

ment house on Brentwood Road. On the sixth floor an old woman opened the door and showed him the way to the room of Mr. Gustave Drouot, flute virtuoso and teacher.

"Mr. Drouot, you have been recommended to me by Mr. Richards, a friend of mine, who says he is one of your students. My name is Walter Kirk and I should like you to give me lessons on the flute," said Walter as he shook hands with the instructor.

"It gives me ze great pleasure, Monsieur Kirk. Allow me to take ze hat and ze coat. Have you taken lessons before? Très bien, monsieur, you have ze flute, we start at once."

Walter drew from its blue velvet cover an old flute with its ivory head piece and silver keys carefully polished up.

"Sacre bleu! monsieur; you have not really come to take ze lesson zat flute. Tell me, monsieur, how is it, you are in possession of an instrument like zat?"

"This flute," replied Kirk, "belonged some years ago to our neighbor in Portland Junction. He came from Europe long before the Civil War and brought this flute with him. He started to teach me how to blow the scale on it just before he died. It's nearly four years ago now. His daughter gave the flute to me, and I thought when I would come to Boston someone would teach me how to play on it."

"Ah, but monsieur does not tell me zat anyone could play ze music on a curiosity like zat?"

"Mr. Preister could play some fine pieces on it," answered Walter.

"It would be what you call it—ze witchcraft. No one today plays on a flute like zat. Zat flute, monsieur, is as old as ze mountains. My memory tells me, monsieur, it was Noah who told his sons to crack zeir faces on an instrument of zat kind. It would be a punishment, ze torture, to try and play on it. You must have ze grande flute, ze modern flute, ze flute made wiz silver, enfin ze flute you can make all ze music wiz. Certainement, ze flute must be made wiz silver, ozzerwise it is not ze modern flute. Mais oui, zey make only ze coffins of wood today; zey do not use ze wood anymore to make ze—comment appelez-vous ze—ze cereals for ze breakfast. Apropos, you can play ze notes on zis flute? If you please I wish very much to hear."

423

Walter complied with this wish and blew the entire diatonic scale. The instructor was amazed.

"Mon cher, c'est magnifique, you have ze tone of ze great virtuoso. If you will start now, zis moment, you will be ze great successor to ze grande Taffanel wizout ze doubt. Now you will go buy ze new system instrument. I shall be very proud to teach you. Zat is all I can tell you today, and after you come back to me next Monday evening at six o'clock we will start at once."

Walter left the instructor after having promised to do as suggested, and next evening sneaked from the office five minutes ahead of time and into the store of Zimmer & Schmidt and asked to be shown a "new system silver flute with a closed G-sharp key."

"One hundred and fifty-five dollars," the salesman said.

Walter's heart sank into his shoes. He said he would think it over. On the way home his hopes rose once more. He would write home for some money. Consequently he wrote, telling of the glowing account his teacher had given of his wonderful tone, and the next letter from home brought with it a money order for forty dollars and a letter to his employer, an old friend of the father, asking for his assistance in the matter.

With ninety dollars in cash and a note properly endorsed for the balance, our hero found himself the next evening in possession of an instrument that reflected the rosiest prospects from every point of view.

Walter's lessons commenced. His teacher seemed to be interested in his progress. After the next lesson, the eighth, he was to be tried on an easy duet by Terschak. The next Monday evening his hopes for a speedy mastery of the instrument rose with every one of the steps in the five flights to his teacher's floor. At the door he was met by the landlady, who informed him that Mr. Drouot had suddenly left after accepting a position out West in a "Philharmonica Band."

After this cheerful bit of news he quietly walked back to his room, and soon it dawned on him that another teacher would have to be found at the earliest opportunity. Accordingly he set about to inquire, and a few days later found himself in the presence of Professor Karl Gelzenan.

424

"Very vell, ve start right away," said the new teacher, as he turned over some exercises on the rack. "Ve vill dry on dis und see how far you is."

Turning around to Walter, who was standing ready, flute in hand, the professor apparently seemed to be in great despair and ready to faint.

"Du himmel," said he, after having passed his finger behind his collar to remove some of that tightness there. "Dot I should alvays have de luck to haf such 'pech vogel' come to me. I only teach how to blay on der wood flute. I am an honest man und if I gannot do you goot, I don'd take your money."

"But," interposed Walter, "my former teacher, Mr. Drouot, distinctly told me that wooden ones were out of fashion. I had a wooden flute when I went to him, and changed it for this."

"You should know better dan dot, yourself. Did you effer see a fiolin made of anyding else dan voot? Iss not der flute a voot vint instrooment? Did you effer see any odder voot vint instrooment, der oboe, der fagott, der clarinet, made of brass or any odder medal? No, mein Herr, you neffer did under you neffer vill. Der first dime you do come to me and I vill deach you for nodding. I vill not deach you on der silfer flute if I should starfe. Change dot ding for a real flute and den I shall dry to see vot I gan do for you. No, no, I gannot do it, it is against my reputation."

The man behind the counter said, "Thirty-five dollars" for the exchange.

Walter was in a nice fix. With a flute that was not of the right kind and his salary hypothecated, he was blocked in every move. A vacancy that occurred in the New York office of his firm gave him an opportunity to get transferred to that branch. There he found a teacher who was not particular whether the instrument was made of wood or silver but who said to him, "I hope that before long the perfect flute will make its appearance, that the question of this or that system or this or that kind of an instrument may then be set aside. Someday someone will use a superior material, different from anything used before. But, for the present you must get that closed G-sharp key changed to an open G-sharp key, otherwise you will have trouble with the high E."

425

"If I only could get my money back and get someone to teach me to play that old flute as Preisler did," said Walter.

*   *   *   *

Two important sociological questions answered by a flutist-philosopher. . . .

An old, long-retired flutist of note who was also known as "The Octogenarian Flutist and Philosopher" was asked in February 1948 what he thought of the possibility of a third World War which so many think unavoidable when the scars of World War II have hardly begun to heal. His answer was: "How right was Da Vinci centuries ago when he classified war as a *pazzia bestialissima.*" (utter foolish frenzy) He continued further: "The trouble lies in the fact that the professional soldier is always glorified with the highest honors, instead of being ridiculed, treated with contempt and called a parasitic destroyer of things, a professional murder on a colossal scale. These dangerous people want an America as militaristic as Germany ever was because—as they put it—'that is the only way to avoid war!' Was there another nation more prepared for war than Germany was? Look at her now! Has war ever settled anything? After each war they all prepare for the next one!"

This "philosopher"—who had held responsible positions for many years in opera, symphony and music schools—was highly esteemed. Only once in his life had he attempted composition. He was thirty-five years old when he wrote what he called a *Scholastic Quartet* for four flutes. Beautifully written in the classical style of Reicha and Kuhlau, it was urged publication by his pupils and admirers. The professor-philosopher first refused because, he said, there was not enough profit for any publisher to risk the required expenses. However, the score was sent to three different firms. The first two returned it "with regret." The third, and last, publisher to whom the score was sent, suggested that the composer pay all the expenses of publication, following which he would receive a royalty of twelve cents on the dollar of the net profit after the first one hundred copies were sold! Needless to say, the score has enjoyed an undisturbed rest ever since.

426

The second question, as important as the first, was disposed by the old flutist, in a few words. "Why," a young man asked, "is sex appeal in all humans, animals, insects and plants, of such tremendous importance that all other matters are insignificant in comparison?" The old flutist-philosopher's brief answer was, "Because of the terrific urge of the unborn to come to life!" The professional soldier, always with his microscopic mind on the next war, worries of low births, not even thinking that the atom bomb has knocked out the entire so-called *art of war*. Such behavior is not of a civilized race but, instead, of a race of idiots. Now that people live longer, "fewer and better children" should be the motto. N.B. In time to come the nations which have erected the tallest monuments to soldiers will be mostly ridiculed!

Another boy of about fifteen who had been a poor flute student the previous year with the old flutist-philosopher expressed the wish to ask a question. He raised his hand and said: "I should like to ask a question but . . . I think, I mean it is difficult to answer!" "Well, go ahead," said the old philosopher impatiently, "there isn't a question I can't answer." "I should like to ask, how does it feel to be dead?" The old flutist chased him out of the house saying, "That is not an intelligent question," to which the boy grumbling said, "Huh, but he couldn't answer it though."

"Professor, will you have a cigarette?" one of his new pupils asked him. "You know or ought to know that I don't smoke," he answered. "I got rid of that abominable and detestable vice years ago, after a long struggle." "Is smoking really bad, professor? I know many wonderful persons, writers, composers, professors of universities, scientists and many beautiful and highly intelligent women, besides some very young and bright boys and girls who smoke." "Unfortunately, that is a sad truth. However, smoking is not only foolish, but dirty, expensive, unhealthy and the cause of many disastrous fires which cost every nation in the world untold millions of dollars in property and numerous lives every year. As much as I hate dictators, yet there should be a law allowing only ugly women with bow legs to smoke and wear short skirts in order to attract the attention of the (unintel-

427

ligent) opposite sex. The result would be similar, I think, to that theatre manager who, having received many protests against women's large hats, announced that only women of advanced age would be permitted to keep their hats on, with the result that at the next performance there wasn't a woman's hat to be seen anywhere in the theatre. I take my hat off to the only city in the world that has a club or society of non-smokers, it is London, England. Smokers, once tightly in the grip of the nicotine, the poor devils, fools or genius, seldom escape. Do you know that within few years apart, Puccini died with cancer of the throat and Marconi with the same malady of the tongue, because of constant cigaret smoking? In our days only the unusual person does not smoke. The two world wars increased smoking, misery and immorality 300%, therefore, war, vice and barbarism all go hand in hand. However, the future generations will not only have gotten rid of these pests, but will laugh at us for behaving so unintelligently. The majority of *great flutists* avoided smoking and requested their talented pupils to do likewise for the benefit of their sensitive lips, beautiful tone and health in general."

Is it not a farce that the majority of sociologists worry because of the abnormal increase of the population of the world while professional soldiers and religious people who—what a paradox —in time of war go hand in hand in excommunicating the enemy and bless their soldiers to destroy the enemy with whom there has been no reason for hate; preach continuously for more and more children? However, if a professional soldier is successful in a battle at a cost of 100,000 lives and another has sacrificed one-half million souls—the majority of whom never knew what they were fighting for—the second soldier who sacrificed the most lives gets the highest honors and, most likely, the tallest monument!

World War III? If that should happen, not only civilization, but the planet itself will be destroyed.

Now that people live longer (thanks to medical science), the motto should be "fewer and better children" and, most important, not to be allowed that the morons or unintellectual class, outnumber for military or religious reasons the intelligentsia!

428

II Personal Recollections of Some Great and Near-Great

GIACOMO NIGRO

Giacomo Nigro, my first teacher, taught the flute in my native town for about fifty years. He was the son of fairly well-to-do and honest farmers who wanted him to be more than a peasant and so sent him to a school about fifty miles from Viggiano, where he could acquire a good literary education and also a profession. He came out a flutist with a good knowledge of solfeggio and theory which enabled him to teach if he so desired.

However, he had other plans. He persuaded his parents to permit him to go to America where he hoped to achieve big things. He was about seventeen years old when he landed in New York but, although many former school mates and friends were there, he found it very difficult to make ends meet after the good sum of money his father had given him was gone.

He had learned that many of the young men of good families who had come to the New World expecting to become rich in a short time, finally had to work on the piers as common laborers, carrying heavy loads on their backs. Among these were sons of the *galantuomini* or aristocrats who instead of going to a university to become a doctor, lawyer, or priest, as their parents desired, had succumbed to the lure of America.

Many times Giacomo was so discouraged he wanted to write his parents to send him money for his return. However, little at a time he had a cheap job here and there, playing at picnics, religious processions, funerals and he even played for a dance from nine until five A.M. for $3.00! After nearly four years in New York he received the sad news that his father had passed on and that he must now return as his mother and sister needed his assistance in the management of the property and crops.

Preoccupied with these thoughts while walking to the home of a flute pupil, he absentmindedly fell into a large hole where coal had just been delivered. Rescued by a policeman, fortunately unhurt, he was released at the police station after much questioning. Homesick for his mother and sister and with nearly a thousand dollars in savings, he left for Italy.

Upon reaching home he learned that his father's sister had recently married a strange man from Le Puglie, a town near Bari. His name was Don Achille, no one apparently knew his full name, and he insisted that the "Don" must not be omitted as he was an important man and boasted of his wonderful virtues.

Within a year or so, Giacomo's mother accepted a proposal of marriage from a man who had lost his wife. He was a fine, hard working farmer with considerable property of his own. Her son had proved neither willing nor capable of managing their property, for he was a gentleman and, too, his training as a musician had not fitted him for country duties.

The news of the marriage was very distasteful to Don Achille who wanted full control of everything. He thereupon created dissension and alarm by telling Giacomo and his sister Franceschella that now their property would be scattered and have to be shared with other children to come and, also, Giacomo would no longer have an excuse and would be called to serve in the army. This was considered a calamity. Don Achille succeeded in persuading Giacomo and his sister to demand most of the property and to sever all connections with their mother and to come and live with him, where, he said, they could all be prosperous, happy and live like *aristocrati*.

It broke the poor mother's heart and to show her good will for her children and also avoid a court case she gave them all the property they asked for, including most of the *titoli* or bonds she still possessed. These demands were engineered by the unscrupulous Don Achille. The old bachelor *zio Vincenzo,* uncle of Don Achille's wife, also lived with them. He had about 20,000 lire in bonds and this, supplemented now with their large property and Giacomo's lessons in solfeggio and flute, seemed to assure a life of ease for Don Achille. He was now in his glory and respected, if not loved, by all the good and simple people to whom he seemed a kind seer. He advised them how to improve their lands, how to save their livestock and even how they themselves could enjoy good health. He assisted at the christening of their babies and was soon called *compare* or god-father by most of the people in that section of the town and even beyond. Upon these occasions he always brought presents of gold; a ring for the baby, a bracelet or earrings for the mother, knowing full well that they would reciprocate tenfold. And so it was. Scarcely a day passed that someone did not bring him a chicken, a kid, a suckling pig or a pot of *ricotta* (a delicious cream cheese), and on holidays, between the *compare* and Giacomo's pupils, a procession filled the house with presents which lasted for months.

To further his hold on these simple folks he whispered in their ears and with great secrecy that he also possessed occult power and consequently could revenge himself upon anyone who displeased him and did not behave well. Giacomo, now a fine, handsome young man, fell desperately in love with the beautiful Rachelina De Cunto. She reciprocated his affections and they decided to inform Don Achille and the rest of the family of their desire to marry. At this news, thunder and lightning broke loose. To bring another woman into this home and disturb its peace and happiness was unthinkable. Giacomo was told that if he insisted on marrying he would have to leave and be on his own. Although he truly loved the girl, he lacked the strength of character to defy them and weakly yielded. He took revenge upon them by making a vow to speak to no member of the family henceforth and for over thirty years he did just that, only addressing his sister in a low disgruntled voice when he needed a clean shirt or his suit pressed.

As a child, I was unaware of the sad story of Giacomo's

431

mother and never knew until I was about fifteen that she was still living and had struggled for years in poverty with her many new children, all girls. Upon this occasion my teacher and I took the usual walk together after his teaching was over. We visited some mutual friends where he indulged in many large glasses of old and exquisite wine. Just as we were about to leave, a tiny, old wrinkled woman came in. As soon as she saw him, she ran to him and putting both arms around Giacomo's big frame cried, "*Giacomo mio, Giacomo mio.*" She was so small she hardly reached his neck. Until then he had been in high spirits telling stories inspired by the much wine he had drunk. He now looked serious and disturbed and putting his arm around her neck said to her in a melancholy tone of voice, "If you had conceived an *ass* instead of *me*, it would have been better!" He then put her aside, bade me follow him and said not a word about what had just happened. Reaching home, I told my mother of the unexpected and startling occurrence and, then relating to me the whole sad story, she said that as it had taken place many years before they had thought it best to say nothing.

At the time I studied solfeggio with Giacomo Nigro, he was forced to teach from early morning to dark to eke out a living. The days when he only accepted a few pupils and enjoyed a gentleman's easy life were long past and this reversal in his fortunes was caused by the unscrupulous Don Achille. Disaster came, at last, swiftly and unexpectedly. Don Achille was arrested together with one of his *compari*, a retired and prosperous neighbor, Tommaso Astrella. This man had married his cousin upon his return from South America where he had collected a substantial sum of money for the church and other religious purposes and had then kept it all for his own use, apparently without trouble. One day Don Achille, wearing his embroidered high leather boots with *speroni lucenti* (shining spurs) set out on horseback for his estate Santo Marco (Saint Mark) on the outskirts of the town. As he passed the house of Tommaso he saw him sitting outside scrutinizing a document in his hand and stopped his horse to greet him. Tommaso showed him the piece of paper which was a promissory note for 50 lire which his wife had received some time back from her father as a birthday present for the youngest of their five children, Giovannino. Inspecting the paper, Don Achille was inspired by the same telepathic thought as *compare Tommaso*, that is, the figure 50 could be made 500, or better still 5000. Surely it was an easy job to alter it by simply adding one, two or more zeros. This seemed very profitable business indeed, so Don Achille, instead of proceeding to Santo Marco, got off his horse and spent considerable time with his *compare*. Later they were seen to visit Don Peppantonio Marsicano, an old foxy notary public, who knew just what they wanted done.

When the paper was presented for payment for the amount of L5000, consternation and dismay struck the home of the Giliberti family, and since they did not have even a fraction of that amount in cash the family was, in a little while, stripped of almost everything they had, including many beautiful hand-made pieces which were part of the dowry of Beatrice, the youngest and only other daughter.

The whole town was shocked and extremely sorry for the plight of the Giliberti family but, apparently, no one thought anything could be done about it. Some there were who said the old father must have been insane to have written such a large amount to his signature when his daughter had long ago been given her dowry. Others winked and shrugged their shoulders. However, matters did not go as smoothly for the two *compari* as they had anticipated. After a few months, the young son of the Giliberti's who was in the army, was informed of their misfortune and that no one had intervened to help them. He applied for an interview with the captain of his company whom he luckily found sympathetic and interested. Within a few days the colonel dispatched a government official to investigate the whole case and the two *compari* were immediately arrested. It was whispered in town that the cunning old Don Peppantonio, the notary public who had altered the promissory note, was also to be apprehended but he had protected himself so cleverly nothing could be done about him.

This imbroglio happened when I had almost finished my course in solfeggio and was, at last, in a few weeks to be given a flute. I was very eager to see how soon I would be able to play upon it but unfortunately my teacher Giacomo had other thoughts on his mind. He and the other three members of the family, convinced of the innocence of Don Achille, decided to use all their financial resources to fight the case against him and engaged the best lawyers in Potenza, the capital of the province where the two *compari* were now safely behind bars.

Don Achille had protested his innocence in the name of the Virgin Mary, saying that his great success and popularity among the simple people had made many enemies who now sought his downfall. Giacomo went back and forth to Potenza. It was long, hard traveling—twenty-four miles of difficult mountain road on the back of a mule—and then long hours with the lawyers. The trial lasted several weeks but they were finally convicted. Don Achille was condemned to one year in prison and deprived of his civil rights. Tommaso, also, with all he had possessed gone, was given three years. He died at the end of the second year, his wife followed him a few months later and her father, old, bitter and worn out died almost at the same time.

All the *titoli* that the grand uncle Vincenzo had owned vanished and weak, past eighty and smoking his inseparable long clay pipe, the shock of the arrest of his beloved Don Achille, killed him.

The several thousand lire which Giacomo possessed were also taken by the lawyers and now with all his money gone he was forced to teach from early morning to dark. He lost also the respect and friendship of the majority of the good people of the town and the *galantuomini*, with whom he had kept company for years, scarcely greeted him now.

The tall, handsome, proud and dignified Italian *"carabiniere"* have an international reputation and with their Napoleonic hats and spotless uniforms are almost irresistible to the gentle sex regardless of their individual, intellectual or moral virtues.

When the *carabiniere* who had arrested and handcuffed Don Achille in his country estate just outside the town, reached the vicinity of the crushed Giliberti family, he made much noise with his long sword and spears to draw the attention of Don Achille's victims and particularly that of the beautiful Beatrice with whom he had apparently fallen in love. One morning, encouraged by her previous acknowledged *Buon giorno* he had dared to whisper to her that she was more beautiful than the "Regina Margherita," who was then young and considered one of the most beautiful women in all of Europe. His audacity frightened and angered Beatrice and she had run immediately to her mother to tell her about the incident. Although he had never again seen her standing at her door looking innocently at the passersby, he was not in the least discouraged. However, neither Beatrice nor her mother came out to look at the unusual spectacle of Don Achille in handcuffs—only the neighbors swarmed about and soon the whole town knew what had occurred.

Don Achille served his full sentence and emerged very little chastened and still a boastful man. There were many who greeted him with derision but soon he began to visit his old peasant *compari* convincing them with his talk of his innocence and "you shall see," he said, "by the holy name of the immaculate Virgin Mary, I shall soon emerge again to be the loved and *respected Don Achille*." However, this proved more difficult than he had thought and, with all his assurance, life was a hard struggle. Gradually it was whispered about that he was a master of witchcraft and that he had many branches in other towns all of whose members were under him. He insisted that his clients call only at night and professed to cure people of anything and especially where doctors had failed. His chief assistant in the preparation of the different mysterious herbs that he alone knew was Giacomo's sister Franceschella, who was the most important person in the family next to Don Achille. Immaculately clean, she was in the habit of washing her hands even after she had handled the whitest and cleanest snow in winter. She did all the cooking and supervised everything that the *compari* brought. The washing was done by the maid who was always at her elbow and the water was provided by a male servant who had to fetch it in barrels on each side of the mule's back a mile or so distant as the town had no water supply. That indispensible luxury came many years later. Giacomo, in the meantime, now found it necessary to accept all the pupils he could teach. He charged five lire per month for his lessons which was the usual price at that time but from his intimate friends he would accept no pay knowing

435

that the presents he would receive on Christmas, Easter and on his name day, San Giacomo, would be double and even triple that amount.

When my six-keyed flute arrived from Milano and my teacher showed me first how to make a sound on the mouthpiece, alone, then to put the three pieces together and then where the fingers should go, I thought I now knew everything. The last thing he showed me that day, I remember, was to call my attention to the chart in the Berbiguier Methode which had come a day or two before the flute. "If you should forget how to finger the few notes I have shown you, just look here." Arriving home, I at once proceeded to blow so many notes, and outblow so many others that mother, although happy for my interest and also because I could make it sound said "Now you be a good boy and go down to your room and close the door. I have a bad headache already."

After two years I played so well that Giacomo said I already played almost as well as he did and would soon be ready for a job. And so it was . . . Later I studied with that prince of a man Alfonzo Pagnotti who must have been very fond of me because even when I hadn't practiced much, he told me *bravo*. I said to myself, "What a difference between the two teachers." Pagnotti had learned the Boehm flute from the great Krakamp and wanted me to do likewise but . . . five hundred lire or one hundred dollars was then an astronomical sum.

This teacher, who had also a good knowledge of the oboe and clarinet and gave lessons on them, acquainted me with much excellent music including all of the Kuhlau's duets which I enjoyed playing with him. He was a very good soul and adored his old teacher Krakamp who had only passed on a few years back, in 1883! At around my fourteenth year when I was practicing many hours a day, inspired by my love for a fair maiden, something seemed to go wrong with me. I was restless, I was heard to scream in my sleep and awakening, startled and frightened, I thought I saw a man with a colored handkerchief around his neck at the foot of my bed. When father came, awakened by my screams, the imaginary figure disappeared through the door. Also, when in proximity to others I unconsciously bumped my elbow against them. My mother, much worried, consulted two women neighbors who insisted that, without doubt, I was a victim of witchcraft! Much alarmed, she told my father that I must be taken at once to a specialist in such matters. But he objected strenuously and said he would, instead, ask Don Vincenzino —Dr. Vincenzo De Cunto—to come and make a thorough examination. He was our family doctor, a very fine and up-to-date physician who every year attended the doctor's convention in Naples or Rome and was, surely, no lazy or sleepy country doctor. He came and his verdict was, "Nothing wrong except mental overwork. Send him to the country and he will soon be normal." My mother was not convinced and, again consulting her two neighbors, who professed to have little faith in doctors, now begged my father to take me immediately to the *orco*, as he was called, the witchcraft man. My father insisted he did not want to make a fool of himself by consulting a dirty, ignorant racketeer who ought to be behind bars, but my mother countered by saying, "You don't believe in anything; you go to church only once in a *blue moon* and yet you would risk the life of one of our children because of your obstinacy." "That is not true," my father answered, "surely you know that I wouldn't hesitate to throw myself into the fire to save my children, but this sort of thing gets on my nerves and as far as not going to church, I make no apology, as I have noticed 'some of the most pious' behave in a scandalous manner." However, mother then told him that if he was not willing to go, then Maria Teresa and Billonia (Apollonia) would gladly accompany her, to which proposal my father then said, "If our son must be treated by that ignorant brute I will take him there but I am positive it is a stupid thing to do. If Don Paolo (my father's cousin, chemist and mayor of the town) should hear of this he will treat me with contempt. He knows they are frauds and so treats them with an iron hand." So to please my mother and also because in his inner heart he wasn't so sure as his loud voice indicated that these bad people couldn't do harm, he at last capitulated and an appointment was made to be there long after dark!

I can still remember the terrible odor as we entered the hut.

437

In one corner, at the farthest end of the room, was a bed. In another corner, lay a goat surrounded by five or six chickens, one sitting comfortably on top of the animal's body. No pig was to be seen, but we knew that, in deference to the expected visitors, the *orco's* wife had taken it out for the time being. The *orco*, thin, short and dirty, took my left hand and put the palm to his nose, and then turning to my father said, "He is well fixed; it requires special herbs which I shall cook in a terracotta pot and bring to your house tomorrow night."

This fantastic occurrence actually took place. He brought the liquid and when sufficiently cool it was thrown on my head and ran over the rest of my body and I was then wrapped in a sheet and jumped in my bed unassisted.

In spite of the fact that my father gave him twenty lire, mother ten and five she had put in my hand to give him when father was not looking, the *orco* had the impudence to ask my father for a loan of 175 lire! Mother saw a "storm" coming and hastened to tell him that we would think it over and dismissed him as quickly as possible. But he received the so-called loan. My poor mother was persuaded that these witchcraft people had the power, when displeased, to enter any home through the keyhole with the aid of a special *inquento* or vaseline they secretly prepared—although my father told her that when Don Paolo had some of them arrested, no one escaped through the keyhole!

This unpleasant treatment proved utterly ineffective and I was then taken to Don Achille. We paid him two visits and upon each occasion he painted my left elbow with some mysterious concoction. I became well immediately although I rather think that the fact that I had in the meantime been forbidden to practice for nearly two weeks had something to do with my recovery. Don Achille was illiterate, he signed his name with a cross X and spoke with the strong dialect of Puglie. I still remember that after he painted my elbow the last time he turned to me and said "you are now in a first class shape. I hear you are leaving soon for America, what a lucky boy!"

It was soon after this that I made my first trip to America

accompanied by two older musicians who had been there for years. I was offered a job at a mineral spring resort for 150 lire —$30.00—a month for three months which I accepted.

It proved to be a healthful one but neither artistically nor financially profitable. When I returned to Italy, after four years, and very homesick for my mother and sisters in particular, I found Giacomo well and in good spirits. He was now again admitted into the circle of the *galantuomini*—with whom he had not been a *persona grata* for a long time—and was jolly and happy except at home, where he continued to be as silent and taciturn as a clam! He had raised the price of his lessons from five lire to seven lire per month—the lira was then twenty cents—and it was understood he could take a vacation whenever he chose.

Giacomo had two comrades, Don Pasquale Spolidoro and Don Ciccio Pisano, and together they made an irresistible and unique trio and had been "Don Juans" in their youth. They were about Giacomo's age, and like him, were bachelors and had been disappointed in love. It was their custom to take a three weeks' vacation together in the valley at the time of the *vendemmia* or gathering of the grapes, a festive period of color and high spirits. The Casino or Villa of Spolidoro, where they stayed, was now a little rundown but it had been an imposing mansion in its day. Back of it lay the vineyard where there was now much activity, but that did not disturb the three friends.

The most important item of the three weeks' holiday was a large barrel of about seventy gallons of the finest red wine not less than ten years old and every day choice foods from town were brought to them mostly on mule back. Maria Rosa, who had been in the household of the Spolidoros for over thirty-five years, was the cook. Now close to seventy, she was still strong and efficient and good-natured, although they often teased her by asking if the *carabiniere* with whom she had had a son when only sixteen had been handsome. She proudly told them that her son, who had lived in New York for years and had five or six children, never failed to send her five dollars at Christmas, Easter and for the *festa della Madonna*. However, they respected her as they knew she had been an innocent girl who had believed her sweetheart when he told her that as soon as he received his discharge he would marry her and take her with him to Northern Italy where he owned much property. He left her without even a goodbye when his term expired.

Maria Rosa's days were now completely occupied preparing meals for the three big paunches gentlemen. They had an enormous capacity for food and wine and although they drank no water during the three weeks and there wasn't a pint of the precious wine left when they were ready to return to town, not one of them had been at any time intoxicated. That was beneath their dignity; they drank to the point of exhilaration but not beyond. Besides, they drank only with their meals. Black, strong coffee followed each meal and none of them smoked or used hard liquor. Breakfast consisted only of a small cup of coffee, black as ink with a little sugar. A walk on the *via nuova* followed comfortably slow, because of their girth. Don Ciccio was enormous, he weighed over 300 pounds. Don Pasquale weighed over 250, and Giacomo almost 200 pounds. Dinner was at noon and they drank four quarts of wine at this meal. At around four, after a good nap, they had a little repast of bread and *caciocavallo*, a strong cheese, not in the shape of a horse as its name would imply but rather resembling a bowl-pin, with at least one quart of wine each. Another walk followed and at around 8:30 another great meal. This lasted between two and three hours and two full quarts each of wine was consumed.

In gay spirits, they teased each other about their gallant, adventurous past. Only Don Ciccio was silent. "Poor man," the other two would say, "he was so slow he never got there on time and when he did, his lady friend saw only his enormous belly." Don Ciccio good-naturedly just smiled and drank another large glass of wine.

Don Pasquale and Don Ciccio were both university men and often after the elaborate meal would recite Latin quotations which Giacomo understood perfectly and then they continued with whole stanzas from Dante, Ariosto, Leopardi, Manzoni and others. At night the snoring of the three was so terrific it almost rocked the house! Maria Rosa, who slept in the farthest part of the house, often complained that she hadn't been able to sleep a wink!

One holy day while I was out with Giacomo and Don Pasquale, Giacomo turned to me and asked if I had ever heard Pasqualino play the church organ. (As they had known each other from childhood, he never called him Don Pasquale.) Don Pasquale was persuaded to demonstrate his ability and, climbing the narrow corkscrew stairs with some effort, he made a motion to the boy to work the bellows and then began a religious tune on the old organ which was used only when Don Pasquale was in the mood. He had studied piano when a boy to complete his general education and, as he was very musical, he was also soon able to play on the organ, to the delight of his pious mother Donna Teresina.

Don Achille passed away during the second year of my army service and his wife, Donna Maria Antonia, who was Giacomo's aunt, followed him in the shadow beyond a few months later. Giacomo and his sister were alone now and his vow of silence was at last at an end.

I returned from Cape Town, South Africa, in May 1907 and was at once prevailed upon to give a concert. Depressed in spirits I consented reluctantly as I had only recently lost my two dearest friends, my mother, the news of whose passing reached me the day after my farewell concert in Cape Town, and Ernesto Koehler. They were born the same year and died the same month. The concert was a great success and this was the program:

I   Overture by Rossini—played by the small local orchestra which I conducted.
II Concerto Op. 97 by Ernesto Köhler (in memoriam) sent to me by the composer from St. Petersburg and which I performed for the first time in Capetown just prior to my leaving. It had the following autograph: "Al caro amico e distinto Flautista Signor Leonardo De Lorenzo, dal suo riconoscente ed affettuoso amico Ernesto Köhler. Pietroburgo li 19 Ottobre 1906."
III Minuetto by Boccherini, orchestra.

441

IV   Trio for three flutes by Kuhlau, Op. 90, with Vincenzo De Milita as second flute and Americo Gagliardi, third flute.
V   My own Fantasia Op. 5 recently published and which I also played for the first time in Capetown.
VI   Strauss' Waltz for orchestra.

The accompaniments were played by Signorina Nunzia Miglionico, whose father, a delightful friend, had been a flutist as a young man but had later established a successful jewelry store in New York. After the performance of my *Fantasia*, Professor Gaetano Argentieri, our respected school principal, asked my first teacher, Giacomo, to stand and he was given an ovation.

Giacomo was now nearing his sixtieth year. He complained that most of his pupils wanted lessons on the "Bohemian flute" and he didn't know a thing about it. He had seen one or two that visitors had brought from abroad but he had never tried to play on one. I showed him mine and when I played it for him he was wide-eyed with astonishment. He was much discouraged at his inability to play it and said, "Too late, I am too old." I succeeded after awhile in convincing him that he was not too old and so Giacomo Nigro, my old teacher, at 60 became my pupil! It was of great help to him in his teaching and at my suggestion he raised his tuition from seven to ten lire a month with lessons only every other day. He died in 1919 and his sister, the "dried old witch," as she was called, although two years his senior, outlived him ten years.

Soon after the concert I left for Naples to continue my studies. I had hoped and planned to study composition with Giuseppe Martucci and piano with Alessandro Longo, but when I arrived at the Conservatory I was told that "Direttore Commendatore Martucci" was too busy to even see anyone. I had come thousands of miles and didn't intend to be turned away so easily. Three days of persistence and perseverence on my part and, at last, the doorman said that the Director would see me at eleven o'clock in his studio. It was the rule of that famous Conservatory that whenever the Director gave an audience or an interview he was to be attired in a Prince Albert coat and striped trousers. It must have been an inconvenience for him to see me, yet the great man was extremely kind and gentle and when I told him

I had come from abroad to study with him he expressed a sincere regret that as the Director of the Conservatory he could accept no pupils. He recommended Professor De Nardis, saying "I think you would enjoy studying with him. He began his career as a flutist." In the afternoon of the same day, I climbed six floors to the apartment of Maestro De Nardis. He was a fine teacher and many composers of Italy studied under him at one time or another. After I had been with him a few months, he expressed a wish to see and hear my *flauto moderno* as he called it. I gladly complied and played for him my *Pensiero Elegiaco* Op. 7, in memory of Ernesto Köhler, which had just been published by Zimmermann. Maestro De Nardis accompanied me. His father-in-law, a distinguished looking gentleman from Abruzzi, was his guest at the time. His name was Dr. Glauco Saverio cav. Strappa and he had been a dilettante flutist. Neither he nor the Maestro had ever seen or heard a *flauto moderno* and they were enchanted. The mechanism, they said, resembled the *tastiera* or keyboard of a pianoforte and the low tones were as mellow and rich as a cello. Maestro Lanciano became my teacher in piano. As Maestro De Nardis had told me that Alessandro Longo taught only advanced pupils, I did not even approach him. Lanciano, who was also an organist in one of the important churches of Naples, must have been disappointed in me in my first lesson. Having evidently heard of my flutistic virtuosity from Maestro De Nardis, he assumed I was equally proficient on the piano, as he said to me when I came in, "I cannot imagine myself giving lessons to an artist like you." I assured him that I had no talent for the piano and I much feared I would be a disappointment to him instead.

Before Dr. Strappa returned to his home, he asked that I play for them once more and at Maestro De Nardis' request for another piece by myself I played my *Fantasia*. At the finish, he thanked me and turning to his son-in-law asked him to please copy for him the melodic part in the finale of this piece and the first theme of *Pensiero Elegiaco*, that he might have it to take home with him. Maestro De Nardis copied in a few minutes the following for his father-in-law:

In the middle of 1909 my studies with Maestro De Nardis came to an end and in November I sailed for America.

* * * *

MELBA AND JOHN LEMMONÉ

My friendship with Lemmoné began soon after I reached Capetown, South Africa, in 1899. Everyone was talking of the great and highly artistic flute playing of John Lemmoné, as he had been there on a tour just before I reached those shores.

A number of his friends and admirers, including the father of a pupil of mine, who also came from Australia, had known him in that distant land. He was, they said, a most modest and amiable gentleman. In spite of his many activities, he never failed to answer any letter he received about flute and flute playing. Thus, his friends, who were also my friends, were instrumental in the beginning of a correspondence which never ceased until before World War II. In 1915 I published one of my most successful pieces for flute and piano *Giovialità*, Valse di Concerto. The dedication read: "Al chiarissimo amico e collega John Lemmoné." A few years later he went one better by sending me a beautiful piece, also for flute and piano, "Wind Amongst the Trees." The dedication read: "To my celebrated friend Leonardo De Lorenzo."

Because of my great interest in him and my avidity for more details of his life, I looked forward eagerly to the reading of

444

Melodies and Memories by Melba. Lemmoné had been her personal manager and flutist on many concert tours and she had given concrete evidence of the fondness and admiration for him. When he was ill and his financial resources rather slim, she gave a benefit concert for John that netted the handsome sum of $10,000 for him—and when she passed on, a few years ago, her will provided that he be given 250 pounds annually for life. It was, therefore, most disappointing to me that Lemmoné, the great and beloved Australian flute virtuoso, who made his debut on the same concert when both were very young, is mentioned only as "my manager who from now on I will call John." There is one exception when Melba relates the amusing story of the crier in a backwoods town announcing, "We also have with us Mr. John Lemon the world's champion fruiterer." True, he was her manager, but he played all her flute obbligatos and also solos on many of her numerous tours. During the tour in America Lemmoné made some fine records, the most famous of which is "Il Vento" by Briccialdi. Not once does Melba tell us that John was a flutist of the first order, and to the readers of *Melodies and Memories* Lemmoné appears a trifle less dignified than a manager when Madam says: "John, I feel a draught, did you close that window?" and . . . many other requests which give the impression that John was, in reality a valet, more than a manager or a great flute virtuoso! And I must confess also that for me there were too many Sirs, Counts, Barons, Marquises, Princes, Kings and their better halves—surely a great flute player is more important to the world. However, the little story about the town crier, mentioned before, makes hilarious reading. Here it is: I shall never forget when, at one town, as dusk was falling, the town crier came to John Lemmoné, my manager, and said, in Irish brogue: "Will you be afther wantin' the bell tonight?" "Certainly," said John. "Roight you are," replied the crier, "You come with me, and listen to how Oi do it." He walked down the street, ringing his bell, and soon a crowd had collected. "Oyez! Oyez!" he cried. "She's arrived. She's here." A little cheer greeted these remarks. "She's nothin' to me, you know," he continued. "I don't know anythin' about her. But when I tell you that she's sung before all the crowned heads of Sydney, she ought to be

445

good enough for this one-horse town." After the audience had assimilated this information, he continued: "We also have with us, Mr. John Lemon, the world's champion fruiterer." (He meant flautist.)

In a letter from Lemmoné in 1915, when I was with the Minneapolis Symphony, he requested me, when he learned that Melba was giving a concert there, that I should greet her and tell her that I was his friend and colleague. Well, after the concert, which was a great disappointment to the not too full house, because, not only had she already been passé for some time, but there was no variety in her program; one song after another, variations on the *Carnival of Venice* and numerous other inartistic stunts. I came to her dressing room—it was open and there wasn't a soul to greet her! If I had been a diplomat and a hypocrite I would have said: "Madam, your singing was marvellous, divine; never heard the like in all my life." But, alas! at that time I was a bachelor . . . After a few words in which she said: "So you had a letter from John, but, tell me, how did you like my singing?" My answer was: "Oh, Madam, I heard you before with the New York Philharmonic!!" I hope I will be allowed to reproduce here the most and best part of an article entitled "After Hearing Lemmoné" published in an Australian newspaper and which has been among my endless clippings for many years:

"Pan, the god of shepherds and the guardian of bees, saw the nymph Syrinx, and desired her. She, loathing his legs and horns, which were those of a goat, fled through the woods from him. He pursued her. Realizing that her flight was vain, she hid among the rushes on the bank of a stream, and prayed to the gods for aid. Whereupon she was transformed into a rush. Pan, disappointed but infatuated, cut the reed, and, piercing it, put it to his lips. Thus came into being the first flute. Lemmoné, it may be, was Pan re-born in human form. Beneath the magic of his breath and fingers the instrument wakes to tell all the hidden secrets of the wood. The rustles of leaves; the shadow, the shine, the airy lightness of a summer zephyr; the purling of a stream; the sparkle of the day, the glamor of the stars; the distant threatening of the storm, the patter of the approaching raindrops; the

446

wren's twitter, the lark's thin song, the nightingale's rich flood of melody. The keenest joy the heart is capable of, thrills, and all the wistfulness that the spirit knows, sighs from the poor tube of wood. It echoes the emotions of the human heart in so subtle and poignant a way as to convey a sense of the unattainable with overwhelming sadness.

"As he travels here and there, from the exclusive homes of culture to the lonely towns on the verge of civilization where existence is too strenuous to allow of the precious hours being granted to study, Lemmoné scatters broadcast a warm and golden largesse of inestimable value. To the cultured, his wonderful art is intellectually refining and elevating. Its technical perfection is all-satisfying, its brilliant spirituality all-sufficing. To those at a distance, out of touch with the great centers of learning, he brings even a dearer message still. Men's heart-strings, which, but for his genius, would have remained forever inert, are touched to a knowledge of a vast and untrodden world of thought and beauty. Glimpses are obtained of a glorious haven whereto all may at least strive, and souls start hopefully onward, glowing with a new resolve.

"Surely, Syrinx, if you but know of the music that Pan in his love has coaxed from your sweet body since he, sobbing, culled the reed from the river-bed, you do not regret that immortal meeting and pursuit!

"Melba and Lemmoné—Paderewski and Lemmoné—Patti and Lemmoné. Might it not as gracefully be written—Lemmoné and Melba—Lemmoné and Paderewski—Lemmoné and Patti? For each is as great as the other."—Vinco.

*   *   *   *

ERNESTO KÖHLER, HIS FATHER, AND ZAMPERONI

When I reached Milan from South Africa in 1907, I had made an appointment with the great artist and prince of a gentleman, Ernesto Köhler, who had been my guiding star for nearly ten years in spite of the distance separating us, he in Russia and I in Capetown. He wrote to me that he would meet me at around

447

11 A.M. in the great Galleria Vittorio Emanuele, where all artists had their rendezvous. When I came there with Albisi we saw no one resembling Ernesto Köhler. Although neither of us had ever met him, I had a good mental picture from a photograph he had sent me. While waiting Albisi mentioned that usually Zamperoni, who had known both Köhler and his father Venceslau Joseph for years, was wont to appear at this hour. Hardly had he finished speaking when a fine looking, tall man came towards us holding out both arms to Albisi, who introduced me to Professor Zamperoni. I was known to him by name because I had sent him a copy of my *Nine Etudes* two or three years previously and which were dedicated to Ernesto Köhler.

How cordial Zamperoni was! He said to me: "Please do not leave Milan without coming to my home; I like to talk flutes and flutists with you." The following evening I was at his home. He seems to have known everybody and I noticed at once a beautiful picture of Verdi with an affectionate dedication. Because Zamperoni, the first oboist, and the first bassoonist had been at La Scala for a great number of years, Verdi, sometimes returning after an absence of several years and always seeing them at their usual places, called them: *"Vecchia guardia"* ("old guards").

There was also a large photograph of Melba and photographs of Ponchielli, Boïto and many other famous personalities. But when the grand old man, Zamperoni, showed me the personal visiting card that Briccialdi had left for him on his birthday, he seemed to have had that closest to his heart. When his great teacher Rabboni died in 1856 (at the age of fifty-six), Zamperoni was only twelve years of age but already a fine player and a star pupil; he had been playing flute since a mere child of five! A few years after, he was given his teacher's post both at La Scala and at the Conservatory.

He was telling me a story about the fact that once in a while the colleagues of the orchestra did not behave in an honorable way; e.g., there was the affair of Giuseppe Martucci who had come from Naples—he was the Director of the Conservatory of Music—to produce his Second Symphony for the first time. After the last rehearsal, Zamperoni said, the first harpist approached the composer and said: "Maestro, it just happens that I am in financial difficulties and I must have some money right now; could you advance the amount due me for this concert?" Martucci, who was an extremely fine conductor and a very gentle and generous soul, said: "Yes, my son, come with me." He took him to the office and told them to advance him the amount. Alas! the harpist never showed up for the concert!!!

Professor Zamperoni had just begun to talk again about flutists: Ciardi, Count Luigi Marini, and others when, suddenly, the electric lights went out. We were left in complete darkness and, waiting for the lights to be restored, there entered Signora Zamperoni with an oil lamp. As soon as she saw me she said: "My dear sir, if you are going to listen to that old man talk about the flute, you will surely be here until tomorrow morning." I told Zamperoni that I expected to meet Ernesto Köhler, who was to stop in Milan on his way from St. Petersburg to his relatives at Modena, which was not far from Milan. Zamperoni knew his father very well and called him Papa Köhler. He was from Bohemia and came to Italy as solo flutist to the Duke of Modena. There he married an Italian lady with whom he had three fine children: Ernesto, Ferdinando, an excellent pianist, and Amalia, whose son, Captain Palmieri, was in the 36th regiment when I was there. It was through Captain Palmieri and Maestro Moranzoni, the director of that fine band, that my correspondence with Ernesto Köhler began a little while after my discharge from the army. Zamperoni also told me that when he resigned from both the Opera and the Conservatory he was pleasantly surprised to see Boïto and Toscanini come to his home the next morning and beg him to reconsider his step because he was still doing such beautiful work that they felt he was yet in his prime. The answer was: "I feel flattered for your compliment and for your visit but I have definitely decided to retire with my reputation in full. It took, as both you well know, many years of intelligent and careful living and I desire to take with me the little reputation I have when I pass on. He was very modest and had in mind the affair of Beniamino di Torino. It was an unforgettable visit! Zamperoni died in 1909.

To return to Ernesto Köhler. Our friendship began when I

forwarded the manuscript of *Six Etudes* of mine from Cape-town which, for my own pleasure and entertainment I had written during the hours of *silenzio* (rest) in the army from 12 noon till 2 o'clock. In the summer time the whole regiment, often including the excellent band, used to drill very early in the morning or march twelve or fifteen miles starting at midnight. Therefore, from twelve noon to two, instead of going to bed and resting I used to retire to the music room and write. Köhler, who knew of me when I was in the army through Maestro Moranzoni, was wondering where I had gone after I was through with nearly three years of military service and was pleasantly surprised to hear from me from a distant and—he thought—the uncivilized land of the Zulus. In returning my manuscript he said, to my surprise, that the *Etudes* had original ideas and were very beautiful and interesting, but would meet with success only if I would add two or three more numbers in a melodic or cantilena style. "However," he said, "the six you sent me require the fingers of a young devil to play!! Of course," he continued, "with the modern flute which you are using, they must be more practical than with my old instrument." I felt flattered but, at the same time, I said to myself, it is about time to change to the Boehm flute; and I did!

In this change, guided only by an old English method by Clinton, I confess that I was not as successful as Briccialdi who astonished his friends by appearing in a concert, with the new flute, after only two weeks! But Briccialdi's change had been to the closed G-sharp, just devised then by the Frenchman Dorus; while I had decided to change to the original open G-sharp key. The first ten or twelve days I used to take both flutes to the Tivoli Theatre and Sunday popular concerts, but the old flute was soon discarded for good. Fortunately it was summer and there were no symphony concerts. On these Sunday concerts, by the way, paid admission was not permitted and so the public, which was plentiful and eager, went through a narrow space, one person at a time, and dropped into the large tray the amount it wished to contribute. The members of these open air Sunday concerts were requested to boost them by appearing as soloists

450

without extra remuneration. I did my share handsomely by playing flute obbligatos and grand solos!

I feel I must say a few words as to the peculiar final parting with my old flute, an almost inseparable companion for nearly fifteen years! A theatrical company at the Tivoli Theatre in Capetown was playing one act of a Charles Dickens play. As one of the actors had to appear playing the flute, I was requested to play a little tune while he held the flute in position. Also, the actor said he would be extremely grateful, in case I had an old extra flute, to lend it to him just for that week. I did so and that was the last I saw of my dear old flute. I reported the affair to both the conductor of the orchestra and the manager, but nothing came of it.

When the *Six Etudes* became nine, having added two slow numbers and another more technical, I forwarded the whole to J. H. Zimmermann of Leipzig, Germany, to whom Köhler had recommended me. The editor, who was then publishing more flute music than probably any other firm, wrote that he would publish my *Etudes* at my expense. There would be around forty pages and the cost would be $200!! I wrote this bad news immediately to Ernesto Köhler who advised me, if I could spare the money, to pay the amount, because, he said, if the work is successful, Zimmermann would then buy the rights from you and thus you would make a good start. I only had $300 in the bank when I made the draft to Germany. It proved as my friend had said. After only a few weeks Zimmermann wanted to know how much I wanted to give him the exclusive rights to make a new edition of his own. I wrote immediately that all I wanted was to recover my $200. The money reached me with the encouraging request that from then on that firm would be glad to publish my other works and would pay a little sum in advance for each.

Soon after my *Etudes* were published I received numerous letters not only from great flutists and teachers but from dilettanti as well. One of these was from the Attorney Libero Stradivari of Cremona, an enthusiastic flute dilettante and a great grandson of the renowned Antonio Stradivari. This led to an

451

interesting correspondence. He had been a friend and admirer of Zamperoni and in one of his letters wrote: "They say that the young man who replaced Zamperoni is fine and very able, but to me the tone of his modern flute, compared with that of Zamperoni, sounds like an ocarina! The Stradivari family was also musical; his wife played piano, his daughter, cello, and his son, violin. When this bit of information was conveyed to Ernesto Köhler his interest was aroused and he composed a charming piece for them, and thus I was instrumental in bringing about their friendship.

After the publication of my second work, *The Two Virtuosi* for two flutes, Köhler dedicated his *La Capriceuse* Op. 94 for flute and piano (or orchestra) to me and gave me the golden advice: "Now write something easy and melodious for flute and piano. After all, you must allow the dilettanti to play your music." The result of this advice was *Six Easy Pieces* and *Sixteen Melodious Pieces* published by Zimmermann and Carl Fischer respectively a few years later. Alas! my meeting with Ernesto Köhler was destined never to take place. Only fifty-eight years old, he had died in Russia, just when he was expected in Milan and soon after his resignation from the Imperial Opera where he had been in the service of the Czar for thirty-five years. This was in 1907.

My next piece was *Pensiero Elegiaco* Op. 7 in Memoria dell' Artista Ernesto Koehler and dedicated to Köhler's friend Antonio Zamperoni. This I sent to Zimmermann with the request to forward a copy to Madam Koehler as soon as it was published. A few weeks later a beautiful and touching letter in Italian reached me from Köhler's Russian wife!

Another man of great reputation both of letters and music was Luigi Hugues. His four books of progressive duets for two flutes, Op. 51, the three advanced and beautiful duets with modern harmony, Op. 109, many solos and sonatas, his Scherzo for two flutes, oboe, clarinet and bassoon from his quintet, many of the excellent etudes, especially the Op. 32 and religious music, gave me the feeling that, if it was possible, I would very much like to meet him. But, unfortunately, only a few days before I reached Milan, I had been told in London that Luigi

Hugues had died two years before, in 1905! However, Hugues was very much alive then and, having retired from the professorship of geography from the Turin University, was living very close to Milan. This I learned years later in New York. Hugues died in 1913.

*   *   *   *

ITALO PIAZZA

I came to know Professor Italo Piazza, not through his flute compositions, because these had been few and were out of print, but through his erudite contributions on musical subjects, e.g., *Proemio ad una storia della musica; Del quartetto de 'legni nel moderno strumentale; Musica celeste* (riflessioni oscure); *Riforme ai Conservatorii di musica?; Un progetto.* The five chapters are under one cover. They are extremely well written and original.

Breve dissertazione storico-critica sul flauto. In this interesting brief history of the flute, written in 1890, Professor Piazza has harsh words for the Boehm flute chiefly because it is mostly of metal which he did not approve.

Il flauto Giorgi. In this pamphlet Piazza launched a ferocious attack on the Giorgi flute. This flute, which was played vertically, as in the olden days, was invented by Carlo Tommaso Giorgi, a pupil of Briccialdi. The inventor claimed that any music written for either the old or Boehm flutes could be played on it with ease and avoidance of all cross fingers. This Piazza discounted vehemently.

Un documento strano. A translation from the Chinese of a pamphlet on parchment paper written by a full-blood Chinese. It is an attack on the European and Occidental music in general. It makes hilarious reading especially when he says that: "When the composers meet with serious problems they solve them simply by the use of a Chinese instrument, the Tam tam!"

It was in 1907 that I first personally met Italo Piazza at the Conservatory of Music in Naples where he had taught the flute and wood-wind ensemble for many years. As he greeted me he said, "So you are the young man who wrote those *Nine Etudes,* a youthful sin to be sure."

He had been described to me as a "veritable bear" but that I found to be an exaggeration. He had grown a long beard since the loss of his beautiful wife a few years ago, at which time his friends dissuaded him from entering a religious order. He now was living alone in an apartment on the seventh floor of an old and dilapidated building. When a visitor sought to see the Professor, the janitor would ring what looked like a cowbell by pulling a long rope, upon which he made his appearance high up with a rather disgruntled expression at the disturbance. Then, when informed there was a visitor he reflected a moment before deciding to admit the intruder.

When I again called on Professor Piazza many years later, in 1926, to be exact, he was not only more hospitable but presented me with the scores of two short compositions: his *Andantino* for string quartet and *Preludio Mistico* for strings, harmonium and harp, also a song (with piano) with the lugubrious title *To a Dead Lady*. Knowing that I came from America he inquired about a number of his old pupils. I told Professor Piazza that I had met, a few years back, in New York three of them whose names I recalled as: Raffaele Esposito, Pietro Caso—who at one time toured with Madam Tetrazzini—and . . . Longo! I could not recall his first name but Piazza immediately said "Francesco!" "Longo," he said, "how is he?" He had great talent also as a pianist. When Longo graduated as flutist he performed the unusual feat of playing on the piano Chopin's great *Polonaise in A-flat*.

When I met Longo in 1910 in New York he was playing piano in one of the several orchestras at the Hotel Waldorf-Astoria. As a flutist, he told me, the situation was hopeless for him. He could not secure a job and was discouraged. Knowing that I was doing some teaching Longo asked me to try and sell his Rudall-Carte flute for $100.00 cash. I sent him a Greek flute player who was looking for just that particular instrument. The Greek came back to me saying he liked the flute but did not have the whole sum in cash and Longo would not accept his offer of $25.00 cash and $5.00 per week for the balance. He begged me so much to help him get the flute before someone else bought it that, hoping to make two people happy, I gave Longo

454

my personal check and gave the flute to the Greek. I was lucky when, after over a year and one half I received the last five dollars. He told me more than once that the jobs were scarce and . . . I must wait!

Little did Professor Piazza realize that his talented pupil would take his own life in a moment of despondency in 1932.

A year or two later I sent him two works of mine: *Vade Mecum* and *Il Non Plus Ultra*, recently published. These he acknowledged by writing me that while he admired the works and my apparently inexhaustible activity, he could not refrain from telling me that in the last two numbers, XVII and XVIII of the *Il Non Plus Ultra*, to quote, "you surpassed yourself with so much ultra-modernism that I suspect you were either not in your right mind, or, getting along in years, you seek to impress us as still a young man!" However, in a postscript he says: "This was not meant as an offense and I am forwarding you the manuscript of a flute quartet of mine *Novena* which, probably, you could use in your class." As the title indicates, the composition is of religious character, not difficult and I, myself, have used it on several occasions.

*   *   *   *

TOSCANINI AND ALBISI

Aberlardo Albisi is known in America by flutists only through his excellent *Second Suite Miniature* for three flutes. His *Albisiphone*, the bass flute in C, played vertically, made quite a hit when it first came out at the beginning of this century. Many famous composers introduced it in their compositions, especially those who heard Albisi himself play on it. There were several Albisiphones in Germany and my friend Ary Van Leeuwen also has one. To my knowledge there is only one other in America. It is in the Dayton C. Miller collection in the Library of Congress. The reason this huge instrument has not progressed in popularity has been because of difficulty to produce a satisfactory sound. Its inventor seemed to have been the only one who could play on it with considerable surety. The last of our friends to hear Albisi play on that mastodontic grandpapa of our family

455

of flutes was Joseph LaMonaca. He said that Albisi played it with considerable ease, but that he himself could not produce a sound on it. Albisi made also a contrivance by which one could play the high F-sharp by keeping the thumb on the B-flat key of the flute.

When I first met Albisi in 1907 he was young, handsome and with tremendous ambition. He was very proud of the fact that it was Toscanini who brought him to the famous La Scala Opera House because the veteran Zamperoni had resigned on account of old age. Albisi was very happy because of Toscanini's apparent friendship and liking for his playing but although he felt flattered he was a bit nervous at first to step into the position of that remarkably great player Antonio Zamperoni! He confessed to me that if everyone could play on the old system flute as Zamperoni played it, there would have been no reason for a Boehm flute! The perfect intonation in the whole register of the instrument and, particularly, its marvellous tone, were little short of miraculous!

However, everything was going so well with Albisi that he was in high spirits when I met him and begged me to come to his home for a ravioli dinner that night. Suddenly, only a few years after, at a rehearsal one morning—was it at the Opera or at a symphony? I do not know—after an important flute solo Toscanini stopped the orchestra and said: "Albisi, I don't like the way you play that solo!" Albisi answered, "I am sorry, Maestro, I did my best." After it was played a second time, Toscanini, who must have been in one of his dangerous moods, again stopped the orchestra and said: "Your playing is terrible this morning; what is the matter with you?" Albisi, crushed and humiliated before all the orchestra, said: "I guarantee you, Maestro, that I have never tried as hard to please you as I do now!" Once more they started from the same place and after the solo was played for the third time Toscanini burst into one of his famous tempests which made Albisi see red and, losing his temper, he got up from his chair, insulted Toscanini and at the same time threw at him first the foot joint, then the middle piece and last the head joint of his flute and ran out of the hall! Poor

456

Albisi; what a scandal! He not only had to leave Milan; he had to leave Italy immediately, and he repaired to Switzerland. There he was soon engaged to teach in both Zurich and Lucerne and was also active as a player.

Albisi's sad experience with Toscanini reminds me of another victim of our instrument. That happened around 1895 when Toscanini was invited to give some concerts in Turin. He had come from Parma and, to the same orchestra where the veteran and famous flutist Beniamino had played so many years with great success and from which he had intended to retire just that year. He was urged to play at least the season because they had just invited the young and already famous Toscanini! He consented. At the very first rehearsal, after a not too important flute passage, Toscanini stopped the orchestra and, in a sarcastic tone, said: "Well, are you the famous flutist of whom I have heard so much?" The veteran player, who was esteemed and loved for his beautiful tone and was called "Beniamino di Torino dalla gran bella cavata" (of the beautiful tone and phrasing), without saying a single word put his flute in the box and slowly walked out. Thus ended the career of a famous flutist who had been an esteemed friend of many colleagues and to whom Krakamp had dedicated a beautiful solo in tribute to his masterly flute-playing.

No wonder, then, that when the writer was in Alessandria, only two hours from Turin, on compulsory military duty in 1897, and wanting to meet the man who had known the famous teacher of my teacher, Krakamp, he wrote me a beautiful letter but said that on account of the unpleasant experience with Signor Toscanini, he did not care to make new friends and, he said: "I suggest younger and still active ones." I still have his letter; it was written the year that Brahms died as well as Antonio Bazzini, who had been one of the few pupils of Paganini and was director of the Milan Conservatory of Music.

Returning to Albisi: At one time, during the beginning of his career, he made the application for the position as first flute at the Opera of Torino and also as teacher at the Royal School of Music, whose director was the well known composer Giovanni Bolzoni. He, by the way, is known in America only through his famous *Minuetto* which almost every orchestra plays.

Albisi had prepared a concerto and a short piece for flute, to be played with the left hand only, with piano accompaniment. This was one of his own compositions and, unfortunately, he made the mistake to play that first. When he finished, Bolzoni said to him: "My dear Sir, the flute, like all other orchestral instruments, is difficult enough to play with both hands; therefore, you are not the man we are looking for." The piece in question, while clever, was only a stunt; and it seems incredible that a man with Albisi's intelligence should choose to play a stunt for a serious and severe man of Bolzoni's caliber!

I received a manuscript copy of the *one hand* piece from Albisi who had a most elegant writing calligraphy. As this was the most beautifully written manuscript I had in my library, an enthusiastic flute dilettante of Los Angeles who knew about it, asked me that I send it to him for a few days, upon my return to Minneapolis, with the Symphony orchestra with which I had paid my first visit to California. In spite of my reluctance to send him the piece by mail, this man, who had most convincing and polished manners, made me promise that I would do so. I sent it by registered mail and in about three weeks a letter reached me that it had just been returned also by registered mail, but, alas! it never reached me and . . . was never heard of again. Besides the fact that it was an unusually beautiful manuscript, it had an elaborate dedication to me! Albisi died in Switzerland in 1939.

*　*　*　*

CARL WEHNER (1838-1912)

I reached New York for the second time at the end of 1909.*
Two great flutists then living in New York, Carl Wehner,

---

* I came to America for the first time in 1892 and remained until 1896, when I had to go back for the compulsory military service. The first engagement, with an ensemble of four musicians, was at Cerulean Springs, Kentucky. The pay was, also for the violinist leader, $30.00 per month. The duties were: playing one hour each time for breakfast at 5:30 A.M., 12:00 noon, and 6 P.M. for dinner. Also playing for dancing three nights per week from 9 to 12. The third, and last month of that

458

who was past seventy, and Georges Barrère, in his early thirties, were already known to me through fame. I was anxious to meet both of them and called first on Carl Wehner. When I entered his studio and presented my card, he, reading my name, at once asked me if I was the man who had written the *Tarantella* Op. 8, which happened to be on his music stand. He was most cordial to me, and most happy when, a few days later, returning my call, I showed him five original letters by his famous teacher Theobald Boehm, in one of which his name was mentioned. I also showed him my collection of photographs of famous flutists, which included Ernesto Koehler—whom he had known in St. Petersburg early in his career—Büchner, Lemmoné, John Finn, W. L. Barrett, Edward deJong, Van Leeuwen, Wetzger, Safranoff, Tillmetz—who studied with Boehm at the same time as Carl Wehner—Franceschini, Manigold, Goldberg, the Berlin millionaire of the famous collection of flutists, and many others. However, nothing aroused his interest more than a program of a concert in which Sebastian Ott, playing first flute, Carl Wehner, second, and the master, third, played a Kuhlau trio. The date was March 28, 1857; fifty-two years before! The concert, in which a number of other artists—playing English horn, two viola d'amour, gamba,* mandoline and mandora,— took part, was arranged by Boehm for Ott who was also studying with him. Ott, in the second part of the concert, played Boehm's *Andante and Rondo*. The five letters of Boehm, all addressed to Ott's father, and many other documents, were presented to me by Sebastian Ott's daughter, Mrs. Hartman, who by a happy coincidence was my next door neighbor in Capetown in 1902!

We became close friends and in his enthusiasm, Carl Wehner offered me his collection, saying: "I wish very much to add mine to yours, because who would appreciate and make use of it more than you? Besides," he added, "I shall soon die and, most

---

memorable first summer engagement, we did not receive any pay because, the manager said, business had been bad! And we had to pay our own fares from New York and back. I was advised not to remain in New York because there were too many musicians.

* I think it should be "viola da Gamba" and, later, "mandola."

likely, it would be thrown into the wastebasket!" Carl Wehner's addition to my collection was, flutistically speaking of course, priceless. It included eight excellent lithographs of Kuhlau, Briccialdi when a young man, Tulou, Philipp Fahrbach, Boehm, Berbiguier, A. B. Furstenau and Ciardi. The first, Kuhlau, is dated 1838 and was made in Copenhagen. It has a most interesting musical enigma on it thus:

No musicologist whom I have asked has been able to decipher its meaning. Ciardi's has a fine dedication to Carl Wehner in Italian with no date, but it was given to him in the early sixties when both were living in St. Petersburg. Besides the eight mentioned lithographs in Carl Wehner's collection, there were a number of small photographs such as : Boehm, Berbiguier, Franz and Karl Doppler, de Vroye—to whom Saint-Saëns dedicated his famous *Romance* Op. 37—W. Popp, Sauvlet, Emil Behm, Tillmetz, as a young man, Barge, Nicholson, Belcke, Lobe, Drouet, Cesare Pugni, a conductor, Masini, Manna, Heindl, Gabrielski, Ott, Dulon, blind flutist-composer, P. Fahrbach, Reichert, Terschak, A. B. Furstenau and his son Moritz, Andersen, Soussman, Galli, Count Luigi Marini, Ciardi, Rabboni, Wehner at 36, Krakamp, Venceslau Köhler, Ernesto's father, Wehner at 24 with heavy fur coat and cap with a pistol on his belt on a tour in Siberia. Ernesto Koehler with a pupil, Cavallini, famous clarinetist, Wehner with a pupil, Heinemeyer and a large picture of Walkiers made in 1864. Beautiful dedications to Carl Wehner on these photographs are by Franz Doppler, de Vroye, Popp, Sauvlet, Behm, Tillmetz and Barge, to whom Reinecke's excellent Sonata *Undine* is dedicated. Also an interesting composition by Ciardi, *Canto Elegiaco* for violin, flute, cello, harp, piano and harmonium, published in Russia, has the following inscription: "Al distinto artista e collega Carl Wehner, *Ciardi*, St. Pietroburgo 27 Febraio 1870." The printed dedication of the *Canto Elegiaco* reads thus: "A sua eccellenza il Signor Principe Kourakin." The re-dedication to me is: "To my dear friend Leonardo De Lorenzo, from Carl Wehner, New York, September 18th, 1910."

I regret to say that Carl Wehner's hatred for the metal flute was excessive and exaggerated. In spite of his financial difficulties in his last years, he would neither hear nor teach anyone with a metal flute!

* * * *

GEORGES BARRÈRE

It was at the end of Carl Wehner's career that Georges Barrère was brought to America by Walter Damrosch. Wehner had earned his great reputation, not as a performer of brilliant solos, but as a master player in symphony and opera orchestras and as a teacher, a field in which he reigned supreme for many years. His greatest asset was his beautiful and matchless tone and, because he had been one of Boehm's finest pupils, no one dared contradict him in any discussion concerning the flute and flute playing.

When Barrère reached New York the grand old man still enjoyed considerable prosperity because of his large class of pupils. That, however, did not last long because Barrère's immediate success was so great that, as far as flute and flute playing was concerned, there was one, and only one—Barrère! With very few exceptions, all the pupils of Carl Wehner left him, changed their flutes from wood to silver, and a number of them, knowing nothing of the fact that the origin of the Boehm flute was logically an open G-sharp key instrument, even changed from open to closed G-sharp key flute!

Barrère, I am convinced, never was aware of the adverse effect his success had on Carl Wehner, who very often thereafter, did not have ten cents for a shave and his hand was too shaky to shave himself.

The success of Barrère was not alone because of youth. He was a great artist, with a genial, ingratiating personality and wit. He became in no time the idol not only of Damrosch, who took advantage of every opportunity to tell his audience what a rare

461

artist Barrère was, but also of the public. I have been assured that a number of people attended the Damrosch concerts not because of love of music but just to see Barrère!

There could not have been a greater contrast in two men than that between Carl Wehner and Georges Barrère. The former was old, heavy and clumsy, while Barrère was young, elegant and handsome and his French accent was irresistible. In later years, when reminded that his manner of talking had not changed in all those years, Barrère confessed that he had taken care not to do so because his accent and he were legendary and inseparable!

Soon after Barrère reached New York, Carl Wehner was induced, after much persuasion, to attend a Barrère concert and hear him in a Mozart Concerto. Carl Wehner, who was not well disposed towards the performer, walked out in the middle of the first movement! I should like to compare Barrère to Heifetz and Carl Wehner to Ysaye.

In 1912 I was engaged by the New York Symphony as the newly formed Barrère Ensemble necessitated much travel on Barrère's part, and it was important that someone be on hand to replace Barrère during his absences. One day I was approached by a flute player who said: "Please tell me your honest opinion of Georges Barrère." I answered: "Georges Barrère is not only a great artist but an unusually fine musician and a very fine gentleman." The man turned his back and never spoke to me again. I later learned that he was one of the few faithful pupils of Carl Wehner.

It was a mistake, I think, for Barrère's manager to advertise him as "the greatest flutist in the world." The world may seem small to a manager but, at that time, about 1910, the same claim was made for Emil Prill by Germany, for John Radcliff by England, for Ary Van Leeuwen by Holland, for Abelardo Albisi by Italy, for Louis Fleury by France, for Viktor Safronoff by Russia, for Duque Estrada Meyer first and later for Ferruccio Arrivabene by Brazil, for John Lemmoné by Australia and for John Amadio by New Zealand. Therefore, "one of the greatest" covers tremendous territory. At another time, a few years ago, a statement was published that Sibelius was the greatest composer

462

since Beethoven; Rachmaninoff the greatest pianist since Liszt, and Heifetz the greatest violinist since Paganini! What nonsense! Sibelius was well matched by a few of his contemporaries; Richard Strauss, Schoenberg and Stravinski, without disturbing the memory of Brahms! The piano playing of Rachmaninoff could be matched by several living pianists although this great man's soul was in creating masterpieces. When I was listening to Rachmaninoff's playing I always had in mind that that was the same man who created the Second Symphony in E minor, the *Isle of the Dead* and the four great piano concerti.

When Barrère changed from silver to a gold flute, a number of the more prosperous flutists did likewise. But, a few years later, the flutistic world was startled to hear that Barrère was now playing on a platinum flute! Only one was able to imitate him that time. The rare material and the prohibitive price prevented the others. The idea of a platinum flute Barrère got from Dr. Dayton C. Miller, who was constructing one for scientific purposes and also to add to his great collection of flutes. That was at the beginning of World War I. But due to the scarcity of this precious metal and the exigencies of the war, it was abandoned.

I should like to include here an article written a number of years ago by Dr. Frank Crane in the *New York Globe*. I think it will be enjoyed by every lover of the flute, although they will never agree to the statement that: "The flute is not considered a dominant instrument. It has rather a humble place in orchestration." Dr. Crane's tribute to Barrère and his flute follows:

"I went to a concert the other day given by the trio de Lutece. This consisted of three musicians. One played the harp, another played the cello. And George Barrère played the flute. Do you know who George Barrère is? Well, he is one of those persons who can do something better than anybody else in the world can do it. When you hear of that sort of a man he is worth going miles to see whether the thing he does be laying brick, painting a picture, acting upon the stage or aught else. There is something about mastery that stirs one to the depths. Just to witness a thing, anything, done with consummate perfection, somehow arouses all the hero feeling in you. It makes you feel great and divine yourself for a moment. The master is the

463

thousandth man, maybe the ten thousandth man. The flute is not considered a dominant instrument. It has rather a humble place in orchestration, and individually the fiddle is more of a vehicle for virtuosity. The horn has been more interpretative of our rampant passions on the hunting field, whether hunting foxes or fellowmen. The flute is the violet in the nosegay of music-making instrument. It is modest, delicate, unobtrusive as a sweet young girl. And when George Barrère plays the flute, it is more than that. It is a fairy piping in the moonlight. It is an elf calling in the woodland. It is the voice of some little other-world creature, a bodiless plaint, a bit of heart-break embroidered with fanciful ecstasy. You get a curious impression. The man looks like a professor of Greek in some Wesleyan university. He is no curly-haired musician type. He might be a Baptist preacher from Indiana. He has no preenings nor professional tricks. He just takes up his silver flute and straightway his spirit enters into it, and you understand how the Deity "breathed into man's nostrils the breath of life and man became a living soul." It is all smooth and equal. The high notes do not shriek nor the low ones sound windy, one is as mellow as another, and the tones have that peculiar human timbre of the cello."

*   *   *   *

FLEURY, GAUBERT, BARRÈRE

A few years before Barrère's death, which took place on June 14, 1944, I wrote to him thus:

"I thought I had heard you in your prime over thirty years ago, but your playing this afternoon was so extraordinary that I feel I must write to you about it, and also ask you, 'What is the secret of your perennial youth?' Evidently these few words of mine, which he knew were sincere and spontaneously written, must have pleased him very much for he answered:

Woodstock, N. Y., Sept. 23, 1939

Dear Colleague and Friend,

If I didn't answer immediately your very lovely letter any sooner it is because I wanted to locate your composition in order to announce its arrival to you. But your *Divertimento Flautistico* was in my apartment in New York and as I contemplated moving I had it very carefully packed before the summer. Thus the delay for which I apologize. First of all I want to thank you very sincerely for your kind words of praise, not only on my playing, but on my age . . . Unlike you I am not in a position to retire in a beautiful Villa in California and I think I shall blow until I disappear. I am very happy that such a prominent judge as you does not detect in my playing that my 63rd birthday comes next month. But I think your retirement was much hurried and you had many years to your credit for keeping up with us. I am sure that you enjoy music now perhaps better than during your long and brilliant career, because you can make music at will and not to order. My congratulations. I may go to California next winter and shall do my best to come up to Villa Pan to present my compliments.

By same mail I send you your MS., though I am wondering if there is a corner in Europe where they would consider nowadays a Concertante for as many as five flutists, while they cannot find the same number of nations willing to go "Concertante";

With again my sincere thanks for your kind letter I remain,

Very sincerely yours,

(Signed) Georges Barrère

According to Darius Milhaud, who wrote Louis Fleury's obituary in the *Chesterian* of July-August 1926, Fleury was scarcely forty-nine that summer when "he succumbed from a sudden and incurable malady." Louis Fleury was one of France's most accomplished and cultured flutists. He toured America with the famous singer Emma Calvé and he was very popular in England where he visited and played frequently. Fleury contributed a number of interesting articles pertaining to the flute in the Chesterian and I should like to be permitted to quote part of one entitled *Song and the Flute* of the January-February issue:

"The combination of the voice and the flute generally conjures up in the mind the appearance on the stage at the Albert Hall of a mature and plump lady, who emits little bird-like notes, whilst a gentleman, younger and of lesser substance, produces corresponding sounds from a wooden or metal pipe. The whole thing concludes with a marriage, not necessarily that of the singer to the flutist, but rather the union of their two voices which should, according to rules, become one in the course of the final cadenza. This union does not always come about without trouble. If the flutist is not of the first rank, the singer gains an easy triumph at his expense, for nothing is more delightful than a beautiful voice and nothing more displeasing than a bad flute tone. In the opposite case the risk lies on the side of the singer. Although the voice is the most beautiful of instruments, it is also the most sensitive. If the singer is not in good form, the clearness of the tones produced by the good flutist will unmercifully show up her imperfections; in this it is the flutist who triumphs. It is true that he then runs another risk, that of never being reengaged by his jealous partner. That happens more often than one may be aware of."

Philippe Gaubert was, like Barrère and Fleury, first Prix of the Paris Conservatory and a star pupil of the illustrious Taffanel. What distinguishes Gaubert from the other two friends and colleagues is his excellent compositions. These are many and of great variety: sonatas for flute and piano, operas, orchestral works and chamber music. He was also director of the famous Paris Opera. Gaubert toured America with the Paris Symphony Orchestra as solo flutist during 1917-18.

Gaubert and Fleury suffered a great deal in the trenches of World War I. In World War II, when France was crushed in a few weeks by the Germans, who became its masters, Gaubert could not survive the catastrophe and died in 1941 at 62 years of age!

*　　*　　*　　*

MAHLER, BUSONI AND DAMROSCH

At the end of 1910 Gustav Mahler, then conductor of the New York Philharmonic Symphony, one morning was rehearsing Busoni's *Elegy* for orchestra, recently composed on the occasion of the death of his mother, Anna Weiss-Busoni. The pianist-composer, at that time in his prime and on a tour of this country, attended the rehearsals. The third and last of these, Busoni himself conducted because Mahler, already a sick man, was unable to attend. One could see that Busoni was not satisfied with Mahler's tempi. They were much too slow and dragging. He was handsome with great bushy hair and extremely pleasant; the opposite of Mahler who, in spite of being only fifty years old, looked over sixty and the least excuse irritated him beyond control. He shouted at every section of the orchestra, even at individuals and whether the man was leader or last in the section. At one time Mahler lost his temper with the double bass section, calling them nasty names and unworthy of being in the symphony. However, in the intermission we saw him shaking the hands of one of those players affectionately. He was L. Manoly, an old schoolmate of his from whom he felt the warmest friendship.

Theodor Spiering, the concertmaster, was another with whom Mahler shook hands after he had made a scene with the first violin section. Again, in the finale of Beethoven's Fifth Symphony, Mahler got furious to such an extent that I heard the solo piccolo player, considered one of America's finest, tell his nearest colleague, the third flutist, "If he insults me again like that, I will hit him." Mahler had told him, in German, that "he wasn't fit to play in a street band!"

The bass clarinet player, to whom Mahler addressed a request to play a difficult passage *alone,* answered meekly in German: "Herr Kapelmeister, this particular passage sounds better in company." However, one of his great favorites, besides the cellist Leo Schulz, was the queer looking X. Reiter, solo French horn, who had played and had been praised by no other than Richard Wagner himself! When old Reiter played a difficult passage without a break, Mahler would shout on top of his voice, "bravo-o-o" but, when the old horn player failed miserably, which was quite often, Mahler was busy looking in the score, making believe he never heard the unpleasant crash!

During that season, 1910-1911, Xaver Scharwenka appeared as soloist in a double pair of concerts. On the first pair, an all-Beethoven program, he played the Concerto No. 5 in E-flat major, Op. 73. On his next appearance Scharwenka performed for the first time his newly composed fourth concerto. Evidently there was no love between Mahler and Scharwenka because neither during rehearsals nor after the performance of the concerti did the two men shake hands, as is usually the custom, nor did they look at each other. In spite of the fact that he was quite old and far from handsome, Scharwenka was extremely elegant and his appearance was that of a *grand seigneur!*

Before I joined the New York Philharmonic, Mahler had made two excellent flutists his victims. At that time the orchestra manager was a double bass player by the name of Felix F. Leifels who, being an old friend of Carl Wehner, told him that the best flutists in New York were not eager to accept the position of solo flute under Mahler. Carl Wehner, who had shown much affection for me in the little time I had known him, came to see me and said: "The position of solo flute with the New York Philharmonic is yours if you want it but, you must promise me *never to answer back Mahler.* He is a sick man and very unpleasant." The only time I answered Mahler was when he called me Lorenzo (my name on the program was spelled with a small "d"). I said: "De Lorenzo, please, Maestro." However, I have no pleasant recollections of Mahler, nevertheless, I feel thankful to have had the opportunity to know and play under that great man, who died only a few months after, at fifty-one years of age.

A couple of years after this I found myself with the New York Symphony Society and Walter Damrosch. In the three years with that orchestra I cannot recall that Damrosch lost his temper a single time. He had a smile which, coupled with his extraordinary personality, handsomeness and impeccable English phraseology, turned the heads of all the ladies, young, old, beautiful and . . . all the others! Damrosch was not popular with the musicians in spite of the fact that he treated everyone with apparent kindness and an irresistible smile. He was not admired as a conductor. However, he gave wonderful concerts with his fine orchestra and, most of the time at the next rehearsal, he would say: "A lovely concert yesterday, thank you, gentlemen."

It was well known that Damrosch paid his musicians the minimum salary possible. The moment anyone asked for a raise he was not *persona grata* any longer. However, there was one man in the orchestra who was never troubled in regard to money matters, he was given all he wanted without asking. This man, one of the trilogy which formed that institution (1. The

New York Symphony Society; 2. Walter Damrosch and 3. Georges Barrère) was indispensable; one could not think of excluding him in any activity whatever, not even when he was on tour with his Ensemble (one of the main reasons for my being there) it was felt that he was there in spirit. At one time, I cannot recall the occasion, on the intermission of an afternoon concert in Carnegie Hall, Damrosch had requested Andrew Carnegie to deliver a short address. The famous old millionaire, who was very close to the flute section and spoke longer than he should and not very interestingly, made an unfavorable impression, at least to the orchestra personnel, as a speaker. After he finished, Barrère asked, "What is the equivalent in Italian of "silence is golden?" "Il silenzio è d'Oro," I answered.

One morning, in the intermission, the orchestra manager announced that Damrosch wished the entire orchestra at his home that evening at eight o'clock. We found out later that it was his fiftieth birthday. On the stairs in his home there were autographed pictures of Wagner, Brahms, Liszt, and many others whom he had known when very young. We all had a memorable time!

* * * *

LOUIS MAURER

Louis Maurer, artist, painter, lithographer, carver and flute dilettante, celebrated his 100th birthday on February 21, 1932 —an event of particular interest to the flute world.

Maurer came to America from Germany at the age of sixteen years. A most charming, modest man, he gave one no impression of old age. He was in this respect quite phenomenal and proved conclusively that it is possible for a man to reach 100 years in full command of his faculties, vivid, alive with interest in his fellowmen, still young at heart and younger in appearance than many a man of 70 years. His memory was remarkable and he recalled events of his entire lifetime from two years of age.

When I met Maurer for the first time, in 1910, he had played the old system flute for 65 years. He was anxious to know if I thought it advisable for him to change to the new system or

469

Boehm flute—adding naively that he was 79 years old but he didn't believe that would make much difference. He was so earnest I decided he could do it and lessons began immediately lasting five years or until my departure to join the Minneapolis Symphony Orchestra.

He was a model pupil, rain or shine he was there at the appointed hour and if on a particularly cold and blustery day I would suggest a postponement, or offer to come to him, he refused, saying it was good for him to be out.

He at first played on a wood flute, but I later advised him to use one of silver as it would be easier to play and require less care. He bought a silver flute with an especially built ivory headjoint, a beautiful instrument in appearance but after the headjoint had split several times he resigned himself to a complete silver flute. We became very devoted to one another and when the time came for me to leave New York he sadly said that his flute playing days were over. But it was not so. He kept on playing and despite his advancing years whenever I made an infrequent visit to New York we always had a musicale, beginning with a flute solo played by him and accompanied by his charming daughter, Mrs. Karl Furstenberg, and followed by duets, etc.

After one of his lessons Maurer informed me he was going to the hospital on the morrow to undergo a minor operation. "Even so," he said, "it may be the last time we see each other. I have attended to every detail in case the time for my departure has come, but I feel it is not yet." It was a bladder operation and not as minor as he thought. His surgeon remarked afterwards that only one man in a thousand, at his age, survived such an operation. He was then past eighty. A few years later he was run down by an automobile near his home but, although considerably shaken up and hurt, he was soon up and about and busy at his numerous activities. He was an early riser and preferred to paint and play in the morning. He has shown his love for the outdoors and for animals in many strikingly interesting canvases. He was especially fond of horses, not only as a subject for his art, but as a fine horseman. He took prizes as a sharp shooter. He had one of the most remarkable collections of seashells in the world, a collection begun when a boy. In it were many rare and expensive specimens and all of interest and beauty. It was a hobby very dear to Maurer's heart and he enjoyed explaining the mysteries of his treasures. As an artist he was a painter, lithographer, and a very fine carver in wood and ivory.

As his connection with the firm of Currier and Ives has been dwelt on at length in magazine articles, I only mention it in passing. There were a couple of erroneous statements in those articles which I should like to correct at this time. It was said that he had never seen a camp fire. He was quite indignant over that. He had been a member for twenty years of the "Camp Fire Club" and here he met many famous men, including Theodore Roosevelt and Buffalo Bill.

The statement was also made that he had taken up flute only when he learned that Leonardo da Vinci had been a proficient performer on that instrument. As a matter of fact, he had his first flute lesson in 1841 when he was nine years old. His teacher was Joseph Schneider, a fine musician and leader of the military band of his native town, Bierbrich on the Rhine. Maurer's son, Alfred, was the well known modernist painter. He lived in Paris several years before the war and after his return to America won the Carnegie medal and prize of $1500.00. Although the most harmonious relation existed between father and son there was no admiration for each other's art—the gulf between the old school and the new was too wide to bridge.

One day in 1912, I stepped into the Carnegie Library, New York, where my attention was soon drawn to a rather large picture. I was pleasantly surprised to find that "Old New York," as the picture was named, was by Louis Maurer. While I was admiring its details an old guard approached me and said, "That picture seems to interest you, probably you would be much more interested if I told you I know the man who made it." "Indeed," I replied, "and probably you would like to know that I played flute duets with him yesterday." The picture was made when Maurer was twenty-two.

It is my good fortune to possess two unusually fine and original pictures by Maurer, both not only musical but also flutistic

471

in subject. The large one was inspired by the performance in his home of a manuscript of mine entitled *Giovialità*, Valse di Concerto. In the foreground are two charming girls dancing to the music produced by one boy playing a vertical flute, another a double flute and a girl, the lyre. Pan with his pipes sits on the left side and in the background is an imposing temple. It was made in 1914. Dr. Dayton C. Miller says of this picture, which is also used on the cover of *Longevità*: "Mr. Maurer's picture on the cover is rather suggestive. It seems to indicate that the modern flute player is somewhat disturbed by the classical music of the Pan pipes. I have in my office a bronze statue—a replica of a large marble which is in the Louvre, in Paris, which expresses the opposite idea, namely, that a shepherd player has hung his Pan pipes on a stump and is finding special delight in the modern flute." I have an excellent reproduction of this picture in my studio sent to me by Dr. Miller. The other original picture by Mr. Maurer in my possession, though small, is a gem of humor and whimsy. It depicts an orchestra of frogs all, with the exception of the double bass player, seated on mushrooms. The title on the back reads: "Grand Serenade" by the Philharmonic Orchestra of Hackensack Swamps." Vocal duet by Miss Malbrouse and Mr. Grimalkin. The conductor (who has a dead rat hanging on his belt) and vocalists are cats. It was made in 1911.

Maurer never missed a concert if there was good flute playing on the program and had been an active member for years of the New York Flute Club. Maurer's nephew, Frederick Maurer, of Berkeley, California, has been one of California's finest pianists and composers. He has some excellent songs to his credit. He enjoyed the friendship of Edward MacDowell who held him in great esteem. A number of years ago he composed a quaint but charming piece for flute and piano which I played at his home with the composer at the piano.

1832, the year of Mr. Maurer's birth, was an interesting one musically, historically, and flutistically.

The Boehm flute was first given to the world in 1832. Goethe died in 1832. Germany celebrated the first centenary of Haydn's birth in 1832. In 1932 the famous University of Poitiers,

France, celebrated its 500th anniversary. It was founded in 1432 by Charles VII. Lewis Carroll, who gave us that classic of non-sense *Alice in Wonderland* and *Through the Looking Glass*, was born in 1832. Gustav Doré, who illustrated Dante's *Inferno*, Cervantes' *Don Quixote* and the *Bible* and who was also painter, sculptor and played violin, was born in 1832. In 1832 Morse developed the idea of transmitting intelligence instantaneously at a distance by means of an intermittently charged electro-magnet.

Kuhlau died at Copenhagen, where he was musical director for the King, in 1832, at the early age of forty-six and of sorrow over the irreparable loss, by fire, of a full case of unpublished manuscripts, which comprised another set of flute duets, trios and a quartet for four flutes, sonatas and an opera.

Goldmark was born in 1832. Clementi died in 1832. Johann Christ. Fried. Bach, famous composer and son of the great Johann Sebastian, died in 1832. Garcia, Manuel del Popolo Vicente (father of Manuel, singing teacher and in-ventor of Laryngoscope, whose sister was Maria Malibran) tenor, composer, and conductor, died in 1832. Maria Milanollo, a genius of the violin and who died at the age of sixteen, was born in 1832. Bellini's famous opera *Norma* was first given in 1832. Donizetti's famous opera *Elisir d'Amore*, composed in the incredible short time of fourteen days, was given first in 1832. Charles Lecoque, distinguished French composer of light operas, was born in 1832. In 1832 Italy celebrated the first cen-tenary of Pergolesi's delightful opera *La serva padrona*, first given in 1732 and which still holds the stage. The Netherlands, in 1832, celebrated the 300th anniversary of the birth of Orlando di Lasso who, after Palestrina, was the greatest composer of the 16th century. He was born in 1532. Walter Scott died in 1832. Napoleon II, only son of Napoleon I, died in 1832, and Amer-ica celebrated the first centenary of Washington's birth the day after Maurer was born.

A few years ago, when I published a series of melodious pieces for flute and piano, the first one *Serenata* was dedicated to Maurer and so when I wrote him that I had composed two short pieces for flute and piano *Longevitá*, Andante and Valse, for his

473

100th birthday celebration he replied in quite excited vein, showing tremendous interest and hoping they were not too difficult for him to play. What a young man he truly was!

In reference to this occasion, I am quoting in full an article published in the Buffalo *Times*, Friday, May 27, 1932, written by Kate Burr:

In New York the other day a musical composition was played to the man to whom it was dedicated. "Ah, that is a beautiful piece!" he said. "I hope I am worthy—now I shall play something." Stepping briskly across the room he drew a silver flute from its nook behind a bookcase. And to the poem in sound he had just heard, he responded with another.

The incident was full of charm—music making answer to music— a musical honor given and acknowledged in manner so finely befitting the occasion, the giver and the recipient.

But the response to Leonardo De Lorenzo's *Longevitá*, Andante and Valse, takes on the glamour of the marvellous when it is known that the player of the silver flute is one hundred years old. He is Louis Maurer, famed designer of prints.

Don't imagine that Mr. Maurer in his capacity as a musician chose some light and easy tune. No, the selection he played was an air from *Lucrezia Borgia*. His interpretation was that of a master. His handling of the instrument's complex keys was sure, the execution perfect. Admirable for any player—tenfold wonderful for a man a hundred years old.

But to my mind the marvel of the recent occurrence is surpassed by its origin. For Mr. Maurer was seventy-nine years of age when he entered the music department of Mr. De Lorenzo as a pupil. He was the kind of student that gladdens a teacher's heart. Wild weather or fine, always found him present. He applied himself, at seventy-nine, to music with the same energy and zeal he had shown in youth in learning the arts of color and design.

Think of what it takes to master a profession, even when life is young and the world is all before one. Then imagine what it means to do the same thing, when far advanced in years. Courage, faith, hope, patience must have flamed at their highest in the soul of Louis Maurer when he enrolled himself in the music class at the age of seventy-nine.

But these qualities brought their reward. Among the most pleasant sequels of the veteran Maurer's musical initiative were meetings in which social converse and art enthusiasm were happily united. Whenever his teacher, De Lorenzo, visited New York, master and erstwhile pupil had a musicale, of which a feature was a solo executed by Maurer.

The facts sum up in a musical career, begun at seventy-nine, and now, after twenty-one years, going strong. If anybody knows a parallel to that, let's hear about it! Someone has said that to everyone some great field of ambition, earnestness, acquirement, achievement, must remain unknown. If heard of at all, only with the faintness of a distant echo, falling for the most part on unheeding ears.

It's a sad and sobering thought. The more so because its truth was never so poignant as now when knowledge has put forth so many branches that no one can catch a glimpse of all of them, to say nothing of plucking the fruit.

But much that life contains is within reach. The richly freighted branch can be grasped if there is the will to grasp it. It was such a branch that Louis Maurer attained when he added to his career as a designer a career as a musician.

There are no words more often used unadvisedly than "too late." It was not too late for Louis Maurer although he was seventy-nine years old.

He died July 19th, 1932.

*　　*　　*　　*

CARLO TOMMASO GIORGI

While at the seaside resort town of Viareggio, Italy, in 1926, I met Carlo Tommaso Giorgi, inventor of the famous keyless flute. As a memento to our meeting he said he would send me the original manuscript of a Concerto by Giulio Briccialdi, who had been his flute teacher. Unfortunately he found that he no longer had it as he had loaned it to some flutist who never returned it, and he thereupon sent me, instead, after my return to Rochester, New York, two large beautifully bound books which contained a collection of eighteen solos for flute and piano by Boehm, Briccialdi, Marini, Krakamp, De Pauli, Fumagalli, Rabboni and Ciardi. These were mostly on operatic themes and variations which were popular a century ago. The

475

bulky piano part had 291 pages and the flute 159. In the piano book, on page 181, there is a *Divertimento variato* on the opera *Oriazj e Curiazj* by Mercadante and dedicated by its composer, E. Krakamp, to his pupil, IL SIGNOR MARCHESE di CASTELLUCCIO. However, what was of special interest to me was that on the upper right hand of the frontispiece there was the following, written in Krakamp's own handwriting "In segno di stima, l'autore al Signor Raffaello Galli." Evidently this piece must have been given to the famous banker-flutist-composer by Krakamp on one of his visits to Florence from Naples, before the piece was included in that collection. It was published by Giovanni Ricordi, the grandfather of Giulio Ricordi at around 1850. It couldn't have been much later because the piece, being Op. 65, must have been composed at about the same time as his *Luisella* mentioned in another chapter and which is Op. 63 and dedicated to Giuseppe Rabboni who died in 1856. Rabboni, by the way, exchanged the compliment by dedicating to Krakamp one of his most beautiful duets, the Op. 47. The whole collection, therefore, of the eighteen soli sent to me by Giorgi and engraved on rag paper of the finest quality, must be close to one hundred years old with some pieces, as for instance the first one by Boehm, *Variations on a Tyrolien Air* Op. 20, passing the century mark by many years.

The different editors are the following:

B. Schott and Sons, Mayence et Anvers.

F. Lucca, Milano.

Giovanni Ricordi, Milano.

Giovanni Canti and Company, Milano.

Ferdinando Lorenzi, Firenze.

The piece by Ciardi was composed long before he went to Russia, that is, when he was in the service of His Imperial and Royal Highness the Grand Duke of Tuscany. It is dedicated to SUA ECCELLENZA LA PRINCIPESSA CATERINA WSEVOLOYSKY.

A piece by Briccialdi is dedicated to Boehm.

One by Count Marini dedicated to Briccialdi and a short and original one *Il Pollo* (The Chicken) by Polibio Fumagalli, umilmente dedicato to his teacher, Giuseppe Rabboni, solo flutist at the opera La Scala, Professor at the Conservatory and honorary

Professor of the PONTIFICIA CONGREGAZIONE ED ACCAMEMIA DI SANTA CECILIA, ROMA.

* * * *

ARY VAN LEEUWEN

This Dutch artist is one of the most famous and accomplished of all living flutists. Holland has contributed many great artists to the flute playing world, among whom were Drouet; Demersseman, Edward and Jacques de Jong, Fransella, Sauvlet. Edward de Jong lived in England many years and was, for a long period, conductor of the Hallé Orchestra of Manchester. I made his acquaintance in 1904 when he toured South Africa with the noted English singer Ben Davis. De Jong was sixty-nine years of age then, but still vigorous and an excellent player. We played many duets together including the new manuscript of my *The Two Virtuosi*. Fransella also made his home in London and enjoyed great popularity as teacher, soloist and symphonic performer. Van Leeuwen made his home in Vienna for a number of years where he taught in that famous Conservatory and occupied the principal position in both the Opera and symphony orchestras when Gustav Mahler was the dominant figure in that great art city. Mahler held Ary in great esteem.

Van Leeuwen has edited and also made many transcriptions for flute of works by the great masters, some of which were little known and still in manuscript in some European library. One, in particular, a magnificent work and which should be in every flutist's library is a sonata for two flutes and piano by W. F. Bach. When Van Leeuwen first reached California it afforded me much pleasure to give a soirée in his honor in my "Villa Pan" in Beverly Hills. Upon this occasion Van Leeuwen and myself, and with my wife at the piano, played this sonata to the delight of all those present. During this period Ary had some leisure and so almost every day we had a wonderful time playing numerous duets by Kuhlau, Briccialdi, Doppler, Drouet, Tulou, Romanino and many others. I had not played so many duets and with so much enthusiasm since my student days. We also played my newly composed *Suite Moderna* for two flutes which, needless to say, Van Leeuwen read magnificently at sight.

477

One day Van Leeuwen came to the house earlier than usual and, with a broad smile, handed me a new piece of music, his own composition, just published. "This," he said, "is with my compliments and best wishes in exchange for an old compliment of yours over thirty years ago. Is it not better late than never?" The music he handed me was *Sonatina in the Old Style* for three flutes. The dedication read: "To my dear colleague Leonardo De Lorenzo." A charming composition, and not too difficult.

I wish to mention here that before coming to California Van Leeuwen was first flute with the Cincinnati Symphony Orchestra for many years, and Eugene Goossens, who admired Ary, dedicated his *Three Pictures* for flute and piano to him. Besides being a great flute virtuoso Van Leeuwen plays fine piano, sings well, and is an excellent composer.

*   *   *   *

MADAME FRANZ WERFEL

At our "Villa Pan" in Beverly Hills, one evening in 1943, we enjoyed two excellent recordings: Mahler's Fourth Symphony and the same composer's *Song of the Earth*. The latter, as everyone knows, is called a "Symphony of Song on a Chinese Tragic Poem." The day after, while reading *The Song of Bernadette* by Franz Werfel, our door chimes played its little eight-note tune. Answering its summons, I found a very handsome lady with her chauffeur, who told me she was Madame Franz Werfel. After my first surprise I said: "Madame Werfel, were you not Madame Gustav Mahler a number of years ago?" She said, "Yes, I was." "Then," I said, "I used to see you every morning at rehearsals of the New York Philharmonic in Carnegie Hall thirty years ago." "It was thirty-three years ago," she said. For me it was a memorable visit and brought back many memories of Gustav Mahler's last season as conductor of the New York Philharmonic Symphony Orchestra. He was a sickly and, consequently, very irritable man. He wanted to produce his grandiose Symphony No. 8, called the symphony of a thousand—but, the ladies committee, to whom Mahler had to submit his programs, told him that it would take too many rehearsals and the cost

478

would be prohibitive! Later he was allowed to perform his Symphony No. 4 and part of Song of the Earth. This same committee requested Mahler to play much Tchaikovsky, whom he hated! One morning while rehearsing the Pathetic he was in a particularly bad humor and one of the musicians played a wrong note. Mahler, instead of jumping and losing his temper as was his custom, said: "That is all right, it doesn't really matter. This music is better without a conductor, anyhow!" Mahler did not even finish the season—1910-1911. One pair of concerts was conducted by Ferruccio Busoni—who was on a tour in America at that time. We played his Elegy, a composition in memory of his mother who had recently passed away. The rest of the season was conducted by the concertmaster Theodore Spiering. Mahler died in Vienna a few months later at the age of fifty-one. I do not recall to have seen Mahler smile a single time at rehearsals. The only time he would smile was at the intermission when he saw his young and very beautiful wife and their little girl of about two years of age. His wife was in her early twenties and he past fifty.

That was an unforgettably sad season for the first clarinetist, a Frenchman and a refined artist, and myself. Between the bad humor and irritability of Mahler and the almost unbelievable unkindness of some of my colleagues, I was most miserable. It took many years to regain only a fraction of the good reputation lost in that season. To return to Madame Werfel's visit, a result was the acquisition on our part of the Verdi: The Man in his Letters—the self revelations of a genius, published in English for the first time, edited with a preface by Franz Werfel.

We are honored to have the following inscription on the flyleaf: "A Leonardo e Modina De Lorenzo, dedicato colla più grande stima di Franz Werfel, B. Hills, Calif. 1944—Alma Mahler Werfel." It is an extremely interesting book, masterly and sympathetic in its treatment of the subject. Franz Werfel has written also a novel on Verdi. No musician should miss reading this book. The psychological aspects of the Wagner-Verdi controversy are brought out most vividly, and with deep insight.

479

An Illustrious Flute Pupil of Franz Doppler

One day, to be exact, on April 21st, 1948, we had as our guests, Dr. and Mrs. Joseph G. Breco from Hollywood Riviera, a community adjacent to Palos Verdes. The good doctor, a delightful and very amiable man had recently retired after forty-nine years' practice, during which he had delivered nearly 7000 babies. He had had his own hospital in a town in Oklahoma and he was relating some of the interesting experiences of his long career. When he mentioned that often, when an emergency call came during the night, he would jump into his car clad only in his night shirt, reaching the patient many times before the ambulance, even saving a life by immediately amputating a hanging limb and using oftener than any other kind of spinal anaesthesia which he thought was one of the greatest boons in medical science, I said to him, "Doctor, that recalls to my mind an interesting incident. It concerns the doctor who discovered what has been regarded for many years as a veritable 'miracle of science.'" The story which I told Dr. Breco is the following: One early afternoon in October of 1910 I was at the flute counter of Carl Fischer's music store on Cooper Square, New York, waiting for some proofs to correct from my *L'Indispensabile* which that firm was then publishing when an elegantly dressed gentleman of middle age and height approached me. "Mr. De Lorenzo, I presume," he said. "That is my name," I answered. "My name is Corning, Dr. Corning," he repeated, handing me his card and adding, "I have studied flute with Franz Doppler who also dedicated a piece to me for two flutes and piano on the opera *Rigoletto*." It just happened that I had with me, under my arm, a large envelope containing a number of photographs. I pulled out an autographed picture of Franz Doppler, given many years before by that great artist to Carl Wehner who, in turn, had recently given it to me and showed it to him. Looking at the picture, Dr. Corning said, "Yes, that is he, that was my flute teacher." Then he continued, "When is your *L'Indispensabile* coming out? I received an advance announcement quite some time ago and I am eager to see it. But you should also compose an operetta full of fun and good

480

melodies which everyone could sing, whistle or hum." I answered that that was not in my line but Dr. Corning insisted that "if you will but set your mind on it you will succeed for you have a facile melodic gift which you have shown in a number of your pieces."

When I reached home I looked at his card again, it read: "Dr. James Leonard Corning." How could I have guessed then at that time that years later—in 1938—his Spinal Anaesthenia would be used on me and that to my amazement I would be able to lie on an operating table for nearly three long hours, conscious of what was going on and yet with not the least discomfort or pain!

Dr. Corning, American physician, was born at Stamford, Connecticut on August 26, 1855 and died in Morriston, New Jersey, the day before his sixty-eighth birthday, August 25, 1923.

It is said that some people get new ideas sitting on a comfortable arm chair looking at the rings of their cigarette smoke. However poor that excuse may be, it is a fact that Dr. Corning was inspired in his many discoveries not by smoking numerous cigarettes but by playing the flute walking in his laboratory. He studied at Heidelberg and Wurzburg in Germany and was graduated at the latter. He had an international reputation as an expert neurologist and as the discoverer of spinal anaesthesia in 1885 (which was not appreciated or understood at first and put aside for a few years). He was the first to inject liquid paraffin into the tissues, there to solidify; he also demonstrated that the action of stimulants, sedatives and certain other medicinal substances may be increased if the subject remains in compressed air. As consulting neurologist he served various New York hospitals and, besides his contributions to the medical press, wrote *Carotid Compression* (1882), *Brain Rest* (1883), *Local Anastesia* (1886), *Hysteria and Epilepsy* (1888), *Pain in its Neuro-Pathological and Neuro-Therapeutic Relations* (1894), *Experimental Researches Regarding the State of Mind in Vertigo* (1895). Under the pseudonym of Roland Champeon he wrote a romance entitled *Princess Ahmedee* (1900).

A *Letter from Okinawa Shima*

An unusual and interesting airmail letter reached me from Okinawa Shima February 16, 1946, written by an unusual young man who is a botanist and algologist (marine plant life) and an enthusiastic flute dilettante. Here it is:

February 6th '46
From Okinawa Shima

Dear Mr. De Lorenzo:

Forgive, I had not answered your card from "Villa Pan by the Sea." Thanks for your well wishes. Perhaps they have helped one with the good luck that has stepped one's way in the past weeks.

I must admit your postcard with the tinted photo of the Plaza stirred me a good bit. I miss the scene very much. But it won't be so very long . . . Time passes so very rapidly out here. It's mutual, I'm very eager to meet you after the introduction my family have given me.

Though I make myself a bit unpopular with my practicing (cuz it's not in a popular vein!) and our work has been so pressing one's practice hours have been cut down, I'm still deriving a keen satisfaction out of my music. There is one (though many no doubt) technique that baffles me. I'm afraid my tonguing and emboucher is quite wretched. Occasionally one can compare with a recording broadcast from Australia or Moscow . . . and the comparison is most depressing. However, there is still the joy of recreating a Handel Sonata or a Mozart Concerto, crude though it be, that sustains our enthusiasm. I hope I shan't disappoint you too much. Your offer is very generous. It has been some time since playing with an accompaniment. The best gains seemed to be when studying with another.

One thing that takes my curiosity since being among Orientals has been their flute music. The Philippinos, for instance, have a very quaint though entrancing flute literature. On occasion I used to wander at dusk through the rice paddies and hear the native flute players stirring the sunset air with their plaintive notes. My regret is that in my short stay I was unable to procure any of this magical music.

On Okinawa there are flute players but they are, oh, so scarce. Their music is an assortment of Chinese, Korean and Japanese . . . all pentatonic, yet I understand they have a literature indigenous to the island. I am hoping to unearth some of it before leaving.

A charming Japanese girl, a close friend of mine at the University

482

of Hawaii, first interested me in legendary and classical Japanese flute and string music. Since then I've had my ear and eye out for this illusive art. It takes an Oriental ideological approach to attain the esthetic enjoyment associated with this music, it is said, but as a believer in the recognition of beauty in any guise if the ear and eye are keen and in tune, I have found no want of a preliminary other than an open and inquiring interest. The appreciation follows. Much of their music is symbolic and as such has suffered the stereotyped judgment of Occidental viewpoints. However, it is just such a symbolism as one finds in a "natural" language . . . The basis is "organic" and not affected. Just as our philosophy in the Occident may be refreshed by Oriental metaphysics and Oriental intuition (which is a struggle to comprehend!) so may our concepts of the art of harmony and melody be broadened by contact with Oriental musical concepts.

A very interesting school of thought is developing at present in modern Chinese and Philippine music circles with the development of homophonic, octagonic, symphonic composition. Perhaps you have heard some of these curious things. I find them most amazing. It is still a question as to their ultimate "sincerity," but the composers are treading the path of experimentalism in an attempt to use the great music forms of the West (Fugual, Sonata, Variation, song form, etc.) applied to Oriental harmonies and scale eccentricities. The folk music and incidental chamber works of the Orient have a vast literature with exhaustless possibilities for the transcriber, but it will no doubt take a mind well schooled in the ways and turns of Oriental thought and insight to propound their musical ideas in the new gloss of our more colossal art forms.

Shortly, I am to make a trip to Shanghai, China. The possibilities of picking up sheet music, I understand, are good, very good. Of course my eyes will be out for the unobtainable scores of European masterpieces, but in particular I hope to find a fair selection of Chinese and other Oriental compositions. A visit to the Shanghai University should help out in this search. My other aim is to seek Oriental philosophical works . . . rare or unobtainable in the States. I have been given some good sources by various contacts in this area and am eager to get on the trail.

In a week or two my duties for the Navy come to a temporary halt. My thirty days leave (usually taken at home by the sane young men in the service) will commence and for thirty luscious days we shall be collecting wild life on the island. Shortly after this excellent sojourn my discharge will be due and I'll probably see you some time around the middle of May. My intentions are to return to college next fall. Most probably, I'll be around P. V. for several months after my return. At that time you may have a very eager though not always exacting student in your charge.

Please give my best regards to Mrs. De Lorenzo and thanks again for your attention and respects. I trust all is well with you. To my family you have been a source of much kindness and friendship. As a son away from home for such a long period, I cannot thank you enough for being what you are to them.

Your Friend,
Townsend Conover.

CONOVER, MARY CHASE (contemporary), a flute amateur of talent. Her enthusiasm and love for the instrument is an inspiration and entitles her to special mention. She studied piano three years and, because she wanted also to play in a school orchestra, was given a flute on which, not knowing any better, she began to play on the left instead of on the right. However, a local shoeworker, John Rafferty, who was also the only flute player in the vicinity of Auburn, Maine, corrected that mistake and guided her study for the next four years. In 1946 she was doing graduate work in mathematics and education at the University of Colorado. Her flute accompanied her wherever she went—on foot or bicycle, by train, plane or boat—and brought her much pleasure in the opportunity to play in high school and college orchestras. It also served a very practical purpose in earning money with which she could pay her first year's tuition at Bates College. It was the common interest of the flute that first drew Towne (Townsend Conover) and her together in Northfield a year and a half ago (1947). During the past fourteen years, from 1934, the flute has been her inseparable, indispensable companion. Its notes have been heard in the woods or on the rocks along the shores of Casco Bay on the rugged Maine coast, on board a ship's concerts, in the moonlight in the Pyrenees, where people of nine nations were joined in helping build a youth hostel and orphans' home and school, in the firelight of the high-arched kitchen of an old castle high on a Luxemburg hill, in the big hall at Loch Lomond youth hostel in Scotland for the delegates from 24 different countries to the first postwar youth hostel conference. At the wedding of Mary Chase and Townsend Conover, the march was *Loch Lomond* played by a favorite professor at Bates, Seldon Crafts. Also, the two flutes of the newlyweds were heard in *Two Scotch Folk Tunes.*

*   *   *   *

A Glimpse of Viggiano

Probably it will be interesting to know that around 1775 every town in Southern Italy had its autocratic nobleman who not only owned most of the land, but dominated everything and everybody with such brutal power unthinkable to us in our day.

The master and lord of my native town at that time was the *Principe di Viggiano*, whose power was such that he had the right to the first night of every *newly married bride!* The following tragic and dreadful story was told me by a peasant who lived with us and who took care of our country property for nearly half a century and who died at an advanced age at the beginning of this century. He had learned the details from his father, who had been in the service of the *Principe* in one of the three great castles, each castle was a powerful fortress (one was on the highest spot of the town, one in the center of the town and another in the valley, where most of the property, including huge vineyards supplying all necessities, were located). The three castles had underground communication for, in case of trouble, they could hide or flee until reinforcements came to subdue the rebel. I have a vivid recollection of the remains, or ruins, of the three great castles, in particular the one on the highest part of the town, near St. Peter's church. That was the only one of the three completely abandoned. It was impressive to us children to throw a stone in a small opening hole and hear the almost terrifying rumble below—there was no sign of a building to be seen above ground, the ravages of weather and time had covered it all but most of the superstitious peasants were certain there were numerous ghosts. At one time this beautiful and great "Castello del Principe," as it is even now called, had magnificent loggias and balconies. The other two *castelli*, the one in the center of town had been converted into several dwelling houses and that in the valley, was in the hands of a number of farmers who paid tribute to Don Pasquale Nigro (later cavaliere Nigro, who died around 1935), the representative of the *Principe di Viggiano*, whose heirs live in Northern Italy.

One morning, the prince was inspecting his property in the valley when, seeing two young men working, he stopped. "You two seem to enjoy life and be in good health," he said. "Do you live with your parents or have you a family of your own?" The elder of the two said: "Your Highness, we are brothers and are both unmarried." "But," the prince said, "you are both young, vigorous and good looking. Why, then, don't you get married?" "Your Highness," answered the younger, "I would have married but, the thought of giving my bride . . ." The prince said: "If that is the only reason, I will forego the privilege if you marry within two weeks." The young man married his husky and *bella contadina* (beautiful peasant girl) before the two weeks elapsed. However, whether the prince forgot to give counter orders to his two bravi, whose duty it was to bring to the palace the good looking and healthy maidens, was never known, because she was seized after the church ceremony and taken away and no power could save her.

The prince and his family never mingled with the populace at the numerous religious processions of the different saints. They had their chapel and priest and attended service daily and twice on Sunday. However, now and then the prince would mingle incognito, and listen to what the peasants had to say to each other. At noon, after one of these processions the prince, not long after the bride was kidnapped, looking up at his great loggia, he saw a ghastly and dreadful sight. His wife and his daughter were hanging nude by their feet, disemboweled and the two sons were on each balcony in the same position! The prince was never seen after that. From that time on the Viggianesi, feeling free, began to emigrate to North and South America, England, Australia, and even . . . Russia, the peasants as laborers and many others as wandering musicians playing on a small peg harp, or violin and flute.

These latter were, to a certain extent, successful in sending considerable sums of money to those of their families left behind. As a result, more and more learned to play the harp, the violin and the flute, so that they could be seen almost everywhere. A poet from the same province made himself known when, in a poem, he said:

"Arpa in collo son viggianese
Tutto il mondo è mio paese."

(With the harp on my back I am from Viggiano and the whole world is my country.)

This lasted until the beginning of this century.

When *tatta Prospero* (the old peasant who told us this story), whose wife had been a wet nurse to my brother Nicola, became very old, blind and bedridden, he said to our sister Vincenzina, who took care of him: "Vincenzina, you see how stupidly useless I am, do me the great favor of contracting a mixture of something in order that I will not linger any longer and continue to be of such trouble to all of you. God, I know, will bless you and I will enjoy peace and rest." "My dear tatta Prospero," Vincenzina answered, "You have been such a wonderful worker, so faithful and of such great help to us for so many years that the least we can do for you now is to take care of you."

In 1899 there were in Viggiano several courageous young men who wanted and demanded an improvement in the administration of the town.

True, in a way, everyone felt free and could breathe the wonderful mountain air without tax or interference. The terrible autocracy of the prince had been done away with long ago and it was now only a nightmare, a legend which some refused even to believe in spite of unmistakable and tangible evidence. At the head of the many Socialists (the *contadini* or peasants, had never heard that expression before) were two sympathetic young men of about twenty. One, Nicola Basile, was a schoolteacher just graduated. He was the son of a much loved married couple imported from central Italy to teach school in Viggiano. The other was Vincenzo De Milita, a flutist who had recently returned from abroad and both were regarded by the peasants as veritable

487

heroes. The *galantuomini*, of course, were annoyed and called them *scostumati malandrini* (bad mannered rascals).

The peasants were radiant with happiness because, they said, "At last Providence has sent us two wonderful boys who, not only fight for us underdogs but can discuss with those arrogant persons any subject and, best of all, they can read and write as well as the most cultured of them."

The whole affair became interesting but serious at the same time. The two leaders who were making speeches as often as they could were now devoting all their time and attention and intelligence to what they thought was a good cause.

A little later, encouraged by many, they demanded at the municipio (court house) to be shown the administrative books. That was too much for the old veteran employees, at the head of whom was Don Ciccio Pisano, who made a complaint to the mayor Don Paolo De Lorenzo, his brother-in-law, asking for the arrest of the two scoundrels. However, at the carabinieri headquarters it was said that there was not a reason sufficient for arrest. A few months later a pretext was found or invented, and the two were arrested soon after they had discovered that the town's taxes were being paid only by the *contadini*.

After a few days in prison, the two leaders were released and came out triumphant and with higher prestige because their unquestioned integrity, sincerity and honesty had been vindicated.

The following incident will illustrate how badly Socialism was interpreted by the *contadini*. Don Vincenzino De Cunto, the doctor, inquiring of one of the workingmen if it was understood that he was to work for him on the next day, answered, "Well, since now I am a Socialist, you had better do the work yourself."

In spite of the fact that Viggiano enjoyed considerable prosperity because its wandering sons sent money from abroad, the *galantuomini*, with but few exceptions, looked down on the musicians. However, it was no secret that no family of the upper class, or *aristocrati*, did not have musicians as close relatives. A few years later most of the musician's children were either sent to Conservatories of music or became lawyers, doctors, engineers, priests, etc. Long before a student of law or medicine was gradu-

488

ated, relatives were hunting all over, even in distant towns, for prospective marriageable girls with handsome dowries.

The young people themselves were seldom consulted until the transaction of property and cash was satisfactorily concluded. But, one may ask, how about the feelings, character and love of the two most concerned? That was seldom discussed; it was not important.

However, going back to serious music and the flute in particular, the most eminent musician and one of the finest contrapuntists of his time, the province of Basilicata (now Lucania) ever produced, was Vincenzo Ferroni (1858-1925).* As a teacher at the Milan Conservatory, pedagogue and composer of symphonies, operas, etc., Ferroni was the only one from this section to reach such eminence. He was born in Tramutola, a few miles from Viggiano, and began his career as a flutist.

$$* \quad * \quad * \quad *$$

JAMES K. GUTHRIE

I invited Guthrie to take part in my "flute ensemble" which I hoped to re-establish as soon as the war was over and in reply to me he wrote: "You know, getting a letter from you is like getting a letter from some legendary figure out of a book." I felt like 300 years old instead of the proverbial three score and ten! He continues: "Ever since I began the study of the flute—I think I was about twelve years old—I have heard about Leonardo De Lorenzo as one of the great figures in flute. My teachers, Jay Plow and Julius Furman, were both great admirers of yours."

"Since I have been conducting seriously—from about 1936— I have had very little time for my flute, although I still practice when I can and now and then I play a job."

Young Guthrie is really a very busy man. Besides playing flute and conducting concerts and grand operas, as he did in 1948, when he conducted Aïda at the Hollywood Bowl, he teaches at the Redlands University and is co-editor of the San Bernardino

---

* See *Dizionario dei Musicisti Italiani* by Alberto De Angelis (Roma 1922).

Sun and Evening Telegram which his father owns. Guthrie's ambition, I understand, is to establish a first class symphony orchestra for both San Bernardino and Redlands and to be its permanent conductor.

*   *   *   *

An Acknowledgment

I wish to acknowledge here my gratitude to an extremely fine and modest gentleman, Dr. Joseph G. Breco. His generosity has made it possible to publish this book and, therefore, I want to tell you a little about him.

Dr. Breco's father, Jacques Bricault De La Marche, came to St. Lin, Canada from France at the age of seven. When he was eighteen years old, he left Montreal for New York with other young men to work at his trade of cobbler, but, when they reached Albany, the entire party was drafted into the army to fight in the Civil War. No one of them could speak English and at the first opportunity they all deserted. They were soon caught, but an understanding French-speaking officer advised them to enlist with him and he would take care of them.

Jacques served through the war under General Sherman and upon his discharge, made his way to Texas where he found work and also attended school to learn English. Soon he acquired two hundred acres of virgin land and took unto himself, as wife, a buxom Irish girl, Mary Wheat. Together they labored to clear part of the land and he also worked as a cobbler to increase their scanty income as the family was growing.

Joseph, their first son, was born in Canton, in 1877. He attended the first school built in that lonesome area of Texas. It was on stilts and had a floor of wide planks with wide cracks between

491

each plank. During the winter the schoolroom was heated with a wood-burning stove and there was always a kettle of boiling water on it. The wild pigs sought refuge from the cold winds under the schoolroom floor and, when the teacher was not looking, the pupils quickly took advantage and poured boiling water down the cracks and the ensuing terrified squeals and squeeks of the poor pigs was a source of unending amusement to the youngsters. Pity the poor teacher who had to contend with this situation almost daily.

Joseph was early taught his father's trade as well as saddle-making and as he was an alert, ambitious lad, he soon became the owner of a first-class saddle business. This, however, did not long satisfy him and he yearned "to put some other knowledge into the upper part of his body" as he tells it. With this thought in mind and working ever harder, he was, at last, able to satisfy his ambition and he entered the University of Fort Worth as a medical student. At the age of 21, he married Miss Sudie Andrews, also from Canton, Texas, and after his graduation they settled in Ada, Oklahoma and here he began his long career as a doctor of medicine. His practice grew and prospered and eventually he built his own hospital. In the forty-six years of his practice, Dr. Breco was not only loved and admired by young and old, rich and poor alike because of his vivid and kind personality, but he was esteemed as one of the most able and eminent surgeons of his state with one of the highest records of distinguished service in the history of Oklahoma.

Dr. Breco was also very interested in farming and until he became too busy he found joy in the care of his Holstein cow who yielded the incredible amount of nine gallons of milk every day. This went on for a considerable length of time when he himself milked her, but, later, when he was forced to put that wonderful and precious animal into other hands, production dropped to a mere three gallons!

In 1945 Dr. Breco retired, and he now lives with his dear, devoted wife in a beautiful home in Hollywood Riviera, California, adjoining Palos Verdes. He is a horticulturist of the first order and his wonderful garden is the admiration of his numerous friends whom he generously supplies with the most glorious roses, dahlias, chrysanthemums, etc., fruits, berries and vegetables of all sorts, including the famous Oklahoma black-eyed peas and most wonderful sweet potatoes in the world!

Although Dr. Breco is a patron of musical activities, he frankly admits he does not understand what it is all about. Long a slave to his profession, there was neither time nor opportunity for him to learn about the art of sound. The first time he and Mrs. Breco came to our home my wife played for him Scarlatti, Chopin, Brahms, Respighi—and when she finished he said, "Well, I guess it was fine and it must have taken you a long time to get those fingers of yours to work so fast and with no music before you, but, frankly the only tune I can distinguish is 'Turkey in the Straw.' Your so-called classical music sounds to me like a glorified racket but jazz is an infernal racket—now, Mr. De Lorenzo, what is your definition of music?" "That is simple," I replied. "Music is the only international language and the eternal, divine expression of God; and someday, my dear heretic, you too will agree with me and change your infidel opinion." "Possibly," he said, "but don't forget you and I are already as old as God's grandmother." At another time, when Joseph Piastro and my wife gave a violin and piano recital at the Hollywood Riviera Club, Dr. and Mrs. Breco bought twelve tickets only because they wanted some of their friends to hear my wife play the piano. After the concert, Dr. Breco said: "We enjoyed the playing of Mrs. De Lorenzo very much and also the fiddle playing. However, I was thinking that if any guy can play as well as he did with his eyes closed, how much more wonderful he would play with his eyes open?" However, as I am succeeding in making an enthusiastic flute dilettante of the 64-year-old hero and retired Navy Captain, Ole Erikson, who did not know a note of music and never played a musical instrument, I suggested to Dr. Breco that I should like to do likewise with him. It would be a lot of fun, I told him and he smiled contentedly.

My Complete Story of the Flute

ADDENDA I
ADDENDA II
ADDENDA III

Note: Following are page 496 to 594. These pages are facsimile reproductions and bear their original page numbers.

TO MODINA

ADDENDA TO

"MY COMPLETE STORY OF THE FLUTE"

ABOUT 100 THUMB-NAIL BIOGRAPHIES
AND OTHER INTERESTING MATERIAL

FOREWORD

The material originally gathered and prepared for this book would have filled three volumes of the same size . . . . I had, therefore, to submit reluctantly to a surgical operation of vast dimensions, if the book were to be published at all.

Eventually, the material in this booklet with many photographs of pioneers and young flutists, will be an Integral part of a new edition of "My Complete Story of the Flute."

I gratefully acknowledge the numerous letters of appreciation that I have received from many countries. These were not only from average flute dilettanti, but from eminent people whose time was valuable and, of these, the most were from Doctors of Medicine. Others were from Doctors of Music, of Law, of Philosophy, and engineers, inventors, psychologists, scientists, physicists, businessmen, etc.

L. D., August 1954
Palos Verdes Estates, California

ADDENDA TO

"MY COMPLETE STORY OF THE FLUTE"

ABOUT 100 THUMB-NAIL BIOGRAPHIES

AND OTHER INTERESTING MATERIAL

By Leonardo De Lorenzo

TABLE OF CONTENTS

THUMB NAIL BIOGRAPHIES

THUMB NAIL BIOGRAPHIES

ADENEY, RICHARD E.: (contemporary)
For many years principal flutist of the London Philharmonic Orchestra. In 1954 he performed Malcolm Arnold's Concerto for Flute and strings, dedicated to Richard Adeney.

ALBANO, GIUSEPPE: (1813-1889)
A Neapolitan flutist of the *gran cavata* or very beautiful tone, on account of which he was so popular with the audience of the famous San Carlo Opera House of Naples, that whenever he played an incidental solo in the orchestra, they shouted, *bravo, bravo.*" Albano was solo flutist at the San Carlo for 56 years.

ALFIERI, SALVATORE: (contemp.)
An excellent flute virtuoso, Alfieri graduated first from the Pesaro Conservatory, where he studied with Prof. Crespi, and also from Santa Cecilia, Rome, where he studied with Prof. Tassinari. Other students of Tassinari of the younger generation of virtuosi of equal eminence are: Gastone Tassinari, (his nephew) Severino Gazzelloni, Giovanni Gatti and Ferdinando Staiano.

DORIOT, ANTHONY: (contemp.)
One of the most talented of all the American women flutists, Doriot Anthony, formerly with the Los Angeles Philharmonic, is the solo flutist of the Boston Symphony since the 1953-54 season.

BAFONDA, ANTHONY: (contemp.)
Of Italian extraction, Bafonda is an excellent musician and plays equally well flute, piano and the Hammond organ. He is also a fine teacher and has composed some songs with flute obbligato. As a sergeant in a West Point Military Band for nine years, he resigned that position in 1947 and in 1951 he made his home in Los Angeles.

BAKER, FREDERIC: (contemp.)
An able flutist of the younger generation. Baker was the solo flutist of the Denver (Colorado) Symphony.

BARWAHSER, HUBERT: (contemp.)
At the festival in Amsterdam, Holland, in 1952, Barwahser performed, for the first time anywhere, Sem Dresden's new flute Concerto with orchestra admirably and with fine success.

BENTZON, JOHAN: (contemp.)
This bearded and popular piccolo player is also Chairman of the Danish National Orchestra's five men governing board. King Frederick IX and Queen Ingreed are warm supporters of the Symphony and the American tour of 1952 was under the King's patronage.

BEVER, MICHAEL: (contemp.)
Dr. Bever, who is a teacher at the Massachusetts Institute of Technology, is a dilettante flutist who studied with James Pappoutsakis of the Boston Symphony. In a letter dated October 8th, 1949, he says: "I am interested in acquiring a Bass Flute

pitched one octave below the concert flute. I have only been able to learn of one such piece, a trio for Bass Flute, Viola and Keyboard by Ph. E. Bach, of which you have probably heard. As you may know, this piece was performed in this country by A. Van Leenwen."

BRUGNOLI, GIUSEPPE: (1870?-1935?)
An excellent flutist brought to the Metropolitan Opera House by Toscanini in 1912. He returned to Italy after a few years, where he died.

BRUN, FRANCOIS JULIEN: (contemp.)
Is the conductor of the famous Concert Band *Musique de la Garde Republicaine* which recently has added 43 string players to its original 83 wind players. Maestro Brun graduated from the Conservatory in flute and in 1938 was appointed principal flutist of the band of which he is the Conductor.

BRUSCALUPI, VIRGILIO: (contemp.)
Flute teacher of the Conservatory of Florence and also bandmaster.

CARTAGE, FERNAND: (contemp.)
An excellent French artist, Cartage, with Charbonnier at the harpsichord, made fine records of J. S. Bach's sonatas. Soloist Opera Comique and Conterts Lamoureux.

CASTAGNER, J.: (contemp.)
Is the splendid flutist with the Woodwind Quintet of Paris, France.

CID, LOPEZ del: (contemp.)
This excellent Spanish flutist is also a fine teacher and resides in Madrid.

COLE, ROBT. (contemp.)
An excellent artist, Cole is a member of the Philadelphia Symphony and solo flutist with the Robin Hood Dell summer concerts, Philadelphia.

CLARKE, HAROLD: (contemp.)
A member of the Royal Opera House (Covent Garden), London, is also professor of the flute at the Trinity College of Music, London.

COLEMAN, WALTER: (1907-   )
Flutist, cellist and mathematician, Coleman studied flute with Barrére and Kincaid. After 17 years as a student and teacher of mathematics (M. A. Harvard, 1936), returned to the music profession in 1947. B. Mus., 1949, M. Mus, 1950 both from the University of Texas. Cellist and flutist with the Austin Symphony since 1946. Cellist in the San Antonio Symphony the 1948-49 season. Instructor in "flute and lower strings" at the University of Texas since September 1950.

CRESPI, STEFANO: (contemp.)
An excellent flutist of the younger generation. Crespi is teacher at the Conservatory of Pesaro.

1

CRUNELLE, GASTONE: (contemp.)
Studied with La Fluerance, Hennebains and Gaubert. In 1920 he received his Premier Prix. Crunelle is one of the finest French flutists of the new generation. He lives in Paris.

CURRAN, KATHERINE: (contemp.)
Wife of Tom Curran. Studied with Donald Mac Donald and Kincaid. Third flute with San Antonio Symphony 1949-50, second flute 1950-51.

CURRAN, TOM (contemp.)
Studied with Arthur Lora. Second flute with San Antonio (Texas) 1947-50. Stopped playing professionally to devote his entire time to his commercial art business in San Antonio.

DAWES, CHARLES G.: (1865-1951)
Was born in Marietta, Ohio, August 27th, the descendant of a long line of Americans, including William Dawes, the "patriot" who rode on the midnight ride with Paul Revere. Besides his fine flute playing—some of his friends, and in particular, his mother called him "the flute virtuoso"—he was remembered by many music lovers as the composer of the beautiful "Melody in A Major." Dawes served as Vice-President under Calvin Coolidge from 1925 to 1929. His familiar characteristic was to be seen with his famed upside-down pipe. He used words so forceful they had to be deleted from the Congressional Record. He actively sought only one election office, a seat in the Senate, and failed in that bid; but was virtually "drafted" for the Vice-Presidentcy and was in public life for more than three decades. Dawes borrowed $100.00 to get married in 1889 and 43 years later borrowed $80,000,000 to keep his banks from economic ruin. During World War I, he went to France with the rank of Lieutenant Colonel and by the end of the war was General Purchasing Officer of the A.E.F. An officer sent a wire to Charles Dawes: "Exigent we have crossties. Move heaven and earth to get them by Saturday." The same day Dawes answered: "Raised hell and got them today." When Dawes went to the Court of St. James, he was asked if he would wear knee breeches, as court custom dictated. "Hell, no," he replied, and he didn't. Dawes was awarded the 1925 Nobel Peace Prize for his famous German Reparations Dawes Plan in 1922. He died in Evanston, a suburb of Chicago, April 23, 1951.

DIETL, ALFRED: (contemp.?)
Born in Worms, (Rhine), was the successor of the solo flutist Max Schmiedel in Heidelberg, Germany, but disappeared during the second World War. He was known for his outstanding playing of the Piccolo and popularly called the "Kolibri" (hummingbird) of the orchestra. It is not known whether he is still living.

DORAN, MATT H.: (contemp.)
Another of Los Angeles flutists and composer of the younger generation is Doran. He wrote a flute concerto, a quintet for Woodwind, a trio for flute, cello and piano and other works. Has given sever flute recitals. A. Van Leeuwen has been one his many flute teachers and Ernest Toch one his several teachers in composition. Doran's ac demic degrees from S.C. are BM, BA, MM, an Dr. of Musical Arts. Doran is teaching flute, ha mony, and counterpoint at Del Mar College, Co pus Christi, Texas, and plays solo flute in th Symphony.

DAYTON, IRVING: (contemp.)
Dr. Dayton, an enthusiastic flute dilettante, is physicist at Cornell University, Laboratory Nuclear Studies, Ithaca, New York. He, like D D. C. Miller, collects everything pertaining the flute.

DVORAK, CECILIA: (contemp.)
Talented singer and flutist, she claims to teac both from beginning to artistic finish. Miss Dvora is also a member of Local 47 Woman's Club, whic is a branch of the American Federation of Mus cians, Los Angeles.

EITLER, ESTEBAN: (1913-   )
Was born in Austria and studied flute , piano an cello at the Royal Music University of Budapest. I 1934 Eitler graduated with distinction as a flut virtuoso and in 1936 settled in Buenos Aire Argentina, where he was appointed solo flutis with the *Filarmonica Metropolitana*. In 194 he became a *Naturalizou—se cidadae argentin* (Argentinian Citizen). Eitler has made a grea reputation in South America not only as a flut virtuoso but also as teacher and composer wh publishes his own works. His recitals in Santiag Rio de Janeiro, Sao Paulo, Buenos Aires, Las Pa etc., have been and are a great success and tribute to his artistry.

ERICKSON, CAPT. OLE (contemp.)
Capt. Ole at 64, retired with honors from the U.S Navy Coast Guard. With a good pension and large gold medal for having saved the live of several people in World War II, Capt Erickson did not find life very interestin just *doing nothing!* Being very fond of music one day he said to me, "if I could only play musical instrument!" These words were, I fel directed to me. "I will teach you to play flute, I said, on "three conditions: you will have t have a lesson every other day, which means driv ing nearly 60 miles for every lesson. I will accep no remuneration and no presents and last, you will have to attend all the Symphony and Cham ber concerts possible. "Your conditions are won derful," Capt, Ole said, "however, I do not lik to be deprived to show you my appreciation and I must warn you, that I will not be a good stu dent, not only because I don't know the difference from one musical note to another, but I am no quick at grasping things." The following day I broke my vow not to teach anymore, and lessons on solfeggio continued for about three months. Capt. Ole is tall, kind, generous, and the gentle sex thing he is also handsome! To this a friend

emarked: "How can a man with a head like a billiard ball be handsome?" Let us not forget that Capt. Ole, in that respect, is in good company. Pablo Casals is one, Dimitri Mitropoulis another, and the Italian poet, Gabriele D'Annunzio, who was irresistible with the gentle sex, in regard to his lack of hair said: "Hair? I hate hair; when I find one in my soup, it turns my stomach!" "Why is it," Capt. Ole once asked, "that modern or ultra-modern music, even that which is composed, by an acknowledged genius, does not enter my head and leaves me cold, while Schuman, Mendelsohn, Chopin and many others, melt my soul and delight me to ecstacy?" "Because," I answered, "those are geniuses of the great romantic school who will last as long as our planet will!

Capt. Ole now (summer of 1954) is visiting in his native Norway, and upon his return will resume flute lessons with Mr. Hullinger, with whom he has been studying for the last two or three years.

FAULKNER, RONALD: (contemp.)
An excellent flutist and teacher from Greeley, Colorado. He is very modest and retiring about his talent. Taught instrumental music at Greeley High School and at the College. He is known there as a splendid artist.

FISHBERG, ISAAC: (1851-1951)
Flutist since childhood and a patriarch who counted 43 musicians among his immediate family of more than 150. Fishberg died February 1951 at 100 years of age, flute in hand at the Warschauer Haym Solomon Home for the aged, in New York.

GOLLAND, HARRY: (contemp.)
The Cleveland Chamber Music Ensemble is formed of the following musicians: Harry Golland, flute; Kurt Loebel, violin; Muriel Carmen, viola; Bonita Potts, cello; and William Kurzbe, piano.

GUENTHER, RALPH: (contemp.)
Dr. Guenther teaches flute at the University of Ft. Worth, Texas.

GILBERT, GEOFFREY: (1914-   )
English flutist who performed Ibert's flute concerto the first time given in England with Georges Enesco conducting in 1948. An excellent oboist in his early career, he became proficient in both the oboe and the flute. Gilbert was born in Liverpool and studied at the Royal Manchester College of Music of which he was made a Fellow in 1951. Because of his unusual talent and popularity as a flute virtuoso, the oboe was abandoned early in his career. Gilbert studied with René Le Roy and has been with the BBC since 1948. He plays on a platinum flute. His father, who died in 1953 was first oboist with the Liverpool Philharmonic where the other son Thomas is now first clarinettist.

GILMORE, PATRICK SARSFIELD: (1825-1892)
When "The Fabulous Bandmaster," as Gilmore was called, was 16 and employed with a bottling concern, because he was extremely fond of music, his employer contributed some extra shillings towards the purchase of a flute. That was in Ireland in 1836. However, after only a few months of enthusiastic and intense studying, mastering the instrument in a way that it would have taken many others more than twice as long, he applied for a position with the Athlone Band, was told that there was no vacancy for flute! After only three months, on the advice of the band master, returned with a cornet, to the amazed conductor, and was accepted as a member of the band!

GIORGI, CARLO TOMMASO: (1856-   )
In another chapter I wrote about Prof. Giorgi whom I met at Viareggio, Italy, as the youngest man of over three score and ten I had ever seen. Well, the correspondence between us lasted until the start of World War II; then we lost track of each other. In January 1951, after 25 years, a friend from Boston forwarded a clipping from the Christian Science Monitor saying that a man 95 years old in Italy had written a book about music in which he claimed that the composing and performing of the music, as we have known it, is all wrong and, therefore, Bach, Beethoven and Rossini he considered as "Musicisti Orecchianti"— "Musicians who made music by ear." The name of this courageous nonagenarian was Carlo Tommaso Giorgi. "No," said I, "Giorgi is not dead as I had thought, he is very much alive." So without losing time, I dispatched an airmail letter to him in Viareggio. I did not have to wait long for an answer of four pages in his clear and beautiful handwriting. He said my letter was more than welcome and continued: "The book of which you speak was originally of one hundred pages and I wrote it while on a visit to a nephew of mine in Genoa while that City was bombarded during World War II. All the publishing firms to whom I sent it refused to publish it even at my own expense. However, an American officer showed considerable interest and said he would try to have it published in America. I have never heard a word from him since. Lately, I have reduced the one hundred pages to only ten, and even now I cannot find a publisher to put it in print also, because the paper is so scarce. Nothing is published but the very essential." Then he says: "My health is fine. I haven't had a cold in years, I sleep as when I was 25, read and write without glasses and most of the people here think I am a phenomenon. I was born December 21st, 1856, therefore, your promise 25 years ago of composing a piece for my hundredth birthday, without double sharps or double flats, is fast approaching; and I know I will be able to play it in public."

HAKAN, EDLEN: (contemp.)
A talented flutist who has recently made his home in Los Angeles. On April 8, 1951, he gave a recital at the Hancock Auditorium with Ingolf Dahl at the piano, and on May 13th, with Lillian Steuber at the piano, a second recital was given at the Los Angeles County Museum.

HALE, JONATHAN: (contemp.)
One of the most enthusiastic flute dilettanti, Hale

is a character artist in Hollywood. He is the owner of the beautiful gold flute of the late I. L. Lockney of Walla Walla, Washington.

HIGBEE, DALE S.: (contemp.)

Dr. Higbee from Austin, Texas, writes: "I am a clinical psychologist and amateur flutist and was delighted with your book about our beloved instrument. Thank you for writing and publishing it." Dr. Higbee is also a book hunter and requested me to help him find all the books written on the flute.

HOBERMAN, ARTHUR (contemp.)

The tallest of all flutists in Los Angeles, is an artist of the first rank. Hoberman showed his artistry on several occasions, soon after he reached Los Angeles from Seattle, but in particular at a concert of the Flute Club where he performed with consummate skill the writer's "Suite Mythologique."

HRABAK, ALOIS: (contemp.)

The Hrabak flute group of Pittsburgh, Pennsylvania, is composed of Alois Hrabak, William Hagar, Florence Mundy, Dr. Russell Cook and Ernest Deutch. They are, of course, all members of the Pittsburgh Flute Club of which the following are some of the one hundred members: Bernard Elbaum, Stanley Levin, Jeanine English, Ethan Stang, the outstanding solo piccolo of the Pittsburgh Symphony who performed Paganini's Theme and Variations (Caprice number 24) with Gloria Hieger at the piano.

JESSEN, WOLF E.: (contemp.)

An architect by profession, Jessen is an excellent amateur flutist. Has played with the Austin Symphony (Texas) since it was founded in 1938.

LA DUCA, GIUSEPPE: (1847-1920?)

Flute teacher at the Palermo Conservatory from 1882 to 1919, had a great number of noblemen studying flute with him amongst whom were: Count Ranchibile, Prince of Belmonte and Prince Formosa.

LEVY, G.: (contemp.)

Is the excellent solo flutist with the *Orguesta Sinfonica* de Buenos Aires, Brazil.

LICHTER, ADOLPH L.: (contemp.)

A successful retired business man from Detroit. Lichter was born in Russia and came to this country at the age of 15. Soon after he acquired a fife and also an old-system flute which he played without the least instruction. The love for our instrument increased to such an extent that now he said: "If a person would suggest that I gave it up for a million dollars, I would say, 'You keep your million dollars while I continue to play my beloved flute which gives me so much pleasure and, besides, keeps me ever young'." He read at sight creditably well the second book of duets for two flutes and piano Op. 65 by F. Buchner, with myself playing second flute and my wife at

the piano at Villa Pan, February 5, 1952. Lichte is the owner of a number of valuable flutes whic includes two gold flutes and two (yes, two platinum flutes. In parting from a delightful vis to Villa Pan we all had a jolly and a hearty laugh when he said: "Now I must buy a new and a ver large hat because, having known you personall and having played duets with you, I feel my hea swelling to such proportions that my friends i Detroit will not know me." He bought twent copies of my book for his friends.

LOCKNEY, I. L.: (1875-1951)

American flutist and teacher at Whitman College Conservatory of Music at Walla Walla, Washing ton. In a letter dated April 28th, 1951, Lockne says: "Upon my next visit to California I wil call upon you and show you my recently acquire solid gold flute made on Dayton C. Miller's theor of density of that metal. Its tone is beautiful. W have been using your "L'Indispensabile" Part I and II and also your "Neun Grosse Kunstler Studien' here for many years." Alas, Mr. Lockney died th summer of 1951 while on his vacation in Canada

LONGO, LUIGI: (contemp.)

This excellent artist, after many years of teaching at the Milan Conservatory, has been transferred to the Venice Conservatory.

MacDONALD, DONALD: (contemp.)

Solo flutist Buffalo Philharmonic.
A young and talented flutist who graduated from the Eastman School of Music. He was solo flutist with the San Antonio (Texas) Symphony from 1947 to 1949. M M degree in 1952.

McKENNA, DANIEL J.: (contemp.)

"My Complete Story of the Flute" is one of the most interesting books I have ever read. Also, your wonderful "L'Indispensabile" which I bought in 1914, I am still using. I became particularly interested in the Giorgi Flute as described in your book and I was able to obtain a photostatic copy of United States patent No. 594,735 which was issued to Giorgi on November 30, 1897. The patent contains a scale drawing showing the flute, the arrangement of the holes, the mouth-piece, etc. I have been thinking of making one out of a tube of polystyrene or some similar plastic material.
Dr. McKeena is an enthusiastic flute dilettante and teacher of law at the University of Detroit, Michigan.

MANCINI, LORY: (contemp.)

As a young man, Mancini was an expert cabinet maker, having learned the trade to a finish near Rome, Italy, where he was born. However, having emigrated to America at the beginning of this century and being unusually fond of music, studied flute and oboe well enough as to become professional for many years in Los Angeles, California until an era of bad times with the advent of music machines which supplanted living musicians. This owever, did not discourage the still young Mancini who suddenly discovered that he was an inventor. From several household gadgets he earned enough money as to visit frequently his beloved Rome and relatives there. Now, 1954, and since 1952, Mancini is enjoying an excellent government position as a precision worker in a radar base.

MANNING, WARREN F.: (contemp.)
An excellent flute dilettante. Dr. Manning teaches French at the University of West Virginia.

MARTUCCI, ANGEL S.: (contemp.)
One of the most eminent flutists of South America of the younger generation is Martucci. Besides being the solo flutist of the famous Teatro Colon, Buenos Aires, he is also teacher at the National Conservatory of Music. In 1946 Martucci played the first performance of Alberto Wolff's new flute concerto in a masterly fashion with the composer conducting.
The following are some of the noted composers of South America who have dedicated their flute works to Martucci: Alberto Ginastera, Angel E. Lasala, Hector Gallac, Honorio Siccardi, Juan Carlo Paz, Luis Gianneo, Esteban Eitler and Alberto Wolff. The above information was given to me by Esteban Eitler who says in his Italian letter to me: "Your letter of June 1952 was received with great joy as your name has been known to me since my conservatory days. Besides Martucci, a great artist, there are other excellent flutists here, one of whom is H. J. Koell Reutter, flutist and composer. Also, Brazilian colleagues of different regions are: Moacyr Li Serra and Ary Ferreira. Of the younger generation in Europe, I know Ermeler, Redel, Fink, Koroset, Bopp, Hakan Edler, Habschied and a few more." Now, Esteban Eitler, an artist of great reputation and considered a "vital force in Argentine's musical life" does not think that by calling the attention of other worthy colleagues will minimize his own reputation. This great artist and creator of many works, including concerti for many instruments, chamber music for numerous combinations of wind and string instruments and orchestral works, feels as modest and as humble as when, in order to make a living when he first reached Argentina in 1933, played piano and saxophone in a Jazz orchestra! Humility, how wonderful! Eitler ends his Italian letter by saying: "Please keep on corresponding with me as I am your most devoted admirer."

MATTIA, FRANCESCO: (contemp.)
Flute teacher at the Conservatory San Pietro a Majella, Naples.

MESTHENE, EMMANUEL: (contemp.)
Distinguished flute dilettante of New York, teacher of philosophy at Adelphi College and a Bach enthusiast. Dr. Mesthene organized the Bach Cantata Guild.

MICCOLI, ICILIO: (contemp.)
Italian flutist who studied with Italo Piazza at the San Pietro a Majella Conservatory, Naples, from where he graduated in 1907. An interesting "Concerto" for flute and piano by Italo Piazza, whose manuscript is owned by Pietro Caso, another pupil of Piazza, is dedicated to both Caso and Miccoli. The latter has been in America since 1907 and has lived in Los Angeles for a number of years.

MILLER, DAYTON C.: (1868-1942)
Although Dr. Miller has been mentioned more than once in other chapters of this book, the following from a letter to me dated February 26, 1938 will be found of considerable interest. "I have been very busy with scientific work, and writing, and have done almost nothing with the flute, as far as musical performance goes. I am still devoting a great deal of time to the collection of books, music and instruments. However, the collections are reaching the saturation point and new specimens are coming more slowly. I was in Europe last summer and succeeded in finding only ten or twelve specimens; of these perhaps four or five only are important. One of the instruments is a fine glass flute which belonged to the Emperor Joseph, the first emperor of Austria. It bears his coat of arms."

MOORE, T. W.: (contemp.)
This English gentleman has devised a combination of a flute and piccolo in one. Years ago, a combination of a flute in C and flute in D flat was devised and patented by Nicola Alberti. It had an ingenious and scientific contrivance with a revolving inner tube. It was given a gold medal at the San Francisco Exposition of 1915 and . . . soon forgotten! Now I shall have its inventor, Mr. Moore, do the description as published in the July issue of 1953 of Musical Opinion" London, England.
"Some little time before the war the writer began experimenting with a flute that would include all the notes of the piccolo in addition to the normal compass of the flute. It was felt this would be a great convenience to the orchestral player who now sits with the piccolo under his arm or within reach while he plays the flute parts, changing over often without much time to do so, according to the directions in the music. In the model about to be described this can be done simply by a movement of the right-hand thumb and the change over is almost instantaneous. The solo player also would benefit by having an additional octave over which to demontsrate his command and some of the awkward fingering of the upper notes of the flute can be ironed out by simply changing to the piccolo.
A brief description of the mechanical features may be of interest: the keystone of this invention consists of a sliding valve location inside the head of the flute, which is operated from outside, and can be slid to and fro within certain limits and seals off either the flute tube or the piccolo tube. When the flute is played in the normal way the end of the valve acts as the cork or stopper and when it is desired to bring the piccolo tube into

action it is drawn underneath the embouchure, and connects with another smaller tube fitted to the hitherto dead end of the instrument. This small tube carries the note-holes of the piccolo and since it was designed to concentrate on the upper notes of the piccolo a tube was designed to give a fundamental note of A (440). The notes below this down to D can be duplicated on the flute without difficulty and by this means the upper notes of the piccolo can be produced without the effort that is now needed."

MORITZ, ROLAND F.: (contemp.)

This young and talented flutist who graduated from the Eastman School of Music in 1952, is the son of the eminent bassoon player, Frederick Moritz, of the Los Angeles Philharmonic. Young Moritz's academic degrees: BA & MM. He is in U. S. Navy, Now, 1954, with L.A. Philharmonic.

MOSKOVITZ, HARRY: (contemp.)

Prominent flutist and teacher of "The basic elements of fine flute playing." Moscovitz has produced many excellent student-artists and makes his home in New York.

MOSER, PETER: (contemp.)

Amateur flutist from Denver, Colorado. During one of his recent visits to California, Mr. Moser came to see me and presented me with a most interesting miniature piccolo . . . to show, he said, his admiration and appreciation for what I had contributed to the flute and its literature. "Piccolissimo," as I have named it, resembles, on a very small scale, an old flute with an ivory head, and was made by Mr. Moser himself.

MOYSE, LOUIS: (contemp.)

The son of the eminent flutist Marcel Moyse is also a talented musician. He is the pianist of the Marcel Moyse trio in which his wife, Blanch Honegger-Moyse, related to the famous composer, is the violinist. Louis also is an excellent flutist and composer.

NICOLET, AURÉLE: (1926-   )

Born January 22nd at Neuchatel (French- Swiss). Nicolet is considered one of the greatest players of modern times. His first lesson on the flute took place when he was eleven and the teacher was André Jeannet, solo flutist of the Townhalle, Zurich. In 1944, first prize at the National contest at Geneva. In 1945, student of Marcel Moyse, in Paris. First prize in 1947. In 1948, first prize, National Conservatory Geneva and teacher at that Conservatory. From 1949 solo flutist of the Berlin Philharmonic. Nicolet, in spite of his youth, has been called a *phenominal flutist* and has to his credit a number of excellent records which includes Frank Martin's "Ballade" for flute and orchestra, Honneger's "Concerto da Camera" for flute, English horn and strings and "Sonata" for flute and piano and "Concerto" with orchestra by R. D'Alessandro.

OKURA, BARON: (contemp.)

Baron Okura invented the "Okraulos", an instru-

ment which he successfully introduced in 1936 i Berlin, Germany and in Paris, France. Accordin to Prof. Moyse a great improvement of th "Kerbfloete" (Shakuhatsi); as easy to play as th Querfloete, Giorgifloete.

OPAVA, EMIL: (contemp.)

This excellent artist was solo flutist of the Mir neapolis Symphony until the middle of 1951-2 sea son when, because of illness, he was given a leav of absence and came to California to recuperate an rest. Before his departure to rejoin the Minneapoli Symphony in 1953, he and his wife visited us i our Villa Pan by the sea. I then asked him if were true that his parents were Corsicans, as I ha been told and probably then your forbears wer related to Napoleon. We all enjoyed a hearty laug and after the dinner of spaghetti, meat balls an 'vino spumante" Opava said— "The truth is m parents were Hungarians—but after this wonder ful dinner I feel quite sure I am related to th great Napoleon.

PACI, RENATO: (contemp.)

Is the flute teacher of the Palermo Conservatory

PAGENKOPF, WILLI: (contemp.)

Solo flutist of the Stadtorchestra in Meiningen Germany, who has published an illustrate booklet (pamphlet) "Geschichte Der Floete (Story of the Flute). He also invented a "Block floetenmundorgelspiel" for ensemble playing. Hi address is Ernestinerstrasse 8 in Meiningen, Ger many.

PALANGE, LOUIS (1917-   )

Born near San Francisco of Italian parents fron Abruzzi. An excellent composer of Symphonie (for orchestra and band.) operas and chambe music for both strings and wind instruments Palange is a fine player on the bassoon, flute anc oboe, and I believe he will be a famous composer His brother Joseph is also a flute player and bassoon player.

PARKER, BROOKS: (contemp.)

Talented American flutist who lived a number o years in San Francisco, California. In 1927 he lef for New York where he played at the Capitol Theatre replacing Arthur Brooke. From 1942 t 1947, he toured with Sigmund Romberg. Since 1950, Parker has made his home in Hollywood, California. The 1951-52 season finds him the solo flutist of the Seattle Symphony Orchestra.

PATTI, SALVATORE: (contemp.)

Flute teacher at the Foro Italico, a branch of Santa Cecilia, Rome.

PELOSO, GIUSEPPE: (contemp.)

Solo flutist of the famous La Scala Opera House, Milan, Italy.

PIARULLI, CARLO (contemp.)

Flutist, pianist, teacher and Hammond organist,

s of Italian parentage. He was born in Rochester, N. Y., and studied flute at the Eastman School of Music and piano with Modina De Lorenzo.

PINTORNO, VINCENZO (1862-   )
A Nonagenarian and an excellent flute virtuoso in his early career, Pintorno was also a successful orchestra conductor for twenty years and a voice teacher for thirty years at the Milan Conservatory. On January 31, 1951, *Grande Ufficiale* Vincenzo Pintorno, celebrated his 90th birthday with numerous friends, relatives and admirers at his native Cefalú, Sicily.

POTTER, ROBERT W. F. (1898-   )
Medical School, Liverpool University; collector of gramophone records since 1923, and contributor to "THE GRAMOPHONE" (1930-39). Took up music and the flute at the age of 46, joining five amateur orchestras at 50. First lessons from Eileen Naisby, (Flute scholarship winner), later from Harold Hill (Liverpool city Police Band.) And orchestra training under Eugene Genin, (late of the Liverpool Philharmonic). Became enthusiastic dilettante for everything flautistic. Has learned much from all his flute friends and colleagues, and from accompanying orchestral records."
I have had a delightful correspondence with Dr. Potter in regard to "My Complete Story of the Flute."

RAMPAL, PIERRE: (contemp.)
In a recital that was pronounced highly successful, Rampal played: Bach, sonata for flute alone; Beethoven, sonata in B flat; Hindemith, sonata Honegger, Danse de la Chievre; Dukas; La Plainte; au Loin du Faune; and Roussel's Andante and Scherzo, Op 15., in New York.

RANKIN, I. EDWARD (contemp.)
Violinist, teacher and enthuiastic flute dilettante for nearly fifty years from Yakima, Washington. He says: "I learned to play flute first from some old Howe Corresponding Lessons; also a great deal from Arthur Brooke Method, but particularly from your *L'Indispensabile,* which has been my bible and constant guide."

RATCLIFFE, HARDIE (contemp.)
He is secretary of the British Musicians' union which has a membership of 28,000. Ratcliffe plays both flute and clarinet and because of his power, is called England's Petrillo.

RISPOLI, PASQUALE: (contemp.)
An excellent artist who visited America in December 1950 with the "Virtuosi di Roma." Studied at Santa Cecilia, Roma, with Prof. Arrigo Tassinari.

SAURINI, ALBERT: (contemp.)
Was born in Rochester, New York, and studied first with his cousin Carlo Piarulli and later at the Eastman School of Music from which he graduated. Since 1952 solo flutist with the Indianapolis Symphony.

SALIMENT, GEORGE EDWARD:
(1770-1830)
An American flute virtuoso much esteemed in New York between 1785 and 1825.

SAVAGE, A.T. (contemp.)
In spite of his bellicose name, Mr. Savage, a dilettante flutist, is one of the finest and most gentle spiritual souls I have ever met in my life. A mystic in the very sense of the word, Savage's knowledge of astronomy in conjunction with astrophysics and astrology is remarkable. He is a veritable Mahatma Gandhi of the flutistic world. "Most of the ills, sorrows and tragedies of the human race could be conquered" he placidly says, "with love, kindness and spiritual understanding. It will take time to evolve and develop such a race of human beings, but I haven't a doubt that it will be accomplished. War, armies, policemen, jails, dishonesty, immorality and filthy books, bad health and what goes with it, will be a thing and a disgrace of the past." Mr. Savage's letters are mostly signed: "In wholesome sincerity, A. T. Savage." Mr. Savage resides in a suburb of Los Angeles.
N.B. Mr. A. T. Savage is my *mentor* and my faithful *spiritual advisor.*

SCHMIEDEL, MAX: (contemp.)
For many years solo flutist in Heidelberg, Germany, using "Reformfloete" devised by his teacher M. Schwedler, who died in 1949 at 96. Schmiedel, has a very large and interesting collection of rare flutes.

SELDERS, RAYMOND E.: (contemp.)
Dr. Selders is a prominent M.D. of Houston, Texas, and makes flute playing his fondest hobby. He says: "I am just an amateur but I have studied the flute seriously and have practiced diligently. About 1914, I bought a copy of your "L'Indispensabile" which I worked on until I wore the book out. I had it rebound at the University of Oklahoma book bindery and now (1952) I have worn it out again. In 1914 I studied with Alfred Quensel, and in 1925 with Barrére. I can play the Mozart Concerto in D satisfactorily." Dr. Selders owns three flutes; a silver, a gold and a platinum flute. Dr. Selders says: "My flute has been a source of pleasure and relaxation all my life, and I intend to devote more and more time to it as I gradually retire from the practice of medicine."

SHAEFFER, ELAINE (contemp.)
This talented A m e r i c a n young woman formerly solo flutist with the Houston (Texas) Symphony, has been concertizing in Europe lately. At the Festival of Venice, Italy, in 1954, she performed for the first time Virgil Thompson's flute Concerto with orchestra.

SHAW, PHINEAS S.: (contemp.)
A dilettante flutist from Greensboro, North Carolina, says: "There must be a sort of Freemasonry among flute players, even though they have never met. The love of the instrument and the great love of much of that which is good in flute music forms, at least for me, a

7

tangible—though abstract, bond of fellowship. Possession and reading of your book has seemed to extend this bond of Fellowship backwards through the recent century, so that in the living company of the Flute Fraternity down through the years. I was born in London, England, and I have played Flute for many years and some of the names in your book brought back to me nostalgic memories. Usually I have been disappointed in what books I have been able to read on the flute, but your is indeed surprising both in the amount of information it contains and the amount of pleasure one gets from it. I feel strongly that it will, like Dicken's Novels, furnish increased pleasure and education with each reading. For that reason, I shall read your book over and over again."

STUART, A. BENTON (contemp.)
1887-1942
An excellent and much beloved flutist and teacher, Stuart received his training mainly from Karl Hodge of Cleveland and Frank Borstadt of Chicago. Before going to Denver, he received profession band and orchestra experience in Detroit, Seattle, San Francisco and with traveling bands. He conducted the junior students orchestra at Denver College of Music, and was a member of the Denver Woodwind Quartet. He died in Denver at the age of 55.

SYMONS, E. N.: (1870?-1950)
A great friend of John Lemmoné for many years, Symons was born in England. During his boyhood, he played a fife, and at the age of ten he was a member of the Dalton-in-Furness drum and fife band. Symons, who was called by Lemmoné "one of the greatest amateur flustists in the world," lived most of his life in Rockhampton, Queensland, (Australia), in which city he put all his soul and enthusiasm in its musical activity with the Orpheus Club Orchestra, of which he was one of its founders in 1906. Symon's daughter, Miss Rita Symons, is also an enthusiastic flute amateur and again like her father, a professional pharmacist chemist by profession. At Symon's passing in 1950, the following was a loving tribute to a rather-lengthy memorial:
> "There is nothing to be added to the dignity of his life, and there is nothing that can be taken away — good and profound in its noble sense, full of that human charity and utter renunciation of self; that was my friend, E. N. Symons.
> "Great nature had a million words,
> In tongues of trees, and songs of birds,
> But none to breathe the heart of man,
> 'Til music filled the
> "Pipes O' Pan"

Henry Van Dyke

THOMAS, JOHN: (contemp.)
Flutist and organist, Thomas is a graduate of Eastman School of Music. He was solo flute with the San Antonio, (Texas), Symphony 1947-1949.

TORCHIO, BALDASSARE: (contemp.)
An excellent artist of the younger generation Torchio is the flute teacher at the Milan Conser vatory.

TROWBRIDGE, CHARLES RUSSELL: (contemp.)
A government employee of Denver, Colorado Trowbridge is one of the best flute dilettanti o that city. He studied with A. Benton Stuart. Denver University and has also a fine knowledge of the Italian language. At a Musicale in which several flutists took part soon after the appear ance of "My Complete Story of the Flute," beside discussing the new book, several compositions o Leonardo De Lorenzo were performed which in cluded "Giovialitá", "Melodia" and "Il Velivolo." This last piece, unaccompanied, was played by Trowbridge in almost one and one-half minutes which closed a very pleasant evening, the summer of 1951.

TURKEYLEGS, JOHN: (c. 1850-?)
The noted American composer Thurlow Liurance's Researches in Indian Song was published in Musical America of April 26, 1919. Of the many flutes and flageolets, Liurance said: "I am convinced that the American Indian has a theme for every activity and characteristic of his life. His best songs are spiritual songs, and his flute or flageolet is his only real musical instrument. There are four toned and six toned Hopi flageolet made from hollow bone, a kiowa six toned flute, some Pueblo flutes which showed marks of civilization, having been made by a Ute Indian, from a piece of gas pipe. The tone was produced by blowing on the rim. Some of the Southern Pueblo Indians played on exquisitely beautiful flageolets. A flute which an Indian had made by pounding together silver dollars, showed what splendid silversmiths these Indians were, belonged to John Turkeylegs, a shrewed Cheyenne Indian, whom Liurance called "the best flutist in America". Turkeylegs inserted a goose-quill into the chamber of his flute to make a tremolo.

VINCENT, HENRY: (1793-1880)
An excellent and cultured flutist, Vincent came from a family of famous English musicians. The family of Vincent, who were all recognized composers and performers during the early part of the 18th century, were Richard Vincent, Thomas Vincent, James Vincent and Thomas Vincent, Jr. The Vincent family of a later period were still musical. Dr. C. Vincent, another descendant of Henry Vincent, a grandson of Thomas, died in London in 1880, aged 87.

VINCI, DOMENICO: (contemp.)
An artist of the younger generation, Vinci is the flute teacher at the Conservatorio Paganini, Genoa.

WEBER, LOUIS: (1859-1935)
Dr. Weber was a fine and erudite gentleman, kindly and considerate as well as a noted physician

nd psychiatrist. He, as well as his daughter Agnes, studied flute with Harry Baxter. Besides flute playing Dr. Weber had another hobby, that f collecting paintings and sculpture, and as a young man, played zither very well. He became an intimate friend of the noted painter Paul Lauritz to whose home he used to go often, and never without his beloved flute. Dr. Weber's admiration for Lauritz is well-known because he owned forty paintings by that artist. Dr. Weber was a member of the Los Angeles Flute Club of which he seldom missed a meeting. Another daughter of Dr. Weber married Victor Schertzinger, (1870-1941) noted motion picture director and composer of Hollywood. Dr. Weber was born in Roaring Creek, Pa., Dec. 25, 1859, and died in Los Angeles, January 26, 1926.

WADE, ARCHIE, (contemp.)
Of the younger generation of flutists in Los Angeles, Wade is one of the finest and most accomplished. At one time solo flutist of the Los Angeles Philharmonic and more than once President of the Los Angeles Flute Club, Wade, because of his kindness, fine personality and excellent musicianship, is loved and held in high esteem. Wade's beautiful playing in Debussy's Sonata for flute, viola and harp, able assisted by Harry Blumberg, viola, and Dorothy Remsen, harp, has been a delight to listen to both at the Flute Club and at the Los Angeles County Museum. Wade is also one of the most active members in the Flute Club; ready at any time to fill a gap whether for a 4th flute in a quartet or a difficult solo part in any other combination.

WHITTEMORE, LEWIS BLISS Rt. Rev.: (contemp.)
The cover of "The Churchman", oldest Religious Journal in English speaking world, dated March 1, 1939, New York City, had an excellent photograph of Lewis Bliss Whittemore, Bishop of the diocese of Western Michigan, playing the flute. He first demonstrated his ability as a flute soloist at a Rotary Club Hobby, held in Grand Rapids many years ago. The first sermon ever heard over the radio was one he preached January 2, 1921 when Station KDKA broadcast the service from Calvary Church, Pittsburgh.

WIDNEY, J. P.: (1842-1938)
Dr. Widney was fond of the flute and played it often and creditably. He came to California in 1862 after studying at the Toland Medical College, San Francisco, and serving for two years in Arizona as assistant surgeon in the United States Army. He aided his brother Judge Widney, at the time of the Chinese riots in Los Angeles in 1871 in checking wholesale slaughter. In 1868, settled at Los Angeles where he practiced medicine and was one of the promoters of the University of Southern California. He wrote an interesting book "Life History of the Aryan Race". Dr. Widney was born in Miami County Ohio, and died in Los Angeles, California, July 4,

1938, at the age of 96.

WILT, THOMAS: (contemp.)
This young American flutist, accompanied by his wife, played Prokofiev Sonata Op. 94 and Schubert's "Introduction and Variations" Op. 160 at a New York Flute Club in February, 1951.

WOLF, ANTON: (contemp.)
This young and talented flutist - composer graduate of the New England Conservatory, studied with G. Laurent.

WREN, LORNA: (contemp.)
A talented young woman professional flutist living in Glendale, California.

* * *

OTHER EMINENT
YOUNG EUROPEAN FLUTISTS

Josef Niedermayer (Vienna Philharmonic)
Kurt Redel (Detmold, Germany)
Dr. Herbert Kolbel (Cologne, Germany)
F. B. Chapman, (England)
Dr. Gustav Scheck (Freiburg Germany)
Krefeld; flutist and lutenist (Germany)
Zanke (Wurzburg, Germany)
Zucca (Essen, Germany)
Bobzien (Hamburg, Germany)
Theurer (Munich, Germany)
Rolf, Ermeler (Germany)
Ferdinand Conrad (Germany)
Josef Bopp (Switzerland)
F. R. Rampell (France).

* * *

9

OTHER INTERESTING MATERIAL

HE AFFINITY OF THE AMERICAN INDIAN
IN RELATION WITH HIS RELIGION
AND THE FLUTE

flute student who had read "My Complete
tory of the Flute" asked what he thought an im-
ortant question and added, "no one has yet given
ae a satisfactory answer". The question: "How
nany tribes of Indians are there in America and
vhy are so many of them interested in flute-play-
ng?" The answer: Music is an integral part of
he Indian religion and the flute is one of their
avorite instruments. The Indian of North and
outh America are divided into 16 main stocks:
Algonquian, Athapascan, Eskimayan, Iroquoian,
Mayan, Mushkogeyan, Siouan and Ute-Atzecan in
North America. Araucanian, Arawakan, Aymaran,
Cariban, Chibchan, Tapayan, Tupian, and Quech-
nan in South America. At one time there were
1500 tribes of Indians who lived in the vast area
netween Hudson Bay and Cape Horn. North
America has about 36,000 Indians. Canada 100,000.
Mexico, 2,000,000. Central American 2,000,000
and South America 6,500,000. So many Indians
love and play the flute, because their God and the
flute go hand in hand in all their religious
rituals. The following, taken from p. 27 of "My
Complete Story of the Flute" will illustrate . . .
"God of the flute-Blue flute people - Flute and
Prayer of the desert God - Reed flutes and flutes
of high Mystery - The Spirit leader of the Flute
ceremony - The Secret order of the Flute instituted
- Prayer Flute of the far desert - The Sign of the
Flute of the Gods - The Worship of Pan - *The
Music of the desert gods is the music of the flute;*
let it not be silenced by trumpets of brass made
by white men who conquer". However, not all
Indians occupy their time with just religion, superstition and flute playing. There were ingenious
Indians in what is now Colombia, that water-
proofed their clothing by reinforcing them with
juice of wild rubber trees, long before Columbus
discovered America.
To two noted American composers, Thurlow Lieu-
rance (1878) and Charles W. Cadman (1881-
1946) goes the credit for spending many years
with the American Indian in research and recording native music. As everyone knows, however,
that the flute did not attract just unlearned and
wild Indians. It also attracted many historical
personages of the past and present: Pharaohs,
Emperors, Kings, Princes and other noblemen,
Philosophers, Doctors, Generals, Poets, Statesmen,
Scientists, famous composers, men of affairs, etc.
Some of these enthusiastic dilettanti were excelled
performers. About 1200 languages are spoken by
American Indians, many of them by only a few
hundred people.

THREE MUSICAL LITERARY GENIUSES
DANTE, ALIGHIERI (1265-1321)
Was a very musical soul. His whole work sparkles
with musical feeling. In his immortal "Divina

Commedia," in his matchless lyrics, and other
works including "Vita Muova" various musical
instruments, including the flute are mentioned. The
following, often quoted in musical and especially
instrumental works is typical:
. . ., se la voce tua sarà molesta
Nel primo gusto, vital nutrimento
Lascerà poi, quando sarà digesta.
                    Paradiso, Canto XVII
(. . . . if thy voice be grievous at
first taste, yet vital nutriment shall
it leave thereafter when digested.)

SHAKESPEARE, WILLIAM (1564-1616)
Of all the world's greatest poets the one who
honored the flute most is Shakespeare. It will
suffice, to quote only the following, from "Ham-
le" to illustrate the interest and knowledge of
Shakespeare in the flute:
"Will you play upon this pipe?
Govern these ventages with your
Fingers and thumb, give it breath
With your mouth, and it will discourse
Most eloquent music."

CERVANTES, MIGUEL de SAAVEDRA (1547-1616)
When a young man, Cervantes became a soldier,
lost an arm in a battle and was taken prisoner
in 1576 by the Barbary pirates, and wrote part
of his immortal novel "Don Quixote" in jail.
Cervantes, like Dante and Shakespeare, was very
musical. I have a volume of "Don Quixote"
illustrated by Gustav Doré. There are several
illustrations in reference to musical episodes, as
for instance, one in which Don Quixote plays
some kind of a mandola. In another, several
people play on long Egyptian-like trumpets and
one on a horn. An interesting but rather gruesome illustration depicts a troup of musicians
seated on an ornate wagon and playing mandoline,
horn, oboe, tambourin and, in front of them all,
a flute player! The figure of death stands in
the rear, and the procession is accompanied by
hooded figures carrying lighted candles. The
most interesting picture, to me, is one in which
Don Quixote becomes a shepherd and plays on
a large Pan pipes while Sancho Panza blows on
a huge bag pipe. Cervantes died the same year
as Shakespeare, 1616.

* * *

THREE UNMUSICAL LITERARY GENIUSES
GOETHE, JOHANN WOLFGANG VON (1749-1832)
In my list of detractors of the flute, I have mentioned Goethe. He was so unmusical that he was
unable to comprehand and appreciate the genius of
his illustrious friend Beethoven, although his
grandson, Walter Wolfgang (1818-1885), was
known as a composer of operettas and songs.
When Schubert, who admired him greatly and had
already set numerous of his lyrics to music, visited him one afternoon, Goethe's only comment to
a friend was: "That insignificant little Schubert

visited me the other day. I had the impression that he came to spy on me, because he wore spectacles so he would not miss the minutest details and objects in my studio and other parts of the house!" Poor Schubert; he was so near sighted that he wore thick glasses not to spy on anything or anybody but through forced necessity. How can one, musically speaking, take Goethe seriously when his attitude towards the two geniuses, Schubert and Weber, was so uncomprehending. He would rather listen to music by an insignificant and unknown composer whose name no one remembered than the inspired songs of Schubert written to his own lyrics. As to Weber, Goethe left the Opera house after the second act of "Oberon" saying "A lot of noise for nothing" and when these two great composers each paid their respects to him, the poet's behavior left little doubt of his hostile feeling towards these two gentle but great souls! Both departed from Goethe's house broken hearted.

HUGO, VICTOR MARIE (1802-1885

It cannot be true that poetry and music go hand in hand when a genius of Hugo's calibre says: "Why do people lose their time listening to music?" He was so unmusical he could never distinguish one tune from another and was usually gruff and ungrateful to the composers who asked to set his plays to music, even to Verdi with "Ernani" and Rigoletto" but evidently this unfortunate characteristic of Victor Hugo was not known to Delibes. He had been requested by a special committee to compose the incidental music to one of Hugo's plays and conducted the music while Hugo, in person, supervised rehearsals.

Delibes thought he had composed some of the finest music he was capable of and could not understand why Victor Hugo did not even once take notice of him or hint that the music pleased him. Finally, the composer-conductor, unable to restrain himself longer went to Victor Hugo and asked if the music met with his approval. Victor Hugo answered: "Your music did not annoy me". Although one of Hugo's poems is entitled "Viens une flute invisible" and has been set to music by Sains-Saens, he was not musical. Also Theophile Gauthier (1811-1872), another famous French writer, and a disciple of Victor Hugo, considered music "The most expensive of all noises".

CARLYLE, THOMAS (1795)-1881)

The unmusicality of Goethe and Hugo is even surpassed by Carlyle. Music is almost entirely ignored throughout his immense writings. The huge biography of Frederick the Great, his opus magnus, contains not a word of that sovereign's musicianship, his fine flute-playing, his compositions comprising over a hundred sonatas for his favorite instrument and his opera "Il Re Pastore". N. B. The above material is from Leonardo De Lorenzo's unpublished chapters in "My Complete Story of the Flute".

"ODE TO A GRECIAN FLUTE"

EDGAR ALLAN POE: (1809-1849) The noted American author and poet was a highly gifted but ill-balanced man of genius. On his father's side h claimed descent from an old Italian family wh had long lived in England. I very mucht doub that his ancestor's name was Poe, which is no Italian but may, rather, have been Po, lik the name of the Italian river in Northern Ital and with which the American soldier is familiar The relation of Poe to the flute is for me purely a fanciful one. Among my clippings I have one yellow with age, of Poe's poem "The Raven" with a reproduction of a painting by Carling. He depict Poe, with a tortured expression on his face, seate in front of an easel with a painting of his wife o it and playing the flute. The raven is beside him and a bottle on the floor. At the top. above two lines of music, is a vision of Poe, and Lenor huddled against his side. Also, in 1845, when Poe was editing the "Broadway Journal", a young writer. Richard Henry Stoddard, sent his first poem "Ode to a Grecian Flute" to him for publication. When, after several weeks the poem had not been published and no word received, he took courage and went to see the editor who was then living on East Broadway near Clinton. I shall quote from Stoddard's own words his subsequent experience with Poe. "I knocked at the street door, and was presently shown up to Poe's apartments on the second or third floor. He received me with the courtesy habitual with him when he was himself. I told my errand, and he promised that my ode would be printed next week. I was struck with his polite manner toward me, and with the elegance of his appearance. He was slight and pale, I saw, with large luminous eyes, and was dressed in black. When I quitted the room I could not but see Mrs. Poe who was lying on a bed, apparently asleep. She too was dressed in black and pale and wasted. Poor lady, I thought, she is dying of consumption. She never stirred, but her mother came out from the back parlour, and introduced to me by her courtly nephew. Breathing a benediction upon the three, I stole downstairs, and rambled slowly home.

In the next Broadway Journal the ode was mentioned as follows: "To the author of the lines on the 'Grecian flute'. We fear that we have mislaid the poem'. And a week later, this: 'We doubt the originality of the 'Grecian flute', for the reason that it is too good at some points to be so bad at others. Unless the author can reassure us we decline it'. When I came back to see him he was in a morose mood. 'Mr. Poe', I said, 'I called to assure you that I did write the Ode' — Poe started, and glared at me, and shouted, 'You lie, get out of here, or I will throw you out.' After my indignation and astonishment, when I came to consider the matter I was rather flattered than otherwise, for had not the great Poe declared that I did not write the poem, when I knew that I did? What a genius I must be! Stoddard came to the conclusion, and which he maintained throughout that Poe was not a good "critic!" It would be interesting and enlightening if I could reproduce here the "Ode to a Grecian Flute."

*   *   *

11

BEETHOVEN'S FATHER PLAYED FLUTE. Beethoven's grandfather was also a musician. He was honest, sober and proud. It was he who first discovered the spark of genius in the grandson, who, like him, was named Ludwig Van Beethoven. His mother was a good, hard working and kind German woman. She was frail, meek, pious and constantly pregnant! Beethoven's father was an inveterate drunkard. At home, during sober periods, he played flute or oboe accompanied by his gifted son and people passing by were wont to stop and exclaim "How beautiful!" Beethoven hated his father for his brutal behavior and remarked "What a difference between Mozart's father and my father!"

* * *

NEW YORK FLUTE CLUB OFFICERS — 1954

Mildred Hunt Wummer, President.
Lewis Bertrand, Harry A. Weill, Dr. Maurice S. Rosen, Emil Stock, Lawrence D. Taylor, and Thomas Benton.

* * *

LOS ANGELES FLUTE CLUB OFFICERS — 1954

William Hullinger, President.
Haakon Bergh, Elgin Asbury, Sylvia Rudeman, Mary Claire Hardwick, Harold Lewis, Elsie Moennig, Sheridan Stokes and Arthur Hoberman.

* * *

On December 19, 1926 the New York Flute Club performed for the first time a composition by Giulio O. Harnisch, Protoplasmer Postlude "When she passed by" for nine flutes, violin, cello and triangle.
The composer, who was then a viola player with the New York Philharmonic, conducted.
February 6, 1933 on a program of *Pan American Association of Composers* the final number was a "Concerto for Flute" with an orchestra of . . . ten flutes by Henry Brant (composer of chamber music and radio music.) The performers were:
GEORGES BARRÉRE — *Soloist*
Flutes—
Victor Harris
Milton Wittgenstein
Sarah Possell
Valentine Dike
Robert Bobles
Alto Flutes—
Paul Siebeneichen
John Petrie
Piccolos—
Frederick Wilkins
Carl Moore
Harry Baugh

On January 26, 1936 the last number on a concert of the New York Flute Club was a "Suite for Nine Flutes" by Arcady Dubensky: Prelude,

Menuetto, Angelus, Etude, (Song of the Wind) Allegro Barrèrissimo. The players: Georges Barrère, Frances Blaisdell, Julia Drum, Lorna Wren, James Hosmer, John Kiburz, Paul Siebeneichen, Frederick Wilkins, Milton Wittgenstein.
The above information I owe to Milton Wittgenstein, vice-president of the New York Flute Club.

NEW YORK FLUTE CLUB
Sunday, January 26, 1936
RECITAL OF
Original Compositions for Flutes
in Solo; Duet and Larger Groups
GEORGES BARRÉRE
Assisted by
Misses: Frances Blaisdell, Julia Drum, Lorna Wren.
Messrs: James Hosmer, John Kiburz, Paul Siebenechen, Fred Wilkins, Milton Wittgenstein.
PROGRAMME
1. Sonata in A Minor ....J. S. Bach
    (Flute and piano)
    Allemanda
    Sarabande
    Courante
2. Allegretto and Menuetto ....Beethoven
    (Two Flutes)
3. Trio Op. 90 in B Minor ....Kuhlau
    (Three Flutes)
    Allegro non tanto
    Scherzo
    Adagio
    Finale
4. Rondo Capriccioso ......Robert Russell Bennett
    (Four Flutes)
5. Divertimento Flautistico, Leonardo De Lorenzo
    (Five flutes with flute in G and piccolo)
    I Mattinata
    II Serenata a Pan
    III Allegro finale
6. Suite for nine flutes ....A. Dubensky
    (new, first performance)
    Prelude
    Angelus
    Menuetto
    Etude (Song of the Wind)
    Allegro Barrèrissimo
    * * *

12

A SHORT FLUTISTIC STORY for the "Los Angeles Flute Club" concert Oct. 25, 1953 at the Hancock Auditorium of the University of Southern California, on the occation of De Lorenzo's gift to that University.

This is an excellent time and place to tell you a short flutistic story. However, before the real story begins, I wish to tell you what this particulat lady thinks of the delightful gentleman, her husband whom, she calls *an incurable dilettante*.

"Mr. De Lorenzo," she asked me one day when I was their guest, "I wish to know if all other flute amateurs love their flute as my husband does! — I think he is unique in the whole world. Do you know, Mr. De Lorenzo, that my husband actually takes his flute with him even when he goes to the bathroom?" . . . Now here is a letter from this *unique* lover of the flute.

"My dear friend", he writes: "I have great news for you. My charming and sweet wife has just presented me with the third set of twins! . . . We are, believe it or not, extremely happy about it. "I guarantee you that if all these darling children will inherit only a small part of the love for the flute from their father, we shall have a band of seven flutists in our home in the near future! Their names? Oh yes, I knew you would be interested. Well, the first set, two girls, are called *Kate* and *Duplicate*. The second set, two boys, are *Pete* and *Repeat*. The third set, also boys, we have just named *Max* and *Climax!*
*   *   *

Here followed an interesting program beautifully performed.
Assisting Artists

JOSEPH RIZZO	Oboe	GREGORY BEMKO	Cello
FRANKLYN STOKES	Clarinet	ANDREE BRUN	Piano
WENDELL HOSS	French Horn	MILDRED PORTNOY	Piano
ADOLPH WEISS	Bassoon	ETHEL ZIMMERMAN	Piano

HANCOCK AUDITORIUM   HANCOCK FOUNNDATION
University of Southern California
University Avenue at 36th Street
SUNDAY EVENING, OCTOBER 25, 1953   —   8:30 P.M.
P R O G R A M

Prelude and Fugue No. 8 . . . . Bach-Weiss
From the Well-Tempered Clavichord, Book No. 1
The New Music Ensemble

Seconda Suite Miniatura . . . . Albisi
La Campanella   Barcarola   La Sorgente
Sylvia Ruderman   Ruth Benno
Elsie Baxter Moennig

Trio in G Major . . . . Beethoven
Allegro   Adagio   Andante
Lorna Wren — Flute   Gregory Bemko — Cello   Andreé Brun — Piano
Sonatine for Flute and Piano . . . . Dutilleux
Roger Stevens — Flute   Ethel Zimmerman — Piano
Due Divertimenti Brillanti, Opus 24 . . . . De Lorenzo
Sheridon Stokes — Flute   Franklyn Stokes — Clarinet   Adolph Weiss — Bassoon
PRESENTATION by the Los Angeles Flute Club of the
Leonardo De Lorenzo Flute Collection to the University
of Southern California. Acceptance by Dr. Raymond
Kendall,, Dean of the School of Music.
I N T E R M I S S I O N

Rondo Capriccioso . . . . Bennett
Sylvia Ruderman   Harold Lewis   George Poole   Don Lazenby
Conducted by William E. Hullinger
Sonata for Flute and Piano . . . . Martinu
Allegro Moderato   Adagio   Allegro poco Moderato
Arthur Hoberman — Flute   Mildred Portnoy — Piano
Perpetual Motion . . . . Paganini-Bergh
Haakon Bergh   Arthur Gleghorn
Temas de Guia Pratica . . . . Villa-Lobos
Acordei de Madrugada   (Reception of the Dawn)
O Anel   (The Ring)
O Bastáo ou mia Gata   (The Naughty Cat)
Senhora dona viuva   (The Merry Widow)
The New Music Ensemble

13

Serenade, Op. 25 . . . . Beethoven
   Ethyl Guyon — Flute   *Frederick Clint — Violin*   *Zahr Bickford — Viola*

Scene des Champs Elysees, from "Orpheus" . . . . Gluck
   Molly Michel — Flute   *James Hopkins — Accompanist*

Le Carneval Russe . . . . Ciardi
   Ethyl Guyon — Flute   *Zahr Bickford — Accompanist*

Trio for Flute, Cello, and Piano . . . . Matt Doran
   Allegro   Andante   Allegro
   Archie Wade — Flute   *Joseph DiTullio — Cello*   *Selma Kramer — Piano*

Miramar, a Serenade for the Flute Family . . . . La Monaca*
   Piccolos — Ruth Benno, Archie Wade
   C Flutes — Sylvia Ruderman, Harold Lewis, Elsie Moennig
   Bass Flute — Harry Klee   *Piano — George Covell*
   Conducted by William Hullinger

Suite in Olden Style for four Flutes . . . . Lovelock**
   Sylvia Ruderman   *Harold Lewis*
   Harry Klee   *Archie Wade*

*Composed for and dedicated to the Los Angeles Flute Club by Joseph La Monaca, octogenarian, retired flutist of the Philadelphia Symphony Orchestra.
**Composed for and dedicated to the London Flute Club.

BEETHOVEN THE ILLEGITIMATE SON OF A FLUTIST MONARCH?: At around 1805 there was at first a whisper in Vienna that Beethoven might be the illegittimate son of Frederick the Great! The story started when some one made the startled discovery that the composer, stocky, powerfully built and unusually proud and arrogant, resembled that monarch.

After a while the whisper changed into a loud talk. English and French encyclopedias printed the story: The king was known to have been not only impotent but had never been in Bonn. The affair with a musician's wife was supposed to have taken place when that sovereign was over sixty years old. When the story was told to Beethoven by his friend Wegeler, who was indignant about it, he felt neither amused nor offended and replied that he had known it for a long time. Why shouldn't the people think he was descended from a King, and wasn't he better than any of them? He was indeed the King of them all! There were, he told some of his few trusted friends, many Kings but . . . only one Beethoven!

At any rate, Beethoven's attitude toward this strange story is peculiar indeed as he never uttered a word of denial in the matter at any time.

* * *

UNUSUAL FLUTE RECORDS

Carl Philip Emanuel Bach's Sonata, D Major, for flute and continuo. Trio, B Minor, for flute, violin and continuo; Duo, E Minor, for flute and violin; and quartet G Major, for harpsichord, flute, viola and cello. The excellent flutist is Kurt Redel. (London OL 50017)

* * *

CLASSIC EDITIONS
ANTHOLOGY OF *RECORDER* MUSIC

La Noue Davenport, recorder; Jesse Tryon, violin; Earl Schuster, oboe; Patricia Davenport, harpsichord. Marjory Neal, cello. Alessandro Scarlatti; Loeillet; J. S. Bach; Teleman. (Classic Editions CE 1051)

* * *

WORKS WITH FLUTISTIC TITLES

The Flute Player (painting by Meissonier)
The Delight of Pan (book by Lord Dunsany).
The Half-naked Pan (in Franz Werfel's last book "The Star of the Unborn").
Still-Life with Flute (painting by Harley Perkins).
Flute Player (bronze sculpture by Bernard Rosenthal).
The Great God Pan (A biography by the Tramp, Played by Charlie Chaplin. Book by Robert Payne).
The Great God Pan (An Encyclopedic, Hermetic, Qabbalistic and Rosicrucian Philosophy by Manly P. Hall, Los Angeles).
La Flute de Pan (voice and piano, by Dubussy).

History of the Flute (book in French by Adrien Gerard, 1953.)
Pan the Piperess (painting by R. Hinton Perry).
Musical Interlude (painting by Andree Ruellan).
Der Pfeifer (painting by Edouard Manet).
The Amorous Flute (pamphlet of 1948 by John Maribold).
The Flute of Krishna (pamphlet by L. Adams Beck).
Le Faune (water color by Gaston La Touche).
Idyll (nude boy sitting on a wall playing on a double flute; a goat streched on ground, painting by Fortuny).
The lost flute of Jade (flute, narrator and orchestra, chinese music, by Alexander Tcherepnin, 1954).

LE JOUEUR DE FLUTE (Radio Ballet on the legend "Le charmeur desats de Hamelle" for 16 instruments, children choir, basso and a reciting voice. Conducted by its composer, Marius Constant. Rome, Italy, 1954).

* * *

DR. STEINIGER

A letter from J. Heywood, the English who uses a special flute to lure the rats to their destruction, informs me that Dr. F. Steiniger of Hannover, Germany, invited him to give a public demonstration there.

The success was such that Heywood was given an ovation in the great square and was invited to many other countries including Austria. Professor Steiniger, an authority on public health, etc., wrote a whole article and a biography of Heywood in July of 1954.

* * *

SELF GLORIFICATION

A flute player who happened to be the solo flutist in a first class "Symphony Orchestra" more by luck than by merit, not many years ago, told his pupils not to miss that afternoon's concert because he had an important solo in Ravel's "Daphne and Chloe" to perform and that there was much to learn by hearing him play it".

After the concert, before the pupils could open their mouths, he told them: "Wasn't that the most marvellous flute-playing you ever heard? Didn't that make your hair stand up on your head?" "Needless to say, however," he went on "none of you will ever achieve such mastery and finish on the flute as you have heard this afternoon!"

Can one imagine a real artist behaving that way?

* * *

BÖHM and PAGANINI. In 1828 Böhm was in Vienna for a short visit and at that time Paganini, who had given the twelfth concert was exciting to ecstacy the music loving Viennese. Bohm was so transported with Paganini's magical playing that

15

he tried to get him over to Munich. When Böhm was presented, the great genius of the violin was lying on a sofa, wrapped up in rugs, like a corpse. At first he would not consider it because he thought the city too poor, but a year later, in 1829, Böhm induced Paganini to go to Munich in which city he created a tremendous furore.

THREE PLUS THREE
FRIEDRICK WILHELM NIETZSCHE

Nietzsche, one of the greatest minds of the XIX century whose philosophy was wrongly interpreted for many years, is known to the world in particular for his "Also sprach Zarthustra," on which Richard Strauss composed one of his greatest symphonic poems asked a friend the following:

"What do you think is the chief interest of the majority of the people of most nations?" His friend replied, "The majority of the *quasi educated people* (neither educated nor illiterate) apart from food, sex and tobacco, have three other interests: Reading immoral books; liquor; toy guns and tin soldiers for the amusement of their children."

Nietzsche, whose ideal was the development of a superman, said: "Now I know why *man* is the only animal that laughs!"

A bill to ban the manufacture, importation, or sale of war toys was introduced in the Italian Chamber of Deputies in 1953. Mary Chiesa-Tebaldi, Republican, who presented the proposal with nine other legislators, said: "Children who play with war toys are subject to grave moral damages."

Things, however, haven't changed much in the last three quarter century—incidentally the great philosopher, who was vindicated only nearly fifty years after his passing in 1900, was a musical soul and was more fond of the flute than any other orchestral instrument.

* * *

MY ALBUM: I began to gather the material, not just flutistic, but of general interest in 1902, in Cape Town, South Africa. The 250 large pages full of interesting reading matter and with many illustrations was presented with much other material on the behalf of the Los Angeles Flute Club, to the University S.C. in 1953. To mention a few items: An original stamped letter by Theobald Böhm of March 29, 1857. A program of a "Concert" given by Sebastian Ott, a pupil of Böhm, dated August 12, 1855. One of the very last letters, written by Louis Maurer at the patriarcal age of 101 and dated May 25th 1932. A caricature of Giacomo Puccini by his friend Enrico Caruso. A chronological list of Musicians, by Julia E. Williams, from about 130 A. D. Numerous small pictures of famous composers from Guido D'Arezzo to Arnold Schoenberg, Edgar Varesè, Italo Montemezzi, Dimitri Shostakovich. A whole large page of *Palindrome* in many languages. Science in animal and plant life. Pictures of many great philosophers including Socrates, Plato, Spinoza, etc. Picture of a group of seven outstanding men in history: Archimedes, Beethoven, Michelangelo, Dante, Shakespeare, Newton, Aristotle. An excellent photograph of "The Los Angeles Flute Club", with its thirty members, names and holding their flutes. Autographs of: Theobald Bohm, Carl Wehner, Rudolph Tillmetz, Cesare Ciardi, Ernesto Kohler, Ferdinand Buchner, Emanuele Krakamp, Franz Doppler, Wilhelm Popp, Paul Wetzger, W. L. Barrett, Maximilian Schwedler, Roman Kukula, Leopoldo Pieroni, Antoin Sauvlet, Edward de Jong, Adolf Burose, John Finn, Abelardo Albisi, John Lemmoné, Julius Manigold, Filippo Franceschini, Albert Fransella, Adolph Goldberg, Vittorio Beniamino, Emil Prill, Paolo Cristoforetti, Wilhelm Barge, Emil Behm, A. deVroye, Louis Maurer, Fred Lax, Italo Piazza, Georges Barrère, Ary Van Leeuwen, Libero Stradivarius, Ferruccio Arrivabene, Victor Safronoff, Macaulay H. Fitzgibbon, Alberto Veggetti, Count Gilberto Gravina, Antonio Zamperoni, Emil Medicus, Christopher Welch, Dr. Dayton C. Miller, Camillo de Nardis, (who started his career as a flute prodigy), George Eastman (a flute dilettante as a young man), John Townsend Conover, Dr. Lloyd R. Watson, Alfonzo Pagnotti, Giacomo Nigro, Ulrico Virgilio, Arthur Lora, Joseph La Monaca, Carlo Tommaso Giorgi, Lambros D. Callimahos, Fortunato Sconzo, Sandor Vas, Elaine H. Clark, and the Rt. Rev. Lewis Bliss Whittemore (Bishop of the diocese of Wisconsin.) Autographs in my possession of non flutistic personalities of note are:

Arturo Toscanini, Wilfried Wagner, Jacques Ibert, Arnold Schönberg, "G. B. S." Sir Thomas Harty, Fritz Reiner, Selim Palmgren, Emil Oberhoffer, Bernardino Molinari, Madam Alma Mahler Werfel, Franz Werfel, Giuseppe Martucci, Sigfrid Karg-Elert, Howard Hanson, Wesley LaViolette, Eugene Goossens, Giovanni Bolzoni, Alfred Maurer, Onorio Ruotolo, Antonio Calitri, Grisha Goluboff, Giovanni Moranzoni, Adolph Weiss, Felix Winternitz, Gustav Tinlot, Cesare Sodero, Gustav Arlt, Donald N. Ferguson, Cesare Pugni, Alberto Salvi, Joseph Piastro, Arturo Giovannitti, Otakar Sevcik, Eugenio Pirani, May Engstrom Hoss, Radie Britain (Mrs. Edgardo Simone), Frederick Jacobi, Bernard Rogers, Paul White, Vittorio Giannini, Dusolina Giannini, Alma Vitek, Antonio De Grassi, Hazel Littlefield Smith, Edgar Varése, Madame Wouters (widow of Adolphe F. Wouters) Mario Castelnuovo - Tedesco, Mario Pilati, Richard Jates Sturger, Richard Czerwonky, Ario Flamma, Gustave Langenus, Gustave Saenger, Carl Fischer, Walter S. Fischer, David Stanley Smith, Count Chigi, Principe Alessandro Grimaldi, and others.

ARISTOS

In the "Los Angeles Examiner" of June 18, 1946, Robert Ripley in his "Believe-it-or-Not" had an excellent drawing of a Roman playing on a double flute scattering musical notes which spelled the name of Petrillo, the president of the American Federation of Musicians, because of the threatening musicians strike. The picture of the double flute player had the following comment: "Musicians were the first strikers". "Aristos, a greek flute player in charge of a flute orchestra in the Temple of Jupiter called out his men because they were barred from eating lunch in the temple". (309 B. C.)

THE FLUTIST IN LEISURE HOURS

I   Excerpts of Philosophy

II   Music Appreciation

III   Wit and Humor

EXCERPTS OF PHILOSOPHY:

SOCRATES: B. C. 469-399.
One thing only I know, and that is that I know nothing.

* * *

PLATO: B. C. 427-347.
What is generated from life? Death! and from Death? Life! Purity, knowledge?: separation and release of the soul from the body!

* * *

ARISTOTLE: B. C. 384-322.
Political science does not make men, but must take them as they come from nature. Man, when perfected, is the best of animals; but when isolated he is the worst of all. To live alone one must be either an animal or a god.

* * *

EPICTETUS: A. D. Circa 118.
Nature hath given men one tongue and two ears, that we may hear from others twice as much as we speak.
Give me by all means the shorter and nobler life, instead of one that is longer but of less account!
No man is free who is not master of himself. Freedom is the name of virtue: slavery, of vice . . none is a slave whose acts are free.
The anger of an ape—the threat of a flatterer: these deserve equal regard.

* * *

MARCUS AURELIUS: A. D. 121-80.
From Rusticus I received the impression that my character required improvement and discipline.
From my brother Severus, to love my kin, and to love truth and to love justice.
From my father, mildness of temper, no vainglory and a love of labor and perserverance.

* * *

BACON: (1561-1626)
Men are not animals erect but immortal gods. Everything is possible to man. Man must fight man, but must make war only on the obstacles that nature offers to the triumph of man.
Learning conquers or mitigates the fear of death and adverse fortune.
Fig-leaf phrases used to cover naked ignorance.

* * *

SPINOZA: (1632-1677)
To hate is to acknowledge our inferiority and our fear.
Conceit makes men a nuisance to one another.
Humility is either the hypocrisy of a schemer or the timidity of a slave.
Democracy is the most reasonable form of government.
The defect of democracy is its tendency to put mediocrity into power.
Minds are conquered not by arms but by great-

ness of soul.
It is unreasonable to wrap up things of little or no value in a precious cover.
Is God a person? Not in any human sense of this word . . . You know not what sort of God mine is. I believe that a triangle, if it could speak, would in like manner say that God is eminentaly triangular, and a circle that the divine nature is eminently circular.
He who wishes to revenge injuries by reciprocal hatred will live in misery.

* * *

VOLTAIRE: (1694-1778)
Conscience is not the voice of God, but the fear of the police. All action is dictated by egoism self-love.
Virtue is egoism furnished with a spy-glass.
Like the ass, which died of starvation between two bundles of hay, not knowing which to choose.

* * *

JEAN JACQUES ROUSSEAU: (1712-1778)
Nature is good, civilization bad. By nature all men are equal, becoming unequal only by class-made institution. The law is an invention of the strong to chain and rule the weak.

* * *

KANT: (1724-1804)
Truth for the most part is unpopular, and the proof of this statement lies in the fact that it is so seldom told.
The statement that man is the noblest work of God was never made by anybody but man, and must therefore be taken "cum grano salis."
Who am I? What am I? What can I do? What can I know? The answer to number four is that I cannot know anything . . . that is to say, the wise man is the man who knows that he does not know.
Does death end all? No, there is the litigation over the estate.
A man is miserable without a wife and is seldom happy after he gets one.

* * *

SCHOPENHAUER: (1788-1860)
A life devoted to the acquisition of wealth is useless unless we know how to turn it into joy; and this is an art that requires culture and wisdom. Only the young can live in the future, and only the old can live in the past. The character of will, is inherited from the father; the intellect from the mother.
The intellect tires, the will never; the intellect needs sleep, but the will works even in sleep.
We are unhappy married and unmarried we are unhappy. (Schopenhauer and Kant are an authority only in the second half of that sentence . . . L.D.*)
Only a philosopher can be happy in marriage, and philosophers do not marry.
Happiness depends on what we have in our heads rather than on what we have in our pockets.

THOREAU: (1817-1862)

Nothing should be claimed as truth that cannot be demonstrated.

As a whole, this world is better adapted for the production of fish than genius. Man is only the tool or vehicle—Mind alone is immortal—That is the thing.

* * *

WILLIAM JAMES: (1842-1910)

I firmly believe, myself, that our human experience is the highest form of experience extant in the universe.

I believe rather that we stand in much the same relation to the whole of the universe as our canine and feline pets do to the human life.

* * *

NIETZSCHE: (1844-1900)

It is not given to man to love and be wise.

Men are not equal; we wish to possess nothing in common.

Nothing could be more unfortunate than the supremacy of the masses.

Given good birth and eugenic breathing, the next factor in the formula of the superman is a severe school.

* * *

DEWEY: (1859-1952)

Ignorance is not bliss, it is unconciousness and slavery; only intelligence can make us sharers in the shaping of our fates.

Not perfection as a final goal, but the ever-enduring process of perfecting, maturing, refining, is the aim in living.

* * *

BERGSON: (1859-1950)

Mind is not identical with brain. Consciousness depends upon the brain, and falls with it.

Telepathy is overwhelming. There is no doubt about the sincerity of Eusapia Palladino.

* * *

SANTAYANA: (1863-1952)

I dislike the ideal of equality. The equality of unequals is inequality.

Civilization has hitherto consisted in the diffusion and dilution of habits arising in privileged centers. It has not sprung from the people. I despise above all the chaos and indecent haste of modern life.

* * *

CROCE:* 1866-1952)

Knowledge has two forms: it is either *intuitive* Knowledge or *logical* knowledge.

Man is an artist as soon as he imagines, and long before he reasons. I prefer art to metaphysics and to science: the sciences give us utility but of the thing perceived.

I believe that we shall never know exactly why a thing is beautiful.

* * *

RUSSELL: (1872-   )

There is nothing that man might not do if our splendid organization of schools and universities were properly developed and properly manned, and directed intelligently to the reconstruction of human character.

It is better to err on the side of hope than in favor of despair.

The ability to read in this age of subsidized newspapers is an impediment to the acquisition of truth.

I have come to realize that the white race isn't as important as I used to think it was.

* * *

N. B. A study of the flute shows that the wind necessary to play the instrument must have a velocity of more than 75 miles an hour.

* * *

*These two confirmed old bachelors, Kant and Schopenhauer, repeated what was said by Socrates, better and in a fewer words many centuries before, to a young farmer who asked his advice as to marry or remain single, he said: "My son, do as you want, you will repent."

*Benedetto Croce, the beloved Italian Philospher whose name means HOLY CROSS, was an agnostic.

MUSIC APPRECIATION

The musician is one who has seen the most of truth. —Socrates

Music and measure lend grace and health to the soul and to the body. —Plato

Did ever any man believe in flute-playing and not in flute players?—Plato

This is the voice which I seem to hear mourning in my ears, like the sound of the flute in the ears of the mystic. —Plato

Music is a moral law. It gives a soul to the universe, wings to the mind, flights to the imagination, a charm to sadness, gayety and life to everything else. —Plato

The man who has music in his soul will be most in love with the loveliest. —Plato

Music produces a kind of pleasure which human nature cannot do without. — Confucius.

If the king loves music, there is little wrong in the land. — Mencius

Music to the mind is as air to the body —Plato

The man that hath not music in himself, and is not moved with concord of sweet sounds, is fit for treason, stratagems, and spoils; let no man trust him. — Shakespeare

Music is a more lofty revelation than all wisdom and philosophy. — Beethoven

Music is truth — Wagner

Truthfulness is an indispensable requisite in every artistic mind, as in every upright disposition. — Wagner

Life without music would be a mistake. —Nietzsche

Such sweet compulsion doth in music lie. —Milton

To the true artist music should be a necessity and not merely an occupation; He should not manufacture music, he should live in it. — Robert Franz

Were it not for music, we might in these days say, the Beautiful is dead. — D'Israeli

Music is a shower-bath of the soul, washing away all that is impure. — Schopenhauer

It would indeed be wonderful if music were found where there is no taste for it.—Mendelssohn

Music is the only one of all the arts that does not corrupt the mind. — Montesquieu

Music is almost all we have of heaven on earth. —Addison

What is the musician's calling? Is it not to send light into the recesses of the human heart? —Shumann

Those who bring sunshine into the lives of others cannot keep it from thmselves. — Barrie

A man often forgets his friends, his native land, and sometimes his language, but the songs of childhood and youth never fade from memory. —Anon

Music would have no right to exist as an art, if that which it expresses could be painted in oil or rendered by so many words. — Hiller

Melody alone constitute the essence of all music. — Raff

Of all the liberal arts, music has the greatest influence over the passions, and it is that to which the legislator ought to give his greatest encouragement. — Napoleon I, at St. Helena

Music washes away from the soul the dust of every-day life. — Auerbach

Music is Love in search of a word. — Lanier

Music means harmony, harmony means love, love means God. — Lanier

To play in time is the politeness in music. —Anon

Where words leave off, music begins. — Heine

Music is fundamental — one of the greatest sources of life, health, strength and happiness. —Burbank

Art of arts; surpassing art. — Shelly

Music can invariably heighten the poignancy of spoken words, but words can rarely—in fact, I doubt whether they can ever—heighten the effect of musical declamation. — MacDowell

Music, that gentler on the spirit lies—than tired eyelids upon tired eyes. — Tennyson

Genius is the agency by which the supernatural is revealed to man. — Liszt

"Fair trembling Syring fled, Arcadian Pan, with such a fearful dreat;" —Anon.

And when she passed it seemed like the ceasing of exquisite music. — Longfellow

Music cannot happily reproduce that which is inanimate and which does not appeal to the heart. — Voltaire

"There is music in the sighing of a reed." —Byron

Symphony of fine musicians, or sunset, or sea waves rolling up the beach— what do they mean? They bring to the soul joy in what cannot be defined to the intellectual part or to calculation. —Whitman

Music is not a mere pastime. Its effect are both powerful and beneficial, not only upon the cultured few, but upon the (uncultured) many. —Haweis

Perfection should be the aim of every true artist. — Beethoven

The human voice is really the foundation of music. —Wagner

A song will outlive all sermons in the memory. — Giles

It seems strange to thing my violin was once a tree. It must be centuries old, and through all these years it was listening and learning and weaving in with its growth the forest melodies. — Reed

To be a true artist you must be a true man. —Weber

Every difficulty slurred over will be a ghost to disturb your repose later on. —Chopin

The one and only form of music is melody; no music is conceivable without melody and both are absolutely inseparable. — Wagner

Music is a heavenly art; nothing supplants it except true love. — Berlioz

The effect of good music is not caused by its novelty. On the contrary, it strikes us more, the more familiar we are with it. — Goethe (1)

Music is well said to be the speech of angels. —Carlyle (1)

Who among us has not sought serenity in a song? Hugo (1)

Music requires inspiration. — Gluck

It is in music, perhaps, that the soul most nearly attains the great end for which, when inspired by the Poetic Sentiment, it struggles—the creation of supernal beauty. — Poe

Music is the medicine of the breaking heart. —Hunt

Of all the pleasures of the senses, there is none which less corrupts the soul than music. —Montesquieu

Music changes; it is a matter of taste and fashion: but the human heart does not change. — Voltaire

Art has no fatherland, and all that is beautiful ought to be prized by us, no matter what clime or region has produced it. — Weber

Love is the spirit of life, and Music the life of spirit. — Coleridge

To me it is the most beautiful among the languages I know . . . It is above all in the silence of night that music is expressive and delicious. —Diderot

All music is national; it draws its character in the main from the language, which is its own, and it is the prosody of that language which gives its characted. — Rousseau

Show me the home wherein music dwells, and I shall show you a happy, peaceful and contented home. — Longfellow

There is no feeling, perhaps, except that extremes of fear and grief, that does not find relief in music—that does not make a man sing or play better. — George Eliot

Where there is no heart, there can be no music. —Hauptman

The first conception is always best and most natural. Reason may err, but feeling never. —Schumann

Every day that we spend without learning something is a day lost. — Beethoven

What is the musician's calling? It is not to send light into the deep recesses of the human heart? — Schumann

True art endures forever, and the true artist delights in the works of great minds. — Beethoven

To be really impressed by music we should, as it were, actually feel the vibrations of the instruments and voices.—Berlioz

Music is a language which genius invented for love. — De Musset

(1) At one time or another in their careers, even these "Three unmusical literary geniuses" were seduced by the fascinating and irresistible charm of the "Art of sounds."

The language of music is common to every generation, and all understood because we understood the heart. — Rossini

Music retains its divine (aspiration) and its inviolable virginity. Without melody, music becomes the most insufferable of noises — Méry

Which of the two powers—love or music—is able to elevate man to the sublimest height? Why separate one from the other? They are the two wings of the soul. — Berlioz

I know nothing more touching that a beautiful musical creation. Ah, what happiness to be able to understand this divine language! — Gounod

Let there be life, life everywhere, even in the infinity of song! — Zola

New music? New inspiration?—Go back to the old masters! — Verdi

As a rule men of letters have a horror of music (1) . . . As for my self, I enjoy any kind of music: eccentric, learned and naive. — Alphonse Daudet

The mass of the public enjoys works in poor taste. Such there have been in all ages, since they conform to a need, and for all that one may do they cannot be suppressed. — Debussy

Music and night are two sombre goddesses — Madam de Noailles

Music is ominipresent. —Lamaitre

What love is to man, music is to the arts and to mankind. — Weber

We cannot imagine a complete education of a man without music. — John P. Richter

Music is pure sentiment itself, dispensing entirely with the language of words, with which alone the intellect can operate — Liu Yutang

The language of music is infinite; it contains all; it is able to express all. — Balzac

"The soft complaining flute
    In dying notes discovers—
        The woes of hopeless loves,
Whose dirge is whispered by the warbling flute."
                                            —Dryden

"E'en Apollonius might commend his flute,
    The music, winding through the stops, upsprings
        To make the player very rich." — Mrs. Browing

* * *

WIT AND HUMOR:

It's a good thing to think twice before you speak and then keep right on thinking—

Trouble begins at the cradle and ends at the grave. At least we hope it does.—

Modern furniture often becomes antique before it is paid for.—

Drink is dangerous to married men. It makes them see double and feel single.—

The modern bathing girl is being vaccinated on her face so it won't be noticed.—

When a politician talks of the people, it is sometimes hard to tell whether he says "the masses" or "them asses."—

20

The really happy man is one who has mastered the art of listening to his wife and radio at the same time.—

A girl is never happy until some boy comes along and makes her miserable.—

The poorest man in the world is he who has nothing except money.—

The head never begins to swell until the mind stops growing. —

Even though she refuses him, a woman always admires the good judgement of the man who proposes to her.—

A child prodigy usually reaches maturity and obscurity about the same time.—

(1) One of these, *Théophile Gautier saids "Music is the most costly of noises."*

It would help us all if we had some of the common sense we think the other fellow ought to have.—

Work is a fascinating thing; most people can sit and look at it for hours.—

It is often the case that love at first sight doesn't survive a second look.—

The only way to get along with some people is to carefully conceal your opinion of them.—

A man has to be a little foolish now and then to keep from going entirely crazy.—

You may fill a man's head with education, but still his ideas will depend on how full his stomach is.—

Some people are healthy only because no self respecting germ would go near them.—

Even an honest man will steal a glance when a pretty girl passes by.—

Some remarks are like medicine—not so bad if they are swallowed quickly.—

Many a woman has married for a living and starved for love.—

Others loaf, but you merely take a rest—

The people who live longest are those who have too much sense to worry and those who haven't enough sense to worry.—

A girl is considered beautiful these days if she looks as good after washing her face as she did before she washed it.—

The fellow with the inferiority complex sometimes has a pretty good sense of values.—

Lots of people actually believe that their troubles are interesting to others.—

One reason why the talkative person knows so little is because he can't listen and learn.—

Only a fool will open his mouth and shut his eyes when engry.—

If some persons really knew themselves, they would be ashamed of the acquaintance.—

Is isn't always what we think we are—it's what other people know we are.—

It costs nothing to think, as long as you don't think out loud.—

Men who have nothing else to apologize for should apologize for being on earth.—

If your heart prompts you to do a good deed, do it immediately before you have heart failure.—

Wisdom is merly common sense in a uncommon degree.—

If we could only borrow money on our good intentions, "poverty" would soon be an obsolete word.—

Possibly the explosion of the theory that two can live cheaply as one is responsible for a good many divorces.—

Many a man's self-conceit is due to ignorance.—

Some men are satisfied with half a loaf, and some loaf all the time.—

The pessimist has an ingrowing grudge against humanity in general and himself in particular.—

Give a pessimist a piece of rope and he will . . . hang himself with it. Give an optimist a piece of rope and he will . . . start a cigar factory.—

No artist can paint a self-made man as big as he thinks he is.—

The man who has no secrets from his wife has either no secrets or no wife.—

Better praise a man while he is alive and abuse him after he is dead than reverse the order.—

There seem to be more blockheads in the world than wooden legs.—

Some men are never happy unless they are in a position to make others miserable.—

Many a man that "rises to the occasion" doesn't know when to sit down.—

An optimist is a cross-eyed man who is thankful he isn't bow-legged.—

It is better to remain silent, at the risk of being thought a fool, than to speak and remove all doubts.—

Any dead fish can float down stream but it takes a live one to swim up.—

A wise man makes more opportunities than he finds.—

Don't rest on last year's laurels—they won't pay this year's bills!

I am a great believer in luck. The harder I work the more of it I seem to have.—

Did you ever notice that the quietest thing about a busy man is his tongue?—

A bachelor is an incomplete animal, and useless as an odd half of a pair of scissors.—

* * *

SOMETHING IN A NAME

SOCIALISM—You have two cows and give one to your neighbor.

COMMUNISM—You have two cows; the Government takes both and gives you the milk.

FASCISM—You have two cows; the Government takes both and sells you the milk.

NAZISM—You have two cows; the Government takes both and shoots you.

NEW DEALISM—You have two cows; the Government takes both, shoots one, milks the other and throws the milk away.

CAPITALISM—You have two cows; you sell one and buy a bull.

—*New York Times.*

MY COMPLETE STORY OF THE FLUTE
QUASI INDEX

* * *

ENTHUSIASTIC ACCLAIM OF THE FIRST EDITION OF "MY COMPLETE STORY OF THE FLUTE"

Your book is the most glorious contribution to Flute Literature and History." — E. W. Garside, President of Sydney Flute Club, Australia. (An intimate friend of John Lemmoné and Dame Nellie Melba.)

* * *

"Every time I need inspiration and encouragement, I read a few pages from your wonderful book, "My Complete Story of the Flute." — Kay Kennedy (Sixteen year old girl of great talent, being solo flute of the Tulsa, Oklahoma University Symphony Orchestra. She is giving a full flute recital every year.)

* * *

"Your book continues to be an inspiration to me every time I read a few pages." — Charles Russell Trowbridge, Denver, Colorado. (Flute dilettante)

* * *

"Your book is really terrific . . . and I can see many pleasant hours reading and reviewing it." — J.M. Grolimund, Elkhart, Indiana. (Flute dilettante and President of the Selmer Musical Instrument factory)

* * *

"My Complete Story of the Flute" fascinated us to such an extent that even our meals were forgotten. Your book has been given the place of honor, next to our Harvard Dictionary of Music in our new book case." — Edna Walraven, Oroville, Wash. (Mrs. Walraven's son constructed an interesting clay flute on which he can play several tunes)

* * *

"I feel that your book should be in every flutist's library and I will do all I possibly can to popularize it." — Emil Stock, New York. (Treasurer New York Flute Club and 50 years with Carl Fischer Inc.)

* * *

Dear Mr. DeLorenzo,
I am disappointed that my mother's interesting letter on page 419 appears anonymously in your fine book. You have my permission to sign her name to what she wrote there in any future edition of your book. — Marcelline Hall Sanford. (Daughter of Grace Hall Hemingway and sister of Ernest Hemingway)

* * *

"My Complete Story of the Flute contains a wealth of material which makes it a most important contribution to music literature." — Arthur Henderson, Chicago, Ill. (A musician and flute dilettante)

* * *

Thank you for including me in your very wonderful book. — Matt. H. Doran. (A Los Angeles young flutist, composer and teacher of composition and history)

"I wish to congratulate you for your wonderful achievement—namely, your great book on the history of the flute." — Anthony Bondi, M.D., Rochester, New York.

* * *

I am very proud and happy to have your book autographed by both of you — Serena Cummings, Redondo Beach, California. (A lady patron of the art)

* * *

"Mr. De Lorenzo's book, "My Complete Story of the Flute" is certainly a masterpiece, and without you, Dr. Breco could not have been given to the world. It is a rare book for all times, and one which can be enjoyed by everyone as well as musicians." — Lida Ross Conover, Palos Verdes Estates, California. A great lover and patron of music whose son, Townsend and his wife Mary, are enthusiastic flute dilettanti.)

* * *

Your great book has immortalized you. — Vincenzo Pezzi. (Bassoon virtuoso, teacher at the Eastman School of Music and soloist for many years with the Rochester Philharmonic)

* * *

"I have just finished Mr. De Lorenzo's fascinating book and in learning of your part in the publication, dear Dr. Breco, I think a word of appreciation is due you, as well as the author." — Elizabeth D. Fisher, Rolling Hills, California. (A musician graduate from Oberlin Conservatory and a Patron of the Arts.)

* * *

Now, besides your other accomplishments, you are an author. How proud we are of you. — Beatrice Peterson, Granada Hills, California. (Noted Kindergarten teacher, Minneapolis, Minn.)

* * *

"As an enthusiastic, though unskilled amateur flute player, I have always been interested in the history and cultural aspects of the flute. I am writing this little note to tell you how much I enjoyed your book, for I found all sorts of new and interesting facts in it." — Irving E. Dayton, Cornell University Laboratory of Nuclear Studies, Ithica, New York.

* * *

It is with much satisfaction and pleasure that I now possess your colossal work "My Complete Story of the Flute." I find it most interesting as well as profitable reading. It should be in the private library of every flutist as well as all public libraries. — Wm Hullinger, Los Angeles, Calif. (Noted flute teacher and President of the L.A. Flute Club)

* * *

"A wealth of information, gay spirit, and the story of your own courageous life makes your book a treasure. I have had hours of delight in reading it. May I bring it for your autograph? I am perfectly delighted to hear about the Order of Knighthood of Merit bestowed on you by the Italian Government. It is an honor you so well deserve and I hope it is a matter of real satisfaction to you to have your beautiful book recognized in this way." — Hazel Littlefield Smith, Palos Verdes Estates, California. (A Poet and Musician and Patron of the Arts.)

* * *

"Congratulations to you. You should feel repaid indeed for the work of many years. How good of you to let me know of the "Ordine dei Cavalieri." Really, it is splendid and mother joins me in felicitations." — Elaine H. Clark, Rochester, New York. (An enthusiastic flutist dilettante of unusual culture.)

* * *

"I have read your book and I think it is a wonderful work. The years that it took you to compile . . . . one shudders at the thought of it. Please let me know where I can obtain a copy of your "Nine Etudes" published in Germany, many years ago?" — John Wummer (Solo Flutist, New York Philharmonic, New York.)

* * *

"I wish to express my great admiration for your magnificent book, it is a veritable masterpiece and I will tell you so in person in a few days." — Ary Van Leeuwen, Los Angeles, California. (One of the world's most famous and accomplished flute virtuosi)

* * *

"Bravo De Lorenzo. Your book, a great job well done." — Arthur Lora, New York. (One of the finest musicians and composers among flute players; for many years solo flutist Metropolitan Opera, N.B.C. Symphony and Teacher, Julliard School of Music.)

* * *

"The Division of Music Library of Congress, Washington, D. C., requests me to write a book review on "My Complete Story of the Flute" and in order to do a good job, I took time off and read the entire work. I enjoyed it very much and trust your labors will be appreciated in a substantial way. Many congratulations for a very interesting and instructive book, which all flutists should appreciate." — Emil Medicus, Ashville, North Carolina. (Noted all over the world, also because of his "The Flutist" Magazine.)

* * *

Only by chance I came across your very excellent book. The particular person who had a complimentary copy of your beautifully autographed book, said thoughtlessly to an enthusiastic friend, "why should you buy a copy when you can read mine?" I think that a person thus honored should,

instead, purchase an extra copy to present to h neighborhood library or to a friend.
Ed Wadleigh, Manhattan Beach (a young man c good culture, interested in books and the arts) Flute Player (painting by Cornelia Rultenberg The Flute Player (drawing by Charles Bargue The Infant Pan (oil painting by Guido Bach Still-Life with Flute (painting by Harley Perkins Le Foueur de Flote (price radio ballet — I charmeur des rats de Hamelle — by Marius Constant, 1954).
"I must tell you again and again how much am enjoying your book. I am so familiar with s many of those names, I feel I know them personal ly." — Edward J. Rankin, Yakima, Washington (Teacher of violin and flute for many years.

* * *

"Your book is not only very attractive looking, i is most enjoyable, very lively and entertaining. think the work has turned out beautifully." — Wendell Hoss, Glendale, California. (One of th finest French Horn players, teacher and con ductor, and President of the Los Angeles Frencb Horn Club.)

* * *

"My warmest and sincerest congratulations for your colossal book. It is a monument to you and to your charming wife who collaborated so wonderfully and beautifully." — Joseph La Monaca Philadelphia. (Composer of numerous works for orchestra, band, chamber music, including flute quartets and a grand Opera. Thirty years member of the Philadelphia Symphony.)

* * *

"I have seen a copy of your new book, "My Story of the Flute" and I think it is very interesting. Dr. Vincent, who is a flutist himself and who owns a copy of it, commented to me very highly on it the other day." — Gustay O. Arlt, University of California. (Dr. Arlt, musicologist, organist and oboist, is Dean of the Graduate Division, Los Angeles, California, and translator of Franz Werfel's last book "Star of the Unborn.")

* * *

"I could hardly wait to devour the pages of your beautiful book, which shows a lifetime of research. The Photograph of Edgardo's "Pan" is excellent and I am pleased that you included it." — Radie Britain Simone, Hollywood, California. (Noted woman composer, pianist and teacher)

* * *

"Dear Dr. Breco: I took the book, "My Complete Story of the Flute" home and found it very interesting, especially your comment regarding classical music and jazz. I am sure you have a lot of kindred sympathy. The book is now in the College Library." — Oscar L. Parker, East State College, Ada, Oklahoma.

● ● ●

24

"Your book is a real accomplishment and the contents represent tremendous research. I like the style, informal, and easy to read. Also, the various incidents and episodes keep the reader interested and amused." — Lloyd R. Peterson, Minneapolis, Minnesota. (Prominent Attorney . . . plays piano, banjo, and is fond of jazz, football and fishing.)

* * *

"I read your book with great interest. It certainly taught me a lot I never knew about my favorite instrument and the men concerned with it. — David Colvig, Houston, Texas. (Flutist with the Houston Symphony.)

* * *

"I read your book with enthusiasm and the chapter on my father is wonderful tribute. Let me congratulate you on the monumental achievement. I remember vividly the many times you graced our home with your warm personality and superlative talents." — Eugenia Maurer Fuerstenberg, Stoneham, Massachusetts. (Daughter of Louis Maurer, the artist who played the flute at one hundred years.)

* * *

"Just read your splendid book. All congratulations on completing such a tremendous task." — Edward Mellon, Austin, Texas. (Music teacher, University of Texas.)

* * *

"In 1914 I bought your L'Indispensabile, which I worked on until I wore the book out. Now the third copy is falling to pieces. Your new book on the history of the flute is most interesting and instructive." — Raymond E. Selders, M.D., Houston, Texas (Dr. Selders has an unusual personality in the world of fine flute dilettanti. He owns several flutes, including two gold and one platinum . . . Dr. Selders has met most of the eminent flute virtuosi in America.)

* * *

"Mr. Compton Mackenzie, the celebrated novelist and writer and editor of the "Gramaphone" invited me, last autumn to write an article on the flute from the point of view of the gramaphone records, and I should like to take the opportunity of mentioning Mr. De Lorenzo's fascinating and most interesting book, when I can bring myself to prepare the material for the article." — Robert W. F. Potter, Cheshire, England. (This long and interesting letter from Mr. Potter of the Medical School, University of Liverpool, was written to "The Citadel Press, New York.)

* * *

"The changing consciousness gives a pre-glimpse of your future, Mr. De Lorenzo. I had thought that you had reached the Top in Music, but not yet. Your present marvelous achievements are not a preparation for that which is to be at a later time. All humanity is to learn to love you. You will have earned it, and the quiet ever good in you will be free and unfettered by all acclaim

that will come to you." — Archie Savage, Fallbrook, California. (Mr. Savage, the Gandhi of the flutistic world, has been the writer's spiritual Mentor for a number of years.)

* * *

"Your beautiful book, which gave me great pleasure, I am presenting to the University of Heidelberg. Two young lady flutists wanted so much to buy a copy, but its price is beyond their purse. If you could only allow a discount, many I am sure would want to have your book here." — Walter Mang, Heidelberg, Germany.

* * *

"Allow me to congratulate you on your book. No one knows better than I, the vast amount of work and research that has gone into it. Please accept my sincere admiration for what you have accomplished." — L. A. Haynes. (Mrs. William S. Haynes, Boston, Mass.)

* * *

"Your beautiful book is an excellent piece of work in every way. I am delighted to be a part of it." — Wesley La Violette. (Dr. LaViolette is noted as a composer, writer, teacher and President of the American Operatic Laboratory Inc., Los Angeles, California)

* * *

"Your excellent book of much historical value is surely most impressive. You have done us a great honor by including our Philharmonic Woodwind Quintet. I am sure it must have given you real pleasure in preparation of it, altho the research work required, must have been somewhat exhausting. Heartiest Congratulations." — Arthur M. See, Executive Director, Rochester Civic Music Association, Rochester, New York.

* * *

"I wish to express my appreciation for the great pleasure reading your book gave me. It holds a prominent place in my library. — Chester V. J. Anderson, Dallas, Texas. (|Dilettante flutist, well versed in flute matters.)

* * *

"I congratulate you on your excellent book. However, many are disappointed here, that you did not accord more prominence to one of England's greatest Flutists, Geoffrey Gilbert, Principal of the B.BC. Orchestra." — Arthur P. Smith, London, England. (A flute dilettante who is in the music publishing and wholesale music trade, the second person to call my attention to Geoffrey Gilbert. Mr. Smith also calls my attention on two omissions: Harold Clark, Professor of Trinity College of Music, London and member of Covent Garden Opera Orchestra, and Richard Adeney, at one time Principal London Philharmonic.)

* * *

"As an admirer of your personality and of your book, "My Complete Story of the Flute" I shall treasurer an autograph of you. You will make me happy in sending it to me." — Ernest F. Manfred, New York. (Dilettante flutist)

* * *

"Can't tell you in words how much I have enjoyed your wonderful book, and so have several of my friends who are reading it." — Florence Jepson, Wayzata, Minnesota. (Writer, lecturer and Patron of the Arts.)

* * *

"You, and only you, Maestro De Lorenzo, could have conceived such a precious book, which is indispensable to every lover of the flute, throughout the world." — Rodolfo Cafaro, Rome, Italy. (Enthusiastic flutist and business man.)

* * *

"As soon as we got your book, we found it of such interest that Mario and I practically snapped it from each other's hands, with much fun." — Elise Frosali, Los Angeles, California. (Mario Frosali, Elise's husband, an excellent musician, graduate from the Conservatory of Milan and who enjoyed the friendship of Puccini, is also an excellent liutaio, maker of violins, violas and celli.)

* * *

"We were delighted with the beautiful and elegant edition of your "Story of the Flute" and its interesting material throughout." — Principe Alessandro Licastro Grimaldi, Rome, Italy. (A young nobleman of great culture, who is also a poet, writer and Patron of the Arts.)

* * *

"Your book will be a treasured source of reading long after many of the present day "best sellers" have been forgotten." — Mrs. Clara Meyer (Public Stenographer, Redondo Beach, California, who worked with me in writing my book.)

* * *

"I wish to express my appreciation. Your book is one of the treasured volumes of my library. — Auten F. Bush. (Noted City Attorney of Hermosa Beach, California.)

* * *

"Thank you for your autograph in "My Complete Story of the Flute." You surely must have had a fabulous career in meeting and associating with so many world famous personalities." — John Vincent, University of California, Los Angeles. (Writer, composer, educator and conductor. Dr. Vincent started his career as a professional flutist in Boston.)

* * *

"Louis Albert Clavero Contreras is honored to salute the famous artist, Leonardo De Lorenzo, who has created a great and inspiring book for all lovers of the flute." (Professor Clavero is a noted flute virtuoso, composer and teacher at the Conservatory of San Diego de Chile.)

"A pupil of mine just arrived from London showed me your great book on the history of the Flute which delighted me. Hearty congratulations." — André Neumier (Professor at the Conservatory, Verviers, Belgium.)

* * *

"My sincerest congratulations for your wonderful book, which is a "Dictionary of the Flute." Most of the new American flute compositions, I do not know. Are they all published? Some of the outstanding new flute works here are; Frank Martin's "Ballade" for flute and string orchestra. Honegger's "Concerto da Camera" for flute, English Horn and strings; R. d'Alessandro, "Sonata" and "Concerto" with orchestra." — Auréle Nicolet Berlin. (Nicolet was appointed solo flute with the Berlin Philharmonic in 1949 at the age of 23. He is known there as the phenomenal flutist.

* * *

"Your, "Complete Story of the Flute" is completely different from what we expect from a book about one special musical instrument, because it covers a tremendous variety of interesting stories in addition to the history of the "Flute," its "Music" and the "Performer:" Starting with Confucius (who played melancholy tunes on the flute.), the old Chinese, Egyptians, Greeks, up to "Exotic Lands," "Europe" and the "Americas." Recently I mailed a copy of your book as a "birthday present" to one of my friends in Atlanta, Georgia." — Paul Stoye, Palos Verdes Estates, California. (Professor Stoye, concert pianist, composer and teacher, was head of the Piano Department for 28 years at the Drake University.)

* * *

"The next edition of your book, I sincerely wish from a flute-player's physiologist viewpoint at least, that you will mention "Physiology in Relation to Playing the Flute" by J. Roos. It was published in Holland in 1935 and its author died in a concentration camp in 1938." — Francis Edward Picklow. (A Physiologist student with a Masters Degree and working for his Ph. D., at the Columbus Ohio State University.)

* * *

"I read your great book from cover to cover in one day. I simply couldn't put it aside without finishing." — Carlo Tommaso Giorgi, Viareggio, Italy. (Professor Giorgi, writer, musician, flutist, and world famous since his Giorgi flute of over 70 years ago, is now 97 and lives in Viareggio, a seaside resort near Pisa. He reads and writes without the aid of glasses and, he says, sleeps like a young man of 25.)

* * *

"My Complete Story of the Flute" is one of the most interesting books I have ever read. Also, your wonderful "L'Indispensabile" which I bought in 1914, I am still using. — Daniel J. McKenna, University of Detroit, School of Law. (Dr. McKenna, teacher of Law, is an enthusiastic flute dilet-

ante and an admirer of Giorgi and his keyless
lute, is now (1954) constructing one of polystyrene plastic material.)
* * *

Your book is indeed surprising, both in the
amount of information it contains and the amount
of pleasure one gets from it. I feel strongly that it
will, like Dicken's novels, furnish increased pleasure and education with each reading. For that
reason I shall read your book over and
over again." — Phineas S. Shaw, Greensboro
North Carolina. (A succssful business man, writer
and an able dilettante flutist since childhood. Mr.
Shaw was born in London, England. He has also
written an interesting script on my book which we
hope will be filmed.)
* * *

"I don't know when I have enjoyed a book as much
as your "My Complete Story of the Flute;" it is
precious." — Mildred Mooney, Palos Verdes
Estates, California. (Pianist, teacher, and authority
in Chinese culture, through her long sojourn in
that country where she was born.)
* * *

"Please allow us to express our admiration for
your great book and your new flute quartet in
which we were privileged to play. You seem to
have the power to create things which can never
die! The freshness of spirit and vitality which they
display seem to live and draw us into a central
spirit where all sense of passage of time is lost."—
Mr. and Mrs. Arthur C. Lytle, Jr., Palos Verdes
Estates, California. (Mr. Lytle is an able engineer
and his wife often plays duets with him, while he
is away, with a prepared tape recording the other
flute.)
* * *

"Your book is an accomplishment of the first
order. It honors the whole flutistic world, Italy,
and the great land of which you are a citizen.
The Minister of Education, also had words of high
praise for your beautiful book." — Arrigo
Tassinari, Roma, Italia. (Professor Tassinari, well-
known all over Europe, is the esteemed flute teacher of Santa Cecila, Rome, from which Severino
Gazzelloni, one of the most accomplished flutists
of the younger generation graduated recently.
Gazzelloni plays on a platinum flute.)

A FEW CORRECTIONS:
Following page 305 the French horn player and
the Oboist (standing) should read Fred Klein,
Robert Sprenkle. Three pages later should be Lambert C. Flack.
305, Nillson should be Nilsson.
337, Nikish should be Nikisch.
353, Haydn died 1809, not 1890.
353, Mozart born 1756, not 1765.
359, Pijer should be Pijper.
359, Ibert born 1890 not 1900.
477, Davis should be Davies.

27

TO MODINA

On My 80th Birthday (August 29, 1955) And Our 41st Anniversary
With Gratitude

ADDENDA NUMBER II TO

"MY COMPLETE STORY OF THE FLUTE"

THUMBNAIL BIOGRAPHIES AND OTHER MATERIAL

BY LEONARDO DE LORENZO

FOREWORD

"What is your definition of Music?" I will endeavor to submit three answers from three different sources:

"Music is an expression of the dignity of man, the potential greatness and worth of the individual. To us in liberal education, it may be a liberating force freeing the spirit of man for its greatest intellectual, aesthetic and moral achievements, a means of ridding the mind of the nonessentials, or of developing a kind of objectivity.

"Music expresses the outreach of man's mind and the yearning of man's heart, and seeks to express perfection and depth of feeling. It possesses a universality in its language and appeal transcending time and space, and is therefore a socially uniting factor."
                —Dr. Arthur G. Coons, President of Occidental College

*   *   *

"Music is one of the greatest blessings of mankind, and to be without musical training is almost equal to being illiterate—we are just living in the age of music today. It is pumped into our houses via radio like water and electricity. And the more people understand it the more they are able to enjoy it. Music is inspiring! And anything that is inspiring is elevating."
                —Professor Paul Stoye, Teacher, Composer, pedagogue;
                28 years head of the Piano Dept., Drake University.

*   *   *

"Music is the only international language and the eternal, divine expression of God."—Leonardo De Lorenzo.

*   *   *

N.B. This pamphlet is not for sale. It has been written in gratitude to all those who have sent me their beautiful letters of encouragement in regard to "My Complete Story of The Flute."

TO MODINA

On My 80th Birthday (August 29, 1955) And Our 41st Anniversary
With Gratitude

ADDENDA NUMBER II TO

"MY COMPLETE STORY OF THE FLUTE"

THUMBNAIL BIOGRAPHIES AND OTHER MATERIAL

BY LEONARDO DE LORENZO

TABLE OF CONTENTS

THUMBNAIL BIOGRAPHIES

THUMBNAIL BIOGRAPHIES

BAKER, JULIUS: (Contemporary)
Member of the Bach Aria Group. One of the finest and most brilliant flute virtuosi is Julius Baker. His many records, in ensemble and solo, in particular the Ibert Concerto with Orchestra, places Baker on a pedestal all his own.

BERGH, HAAKON: (1913-)
Born in Gregory, South Dakota, Bergh is an excellent flutist and composer. Came to Los Angeles in 1927. Studied flute with Julius Furman and music and theory with Ernest Toch, Joseph Schillinger and Harold Byrns. Was with the NBC Symphony (Toscanini) and has been with the RKO Orchestra from 1948 to 1954 in Los Angeles. In the Army from 1943 to 1946 he was in charge of bands in New York. Bergh is a member of Fine Arts Winds Players, Los Angeles. Also the Los Angeles Chamber Symphony and played many obbligatos and made records with Jeanette McDonald, Rise Stevens, Katherine Grayson and Diana Durbin. Bergh was many times soloist on ABC New York, also on National Hookup and "Music of Today." His excellent transcription of Paganini's "Moto Perpetuo" for two flutes and piano was performed with great success for the first time at the annual "Flute Club Concert" at the University of Southern California, October 25, 1954, with Arthur Gleghorn as his able assisting colleague.

BERGNER, CARL: (Contemporary)
On December 19, 1954 at the Carl Fischer Hall. New York, a program of eighteenth-century masterpieces was offered by Mr. Bergner and Mr. Puyana, under the auspices of the New York Flute Club. Together, they performed the Handel Sonata No. 3 for Flute and Harpsichord; a Sonata by Giardini; and two marvelous pieces by Francois Couperin, the "Musette de Choisi" and the "Musette de Taverni." Mr. Bergner played Franchetti's "Dirge" for flute alone (the only modern work on the program). Mr. Puyana (whose full name is Raphael Antonio, too long for headings) performed sonatas for harpsichord by Scarlatti, Freixanet, and Albeniz, and works by Rameau and Couperin. Mr. Bergner, who is Chairman of the Woodwind Department of the Hart College of Music in Hartford, Conn., played with admirable taste and musicianship. And Mr. Puyana,, one of the most talented pupils of Wanda Landowska, proved himself not only a vivid and original musical temperament but a real master of his instrument. (from Musical America).

BUCCI, BELISARIO: (1873-1947)
Savant, scholar, poet, scientist, musician, etc., whose vast knowledge on almost any subject under the sun, was positively fabulous! Bucci lived in Naples next to an old, large and rather mysterious castle. When the noted sculptor Onor Ruotolo's saintly mother decided to send her gift son to Bucci for private instruction, she impress upon the little boy of nine the importance addressing the great man not by name, whi would lack reverence, but as Maestro and a that he must be alert and attentive to ever word his teacher spoke. Also, she said, he has a infinite variety of things to teach you besid Latin, if you are worthy.

When the portone or huge front door clos behind the lad as he went for his first lesson, I had to cross a large patio of cobble stones cover with weeds. Before reaching one of the thr large stone stairs, dark and gloomy, he w terrified by a creeping noise close by—it was snake! But as he started, trembling, to ascend th interminable six flights of stairs, all fears we forgotten as he heard heavenly music. It w Maestro Belisario Bucci playing the flute to h birds. He instructed them patiently every da for two hours until they became proficient. The he set them free, well knowing that most c them would soon return and sing for him h favorite tunes from the window or other place to show their gratitude. He went to the marke regularly every week to select his birds, for som of which he had to pay a big price.

Bucci was indeed a remarkable personality i the long list of flute dillettanti and I am happ to add him to my list. I learned about him fror a booklet entitled "Il Mio Primo Maestro, (Poemetto) by the noted sculpture, writer an poet Onorio Ruotolo, whose teacher in his ar was another artist of international fame, Vincenz Gemito. An interesting book "Ruotolo" Man an Artist, with more than 100 beautiful reproduc tions and with an unusually sympathetic "Appre ciation" by Frances Winwar and published b Liveright, New York, is worth having in one library. John Macy's great book of 672 page entitled "Story of World Literature" is beautifull illustrated by Onorio Ruotolo.

BROOK, PAIGE: (Contemp.)
On Feb. 12, 1955 in New York at the Kaufma Auditorium the "Philharmonic Chamber Ensem ble" gave an excellent performance of the work premier of Paul Creston's "Suite" for piano, flut and violin. The composer was at the piano, Paig Brook the able flutist and David Kates the violinst.

CAFARO, RODOLFO: (1890-)
One of the most enthusiastic flutists of any time anywhere is Cafaro. In his younger days Cafaro was a professional flutist occupying prominen positions not only in Italy but also in England Scotland and South America. However, for a number of years Cafaro has retired from active participation and devotes his time to a stationery

ore in Rome, Italy. Because of his extensive
musical library and affable personality it should
e a rendezvous for all flutists near and far. He
speaks English well. So my colleagues, in Rome
to not fail to call on Mr. Cafaro, at Via R.
razioli Lante N. 8 (angolo Piazza Giovane
talia) Roma.

CARATGE, F.: (Contemp.)
solo flutist at the Opera Comique, Paris and also
if the Concerts Lamoureux.

CARMIGNANI, MARIO: (1910-   )
Born in Roma and graduated from the Conserva-
ory of Santa Cecilia, Carmignani studied with
Alberto Veggetti. He is solo flutist at the "Teatro
ell' Opera," Roma, Italy.

CHAPMAN, FREDERICK BENNETT
    (1887-   )
English flutist, teacher and writer of the pamphlet
'Flute Technique" (Oxford University Press,
London). Chapman graduated in Science at Lon-
on University before studying the flute with
Robert Murchie. At one time he taught flute at
Reading University.

CLERICI, SILVIO: (Contemp.)
This excellent flutist who studied at the Santa
Cecilia Conservatory, Roma, with Alberto Veggetti, is the flute teacher at the Torino Conserva-
ory.

DEFRANCESCO, EDMUND:
    (Contemp.)
Professor of flute at the Conservatory of Lausanne,
Switzerland, and first flute in the Lausanne
Chamber Orchestra.

DELANEY, CHARLES: (1925-   )
Flutist, composer and teacher at the University
of Illinois. Has studied flute with Lamar Stringfield, Rex Elton Fair, Alfred Fenbuoque and
Marcel Moyse. He says: "You might be interested
to know that we have a Flute Club here (30-40
members) and give six concerts a year. Also, in
the summer I teach at Transylvania Music Camp
(near Asheville, N. C.) and know Emil Medicus
and Lamar Stringfield (my teacher) well. Every
now and then they come over for concerts and
we have a good time. My pupils and I have enjoyed your book immensely." DeLaney's academic degrees: B.S. (Psychology) and M.M.

D'INVERNO, ARMANDO: (Contemp.)
This excellent flutist and teacher was for a number of years Principal at the San Carlo Opera,
Naples. Now because of his age he has been replaced by a younger flutist. However, D'Inverno
is still a member of the San Carlo, playing second
flute.

DUFRENE, FERNAND: (Contemp.)
He is the excellent flutist of the Wind Quartet of
the French Radio Orchestra. The other members

are: Jules Goetgheluck, Oboe; Maurice Clinquen-
ois, clarinet; Renè Plessier, bassoon and Louis
Courtinat, French horn. They make recordings
for Engel disks in the twentieth-century works
for woodwinds.

EMMETT, DANIEL DECATUR:
    (1815-1904)
Born Oct. 29th, Emmett played both violin and
flute and is the composer of "Dixie." An Ohio
Yankee, he was a versatile person as musician
and man. The composer of the marching song of
the Confederacy and also composed "Old Dan
Tucker" when he was only 15. One morning in
1859 Bryant, with whose minstrel show he was
touring, asked Emmett to make up a tune for the
show's "Walkaround" and he produced "Dixie"
in one afternoon. Its popularity was prompt and
wide. The Ohio memorial to him is fitting, though
he really needs none besides the constant popularity of "Dixie."

FAHLBUSCH, AGNES: (Contemp.)
This unusually talented flutist from Leipzig whom
I met in New York in 1913 on her short visit to
America, was an enthusiastic pupil of Schwedler
and, of course just as against the Böhm flute for
no other reason than to be faithful to her beloved
teacher. In her long letter to me in 1955 (42
years after our first meeting) because she had
seen a copy of "My Complete Story of the Flute"
she was as enthusiastic as ever in regard to flute
and flute playing.

FRENZ, HANS: (Contemp.)
One of the finest and most accomplished flute
virtuosi of present Germany is Frenz. He has
taken over all the artistic activities of the late
and much admired Emil Prill, with whom Frenz
studied. He lives at Charlottenburg, near Berlin.

FRITZSCHE, REINHARD: (Contemp.)
From this excellent musician, flutist and teacher
of whom I wrote on page 234, I received in
January of 1955, an extremely interesting flute
composition in beautiful manuscript, like print.
It is in appreciation of "My Complete Story of
the Flute." It says: To Leonardo De Lorenzo,
Tre pezzi per Flauto Solo 1. "Improvvisation,"
2. "Capriccio," 3. "Epilog." It is very original,
modern and not too difficult.

GILBERT, DAVID: (1936-   )
Born in Huntingdon, Pa. Studied flute with
Harold MacDougal, Donald Adcock, Earl Slocum.
Also with Charles DeLaney, Walfrid Kujala and
Joseph Mariano. Gilbert is member of the Rochester Symphony and Civic Orchestra with which
he has been soloist. He is now, 1955, majoring in
composition at the Eastman School of Music and
has to his credit a string quartet, a trio in three
movements for flute and two clarinets and a suite
in three movements for two flutes.

HAGEMANN, PAUL: (1875-1932)

A nobleman and a banker from Copenhagen, Denmark. Hagemann is one of the most distinguished flute dillettante of Europe. Paul Hindemith has dedicated his "Canon" for two flutes to him and Igor Stravinsky, among other composers, has dedicated one of his flute pieces to Hagemann.

JACCHIA, AGIDE: (1875-1932)

Born in Lugo, Italy, and died at Siena. He studied at Parma Conservatory, with Cristoforetti, and graduated with honors in 1896. Won many prizes as a flute protegè. However, his love for conducting which he studied with Mascagni at Pesaro, soon made him give up his flute. Jacchia's career as conductor was brilliant. He made his debut at Brescia and, soon after, Ferrara followed. In 1902 he toured America with Mascagni. Back in America after conducting in Milano, Torino, Livorno, Siena, etc., Jacchia conducted the Montreal Opera Co., the Century Opera Co., New York, and, for a number of years, the "Boston Pop" Concerts.

KNOWLAND, L. M.: (Contemp.)

A fine flutist and teacher from Kansas City, Missouri, Knowland has written some good and original daily exercises for the flute and has played obbligatos to Miss Margaret Truman, the charming and talented daughter of the ex-president of the United States of America.

MESS, CARL FRIEDRICH: (Contemp.)

The following is taken from Musical America: Bach: "Coffee" Cantata, No. 211. Friederike Siler, Soprano (Lieschen); Johannes Feyerabend, tenor (Narrator); Bruno Muller, baritone (Schlendrian); Karl Friedrich Mess, flute; Helmut Reimann, cello; Helma Elsner, harpsichord; Pro Musica Orchestra, Stuttgart, Rolph Reinhardt, conductor. "Amore Traditore," Cantata No. 203. Bruno Muller, baritone; Helma Elsner, harpsichord.

KRELL, JOHN: (Contemp.)

An excellent flutist and teacher, Krell is a member of the Philadelphia Symphony.

KUJALA, WALFRID: (Contemp.)

An excellent flutist, Kujala studied at the Eastmann School of Music and is now (1955) member of the Chicago Symphony.

MONTEUX, CLAUDE: (Contemp.)

Flutist and conductor, Claude is the son of the eminent and world famous Pierre Monteux. The following is from Musical America, February 1, 1955. Columbus, Ohio—Claude Monteux appeared in the double role of conductor and flute soloist in a concert by the Columbus Little Symphony

on Dec. 17, in Mees Hall. The premiere w given of a "Concerto Antoniano" for flute a orchestra by Nicholas Flagello, who came fro New York to conduct his work as guest, wi Mr. Monteux as the soloist. The latter l Mozart's Overture to "Cosi fan tutte," a Andante for Strings by Tartini, and the Beet oven Second.

PANICO, GIUSEPPE: (1907-   )

Studied with D'Inverno and was soloist at th "Sala degli Artisti," Napoli, and also with th Orchestra da Camera dell 'Associazione Artistic Internazionale. For many years solo flutis "Banda del corpo delle Guardie di Pubblic Sicurezza," Roma.

POWELL, ED. E.: (Contemp.)

This splendid flutist, the son of the popular flut manufacturer in Boston, is the solo flutist of th "Telephone Hour Symphony Orchestra," Nev York.

REZNICEK, HANS: (Contemp.)

The following is taken from Musical America Bach: "Brandenburg" Concertos. Chamber Or chestra of the Vienna State Opera, Felix Pro haska conducting. Jan Tomasow, violino piccolo. Jan Tomasow, Rudolph Steng, and Alfred Jilka violins; Paul Angerer, Wilhelm Hübner, Edwar Rab, and Ernst Kriss, violas; Richard Harand Günter Weis, and Ludwig Beinl, cellos; Nikolau Harnoncourt and Beatrice Reichert, violas d gamba; Otto Rühm, contrabass; Karl Mayrhofer oboe; Hans Reznicek, flute; Helmut Wobisch trumpet; Karl Trotzmuller and Paul Angerer recorders; Anton Heiller, cembalo; and others. (Bach Guild, BG 540, 541, and 542, $14.94)***

SCHMIEDEL, MAX: (Contemp.)

Solo flutist of the State Orchestra in Heidelberg for many years. He studied with Schwedler. Now (1955) at 82 in Leipzig wants to know what will become of his fine collection of flutes and his large library of music! He says that when he returns on this planet (evidently Schmiedel is a convinced believer in reincarnation) he will begin to play his beloved flute as soon, or sooner, than his diapers are on.

SCHWEDLER, MAXIMILLIAN: (1853-1940)

This world famous flutist, teacher and pedagogue, of whom I wrote at length in another chapter, and who enjoyed the friendship and esteem of most of the great musicians of his time, was known also because of the Schwedler flute. This has been one of the numerous variations of the old flute antagonistic to the Boehm flute in a losing war against the modern instrument. Schwedler enjoyed fame and prosperity in his long career as soloist and teacher at the Gwandhous, Leipzig. However, at the end of the second World

ar, old in years, his funds wiped out, with
arcely enough food to live on and no heat in
e severe cold weather, at 86 with no hope in
ew, he took his own life. Thus ended in tragedy
e life of one of the most noted flutists of modern
mes!

TOKES, SHERIDON: (Contemp.)

ne of the younger generation of flutists in Los
ngeles. A talented and enthusiastic lover of
usic and everything pertaining to the flute, he
President of the Los Angeles Flute Club (1955)
signal honor for one so young. Stokes has ap-
eared in many concerts as soloist and in en-
mble with fine success.

ITA, MICHELE: (1895-1913)

have mentioned this remarkable young man of
perior talent on pages 284 and 323. Vita, which
eans life, should have been, instead, Vitabreve,
s he came all the way from far New Zealand
o study flute with me in New York, 1910. He
assed on at 18 years of age in 1913 and is still
ividly in my mind. One day he also brought with
im a sheet of paper on which were written many
ueer words. He wanted me to help him with the
neaning, if not the pronounciation, because some
vere almost impossible to pronounce. We worked
iligently together and were having lots of fun
erusing various dictionaries, encyclopedias, etc.,
tc. The work was about one half done when, a
igh power took him, probably to perform duties
eyond the possibility of our plane! Here follows
ome of these words: "Aaron" elder brother of
Moses and high priest of the Jews. "Antofagasta"
eaport of Chile. "Baalbek" former City of
yria. "Babirusa" curious animal of the same
amily as the pig. "Caiaphas" Jewish high priest,
took leading part in trial and condemnation of
esus. "Calaealaria" germ of herbs and shrubs.
'Deuteronomy" Fifth book of the Old Testament.
'Didymium" very rare metallic substance. "Eclip-
tic" apparent annual path of the sun. "Ecology"
section of botany and zoology. "Euthanasia" death
without pain. "Jig" Irish National dance. "Jocasta" in Greek legend the mother of Oedipus.
"Formaldehyde" oxidation products of alcohols.
"Foxglove" any plant of a genus or perennial
herbs. "Grampians" mountain range of Scotland.
"Groat" Old English silver coin, the value of
fourpence. "Hausa" Negroid people living in the
Sudan and Nigeria. "Hawkweed" a plant of the
large genus of milk-juiced herbs. "Iridium" metallic element found in nature associated with
platinum. "Irkutsk" District of Siberia. "Jodhpur"
Native state of Raiputana, India. "Kahoolawe"
Island of the Hawaiian Island. "Kaluhari" Desert
Plateau of S. W. Africa. "Laccolith" In geology,
an intrusive igneous rock in molten state. "Dnepro-
petrovsk" Town and river port of Ukraine. "Kan-
kakee" County seat, 56 miles from Chicago.
"Karakorum" ruins of ancient cities of No. Mongolia. "Lamaism" religious system prevalent in
Tibet, Mongolia and Sikkim. "Maccabees" Jewish
family distinguished in the revolt against Syrian
tyranny, 2nd Century B.C. "Macgillicuddy's"
Reeks highest mountain range in Ireland. "Nam-
ugualand" District of South Africa. "Nebuchad-
nezzar" King of Babylon. "Obadiah" Hebrew
minor prophet. "Ocelot" handsome American cat,
Texas to Patagonia. "Odoacer" (434-493) Italy's
first barbarian ruler. "Pandora" in Greek mythology, a beautiful woman upon whom the gods
lavished their choicest gifts. She was the wife of
Epimetheus, the brother of Prometheus. "Paleo-
zoic" division of geological time. "Palladium"
rare metallic element unaltered by exposure to
air but slowly attacked by nitric acid. "Parteno-
genesis" in biology, a method which an individual
is developed from an infertilized egg cell.
"Quagga" extinct variety of the zebra. "Quetzal"
a tropical peruvian bird ranging from Guatemala
to Panama. "Ra" sun God of the Egyptians with
the head of a hawk. 'Rama" one of the incarnations of Vishna, in Hindu mythology. "Saigon"
Port and capital of Cochin-China. "Saki" kind of
small monkey in South America and forests of
the Amazon. "Sokotra" Island in the Arabian sea
to the Gulf of Aden. "Taal" volcano on Bombon
Island, Philippine. "Taihoku" Capital of Formosa.
"Ucagali" river of Peru, 1200 miles long.
"Ulfilas" Christian apostle among the Goths.
"Ur" ancient Sumerian city. "Verendrye" national
monument in North Dakota. "Vesteraalen" island
off the coast of Norway. "Waccamaw" river of
North and South Carolina, over 500 miles long.
It empties into the Pee Dee river. "Wahhabis"
Mohammedan sect, followers of Ab-el-Wahab.
"Wallachia" division of Rumania, between the
Carpathians and the Danube. "Wampanoags"
members of an Algonquian tribe of American
Indians. "Xingu" river of Brazil flowing for 1300
miles into the Amazon. "Xanthippe" Wife of
Socrates, was noted for her peevishness and ill-
temper. "Yazoo" river of Mississippi, 300 miles
long. "Zloty" Monetary unit of Poland, worth
about 11¼ cents. "Zombi" in voodooism, a corpse
believed to be animated without a soul. "Zoro-
aster" religious teacher, also known as Zarathus-
tra, 800 B.C. "Zwingli" Swiss reformer, born
1484, killed 1531. "Zygote" in biology, the cell
which results from the fusion of two others and
from which a new individual develops. Michele
Vita was also interested in Palindromes; however, he did not live long enough to finish his
job. The brief list is as follows: "Abba" (Aramaic
for father or God) "Ada" (County seat of Ponto-
toc Co., Oklahoma). "Akka" Negroid race of
pigmies discovered in some forests near the
Congo in 1869). "Anna" (Also Indian coin, divided
into 12 pie, worth about two cents). "Akaka"
(name of guitar player). "Ahavana" (Symphonic
poem by David Diamond). "Aerea" (Italian for
Air Mail). "Egge" (Norwegian composer). "Asa"
King of Judah, son of Abijah, known for his
vigorous measures against idolatry). "Ara"

(Altar). "Eze" (Young African chieftain, from Nigeria, of great culture). "Gig" (a light carriage or a long light ship's boat). "Kazak" (Republic of Soviet Russia in Central Asia). "U-nu" (name of Prime Minister of Burma). "Utu" (a religious Sumarial name). Also:

ala, afa, aga, eve, ere, ewe, sees, nun, noon, etc. ad infinitum. The following four Czeck words are without vowels and almost impossible to pronounce except by Czecks. The last is also a Palindrome. "Strc" stick "Prst" finger "Skrz" thru "Krk" neck. One more similar instance of a word without vowels is used by the Sherpas, a Himalayas tribe living close to Mount Everest: CWM (pronounced Koom) meaning Western Valley.

WILLSON, MEREDITH: (Contemp.)

Soon after the appearance of "My Complete Story of the Flute," a letter reached me from Meredith Willson who at that time was in New York; he said: "Every flutist I know here speaks of your book. I haven't seen it yet but I will get a copy eventually. However, I hope you have mentioned the wonderful flute lesson you gave me in Mason City, Iowa, a number of years ago, when you told me "never play F# with the middle finger of the right hand except in rapid passages." The story Willson refers to is the following: Many years ago, to be exact it was in 1916 when, on the usual spring tour with the Minneapolis Symphony we played a matinee concert in Mason City, Iowa. After the concert, a nice boy of about 13 came to me and said, "Mr. De Lorenzo, I never thought the flute solo in William Tell could be played as beautifully as you did." "I also play flute a little and I would like to have a lesson from you." "My dear boy," I answered, "We have had a rehearsal this morning, a concert this afternoon and another toight, therefore, there is hardly time enough to eat a bite and change for the next concert." "I shall be very disappointed and so will the Mayor, who is interested in me and who suggested I see you about a lesson," he replied. How could I refuse? Many years after, when the Rochester Philharmonic and the Opera Co. went to New York, before the rehearsal of a Mozart Opera in which Eugene Goossens was the Conductor, an elegantly dressed and good looking young man with a flute case under his arm, came to me and said: "Mr. De Lorenzo, I wonder if you remember me. You gave me a flute lesson a number of years ago in Mason City, Iowa, and now I shall have the great pleasure to play next to you. "Probably," the young man continued, "you will be interested to know that I am the assistant solo flutist with the New York Philharmonic." When John Phillip Sousa, the famous Bandmaster, took his band to Europe, Meredith Willson was the solo flutist. It just happened that my Cadenza for solo flute, two flutes and flute and clarinet on Liszt's "2nd Rhapsody" had just been issued by Carl Fischer. Willson played it for Sousa an asked him if he should not make a cut on accou of its length. Sousa answered: "Play every no and every time." The "Rhapsody" was performe every day and often twice in a day!

BETWEEN COMPOSERS

DEBUSSY: (1862-1918)

It would have been a blessing to the world of music if Saint Saëns had remained in Africa all his life and never composed a note of music!

BRAHMS: (1833-1897)

Sharing the same box at the Opera house with Tschaikovsky for the latter's first performance of his 5th Symphony in Germany, the composer, surprised at the lack of comment from Brahms, asked him how he liked his Symphony. The answer was: "I did not like it." From that time on Tschaikovsky refused to listen to any of Brahms' music.

BEETHOVEN: (1770-1827)

The English composer and mystic, Cyril Scott, said that "All of Beethoven's music is cheap trash." A musician who loved and revered Beethoven remarked: "Long after that mystic and composer has decomposed, Beethoven will be growing higher on his tall pedestal!"

MOZART: (1756-1791)

His father, Leopold, also an excellent musician and a fine man, warned his son, to whom he was devoted, to hold his tongue because he talked too freely against almost everyone including his patrons, to the detriment of his career. It was the custom at this time when two prominent musicians performed in the same town to engage in a contest. After such an event with Clementi as his adversary—each was asked his opinion of the other. Clementi, who was a greater virtuoso said of Mozart, "He is one of the most extraordinary geniuses in the world." But Mozart, forgetting his father's admonition, and the kindness of Padre Martini, commented "Clementi is a great bluff and a charlatan as are all his countrymen." Is it any wonder then that Mozart suffered constant poverty in spite of his colossal genius?

TSCHAIKOWSKY: (1833-1893)

When he presented the manscript of his famous piano Concerto Number Two in B Flat Minor to Nicholas Rubinstein, thenDirector of the Moskow Conservatory and to whom it was dedicated, Rubinstein returned it the following day with the remark: "Piotr Ilich, your Concerto is nothing but trash from the first page to the last. It lacks melody, the themes are miserable and it is unplayable. Throw it in the waste basket and try again. The composer tore off the dedication and sent it to Hans Von Bulow who gave the first performance in Boston with huge success!

Poor Tschaikovsky, the identical thing happened to him with his violin Concerto. This time it was Prof. Leopold Auer, the famous teacher of Heifetz, Elman, Zimbalist and numerous others who told Tschaikovsky, "Your Concerto is positively unworthy; no melody, no form and, worst

of all, badly written and unplayable!" Tschaikovsky didn't change a note, he tore off the dedication and sent it to the violinist Adolph Brodsky (1851-1927) who performed it with huge success!

WAGNER: (1813-1883)

When one of his operas was being rehearsed in Italy, the composer, teacher and pedagogue Mugellini said: "Horrors, Wagner doesn't know how to write for the orchestra!"

SIBELIUS: (1865-   )

I enjoy the music of many composers, however, I never did like the music of Ravel."

VERDI: (1813-1901)

When Von Bulow was requested to conduct the first performance of Verdi's "Manzoni Requiem" in Germany, which had already been performed in many countries, Von Bulow replied "To conduct a piece by Verdi is beneath my artistic dignity!" Next morning Brahms, sipping his black coffee and reading as usual his morning paper, was shocked to see in capital letters "Von Bulow insults Verdi." Brhams immediately dispatched his servant to the music store for the score of Verdi's "Requiem." After reading the score, Brahms again dispatched his servant to fetch Von Bulow. "Hans," Brahms said to him holding the score in his hand, "You made an ass of yourself." "Only a genius can write such music. I request that you go to the nearest telegraph office and dispatch an apology to Verdi," which Von Bulow humbly did!

BERLIOZ: (1803-1869)

No one admired him more than Paganini, in spite of the fact Berlioz was then called "the over temperamental and lunatic musician." Paganini, in order to encourage Berlioz who was in financial straits, presented him with the magnificent sum of 20,000 francs, which at that time was considered a small fortune.

CHERUBINI: (1760-1842)

This great and venerable man, so much admired by all and particularly Beethoven, was the Director of the Paris Conservatory at the time when Berlioz was a student there. The antagonism between these two unusual men is historical. Cherubini, serious and probably over conservative could not appreciate the too temperamental Berlioz who was breaking all the standard rules in composition. Therefore, when they met, which was very often, violent epitaphs were exchanged between them.

SAINT SAENS: (1835-1922)

When Tachaikowsky was planning a tour to conduct his works, he was requested to include Paris. Tschaikovsky said that Paris was one place he had made up his mind not to go. The idea of being compared with their Saint Saëns, is offensive to me to say the least!

WAGNER: (1813-1883)
"Verdi's orchestra sounds like a huge guitar!"

VERDI: (1813-1901)
I do not admire Wagner as a man. However, the greatest opera ever conceived by a human mind is, to my thinking, Wagner's "Tristan and Isolda."

VIVALDI: (1675-1743)
"One of the great composers of all time, a man of prodigious productivity, was for more than a century after his death known principally as a humble purveyor of source material to Bach, one of the most ruthless scavengers of other men's ideas whoever put pen on paper." The above startling insult to the memory of Bach was, I thought, positively sacrilegious. Bach was much too great a genious to be accused of plagiarism or of stealing other people's ideas. True, in his numerous transcriptions of Vivaldi's music, Bach often forgot to mention Vivaldi's name but, that was without doubt, because of the hurry in which Bach worked on transcriptions. I confess that I was so shocked at what I read that I dispatched a short letter of protest to Ewing Poteet, the writer of the Program Notes for the "New Orleans Symphony Orchestra." No answer ever reached me.

D'INDY: (1857-1931)
Composer, writer, teacher and pedagogue. Famous also for his biting and derogatory remarks. D'Indy was nicknamed by a few of his friends and many others "The Cyclops" because he too, like the Macedonian King Antigonus (382 B.C.) early lost an eye. The flutist world is proud of its distinguished Cyclops Frederick Kuhlau. Now back to our teacher, writer and pedagogue. D'Indy used to express his opinion on music and musicians thus: "With few exceptions, in which of course is included Bach, I do not like German music. Also, in regard to the Italian composer, some enjoy undeserved success." To this an answer was given by two Italian musicians. The first: "Probably D'Indy had in mind Palestrina, Monteverdi, Vivaldi, Alessandro Scarlatti. The second: No, I think he had in mind those of his own generation, Verdi, Puccini, Mascagni, Pizzetti, Castelnuovo-Tedesco.

MAC DOWELL: (1861-1908)
This American composer of great talent had a special dislike for Brahms music. He often expressed himself thus: "Brahms' themes are poor, his melodic line uninteresting and his whole structure positively miserable!" These derogatory remarks were uttered when MacDowell was in Germany while Brahms was still alive. It lost the American composer many friends.

RUBINSTEIN: (1829-1894)
At the end of Antoin Rubinstein's career he was asked whom he thought were the best pianists of the day. After mentioning only a few, one o whom was Busoni, he said: "Both D'Albert and Rosenthal are not musical!"

SCHOENBERG: (1874-1953)
The famous violinist Kreisler, on his 80th birth day, speaking of Schoenberg said: "Many years ago, when we were both young we saw each other often, confided in one another, and not only on matters musical. At that time Schoenberg wrote some beautiful music. The String Sextet the Gurre Lieder, which reminded me of Parsifal. It is a fine work. However, many years later I attended a concert of all his latest compositions. After the concert I saw Arnold and told him there was only one song I liked. Schoenberg, who could be sharp tongued said, "Have I fallen so low in my art that Fritz Kreisler likes any part of it?" Some time later, when a correspondent asked Schoenberg what he thought of Kreisler, Schoenberg said, "Fritz, I loved him dearly, but now that stinker does not want to follow me." When I first met Schoenberg in 1936 I told him that his String Sextet, which I had recently heard at the Eastman School of Music, impressed me as one of the greatest musical compositions I had enjoyed in my life. Schoenberg smiled and said, "Old stuff."

OFFENBACH: (1819-1880)
On a visit to Paris, Wagner was astonished at the popularity of the operetta composer Offenbach. Although Wagner did not and could not admire Offenbach, nevertheless, he sent him with his compliments the score of "Tristan and Isolda." The following day, Offenbach dispatched a short note to Wagner saying: "Thank you for the score. However, I regret to state that I couldn't for the life of me, find any music in it! You surely have mistaken your profession!" A few months later Wagner sent Offenbach his newly published book in which he unmercifully attacked the Jews (including his benefactor Meyerbeer). Offenbach promptly returned the book saying: "You haven't the least talent for writing; you had better go back to music!"

ROSSINI: (1792-1869)
His father Giuseppe, of irrepressible good humor, was famous among his friends as a joker, town-trumpeter and inspector of slaughter houses. Gioacchino's harpsichord teacher, Prinetti, who played scales with two fingers and combined his music with the sale of liquor, had the convenient habit of sleeping as he stood! Young Gioacchino's incorrigible love of mimicking his master compelled his father to take him from Prinetti. He apprenticed him to a black smith. Young Rossini, ashamed and repentant, resolved to amend his ways and apply himself diligently.

Many years later, when Rossini was enjoying fame and great popularity, he visited London. While he was walking on a crowded street, he saw Sir Henry Rowley Bishop. The noted English composer (1786-1855) wrote many compositions, several of which were songs with flute obbligato, the most famous being "Lo! Hear the Gentle Lark" so well-known to singers and flutists. Rossini had met Bishop on a previous visit to London but, try as hard as he could, it was impossible to remember the Englishman's name. However, as Bishop approached, Rossini said: "Sir . . . and at the same time began to whistle one of his songs, to the amusement and delight of Bishop! At another time in Paris an illustrious friend of the Maestro, a Duke, visited Rossini one morning and found him in bed reading the score of Wagner's "Tristan and Isolda" upside down! "Maestro" said the Duke quite alarmed, you must be very tired and overworked. Do you know that you are reading that score upside down?" "Yes, I know," answered Rossini, "but do you know, my friend, that I spent the best part of the night reading it the usual way, and for the life of me, I couldn't make head or tale of it, so I thought I would try it the other way!"

MEYERBEER: (1791-1864)

Rossini and Meyerbeer, to the eyes of the world were supposed to be great friends because whenever they met they embraced and lavished the most extraordinary compliments on one another. The truth, however, was that they were extremely jealous of each other. At one time when Rossini was walking arm in arm on one of the Paris Boulevards with the young composer of popular songs, Paolo Tosti, the Maestro suddenly doubled up, screaming in pain. Tosti, alarmed, said: "What is it Maestro, shall I call a Doctor?" Rossini, still in contortions whispered: "It is nothing, you see Meyerbeer is coming towards us, and if he sees me in pain he will be very happy!" Rossini was the more popular and wittier of the two with fun making proclivities and improvising jokes. Meyerbeer, a millionaire and an aristocrat was, of course serious and dignified. Neither of them excelled as pianists. One evening at a great party where many of Paris aristocracy were invited, a Baroness had the bright idea of suggesting that both Rossini and Meyerbeer compose one short piano piece and each play the composition of his opponent first and his own last. Meyerbeer was first. In his own piece, everything went smoothly, but in Rossini's, an equally easy one, he played it well except the last chord, in which there was a note that couldn't be reached and Meyerbeer promptly said: "This last chord no one can play, it is badly written!" Now came Rossini's turn. He played his friend's piece without a slip as it was very simple. In his own, all were interested to see what he would do in regard to the last chord. When Rossini reached it, he deliberately leaned over and played the unreachable note with . . . his nose! The hilarity was extraordinary. Meyerbeer, who also had had a grand time and appreciated the joke, went to

Rossini, embraced and kissed him on both cheeks, saying: "I hope I will be spared Marsyas' faith in this contest."

When Meyerbeer died, his nephew, equally wealthy and aristocratic, and an amateur musician and composer, went to Rossini with a bundle under his arm. "Maestro," he said, "Knowing of the great love and admiration between you and my dear lamented Uncle I, in the sorrow of his passing, was inspired and wrote a funeral march in his dear memory! Will you be so good as to peruse my score, telling me what you think of it?" Rossini, after glancing at the manuscript said: "My dear young man, I admire your love for your illustrious departed Uncle and sympathize for your sorrow. However, in regard to the funeral march, I think it would have been far more successful if it had been written by your Uncle . . . for you!"

BERLIOZ: (1803-1869)

While Mendelssohn, Schumann and Schubert with reservations, and other great composers agreed that, regardless of his faults and weaknesses, Rossini was an undisputed genious, Berlioz said: "Every note of Rossini's music should be burned, together with all his followers!"

MASSENET: (1842-1912)

Massenet was loved by everyone who had the privilege of knowing him, not only because he was a great musician but for his kindness and very beautiful character. He never expressed an unkind remark of his numerous colleagues. Massenet's "My Recollections" is a delightful book. The following is an incomplete list of the noted composers he met during his long and brilliant career: Meyerbeer, Rossini (whom he met at the end of their careers, as they belonged to an earlier generation), Wagner, Verdi, Liszt, Berlioz, Halevy, Gounod, Franck, Saint-Saëns, Thomas, Reyer, Reber, Dubois, Delibes, Charpentier, Leroux, Carafa, Godard, Lecocq, Lalo, Cilea, Pedrotti, Schmitt, Ropartz, Hahn, Giordano, Mascagni, Leoncavallo, Puccini. However, one may ask, where is Debussy, Ravel, Satie, D'Indy, Roussell, Mahler, Varèse, Stravinsky, Schoenberg, and a few others of the ultramodern idiom? These were entirely ignored in his book, why? They didn't talk the same language, musically speaking and, therefore, had nothing in common, not even friendship. In the second list I have purposely omitted "Les Six" Milhaud, Auric, Honegger, Taillefere, Poulenc, Durey and also Ibert, because these belong to a younger generation.

Massenet had great love for his Master Ambrois Thomas and on both Wagner, whom he met in 1861, and Verdi at the Palazzo Doria in Genoa, he lavished great tributes of admiration. The last chapter, XXIX, in "My Recollections" is titled "Thoughts After Death." It is interesting beyond words!

GOUNOD: (1818-1893)

In 1892, Eugenio Pirani, Italian pianist, composer, teacher and pedagogue of international reputation who lived for a number of years, in his later life, in Brooklyn, N. Y., was correspondent for several German musical magazines. His chief occupation at that time was to interview famous composers and write their experiences. Gounod at that time, the year before he passed on, was old and not well. Pirani, who had known him before, was interviewing the great composer when a very beautiful young lady was announced. The old Maestro made a sign for her to come in. She introduced herself, in very poor French, and in a few words explained that she was a pianist just graduated from the class of Leschetisky and the purpose of her visit was that of securing an autographed photograph of Gounod. When the famous composer heard this, in a rage he said: "No, positively not. I have been pestered so many time to give my autographed picture that I am very tired of this nonsense, besides, I haven't another picture left and it cheapens me. Who cares about my autograph when so many people have it? "After this outburst, Gounod expected the young lady would reluctantly leave. Nothing of the kind happened. Although it was evident that she was discouraged and near tears, the young woman approached the Maestro and, mustering a coquettish smile, put her arms around his neck and kissed him on the mouth with such fervor that Gounod, after several attempts to free himself, begged her to release him. Finally he reached for the bell with one hand and said to the maid who appeared immediately, "Bring one of my photographs!" Gounod, exhausted, scribbled his name on it and, in a few seconds, the Maestro's studio became the calm and placid place it had been a little while back! Pirani taught piano and composition in Brooklyn; wrote for several periodicals and musical papers. His interesting book "Secret of Success of Famous Composers" published by Theodor Presser, Philadelphia, increased his already fine popularity. He was a handsome man of high culture and a linguist. Pirani left America for Berlin, where his German family was living and died there in 1938 at 88 years of age.

STRAVINSKY: (1882-   )

In his youth Stravinsky, on a visit to Rimsky-Korsakov, whom he greatly admired, played some of his revolutionary music for the Master. After he finished, Rimsky-Korsakov wasn't sure that he liked the young man's music. However, he hesitated to pronounce himself against it. He said that never before in his life had he heard that kind of music. Young Stravinsky wasn't at all disturbed by the lukewarm reception of the famous Master and a week later he returned to Rimsky-Korsakov with another bundle of music under his arm, begging the Master to *please hear*

some more of his works and immediately seated himself at the piano and began to play. After only a few minutes, Rimsky-Korsakov abruptly got up and requested the young Stravinsky to *stop playing* because, he said, "there is danger I may begin to like that sort of music!" Shortly after, the world of music in Paris was startled delighted and puzzled at Diaghileff's Ballets with Stravinsky's new, revolutionary music. There were many fights between the two factions which lasted considerable time. Meanwhile the public was aroused and the publicity was extraordinary Stravinsky became so popular, not only in Paris but all over the world that he dimmed, for a time at least, the great reputation of Debussy!

OTHER MATERIAL

OTHER MATERIAL

* * *

In the summer of 1954 Charles De Laney, teacher of flute at the University of Illinois and organizer and President of the Champaign-Urbana Flute Club, discovered in an old southern mansion in Georgia a large trunkful of early 19th Century flute music. Well preserved it consisted of solos with and without piano, duets, trios, etc. DeLaney thinks it is one of the most complete collections of 19th Century flute music known. It belonged to an American General before the Civil War, who was an enthusiastic flute dilettante and who collected all this during his stay in Europe.

* * *

A "Flute" is the name of a French Naval vessel of the 17th Century.

* * *

In Gretry's three act opera "Andromaque" (Trojan heroine, the wife of Hector) the principal role is accompanied throughout by *three flutes* in harmony. "Andromaque" was first produced in 1778.

* * *

The "Oratorio Society" of New York's principal musicians in Bach's B minor Mass, given at the Hunter College Auditorium on March 15, 1955, were: Lois Schaefer, flute; Lois Wann, oboe; Marilyn White, violin; Bruce Prince Joseph, harpsichord; and Joseph Coutret, organ.

* * *

The wind ensemble of the Aspen Festival, Aspen, Colorado, June 27th to August 27th, 1955 is composed of the following members: Albert Tipton, flute; Lois Wann, oboe; Reginald Kell, clarinet; Harold Goltzer, bassoon; Joseph Eger, French horn; and Wesley Kindskoog, trumpet.

* * *

The "Bach Aria Group," New York, of which the very able flutist is Julius Baker, will appear at the Prades Festival under the direction of Pablo Casals, July 2 to 18, 1955.

* * *

In Verdi's masterpiece, the "Manzoni Requiem" the wood wind, as all other parts in fact, have remarkable work to do. After the very beautiful trio for soprano, mezzo soprano and tenor, in the "Dies Irae" there is an obbligato for bassoon solo which is extremely beautiful. Also, the solo flute has much fine work. However, at the end of the "Agnus Dei" Verdi surrounds the vocal line with a remarkable web of instrumental counterpoint, played by *three solo flutes!*

* * *

A friend of mine wanted to know if the American composer of Italian extraction Dello Jojo who, by the way has also written a concer-

tino for flute and orchestra, was any relation to the Prime Minister of Indonesia, Ali Sastro-amidjojo. "I thought" my friend said, "that the composer, having been born in America, he might have shortened his name." It is true that "Dello" means "of the jojo" (pronounced yo yo), however, it is a neapolitan name, not an Indonesian one.

Another gentleman, also from Indonesia, the Counselor of the Indonesian Embassy, whose name is just as difficult for us is: Sujono Surjot-jondro!

* * *

Lord Dunsany, the noted English nobleman poet, author and playwright has written a book on a flutistic subject "The Delight of Pan." It is a fascinating tale of the lure of Pan's pipes on the simple folk in an English countryside. Lord Dunsany has visited California several times the past years, giving many lectures and has been a house guest of Dr. and Mrs. Dennis Smith of Palos Verdes Estates. We had the pleasure of entertaining him twice in our "Villa Pan" at a musical tea. He has a particular preference for Beethoven. Norman Dello Jojo, American composer of Italian extraction has written an opera based on Lord Dunsany's book "The Ruby."

* * *

An American composer of the new generation, Robert Moevs, living in Rome, Italy, and a 1952 winner of the "Prix de Rome" has composed a "Cantata Sacra" written for men's chorus, solo voice, flute, three trombones and timpany. The work is considered impressively individual, stark and powerful.

* * *

The Chicago Symphony Woodwind Quintet of which Ralph Johnson is the flutist, toured six midwestern states—Illinois, Indiana, Michigan, Ohio, Minnesota and Wisconsin, during May of 1955. The other members are: Robert Mayer, oboe; Jerome Stowell, clarinet; Wilbur Simpson, bassoon; Phillip Farkas, French horn.

* * *

Albert Tipton, the distinguished solo flutist of the St. Louis Symphony, is also the conductor of "Synfonietta," an ensemble of fine instrumentalists. Mrs. Tipton, who is a member of the ensemble, is an excellent pianist.

* * *

John Francis is the flutist in the Sylvan Trio, London, England, and specializes in older music of the XVII and XVIII centuries.

* * *

Dr. Herbert Kolbel, is the author of a 230 page book "Von der Flöte," published in 1951 by Staufen-Verlag, K. G. Cologne, Germany.

Krefeld is the able flutist and lutenist of the Collegium Musicum, in Germany.

* * *

In response to several requests for the names of the most noted flute manufacturers, I submit the following:

Wm. S. Haynes Co., Boston, Mass.
Edward Powell, Boston, Mass.
Bettoney & Co., Boston, Mass.
Selmer, Elkhart, Indiana
Armstrong, Elkhart, Indiana
Rudall-Carte, London, England
Louis Lot, Paris, France
Buffet, Paris, France
Sonneville, Paris, France
Pensell & Müller, New York
Moennig, Germany
Mollenauer, Germany
Adler, Germany
*N.B.—Milano, Italy, had several woodwind factories, but they were destroyed during World War II.

* * *

When Alfred Quensel, the noted and brilliant solo flutist of the Chicago Symphony for many years, was retired with a good pension a quarter of a century ago, he decided to spend the last years of his life in his beautiful Germany in peace. The first World War had just ended to do away with all wars of the future!

However, Quensel's peace of mind was possible only for a few, too few years, because during World War II, one morning while on his usual walk, he was instantly killed by a bomb!

The same fate awaited also to beautiful Lina Cavalieri, killed by a bomb in her own villa at Florence, Italy.

* * *

CHINA AND THE FLUTE

John H. Levis, in his splendid "Foundations of Chinese Musical Art," page 65 says:

"The flute is one of the most ancient and indigenous musical instruments of China. There are two types: the vertical and the horizontal. Both are regarded as fine instruments, but the vertical has long been the common friend of all scholars, both male and female.

While all scholars mastered the flute as they did the brush, there was also general use of this musical instrument among all classes of people. The farmer, rickshawman and the soldier found recreation in its plaintive notes, and comfort too. China has paintings showing the cowherd playing his flute on the back of his water-buffalo. The scholar plays his in his study or in a wooded place or garden.

In the present-day Chinese flute, the ground note on the Hsiao (vertical flute) approximates to "D", while on the Ti-Tzu (horizontal flute), it approximates to "A" . . . "

THE ETRUSCANS AND THE FLUTE

The pre-Roman Etruscans left traces of a remarkably high civilization. To this day it is not known from where they originated. Where Tuscany is, that was where the Etruscans made their homes long, long ago. The sculptured tombs and the paintings found on vases and other pottery display not only a keen artistic sense, but also the possession of gold, silver and other metals used for decorative purpose. The Etruscans were well acquainted with music. The double flute and the transverse flute are often seen in their excavated works of art. Rodolfo Cafaro of Rome, Italy, the only man in captivity who knows all about flute music and flute composers, has sent me a most interesting clipping from a Milano newspaper of May 1955, headed "Col Flauto gli Etruschi cacciavano il cinghiale" (The Etruscans hunted wild boars with the flute).

It tells us that in the XII chapter of "Story of Animals" Eliano writes about an old legend of an *expert flute player* whose enchanted sounds were so irresistible that the wild boars and deers came out from their retreat and . . . were captured! The Milano May Fair of 1955 was enriched as never before with unusual pictures of an Etruscan playing some enchanted melodies on the flute and many other works of art recently excavated.

* * *

NEW FLUTE MUSIC

HENRY BRANT: "A Symphony for Voice, Eight Flutes, and Cymbals."
ALEXANDER TCHEREPNIN: Trio for *three flutes* and Quartet for *four flutes;* first performed in Paris in 1951.
MATT H. DORAN: "Concerto" for flute and orchestra; "Trio" for flute, cello and piano; "Quintett" for flute, oboe, clarinet, bassoon and horn.
MARK WESSEL: Besides many other compositions of real worth, this splendid composer-pianist has to his credit an extremely fine "Concertino" for flute and orchestra. The first performance was played in Chicago by David Van Vactor and the second performance was given soon after by the Rochester Philharmonic under Dr. Howard Hanson and myself as soloist.

* * *

ESTEBAN EITLER: On December 13, 1954, in the National Conservatory of Music, Santiago de Chile, the following compositions by Eitler were performed for the first time:
"Sonatina" (1951 for flute and piano.
"Music for Cello" (1949) unaccompanied.
"Musica da Camera" (1948) for flute and piano.
"Sonatina" (1952) for flute and clarinet.

"Divertimento" (1953) for piccolo, clarinet, viola and piano. The players: Esteban Eitler, flute and piccolo; Rodrigo Martinez, clarinet, Raul Martinez, viola; Hans Loewe, cello; Free Focke, piano.

* * *

Of the three concerts at the *Instituto Chileno* given September, October and November 1954, the following compositions, in which the flute is predominant, are listed with the same players with the addition of another flutist, Heriberto Bustamante nd a bassoon player, Hans Loewe.

WILLIAM ALWYN: "Suite" for flute, unaccompanied.
MAURICE JACOBSEN: "Suite" for flute, cello and piano.
ADOLPH WEISS: "Sonata" for flute and viola.
HERNAN MORALES: "Three monodias" for flute, unaccompanied.
J. NEP. DAVID: (1943) "Sonata" for flute and viola.
JEAN BINET: "Sonatina" for flute and piano.
LEONARDO DE LORENZO: "Due Divertimenti" for flute, clarinet and bassoon.
CARLOS ISAMITT: "Suite" for flute, unaccompanied.
WALLINGFORD RIEGGER: "Tres Canones" for flute, oboe, clarinet and bassoon.
"Suite" for flute alone.
The last in this list of concerts at the "Instituto Chileno" is entitled Festival Tri-partito dedicado a *Holanda Austria e Israels* (Admittance by invitation only).
I. Holanda: JAN MASSENS: "Introduction and Allegro" for oboe, clarinet and piano.
HENRY ZAGWIYN: "Capriccio" for flute and piano.
WILLEM PIJPER: "Sonata" for piano.
II. Austria: ALBAN BERG: "Four pieces" for clarinet and piano.
ANTON WEBERN: "Variations" for piano.
III. Israel: JEHOSHUA LAKNER: "Sonata" for flute and piano.
P. BEN HAIM: "Tres canciones sin Palabras" for oboe and piano.
ABRAHAM DAUS: "Songs of Rahel" for voice, flute and viola. The interpreters are: Zivia Klein, voice; Esteban Eitler, flute; Hans Loewe, oboe; Rodrigo Martinez, clarinet; Raul Martinez, viola; Free Focke, piano.

* * *

N.B.—For th benefit of those who may want information in regard to the above new flute music from the Concert of December 13th, the address of Esteban Eitler follows: Casilla 1214, San Diago, Chile.

* * *

ESTEBAN EITLER: (1955) "Trio" for flute English horn and viola.

HAAKON BERGH: "Three Preludes" for flute alone.
Paganini's "Moto Perpetuo" for two flutes and piano.
LEONARDO DE LORENZO: "19 Preludii e Preludietti" (flute alone).
"Suite Moderna" in four movements for two flutes.
"Divertimento quasi moderno" for flute, oboe and clarinet.
"Capriccio eccentrico" for flute, clarinet and bassoon (dedicated to Adolph Weiss).
"Two Etudes" for four flutes (Fantasietta-Scherzino).
"Divertimento Fantastico" for flute, oboe, clarinet and bassoon.
"Divertimento Flautistico" for five flutes with flute in G and piccolo.
EDUARDO MATURANA: "Trio" for oboe, flute in G and bassoon.
"Quartet" for voice, flute, viola and percussion.
ZEBRE DEMETRY: "Trio" for flute, clarinet and bassoon.
JAN MASSEUS: "Fantasia" for flute in G and piano.
BENIGNO QUINTELA: "Four pieces" for flute alone.
ALEX GRIMPE: "Suite miniatura" for flute alone.
RODRIGO MARTINEZ: "Three preludios" for flute and clarinet.
LUIS ALBERTO CLAVERO: (1950) "Three pieces" for flute alone.
ESTEBAN EITLER: "Trio" for flute, oboe and alto saxophone.
"Quartet" for flute, violin, viola and cello.
"Seven bagatelas" for flute, flute in G, viola and cello.
PAUL HINDEMITH: "Sonatina canonica" for two flutes.
ERNEST KRENEK: "Sonatina" Op. 92 for flute and viola.
WALTER PISTON: "Three pieces" for flute, clarinet and bassoon.
KARL WIENER: "Three pieces" for flute, English horn and clarinet.
RENE AMENGUAL: "Suite" for flute and piano.
ANTONIO LORA: "Improvisation and Burlesca" for flute and piano (Published in New York).

* * *

TWO OUTSTANDING FLUTE RECORDS
The New York Times, Sunday, May 1, 1955 says: "Outstanding among recent discs devoted to VIVALDI is MUSIC OF VIVALDI Volume 3, the third of a series made for Decca by the VIRTUOSI DI ROMA. Here the outstanding work is the flute concerto known as LA NOTTE, ravishingly played by GESUALDO PELLEGRINI.
The other, of equal importance, is the Concerto for two flutes by CIMOROSA played by ARRIGO TASSINARI and an artist pupil of his.

SCIENCE AND ART

The planet, Pluto, revolves around the sun in 248 years.

* * *

Evaporation from the surface of the Dead Sea is estimated at from 6½ to 17 feet annually.

* * *

The gold funerary mask of King Tut-Ankh-Amen is in the Egyptin Museum at Cairo.

* * *

Ostrich eggshells were used for water containers as early as 5000 B. C.

* * *

The tongue of a 90-foot whale may weigh as much as 3¼ tons.

* * *

Although the banana plant probably originated in Asia, most bananas used in the United States come from the Western Hemisphere.

* * *

In 1940, Korea was the world's fourth largest rice producer.

* * *

It is possible for as many as 40,000 cicadas to emerge in a single night from under one tree.

* * *

The recorder, a flute-like instrument, is now being played by approximately 250,000 people.

* * *

Scientists believe that insects have existed for about 250 million years.

* * *

A female fly can lay its first batch of eggs less than a week after its birth.

* * *

When the Romans conquered Egypt in 26 B.C. they collected part of the tribute in the form of Egyptian glassware.

* * *

About 1,200 languages are spoken by American Indians, many of them by only a few hundred people.

* * *

The female bullfrog is slightly larger than the male and usually is silent.

* * *

Donkey milk has been used for human consumption for countless centuries.

* * *

The Roman Colosseum was sometimes flooded for sham naval battles which sometimes resulted in deaths among the participants.

* * *

The 19,344-foot Cotopaxi cone in Ecuador is the world's highest active volcano.

* * *

Helium gas, once valued at $2500 a cubic foot, now is produced for less than one cent a cubic foot.

* * *

In ancient Egypt, cats were used as retrievers.

Ancient Rome built a road system that stretched from northern Scotland to the Euphrates river in Asia minor. Parts of it are still in use.

* * *

One variety of termite will eat through lead or concrete in search of wood.

* * *

Wire worms, army worms and grasshoppers are among the insects pestering Kentucky farmers.

* * *

Gunpowder is a mixture of saltpetre, sulphur and charcoal.

* * *

The hornbill, a bird of Borneo, Java and Sumatra, seals his wife up in a hollow tree at nesting time and feeds her through a small opening.

* * *

Scientists believe that birds developed from reptiles.

* * *

Territory claimed by Australia on the Antarctic Continent is almost as large as Australia itself.

* * *

The largest species of bamboo reach a height of 120 feet.

* * *

A rose petal is about five thousands of an inch thick.

* * *

In proportion to their size, whales have a larger amount of blood than other mammals.

* * *

The Coptotermes niger termite has been known to eat through nearly five inches of concrete.

* * *

United States cows produce about 115 billion pounds of milk a year.

* * *

Small killer whales often will attack a large whale in packs, force its mouth open and eat its tongue.

* * *

Cats were sacred animals in ancient Egypt.

* * *

The famed, ancient Colossus of Rhodes was a 105-foot bronze statue of Apollo.

* * *

Several orchids are among the nearly 500 varieties of wild flowers, ferns and shrubs growing in Canada's Yukon territory.

* * *

By the use of Radar, the ending as well as the beginning of rainstorms in a given locality can be predicted accurately from 4 to 6 hours in advance.

* * *

The blue whale is the world's largest animal.

— 13 —

The compound eyes of some fossil trilobites had as many as 15,000 lenses.

* * *

Galileo demonstrated in 1632 that the earth revolved around the sun.

* * *

Some octopuses will lay 45,000 eggs at a time, each about half as big as a grain of rice.

* * *

For centuries, people have tried to find the body of Alaric I and the treasure believed to have been buried with him 1,500 years ago under the waters of the Busento river in southern Italy.

* * *

The Antarctic Continent is known to contain huge deposits of coal and other minerals.

* * *

Indian elephants have a single finger-like projection on their trunks while African elephants have two.

* * *

A million mutton birds land on Heron Island, near Australia, the same day each October.

* * *

A number of sea animals swim by jet propulsion.

* * *

The eggs of the tiny Brine Shrimp, found in the Great Salt Lake, Utah, are so minute, it take about 85 million eggs to make one pound.

* * *

The jet stream is a current of air moving from 100 to 500 miles per hour about eight miles above the earth.

* * *

Packs of wild dogs in Indochina, Malaya and India are reputed to be so ferocious that they drive tigers away from their kills.

* * *

There are records of more than 1000 comets, only a fifth of which could be seen without a telescope.

* * *

Bethlehem, Nazareth, Egypt, Emmaus and Lebannon are all towns in Pennsylvania.

* * *

Some comets have been detected which are apparently heading into outer space, never to return.

* * *

Men do not know where cosmic rays come from.

* * *

The population of Tokyo has reached 7,825,810.

* * *

The octopus can walk or propel himself by using jets of water.

* * *

Cosmic rays are mysterious streams of electrical particles striking the earth from unknown sources.

The toad's tongue is attached in the front of its mouth.

* * *

Homer—famous for the Iliad and the Odyssey, could neither read nor write—he was blind!

* * *

The planet Pluto is 3,700,000,000 miles from the Earth.

* * *

The first-known written reference to coal was made by a Chinese who died 2,100 years ago.

* * *

Polar bears have been seen swimming in the sea 200 miles from land.

* * *

As many as 20 species of mosquitoes have been reported in the Arctic.

* * *

In an abandoned citrates plant in Santa Teresa Riva, Italy, a new fabric is being produced by Engineer Enrico Mortillaro from the petrified refuse of fiery Mt. Etna—lava!

* * *

Haley's comet which put on a spectacular show in 1910 is again to be visible from the earth in the mid 1980's.

* * *

Some people's blood pressure will increase to almost three times normal in a severe fit of coughing.

* * *

Although the planet Pluto was not discovered until 1930, its position and orbit was predicted by astronomers in 1914.

* * *

The Library of Congress in Washington has more than 10 million books.

* * *

It is possible to lose consciousness in a severe fit of coughing.

* * *

Long distance power transmission in Sweden uses 380,000 volts.

* * *

"Tezcatlipoca," a leading god of the Aztecs. He was worshipped as the supreme creator, and god of music and dance.

* * *

"Sequoyah," the Indian who invented the Cherokee alphabet.

HUMOR

A sense of humor is the rarest of all human virtues, it means the ability to laugh at yourself and still go on doing the best you can in an admittedly imperfect world."

* * *

An English woman who was critical of American soldiers stationed in England said her reasons for feeling as she did were: "They are overbearing, oversexed and . . . besides they are over here!"

* * *

Philosophy teaches one to be . . . unhappy intelligently.

* * *

Better belly burst than good meat lost.

* * *

Two old maids went for a tramp in the woods. The tramp escaped.

* * *

Woman's faults are many, Men have only two: Everything they say, and everything they do.

* * *

The average bachelor would get married if he could find a girl who loves him as much as he does.

* * *

"All of you men who are fond of music," the top sergeant called out, "step forward two paces." Six men responded. "O.K.," said the sergeant, "you six mugs get busy and lug that piano up to the top floor of the officers' quarters."

* * *

Two men met on the street and one asked the other for a cigarette. His friend gave him the cigaret, commenting, "I thought you had quit smoking."

"I'm just at the first state," replied the other. "I've quit buying."

* * *

A newly-rich woman returned from her first trip to France and was making it known as widely as she could. "And Paris," she gushed, "Paris is marvelous. The people are all so educated and cultured, nothing crude as in this country. My dear, even the street cleaners speak French."

* * *

Many a live wire would be a dead one if it weren't for the connections.

* * *

Herodotus says that the ancient Egyptians kneaded their dough with their feet and their clay with their hands.

* * *

He was so lazy he wouldn't even exercise discretion.

* * *

A good secretary laughs at the jokes her boss spills, not because they are clever, but because she is.

Eve: The first chicken to ruin a man's garden.

* * *

The Duke of Clarence—condemned to die for treason, was given his choice as to the method. His request—to be drowned in a barrel of wine! (England, 1475).

* * *

The little child ended his prayer earnestly: "and please, Lord, can't you put the vitamins in pie and cake instead of in cod-liver oil and spinach. Amen."

* * *

A government worker sat at the table after breakfast one morning, engrossed in a magazine for over an hour. Finally he asked for another cup of coffee.

"Coffee!" echoed his wife. "But look at the clock. Aren't you going to the office today?"

"Office?" exclaimed the startled man. "Heavens! I thought I WAS at the office."

* * *

Frederick the Great cured his soldiers of wiping their noses on thier sleeves by placing rows of buttons on the sleeve—a custom prevailing to this day, but only for decoration.

* * *

Joe, charged with theft, was on the witness stand, and the judge sought to discover if he knew the value of an oath. He said, "Joe, if you tell a lie under oath, do you know what happens?"

Joe said: "Yessir, Judge, I don't go to heaven."

"And if you tell the truth?" persisted the judge. "I go to jail," said Joe.

* * *

It takes face powder to get a man and baking powder to keep him.

* * *

Scientists say that a distant cluster of stars is speeding away from the earth at 15,000 miles a second. Can you blame it?

* * *

In free America, a street sweeper can become a professor, providing he's willing to make a financial sacrifice.

* * *

He: "I'm thinking of getting married." She: "That's a great idea, if you ask me."

* * *

"To err is human, but if the eraser wears out before the pencil, you're overdoing it a bit."

* * *

"Will the operation be dangerous, Doctor?" "Don't be silly. You can't buy a dangerous operation for $50."

* * *

Don't believe the world owes you a living. The world owes you nothing—it was here first.

* * *

On a small service station out on the edge of a western desert hangs this sign: "Don't ask us for information. If we knew nything, we wouldn't be here."

"Does your wife pick your suits "
"No, just the pockets."

* * *

Judge Gruff: "Aren't you ashamed to be seen here in court so often?"
Prisoner: "Why no, your Honor. I always thought it was a very respectable place."

* * *

Steno: "I have an awful cold in my head."
Boss: "Well, that's something at least."

* * *

A boy becomes a man when he stops asking his father for money and requests a loan.

* * *

By studying diligently from the age of 16 to 80, a person can learn about half as much as he thought he knew at 18.

* * *

Everybody is of some use in the world, even if only to serve as a horrible example.

* * *

Income tax is a form of hide-and-seek—the tax collector seeks your hide.

* * *

WHY WORRY?

There are only two reasons for worry: either you are successful or you are not successful. If you are successful there is nothing to worry about, if you are not successful there are only two things to worry about. Your health is either good, or you are sick. If your health is good there is nothing to worry about; if you are sick there are only two things to worry about. You are either going to get well or you are going to die; if you are going to get well, there is nothing to worry about; if you are going to die there are only two things to worry about. You are either going to Heaven or you are not going to Heaven; and if you are not going to Heaven there is nothing to worry about; if you are going to the other place you'll be so busy shaking hands with old friends you won't have time to worry, so WHY WORRY?

* * *

PESSIMISM ON THE LOOSE

" . . . Life is just one damn thing after another. Man comes into this world without his consent, and leaves it against his will. During his stay on earth, his time is spent in one continuous round of contraries and misunderstandings. In his infancy he is n angel; in his boyhood he is a devil; in his manhood he is everything from a lizard up (including a skunk). In his duties he is a fool. (If he raises a family, he is a chump; if he raises a check, he is a thief; if he raises a million by stock juggling, he is a financier.) If he is a poor man, he is considered a bad manager, and has no sense; if he is a rich man, he is considered dishonest but smart. If he is in politics, he is a grafter and a crook; if he is out of politics, you can't place him, as he is a useless citizen. If he goes to church, he is a hyprocrite; if he stays away, he is a sinner. If he donates for foreign missions, he does it for show; if he doesn't, he is stingy. When he first comes into the world, everybody wants to kiss him; when he goes out, they want to kick him. If he dies young, there was a great future before him; if he lingers before dying, he is in the way. Life is a funny proposition . . . "

* * *

What too many of us are seeking theseg days is less to do, more time to do it in, and more pay for getting it done.

* * *

If you want to forget all your troubles, wear tight shoes.

* * *

Garage Owner: "Fifty dollars? That's outrageous. I wouldn't pay Michelangelo that price to paint my garage!"
Painter: "If he does it for less we'll picket the place."

* * *

A boy sought a job at a drugstore and was asked his name by the pharmacist.
"Alexander Graham Bell."
"That's a pretty well known name, isn't it?"
"It ought to be," the boy replied, "I've been delivering groceries around this neighborhood for two years."

* * *

Psychiatrists say we are all a little strange in our behavior. In other words: I am original. You're eccentric. He's nuts.

* * *

One early afternoon a distinguished friend called on Rossini. The maestro was busy preparing his famous Rossini spaghetti sauce and was attired in a large white chef's hat. His guests that evening were to be two elegant couples from the cream of Paris aristocracy.
It just happened, however, that that day Rossini had a bad cold and, in uncovering the pan, his nose leaked and some drops fell in the precious preparation! His friend, shocked and alarmed at what he had seen, told the maestro who placidly answered: "I know, but it doesn't matter because I don't like my guests; they practically imposed themselves on me this time."

* * *

When the French government unveiled a monument of Rossini while he was still alive, his numerous friends congratulated him for the unusual honor! Rossini said: "The French government trusted me."

LEONARDO DE LORENZO'S
80th BIRTHDAY PROGRAM OF HIS WORKS

Sunday, August 28th, 1955 at 5:30 p.m.
"Villa Pan By The Sea"
721 Cloyden Square, Palos Verdes Estates, California

I   "Longevità" Valse di Concerto, for flute and piano.

II   Duet, 1st movement, from "Suite Moderna,"
for two flutes in four movements.

III   "Capriccio Eccentrico" for flute, clarinet and bassoon,
in modern idiom. (dedicated to Adolph Weiss).

IV   "Fantasietta," in modern idiom, for four flutes.

V   "Serenata a Pan" for five flutes including bass flute solo.*

VI   "Divertimento Flautistico" for five flutes
including flute in G and piccolo.
    (a) "Mattinata," Andantino - Allegro moderato
    (b) "Serenata breve a Pan"
    (c) "Allegro finale"
Performers: Haakon Bergh, Arthur Gleghorn, Archie Wade, Sheridon
Stokes, Sylvia Rudeman Glass (3rd flute and piccolo),
Harold Lewis (flute in G), Harry Klee (bass flute), Ugo
Raimondi (clarinet), Adolph Weiss (bassoon), and Modina
DeLorenzo (piano).

* As this program includes the whole family of flutes, the "Serenata a Pan" (3½ minutes)
will be played twice, first with bass flute solo and in the "Divertimento Flautistico"
(second movement), with flute in G solo. The ensemble of four and five flutes will be
conducted by Haakon Bergh.

Flauto solo   Preludio Amabile   Leonardo De Lorenzo

AUTHORITIES ON MUSIC ACCLAIM
"MY COMPLETE STORY OF THE FLUTE" . . .

"Your book will be a revelation to all its readers, professional musicians, as well as music lovers in general."—Mario Castelnuovo-Tedesco, Beverly Hills, Calif. (World-famous Composer).

*　*　*

"Your book is superb. Besides the flute and fiute-playing, it has romance, love, comedy, and tragedy, with numerous other items of great interest."—Josef Piastro, Hollywood, Calif. (Famous violinist, conductor, and composer).

*　*　*

"Maestro De Lorenzo knows not only all about the flute, but also all about the flute players of yesterday and today."—Adolph Weiss, Beverly Hills, Calif. (distinguished composer and bassoon viruoso).

*　*　*

"A veritable cornucopia of wonderful material." —David Ewen, New York (well-known writer on music).

*　*　*

"A remarkable book. It should be found in every public library."—Henry Woempner, Los Angeles, Calif. (eminent flute virtuoso).

*　*　*

"Your book, in conjunction with the flute, combines history, tragedy and anecdotes in an admirable way."—Prof. Ernest Hoffzimmer, Redondo Beach, Calif. (distinguished pianist, teacher and pedagogue. 21 years head of the piano department of Blumington, Indiana University, and one of the most enthusiastic followers of Ferruccio Busoni).

*　*　*

"A magnificent work . . . "—Dr. Wesley La Violette (writer, composer, philosopher, and President of the California Association of Vocational Schools).

*　*　*

"It was refreshing, after so many years, to read your great book and also get news of you. A bravo from my heart." — Agnes Fahlbusch, Leipzig, Germany (a distinguished professional woman flutist).

*　*　*

"Your book is considered "Opera pregevolissima" (valuable-worthy)—Dr. Pasuale Bandiera (Manager of the Publishing firm Fratelli Bocca, Rome and Milano, Italy.

*　*　*

"Congratulations for your precious notes and education for one eager to know or refresh himself reading your great book."—Dr. Bertrand B. Machat (Santa Barbara, Calif.).

*　*　*

"How I have enjoyed "My Complete Story of the Flute" and also the Addenda. It is not only educational but entertaining as well."—Felice Kubelik Jordan, Palos Verdes Estates, Calif., (Grand daughter of Jan Kubelik, teacher, musician and patron of the arts).

"Your book has been delightful, instructive and marked with the author's originality and sense of humor. I particularly enjoyed your correspondence with G.B.S."—Frances Winwar, New York, (noted writer and a great lover of music).

*　*　*

"Thank you for having written such a delightful and inspired book. I shall endeavor to talk and write about it all I can. It should have a phenomenal success! I also thank Dr. Breco for helping you in publishing it."— Onorio Ruotolo, New York, (famous sculptor, writer and poet).

*　*　*

"I am extremely grateful to you and to Mr. Pezzi for having mentioned me to you, and I hope that I may prove worthy of your interest to include me in your great book."—David Gilbert (a flutist and composer of the younger generation of great talent who is member of the Rochester Philharmonic).

*　*　*

"Thank you for including me in your very wonderful book."—Matt H. Doran (Flutist, composer nad teacher of harmony nd counter-point at Del Mar College, Corpus Christi, Texas).

*　*　*

"I wonder how many Americans, outside of the musical circles, realize what a great service you have rendered. Both your book and the Addenda are, I think, unique. You have probably been deluged with letters of appreciation. Permit me to add one more to that vast number."—Sonia H. Davis, Los Angeles, Calif. (writer and Patron of the Arts).

*　*　*

"I have the honor of being mentioned in your great book." — Frank Horsfall, Seattle, Wash. (Flute teacher and 46 years solo flutist with the Seattle Symphony).

*　*　*

"Your admirable book is fascinating because of the combination of knowledge and information of great interest. It is indeed a valuable addition to my library."—Bruno Zirato (Manager New York Philharmonic Symphony Society).

*　*　*

"Your beautiful book, which has become one of my treasures because of its educational value, is precious." — Dorothy Simpson Smith, Whittier Calif. (An excellent concert pianist and Patron of the Arts).

*　*　*

"Just returned from an unforgettable visit to Europe. The masterly descriptions in your wonderful book of the many museums, churches, etc., was a delight and it made things considerable easier for us to locate what we were looking for.—Mr. and Mrs. Ulan Hill, Dallas, Texas (enthusiastic Patrons of the Arts and the Dallas Symphony Orchestra, of which Mrs. Hill is on the Executive Committee).

"Mrs. Truman and I are reading your complete story of "The Flute" with a lot of interest."—Harry S. Truman, Kansas City, Missouri, (The Honorable ex-President of U.S.A.).

*   *   *

"YOUR BOOK IS INSPIRED"

Alberto Salvi, one of the world's greatest harpists and his charming wife Annina, who, incidentally is Leonardo De Lorenzo's niece, flew from Wilmette, Illinois in August, 1955, to spend a delightful vacation in Palos Verdes Estates at Villa Pan by the Sea.

*   *   *

PERENNIAL PEACE AND PROSPERITY FOR EVERYONE—A young American philosopher of the new generation says: "Now that we have the Atomic Power at our command, the world will enjoy perennial peace and prosperity only if it can learn to stop glorifying the destructive cancer of militarism and the utter senseless bestiality of war!"

A FEW OF THE OUTSTANDING CHAPTERS IN
"MY COMPLETE STORY OF THE FLUTE"

TO THE NINE MUSES

One of whom "Euterpe" Goddess of Music, is also given credit
for being the inventor of the transverse flute

ADDENDA NUMBER III TO

"MY COMPLETE STORY OF THE FLUTE"

THUMBNAIL BIOGRAPHIES AND OTHER MATERIAL

BY LEONARDO DE LORENZO

EX LIBRIS

G·RICHTER

MODINA and LEONARDO DE LORENZO

LEONARDO DE LORENZO
Villa Pan
1339 Mission Ridge Road
Santa Barbara. California

Printed by

MULKINS PRINTING

Redondo Beach, California

FORWARD

In Greek mythology, the Nine Muses, presiding over different kinds of poetry, arts and sciences, were the daughters of Zeus and Mnemosyne and the companions of Apollo. Euterpe is represented with a lyre and sometimes with a transverse flute. It does not matter which of the two instruments as both are of the same period of antiquity, as is illustrated by the famous contest between Apollo, on the lyre, and Marsyas, on the Pan pipes. It is well known that the unfortunate Marsyas was skinned alive by his victorious opponent Apollo. The credit for the invention of the Pan pipes is given both to Pan himself and to Marsyas' father.

THE NINE MUSES: "Euterpe" who is also called the enchanting Muse in a French printing of the XVIII century by Audoin and Dubois from which the painting of Le Sueur is made, is represented playing the transverse flute with a crown of flowers on her head. "Clio", Goddess of History"; "Thalia"; Goddess of Comedy and idyllic poetry "Melpomene", Goddess of Tragedy, wearing a sword and the cothurnus; "Terpsichore," Goddess of Dance and Song, represented with the lyre; "Erato," goddess of erotic poetry, also with a lyre; "Polymnia," goddess of the hymn; "Uranio," goddess of Astronomy, represented with a staff pointing to a globe; "Calliope," goddess of epic poetry, represented with a tablet and stylus. Mount Helicon, with its sacred fountains, and Mount Parnassus were sacred to the Muses.

Now I will add another name to the above Nine Muses; "Penelope", she is not a goddess but I will call her *goddess of Virtue:* The following will illustrate:

"Penelope", again in Greek legend, was the wife of Ulysses (Odysseus). During the protracted absence of her husband she was besieged by suitors, but she told them she must finish the robe she was making for her father-in-law. She worked at this all day and at night undid all she had done during the day, thus prolonged her fidelity interminably.

A number of operas have been composed on Penelope from time to time. The latest is by the Swiss ultra-modern composer Rolf Lieberman, who is known for composing a piece for jazz band and a symphony orchestra in 1956.

L. D. Santa Barbara, Calif. 1957

TO THE NINE MUSES

One of whom "Euterpe" Goddess of Music; is also given credit
for being the inventor of the transverse flute

ADDENDA NUMBER III TO

"MY COMPLETE STORY OF THE FLUTE"

THUMBNAIL BIOGRAPHIES AND OTHER MATERIAL

BY LEONARDO DE LORENZO

Addenda Number III

Table of Contents

THUMBNAIL BIOGRAPHIES (ADDENDA NUMBER III)

LESSANDRO, DRISKO RUTH (Contemp.)
his fine flutist of both the Oklahoma City Symphony and the San Antonio (Texas) Symphony married its able and ambitious conductor Victor lessandro in May of 1955. They make their home a San Antonio whose Symphony officials feel appy to have Victor Alessandro as its conductor.

* * *

OVONE FORTUNATO (contemp.)
or many years solo flutist with the Chicago opera. tudied with Italo Piazza at the beginning of the entury. He retired to Italy many years ago.

* * *

)AFNI, BRUNO: (Contemp.)
An excellent flutist who, at the Circolo Artistico 'riuliano, Udine, gave with great success the first erformance of "Egloga" for unaccompanied flute nd "Pastorale e Burlesca." for flute and piano by Inrico De Angelis Valentino, in May, 1955.

* * *

)ENECKE, JULIA: (Contemp.)
This splendid flutist, who was with the Minneapolis Symphony for a number of years, is the vife of Henry Denecke, the Conductor of the 'edar Rapids (Iowa) Symphony who also studied he flute at one time. Mrs. Denecke wrote an nteresting account of "My Complete Story of he Flute" in the Minneapolis Star of July 15, .951.

* * *

DI NARDO, GIOVANNI: (Contemp.)
This fine flutist studied with Italo Piazza, D'Inverno and Bossi at the Naples Conservatory. He is a member of the Scarlatti Chamber Orchestra with which he has played many concerts.

* * *

DI TULLIO, LUISA: (Contemp.)
The daughter of a prominent Los Angeles cellist is one of the youngest and most promising of the new generation of flutists. In one of the Los Angeles Flute Club concerts she performed Griffes 'Poem" most creditably.

FALIERO, DOMENICO: (Contemp.)
An excellent and memorable concert was given at Salerno, Italy, in the *Casino Sociale*, già Casino dei Nobili, in April, 1956. One of the numbers in particular, Bach's Branderburg Concerto No. 5, in which the three soloists were Raffaele Ronga, pianist; Giuseppe Prencipe, violinist and Domenico Faliero, flutist, met with great success. The orchestra stabile da camera of the Liceo Musicale Giuseppe Martucci was conducted by Maestro Domenico Stabile.

* * *

GIESE, W. RICHARD (1924-)
Another American fine flutist. He studied with Georges Laurent and makes his home in Los Angeles. Giese was associated with Berkshire

Music Center; Longines Symphonette; Ballet de Paris (1954); Baltimore Symphony; Sadlers Ballet from 1953 to 1956.

* * *

GRAF, PETER LUCAS: (Contemp.)
In Bach's Suite No. 2 in B minor for flute and orchestra, known to all flute virtuosi, Graf is the soloist in this new record with the Winterthur Symphony Orchestra conducted by Clemens Dahinden.

* * *

GRASSO ELVISIO: (Contemp.)
Is the flutist of a new and original quartet recently formed in Italy for piano, flute. oboe and bassoon. The others are: Enrica Parodi, pianist; Elia Owcinnicoff, oboe; Virginio Bianchi, bassoon.

* * *

GRAVINA, GILBERTO: (Contemp.)
Count Gravina is directly related to Cosima Wagner, von Bullow and Liszt. His father married the daughter of von Bulow and Cosima. This splendid musican conducted an interesting symphony concert in Firenze, Italy, in which an early work of Wagner, a symphony, never before heard in Italy, was the novelty in which the conductor-flutist scored a fine success. It will be remembered that Gilberto Gravina composed a "Preludio e Fuga" for 12 flutes dedicated to this writer. The score of this original work, performed at "Villa Pan" and at the "Los Angeles Flute Club," was presented by Leonardo De Lorenzo to the Los Angeles Flute Club, together with his own "Serenata Breve a Pan" for five flutes, including bass flute solo.

* * *

HABSCHIED, JOSE: (Contemp.)
Born in Yugoslavia he studied first at the School of Music in Belgrado. He then completed his flute study at the Vienna Conservatory under Prof. Wanausek and Resniczek. Returning to Belgrado Habschied was given the position of solo flute in the orchestra of the Royal Guards and also of the Philharmonic Orchestra of the Capital. Has also taken part in the Vienna Philharmonic and later founded the Belgrado woodwind quintet giving there numerous concerts. In 1949 he was offered a position to teach at the Universidad Nacional de Cuoy and solo flutist of the Orquesta Sinfonica de la Universidad of that Argentina City. Habschied performed for the first time"Impresiones de la Puna" by the famous Argentina composer Alberto Ginastera.

* * *

HAGEMANN, PAUL: (1882-)
A distinguished and internationally known flute dilettante is Paul Hagemann, a banker of Copenhagen, Denmark. I think he could be compared with the Florentine Raffaello Galli (1824-1889), also a wealthy banker who devoted his life, talent, and his enthusiasm to his beloved flute, for which he composed many pieces, etudes and a fine method. Hagemann, in his younger days, when he was working in a bank in Paris, studied with

— 1 —

Taffanel and also with Hennebains. Hagemann's artistic playing met with the approval of Joachim Andersen (1847-1909) who encouraged him to appear in public both as a soloist and in ensemble. This he did with many noted musicians including Henry Marteau who dedicated to him his "Divertimento" for flute and violin and also a "Partita" for flute and viola. A number of composers from South America have dedicated "Suites" and "Sonatas" to Hagemann, among these are Becerra, Quintela, Maturana, and an extremely fine piece for flute alone by Esteban Heitler. The Swiss composer, Eric Schmidt, dedicated an interesting trio for flute (Hagemann), violin (G. Baccarotti), and the composer (at the piano), performed a number of times with fine success. Hagemann, when in Berlin, enjoyed the friendship of Adolph Goldberg (probably one of the very wealthiest of all flute dilettanti) and Emil Prill, to whom Goldberg presented a gold flute (now the property of Alfred Lichtenstein). Other famous composers who dedicated their flute works to Hagemann are the following: Joseph Lauber, 10 works, including a beautiful quartet for four flutes. P. V. Kleneau, 2 works. Karl Hasse, 1. Marteau, 2. Hindemith, 1. Joh. Nep. David, 2 Renê Baton, 1. Esteban Eitler, 1. Willy Schneider, 3.

Hagemann, in his letter to me, was evidently thrilled in regard to "My Complete Story of the Flute" and its two Addendas. He writes at length about the different makers of flutes and which is the best material. He is unacquainted with American flute firms and I supplied him with a list. Of the several flutes he has, the best one made of wood, is a Louis Lot, No. 7300. He thinks that a metal flute made of pure silver is superior to that made of gold.

* * *

IANELLI, ALFREDO: (Contemp.)
The first performance in South America (Buenos Aires) of the North American critic and composer Virgil Thomson's Concerto for flute and orchestra, was brilliantly played by Alfredo Ianelli. The composer conducted.

* * *

KLEMM, KONRAD: (1925 -)
An excellent performance of Jacques Ibert's Concerto for flute and orchestra was given by Konrad Klemm in Rome, December 1955 with Jean Martinon conducting splendidly.

* * *

LICHTENSTEIN, ALFRED: (Contemp.)
This young and talented flutist was soloist at the festival in Woodstock, New York on August, 1956.

LOLYA, ANDREW: (Contemp.)
Flutist of an excellent ensemble which has given fine concerts in Carnegie Hall, N. Y. The other members are: Margaret Hills, conductor; Grant Williams, tenor; Ronald Kutik, trumpeter; Melvin Kaplan, oboist; Harold Kohon, Raymond Kunicki, Alban Berg, violinist; David Uchitel, violist; Loren Bernsohn, cellist; Harriet Wingreen, cembalist, and others.

MOJICA, GILDARDO: (Contemp.)
In June of 1956 in Mexico City, in one of M[...] zart's numerous commemorative concerts an e[...] cellent performance of the double concerto f[...] flute and harp with an orchestra conducted [...] Antoine de Bavier, was played. The soloists we[...] Gildardo Mojica, flute and Senorita Judith Flo[...] Alatorre, harp.

* * *

PELLEGRINI GESUALDO: (Contemp.)
Recently, 1956, this fine flutist made a record the Concerto for flute and orchestra by Vival[...] called "La Notte." The performance was p[...] nounced "ravishing."

POLITIS, JAMES DIMITRI: (1921 -)
Studied flute with John Wummer. He is no[...] 1956, solo flute with the Metropolitan Oper[...] House of which orchestra he has been a men[...] ber since 1951. Politis was born in New York.

* * *

POLI, NIVES: (Contemp.)
Miss Poli, in November of 1955 at Naples on he[...] debut exhibited mastery of elected and chose[...] dancing and also on playing the flauto dolce e[...] quisitely.

* * *

PUGLIESE, NICOLA: (Contemp.)
Graduated from the Concervatory of Pesaro h[...] studied with Crespi. Pugliese is member of th[...] Teatro dell 'Opera at Rome and first prize c[...] the Rassegna Nazionale Giovani concertisti 1955 56.

* * *

RAPP, ROLF: (Contemp.)
Is the flutist of the newly formed (1955) "Vivald[...] Ensemble," Firenze, Italy. The members are: Lili[...] d'Albore, violin; Ornella Puliti-Santoliquido, piano[...] Rolf Rapp, liuto, cembalo, flauto dolce; Nives Poli[...] flauto dolce, soloists: other members: Massim[...] Amfiteatroff, cello; Giorgio Consolini, Land[...] Cianchi e Mario Barlacchi, violins; Elena Bellon[...] Filippi e Franco Lippi, violas; Fausto Turchini[...] cello; Carlo Coppoli, double bass. The "Vivald[...] Ensemble" specializes in XVI and XVII century music.

* * *

RAMPAL, PIERRE: (Contemp.)
On December 7, 1955, this famous French flutist[...] performed for the first time in Rome a concerto for flute and orchestra by Haydn in D major which was pronounced as fresh as if written recently. Rampal played also Leclair Concerto for flute and orchestra. De Fremment directed.

* * *

RISPOLI, PASQUALE: (Contemp.)
Who visited America with the "Virtuosi di Roma" in 1950, has given up flute playing for conducting, for which he has shown great talent. In a very successful concert in Milano, Rispoli conducted a Symphony by Haydn, an interesting composition for strings by the Venetian composer, Gabriele Bianchi and a Concerto Grosso in F Major for flute, oboe, clarinet, bassoon, horn and strings by Giorgio Federico Ghedini.

CALERA, NICOLA: (Contemp.)
pupil of D' Inverno Scalera is the solo piccolo the famous Teatro S. Carlo, Napoli.

* * *

TAYLOR F. PARKER: (Contemp.)
graduated from the Eastman School of Music. has been solo flute with the U.S. Army Band, Fort Myer, Virginia for a number of years. Taylor appeared a number of times as soloist, playing such artistic compositions as Griffes' "Poem" and others of equal importance.

* * *

URCIUOLO, FRANCESCO: (Contemp.)
This young artist is the new solo flutist of the San Carlo Opera of Napoli. In a first performance of "Concerto" for flute, strings, harp and celesta by Renato Parodi, Urciuolo was acclaimed by the large audience. The conductor, Rudolf Moralt.

URBAIN, JOSEPH: (Contemp.)
This young and able flutist and teacher from Ameries, Belgium, is a graduate "du Concorse International" of Geneva, Switzerland, 1948. Urbain writes that World War II was responsible for the loss of all his flute library, including De Lorenzo's "Nine Etudes," "L'Arte Moderna del Preludio," "Il Non Plus Ultra," "Vade Mecum" and many other works for flute and piano, which I have not been able to replace. "Fortunately, I have been able to procure "My Complete Story of the Flute" which I think is a great work."

* * *

WOLFS, WALTER: (Contemp.)
I cannot recall who sent me an interesting, illustrated musical page from a magazine with eleven "Picture Christmas Cards" from 1939 to 1954. It depicts a handsome musical family of eight with three dogs from Rydal, Pennsylvania. The head of the family, Walter Wolfs, is to be seen in each picture with his inseparable flute, always playing a position with the others performing on different instruments. In each picture they are in different costume, indians, cowboys, firemen, clowns, fishermen, ballet dancers, 19th Century dandies on an overflow English carriage called "break" and owned by a farm at a nearby riding academy. The instruments, besides Papa Wolfe's Flute are: pan pipes, shepherd's pipes, recorder, bassoon (or is it bass flute?), violin, guitar, accordion, ukelele and the players are apparently having a good time. Their names: Walter, Irene, Nicholas, Thomas, Catherine, Lucy, Alexandra and Andrew. The excellent photographer is Lucian Loeb.

* * *

ZEITLIN, SIDNEY: (Contemp.)
One of Los Angeles' young generations of flutists. On October 12, 1956, at the Hancock Auditorium University of Southern California) with Roland Moritz, gave a beautiful performance of De Lorenzo's "Suite Moderna" (4th movement) for 2 flutes. Also, at the same auditorium a few days later, October 21st, Zeitlin, this time assisted by the flutist Eve Dickens, played beautifully Cimarosa's Concerto for two flutes and orchestra under the direction of Ingolf Dahl.

Also a few other followers of Pan who should be mentioned:

ADELE STERRY (Contemp.)
Solo piccolo and flute with the Seattle Symphony. She is also a prominent teacher.

* * *

JULIUS KIMSLER (Contemp.)
Who, with Arthur Gleghorn and Haakon Bergh, played beautifully an excellent "Sonata" for three flutes by Hood at the Los Angeles Flute Club concert of November 11, 1956. Also, on the same program,, a "Sonatina Antique" for flute and cello by our departed friend and distinguished colleague Ary van Leeuwen, was splendidly performed by Arthur Gleghorn and Alexander Borisoff. In the first movement of this scholarly' written Sonata, van Leewen displayed his great love and admiration for Bach.

* * *

WALTER MANG (Contemp.)
A distinguished citizen of Heidleberg, Germany, who is an enthusiastic flute dilettante.

* * *

FRANCIS STOELF (Contemp.)
A young Belgian professional flutist of talent.

* * *

ROBERT E. EASTERN (Contemp.)
An esteemed citizen of Santa Barbara, California, manager of the gas company of the city and an old friend of Harry V. Baxter. He is also an enthusiastic lover of the flute and President of the Community Music and Arts Association.

KARL FRANKEL (Contemp.)
After he had seen and enjoyed a copy of "My Complete Story of the Flute" in Vienna he sent me a beautiful letter in appreciation and a Keyless transverse flute with six holes which he had played in the mountains of Austria for serenades, dances, etc. for many years. This little instrument, called Schwegelpfeife I shall treasure. It figures in delightful fairy stories and legends.

BETWEEN COMPOSERS

FRANCK, CESAR: (1822-1890)

This great master's peculiar charm, the masterly authority of his teaching, his goodness of heart and kindly manner that never grew less during the long years of his professional career, endeared him to everyone. At fifteen he left his native Belgium to enter the Paris Conservatory, then directed by Cherubini. Retiring and modest by nature, César Franck taught for years every day as many as ten pupils one hour each. One wonders where he found the time to create the great number of beautiful compositions he left at his passing. His life was always regular and tranquil, almost that of a Saint. The last thirty-two years of his life were spent as organist at the Church of Sainte Clotilde. His mind, sensitive to all kinds of beauty, open to all innovation, free from all jealousy, welcomed with the utmost warmth the compositions of his contemporaries who, more fortunate than himself, reached world success. He was indifferent to the plaudits of the multitude as Art for Art's sake was his heaven and lived apart from mortals in a superterrestrial world. The central character of his music may be described by the single word "mysticism." César Franck passed most of his time in divine contemplation and under his fingers the organ of Sainte Clotilde conversed with angels rather than men. However, in spite of Franck's great reputation and saintliness, he was severely and unjustly criticized by a number of his contemporary composers who attended the first performance of his Symphony in D Minor. Gounod said: "César Franck showed his impotence and lack of artistic power. Who has ever heard of employing an English Horn in a symphony?" The following are some of the many noted pupils of César Franck: Vincent D'Indy, Henry Duparc, Ernest Chausson, Gabriel Pierné, Augusta Holmes, Guy Ropartz and many others.

* * *

PERGOLESE: (1710-1736)

Pergolese or Pergolesi, which is right? As a matter of fact, both are right because the name derives from Pergola, which is also the name of a town from which the family of the composer originally came. If a person comes from Pergola, he is a Pergolese; if two, they are Pergolesi. Now the composer: In 26 short years this wonderful man composed numerous operas, both serious and comic, oratorios, cantatas, sacred music, instrumental music, etc., etc. His father was a surveyor and his grandfather a shoemaker. He studied the violin with Francesco Mondini and composition with Francesco Feo (C.1685-1740) one of the masters of the Neapolitan school and Francesco Durante (1684-1755) whose pupils included many of the most distinguished of the Italian composers: Traetta, Vinci, Jommelli, Piccinni, Sacchini, Pergolese and Paisiello.

The most famous of his operas is "La Serva Padrona." Many others of equal worth were hissed mercilessly by a public whose mood no one could predict. "L'Olimpiade" (How prophetic was Duni, Egidio Romuoldo (1709-1775) the founder of Opera-Comique in France who, on seeing the score of "Olmpiade" Pergolese's Capo d' opera s: to the composer: "Your music is much too good be successful." When this opera was first giv in Rome with the young composer conductir after a few hisses someone threw a rotten oran which struck the composer's head! The offem was so unexpected and so great that Pergolc never really recovered from that shameful attitu by a supposed civilized public. The above d: gusting episode to a sensitive genius was the tr cause of his premature death, not, as some bi graphers contend that the many love affai shortened his life. It was also after this affair th Pergolese showed the first sign of consumptic and moved to Pozzuoli, devoting his creative pow only to sacred music. There he wrote the famor "Stabat Mater" for which he was promised te ducats but whether this was paid is doubtful, his possessions had to be sold to pay the expens of his funeral which amounted to eleven ducat As to his love affairs, two must be mentioned. Tr first, that he was in love with the daughter Lord Bulwer, British Ambassador Extraordinary the Courte of Naples, is considered a legend an hardly requires formal refutation. The secon Maria Spinelli, of the princely house of Caria was told by her three brothers that unless sr chose within three days a husband who was he equal by birth, they would kill the compose Pergolese, with whom she was in love, and wr returned her affection. After three days the lad decided to enter a nunnery instead, stipulatir that Pergolese was to conduct the mass on occasion of her taking the veil. She entered th Convent of Santa Chiara, and died there a yea later. Pergolese again conducted the requiem fo her. His own death took place little more than year after this and he was buried in the Cathedra of Pozzuoli.

Soon after Pergolese's death, the famous com poser Paisiello made the following unkind re mark: "Pergolese would not have been so mucl esteemed if he had lived longer!" That statemen could as well be applied to Shubert, Mozart Chopin, Mendelssohn, and others. However, i was well known that Paisiello was of a jealou disposition. Pergolese's romantic history has form ed the subject of two operas bearing his name, on by Paolo Serrao (Naples 1867) and the other by Stefano Ronchetti Monteviti (Milano 1857).

* * *

GLINKA, MICHAEL IVANOVICH: (1803-1857)

Years before Debussy was born, to whom credit was given for being the first to use the whole-tone scale Glinka, whom Listz designated the "Prophet-Patriarch" of Russian and who laid the foundation of the modern Russian School of Music, made use of the whole-tone scale in one of his early operas, "Russlan and Ludmilla" in 1842. This Opera, on a subject by the eminent poet and writer Pushkin (1799-1837) would have been much more successful if Pushkin had prepared the libretta, as he promised to Glinka and if he had not been killed in a duel just before he began his sk, at the age of 38. As it was, the libretto was t togther by no less than five others, and proved be a concoction of superstition, romance, wizdy, magic sword, etc. The overture, one of the w elements of the score to come off successfully, to be found often in concert programs. Glinka d Berlioz were born the same year, 1803, from ealthy parents. They became close friends from e first visit of Glinka to Paris and the admiran for each other was mutual and sincere.

* * *

AISIELLO, GIOVANNI: (1741-1816)

ow very little is remembered of this highly talted and very prolific composer who wrote nearly 0 works, which includes about 100 operas, both ria and buffa, symphonies, oratorios, cantatas, c., etc. He was born at Taranto, south of Naples, d studied at San Pietro a Majella. His father as a veterinary surgeon. As a young man his orks were so successful that his fame preceeded im wherever he went. Catherine the Great of ussia secured his service for eight years in which untry he was admired and honored. In Paris apoleon remunerated him handsomely and conrred upon him several decorations. However, in pite of his great success and protection of both atherine the Great and Napoleon, as a man, aisiello was not admired because of his unusually alous disposition. "La Pupilla" and "Il Mondo a ovescio" two successful comic operas written for ologna, where he was summoned after the sucess of his dramatic "Intermezzo" composed while ill at the Conservatory, inaugurated a long series f successes in all the chief Italian towns. "L'Idolo inese" was another successful opera and "Il Marchese di Tulipan" written for Rome in 1792, njoyed for years a European popularity. Another f Paisiello's successful operas was "Molinara" beause its airs were remarkable for simplicity, grace nd charm. The duet of "Nel cor pui non mi ento," immortalized by a number of great composers, including Beethoven who wrote famous ariations on the theme and Paganini used it on ne of his violin solos. In England where it was known as "Hope told a flattering tale" became famous for many years. "Il Barbiere di Siviglia," however, written in St. Petersburg about 1780, one of his finest works, when first performed in Rome soon after his return from Russia, was coldly received, but it ended by obtaining so firm a hold on the affection of the Roman public, that the attempt of another composer to write another "Barber" was regarded as sacrilege, nor would this audience at first give even a hearing to the famous work which finally consigned its predecessor to oblivion. On one occasion when Paisiello, full of success and honors, came face to face with young Rossini recently arrived in Rome to endeavor to produce his "Barber," the elder composer severely reprimanded him by saying, "sbarbatello sfacciato" (impudent beardless young man) for attempting to write an opera on which subject He himself had already composed a successful one.

RIMSKY-KORSAKOV: (1844-1908)
A famous English music critic who was also a contrapuntist and composer of religious music said, when he first heard the name Rimsky Korsakov, " A man with such a name I visualize with great bushy whiskers saturated with vodka and with an unsteady gait." (Probably the English music critic had in mind Moussorgsky whom, it was said, never composed unless under the influence of liquor).

* * *

RAIMONDI PIETRO: (1786-1853)
One of the greatest contrapuntists of all times. Besides 66 operas one, "Il Ventaglio" considered very unusual because of the great erudition throughout. Of his five oratorios, three (Putifar Giuseppe and Giacobbe) after having been performed separately at the Teatro Argentina of Rome, were performed together at the same time. Of his many religious compositions and religious symphonies, in one of these, a "Fuga" in sixty-four parts divided in sixteen choruses is considered a prodigious and unique work. Raimondi was teacher of composition at the Naples Conservatory, director of the Palermo Conservatory and in the last few years of his life, Maestro a San Pietro in Vaticano.

* * *

RANDHARTINGER, BENEDICT: (1802 - ?)
Of the many forgotten composers, Randartinger, who was a close friend of Schubert and one of the very few friends who visited Schubert in the terrible loneliness of his last illness, was an Austrian and probably one of the most prolific. At first he studied for the law and was for ten years at the Court of Vienna as Secretary to Count Széchényi. Soon after he forsook this line of life for music. His compositions are more than six hundred in number, comprising an opera "Kônig Enzio;" twenty masses, 60 motets; symphonies quartets, etc.; 400 songs; 76 four-part songs, etc. A volume of Greek National songs, and the volume of Greek liturgies. He studied composition with Salieri.

* * *

RACHMANINOFF, SERGEI: (1873-1943)
In my Addenda Number II I wrote of the dislike of the American composer MacDowell for Brahms' music. Now let us see what effect MacDowell's music had on Rachmaninoff. In 1906 Rachmaninoff had gone with his family to Dresden, Germany, where he spent the following three years, returning to Russia only for the summer. He had chosen Dresden also because of the impression he had received there on an earlier visit from a performance of "Die Meistersinger." Too, he was delighted at the thought of being able to hear Nikisch conduct the Gewandhaus Orchestra in nearby Leipsig. He enjoyed the opera and was strongly impressed by Richard Strauss' "Salome" and never tired of attending Meistersinger and various oratorios. However, when he heard Teresa Carreño play MacDowell's "D minor Piano Con-

certo" in Leipzig, complained that he did not like the music by someone called Dovel and was so upset by it that he coughed and sneezed for the next three days!

It is interesting to know that when Rachmaninoff's second symphony came out, Nikisch had it on two of his programs but, when he saw that the score was dedicated to S. I. Taneiev, Nikis struck the symphony from his two programs (Berlin and Leipzig) though the symphony w already printed on them. Nikisch's disappointme that the symphony was not dedicated to him w such that he never spoke to Rachmaninoff aft that and even refused to see him!

CASALS, SCHOENBERG and the . . . music of the future!

CASALS PABLO (1876-)

YSAYE, the famous Belgian violinist who was himself esteemed as one of the great masters of the bow, at the beginning of this century said "CASALS is the greatest master of the bow of all time." And the noted Violoncellist Piatigorsky, when CASALS was touring in Russia, traveled 200 miles in bitter cold weather, to hear him play. However, the most astounding thing is that now, in 1957, at eighty CASALS' art is as great as it was fifty years ago. Several biographies have been written on CASALS, the latest of which, is called "Conversations avec PABLO CASALS" by J. M. Corredor and published by the Paris House of Albine Michel.

As one browses through the volume, one is tempted to pause and quote and to marvel too. Can you imagine a quintet with Fritz Kreisler and Jacques Thibaud as the violinists, Eugéne Ysaye as the violist, Casals as the 'Cellist and Ferruccio Busoni as the pianist? These men met and played together in Belgium before World War I—just for their own fun.

Now CASALS and the modern music. "The is nothing sincere about modern music" Pab Casals told an Associated Press representativ "The tragedy is that all modern composers kno it, but can't admit it . . . nobody loves it. It lac all conviction." He then recalled a conversation I once had with Arnold Schoenberg, inventor of tl 12-tone system of composition. Schoeberg told hi he was trying to find out "what was on the ba of the medal which we call music, to discover tl elements of a new kind of music." "Poor Schoe berg," said Casals, " he caught himself in his ov net. He could not find the new kind of musi because what he found was no music. But h many followers and imitators took him at h word and pretended that a new music had bee discovered." Before anybody says, "Maybe it the altitude, let me batten down all the hatches. The above is taken from "Musical America. March 1956. I first met Casals in Minneapolis i 1916. The brief meeting was in Italian, whic language he spoke like a native.

FAMOUS BACHELORS

(Noted men who never married)

VIRGIL (70 B.C. — 19 B.C.)
CICERO (106 — 43 B.C.)
SENECA (4 B.C. — 64 A.D.)
MARCO POLO (1254 — 1324)
BOCCACCIO (1313 — 1324)
MASACCIO (1401 — ?)
DONATELLO (1386 — 1466)
LEONARDO (1452 — 1519)
MICHELANGELO (1475 — 1564)
SAVONAROLA (1452 — 1498)
ARIOSTO (1474 — 1533)
LUTHER (1483 — 1546)
TIZIANO (1477 — 1576)
RAFFAELLO (1483 — 1520)
BOTTICELLI (1444 — 1510)
ERASMUS (1466 — 1536)
GIORGIONE (1477 — 1510)
CELLINI (1500 — 1571)
CERVANTES (1547 — 1616)
GIORDANO BRUNO (1550 — 1600)
VELASQUES (1599 — 1660)
NEWTON (1642 — 1727)
VOLTAIR (1694 — 1778)
HANDEL (1685 — 1759)
QUANTZ* (1697 — 1773)
HAMILTON ALEXANDER (1751 — 1804)
PERGOLESI (1710 — 1736)
KANT (1752 — 1837)
ZINGARELLI (1752 — 1837)
BEETHOVEN (1770 — 1827)
SCHOPENHOUR (1788 — 1860)
THORWALDSEN (1773 — 1846)
TURNER (1775 — 1851)
KUHLAU (1786 — 1832)
CZERNY (1791 — 1804)
COROT (1796 — 1875)
DONIZETTI (1797 — 1848)
KEATS (1795 — 1821)
SCHUBERT (1797 — 1828)
PUSHKIN (1799 — 1837)
BELLINI (1801 — 1836)
THOREAU (1817 — 1862)
WHITMAN (1819 — 1892)
CHOPIN (1810 — 1849)
NICOLAI (1810 — 1849)
DOSTOJEWSKY (1827 — 1887)
BRAHMS (1833 — 1897)
MOUSSORGSKY (1835 — 1881)
GIORGI (1856 — 1953)
OSCAR WILDE (1860 — 1900)
HUGO WOLF (1860 — 1903)
BOÏTO (1842 — 1918)

*Quantz, like his royal pupil Frederick the Great
(1712 - 1786) belongs to this list of famous bachelors because both he and the King were
married in their youth to the wrong person
and the union only lasted a few days.

SOME UNUSUAL SHORT LEGENDS MOSTLY FROM THE LAND OF PAN AND MARSYAS

According to greek legend, Midas, King of
Phrygia was so fond of wealth that in spite of the
fact he was the richest man in the world, asked the
gods that all he touched might turn to gold. His
wish was granted, but when, even his food became
gold, he implored relief and gained it by bathing
in the river Pactolus. At the famous contest between Apollo and Marsyas, Midas was the only one
who voted in favor of Marsyas, and for that he
was given ass's ears! Midas contended the contest
unfair because Apollo made use of two instruments, lyre and voice, against Marsyas' Pan pipes.

* * *

"GORGONS" Three winged female monsters,
according to Hesiod (first of the greek didactic
poets) they were named "Stheno" Eurvale,'' and
"Medusa;" they had snakes for hair, and turned
all who looked upon them to stone. Medusa, who
alone was mortal, was slain by Perseus (the hero
son of Danâê by Zeus) watching her mirrored in
his shield, so that he need not look upon her.

* * *

"CYRENAICA" An ancient country of North
Africa, also called Barca. The capital was "Cyere,"
where lived Aristippus, a pupil of Socrates. He
founded the "Cyrenaic School" of philosophers,
who advocated pleasure as the chief aim of life.

* * *

"PANDORA" A beautiful woman (all gifted)
upon whom the gods lavished their choicest gifts.
She was the wife of Epimetheus, the brother of
Prometheus. Zeus gave her a box in which was im-
prisoned all human ills; this was "Pandora's box."
The woman could not restrain her curiosity, and
against all instructions she opened the box, re-
leasing the ills to scatter over the earth. Hope,
also in the box remained as her only consolation.
A variation of the legend states that the box
contained all the blessings of the gods. including
Hope, and that Pandora allowed all to escape
save only Hope.

* * *

"Tezcatlipoca" A leading god of the Aztecs.
He was worshiped as the supreme creator, and god
of music and the dance. He had many forms and
attributes. His altar at Tenochtitlan was the scene
of human sacrifices, especially of prisoners of war.

* * *

"Aesculapius: Greek god of medicine. He
showed his power by raising the dead and so
aroused the anger of Zeus, who killed him with a
thunderbolt. He is mentioned by Homer and may
have been an actual person.

* * *

"PHIDIAS" greatest of the ancient greek
sculptors, 490 B.C. under Pericles superintended
all the works of art designed to beautify Athens.
His chryselephantine statue of Zeus at Olimpus
was one of the Wonders of the Ancient world. He
died in prison, a victim of jealousy, in 432 B. C.

"HERMAPHRODITE" Individual capable of producing both spermatoza and ova, and therefore possessing the functions of both sexes. The condition is normal in plants whose flowers contain stamens and pistils, although selffertilization is less usual than cross-fertilization. Some invertebrates are normally self-fertilizing, e.g., the oyster and the clam. Earth-worms are both hemaphrodite and colpulative, two individual simultaneously impregnating each other.

*   *   *

"PHAETHON" Son of the sun-god Helios and the nymph Clymene. Attempting to drive his father's chariot his strength failed and he approached the earth so closely as to scorch it. Zeus struck him with a thunderbolt into the river Eridanus on Po. (one of Camille Saint-Saens; 1835-1921, four Symphonic poems for orchestra, is named "Phaethon;" the others are "Le Rouet d' Amphale," "Le Jeunesse d' Hercule" and "Danse Nacabre")

*   *   *

"PRAXITELES" greek sculptor, 400 B.C. During excavations among the ruins of Olympia in 1877 a group of Hermes and Dionysus (only original sculpture by him in existence) was found. He died in 330 B.C.

*   *   *

HYDRA" A nine headed monster haunting the Lerna marsher. Its destruction formed one of the labors of Hercules. As each head was removed two others replaced it, the central one being immortal. Aided by Iolaus, Hercules burned their roots with firebrands, and then severed and buried the central head.

*   *   *

"THETIS The mother of Achilles. She was a Nereid, and married Peleus a mortal. The gods Poseidon and Zeus sought her love, but they abandoned their wooing when they learned that her son was destined to out do his father.

*   *   *

"APHRODITE" The goddess of love. One legend made her the daughter of Zeus and Dione; in another she rose from the foam of the sea, this being the meaning of her name. She became the wife of Hephaestus (Vulcan) and had as her lovers Hermes, Ares, Poseidon and other gods, as well as Anchises, a mortal. By Ares she was the mother of Eros. Aphrodite was regarded as the goddess of Fruitfulness and the ideal of female beauty.

*   *   *

"APOLLO" greek god, god of healing and the father of Aesculapius. He had also the gift of prophecy and to him the famous temple, with its oracle, at Delphi, was dedicated. He was also the god of song and music, and his emblems included the lyre and the bow. The finest existing example is the statue of the Apollo Belvedere in tre Vatican, Rome.

*   *   *

"JOCASTA" The mother of Oedipus and the wife of Thebes. On her husband's death she married her own son Oedipus and bore him children, but on discovering his idendity, she hanged herself.

A FEW UNUSUAL WORDS
AND THEIR MEANING

"ASHURBAMPAL HAMMURABI" King Babylon, sixth monarch of 1st dynasty.

*   *   *

"NIMROD" Son of Cus a *mighty one of th* *earth* and the founder of Babel. Aso a might hunter and warrior.

*   *

"NINEVEH" City of Assyria. After centurie of political activities under Hammurabi and late under Sennacherib and Ashurbamipal, it becam the royal capital. Nabopulassas, King of Babylo brought upon its fall 612 B.C.

*   *   *

MWERU" Lake of Africa, 90 miles to th west of Lake Tanganyyika, discovered by Davi Livingstone in 1867.

*   *   *

"PASSAMAGUODDY" Inlet of the bay o Fundy, between Main and Canada.

*   *   *

"MULLIGATAWNY" The name is a nativ Indian soup, meaning literally "pepperwater."

*   *   *

"MURRUMBIDGEE" River of New South Wales, Australia.

*   *   *

"MUMBO JUMBO" Tribal deity of African Savages.

*   *   *

"SEMACHERIB" King of Assyria (701 - 68 B.C.) conquered Phoenicia, ravaged Judaea and beseiged Jerusalem; built many canals and an enormous palace at Nineveh. Was murdered by his two sons.

*   *   *

"ZOMBI" In woodooism, a corpes believed to be animated without a soul. Such reanimated dead bodies are resurrected for slavery.

*   *   *

"APALACHICOLA" River of Florida, flowing for 90 miles to the Gulf of Mexico. It is formed by the union of the Chattahoochee and Flint Rivers.

*   *   *

'ANU" Babylonian god of heaven. At first worshipped as a local sky deity in Erech, he came to be regarded as supreme in a triad which included Bel of Nippur and Ea of Eridu, who were deemed to rule heaven, earth and sea respectively.

—8—

A FEW OF THE MANY EMINENT NEGLECTED COMPOSERS OF THE PAST

Many countries, including France, Germany, Spain, England and others have had a number of fine but neglected composers in the past. However, I think Italy's list is easily the longest. From the following, which I could double if space permitted the works of the old masters are discovered very often by enthusiastic musicologists to brighten their hearts.

ANIMUCCIA (1495 — 1511)
MONTEVERDI (1567 — 1643)
FRESCOBALDI 1583 — 1644)
CAVALIERI (1550 — 1599)
DONI (1593 — 1647)
NANINI (1545 — 1607)
TURINI (1595 — 1656)
MARENZIO (1525 — 1599)
ZARLINO (1517 — 1590)
GALILEI (C. 1553 — ? 1603)
CACCINI (1558 — ?)
PERI (1561 — ?)
CARISSIMI (1604 — 1675)
CESTI (1620 — 1669)
LEGRENZI (? 1625 — ?)
PASQUINI (1637 — 1710)
CIAJA (1671 — ?)
MARCELLO (1686 — 1739)
CAPOCCI (1674 — 17?)
PERTI (1661 — 1756)
ALESSANDRO SCARLATTI (1659 — 1725
PORPORA (1686 — 1767)
DURANTE (1684 — 1755)
CLARI (1669 — ? 1745)
ALBINONI (1674 — 1745)
PADRE MARTINI (1706 — 1784)
ZIPOLI (C. 1675 — ?)
PESCETTI (1704 — 1766)
CIAMBI (1719 — ?)
GALUPPI (706 — 1785)
NARDINI (1722 — 1793
CIMAROSA (1749 — 1801
*BIANCHI (1752 — 1810)
FIORAVANTI (1764 — 1837)
GENERALI (1783 — 1832)
COCCIA (1782 — 1873)
PARADISI (1710 — 1792)
SACCHINI (1734 — 1786)
SALIERI (1750 — 1825)
ZINGARELLI (1752 — 1837)

*WAS teacher to Sir Henry Bishop. Wrote many operas for Paris and London where he died by his own hand in 1810.

* * *

THE DUKE OF MILANO AND DA VINCI

LEONARDO DA VINCI was called from Florence to the court of Milano not as a scientist or a painter or a sculptor but "because he was such an adept harpist, playing and singing his own compositions." So Leonardo came and led the dance and the tourney; improvised songs and planned the fetes and festivals where strange animals turned into birds and gigantic flowers opened, disclosing beautiful girls. Knowing then, that the powerful Duke was unaware of his other talents and that he had called him solely to entertain his guests, because he was "the most accomplished harpist in Italy," he decided to write the Duke a letter, wherein he commends himself, and in humility tells of a few things he can do. The following is Da Vinci's letter in his original hand writing. This most precious document is now in the Ambrosian Library at Milano.

"I believe I am equaled by no one in architecture, in constructing public and private buildings, and in conducting water from one place to another. I can execute sculpture, whether in marble, bronze or terra cotta, and in drawing and painting I believe I can do as much as any other man, be he who he may. Further, I could engage to execute the bronze statue in memory of your honored father. And again, if any of the abovementioned things should appear impossible or overstated I am ready to make such performance in any place or at any time to prove to you my power. "In humility I thus commend myself to your illustrious house, and am your servant, Leonardo da Vinci."

And the strange part of all this is that Leonardo could do all he claimed or he might, if there were a hundred hours in a day and man did not grow old.

* * *

UNUSUAL CHORDS

At one time long ago, in 1907 to be exact, I brought two unusual chords of the seventh to my theory teacher Camillo De Nardis. He had a great reputation as a scholar and was one of the finest contrapuntist in Europe. I asked him what he thought of them and also I wanted to know if my analysis was correct.
The following were the chords:

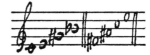

The first, dominant chord of seventh with an augmented fifth and the second, also a dominant chord of seventh with a diminished 5th.
The Maestro, who had a very sharp eye, only said, "those chords were devised by satan, and, therefore, will at all times be able to produce only infernal noise but, beautiful music, never."—Years after, forgetting what Maestro De Nardis had told me about those two chords and, just for fun, I transposed the first chord C, E, G sharp and B flat, a semitone higher for eleven times, thus, including the first, I had produced twelve unusual chords of the seventh. Having done the same with the second chord, F sharp, A sharp, C and E, I added another 12 unusual chords of the seventh to my table of chords. Now, instead of being satisfied with such an abundant table of chords, I trans-

posed the same two chords a semitone lower! Of course I soon discovered that there were numerous repetitions in its inversions etc.—After this mastodondic charts of chords produced from only two original ones, I said to myself: by using many other chords I could keep on going ad infinitum!— Please notice that in all chords there isn't a single one in which two semitones are close to each other such as is found e. g. in the chord of seventh on the first degree of C major:

Formerly one abided by rules which avoided such unpleasant discords but these have been long discarded.—However, I looked at my chart and said: "Now what shall I do with all this *cement foundation?* So I selected four chords, wrote an accompaniment suitable for a second flute and then wrote the piece on top and, vice versa, I selected the tune first on other four chords and then devised the accompaniment.

After several weeks of real hard work, in reading over my accomplishments in composing on only unusual chords, I said to myself: " How right Maestro De Nardis was!" And, too, I wonder how many others did the same thing, that is, devising chords which only satan enjoys?

* * *

MISCELLANEOUS

PROFESSOR Carlo Tommaso Giorgi, world inventor of the Giorgi flute died November 28, 1953 in Viareggio at the age of 97. His niece Signora Luisa Cadaciocchi, Via Luigi Muzzi 31 Prato, (Toscana) Italy, notified me and also, forwarded a booklet, MUSICA - FISICA - CINEMATICA." L' Atomica nella Musica" published by Angiolini and Vissibelli, Lucca, Italy, Via Vecchia S. Marco. The purpose of this pamphlet, which was written a few months prior to his passing is to show that the whole music structure could be in mathematical numbers, abolishing lines, clefs, keys, sharps, flats etc. The phamplet was copywrited in 1952.

* * *

.The Yugoslavian flute virtuoso, Jose' Habschied, who has made his home in De Cuyo, Mendoza, South America, is very proud of the fact that he gave the first performance in that country of Jaques Ibert's difficult concerto with the "Orquesta Sinfonica — Universidad National." The conductor was Aquiles Romani. The flutists of the symphony of that " Escuela Superior de Musica" are Jose' Habschied, Blanca Vicente and Pedro Candito. The concert took place in the Teatro Indipendencia, Wednesday, June 13, 1956, at 10 p.m.

Victor Saudek, President of the Pittsburg Flute Club for over 40 years, retired in San Diego California since 1953, conducted a pop concert an performed Bach's Sonata No. 2 in E flat, with Corinne Du Val Brevin at the piano, May 28, 1956

* * *

Sidney Lanier did not die in Baltimore, a stated by some of his biographers, but on a house on Route 108, one and a half miles north of Tryon 50 miles east, south of Asheville, North Carolina

* * *

The Christian Science Monitor of May 25 1956, besides reproducing a "Short History of the Flute" from My Complete Story of the Flute had a wonderful illustrated article on Stradivarius titled " A Genius Among Artisans" by Nicolas Slonimsky. Then, on the same page, there were two poems on Stradivarius, one by George Eliot (1819 — 1880) and one by Henry W. Longfellow (1807 — 1882). Also there was a poem on the "Maple Bassoon" by Winthrop P. Tryon, Post— "Reaissance Painting" and also a magnificent article in a beautiful Italian, "Il regno dentro di noi." *The Home Forum* page of that date was, artistically speaking, unique, matchless!

* * *

Stromento di Porco: This uncomplimentary and unattractive name was given a musical instrument of long ago originally called Psaltery or Salterio. In an illustration from 15th century painting by Filippino Lippi it represents a "stromento di porco" so-called by Praetorius in his "Organographia" because of its likeness to a pig's head. It was played without a plectrum.

* * *

On one of the Los Angeles Flute Club concerts (June 11, 1956) there was an interesting piece for flute, cello and piano composed for Luisa Di Tullio by Eugene Poddany. The cellist was Frederick Seykora and at the piano, Virginia Di Tullio, sister of Luisa. The composition was beautifully performed and enjoyed by the unusually large audience.

* * *

Two works of mine were performed at the 1956 Los Angeles Flute Club Annual concert at the Hancock Auditorium of the University of Southern California October 12. A young lady mentioned to a friend of ours that she had never seen or spoken to a composer, so at intermission time, our friend told me about the incident and asked me to shake hands with the young girl which I did to her evident delight. I then told her the story of an old farmer who had never seen an opera—so when one of his friends took him as his guest it was a great event. During the curtain calls he noticed one man taking bows with the singers. He was in civilian clothes and so was not a member of the cast. This puzzled him and he asked, "say, who is that guy who hasn't done a speck of work and who is bowing so much?" When he was told that that was the composer of the opera, with incredible surprise he said: "well, I will be darned, I thought all the composers were dead!"

PIGS AND BASSOONS

I have before me an extremely amazing picture of four fat pigs sitting on their hind legs each playing the bassoon, and in front, a baby pig with a piccolo, taken from Musical America issue of August 1956. We have been faithful subscribers to this excellent magazine for over forty years and I have their permission to quote anything I wish.

Genuine comic effects can be produced by certain sound colors. The bassoon, for instance, has been called the clown of the orchestra, a generalization that is too sweeping. The bassoon can be a very serious instrument, capable of singing beautiful cantilenas. But with a certain handling, in certain registers in staccato jumps or quick passages, it sounds definitely funny. It has been used for this purpose innumerable times. D'Albert, for instance, in his opera "Flauto Solo" composed a pigs' quartet for four bassoons, with the piccolo added as the voice of the piglet.

* * *

From musical America of September 1956, we learned that at a concert in Darmstadt, Germany, the first world performance of a new Sonatina for Flute and Piano by Boulez, was perfomed by the Roman flutist Severino Gazzelloni of the platinum flute. The Boulez title might well be ironic, for the Sonatina is of the utmost technical difficulty and is a broad sonata design in four parts, to boot. The flute, has ecstatic and feverish melodic curves of fortissimo and pianissimo in the highest and lowest registers, with flutter-tongue passages and leaps of the ninth. The performance by the Roman flutist Severino Gazzelloni and the New York pianist David Tudor was dazzling, a sovereign achievement. After so bold a style, Schoenberg's Wind Quintet, admirably played by the Cologne Radio Ensemble, seemed classically sedate.

* * *

At a Los Angeles Flute Club concert on September 9th 1956, there was an unusual and distinctive novelty of artistic merit. Its title, "Insect Suite," by the well known Hollywood conductor-composer Charles Previn:
1. Autobiography of a Japanese Beetle
2. Supplication of a Praying Mantis
3. Confessions of an Aphis
4. Lullaby for the Baby Spider
5. Traffic on an Ant Hill
Before the performance the composer gave an interesting synopsis of each number in a manner which was delightfully amusing.

The five artists, each of equal merit and well known, were :
Joachim Chassman, violin
Milton Thomas, viola
Kurt Reher, cello
Stella Castellucci, harp
Sheridon Stokes, flute
The performance of each number was impeccable and enjoyed by everyone present.

* * *

"MARSYAS" On Wednesday, August 1956, an excellent " Prelude and Entract" from "Marsyas" by Diepenbrock (1862 —) was played on the gas hour in Los Angeles by the Concertbouw orchestra of Amsterdam conducted by Edward Van Beinum. The interesting solo flute was masterly performed altho the artist was not mentioned.

* * *

The following interesting collection of flutistic pictures was sent to me from Rome, Italy, in April of 1956, by Panico Giuseppe, who is solo flute with the "Banda del Corpo delle Guardie di Pubblica Sicurezza:"
1. CALLIOPE, EUTERPE, with flute and Talia, three of the nine Muses.
2. "Tre angeli musicanti" by Bernardino Luini.
3. The Angel's Song.
4. "George Biddle Playing the Flute" by Alexander Brook.
5. "Glass Instruments" (Berlin Exposition 1938) picturing flutes, clarinets, oboes, bassoons, cellos etc., all made of glass.
6. "The Flute as it was in the middle of the XVIII century" picturing a nobleman with an enormous wig playing the tranverse flute.
7. "Storekeeper Cullen" Jimmy by night, King by day (playing the flute on the michrophone for an unseen audience).
8. "Concert D'Amateurs" Ladies singing and other performers on violin, double bass, oboe. The flutist is an aristocrat with a wig and a sword on his left side.
9. "Il Minuetto" by Watteau — Besides the dancers there is a lady playing the lute and a flutist.
10. "Suonatore di Flauto" Trieste Museo Civico di Storia ed Arte (Scuola francese XVII century).
11. "Costume de Fou" (XVI° Siecle) Dapre' le chevalier Chevignard. A Mephistofelic flutist.
12. A nude woman under a huge birch tree on top of which Pan plays his double flute unconcerned.
12½. Two barefooted little San Blas girls (Panama) play primitive Panpipes.
13. "The Trio" A violinist, sitting, another very old man with a recorder in his hands and another man, standing, playing on a keyless transverse flute. "First Part of Henry IV." The flutist in this picture is elaborately dressed like a Mousketeer with sword and leather gloves! The King, with a large beer stein is amused.
14. Der frohliche Flotenspieler. Two boys with one flute having lots of fun.
15. A horse carriage with the driver in front, in a forest of tall trees. inside the carriage two lovers, the man's head on her shoulder while on the back of the carriage, outside, a nude boy plays the flute.
16. "Le Concert" a drawing by Michel Moreau (1741 — 1814) four aristocrates: a lady at the harpsichord and three gentlemen, violin, flute and a singer.
17. "The Solo" An oil painting by Paul Sample. An old gentleman standing in front of a music stand plays on his flute. This picture has two articles, one on "The Solo" and a long one entitled "Pastorale on a Flute" by Harriet Patchin Botham, from (The Christian Science Monitor, August 12, 1955).
18. Philippine Folk Musician, A young Hanunoo girl playing a nose flute.

19. Music from Palestine, "Aviva," girl singing, and "Hillel" youngman with mustach playing the recorder.
20. 'Spahis," A tribe of desert Mahomeddan nomads with a band of about fifty playing trumpets and flutes in their beautiful costumes.
21. "Spahis" A band of nomads aristocrats gentlemen of the desert elegantly dressed and playing flute.
22. "The Magic Flute," Then and now. Picturing two Papagenos each with a large cage of birds on their backs, playing on Pan's pipes.

* * *

THE SUDDEN PASSING OF A BELOVED FLUTIST

The sudden and untimely passing of Henry Woempner at Colfax, California, in September 1956, was a shock to all who knew him. He was loved not only for his artistic attainments but also for his kindness. His was a gay, blithe spirit and his playing too was gay and impetuous, but always that of a fine artist. We remember particularly his excellent performance of Dr. Wesley La Violette's beautiful Sonata (recorded) for flute and piano which was composed for Henry Woemper.

* * *

"Vivaldi" lived in peace with himself, so much so that his compatriots allowed him to die miserably in Vienna July 28, 1741. The cost of his funeral was 19 florins and 45 cents and even the bells of the poor were allowed to peal (Gian Francesco Malipiero, "Ricordiana," November 1955).

* * *

ALBERT TIPTON, the solo flutist of the St. Louis Symphony for many years is, since 1956, solo flutist with the Detroit Symphony. Tipton is also the flutist of the Detroit quintet whose other members, first desk players of the Symphony are, Gordon Staples, assistant concert master; Vincent Malidon, clarinet; William Sabatini, horn; and William Prencil, violist.

* * *

PROMINENT SOUTH AMERICAN FLUTISTS

The first of the three, not only because of seniority but because he is an excellent and prolific composer as well, is Esteban Eitler. The second is José Habschied and the third is Angelo Martucci. I received from them news of their artistic activities as soloists teachers etc., besides programs, photographs and biographical sketches. A little while ago (June of 1956) that genial South American genius of the cello Ennio Bolognini who, like Martucci, is of Italian extraction on a visit to Villa Pan, in glancing at the numerous photographs in the large room named " Temple of Pan," suddenly cried: "There is my dear friend Martucci, do you know him? and do you correspond with him?" The flutists of South America evidently are immune of jealousy. Not only they speak of each other with admiration but they seemingly go further. When Eitler heard of "My Complete Story of the Flute" he forwarded money order for three copies and said the other two copies were personal gift for his two distinguished colleagues Habschied and Martucci.

* * *

"MUSIC" AND IN PARTICULAR "FLUTE MUSIC" PROCLAIMS ETERNAL TRUTHS

"IL FLAUTO"
Ascolta:
dolcissimo un flauto lamenta
Ventagli d' aria
muovono il suo pianto
La sua voce
soavemente esala
parole d' amore
Franca Masetti

* * *

NEW FLUTE MUSIC FROM EVERYWHERE

ESTEBAN EITLER:
  Insinuacion (flauta sola)
  Sentimiento indefinido (flauta y piano)
GUSTAVO BECERRA:
  Trio for flute, violin and viola
MARIUS FLOTHUIS:
  Sonata da Camera (flute and piano)
HECTOR GALLIC:
  Pastora Calchaqui (flute and harp)
STEVAN HRISTIC:
  Danza griega (flute and piano)
WOLFGANG JACOBI:
  Trio for flute, violin and piano
ANGEL E. LASALA:
  Poem del Pastor Coya (flute and harp)
JOSEPH LAUBER:
  Suite clasique (flute and piano)
FRANK MARTIN:
  Ballada (flute and piano, or flute and orchestra)
BOHUSLAV MARTINU:
  Sonata (flute and piano)
  Madrigal (flute, violin and piano)
WALTER PISTON:
  Sonata (flute and piano)
HALSEY STEVENS:
  Sonatina (flute and piano)
PETER STOJANOVIC:
  Concerto (flute and orchestra) first performance by José Habschied, Universidad de Cuyo, Mendoza (1955)
HENRI ZAGVIJN:
  Capriccio (flute and piano)
SAVINO DE BENEDICTIS:
  "Pan S'ispira" (flute and strings)
ALEXANDER TCHEREPNIN:
  "The Lost Flute" (narrator and orchestra on Chinese poems)
NED ROREM:
  "Mountain Song" (flute and piano published by Peer International)
WESLEY LA VIOLETTE:
  "Sonata" (flute & piano published by Presser)
GAIL KUBIK:
  "Nocturne" (flute and piano published by G. Schirmer)

EAN FRANCAID:
  Musique de Cour (flute, violin and piano)
KAREL PAHOR:
  Trio (flute, oboe and bassoon)
ESTEBAN EITLER:
  4 pieces (flute, oboe, clarinet, and bassoon)
RIVIER JEAN (1896 —)
  Jean Pierre Rampal at the 1956 Strasbourg
  First performance of his Flute Concerto, fes-
  tival, with L. Martin conducting.

        *   *   *

A few of Leonardo De Lorenzo unpublished works.
Flute and piano:

  "Idillo"
  "Il pastorello Polacco"
  "Fantasia"
  "Capriccio"
  "Allegro di Concerto"
  "Improvviso" (modern idiom)
  "Valse di Bravura"
  "Modina," Tarantella
  "Suite Moderna," for two flutes
  "Trio quasi moderno" (Flute, oboe and clarinet)
  "Trio Eccentrico" (flute, clarinet and bassoon)
    modern idiom
  "Two Etudes," for four flutes (modern idiom)
  "Quintet," for five flutes, with flute in G and
    piccolo

LENNOZ BERKELEY:
  Sonatina (flute and piano)
LEON SCHIDLOWSKY:
  Trio (flute, cello and piano)
ESTEBAN EITLER:
  Trio (flute, english horn and piano)
THOMAS B. PITFIELD:
  Sonatina (flute and piano)
HEITOR VILLA — LOBOS:
  Duet (flute and clarinet)
WALLINGFORD REIGGER:
  Duet (flute and clarinet)
CLAUDIO SANTORO:
  Sonata (flute and piano)
HERNAN MORALES PETTORINO:
  Tres monodias (flute alone)
WALTER PISTON:
  Sonata (flute and piano)
ABELARDO QUINTEROS:
  Three pieces (flute, clarinet and bassoon)
  Tres invenciones (flute and clarinet)
MILENKO ZIVKOVIC:
  Suite (flute and strings)
ESTEBAN EITLER:
  Serie Boliviana (flute and strings)
  Divertimiento (piccolo, clarinet, bass clarinet
    and guitare)
  Divertimiento (piccolo, clarinet, trumpet and
    bassoon)
  Quartet (piccolo, flute, trumpet and tenor
    saxophone)
  Quartet (flute, violin, viola and cello)
N. B. most of the compositions by Esteban Eitler
are published by Heugel & Co. (au Menestrel, Edi-
teurs de Musique, rue Vivienne, Paris).
The above list could have been extended ten fold
if space permitted.

EDWARD HANSLICK (1825 — 1904) One of
the most famous and most feared of musical critics
of last century was Dr. Edward Hanslick, tutor of
aesthetics and music history at the Universities of
both Vienna and Prague. He first studied law but
his great love for music which was fostered at
home, led to its abandonment and under Tomas-
chek he became an excellent pianist. Hanslick was
the terror of many great artists, rich, poor, famous
or unknown, males, females, young, old instrumentalists, singers and composers. Among the latter
Anton Bruckner (1824 — 1896) was abused to such
an extent after the production of each symphony
that he made a direct protest to the Emperor.
Hanslick in his life time, had two musical gods
and they were contemporaries, Brahms and Wagner, but Brahms first.
  The following is what Hanslick wrote after the
first peformance of Tschaikowsky's violin concerto: "The violin is no longer played; it is
yanked about, it is torn asunder, it is beaten
black and blue. I do not know whether it is possible for anyone to conquer these hair-raising difficulties, but I do know that Mr. Brodsky marty-
rized his hearers as well as himself. Fredrich Vis-
cher once asserted in reference to lascivious paintings that there are pictures that "stink in the eye."
Tschaikowsky's Violin Concerto suggests for the
first time the horrid idea that there may be music
that stinks in the ear."

        *   *   *

CORRECTIONS—In one of the programs from
South America there was a composition for flute,
clarinet, English horn and bassoon by the old
Italian composer, Luca Marenzio (1553 — 1599).
I have purposely underlined clarinet because this
instrument was not known at the time as it was invented by the German flutist Johann Christopher
Denner, (1655 — 1707). The composition in question then, could not have been in its original form.

— 13 —

PALINDROMES

"AEREA," Italian for airmail.
"MAM," principal tribe of Guatemala.
"ULLU," name of musical director, (1956)
"AKAKA," name of waterfalls on Hawaii Island.

AVIVA," a woman singer in company of a man playing on a vertical flute, presenting folk music from Palestine.
Music that is the same, played right side up or upside down.

Here are some clever ones by Leigh Mercer, a collector of palindromes.

A man, a plan, a canal—Panama.
*
I saw thee, Madame, eh, 'twas I.
*
Six at party, no pony-trap, taxis.
*
Live not evil.
*
Are we not drawn onward, we few, drawn onward to a new era?
*
No, I save on final plan if no evasion.
*
"Now dine," said I, as Enid won.

"Tis Ivan, on a visit.
*
See few owe fees.
*
"Not New York," Roy went on.
*
Poor Dan is in a droop.
*
Yawn a more Roman way.
*
Won't mists or frost, Simon.
*
Never a foot too far, even.
*
Madam, in Eden I'm Adam.

BACH, FREDERICK THE GREAT
AND THE FLUTE

In a 1956 issue of the Italian magazine "Radio Italiana" published at Torino, there was the following titled story: "The Consolation of war and of music" or "The Flute of Frederick the Great and the Great Bach" by A. M. Bonisconti. Because of the length of the article for which there is no space here, I will reproduce a translation of the most important portion, the letter of Bach to Frederick the Great. "With every humble devotion I have dedicated to Your Majesty an 'Offerta Musicale' in which the best part is written by your illustrious hand. I added to it all my knowledge with the laudable intention to exhalt, altho in a humble field, the fame of a prince whose greatness in the realm of music is on a par with the art of war and peace in which you are acclaimed and admired by all." The theme, which Frederick the Great gave Bach on his visit to the King at San Souci in 1747 Bach developed into a well known masterwork.

Besides the visit to the King, Bach was glad to see his son Carl Phillip Emanuel who was Court musician and whom he had not seen for six years, and also the famous and much loved Quantz, the Kings' flute teacher, who had been one of Bach's most devoted students. When Bach arrived at the palace, the King announced that all other activities be stopped in order that he could devote all his attention to the great master. Bach had the beautiful philosophy of remaining calm, serene and thus he was seldom irritated. However, the only time when he was not at his best was when he was requested by high personages to listen to their performing or even reading the manuscript of a composition with the hope of plaudits from the great man. On one occasion a lesser king performed for Bach who never uttered a word after the piece was over, and being asked what he thought of the performance Bach said, "Well, Kings are usually bad players, but you, Your Majesty, play like a prince!"

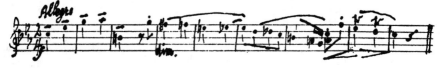

..AN ORIGINAL MUSICAL PROGRAM GIVEN AT THE "LOS ANGELES FLUTE CLUB"

An original and very interesting program was given at the Olive Hill Foundation (Barnsdall Park) by the Los Angeles Flute Club on Monday, March 12, 1956 at 7:30 p.m.

THE PROGRAM

I Stabat Mater ....Palestrina-Burdick
  Echo Song ....di Lasso-Hyde
 (for two antiphonal horn choirs) played by the Los Angeles Horn Ensemble.

II Prelude on "Aberystwyth" ....Rayner Brown
  Scherzo on "Star Dust" ....Rayner Brown
  (for four concert flutes, two alto flutes and bass flute)
  Haakon Bergh, Richard Giese, Harold Lewis, Burnett Atkinson, Sylvia
  Rudeman Glass, Sheridon Stokes and Harry Klee.

III "Trio" two flutes and cello ....Arnold Bergh
  Phyllis George, Luisa Di Tullio, Wendy Brennan

IV "Quartet" two flutes and two French horns ....Abeltschaufer
  Harold Lewis, Burnett Atkinson, Arthur Frantz, Charles Peel.

V "Octet" Los Angeles Horn Ensemble ....Kaun
     Conducted by Wendell Hoss

VI Changes for seven flutes (5 concert flutes, Alto flute & Piccolo)..Maury
  Archie Wade, Slyvia Rudeman Glass, Richard Giese, Harry Klee, Don
  Lazenby, Sheridon Stokes (alto flute) Paul McLarand (Piccolo)

The last number on this unusual interesting program was noval, original and had artistic value. Each player came in front for a short solo accompanied by the rest of its colleagues and there was an irresistible comic touch as one of the players was chewing gum continuously and desisted only during his minute and one half of solo! The ensemble was conducted by the composer, an excellent pianist, with great success.

GUSTAV MAHLER (1860 — 1911) THE EMPEROR AND THE NEW YORK PHILHARMONIC

Francis Joseph, (1830 — 1916) Emperor of Austria-Hungary, offered Mahler the post of general director of all the Opera houses of the Empire if he would first become a convert to Catholicism. Mahler accepted the proposition and became the musical autocrat of the Empire. Etiquette required that the list of operas be presented to the Emperor, for his approval. On one of these occasions, after a protracted season of Gluck and Mozart, the Emperor requested a change to some lighter operas and mentioned some of the lesser composers of whom Mahler did not approve. However when he saw that the Emperor was obdurate, he said to him, "your Majesty: I will obey your orders but I do not admire your taste."

Later, at the height of his career, Mahler was invited to conduct the Metropolitan opera of New York and the following year to head the New York Philharmoic. It was then that Mahler wanted to perform for the first time his colossal symphony No. 3, usually called "Symphony of a Thousand," so named because it required one thousand persons to perform between a huge orchestra and many choruses. However, when the women committee of that institution, to whom the programs had to be submitted, learned that the preparation

of that colossal work required a whole month or probably two months of rehearsals at a terrific cost, it reluctantly refused to consent to its performance. When Mahler, the all powerful, was given the bad news, he could not believe it! "To think" he said, "that a group of women would dare to contradict my wishes!" It was too much for him to take but he reluctantly agreed to give the fourth symphony instead, which required only a few singers in the finale and no choruses. The New York music critics did not approve of this work and the all powerful Mahler's health began to show signs of failure and he died after a few months in Vienna only 51 years old.

The symphony of a Thousand was performed a few years later after months of preparation, by Leopold Stokowsky and the Philadelphia Symphony Orchestra.

*   *   *

WAGNER (1813 — 1883) and BERLIOZ (1803 — 1869) The only thing in common between these two wonderful men was music. But even in this, if there was a spark of mutual admiration, no one was aware of it: evidently it was a well kept secret. Wagner, in his many visits to Paris, had met Berlioz once or twice at a social gathering. However, the effort both made to avoid one another was a tragic comic affair. Wagner had heard too many times before from Berloiz's admirers that the latter was able to read at sight the most complicated orchestral score on the piano. "It was positively fabulous . . . unbelievable," they said.—Berlioz, like his great antagonist Wagner, was not a brilliant pianist. In his younger days he apparently found time to amuse himself by playing on the flute and guitar, two instruments which he loved. On the piano he became proficient only through his love of reading all the orchestral scores possible. The great Wagner, on an occasion when he knew that Berlioz would also be present, took with him the score of his "Tristan and Isolde." The time soon came when all the guests were aware Wagner had brought his *terrific score*. However, it was arranged in a diplomatic way that no other than Wagner himself should request Berlioz to read the score which at that time was little known. When both Wagner and Berlioz walked to the grand piano, Wagner handed Berlioz the score who seated himself at the instrument and opened the score. After glancing at it a few moments he turned to Wagner and said: "In what key do you want me to play it?"

* * *

'PLAYING FOR LOVE"

The New York Times of August 12, 1956 (Sunday) had an unusually interesting article with the above title written by Ross Parmenter, who claims that there are 27, 650,000 Americans who play one musical instrument or another. The great majority of the instrumentalists are pianists, they account for 20,000,000 of the total. Guitarrists are the next largest group with 4,000,000 of them. Violinists, violists, cellists, and *bull fiddlers* (double basses) for a toal of 3,000,000, while there are 2,250,000 woodwind players and 2,225,000 brass players. To the objection that these figures combined go well beyond the 27,650,000 total, the reply is that a number of persons play more than one instrument. And it gives these total, for the humbler instrumentalist: 1,600,000 play the ukulele, 1,500,000 the accordion and 4,000,000 the harmonica. A great number of the amateur musicians are school children.

There are now 40,000 American school bands and 20,000 school orchestras. The acceptance of music as part of the school curriculum is now widespread in the United States. Industrial concerts have also increased amateur musical activities and amateur music-making too, has been encouraged and developed by municipalities. Sometimes it has been used in programs to prevent juvenile delinquency, sometimes merely to help adult citizens enjoy themselves. The establishment of music camps has also contributed to the amateur boom. Music in Rural Areas shows that the development of paved roads and the increased ownership of automobiles have helped inhabitants of small farm towns and sparsely settled countries to have more music. In Humbolt County in California, the sixty members of the Humbolt Little Symphony travel 130 miles weekly to attend rehearsals. The picture as a whole is a cheering one, even if the sounds the massed amateur produced have not the luster and the sheen of professional ensembles, it is good to know so many are finding such enjoyment in music. There is comfort, too, in the realization of all that magical sense of fellowship that comes in making music jointly with others. And these things are especially heartwarming when one thinks of all the struggle, rivalry, back-biting and discouragement there is in the world of professional music-making. It is further proof that perhaps the greatest happiness is to be found in doing thinks for love.

Los Angeles Flute Club

PROGRAM 8:00 P.M.   —   FEBRUARY 10, 1957

Serenade for Flute and Viola ....William Presser
Archie Wade, Flute   -   Harry Blumberg, Viola

Chanson et Badinerie ....Pierre Camus, 1913
Richard Giese, Flute   -   Dorothy Remsen, Harp

Theme and Variations for Flute and Harp ....Matt Doran
Archie Wade, Flute   -   Dorothy Remsen, Harp

Introduction and Pavane ....Michel Michelet, 1952
Haakon Berg, Flute   -   Louise Di Tullio, Flute
Sylvia Ruderman Glass, Alto Flute
Sheridon Stokes, Alto Flute   -   Dorothy Remsen, Harp

Suite Breve ....L. Rohozinski
Plus Lent
Tres modere
Assez vite

Los Angeles Flute, Viola and Harp Trio
Archie Wade, Flute
Harry Blumberg, Viola   -   Dorothy Remsen, Harp

LOS ANGELES FLUTE CLUB OFFICERS 1957

President ....Haakon Bergh
Vice-President ....Elise Baxter Moennig
Treasurer ....Elgin E. Asbury
Recording Secretary ....Patricia H. Johnson
Corresponding Secretary ....Mary Claire Hardwick
Program Committee ....Richard Giese, Chairman
June RUSSO, Sheridon Stokes
Librarian ....Archie Wade

HUMOR
A SENSE OF HUMOR IS THE RAREST OF ALL HUMAN VIRTUES, IT MEANS THE ABILITY TO LAUGH AT YOURSELF AND STILL GO ON DOING THE BEST YOU CAN IN AN ADMITTEDLY IMPERFECT WORLD!

The Duke of Clarence — (England, 1475) was condemned to die for treason, was given his choice as to the method—he requested to be drowned in a *BARREL OF WINE!*

* * *

The little child ended his prayer earnestly: "and please, lord, can't you put vitamins in pie and cake instead of in cod-liver oil and spinach? Amen."

* * *

Teacher to a boy: How much is 9 times 8?
The boy: 9 times 8? — 72.
Teacher: Pretty good.
Boy: Pretty good? Hell its perfect!

* * *

"Does your wife pick your suits?"
"No, just the pockets."

* * *

Judge Gruff: "Arn't you ashamed to be seen here in court so often?"
Prisoner: "Why no, your Honor. I always thought it was a very respectable place."

* * *

"How do you spell 'sense'?" inquired the stenographer. "Which one?" asked the boss, "dollars and cents or horse sense?"
"Well," said the steno, like in I haven't seen him sense'."

* * *

Give me sense of humor, Lord;
Give me the grace to see a joke.
To get some happiness from life,
and pass it on to other folk.

* * *

She said: "My husband would never chase after another woman. He's too fine . . . too decent . . . too old."

* * *

Most girls nowadays are on the lookout for a man who is tall, dark, and has some.

* * *

Psychiatrist to patient: "When did you first discover that you enjoyed paying your income taxes?"

* * *

Give me a good digestion, Lord
and also something to digest.
Give me a healthy body, Lord
with a sense to keep it at its best.

* * *

When a boy is born, friends ask,
"How is the mother?"
When he gets married they say:
"wasn't the bride lovely?"
And when he dies, they ask: "How much did he leave you?"

* * *

If some one tells you "you are a cauliflower," that means you are a cabbage with a wasted college education.

Alcoholic: A drinker who drinks between drinks.

* * *

An old prosperous farmer was told by his young son-in-law, "this farm is badly managed, everything is old style. If I were to manage it," the old farmer interrupted him saying, "I know, you would raise hell without roots."

* * *

Mrs. Duff: "I always feel lots better after a good cry."
Mrs. Jawsom: "So do I. It sort of gets things out of your system."
Mrs. Duff: "No. it doesn't get anything out of my husband."

* * *

All the American people expect of a president is that he shall be a combination of Moses, Demosthenes, St. Peter, Houdini and Santa Claus.

* * *

Papa bird is reported to have complained to mama bird: "Can you beat it? Just about the time we get a little nest egg laid away more bills accumulate."

* * *

One Pakistan tribe has a custom of expressing apology by sticking out the tongue.

* * *

Wife: "I asked you to mail this letter a month ago. I just found it in your coat pocket."
Husband: "Oh, yes, that was the day I started leaving the coat at home so you could sew the button on."

* * *

A camel is an animal that looks like it was put together by a committee.

* * *

The old moutaineer was sitting in his favorite cane-backed rocker on the porch of his cabin, slowly rocking east and west. Nearby sat his 42-year-old son, rocking north and south. "Son," drawled the old man, "It's about time you learned not t'wear yerself out thataway. Rock the way the board runs, and save yer stren'th."

* * *

She's an excellent house-keeper. Everytime she gets a divorce she keeps the house.

* * *

Irate Father: "I sacrificed everything I had in order that you could study médicine. And now that you'er a doctor you tell me I have to give up smokin."

* * *

We have known for sometime that "philosophy teaches one to be miserable intelligently," therefore, if you should happen to be smoking in bed and that the ashes might be your own cheer-up, don't be dismayed because D' Annunzio said, death is an extension of life!"

Mrs. Flannagan, stout, wealthy and snubbish, did
not appreciate her modest neighbor who had tried
to be friendly, "good morning Mrs. Flannagan,
you look very charming today." "Oh, oh," replied
Mrs. Flannagan, I wish I could say the same about
you." "Oh yes you could," the neighbor answered,
'if you were as good a liar as I am!"

    *   *   *

"Do you say prayers before eating?" the clergyman asked the little boy. "No, sir, I don't need to,"
replied the child. "My Mother's a good cook."

    *   *   *

AN OLD MAN DISCUSSES MARRIED LIFE

Lord, we've had our little wrangles,
an' we've had our little bouts.
There's tongue's a trifle hasty an'
my temper's apt to fly,
An' Mother, let me tell you,
has a sting in her reply.
But I couldn't live without her,
an' it's plain as plain can be
That in fair or sunny weather
mother needs a man like me.

I've banged a door an' muttered
angry words beneath my breath.
For at times when she was scoldin'
mother's plagued me most to death,
But we've always laughed it over,
when we'd both cooled down a bit,
An, we never had a difference
but a smile would settle it.
An' if such a thing could happen,
we could share life's joys an' tears
An' live right on together
for another thousand years.

Some men give up too easy
in the game o' married life,
They haven't got the courage
to be worthy of a wife,
An' I've seen a lot o' women
that have made their lives a mess,
Coz they couldn't bear the burdens
that are mixed with happiness.
So long as folks are human
they'll have many faults that jar,
An' the way to live with people
is to take them as they are.

We've been forty years together,
good an' bad, rain an' shine,
I've forgotten mother's faults now
an' she never mentions mine.
In the days when sorrow struck us
an' we shared a common woe
We just leaned upon each other,
an' our weakness didn't show.
An' I learned how much I need her
an' how tender she can be
An' through it, maybe,
mother saw the better side o' me.
        Copyright 1919, by Edgar A. Guest.

"Melodia"   Leonardo De Lorenzo

"Scherzino" Leonardo De Lorenzo

Index to the Revised Edition

Because there are many misspelled words in the original text, page numbers are given in the index only after correctly spelled entries. The misspelled entry is followed by a "see" reference to the correct entry. Entries in the index from the Addenda are given as A: page number for Addenda I, B: for Addenda II, and C: for Addenda III. Entries followed by *(RSR)* indicate De Lorenzo took the material from *A Treatise on the Flute* by Richard Shepherd Rockstro.

Andersen, Vigo (brother to Joachim), 214, 323

Anderson, Chester V. J., A:25

Andrews, Sudie (Mrs. Joseph Breco), 419, 492

Angerer, Paul, B:3

Angiolin and Vissibelli, Lucca, C:10

Animuccia, Giovanni (1500–1571), C:9

Annunzio, Gabriele d', 407, 409

Anthoni, Theophile, 214

Anthony, Doriot, 214–15, 338, 344, A:1

Antigenidas (ancient flutist), 311

Antigonus (king of Macedonia, 382 B.C.), B:7

Antisthenes (Greek philosopher), 310

Antonini, Alfredo, 360

Antwerp Conservatory (Belgium), 214

Aphrodite, C:8

Apollo, 22, 41, 43, 311, 314, 400–01, 411, C:iii, C:7, C:8

Apuleius, 309

Araucanian Indian, A:10

Araujo, José Feliciano de, 258

Arawakan Indian, A:10

Arcaro, James, 215, 345

Archimedes, A:16

Ardevol, J., *Sonata* for two flutes and viola, 367

Arditi, Luigi, 150

Ares, C:8

Argentieri, Balilla, 215

Argentieri, Gaetano, 442

Arghool (Egyptian pipe), 153

Ariosto, Ludovico (1475–1533), C:7

Aristippus, C:7

Aristophanes on flute playing, 312

Aristos, A:16

Aristoteles, Joaquim, 258

Aristotle, 20, 312, A:16, A:17

Arlom, Albert, 215

Arlt, Gustav, 111, 284, A:16, A:24

Armer, Robert, 215

Armfield, Gladys, 215

Arming, 155

Armstrong, W. T. (flutemaker), B:11

Arnold, Malcolm, *Concerto* for flute and strings, A:1

Arnaldi, 280

Arrivabene, Ferruccio, illus. f. 144, 215, 264, 462, A:16

Articulation. *See* Double-tonguing; Tonguing

Artworks depicting the flute, 42–44, 400–03, 411, 413, 415, 416, A:10, A:15, A:16, A:24, B:11, C:iii, frontispiece to Addenda II and III; C:3 collection of pictures of, C:11–12

Arx, Deitland von, 215

Asbury, Elgin, A:12, C:17

Asbury Park Orchestra (New Jersey), 208

Ashe, Andrew, 215, 283

Aspen Festival (Colorado), B:10

Assam jungle Andu (head catcher), 35

Assisi, Pedro de, 220, 225, 254, 255–59, 265, 339

Manual do Flautista, 220, 225, 254, 255–59, 265

Assumpcao, Fausto, 255, 257

Astor (flutemaker), 125

Astor, John Jacob, 305

Astrella, Tommaso, 432

Athapascan Indian, A:10

Athene, 43

Athlone Band, A:3

Atkinson, Burnett, 215, 344, C:15

Attaignant, Pierre, 216

Attic (Attica, Greece), 310

Auberty, du Boulley Prudence Louis, 215

Audoin and Dubois (printmakers), C:iii

Audubon, John James, 305

Auer, Leopold, 334, B:6

Auerbach, Berthold, A:19

August the Strong (of Dresden), 78

Augustine, Saint, 52

Aulos, 4

Aurelius, Marcus, A:17

Auric, Georges, B:8
Austin, Texas
  Symphony, A:1, A:4
  University of Texas, A:1, A:25
Australia
  bone flute of, 29
  flute bird of, 36
  Glendale Symphony, 250
  Queensland Orpheus Club Orchestra of Rockhampton, A:8
  South Australia Flute Club, 220
Autograph collection, A:16
Avignon Conservatory (France), 270
Ayala, Manuel, 29
Aymaran Indian, A:10
Azeveda, Aureliano di, 256
Azevedo, Alexis Jacques, 215
Azevedo, Antonio Lopes de, 256
Aztecs, 25, 31–32, 52, 205, C:7
Azzano, Giuseppe, 215

Baccarrotti, G., C:2
Bacchylides (ancient poet-flutist), 310
Bach, Carl Philipp Emanuel, 82–83, 93, 291, 334, 351, C:14
  works of, 334, 353, A:1, A:15
Bach, Guido, *The Infant Pan* (painting), A:24
Bach, Johann Christian, works of, 334, 353
Bach, Johann Christian Friedrich, 473
Bach, Johann Sebastian, 6, 37, 84, 93, 112, 158, 167, 208, 333, 334, 335, 412, 473, A:15, B:7, C:3, C:14
  B Minor Mass, B:10
  Brandenburg Concerti, 352, B:3, C:1
  Cantatas, 369, B:3
  Letter to Frederick the Great, C:14
  Prelude and Fugue No. 8 from WTC, A:13
  Sonatas, 216, 262, 334, 350–52, A:1, A:7, A:12, C:10
  Suite in B Minor for flute and strings, 214, C:1

Bach, Wilhelm Friedemann, flute music of, 334, 337, 353
Bach Aria Group, B:1, B:10
Bach Circle of New York, 289
Bach Gesellschaft Editions, 352
Bach Guild recordings, B:3
Bachelors, famous, C:7
Bachoffen, Johann Heinrich, 215–16
Bacon, Sir Francis, A:17
Badal (Hindu flutist), 216
Baden-Baden Orchestra (Germany), 251
Bades, Paul, 216
Badollet, Frank, 216
Bafonda, Anthony, A:1
Bagni (singer), 280
Bagpipe (*zambogna*), 394, 400
Bajer, Antoine, 216
Baker, Frederic, A:1
Baker, Julius, 216, 360, B:1, B:10
Baldini, Girolamo, 216
Baldwin-Wallace Conservatory (Cleveland, Ohio), 229
Ballard Publishers, Paris, 225
Balleron, Louis, 216
Ballet Russe de Monte Carlo, 223
Baltimore, Maryland
  Civic Summer Symphony, 243
  Park Little Symphony, 243
  Symphony, 222, 238, 244, 270, 290, 344, 375, C:1
Balzac, Honoré de, A:20
Bamboo flutes, 5, 205, 315. *See also* Chinese flutes
Band instrument makers, 263, 273, A:23, B:11. *See also* Innovators and inventors; Makers and manufacturers of flutes
Bandiera, Pasquale, B:20
Bandini, Primo, 391
Bandmasters. *See* Gilmore; La Monaca; Sousa; Willson
Bantock, Granville, songs for flute and voice, 369

Beck, L. Adams, *The Flute of Krishna* (pamphlet), 371, A:15
Becke, Johann Baptiste, 121, 218
Becker, Maria José De Brito, 258
Beckerman, J. H., 277
Becquie, A., 218, 324, 325
  Grand Fantasie et Fugue for flute and piano, 218
Beebe, Carolyn, 209
Beecham, Thomas, 210
Beethoven, Ludwig van, 111, 113, 167, 269, 302, 319–20, 333, 334–35, 463, A:10, A:15, A:16, A:19, A:20, B:3, B:6, C:5, C:7
  Allegro and Menuetto for two flutes, 353, A:12
  Klinger's *Beethoven* (artwork), 413
  Serenade, Op. 25 for flute, violin, and viola, 354, A:14
  Sonata in B-flat for flute and piano, A:7
  Strasse, Leipzig, 412
  Trio for flute, bassoon (cello), and piano, 354, A:13
"Beethoven of the Flute." *See* Kuhlau
Behm, Emil, 218, 460, A:16
Beinl, Ludwig, B:3
Beinum, Edward van, C:11
Belgrade, Yugoslavia
  Museum of Natural History, 30
  Orchestra of the Royal Guards, C:11
  Philharmonic Orchestra, C:1
  School of Music, C:1
  Woodwind Quintet, C:1
Belke, Christian Gottfried, 128, 218, 274, 325, 373, 460
Bellermann, Constantin, 218
Bellini, Giovanni, 43, 409
  Madonna (painting), 409
Bellini, Vincenzo (1801–1835), C:7
  aria from *Norma* (opera), 392, 394, 473
Bemboni, Johannes, 221
Bemko, Gregory, A:13
Benda, Franz, 82, 83, 84, 86

Benda, Karl, 93
Benedict, Sir Julius, 141
Benedictus, Savino de, *Pan S'ispira* for flute and strings, C:12
Ben-Haim, Paul, *Tres canciones sin Palabras* for oboe and piano, B:12
Beniamino, Vittorio, 218, 449, 457, A:16
Benkman, Herbert, 345
Bennett, Harold, 218–19, 345
Bennett, Robert Russell, 13, 375
  Rondo Capriccioso for four flutes, 13, 378, A:12, A:13
Benno, Ruth, A:13, A:14
Bens, Agenor da, 254, 255
Benton, Thomas P., 219, A:12
Bentzon, Johan, A:1
Berbiguier, Benoit Tranquille, 91, 99–101 (RSR), 110, 162, 219, 325, 333, 355, 373, 460
  method of, 398, 436
Berenguer, Manuel, 219
Berg, Alban, C:2
  Four Pieces for clarinet and piano, B:12
Bergamo, Chapelle Santa Maria Maggiore, 96, 286
Bergh, Arnold, *Trio* for two flutes and cello, C:15
Bergh, Haakon, 219, A:12, A:13, B:1, B:12, B:17, C:3, C:15, C:17
Bergner, Carl, B:1
Bergseth, Pauline, 219–20
Bergson, Henri (1859–1941), A:18
Berkeley, Lennox, *Sonatina* for flute and piano, C:13
Berkshire Music Festival (Tanglewood, Massachusetts), 209, 266, C:1
Berlin, Germany
  Academy, 75
  Bilse' schen Concert Orchestra, 273, 275, 286, 288
  Court of, as visited by John Adams, 302

600

601

Tillmetz; C. Wehner; Weimershaus; J. Wilkins; Zaduk; Zink
Boehm system of flute, 35, 37, 103, 114,
115, 120, 134, 135, 136, 151, 152,
158, 167, 184, 207, 213, 214, 223,
224, 300, 336, 385, 386, 398, 443,
450, 453, 456, 472
as applied to bassoon, 318, 321
as applied to clarinet, 321
controversy between Boehm and
old, 188, 322–23, 420–26
flutists who changed to, 38, 103, 134,
261, 320–22, 420, 436, 442, 450–
51
Boehm-Gordon controversy, 37, 38,
114
Boethius, De Institutione Musica, 21
Bohl, John C., 306–07
Bohrer (cellist), 106
Boisdeffre, Charles de, 194
Boito, Arrigo, 448, 449, C:7
Bologna, Italy
Conservatory, 280
Liceo Musicale, 251
Lyrica Theatre, 237
Symphony, 237
Bolzoni, Giovanni, 458, A:16
Bonaparte, Joseph (king of Spain and
brother to Napoleon), 304
Bondi, Anthony, A:23
Bone flutes, 32, 35
of human, 28, 205, 303, 401
Bonecorse, M., 101
Bonisconti, A. M., article on Frederick
the Great and Bach, J. S., C:14
Bonneville (flutemaker), B:11
Bononcini, Giovanni, 73
Bonucci, Arturo, 280, 360
Books with flutistic titles, A:15
Boom, Johann van, 282
Boom, Johannes, 221
Boone, Abram, 221
Bopp, Joseph, A:5, A:9
Bordeaux Franklin Hall, 153

Bordes, Charles, 194
Bordoni, Faustina, (Mrs. Hasse), 73
Bore of flute, 132. See also Conical
bore flute; Cylinder bore flute
Borges, Joventino da Silva, 258
Borgia, Lucrezia, 474
Borisoff, Alexander, C:3
Borjon, Traité de la Musette (book), 65
Borne, François, 221
Borodin, Alexander, 44
Borromeo, Count, 408
Borstadt, Frank, A:8
Bos, Conrad, 180
Bossi, Marco Enrico (1861–1925), C:1
Boston, Massachusetts
Flute Players Club, 201, 249, 260
Pops Orchestra, 375, B:3
Society of Ancient Instruments, 201
Symphony Orchestra, 201, 209, 214,
221, 227, 241, 249, 252, 260, 265,
284, 290, 291, 344, 375, 378, A:1
Boswell, James, 245
Botelho, Manuel, 221
Botgorschek, Franz, 221
Botham, Harriet Patchin, "Pastorale
on a Flute" (article), C:11,
Bothwell, Jean, Little Flute Player
(book), 372
Botticelli, Sandro, C:7
Boulez, Pierre, Sonatina for flute and
piano, C:11
Bove, J. Henry, 221
Bowen, W., Pan in California, 372
Bowles, Paul, Sonata for flute and
piano, 367
Boyd, Woodward, The Unpaid Piper
(book), 372
Braga, Emilio, 257
Brahmins, flutes of. See Noseflute
Brahms, Johannes, 150, 335, 457, 469,
B:6, B:7, C:5, C:7, C:13
Brant, Henry, works of, 367, A:12, B:11
Brass in flutemaking, 345
Braun (flutist), 77

602

603

604

605

607

Cologne, Germany
  Conservatory, 286
  Gurzeich-Konzerte, 286
  Radio Woodwind Quintet, C:11
  State Theater, 286
Colonne Orchestra (Paris), 189, 190,
  192, 193, 194, 195, 200, 227, 260,
  275
Columbia Broadcasting Orchestra
  (CBS), 289, 360
Columbus, Ohio
  Flute Club, 265
  Little Symphony, B:3
Colvig, David, A:25
Combination instruments. *See* Alber-
  ti; Moore, T. W.
Commager, Henry Steele, *Works of Sid-
  ney Lanier* (book), 48
Common flute, 6
Composers
  American, B:10
  neglected Italian, C:9
  views on one another, B:6–9, C:4–6
Concert programs, 375–77, A:12–14,
  B:17, C:17
Concert Spirituel, 90
Concertgebouw Orchestra, The
  Netherlands, 274, C:11
Concertina, 270
Concone, Gioachino, 265
Conducting in the eighteenth century,
  73
Confucius, 19, 56, A:26
Conical bore flute, 158, 169, 322, 410
Conn,Co., C. G. "wonder flute," 16
Conover, Lida Ross (mother of
  Townsend), A:23
Conover, Mary Chase (wife of
  Townsend), 484–85, A:23
Conover, Townsend, 35, 224, 482–84,
  A:16, A:23
Conrad, Ferdinand, A:9
Conservatoire National de Musique,
  Paris, France. *See* Paris (France)
  Conservatory

Conservatories of music, European,
  254
Considine, Stephen, 366,
Consolini, Giorgio, C:2
Consolo, Ernesto, 197
Constant, Marius, *Le charmeur desats
  de Hamelle* for 16 instruments,
  childrens choir, basso, and recit-
  ing voice, A:15, A:24
Constantinople (Istanbul, Turkey), 69,
  145, 271
  Sultan's harem, 271, 342
Contrabass recorder, 54,
Contralto flute. *See* Alto flute in G
Contreras, Louis Albert Clavero, A:26,
  B:12
Convent Garden Opera (known as
  Royal Italian Opera, 1847–92;
  Royal Ballet, 1957+; Royal Opera,
  1969+), 64, 102, 139, 152, 160, 161,
  169, 170, 239, 242, 244, 263, 267,
  268, 269, 285, 287, 289, A:1, A:25
Converse, Fredrick, *The Pipe of Desire*
  (opera), 369
Conzaga, Fausto, 257
Cook, Russell, A:4
Cook, Samuel, 224
Coolidge, Calvin, A:2
Coons, Arthur G., B:ii
Copan ruins, 31
Coppola, Carmine, 210–11, 224–25
Coppola, Raffaele, 225
Coppoli, Carlo, C:2
Corbett, William, 64
Corelli, Arcangelo, 64
Corfu 92nd Regiment Band, 246
Cornell University (Ithaca, New
  York), 284, A:2
Corning, James Leonard, 305, 480–81
Corot, Jean Baptiste, C:7
Corpus Christi (Texas) Symphony,
  288, A:2
Corredor, J. M., *Conversations avec
  Pablo Casals* (book), C:6
Correggio, Heinrich, 225

608

610

611

613

614

Fitzgerald, Francis, 232, 345
Fitzgibbon, Henry Macaulay, 26, 38, 39, 40–41, 232, 294, 372
  The Story of the Flute (book), 26–27, 40–41, 372
Flack, Lambert C., 232–33, illus f. 304
Fladd, Fredrick, 233
Flagello, Nicholas, *Concerto Antoniano* for flute and orchestra, B:3
Flageolet, 11, 65–67, 121, 227, 230, 233, 316, 318, 356, 394, 403, A:8
Flamma, Ario, A:16
Flaubert, Gustave, 44
Flautes traversiennes. See Transverse flute
Flautino, 11
Flauto. See Recorder
Flauto dolce. See Recorder
Flauto traverso. See Transverse flute
Flautone. *See* Bass flute in C
Fleischhack, Johann Adolf, 69–70
Fleury, Louis, 41, illus. f. 144, 233, 332–34, 339, 372, 462, 464–66
Florence, Italy
  Conservatory, A:1
  Instituto Vittorio Emanuele, 267
  National Museum, 403
  Philharmonic Society, 15
  Royal Instituto Musicale, 15, 220, 264
  Vivaldi Ensemble, C:2
Florio, Pietro Grassi, 8, 233
Flothuis, Marius, *Sonata da Camera* for flute and piano, C:12
Fluta, 25
Flute (French 17th c. Naval vessel), B:10
Flute clubs and societies, 342
  Birmingham (England), 253
  Boston, 201, 249, 260
  Champaign-Urbana, B:2
  Chula Vista (California), 342
  Cincinnati, 244
  Columbus, 265
  London, A:14, 264

Los Angeles, illus. f. 144, 217, 246, 254, 261, 372, A:4, A:9, A:12, A:13, A:14, A:16, A:23, B:1, B:4, C:1, C:10, C:11, C:15, C:17
  Louisville, 247, 284
  New York, 248, 288, 289, 360, 371, 472, A:9, A:12, A:23, B:1
  Pittsburg, 242, A:4, C:10
  San Diego, 342
  Seattle, 249
  South Australian, 220
  Sydney, 230, 236, illus. f. 304, A:23
Flûte d'amour, 12
Flute harmonique. See Double flageolet
Flûte-à-bec. See Recorder
Flute-bird (*gymnorlindetibicen*), 36
Flute-douce. See Recorder
Flute-mouth fish, 36
Flute-Piccolo combination instrument, A:5, C:iii
Flutist, The (American journal, 1920–29), 40, 253, 254, 262, 328–30
  excerpts from, 420–22, A:24
Flutistic titles (of all types of artworks), 369–73, A:15
Flutists. *See also* Lady flutists
  in American symphony orchestras, 344–45
  number of in U. S., 341–42
  of South America, C:12
  who died young, 325
  who lived a long life, 325
  young European, A:9
Flutist's Magazine (English), 40
Focke, Free (pianist), B:12
Folia (piece of music), 349
Folk music lore, 173. *See also* Robles, Daniel
Folz, Michel, 233
Fonseca, Arlindo Sodamada, 256
Fonseca, Indalicio Franca, 255, 257
Fontaine, Camille, 233
Fontbonne, Léon de, 233
Foote, Arthur, *Night Piece* for flute and orchestra, 367

616

617

Goethe, Walter Wolfgang (1818–1885), 326, 472, A:10
Goetschius, Percy, 203, 209
Gold flutes, 35, illus. f. 144, 219, 238, 295, 303, 331, 376, 415, 463, A:4, A:7, A:25, C:2
given by Goldberg, 238, 306, 378, 415
Gold keys for flutes, 303, 318
Goldberg, Adolph, 59, 238, 306, 415–16, 459, A:16, C:2
Biographical Sketches and Portraits of Famous Flutists, 306
Goldberg, Bernard, 238
Golding, V., 238
Goldmark, Károly, 473
Goldsmith, Oliver, 238, 293
Golland, Harry, A:3
Goltermann, Heinrich Ludolf, 238
Goltzer, Harold, B:10
Goluboff, Grisha, A:16
Gomes, Dourival, 257
Goncalves, Pedro Vieira, 255
Goncourts, Edmond and Jules, 44
Gonzaga, Fausto, 257
Gonzales-Maestre, Francisco, 238
Gonzales-Val, Eusebio, 238
Goode, B., 238
Goosens, Eugene, 231, 478, A:16, B:5
Gordon, Wilhelm, 37, 38, 107, 114, 238
Gorgons (winged female monsters), C:7
Gosse, *On Viol and Flute* (book), 371
Göthenberg Museum (Sweden), 416
Gounod, Charles François A:20, B:8, C:4
Graf, Arturo, 371
Graf, Friedrich Hartman, 239
Graf, Peter Lucas, C:1
Graham, *The Piper at the Gates of Dawn* (book), 372
Grainer, *Die Flute von Sans Souci* for flute and piano, 371
Graitzer, Murray, 239
Grammophone recordings. *See* Recordings

Gramophone (periodical), A:7, A:25
Granom, Lew C. A., *Plain and Easy Instructions for Playing the German Flute* (book), 238
Granzow, H., 277
Grao, Julio O., 258
Grassi, Antonio de, A:16
Grasso, Elvisio, C:1
Graun, Karl Heinrich (1701–1759), 71, 77, 80, 81, 82, 334
Gravina, Count Gilberto, 239, 304, 358, 377, 378–79, A:16, C:1
Preludio e Fuga in Do for 12 flutes, 358, 377, 378
Grayson, Katherine, B:1
Graz, Joseph, 121
Greek flutes. *See also* Ancient flutes and music
legends and mythology, 236, C:iii, C:7
liturgies, C:5
national songs, C:5
Grenier, Albert, 239
Grenser, Heinrich, 89
Grenser, Karl August, 121, 239
Grétry, André, 334, B:10
Grieg, Edward, 159
Griffes, Charles Tomlinson (1884–1920), 197, 360–61
Poem for flute and orchestra, 59, 215, 360–61, C:1, C:3
Griffith, Frederick, 239
Grimaldi, Principe Alessandro Licastro, A:16, A:26
Grimpe, Alex, *Suite miniatura* for flute alone, B:12
Grisez, Georges, 209
Grisi, Carlotta, 131
Grisi, Guilia, 131, 137, 164
Grolimund, J. M., A:23
Groth, Daniel, 239, 345
Grove's Dictionary, 226
Grutsmacher, Carl, 239
G-Sharp Key. *See* Keys: G-sharp
Guard, William J., 305–06

627

631

632

Meyer, Athos Duque Estrada (son of Augusto), 254, 255
Meyer, Augusto Paulo Duque Estrada, 256, 462
Meyer, Clara, 341, A:26
Meyer model, 300, 386. *See also* Ivory headjoints
Meyer system flute. *See* Simple systems: Meyer
Meyerbeer, Giacomo, B:7, B:8
Miami, Florida
　Symphony, 375
　University of, 227
Miccoli, Icilio, A:5, 330
Michailofsky, Ivan, 259
Michel, Alfonso, 30
Michel, Georg, 259
Michel, Joseph, 218
Michel, Molly, A:14
Michelangelo, 43, 407, A:16, C:7
　Apollo e Marsyas (statue), 372
Michelet, Michel, *Introduction and Pavane* for two flutes, two alto flutes, and harp, C:17
Michigan (Ann Arbor), University of, 286
Midas, King, 20, 309, 311, C:7
Miglionico, Nunzia, 442
Mignolet, Jean, 259
Mignone, Alferio, 259–60
Mignone, Francisco, 260
Milan, Italy
　Conservatory, 232, 237, 251, 265, 268, 290, 408, 448, 449, 457, 476, A:4, A:7, A:8
　Court of, 297
　Duke of, C:9
　Galleria Vittorio Emanuele, 408, 448
　May Fair of 1955, B:11
　Scuola Populari di Musica, 215, 280
　Societa di Mutuo Soccorso Italiano, 290
　State Chapel of, 280
Milanollo, Maria, 473

Milhaud, Darius, *Sonatina* for flute and piano, 357, 465, B:8
Milhouse (flutemaker), 124
Millard, Robert E., 260
Miller, Albert E., 260
Miller, Dayton C., 42, 58, 260, 303, 327, 377, 463, A:2, A:4, A:5, A:16
　Collection, Library of Congress, 29, 58, illus. f. 144, 303, 455
　trans. of Boehm's *The Flute and Flute-Playing* (book), 371
Miller, Edward, 260
Miller, Paul, 260
Million, Ernest, 260
Millöcher, Karl, 44, 260
Mills, Frederick H., 260
Mills Music, Inc., 284
Milton, John, A:19
Mims, Edward, *Sidney Lanier* (book), 46N
Minasi, Nicola, 260
Ming Huang, 29
Minneapolis (Minnesota) Symphony, 178, 206, 210, 214, 220, 227, 250, 260, 263, 269, 288, 289, 345, 374, 446, 458, 470, A:6, B:5, C:1
Miranda, Filho Antonio Branco de, 256
Mitchell, Eleanore, 260
Mitropoulis, Dimitri, A:3
Mitterer, Professor, 121
Mnemosyne, C:iii
Modena, Italy
　Collegio dei Nobili, 246
　Municipal Theatre, 224
Modesti, Julius, 414N
Modifications. *See* Innovators and inventors
Moennig, Elise Baxter, 377, A:12, A:13, A:14, C:17
Moennig, Horst, 218
Moennig family (German instrument makers), B:11
Moevs, Robert, *Cantata Sacra* for men's chorus, solo voice, flute,

638

Peabody Conservatory, 47, 243, 248
Peacock, Harriet, 265–66, illus. f. 304,
    339, 345
Pearl, as used on flutes, 304
Peel, Charles, C:15
Peer International Publishers, C:12
Peichler, Antonio Clemente, 266
Peleus, C:8
Pellegrini, Geualdo, B:12, C:2
Pelleteir, Wilfred, 210
Peloponnesos, 21
Peloso, Giuseppe, A:6
Pena, Feliciano, 30
Penas, Jean Baptiste, 266
Penelope (Greek legend), C:iii
Peneo, 242
Pennacchia, Luigi and Amalia, 395–96
Pensel & Mueller Co., B:11
Penville, Edith, 266
Peoples' Symphony Orchestra (Bos-
    ton, Massachusetts), 283
Percival, Samuel, 266
Percussive techniques, 361
Pereira, Bernardino, 256
Pereira, Coaracyara, 257
Pereira, Guiherme Agostinho, 257
Perforated keys. See French model
    flute
Pergolesi, Giovanni Battista, 473, C:4,
    C:7
Peri, Jacopo, 349–50, C:9
Pericles, C:7
Perkins, Harley, Still Life with Flute
    (painting), A:15, A:24
Perrault, 266
Perry, R. Hinton, Pan the Piperess
    (artwork), 372, A:15
Persia, Shah of, 147, 249
Persiani, 131
Perti (1661–1756), C:9
Peru, ancient civilizations of, 21, 23–
    24, 32, 271
Pesaro Conservatory, A:1, B:3, C:2
Pescetti, Giovanni (1704–1766), C:9
Peschak, Franz, 266

Pessard, Emil, 266
Peter (artist), 43
Peter Pan (book), Barrie, James, 372
Peter's, C. F. (publishers), 351–52
Petersen (19th c. flute maker), 9
Petersen, A. C., 286
Petersen, Alfred, 366, 376
Petersen, Jörgen, 266
Petersen, Peter Nicholas, 111, 266, 355
Peterson, Beatrice, A:23
Peterson, Lloyd R., A:25
Peterson, Maude (Mrs. Leonardo De
    Lorenzo). See Modina De Lorenzo
Petrie, John, A:12
Petrie, W. Flinders, 314
Pezzi, Vincenzo, A:23, B:20
Pfitzner, Hans Erich, Palestrina
    (opera), 411
Phaethon, C:8
Phares, Hale, 266
Phidias (Greek artist), 43, C:7
Philadelphia, Pennsylvania
    Centennial exhibition, 47
    Philadelphia Inquirer, 326
    Symphony, 203, 209, 215, 217, 245,
        248, 252, 281, 291, 232, 362, 364,
        A:1, A:24, B:3, C:15
Philibert, 7, 67–68 (RSR), 266
Phillipines
    flute music of, 482–83
    noseflute of, 22, 44
Philosophers and philosophy, A:17,
    B:21
Philoxenes, 312
Phonograph Co. (London), 262
Phonograph records. See Recordings
Photographs. See Collections:
    Photographs
Phrygian fluteplayers, 309
Piacenza, Pasquale, 266
Piarullo, Carlo, A:6–7
Piastro, Joseph, 493, A:16, B:20
    Trio classique in E-flat for flute,
        violin, and piano, 369
Piatigorsky, Gregor, C:6

641

Piatti, Bortolo, 266
Piazza, Italo, 176, 266, 321, 322, 323,
    398–99, 405, 453–55, A:5, A:16, C:1
    Breve dissertazione storico critica
        sul flauto, 453
    Il flauto Giorgi, 405, 453
    works of, 399, 453–55, A:5
Picco pipe (Sardinian shepherd pipe),
    319
Piccolissimo (instrument), A:6
Piccolo, 207, 318, A:5, A:6, C:11;
    methods for, 233, A:5, A:6
Piccolo music, 225, 364, 376, A:14,
    B:12, C:13, C:15
Piccolo-Flute (combination instru-
    ment), A:5
Piccoloists, 134, 141, 217, 226, 228, 229,
    230, 232, 233, 239, 240, 244, 245,
    246, 250, 279, 281, 285, 295, 364,
    467, A:1, A:2, A:4, C:3, C:15
Picklow, Francis Edward, A:26
Picton, Alfred, 266–67
Pied Piper, works on legend of, 371,
    372, 345–46
Pierné, Gabriel, 194, 200, 369, C:4
Pieroni, Leopoldo, 267, A:16
Piffero, 402
Pijper, Willem, 359, B:12
Pilati, Mario, A:16
Pindar, 311
Pintorno, Vincenzo, A:7
Pipes of Pan. See Panpipes
Pirani, Eugenio, A:16, B:9
Pires, José Alberto, 258
Pisano, Ciccio, 408, 439–41, 488
Pisendel, J. F., 71, 74, 75
Piston, Walter
    The Incredible Flutist (ballet), 370
    Sonata for flute and piano, C:12, C:13
    Three Pieces for flute, clarinet, and
        bassoon, B:12
Pitfield, Thomas B., Sonatina for flute
    and piano, C:13

Pittsburg, Pennsylvania
    Chamber of the International
        Society for Contemporary
        Music, 238
    Flute Club, 242, A:4, C:10
    Symphony, 223, 250, 276, B:4
Pizzetti, Ildebrando, B:7
Pizzo, Joseph, 267
Pizzo, Vincenzo, 267
Platinum flute, 35, 321, 361, 375, 378,
    463, A:3, A:4, A:7, A:25, A:27, C:11
Plato (427–347 B. C.), 20, A:16, A:17,
    A:19
Plessier, Rene, B:2
Pliny, Naturalis Historia (book), 20
Plow, Jay, 267, 489
Plunder, Anton, 267
Plymnia (Greek goddess), C:iii
Poddany, Eugene, Trio for flute, cello,
    and piano, C:10
Poe, Edgar Allan, A:11, A:20
Poetry, A:8, A:20
Poets, 44–49, 52, 78, 218, 220, 232, 237,
    242, 248, 279, 282, 305, 310–11, 365,
    A:11, A:20
Poitiers, University of, 472–73
Poland, King of (1720s), 71, 72, 73, 74
Poli, Nives, C:2
Poliocertes, Demetrius, 311
Politis, James Dimitri, C:2
Polledro, Francesco, 395
Pollister, Alexander, 309
Polo, Marco, C:7
Ponchielli, Amilcare, 225, 448
Pons, Lily, 260
Poole, George, A:13
Pope, Alexander, 52
Popp, Wilhelm (1828–1903), 149, 267,
    328, 339, 460, A:16
Porcuincula, Manoel, 259
Porpora (1686–1767), C:9
Porter, Quincy, Little Trio for flute,
    violin, and viola, 368
Portnoy, Mildred, A:13

Pôrto Alegre (Brazil), Rio Grande do Sur, Conservatory, 254, 256, 258
Porto, Antonio de Oliveira, Jr., 256
Portre, Eugene, 267
Portugal, King of, 147
Poseidon, C:8
Posell, George L., 267
Posell, Sarah, 267, 338, A:12
Posella, Leonard, 210, 267, 277, 330
Poteet, Ewing, B:7
Pott, Ernst, 267
Potter, Robert W. F., A:7, A:25
Potts, Bonita, A:3
Poulenc, Francis, B:8
Poussin, Nicolas, *Pan and Syrinx* (painting), 371, 411
Powell, Edward (son of Verne), B:3, B:11
Powell, Verne Q., 237, 267, B:11
Pozzuoli (Italy), Cathedral of, C:4
Prades Festival (France), B:10
Praetorius, 50, 54, C:10
Prague, Czechoslovakia
    Bohemian Royal Chapel, 290
    Conservatory, 224, 244, 246, 262, 272
    Königlich Deutschen Landestheater, 245
    Royal Theater, 246
    University of, C:13
Pratten, Frederick, 139
Pratten, Robert Sidney, 139–142 (RSR), 154, 160, 267, 287
Pratten, Madame Sydney, 140
Praxiteles (Greek sculptor), 43, 403, C:8
Preisler. *See* Priester
Prencipe, Guiseppe, C:1
Prendeville, Harry, 267
Presidents. *See* U. S. Presidents
Presser, William, *Serenade* for flute and viola, C:17
Presser Publishing Co., Theodore, 339, B:9, C:12
Prestini, Giuseppe, 264

Pretz, Godfrey, *Humoresque* for four flutes, 268
Preucil, William, C:12
Previn, Charles, *Insect Suite* for violin, viola, cello, harp, and flute, C:11
Prill, Carl (brother of Emil), 170
Prill, Emil, 59, 170–71, 267, 268, illus. f. 304, 339, 414, 415, 416, 462, A:16, B:2, C:2
Prill, Paul (brother of Emil), 170
Pritchard, Benson, 268
Prix de Rome, 359, B:10
Pronomus of Thebes, 311
Probost, Franz, 268
Prohaska, Felix, B:3
Prokoviev, *Sonata*, Op. 94, A:9
Prometheus, C:7
Prussia, King of, 75, 78
Prussia, Prince of, 74, 76
Prussia, Queen of, 74
Prussian Court Orchestra, 74–76, 78–81, 274
Pryor's (Arthur) Band, 208
Psaltery (*salterio, stromento di porco*), C:10
Ptah (Egyptian god), 4
Ptolemy Soter (king of Egypt), 311
Ptolomaeus, Claudius, 268
Pucci, Saverio, 268
Puccini, Giacomo, 407, 428, A:16, A:26, B:7, B:8
Pueblo Indian flutes, A:8
Pugliese, Nicola, C:2
Pugnani, Gaetano, 278
Pugni, Cesare, 460, A:16
Pugno, Raoul, 187
Puliti-Santoliquido, Ornella, C:2
Purcell, Daniel, 334
Pushkin, Aleksander, C:4, C:7
Putnam, Barbara, 268, 344
Puyana, Raphael Antonio, B:1
Puyans, Emilio, 268
Pythaules, 20
Pythian games, 20

Qualen, John, 268
Quantz, Andreas (father of Johann), 69
Quantz, Johann Joachim (1697–1773),
    8–9, 57, 67, 69–76 (RSR), 77, 79, 82–
    83, 84, 87, 89, 92, 93, 94, 162, 221,
    230, 234, 268, 324, 325, 333, 339,
    351, 414, 415, C:7, C:14
    D-sharp (E-flat keys) of, 8–9
    Essai, 67, 75, 89
    flute of, 94
    improvements to the flute, 8–9, 57,
      75
    pupils of, 75
    sonatas for flute, 74, 334, 415
    wooden tuning slide invention, 75
    works by, 76
Quantz, Justus, 69
Quarterly Musical Magazine, 116, 125,
    126, 130
Quartino di flauto (military flute in F), 11
Quechua Indians, A:10. *See also* Incan
    flutes; Ancient flutes and flutists
Queens Hall Orchestra (London), 234
Quena (Andean flute), 23
Quensel, Alfred, 268, A:7, B:11
Quercy, Paul, 153
Querflöte. See Transverse flute
Quesnay, Alfred, 268
Quintela, Benigno, B:12, C:2
Quinteros, Abelardo, C:13

Rab, Edward, B:3
Rabaud, Henri, 201
Rabboni, Giuseppe, 176, 235, 265, 268,
    290, 322, 448–60, 475, 476
Rabelais, *The Life of Gargantua* (book), 6
Rachmaninoff, Sergei, 413, 463, C:5–6
Radcliff, John, 148, 151–53, 159, 160,
    268–69, 287, 320, 321, 325, 331,
    339, 372, 462
Radio, 210, 225, 250, 265, 341, 375, B:1,
    B:3, C:11
  broadcasts of flute, 415
  programs
    Borden's Wednesday Night, B:3

National Hookup, B:1
Music of Today, B:1
Gas Hour (Los Angeles), C:11
Prudential Family Hour, B:3
Telephone Hour, B:3
Radio City Music Hall, 210
Radio Italiana (Torino, Italy, journal),
    C:14
Radio orchestras
  ABC, B:1
  CBS, 216, 289, 360
  NBC, 224, 236, 239, 270, 289, 375, B:1
  WOR Symphonietta, 229
  WQXR, 265
Radio Times, 341
Radoux, Nicholas Libert, 269
Raff, Joseph Joachim, A:19
Rafferty, John, 484
Raimondi, Pietro, C:5
Raimondo, Emanuele, 269
Raimundo, Domingos, 257
Rallo, Angelo, 269
Rameau, Jean-Philippe, B:1
Rampal, Jean-Pierre, A:7, C:2, C:13
Rampell, F. R., A:9
Ranchibile, Count, A:4
Randhartinger, Benedict, C:5
Rankin, Edward J., A:7, A:24
Rapée, Erno, 210
Raphael, 420
Rapp, Rolf, C:2
Ratcliffe, Hardie, A:7
Rateau, René, 269, 345
Rauch, Alfred, 269
Rault, Félix, 89–90 (RSR), 91, 269
Ravagli, 135
Ravel, Alfredo, 269
Ravel, Maurice, 12, 369, B:6, B:8
  Daphnis et Chlóe flute solo, A:15
  La flute enchante, flute, voice, and or-
    chestra, 369
Ravenna, Italy
  Academia Musicale, 224
  Institutio Musicale Giusepe Verdi,
    223

Rohozinski, L., *Suite Breve* for flute, viola, and harp, C:17
Rolf, Ermeler, A:9
Romani, Aquiles, C:10
Romanino, Camillo, 265, 271, 477
Romberg, Bernard, 110, 355
Romberg, Sigmund, A:6
Rome, Italy. *See also* Ancient flutes and flutists
  Augusteo Orchestra, 360
  Banda del corpo delle guardi, B:3
  Basilica di Massenzio, 360
  French Academy of Villa Medici, 359
  Quintetto Strumentale, 360
  Rassegna Nazional Giovanni Concertisti, C:2
  San Pietro Vaticano, C:5
  Santa Cecilia, 132, 135, 233, 280, 283, 360, 402, 477, A:1, A:6, A:7, B:2
  Academy of, 132, 135, 477
  Teatro Argentina, C:5
  Teatro dell' opera, B:2, C:2
  Virtuosi di Roma, A:7, B:12, C:2
Ronga, Raffaele (pianist), C:1
Roos, J., *Physiology in Relation to Playing the Flute* (book), A:26
Roose, Conrat van der, 271
Roosevelt, Theodore, 471
Ropartz, Guy, B:8, C:4
Rorem, Ned, *Mountain Song* for flute and piano, C:12
Rorich, Carl, *Burlesca* for three flutes and piano, 376
Rose, John Mitchell, 102, 163, 271
Roselier, Adalberto de Assissis, 255
Rosen, Maurice S., A:12
Rosenthal, Bernard, *Flute Player* (sculpture), A:15
Roseroschewsky, Abt, 71
Rossi, Michelangelo, 271–72
Rossini, Gioacchino, 132, 295, 300, 392, 441, A:20, B:5, B:7–8, B:16, C:5
  operas arranged for flute and piano, 295
  opera excerpts for flute, 300, 392

Rossler, Joseph, 216
Rössler, Otto, 272
Rostock State Theatre Orchestra (Russia), 263
Rouault, Georges, *La Flute de Pan* (painting), 370
Rouchefoucauld, 101
Rousseau, Jean Jacques, A:17, A:20
Roussel, Albert, 205, B:8
  Andante and Scherzo for flute and piano, op. 15, A:7
  "Pan" from *Joueurs de flûte* for flute and piano, 370
Roussier (and LaBorde), *Essai*, 67, 90
Roy, Gabrielle, *The Tin Flute* (book), 371
Royal College of Music (Manchester, England), A:3
Rubens, Peter Paul, 43, 411
Rubenstein, Anton, 138, 150, 328, B:7
Rubenstein, Nicholas, B:6
Rubini, Giovanni-Battista, 131
Rubsamen, Walter, H., 272
Rucquoy, Frédéric, 173, 272, 251
Rudall, Frank, 103, 104
Rudall, George, 101–04 (RSR), 136, 137, 164, 271, 272, 324, 325
Rudall and Rose Co., 102, 140, 271
Rudall, Carte & Co., 50N, 101–04, 148, 223, 232, 233, 272, 454, B:11
Ruderman, Martin, 272, 330
Ruderman, Sylvia (Mrs. Glass), 272, A:12, A:13, A:14
Ruellan, Andree, *Musical Interlude* (painting), A:15
Ruggi, 225
Rühm, Otto, B:3
Rultenberg, Cornelia, *The Flute Player* (painting), A:24
Ruotolo, Onorio, A:16, B:1, B:20
Ruskin, John, 409
Russell, A:18
Russo, June, C:17
Ruykel, C., 69

Ryan, Marah Ellis, *The Flute of the Gods* (book), 27, 31, 34, 372

Saal, Wilhelm, 272
Sabathil, Ferdinand, 272, 339
Sabatini, Renzo, 280, 360
Sabatini, William, C:12
Sacades of Argos, 314
Sacchetti, Antonio, 273
Sacchi, Ann, 223
Sacchini, Antonio, C:4, C:9
Sachse-Meiningen, Duke of, 173
Saenger, Gustave, A:16
Safronoff, Victor, illus. f. 144, 273, 459, A:16
Sagras (flutist), 325
Sagul, Edith, 273
Sahagun, Fr. Bernardino de, 33
Saint Louis, Missouri
    Sinfonietta, B:10
    Symphony, 214, 245, 281, 345, B:10, C:12
St. Paul (Minnesota) Symphony, 259
St. Paulinus of Nola, 52
St. Petersberg, Russia
    Chapel Royal, 128
    Choir School, 278
    Herald, 166
    Imperial Ballet Orchestra, 163, 275, 279
    Imperial Conservatory, 279, 285
    Imperial Court Orchesra, 278
    Imperial Opera, 128, 138, 150, 164, 224, 247, 263
    Imperial Theatre, 128, 165, 167, 273, 285
Saint-Saëns, Camille, 189, A:11, B:6, B:8, C:8
    Romanza, Op. 37 for flute and orchestra, 240, 285, 460
    Viens une flute invisible, for voice, flute, and piano, 370, A:10
Salerno, Italy
    Casino Sociale (Casino Nobili), C:1
    Liceo Musicale, C:1

Salieri, Antonio, 269, C:5, C:9
Saliment, George Edward, A:7
Salituro, Antonio, 256
Salo, Gaspar Brecian da, 296N
Salvi, Alberto, 278, A:16, B:21
Salvi, Annina, B:21
Salzedo, Carlos, 197
Sample, Paul, *The Solo* (painting), C:11
Samuels, Bernard Edward, 273
San Antonio (Texas) Symphony, 236, 281, A:1, A:2, A:4, A:8, C:1
San Bernardino, California
    Sun and Evening Telegram, 49
    Symphony, 490
San Francisco, California
    Art Commission, 375
    Exposition of 1915, 42, A:5
    Mid-Winter Fair (1893), 16
    NBC Orchestra, Western Division, 375
    Symphony, 239, 244, 250, 263, 268, 270, 276, 289, 345, 375
Sanches, Alvaro do Amaral Britto, 255
Sanches, Henrique, 257
Sanchi, Tope Gati, 4
Sandrini, Paolo, 273
Sanford, Marcelline Hall (sister of Ernest Hemingway), A:23
Santa Barbara (California) Community Music and Arts Assoc., C:3
Santa Cecilia. *See* Rome: Santa Cecilia
Santa Cruz, Domingo, *Sinfonia Concertante* for flute and orchestra, 363
Santa Monica (California) Symphony, 228
Santayana, George, A:18
Santiago, Chile
    Instituto Chileno, B:12
    National Conservatory, A:12, B:11–12
Santoro, Claudio, *Sonata* for flute and piano, C:13
Santos, Edgard Pereira dos, 257

Transylvania Music Camp (North Carolina), B:2
Treatises on the flute. *See also* Instruction books; Histories
De Assisi, 220, 225, 254, 255, 265
Finn, 372
Hotteterre, 66–67
Quantz, 65, 75, 89
Rockstro, 242
Schwedler, 275
Sconzo, 275, 372
Skeffington, 276
Tamplini, 280
Tillmetz, 158
Tromlitz, 89
Wieland, 288
Tricot, Eduard, 281–82
Trieste, Italy
Liceo Musicali "Tartini e Verdi," 280
Museo Civico di Storia ed Arte, C:11
Museo Storico Musicale, 251
Triflauto, 350
Trills, 385
fingerings for D-natural, C-sharp, D-sharp, low C to C-sharp, 98
Trio de Lutèce (Barrère), 197, 463
Triple pipe (*triflauto*), 349, 350
Tromlitz, Johann George, 9, 88–89 (RSR), 94, 98, 282, 324, 325
Trotzmuller, Karl, B:3
Troughton, Ella D., 282
Trousseau, Charles Cyprien, 282
Trowbridge, Charles Russell, A:8, A:23
Truman, Mr. and Mrs. Harry S., B:21
Truman, Margaret, B:3
Trumble, Ernest, 354
Tryon, Jesse, A:15
Tryon, Winthrop P., C:10
Tsche, 5
Tuberculosis, 47
Tudor, David, C:11
Tulou, Jean Louis, 90, 91, 99, 104–07 (RSR), 110–11, 118, 119, 135, illus. f. 144, 154, 215, 227, 238, 282, 285, 321, 322, 323, 333, 340, 355, 460

Tulou flute, 321
Tulsa (Oklahoma) University Symphony, A:23
Tuning cork, 98
Tuning slide of Quantz, 75, 98
Tupian Indian, A:10
Turchini, Fausto, C:2

Uchitel, David, C:2
Udine (Italy) Circolo Artistico Friuliano, C:1
Uffizi Gallery, 403
Unger, Adolph, 282
United States
Military, 375
Army Bands, B:1, C:3
Coast Guard, A:2
Navy Band, 375
Presidents and the flute, 302–03, A:2
Uranio, C:iii
Uranium flute, illus. f. 144
Urbain, Joseph, C:3
Urciuolo, Francesco, C:3
Ute Indian flutes, A:8, A:10
Utrecht, Herman, 283

Vacha, Caroline, 282, 344
Vactor, David van, 276, 283, 339, 342, 344, 363, 373–74, 375, B:11
Concerto Grosso for three flutes and harp, 363, 375
Vaillant, P., 282
Vaillant, George C., *Aztecs of Mexico,* 34
Valdovinos, Teodoro Juan Y Puyol, 282
Valente, Jefferson, 258
Valentini (Valentin), Roberto, 282, 349
Valentino, Domingos, 257
Valentino, Enrico De Angelis, C:1
Valerio, Nicholas, 282
Valle, Manoel Marcelino do, 256
Van Beinum, Edward, C:11
Van Boom, Johann, 282
Van Dyck, Anthony, 43
Van Dyke, Henry, "Pipes O'Pan" (poem), A:8

Willoughby, Robert, 288, 344
Willson, Meredith, 339, 341, 373–74, B:5
   And There I Stood With My Piccolo (book), 373
Wilms, Jan Willen, 288
Wilschauer, Adalbert, 288
Wilson, Mortimer, *Pipes and Reeds* for two flutes, two clarinets, oboe, and bassoon, 369
Wilt, Thomas, 288, 345, A:9
Winckler, Anton, 288
Winckler, Carl, 288
Wind quintet. *See* Woodwind quintet
Wing, Frederick, 219
Wingreen, Harriet, C:2
Winkler, Theodor, 288
Winter, Joseph, 92
Winternitz, Felix, A:16
Winterthur, Switzerland
   Music School, 215
   Symphony Orchestra, C:1
Winwar, Frances, B:1, B:20
Witicisms, A:20–21
Witteborg, August, 288
Wittgenstein, Hugo, 288
Wittgenstein, Milton, 265, 289, A:12
Wobisch, Helmut, B:3
Woempner, Carl, 260, 289
Woempner, Henry, 206, 289, illus. f. 304, 330, 365, 366, 374–75, B:20, C:12
Wolf, Anton, A:9
Wolf, Hugo, C:7
Wolff, Alberto, *Concerto* for flute and orchestra, A:5
Wolfram, Joseph, 289
Wolfs, Walter, C:3
Wolke, 94
Wolle, John Frederick, 208
Woltman, Frederick, *Poem* for flute and orchestra, 368
Women flutists. *See* Lady flutists
Wood, W., 277
Wood, Betty, 289

Wood, Daniel, 289
Wood and Company (organ makers), 102
Wood flute, 35, 37–38, 150, 207, 253, 298, 300, 321, 345, 378, 470
   boxwood, 65, 318
   cocus wood, 376
   ebony, 65
   wood versus metal controversy, 56–59, 160, 180, 185, 261, 422–26, 461
Woodstock Festival (New York), C:2
Woodwind Magazine, 216
Woodwind quartets, A:8, B:2 (of French Radio Orchestra)
Woodwind quintets, 155, 156, 209, 342
   American Woodwind-Composer Quintet, illus. f. 304, 342–44
   Aspen Festival (Colorado), B:10
   Belgrade Woodwind Quintet (Yugoslavia), C:1
   Chicago Symphony (Illinois), B:10
   Cologne Radio Ensemble (Germany), C:11
   Los Angeles Fine Arts Players (California), B:1
   Rochester Wind Quintet (New York), illus. f. 304
Words, difficult or unusual, B:4, C:8. *See also* Palindromes
Works with flutistic titles. *See* Artworks with flutistic titles; Statuary depicting flutes
World War I, 226, 243, 271, 466, A:2, C:6
World War II, 226, 275, 466, A:2, B:11, C:3
Wouters, Adolphe F., 357–58, A:16
   Adagio et Scherzando, op. 77 for four flutes, 357
Wouters, Madame Adolphe, A:16
Wragg, J., 289
Wren, Lorna, A:9, A:12, A:13
Wright, Dorothy, 365
Wsevoloÿsky, Princess Caterina, 476

Wummer, John, 41, illus. f. 144, 206–09, 211, 223, 288, 289, 290, 331, 334, 360, A:24, C:2

Wummer, Mildred Hunt, 289–90, illus. f. 304, 338, A:12

Wunderlich, Johann Georg, 90–91 (RSR), 99, 104, 106, 290

Wunderlich, Phillip, 290

Wurzburg, Germany
    Royal Bavarian Cadetcorps, 157
    Royal Bavarian Opera, 157
    Royal School of Music, 158, 174, 281

Wysham, Henry Clay, 290, 325

Xavier, Joao Jupyacara, 258

Xenophon, 312

Yaqui Indians, 29

Young, John Harrington, 290

Ysaye, Eugène, 462, C:6

Yucatan (Mayan ruins), 31

Yugoslavian flute of bear jaw, 30

Yutang, Liu, A:20

Zaduck, Sigmund, 290

Zagwiyn (Zagvijn), Henry, Capriccio for flute and piano, B:12, C:12

Zambogna (zampogne). See Bagpipe

Zamperoni, Antonio, 176, 237, 290, 322, 408, 447–52, 456, A:16

Zandonai, Riccardo, Il Flauto Notturno for flute and orchestra, 371

Zanke, A:9

Zarlino, Gioseffo, C:9

Zeitlin, Sidney, C:3

Zeller, 94

Zelter, Carl Friedrich, 128

Zenker, G., 277

Zentner, Franz, 290

Zerrahn, Carl, 290

Zesewitz, Moritz, 290

Zeus, C:iii, C:7, C:8

Ziegler (flutemaker), 147

Ziegler, Roy, 290

Zielsche, Johann Heinrich, 290–92

Zierer, Franz, 291

Zilmer, A. L., 277

Zimbalist, Efrem, B:6

Zimmer & Schmidt Co. (New York), 424

Zimmerman, Ethel, A:13

Zimmermann, Jules Heinrich, 181, 412
    publishing firm of, 358, 412, 413, 443, 451, 452

Zimmermann, William, 413

Zinck, Hartnack Otto Conrad, 291

Zingarelli, 225, C:7, C:9

Zink, Wilhelm, 291

Zipoli, Domenico, C:9

Zirato, Bruno, B:20

Zither, 316

Zivkovic, Milenko, Suite for flute and strings, C:13

Zizold, August, Jr., 291

Zizold, Wilhelm, 291

Zlotnik, Henry, 291

Zola, Émile, A:20

Zucca, A:9

Zucchi, G., 291

Zulu pipe, 153

Zurich, Switzerland
    Conservatory, 243, 246, 261
    Musik Akademie, 246, A:6
    Tonhallen Orchesters, 215, 246, 278, A:6

Zwerchpfieff, 6

Zybin, Wladimire, 291